Sentence Skills with Readings

Annotated Instructor's Edition

Praise for *Sentence Skills with Readings*

"I am so impressed with this text that I would not only suggest but fight for its adoption."

Dorthea D. Burkhart, Davidson County Community College

"The greatest strengths of the text are the detailed explanations and the numerous exercises. [. . .] I would rate the text as an 'A.'"

Mary Jean Gilligan, Delaware Technical and Community College

"The reading selections are excellent."

Charles S. Pierce, Jr., Tidewater Community College

"The ESL pointers are terrific."

Tracy Peyton, Pensacola Junior College

"This text review is my first exposure to *Sentence Skills with Readings*, and I am very impressed."

Beth Ashburn, Piedmont Baptist College

"The writing assignments are excellent."

Glenda Whalon, Cochise College

"This is truly a good text, and I am so pleased and impressed with the changes."

Judy D. Covington, Trident Technical College

"It is thorough, well organized, well developed, and easy to use for both students and instructors."

Theresa Zeleznik, Cuyahoga Community College, Western Campus

"The appendices, the section on how to use a computer to compose, the walk-through of a student's drafts in a "Brief Guide," and the section on reading really pump this book up. The checklists are very good while the reflective activities add a deeper dimension to the composing process."

Michele Mohr, Morton College

"The greatest strength of the text remains its easy-to-use style."

William Muller, Moraine Valley Community College

"Langan's straightforward goals of effective writing and corollary points have always been and continue to be the strengths of the text."

Kris Acquistapace, Crafton Hills College

"There is enough in here to keep students interested, busy – and learning!"

Sara Jane Richter, Oklahoma Panhandle State University

Sentence Skills with Readings

Second Edition

Annotated Instructor's Edition

John Langan
Atlantic Cape Community College

Boston Burr Ridge, IL Dubuque, IA Madison, WI New York San Francisco St. Louis
Bangkok Bogotá Caracas Lisbon London Madrid
Mexico City Milan New Delhi Seoul Singapore Sydney Taipei Toronto

McGraw-Hill Higher Education 

A Division of The ***McGraw-Hill*** *Companies*

SENTENCE SKILLS WITH READINGS

Published by McGraw-Hill, an imprint of The McGraw-Hill Companies, Inc. 1221 Avenue of the Americas, New York, NY 10020.

This book is printed on acid-free paper.

1 2 3 4 5 6 7 8 9 0 FGR/FGR 0 9 8 7 6 5 4 3 2 1 0

ISBN 0-07-242968-2 (student ed.)
ISBN 0-07-242981-X (annotated instructor's ed.)

Editorial director: *Phillip A. Butcher*
Senior sponsoring editor: *Sarah Touborg*
Developmental editor II: *Alexis Walker*
Marketing manager: *Thayne Conrad*
Senior project manager: *Pat Frederickson*
Senior production supervisor: *Lori Koetters*
Designer: *Jennifer Hollingsworth*
Cover illustration: *Paul Turnbaugh*
Supplement coordinator: *Carol A. Bielski*
Compositor: *Electronic Publishing Services, Inc., TN*
Typeface: *11/13 Times Roman*
Printer: *Quebecor Printing Book Group/Fairfield*

Library of Congress Cataloging-in-Publication Data

Langan, John (date)
Sentence skills with readings / John Langan.—2nd ed.
p. cm.
Includes index.
ISBN 0-07-242968-2 (student ed.) — ISBN 0-07-242981-X (annotated instructor's ed.)
1. English language—Sentences—Problems, exercises, etc. 2. English language—Rhetoric—Problems, exercises, etc. 3. English language—Grammar—Problems, exercises, etc. 4. Report writing—Problems, exercises, etc. 5. College readers. I. Title.

PE1441.L356 2001
428.2—dc21 00-030550

www.mhhe.com

About the Author

John Langan has taught reading and writing at Atlantic Cape Community College near Atlantic City, New Jersey, for over twenty-five years. The author of a popular series of college textbooks on both subjects, he enjoys the challenge of developing materials that teach skills in an especially clear and lively way. Before teaching, he earned advanced degrees in writing at Rutgers University and in reading at Glassboro State College. He also spent a year writing fiction that, he says, "is now at the back of a drawer waiting to be discovered and acclaimed posthumously." While in school, he supported himself by working as a truck driver, machinist, battery assembler, hospital attendant, and apple packer. He now lives with his wife, Judith Nadell, near Philadelphia. Among his everyday pleasures are running, working on his Macintosh computer, and watching Philadelphia sports teams on TV. He also loves to read: newspapers at breakfast, magazines at lunch, and a chapter or two of a recent book ("preferably an autobiography") at night.

THE LANGAN SERIES

Essay-Level

College Writing Skills, Fifth Edition
ISBN: 0-07-228322-X (Copyright © 2000)

College Writing Skills with Readings, Fifth Edition
ISBN: 0-07-238121-3 (Copyright © 2001)

Paragraph-Level

English Skills, Seventh Edition
ISBN: 0-07-238127-2 (Copyright © 2001)

English Skills with Readings, Fourth Edition
ISBN: 0-07-092063-X (Copyright © 1999)

Sentence-Level

Sentence Skills: A Workbook for Writers, Form A, Sixth Edition
ISBN: 0-07-036672-1 (Copyright © 1998)

Sentence Skills: A Workbook for Writers, Form B, Sixth Edition
ISBN: 0-07-037127-X (Copyright © 1999)

Sentence Skills with Readings, Second Edition
ISBN: 0-07-238132-9 (Copyright © 2001)

Grammar Review

English Brushup, Second Edition
ISBN: 0-07-037108-3 (Copyright © 1998)

Reading

Reading and Study Skills, Form A, Sixth Edition
ISBN: 0-07-036440-0 (Copyright © 1998)

Reading and Study Skills, Form B, Fifth Edition
ISBN: 0-07-036413-3 (Copyright © 1994)

Contents

Section 2: Verbs, Pronouns, and Agreement

Section 3: Modifiers and Parallelism

Section 4: Punctuation and Mechanics

Appendixes

To the Instructor

Note: The *Annotated Instructor's Edition* you are holding is identical to the student version except for the answers which are included for all the activities and tests.

Key Features of the Book

Sentence Skills with Readings will help students learn to write effectively. It is an all-in-one text that includes a basic rhetoric and compelling readings and gives full attention to grammar, punctuation, mechanics, and usage.

The book contains ten distinctive features to aid instructors and their students:

1. **Coverage of basic writing skills is exceptionally thorough.** The book pays special attention to fragments, run-ons, verbs, and other areas where students have serious problems. At the same time, a glance at the table of contents shows that the book treats skills (such as dictionary use and spelling improvement) not found in other texts. In addition, parts of the book are devoted to the basics of effective writing, to practice in editing and proofreading, and to achieving variety in sentences.
2. **The book has a clear and flexible format.** It is organized in four easy-to-use parts. Part One is a guide to the goals of effective writing followed by a series of activities to help students practice and master those goals. Part Two is a comprehensive treatment of the rules of grammar, mechanics, punctuation, and usage needed for clear writing. Part Three provides a series of mastery, editing, and proofreading tests to reinforce the sentence skills presented in Part Two. Finally, Part Four presents ten high-interest reading selections, followed by assignments that enable students to transfer the skills they have learned to realistic writing situations.

   Since parts, sections, and chapters are self-contained, instructors can move easily from, for instance, a rhetorical principle in Part One to a grammar rule in Part Two to a mastery test in Part Three to a writing assignment in Part Four.
3. **Opening chapters deal with the writer's attitude, writing as a process, and the importance of specific details in writing.** In its opening pages, the book helps students recognize and deal with their attitude about writing—an

important part of learning to write well. In the pages that follow, students are the encouraged to see writing as a multistage process that moves from prewriting to proofreading. Later, a series of activities helps students understand the nature of specific details and how to generate and use those details. As writing teachers well know, learning to write concretely is a key step for students to master in becoming effective writers.

4 **Practice activities are numerous.** Most skills are reinforced by activities, review tests, and mastery tests, as well as tests in the *Instructor's Manual.* For many of the skills in the book, there are over one hundred practice sentences.

5 **Practice materials are varied and lively.** In many basic writing texts, exercises are monotonous and dry, causing students to lose interest in the skills presented. In *Sentence Skills,* many exercises involve students in various ways. An inductive opening activity allows students to see what they already know about a given skill. Within chapters, students may be asked to underline answers, add words, generate their own sentences, or edit passages. And the lively and engaging practice materials and readings in the book both maintain interest and help students appreciate the value of vigorous details in writing.

6 **Terminology is kept to a minimum.** In general, rules are explained using words students already know. A clause is a *word group;* a coordinating conjunction is a *joining word;* a nonrestrictive element is an *interrupter.* At the same time, traditional grammatical terms are mentioned briefly for students who learned them in the past and are comfortable seeing them again.

7 **Self-teaching is encouraged.** Students may check their answers to the introductory activities and the practice activities in Part Two by referring to the answers in Appendix E. In this way, they are given the responsibility for teaching themselves. At the same time, to ensure that the answer key is used as a learning tool only, answers are not given for the review tests in Part Two or for any of the reinforcement tests in Part Three. These answers appear in the *Annotated Instructor's Edition* and the *Instructor's Manual;* they can be copied and handed out to students at the discretion of the instructor.

8 **Diagnostic and achievement tests are provided.** These tests appear in Appendixes C and D of the book. Each test may be given in two parts, the second of which provides instructors with a particularly detailed picture of a student's skill level.

9 **High-interest reading selections provide opportunities for writing.** The final part of the book contains ten high-interest readings followed by paragraph and essay assignments. These assignments allow students to explore interesting, relevant topics while practicing the basic writing principles learned in Part One and the sentence skills learned in Parts Two and Three.

Changes in the Second Edition

Here are the major changes in this new edition of *Sentence Skills with Readings:*

- Collaborative and reflective activities have been added to key chapters of the book. The *collaborative activities* build on the idea that student interaction can increase learning. Group discussion, team writing, and student-generated examples are all used to lend energy to the classroom and strengthen students' mastery of essential writing skills.

  The *reflective activities* build on the idea that getting students to think about what they are learning can increase mastery. These activities engage students' higher-order thinking skills and encourage them to be active participants in their own learning.
- Many of the sentence skills in the book are in a simpler, more intuitive sequence. This framework, which places related topics in the same section, seems better suited to the way students learn. For example, the first section, "Sentences," begins with the simple sentence and subjects and verbs; the second chapter treats fragments; the third chapter examines run-ons; and the final chapter presents the four basic kinds of sentences and the main techniques for joining sentences (subordination and coordination).

  The second section groups together verbs, pronouns, and matters of agreement, and the third section presents modifiers and parallelism. The final two sections are more traditional: punctuation and mechanics, followed by chapters relating to word use.
- The book includes two new reading selections ("Do It Better!" by Ben Carson, M.D., with Cecil Murphey; and "Papa" by Leo Buscaglia), both highly motivational. There is also one updated reading ("Lost Years, Found Dreams," by Regina Ruiz). Pictures have been added to three readings to increase appeal and interest.
- Another addition to the book is an appendix titled "ESL Pointers," complete with practice activities which address common trouble spots faced by nonnative speakers of English.
- Here are some of the other changes in this revision. There is now a section on the use of computers in the writing process. An appendix on the parts of speech has been added. In select paragraph and essay assignments, a greater emphasis is placed on the importance of prewriting and revising. Practice sentences and passages have been freshened and updated throughout the text, and about 20 percent of the material is new. A section on the importance of regular reading, along with an annotated list of widely popular books, now concludes the introduction to the readings in Part Five. Finally, visual interest has been added to the book in the form of a more student-friendly design.

Helpful Learning Aids Accompany the Book

Supplements for Instructors

- An *Annotated Instructor's Edition* (ISBN 0-07-242981-X) consists of the student text complete with answers to all activities and tests.
- The comprehensive *Instructor's Manual and Test Bank* (ISBN 0-07-242980-1) includes (1) a model syllabus along with suggestions for teaching the course, (2) an answer key, and (3) a complete set of additional mastery tests. The manual is 8½ x 11 inches, so that both the answer pages and the added mastery tests can be conveniently reproduced on copying machines.
- An *Online Learning Center* (**www.mhhe.com/langan**) offers a host of instructional aids and additional resources for instructors, including a comprehensive computerized test bank, the Instructor's Manual and Test Bank, online resources for writing instructors, and more.
- An *Instructor's CD-ROM* (0-07-242984-4) offers all of the above supplements and M.O.R.E. (McGraw-Hill Online Resources for English, also available online at **www.mhhe.com/english**) in a convenient offline format.
- *PageOut!* helps instructors create graphically pleasing and professional web pages for their courses, in addition to providing classroom management, collaborative learning, and content management tools. PageOut! is **FREE** to adopters of McGraw-Hill textbooks and learning materials. Learn more at **www.mhhe.com/pageout.**
- *WebWrite!* is an interactive peer-editing program that allows students to post papers, read comments from their peers and instructor, discuss, and edit *online*. To learn more, visit the online demo at **www.metatext.com/webwrite.**

Supplements for Students

- An *Online Learning Center* (**www.mhhe.com/langan**) offers a host of instructional aids and additional resources for students, including self-correcting exercises, writing activities for additional practice, a PowerPoint grammar tutorial, guides to doing research on the Internet and avoiding plagiarism, useful web links, and more.

  AllWrite! 2.0 is an interactive, browser-based tutorial program that provides an online handbook, comprehensive diagnostic pre-tests and post-tests, plus extensive practice exercises in every area.

You can contact your local McGraw-Hill representative or consult McGraw-Hill's web site at **www.mhhe.com/english** for more information on the supplements that accompany *Sentence Skills with Readings, 2nd Edition.*

Acknowledgments

Reviewers who have contributed to this edition through their helpful comments include

Kris Acquistapace, Crafton Hills College
Beth Ashburn, Piedmont Baptist College
Gary Bennett, Santa Ana College
Amelia Billingsley, Floyd College
Dorothea D. Burkhart, Davidson County Community College
Judy D. Covington, Trident Technical College
LaNelle Daniel, Floyd College
Jeanne Gilligan, Delaware Technical Community College
Adam Kempler, College of the Canyons
Michele Mohr, Morton College
William Muller, Moraine Valley Community College
Tracy Peyton, Pensacola Junior College
Charles Pierce, Tidewater Community College
Sara Jane Richter, Oklahoma Panhandle State University
Drema Stringer, Marshall Community/Technical College
Glenda Whalon, Cochise College
Theresa Zeleznick, Cuyahoga Community College, Western Campus

I owe thanks as well for the support provided by Sarah Touborg and Alexis Walker at McGraw-Hill. And my gratitude goes particularly to an exceptional group of talented and caring professionals. Eliza Comodromos, Susan Gamer, Janet M. Goldstein, Beth Johnson, Paul Langan, and Carole Mohr have all played important roles in helping this book become even more student-friendly than before. With their help, *Sentence Skills with Readings* is a much better book than I could have managed by myself.

John Langan

Sentence Skills with Readings

Part One

Effective Writing

Introduction

Part One is a guide to the goals of effective writing followed by a series of activities to help you practice and master these goals. Begin with the introductory chapter, which makes clear the reasons for learning sentence skills. Then read the second chapter carefully; it presents all the essentials you need to know to become an effective writer. Finally, work through the series of activities in the third chapter. Your instructor may direct you to certain exercises, depending on your needs. After completing the activities, you'll be ready to take on the paragraph and essay writing assignments at the end of the chapter.

At the same time that you are writing papers, start working through the sentence skills in Parts Two and Three of the book. Practicing the sentence skills in the context of actual writing assignments is the surest way to master the rules of grammar, mechanics, punctuation, and usage.

Note: A writing progress chart on pages 700–701 (in Appendix F) will help you track your performance.

1 Learning Sentence Skills

Why Learn Sentence Skills?

Why should someone planning a career as a nurse have to learn sentence skills? Why should an accounting major have to pass a competency test in grammar as part of a college education? Why should a potential physical therapist or graphic artist or computer programmer have to spend hours on the rules of English? Perhaps you are asking questions like these after finding yourself in a class with this book. On the other hand, perhaps you *know* you need to strengthen basic writing skills, even though you may be unclear about the specific ways the skills will be of use to you. Whatever your views, you should understand why sentence skills—all the rules that make up standard English—are so important.

Clear Communication

Standard English, or "language by the book," is needed to communicate your thoughts to others with a minimal amount of distortion and misinterpretation. Knowing the traditional rules of grammar, punctuation, and usage will help you write clear sentences when communicating with others. You may have heard of the party game in which one person whispers a message to the next person; the message is passed, in turn, along a line of several other people. By the time the last person in line is asked to give the message aloud, it is usually so garbled and inaccurate that it barely resembles the original. Written communication in some form of English other than standard English carries the same potential for disaster.

To see how important standard English is to written communication, examine the pairs of sentences on the following pages and answer the questions in each case.

1. Which sentence indicates that there might be a plot against Ted?
   a. We should leave Ted. These fumes might be poisonous.
   b. We should leave, Ted. These fumes might be poisonous.
2. Which sentence encourages self-mutilation?
   a. Leave your paper and hand in the dissecting kit.
   b. Leave your paper, and hand in the dissecting kit.
3. Which sentence indicates that the writer has a weak grasp of geography?
   a. As a child, I lived in Lake Worth, which is close to Palm Beach and Alaska.
   b. As a child, I lived in Lake Worth, which is close to Palm Beach, and Alaska.
4. In which sentence does the dog warden seem dangerous?
   a. Foaming at the mouth, the dog warden picked up the stray.
   b. Foaming at the mouth, the stray was picked up by the dog warden.
5. Which announcer was probably fired from the job?
   a. Outside the Academy Awards theater, the announcer called the guests names as they arrived.
   b. Outside the Academy Awards theater, the announcer called the guests' names as they arrived.
6. Below are the opening lines of two students' exam essays. Which student seems likely to earn a higher grade?
   a. Defense mechanisms is the way people hides their inner feelings and deals with stress. There is several types that we use to be protecting our true feelings.
   b. Defense mechanisms are the methods people use to cope with stress. Using a defense mechanism allows a person to hide his or her real desires and goals.
7. The following lines are taken from two English papers. Which student seems likely to earn a higher grade?
   a. A big problem on this campus is apathy, students don't participate in college activities. Such as clubs, student government, and plays.
   b. The most pressing problem on campus is the disgraceful state of the student lounge area. The floor is dirty, the chairs are torn, and the ceiling leaks.

Continued

8. The following sentences are taken from reports by two employees. Which worker is more likely to be promoted?
   a. The spring line failed by 20 percent in the meeting of projected profit expectations. Which were issued in January of this year.
   b. Profits from our spring line were disappointing. They fell 20 percent short of January's predictions.
9. The following paragraphs are taken from two job application letters. Which applicant would you favor?
   a. Let me say in closing that their are an array of personal qualities I have presented in this letter, together, these make me hopeful of being interviewed for this attraktive position.

      sincerely yours'

      Brian Davis
   b. I feel I have the qualifications needed to do an excellent job as assistant manager of the jewelry department at Horton's. I look forward to discussing the position further at a personal interview.

      Sincerely yours,

      Richard O'Keeney

In each case, the first choice (*a*) contains sentence-skills mistakes. These mistakes range from missing or misplaced commas to misspellings to wordy or pretentious language. As a result of these mistakes, clear communication cannot occur—and misunderstandings, lower grades, and missed job opportunities are probable results. The point, then, is that all the rules that make up standard written English should be a priority if you want your writing to be clear and effective.

Success in College

Standard English is essential if you want to succeed in college. Any report, paper, review, essay exam, or assignment you are responsible for should be written in the best standard English you can produce. If you don't do this, it won't matter how fine your ideas are or how hard you worked—most likely, you will receive a lower grade than you would otherwise deserve. In addition, because standard English requires you to express your thoughts in precise, clear sentences, training yourself to follow the rules can help you think more logically. The basic logic you learn to practice at the sentence level will help as you work to produce well-reasoned papers in all your subjects.

Success at Work

Knowing standard English will also help you achieve success on the job. Studies have found repeatedly that skillful communication, more than any other factor, is the key to job satisfaction and steady career progress. A solid understanding of standard English is a basic part of this vital ability to communicate. Moreover, most experts agree that we are now living in an "age of information"—a time when people who use language skillfully have a great advantage over those who do not. Fewer of us will be working in factories or at other types of manual labor. Many more of us will be working with information in various forms—accumulating it, processing it, analyzing it. No matter what kind of job you are preparing yourself for, technical or not, you will need to know standard English to keep pace with this new age. Otherwise, you are likely to be left behind, limited to low-paying jobs that offer few challenges or financial rewards.

Success in Everyday Life

Standard English will help you succeed not just at school and work but in everyday life as well. It will help you feel more comfortable, for example, in writing letters to friends and relatives. It will enable you to write effective notes to your children's schools. It will help you get action when you write a letter of complaint to a company about a product. It will allow you to write letters inquiring about bills—hospital, medical, utility, or legal—or about any kind of service. To put it simply, in our daily lives, those who can use and write standard English have more power than those who cannot.

How This Book Is Organized

- A good way to get a quick sense of any book is to turn to the table of contents. By referring to pages vii–xi, you will see that the book is organized into four basic parts. What are they?

  Part One: Effective Writing

  Part Two: Sentence Skills

  Part Three: Reinforcement of Sentence Skills

  Part Four: Readings for Writing

- In Part One, the final section of Chapter 2 describes how a ___computer___ can help in the writing process.

- Part Two deals with sentence skills. The first section is "Sentences." How many sections (skills areas) are covered in all? Count them. five
- Part Three reinforces the skills presented in Part Two. What are the four kinds of reinforcement activities in Part Three?

  Mastery Tests

  Combined Mastery Tests

  Editing and Proofreading Tests

  Combined Editing Tests
- Turn to the introduction to Part Four to learn the purpose of that part of the book and write the purpose here: Part Four provides reading selections and related questions and writing assignments to capture students' interest and enlarge students' understanding.
- Helpful charts in the book include (*fill in the missing words*) the spelling list on the inside front cover, the progress charts in Appendix F, and the checklist of sentence skills on the inside back cover.
- Finally, the six appendixes at the end of the book are:

  (A) Parts of Speech, (B) ESL Pointers, (C) Diagnostic Test, (D) Achievement Test, (E) Answers to Introductory Activities and Practice Exercises, (F) Progress Charts

How to Use This Book

Here is a way to use *Sentence Skills with Reading*s. First, read and work through Part One, Effective Writing—a guide to the goals of effective writing followed by a series of activities to help you practice and master these goals. Your instructor may direct you to certain activities, depending on your needs.

Second, take the diagnostic test on pages 663–668. By analyzing which sections of the test give you trouble, you will discover which skills you need to concentrate on. When you turn to an individual skill in Part Two, begin by reading and thinking about the introductory activity. Often, you will be pleasantly surprised to find that you know more about this area of English than you thought you did. After all, you have probably been speaking English with fluency and ease for many years; you have an instinctive knowledge of how the language works. This knowledge gives you a solid base for refining your skills.

Your third step is to work on the skills in Part Two by reading the explanations and completing the practices. You can check your answers to each practice activity in this part by turning to the answer key at the back of the book (Appendix E). Try to figure out *why* you got some answers wrong—you want to uncover any weak spots in your understanding.

Your next step is to use the review tests at the ends of chapters in Part Two to evaluate your understanding of a skill in its entirety. Your instructor may also ask you to take the mastery tests or other reinforcement tests in Part Three of the book. To help ensure that you take the time needed to learn each skill thoroughly, the answers to these tests are *not* in the answer key.

Finally, the readings and writing assignments in Part Four are an important part of the book. The readings will motivate and inform you as well as give you practice in reading comprehension. The related writing assignments are crucial. To make standard English an everyday part of your writing, you must write not just single sentences but paragraphs and essays. The writing assignments will prove to you that clear, logical writing hinges on error-free sentences. You will see how the sentence skills you are practicing "fit in" and contribute to the construction of a sustained piece of writing. In the world of sports, athletes spend many days refining the small moves—serves, backhands, pitches, layups—so that they can reach their larger objective of winning the game. In the same way, you must work intently on writing clear sentences in order to produce effective papers.

The emphasis in this book is, nevertheless, on writing clear, error-free sentences as well as on composition. And the heart of the book is the practice material that helps reinforce the sentence skills you learn. A great deal of effort has been taken to make the practices lively and engaging and to avoid the dull, repetitive skills work that has given grammar books such a bad reputation. This text will help you stay interested as you work on the rules of English that you need to learn. The rest is a matter of your personal determination and hard work. If you decide—and only you can decide—that effective writing is important to your school and career goals and that you want to learn the basic skills needed to write clearly and effectively, this book will help you reach those goals.

2 A Brief Guide to Effective Writing

This chapter and Chapter 3 will show you how to write effective paragraphs and essays. The following questions will be answered in turn:

1 Why does your attitude toward writing matter?
2 What is a paragraph?
3 What are the goals of effective writing?
4 How do you reach the goals of effective writing?
5 What is an essay?
6 What are the parts of an essay?
7 How can a computer help?

Why Does Your Attitude toward Writing Matter?

Your attitude toward writing is an important part of learning to write well. To get a sense of just how you feel about writing, read the following statements. Put a check beside those statements with which you agree. (This activity is not a test, so try to be as honest as possible.)

_________ 1. A good writer should be able to sit down and write a paper straight through without stopping.

_________ 2. Writing is a skill that anyone can learn with practice.

_________ 3. I'll never be good at writing because I make too many mistakes in spelling, grammar, and punctuation.

_________ 4. Because I dislike writing, I always start a paper at the last possible minute.

_________ 5. I've always done poorly in English, and I don't expect that to change.

Now read the following comments about these five statements. The comments will help you see if your attitude is hurting or helping your efforts to become a better writer.

1 *A good writer should be able to sit down and write a paper straight through without stopping.*

The statement is *false.* Writing is, in fact, a process. It is done not in one easy step but in a series of steps, and seldom at one sitting. If you cannot do a paper all at once, that simply means you are like most of the other people on the planet. It is harmful to carry around the false idea that writing should be an easy matter.

2 *Writing is a skill that anyone can learn with practice.*

This statement is *absolutely true.* Writing is a skill, like driving or word processing, that you can master with hard work. If you want to learn to write, you can. It is as simple as that. If you believe this, you are ready to learn how to become a competent writer.

Some people hold the false belief that writing is a natural gift which some have and others do not. Because of this belief, they never make a truly honest effort to learn to write—and so they never learn.

3 *I'll never be good at writing because I make too many mistakes in spelling, grammar, and punctuation.*

The first concern in good writing should be *content*—what you have to say. Your ideas and feelings are what matter most. You should not worry about spelling, grammar, and punctuation while working on content.

Unfortunately, some people are so self-conscious about making mistakes that they do not focus on what they want to say. They need to realize that a paper is best done in stages and that the rules can and should wait until a later stage in the writing process. Through review and practice, you will eventually learn how to follow the rules with confidence.

4 *Because I dislike writing, I always start a paper at the last possible minute.*

This is all too common. You feel you are *going to* do poorly, and then your behavior ensures that you *will* do poorly! Your attitude is so negative that you defeat yourself—not even allowing enough time to really try.

Again, what you need to realize is that writing is a process. Because it is done in steps, you don't have to get it right all at once. Just get started well in advance. If you allow yourself enough time, you'll find a way to make a paper come together.

5 *I've done poorly in English in the past, and I don't expect that to change now.*

How you may have performed in the *past* does not control how you can perform in the *present.* Even if you did poorly in English in high school, it is in your power to make this one of your best subjects in college. If you believe writing can be learned, and if you work hard at it, you *will* become a better writer.

In brief, your attitude is crucial. If you believe you are a poor writer and always will be, chances are you will not improve. If you realize you can become a better writer, chances are you will improve. Depending on how you allow yourself to think, you can be your own best friend or your own worst enemy.

What Is a Paragraph?

A *paragraph* is a series of sentences about one main idea, or *point.* A paragraph typically starts with a point, and the rest of the paragraph provides specific details to support and develop that point.

Consider the following paragraph, written by a student named Gary Callahan.

Returning to School

Starting college at age twenty-nine was difficult. For one thing, I did not have much support from my parents and friends. My father asked, "Didn't you get dumped on enough in high school? Why go back for more?" My mother worried about where the money would come from. My friends seemed threatened. "Hey, there's the college man," they would say when they saw me. Another reason that starting college was hard was that I had bad memories of school. I had spent years of my life sitting in classrooms completely bored, watching clocks tick ever so slowly toward the final bell. When I was not bored, I was afraid of being embarrassed. Once a teacher called on me and then said, "Ah, forget it, Callahan," when he realized I did not know the answer. Finally, I soon learned that college would give me little time with my family. After work every day, I have just an hour and ten minutes to eat and spend time with my wife and daughter before going off to class. When I get back, my daughter is in bed, and my wife and I have only a little time together. Then the weekends go by quickly, with all the homework I have to do. But I am going to persist because I believe a better life awaits me with a college degree.

The preceding paragraph, like many effective paragraphs, starts by stating a main idea, or point. A *point* is a general idea that contains an opinion. In this case, the point is that starting college at age twenty-nine was not easy.

In our everyday lives, we constantly make points about all kinds of matters. We express all kinds of opinions: "That was a terrible movie." "My psychology instructor is the best teacher I have ever had." "My sister is a generous person." "Eating at that restaurant was a mistake." "That team should win the playoff game." "Waitressing is the worst job I ever had." "Our state should allow the death penalty." "Cigarette smoking should be banned everywhere." In *talking* to people, we don't always give the reasons for our opinions. But in *writing,* we *must* provide reasons to support our ideas. Only by supplying solid evidence for any point that we make can we communicate effectively with readers.

An effective paragraph, then, must not only make a point but support it with *specific evidence*—reasons, examples, and other details. Such specifics help prove to readers that the point is reasonable. Even if readers do not agree with the writer, at least they have in front of them the evidence on which the writer has based his or her opinion. Readers are like juries; they want to see the evidence so that they can make their own judgments.

Take a moment now to examine the evidence that Gary has provided to back up his point about starting college at twenty-nine. Complete the following outline of Gary's paragraph by summarizing in a few words his reasons and the details that develop them. The first reason and its supporting details are summarized for you as an example.

Point: Starting college at age twenty-nine was difficult.

Reason 1: Little support from parents and friends

Details that develop reason 1: Father asked why I wanted to be dumped on again, mother worried about tuition money, friends seemed threatened

Reason 2: Bad memories of school

Details that develop reason 2: Boredom; fear of being embarrassed

Reason 3: Little time with family

Details that develop reason 3: About an hour to spend with them between work and school; only a little time before bed; homework on weekends

As the outline makes clear, Gary provides three reasons to support his point about starting college at twenty-nine: (1) he had little support from his friends or parents, (2) he had bad memories of school, and (3) college left him little time with his family. Gary also provides vivid details to back up each of his three reasons. His reasons and descriptive details enable readers to see why he feels that starting college at twenty-nine was difficult.

To write an effective paragraph, then, aim to do what Gary has done: begin by making a point, and then go on to support that point with specific evidence. Finally, like Gary, end your paper with a sentence that rounds off the paragraph and provides a sense of completion.

What Are the Goals of Effective Writing?

Now that you have considered an effective student paragraph, it is time to look at four goals of effective writing:

Goal 1: Make a Point

It is often best to state your point in the first sentence of your paper, just as Gary does in his paragraph about returning to school. The sentence that expresses the main idea, or point, of a paragraph is called the *topic sentence.* Your paper will be unified if you make sure that all the details support the point in your topic sentence. Activities on pages 44–48 in Chapter 3 will help you learn how to write a topic sentence.

Goal 2: Support the Point

To support your point, you need to provide specific reasons, examples, and other details that explain and develop it. The more precise and particular your supporting details are, the better your readers can "see," "hear," and "feel" them. Activities on pages 39–44 and 48–60 in Chapter 3 will help you learn how to be specific in your writing.

Goal 3: Organize the Support

You will find it helpful to learn two common ways of organizing support in a paragraph—*listing order* and *time order.* You should also learn the signal words, known as *transitions,* that increase the effectiveness of each method.

Listing Order: The writer can organize supporting evidence in a paper by providing a list of two or more reasons, examples, or details. Often the most important or interesting item is saved for last because the reader is most likely to remember the last thing read.

Transition words that indicate listing order include the following:

one	second	also	next	last of all
for one thing	third	another	moreover	finally
first of all	next	in addition	furthermore	

The paragraph about starting college uses a listing order: it lists three reasons why starting college at twenty-nine is not easy, and each of those three reasons is introduced by one of the above transitions. In the spaces below, write in the three transitions:

For one thing ______ Another ______ Finally ______

The first reason in the paragraph about starting college is introduced with *for one thing,* the second reason by *another,* and the third reason by *finally.*

Time Order: When a writer uses time order, supporting details are presented in the order in which they occurred. *First* this happened; *next* this; *after* that, this; and so on. Many paragraphs, especially paragraphs that tell a story or give a series of directions, are organized in a time order.

Transition words that show time relationships include the following:

first	before	after	when	then
next	during	now	while	until
as	soon	later	often	finally

Read the paragraph below, which is organized in time order. See if you can underline the six transition words that show the time relationships.

Della had a sad experience while driving home last night. She traveled along the dark, winding road that led toward her home. She was only two miles from her house when she noticed a glimmer of light in the road. The next thing she knew, she heard a sickening thud and realized she had struck an animal. The light, she realized, had been its eyes reflected in her car's headlights. Della stopped the car and ran back to see what she had hit. It was a handsome cocker spaniel, with blond fur and long ears. As she bent over the still form, she realized there was nothing to be done. The dog was dead. Della searched the dog for a collar and tags. There was nothing. Before leaving, she walked to several nearby houses, asking if anyone knew who owned the dog. No one did. Finally Della gave up and drove on. She was sad to leave someone's pet lying there alone.

The main point of the paragraph is stated in its first sentence: "Della had a sad experience while driving home last night." The support for this point is all the details of Della's experience. Those details are presented in the order in which they occurred. The time relationships are highlighted by these transitions: *while, when, next, as, before,* and *finally.*

More about Transitions: Transitions are words and phrases that indicate relationships between ideas. They are like signposts that guide travelers, showing them how to move smoothly from one spot to the next. Be sure to take advantage of transitions. They will help organize and connect your ideas, and they will help your readers follow the direction of your thoughts.

To see how transitions help, put a check beside the item in each pair that is easier to read and understand.

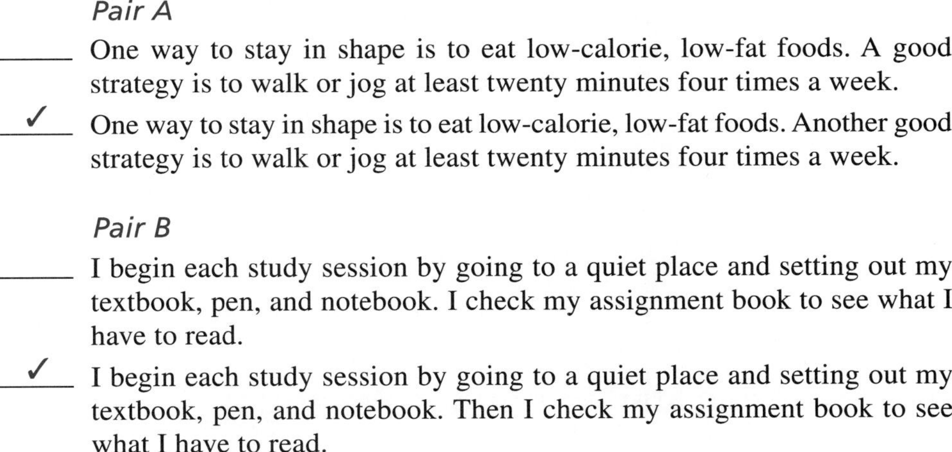

Pair A

_____ One way to stay in shape is to eat low-calorie, low-fat foods. A good strategy is to walk or jog at least twenty minutes four times a week.

__✓__ One way to stay in shape is to eat low-calorie, low-fat foods. Another good strategy is to walk or jog at least twenty minutes four times a week.

Pair B

_____ I begin each study session by going to a quiet place and setting out my textbook, pen, and notebook. I check my assignment book to see what I have to read.

__✓__ I begin each study session by going to a quiet place and setting out my textbook, pen, and notebook. Then I check my assignment book to see what I have to read.

In each pair, the second item is easier to read and understand. In pair A, the listing word *another* makes it clear that the writer is going on to a second way to stay in shape. In pair B, the time word *then* makes the relationship between the sentences clear. The writer first sets out the textbook and a pen and notebook and *then* checks an assignment book to see what to do.

Activities on pages 61–65 will give you practice in the use of listing order and time order, as well as transitions, to organize the supporting details of a paragraph.

Goal 4: Write Error-Free Sentences

If you use correct spelling and follow the rules of grammar, punctuation, and usage, your sentences will be clear and well written. But by no means must you have all that information in your head. Even the best of writers need to use reference materials to be sure their writing is correct. So when you write your papers, keep a good dictionary and grammar handbook nearby.

In general, however, save them for after you've gotten your ideas firmly down in writing. You'll see in the next part of this guide that Gary made a number of sentence errors as he worked on his paragraph. But he simply ignored them until he got to a later draft of his paper, when there would be time enough to make the needed corrections.

How Do You Reach the Goals of Effective Writing?

Even professional writers do not sit down and write a paper automatically, in one draft. Instead, they have to work on it a step at a time. Writing a paper is a process that can be divided into the following steps:

- *Step 1:* Getting Started through Prewriting
- *Step 2:* Preparing a Scratch Outline
- *Step 3:* Writing the First Draft
- *Step 4:* Revising
- *Step 5:* Editing and Proofreading

These steps are described on the following pages.

Step 1: Getting Started through Prewriting

What you need to learn first are strategies for working on a paper. These strategies will help you do the thinking needed to figure out both the point you want to make and the support you have for that point.

There are several *prewriting strategies*—strategies you use before writing the first draft of your paper:

- Freewriting
- Questioning
- Clustering
- Making a list

Freewriting: *Freewriting* is just sitting down and writing whatever comes into your mind about a topic. Do this for ten minutes or so. Write without stopping and without worrying at all about spelling, grammar, or the like. Simply get down on paper all the information about the topic that occurs to you.

Here is the freewriting Gary did on his problems with returning to school. Gary had been given the assignment "Write about a problem you are facing at the present time." Gary felt right away that he could write about his college situation. He began prewriting as a way to explore and generate details on his topic.

Example of Freewriting

One thing I want to write about is going back to school. At age twenty-nine. A lot to deal with. I sometimes wonder if Im nuts to try to do this or just stupid. I had to deal with my folks when I decided. My dad hated school. He knew when to quit, I'll say that for him. But he doesn't understand Im different. I have a right to my own life. And I want to better myself. He teases me alot. Says things like didnt you get dumped on enough in high school, why go back for more. My mom doesnt understand either. Just keeps worring about where the money was coming from. Then my friends. They make fun of me. Also my wife has to do more of the heavy house stuff because I'm out so much. Getting back to my friends, they say dumb things to get my goat. Like calling me the college man or saying ooh, we'd better watch our grammer. Sometimes I think my dads right, school was no fun for me. Spent years just sitting in class waiting for final bell so I could escape. Teachers didnt help me or take an intrest, some of them made me feel like a real loser. Now things are different and I like most of my teachers. I can talk to the teacher after class or to ask questions if I'm confused. But I really need more time to spend with family, I hardly see them any more. What I am doing is hard all round for them and me.

Notice that there are problems with spelling, grammar, and punctuation in Gary's freewriting. Gary is not worried about such matters, nor should he be. He is just concentrating on getting ideas and details down on paper. He knows that it is best to focus on one thing at a time. At this stage, he just wants to write out thoughts as they come to him, to do some thinking on paper.

You should take the same approach when freewriting: explore your topic without worrying at all about being "correct." Figuring out what you want to say should have all your attention in this early stage of the writing process.

Questioning: *Questioning* means that you think about your topic by writing down a series of questions and answers about it. Your questions can start with words like *what, when, where, why,* and *how.*

Here are some questions that Gary might have asked while developing his paper, as well as some answers to those questions.

Example of Questioning

Why do I have a problem with returning to school? My parents and friends don't support me.

How do they not support me? Dad asks why I want to be dumped on more. Mom is upset because college costs lots of money. Friends tease me about being a college man.

When do they not support me? When I go to my parents' home for Friday night visits, when my friends see me walking toward them.

Where do I have this problem? At home, where I barely see my wife and daughter before having to go to class, and where I have to let my wife do house things on weekends while I'm studying.

Why else do I have this problem? High school was bad experience.

What details back up the idea that high school was bad experience? Sat in class bored, couldn't wait to get out, teachers didn't help me. One embarrassed me when I didn't know the answer.

Clustering: Clustering is another prewriting strategy that can be used to generate material for a paper. It is helpful for people who like to do their thinking in a visual way.

In *clustering*, you begin by stating your subject in a few words in the center of a blank sheet of paper. Then as ideas come to you, put them in ovals, boxes, or circles around the subject, and draw lines to connect them to the subject. Put minor ideas or details in smaller boxes or circles, and also use connecting lines to show how they relate.

Keep in mind that there is no right or wrong way of clustering. It is a way to think on paper about how various ideas and details relate to one another. Below is an example of clustering that Gary might have done to develop his idea.

Example of Clustering

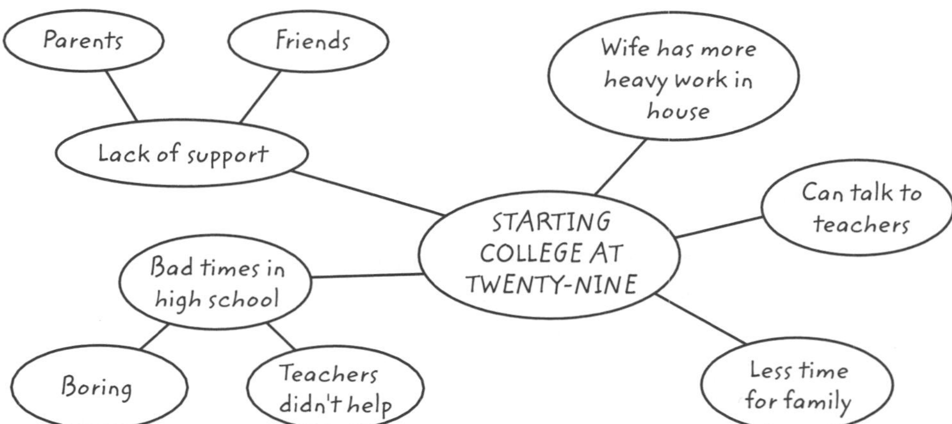

Making a List: In *making a list*—a prewriting strategy also known as *listing, list making,* and *brainstorming*—you make a list of ideas and details that could go into your paper. Simply pile these items up, one after another, without worrying about putting them in any special order. Try to accumulate as many details as you can think of.

After Gary did his freewriting about returning to school, he made up the list of details shown below.

Example of Listing

parents give me hard time when they see me
Dad hated school
Dad quit school after eighth grade
Dad says I was dumped on enough in high school
Dad asks why I want to go back for more
Mom also doesnt understand
keeps asking how Ill pay for it
friends give me a hard time too
friends call me college man
say they have to watch their grammar
my wife has more heavy work around the house
also high school had been no fun for me
just sat in class after class
couldnt wait for final bell to ring
wanted to escape
teachers didnt help me
teachers didnt take an interest in me
one called on me, then told me to forget it
I felt like a real loser
I didnt want to go back to his class
now I'm more sure of myself
OK not to know an answer
talk to teachers after class
job plus schoolwork take all my time
get home late, then rush through dinner
then spend evening studying
even have to do homework on weekends

One detail led to another as Gary expanded his list. Slowly but surely, more supporting material emerged that he could use in developing his paper. By the time he had finished his list, he was ready to plan an outline of his paragraph and to write his first draft.

Notice that in making a list, as in freewriting, details are included that will not actually end up in the final paragraph. Gary decided later not to develop the idea that his wife now has more heavy work to do in the house. And he realized that several of his details were about why school is easier in college ("now I'm more sure of myself," "OK not to know an answer," and "talk to instructors after class"); such details were not relevant to his point.

It is natural for a number of such extra or unrelated details to appear as part of the prewriting process. The goal of prewriting is to get a lot of information down on paper. You can then add to, shape, and subtract from your raw material as you take your paper through the series of writing drafts.

Important Points about Prewriting Strategies: Some writers may use only one of the prewriting strategies described here. Others may use bits and pieces of all four strategies. Any one strategy can lead to another. Freewriting may lead to questioning or clustering, which may then lead to a list. Or a writer may start with a list and then use freewriting or questioning to develop items on the list. During this early stage of the writing process, as you do your thinking on paper, anything goes. You should not expect a straight-line progression from the beginning to the end of your paper. Instead, there probably will be a constant moving back and forth as you work to discover your point and decide just how you will develop it.

Keep in mind that prewriting can also help you choose from among several topics. Gary might not have been so sure about which problem to write about. Then he could have made a list of possible topics—areas in his life in which he has had problems. After selecting two or three topics from the list, he could have done some prewriting on each to see which seemed most promising. After finding a likely topic, Gary would have continued with his prewriting activities until he had a solid main point and plenty of support.

Finally, remember that you are not ready to begin writing a paper until you know your main point and many of the details that can be used to support it. Don't rush through prewriting. It's better to spend more time on this stage than to waste time writing a paragraph for which you have no solid point and not enough interesting support.

Step 2: Preparing a Scratch Outline

A *scratch outline* is a brief plan for a paragraph. It shows at a glance the point of the paragraph and the main support for that point. It is the logical backbone on which the paper is built.

This rough outline often follows freewriting, questioning, clustering, or listing—or all four. Or it may gradually emerge in the midst of these strategies. In fact, trying to outline is a good way to see if you need to do more prewriting. If a solid outline does not emerge, then you know you need to do more prewriting to clarify your main point or its support. Once you have a workable outline, you may realize, for instance, that you want to do more listing to develop one of the supporting details in the outline.

In Gary's case, as he was working on his list of details, he suddenly discovered what the plan of his paragraph could be. He went back to the list, crossed out items that he now realized did not fit, and added the following comments.

Example of List with Comments

Starting college at twenty-nine isn't easy—three reasons

parents give me hard time when they see me
Dad hated school
Dad quit school after eighth grade
Dad says I was dumped on enough in high school
Dad asks why I want to go back for more
Mom also doesnt understand
keeps asking how Ill pay for it
friends give me a hard time too
friends call me college man
say they have to watch their grammar

Parents and friends don't support me

~~my wife has more heavy work around the house~~
also high school had been no fun for me
just sat in class after class
couldnt wait for final bell to ring
wanted to escape
teachers didnt help me
teachers didnt take an interest in me
one called on me, then told me to forget it
I felt like a real loser
I didnt want to go back to his class

Bad memories of school

~~now I'm more sure of myself~~
~~OK not to know an answer~~
~~talk to teachers after class~~
job plus schoolwork take all my time
get home late, then rush through dinner
then spend evening studying
even have to do homework on weekends

Not enough time with family

Under the list, Gary was now able to prepare his scratch outline:

Example of Scratch Outline

Starting college at age twenty-nine isn't easy.

1. Little support from parents or friends
2. Bad memories of school
3. Not enough time to spend with family

After all his preliminary writing, Gary sat back, pleased. He knew he had a promising paper—one with a clear point and solid support. Gary was now ready to write the first draft of his paper, using his outline as a guide.

Step 3: Writing the First Draft

When you write your first draft, be prepared to put in additional thoughts and details that didn't emerge in your prewriting. And don't worry if you hit a snag. Just leave a blank space or add a comment such as "Do later" and press on to finish the paper. Also, don't worry yet about grammar, punctuation, or spelling. You don't want to take time correcting words or sentences that you may decide to remove later. Instead, make it your goal to develop the content of your paper with plenty of specific details.

Here is Gary's first draft:

First Draft

Last fall, I finaly realized that I was stuck in a dead-end job. I wasnt making enough money and I was bored to tears. I figured I had to get some new skills which meant going back to school. Beginning college at age twenty-nine turned out to be much tougher than I thought it would be. My father didnt understand, he hated school. That's why he quit after eighth grade. He would ask, Didnt you get dumped on enough in high school? Then wondered why I wanted to go back for more of the same thing. My mother was worried about where the money were coming from and said so. When my friends saw me coming down the st. They would make fun of me with remarks like Hey theres the college man. They may have a point. School never was much fun for me. I spent years just siting in class waiting for the bell to ring. So I could escape. The teachers werent much help to me. One time, a teacher called on me then told me to forget it. I felt like a real loser and didnt want to go back to his class. College takes time away from my family. ADD MORE DETAILS LATER. All this makes it very hard for me.

After Gary finished the draft, he was able to put it aside until the next day. You will benefit as well if you can allow some time between finishing a draft and starting to revise.

Step 4: Revising

Revising is as much a stage in the writing process as prewriting, outlining, and writing a first draft. *Revising* means rewriting a paper, building on what has been done, to make it stronger. One writer has said about revision, "It's like cleaning house—getting rid of all the junk and putting things in the right order." It is not just "straightening up"; instead, you must be ready to roll up your sleeves and do whatever is needed to create an effective paper. Too many students think that the first draft *is* the paper. They start to become writers when they realize that revising a rough draft three or four times is often at the heart of the writing process.

Here are some quick hints that can help make revision easier:

- Ideally, set your first draft aside for a while. A few hours is fine, but a day or two is best. You can then come back with a fresh, more objective point of view.
- Work from typed or printed text. You'll be able to see the paper more impartially in this way than if you were just looking at your own familiar handwriting.
- Read your draft aloud. Hearing how your writing sounds will help you pick up problems with meaning as well as style.
- As you do all these things, add your thoughts and changes above the lines or in the margins of your paper. Your written comments can serve as a guide when you work on the next draft.

Here is Gary's second draft.

Second Draft

Starting college at age twenty-nine turned out to be really tough. I did not have much support from my parents and friends. My father hated school, so he asked, Didnt you get dumped on enough in high school? Why go back for more? My mother asking about where the money were coming from. Friends would be making fun of me. Hey theres the college man they would say as soon as they saw me. Another factor was what happened to me in high school. I spent years just siting in class waiting for the bell to ring. I was really bored. Also the teachers liked to embaras me. One teacher called on me and then said forget it. He must of relized I didnt know the answer. I felt like a real loser and didnt want to go back in his class for weeks. Finally I've learned that college takes time away from my family. I have to go to work every day. I have a little over one hour to eat dinner and spend time with my wife and daughter. Then I have to go off to class and when I get back my daughter is in bed asleep. My wife and I have only a little time together. On weekends I have lots of homework to do, so the time goes by like a shot. College is hard for me, but I am going to stay there so I can have a better life.

Notice the improvements made in the second draft:

- Gary started by clearly stating the point of his paragraph. He remembered the first goal in effecitve writing: *Make a point.*
- He omitted the detail about his father quitting school to keep the focus on his own difficulties. He remembered that the first goal in effective writing is also to *stick to one point,* so the paper will have unity.
- He added more details so that he would have enough support for his reasons why college was hard. He remembered the second goal in effective writing: *Support the point.*
- He inserted transitions to set off the second reason ("Another factor") and third reason ("Finally") why starting college at twenty-nine was difficult for him. He remembered the third goal in effective writing: *Organize the support.*

Gary then went on to revise the second draft. Since he was doing the paper on a computer, he was able to print it out quickly. He double-spaced the lines, allowing room for revisions, which he added in longhand during his third draft. (Note that if you are not using a computer, you may want to do each draft on one side of a page, so that you see your entire paper at one time.) Shown below are some of the changes that Gary made in longhand as he worked on his third draft.

Part of Third Draft

was difficult.
Starting college at age twenty-nine ~~turned out to be really tough.~~
For one thing
I did not have much support from my parents and friends. My father ~~hated~~
~~school, so he~~ asked, Didnt you get dumped on enough in high school? Why
woried
go back for more? My mother ~~asking~~ about where the money were coming
make
from. Friends would ~~be making~~ fun of me. Hey theres the college man they
reason that starting college was hard
would say as soon as they saw me. Another ~~factor~~ was what happened to
final
me in high school. I spent years just siting in class waiting for the bell to ring.
I was really bored. Also the teachers liked to embaras me. . . .

After writing these and other changes, Gary typed them into his computer file and printed out the almost-final draft of his paper. He knew he had come to the fourth goal in effective writing: *aim for error-free sentences.*

Step 5: Editing and Proofreading

The next-to-last major stage in the writing process is *editing*—checking a paper for mistakes in grammar, punctuation, usage, and spelling. Students often find it hard to edit a paper carefully. They have put so much work into their writing, or so little, that it's almost painful for them to look at the paper one more time. You may simply have to *will* yourself to carry out this important closing step in the writing process. Remember that eliminating sentence-skills mistakes will improve an average paper and help ensure a strong grade on a good paper. Further, as you get into the habit of checking your papers, you will also get into the habit of using sentence skills consistently. They are an integral part of clear, effective writing.

The checklist of sentence skills on the inside back cover of the book will serve as a guide while you are editing your paper.

Here are hints that can help you edit the next-to-final draft of a paper for sentence-skills mistakes:

Editing Hints

1 Have at hand two essential tools: a good dictionary (see page 339) and a grammar handbook (you can use Part Two of this book).

2 Use a sheet of paper to cover your essay so that you can expose only one sentence at a time. Look for errors in grammar, spelling, and typing. It may help to read each sentence out loud. If the sentence does not read clearly and smoothly, chances are something is wrong.

3 Pay special attention to the kinds of errors you tend to make. For example, if you tend to write run-ons or fragments, be especially on the lookout for these errors.

4 Try to work on a typewritten or word-processed draft, where you'll be able to see your writing more objectively than you can on a handwritten page; use a pen with colored ink so that your corrections will stand out.

Shown below are some of the corrections in spelling, grammar, and punctuation that Gary made when editing his paper.

Part of Gary's Edited Draft

Starting college at age twenty-nine was difficult. For one thing, I did not have much support from my parents and friends. My father asked, "Didn't you get dumped on enough in high school? Why go back for more?" My mother ~~woried~~ worried about where the money ~~were~~ was coming from. Friends would make fun of me. "Hey, there's the college man" they would say as soon as they saw me. . . .

All that remained for Gary to do was to enter in his corrections, print out the final draft of the paper, and proofread it (see below for hints on proofreading) for any typos or other careless errors. He was then ready to hand the paper in to his instructor.

Proofreading, the final stage in the writing process, means checking a paper carefully for spelling, grammar, punctuation, and other errors. You are ready for this stage when you are satisfied with your choice of supporting details, the order in which they are presented, and the way they and your topic sentence are worded.

At this point in his work, Gary used his dictionary to do final checks on his spelling. He used a grammar handbook (such as the one in Part Two of this text) to be sure about grammar, punctuation, and usage. Gary also read through his paper carefully, looking for typing errors, omitted words, and any other errors he may have missed before. Proofreading is often hard to do—again, students have spent so much time with their work, or so little, that they want to avoid it. But if it is done carefully, this important final step will ensure that your paper looks as good as possible.

Proofreading Hints

1. One helpful trick at this stage is to read your paper out loud. You will probably hear awkward wordings and become aware of spots where the punctuation needs to be improved. Make the changes needed for your sentences to read smoothly and clearly.
2. Another helpful technique is to take a sheet of paper and cover your paragraph so that you can expose just one line at a time and check it carefully.
3. A third strategy is to read your paper backward, from the last sentence to the first. This helps keep you from getting caught up in the flow of the paper and missing small mistakes—which is easy to do, since you're so familiar with what you mean to say.

What Is an Essay?

An essay does the same thing a paragraph does: it starts with a point, and the rest of it provides specific details to support and develop that point. However, a paragraph is a series of *sentences* about one main idea or point, while an *essay* is a series of *paragraphs* about one main idea or point—called the *central idea.* Since an essay is much longer than one paragraph, it allows a writer to develop a topic in more detail. Despite the greater length of an essay, the process of writing it is the same as that for writing a paragraph: prewriting, preparing a scratch outline, writing and revising drafts, editing, and proofreading.

Here are the major differences between a paragraph and an essay:

Paragraph	*Essay*
Made up of sentences.	Made up of paragraphs.
Starts with a sentence containing the main point (topic sentence).	Starts with an introductory paragraph containing the central idea, expressed in a sentence called the *thesis statement* (or *thesis sentence*).
Body of paragraph contains specific details that support and develop the topic sentence.	Body of essay contains paragraphs that support and develop the central idea. Each of these paragraphs has its own main supporting point, stated in a topic sentence.
Paragraph often ends with a closing sentence that rounds it off.	Essay ends with a concluding paragraph that rounds it off.

Later in his writing course, Gary was asked to expand his paragraph into an essay. Here is the essay that resulted:

For a typical college freshman, entering college is fun, and an exciting time of life. It is a time not just to explore new ideas in classes but to lounge on the grass chatting with new friends, to sit having soda and pizza in the cafeteria, or to listen to music and play cards in the student lounge. I see the crowds of eighteen-year-olds enjoying all that college has to offer, and I sometimes envy them their freedom. Instead of being a typical freshman, I am twenty-nine years old, and beginning college has been a difficult experience for me. I have had to deal with lack of support, bad memories of past school experiences, and too little time for my family.

Few people in my life support my decision to enter college. My father is especially bewildered by the choice I have made. He himself quit school after finishing eighth grade, and he assumes that I should hate school as much as he did. "Didn't you get dumped on enough in high school?" he asks me. "Why go back for more?" My mother is a little more understanding of my desire for an education, but the cost of college terrifies her. She has always believed that college was a privilege only the rich could afford. "Where in the world will all that money come from?" she says. And my friends seem threatened by my decision. They make fun of me, suggesting that I'm going to think I'm too good to hang around with the likes of them. "Ooooh, here comes the college man," they say when they see me approach. "We'd better watch our grammar."

I have had to deal not only with family and friends but with unhappy memories of my earlier school career. I attended an enormous high school where I was just one more faceless kid in the crowd. My classes seemed meaningless to me. I can remember almost none of them in any detail. What I do remember about high school was just sitting, bored, until I felt nearly brain-dead, watching the clock hands move ever so slowly toward dismissal time. Such periods of boredom were occasionally interrupted by moments of acute embarrassment. Once an algebra teacher called on me and then said, "Oh, forget it, Callahan," in disgusted tones when he realized I didn't know the answer. My response, of course, was to shrink down in my chair and try to become invisible for the rest of the semester.

Furthermore, my decision to enter college has meant I have much less time to spend with my family. I work eight hours a day. Then I rush home and have all of an hour and ten minutes to eat dinner and spend time with my wife and daughter before I rush off again, this time to class. When I return from class, I am dead tired. My little girl is already asleep. My wife and I have only a little time to talk together before I collapse into bed. Weekends are a little better, but not much. That's when I try to get my papers written and catch up on a few chores around the house. My wife tries to be understanding, but it's hard on her to have so little support from me these days. And I'm missing out on a lot of special times in my daughter's life. For instance, I didn't realize she had begun to walk until three days after it happened.

So why do I put myself and my family through all these difficulties? Sometimes I'm not sure myself. But then I look at my little girl sleeping, and I think about the kind of life I am going to be able to give her. My college degree may make it possible for me to get a job that is more rewarding, both financially and emotionally. I believe I will be a better provider for my family, as well as a more well-rounded human being. I hope that the rewards of a college degree will eventually outweigh the problems I am experiencing now.

What Are the Parts of an Essay?

When Gary decided to expand his paragraph into an essay, he knew he would need to write an introductory paragraph, several supporting paragraphs, and a concluding paragraph.

Each of these parts of the essay is explained below.

Introductory Paragraph

A well-written introductory paragraph will often do the following.

1 **Gain the reader's interest.** On pages 29–31 are several time-tested methods used to draw the reader into an essay.

2 **Present the thesis statement.** The thesis statement expresses the central idea of an essay, just as a topic sentence states the main idea of a paragraph. Here's an example of a thesis statement.

A vacation at home can be wonderful.

An essay with this thesis statement would go on to explain some positive things about vacationing at home.

What is the thesis statement in Gary's essay? Find that statement on page 27 and write it here:

. . . beginning college has been a difficult experience for me.

You should have written down the next-to-the-last sentence in the introductory paragraph of Gary's essay.

3 **Lay out a plan of development.** A *plan of development* is a brief statement of the main supporting details for the central idea. These supporting details should be presented in the order in which they will be discussed in the essay. The plan of development can be blended into the thesis statement or presented separately.

Blended into a thesis statement: A vacation at home can be wonderful because you can avoid the hassles of travel, make use of your knowledge of the area, and indulge in special activities.

Presented separately: A vacation at home can be wonderful. At home you can avoid the hassles of travel, make use of your knowledge of the area, and indulge in special activities.

Note that some essays lend themselves better to a plan of development than others do. At the least, your introductory paragraph should gain the reader's interest and present the thesis statement.

What is the plan of development in Gary's essay? Find the sentence on page 27 that states Gary's plan of development and write it here:

I have had to deal with lack of support, bad memories . . . and too little time for my family.

You should have written down the last sentence in the introductory paragraph of Gary's essay.

Four Common Methods of Introduction

1 **Begin with a broad statement and narrow it down to your thesis statement.** A broad statement can capture your reader's interest while introducing your general topic. It may provide useful background material as well. The writer

of the introductory paragraph below begins with a broad statement about her possessions. She then narrows the focus down to the three possessions that are the specific topic of the paper.

I have many possessions that I would be sad to lose. Because I love to cook, I would miss several kitchen appliances that provide me with so many happy cooking adventures. I would also miss the wonderful electronic equipment that entertains me every day, including my large-screen television set and my VCR. I would miss the two telephones on which I have spent many interesting hours chatting in every part of my apartment, including the bathtub. But if my apartment were burning down, I would most want to rescue three things that are irreplaceable and hold great meaning for me—the silverware set that belonged to my grandmother, my mother's wedding gown, and my giant photo album.

2 **Present an idea or situation that is the opposite of what you will be writing about.** One way to gain the reader's interest is to show the difference between your opening idea or situation and the one to be discussed in the essay.

The role of computers in schools is constantly growing. Such growth is based on a widespread faith that computers can answer many of the learning needs of our students. Many people believe that it is just a matter of time before computers do all but take the place of human teachers. However, educators should be cautious about introducing computers into curriculums. Computers may interfere with the learning of critical language skills, they may move too fast for students to digest new concepts, and they are poor substitutes for certain real-world experiences.

3 **Tell a brief story.** An interesting incident or anecdote is hard for a reader to resist. In an introduction, a story should be no more than a few sentences, and it should relate meaningfully to—and so lead the reader toward—your central idea. The story you tell can be an experience of your own, of someone you know, or of someone you have read about. For instance, in the following introduction, the author tells a simple personal story that serves as background for his central idea.

I remember the September morning that I first laid eyes on Jill. I'd been calling clients at my desk at work when I heard a warm, musical laugh. There was something so attractive about the sound that I got up to get a cup of coffee and to find the source of that laugh. I discovered the voice to be that of a young, auburn-haired woman we had just hired from a temporary agency. Soon after that, Jill and I began going out, and we spent the next two years together. Only recently have we decided to break up because of disagreements about finances, about children, and about our relationship with her family.

4 Ask one or more questions. The questions may be those you intend to answer in your essay, or they may show that your topic relates directly to readers. In the following example, the questions are designed to gain readers' interest and convince them that the essay applies to them.

> Does your will to study collapse when someone suggests getting a pizza? Does your social life compete with your class attendance? Is there a huge gap between your intentions and your actions? If the answers to these questions are yes, yes, and yes, read on. You can benefit from some powerful ways to motivate yourself: setting goals and consciously working to reach them, using rational thinking, and developing a positive personality.

Which of these four methods of introduction does Gary use in his essay?

method 2

Gary begins with an idea that is the opposite of what he is writing about. His essay is about his difficulties with college life, but he begins with the idea that college "is fun, and an exciting time" for some students.

Supporting Paragraphs

The traditional college essay has three supporting paragraphs. But some essays will have two supporting paragraphs, and others will have four or more. Each supporting paragraph should have its own topic sentence, stating the point to be developed in that paragraph.

Notice that each of the supporting paragraphs in Gary's essay has its own topic sentence. For example, the topic sentence of his first supporting paragraph is "Few people in my life support my decision to enter college."

What is the topic sentence of Gary's second supporting paragraph?

I have had to deal . . . with unhappy memories of my earlier school career.

What is the topic sentence of Gary's third supporting paragraph?

Furthermore, . . . I have much less time to spend with my family.

In each case, Gary's topic sentence is the first sentence of the paragraph.

Concluding Paragraph

An essay that ended with its final supporting paragraph would probably leave the reader wondering if the author was really done. A concluding paragraph is needed for a sense of completion. Here are two common methods of conclusion.

Two Common Methods of Conclusion

1 **Provide a summary and a final thought.** Using wording different from your introduction, restate your thesis and main supporting points. This review gives readers an overview of your essay and helps them remember what they've read. A final thought signals the end of the paper, as in the following concluding paragraph from an essay about personal possessions.

> If my home ever really did burn down, I would hope to be able to rescue some of the physical things that so meaningfully represent my past. My grandmother's silver set is a reminder of the grandparents who enriched my childhood, my mother's wedding gown is a glamorous souvenir of two important weddings, and my photo album is a rich storage bin of family and personal history. I would hate to lose them. However, if I did, I would take comfort in the fact that the most important storage place for family and personal memories is my own mind.

2 **Focus on the future.** Focusing on the future often involves making a prediction or a recommendation. This method of conclusion may refer in a general way to the central idea, or it may include a summary. The following conclusion from an essay about self-motivation combines a summary with a prediction. The prediction adds further support for the central idea.

> So get your willpower in gear, and use the three keys to self-motivation—set goals and work to reach them, think rationally, and develop a positive personality. You will find that a firm commitment to this approach becomes easier and easier. Progress will come more often and more readily, strengthening your resolve even further.

What kind of conclusion does Gary use in his essay?

method 2

In his conclusion, Gary refers to his central idea in the context of the future. He makes hopeful points about what his and his family's life will be like after he gets a college degree.

How Can a Computer Help?

If you don't yet write on a computer, it's time to start. In today's world, word processing is an essential mechanical skill, just as effective writing is a vital communication skill.

The computer can be a real aid in the writing process. You can quickly add or delete anything, from a word to an entire section. You can "cut" material and "paste" it elsewhere in seconds. A word-processing program makes it easy to set margins, space lines, and number pages. It can also help you check your spelling, your grammar, and to some extent your style. And at any point during your work, you can print out one or more copies of your text.

Word processing is not hard to learn. Just as you don't need to know how a car works to drive one, you don't need to understand how a computer functions to use it. Once you have learned a few simple keystrokes, you can begin. You do not even need to own your own computer. Nearly every college has at least one computer center, complete with rows of computers and staff members to provide assistance. Free classes in word processing may be available as well.

Tips on Using a Computer

- If you are using your school's computer center, allow enough time. You may have to wait for a computer or printer to be free. In addition, you may need several sessions at the computer and printer to complete your paper.
- Every word-processing program allows you to "save" your writing by hitting one or more keys. Save your work frequently as you work on a draft. Work that is saved is preserved by the computer. Work that is not saved is lost when the file you are working on is closed or when the computer is turned off—or if there's a power or system failure.
- Keep your work in two places—the hard drive or disk you are working on and a backup disk. At the end of each session with the computer, copy your work onto the backup disk. Then if the hard drive or working disk becomes damaged, you'll have the backup copy.
- Print out your work at least at the end of every session. Then not only will you have your most recent draft to work on away from the computer; you'll also have a copy in case something should happen to your disks.
- Work in single spacing so that you can see as much of your writing on the screen at one time as possible. Just before you print out your work, change to double spacing.
- Before making major changes in a paper, create a copy of your file. For example, if your file is titled "Worst Job," create a file called "Worst Job 2." Then make all your changes in that new file. If the changes don't work out, you can always go back to the original file.

Using a Computer at Each Stage of the Writing Process

Following are some ways to make word processing a part of your writing.

Prewriting

If you're a fast typist, many kinds of prewriting will go well on the computer. With freewriting in particular, you can get ideas onto the screen almost as quickly as they occur to you. A passing thought that could be productive is not likely to get lost. You may even find it helpful, when freewriting, to dim the screen of your monitor so that you can't see what you're typing. If you temporarily can't see the screen, you won't have to worry about grammar or spelling or typing errors (all of which do not matter in prewriting); instead, you can concentrate on getting down as many ideas and details as possible about your subject.

After any initial freewriting, questioning, and list-making on a computer, it's often very helpful to print out a hard copy of what you've done. With a clean printout in front of you, you'll be able to see everything at once and revise and expand your work with handwritten comments in the margins of the paper.

Word processing also makes it easy for you to experiment with the wording of the point of your paper. You can try a number of versions in a short time. After you have decided on the version that works best, you can easily delete the other versions—or simply move them to a temporary "leftover" section at the end of the paper.

Preparing a Scratch Outline

If you have prepared a list of items during prewriting, you may be able to turn that list into an outline right on the screen. Delete the ideas you feel should not be in your paper (saving them at the end of the file in case you change your mind), and add any new ideas that occur to you. Then use the cut and paste functions to shuffle the supporting ideas around until you find the best order for your paper.

Writing Your First Draft

Like many writers, you may want to write out your first draft by hand and then type it into the computer for revision. Even as you type your handwritten draft, you may find yourself making some changes and improvements. And once you have a draft on the screen, or printed out, you will find it much easier to revise than a handwritten one.

If you feel comfortable composing directly on the screen, you can benefit from the computer's special features. For example, if you have written an anecdote in your freewriting that you plan to use in your paper, simply copy the story from your freewriting file and insert it where it fits in your paper. You can refine it then or later. Or if you discover while typing that a sentence is out of place, cut it out from where it is and paste it wherever you wish. And if while writing you realize that an earlier sentence can be expanded, just move your cursor back to that point and type in the added material.

Revising

It is during revision that the virtues of word processing really shine. All substituting, adding, deleting, and rearranging can be done easily within an existing file. All changes instantly take their proper places within the paper, not scribbled above the line or squeezed into the margin. You can concentrate on each change you want to make, because you never have to type from scratch or work on a messy draft. You can carefully go through your paper to check that all your supporting evidence is relevant and to add new support as needed here and there. Anything you decide to eliminate can be deleted in a keystroke. Anything you add can be inserted precisely where you choose. If you change your mind, all you have to do is delete or cut and paste. Then you can sweep through the paper, focusing on other changes, such as improving word choice, increasing sentence variety, eliminating wordiness, and so on.

If you are like many students, you will find it convenient to print out a hard copy of your file at various points throughout the revision. You can then revise in longhand—adding, crossing out, and indicating changes—and later quickly make these changes in the document.

Editing and Proofreading

Editing and proofreading also benefit richly from word processing. Instead of crossing or whiting out mistakes, or rewriting an entire paper to correct numerous errors, you can make all necessary changes within the most recent draft. If you find editing or proofreading on the screen hard on your eyes, print out a copy. Mark any corrections on that copy, and then transfer them to the final draft.

If the word-processing package you're using includes spelling and grammar checks, by all means use them. The spell-check function tells you when a word is not in the computer's dictionary. Keep in mind, however, that the spell-check cannot tell you how to spell a name correctly or when you have mistakenly used, for example, *their* instead of *there*. To a spell-check, *Thank ewe four the complement* is as correct as *Thank you for the compliment*. Also, use the grammar check with caution. Any errors it doesn't uncover are still your responsibility.

A word-processed paper, with its clean look and handsome formatting, looks so good that you may feel it is in better shape than it really is. Do not be fooled by your paper's appearance. Take sufficient time to review your grammar, punctuation, and spelling carefully.

Even after you hand in your paper, save the computer file. Your instructor may ask you to do some revising, and then the file will save you from having to type the paper from scratch.

Chapter Review

Answer each of the following questions by filling in the blank or circling the answer you think is correct.

1. *True or false?* ___T___ Writing is a skill that anyone can learn with practice.
2. An effective paragraph or essay is one that
   a. makes a point.
   b. provides specific support.
   (c.) makes a point and provides specific support.
   d. none of the above.
3. The sentence that states the main idea of a paragraph is known as the ___topic___ sentence; the sentence that states the central idea of an essay is known as the ___thesis___ statement.
4. Prewriting can help a writer find
   a. a good topic to write about.
   b. a good main point to make about the topic.
   c. enough details to support the main point.
   (d.) all of the above.
5. One step that everyone should use at some stage of the writing process is to prepare a plan for the paragraph or essay known as a(n) ___scratch outline___.
6. When you start writing, your first concern should be
   a. spelling.
   (b.) content.
   c. grammar.
   d. punctuation.
7. Two common ways of organizing a paragraph are ___listing___ order and ___time___ order.

8. A thesis statement
   a. is generally part of an essay's introduction.
   b. states the central idea of the essay.
   c. can be followed by the essay's plan of development.
   (d.) all of the above.
9. The words *first, next, then, also, another,* and *finally* are examples of signal words, commonly known as transitions.
10. A computer can help a writer
   a. turn a list into an outline.
   b. find just the right words to express a point.
   c. add and delete supporting evidence.
   (d.) all of the above.

Preview: A Look Ahead

Chapter 3 provides a series of activities to help you master three of the four goals of effective writing: (1) making a point, (2) supporting the point with specific details, and (3) organizing the support. Part Two of this book and a dictionary will help you with the fourth goal—writing error-free sentences. Part Three provides various tests to reinforce the sentence skills studied in Part Two. Part Four of the book presents ten reading selections that will develop both your reading and writing skills.

3 Practice in Effective Writing

The following series of activities will strengthen your understanding of the writing guidelines presented in Chapter 2. Through practice, you will gain a better sense of the goals of effective writing and how to reach those goals. You will also help prepare yourself for the writing assignments that follow the activities.

Your instructor may ask you to do the entire series of activities or may select the activities that are most suited to your particular needs.

1 Understanding General versus Specific Ideas

A paragraph is made up of a main idea, which is general, and the specific ideas that support it. So to write well, you must understand the difference between general and specific ideas.

It is helpful to realize that you use general and specific ideas all the time in your everyday life. For example, in choosing a video to rent, you may think, "Which should I rent, an action movie, a comedy, or a romance?" In such a case, *video* is the general idea, and *action movie, comedy,* and *romance* are the specific ideas.

Or you may decide to begin an exercise program. In that case, you might consider walking, jumping rope, or lifting weights. In this case, *exercise* is the general idea, and *walking, jumping rope,* and *lifting weights* are the specific ideas.

Or if you are talking to a friend about a date that didn't work out well, you may say, "The dinner was terrible, the car broke down, and we had little to say to each other." In this case, the general idea is *the date didn't work out well,* and the specific ideas are the three reasons you named.

The four activities here will give you experience in recognizing the relationship between general and specific. They will also provide a helpful background for all the information and activities that follow.

Activity 1

Each group of words consists of one general idea and four specific ideas. The general idea includes all the specific ideas. Underline the general idea in each group.

Example jeep van truck vehicle sedan

1. salty bitter flavor sweet sour
2. jewelry necklace ring earrings bracelet
3. dime nickel coin quarter half-dollar
4. fax machine copier computer calculator office machine
5. theft murder rape crime holdup
6. cracker snack carrot stick cookie popcorn
7. mascara cosmetic foundation lipstick eyeshadow
8. yes no I don't know answer maybe
9. yard work mowing planting trimming hedges feeding plants
10. job interviews weddings car accidents being fired stressful times

Activity 2

In each item below, one idea is general and the others are specific. The general idea includes the specific ones. In the spaces provided, write in two more specific ideas that are covered by the general idea.

Example *General:* exercises
Specific: chin-ups, jumping jacks, sit-ups, push-ups

Answers will vary. Some possibilities are shown.

1. *General:* pizza toppings
   Specific: sausage, mushrooms, pepperoni, green peppers
2. *General:* furniture
   Specific: rocking chair, coffee table, bed, desk
3. *General:* magazines
   Specific: Reader's Digest, Newsweek, Time, TV Guide
4. *General:* birds
   Specific: eagle, pigeon, sparrow, cardinal
5. *General:* types of music
   Specific: jazz, classical, folk, country and western

6. *General:* cold symptoms
   Specific: aching muscles, watery eyes, headache, sore throat
7. *General:* children's games
   Specific: hopscotch, dodgeball, tag, hide and seek
8. *General:* transportation
   Specific: plane, motorcycle, train, bus
9. *General:* city problems
   Specific: overcrowding, pollution, noise, crime
10. *General:* types of TV shows
    Specific: cartoons, situation comedies, soap operas, talk shows

Activity 3

Read each group of specific ideas below. Then circle the letter of the general idea that tells what the specific ideas have in common. Note that the general idea should not be too broad or too narrow. Begin by trying the example item, and then read the explanation that follows.

Example *Specific ideas:* peeling potatoes, washing dishes, cracking eggs, cleaning out refrigerator

The general idea is

a. household jobs.
(b.) kitchen tasks.
c. steps in making dinner.

Explanation: It is true that the specific ideas are all household jobs, but they have in common something even more specific—they are all tasks done in the kitchen. Therefore answer *a* is too broad, and the correct answer is *b.* Answer *c* is too narrow because it doesn't cover all the specific ideas. While two of them could be steps in making a dinner ("peeling potatoes" and "cracking eggs"), two have nothing to do with making dinner.

1. *Specific ideas:* crowded office, rude co-workers, demanding boss, unreasonable deadlines

   The general idea is:

   a. problems.
   (b.) work problems.
   c. problems with work schedules.

2. *Specific ideas:* cactus, rosebush, fern, daisy

   The general idea is:

   a. plants.
   b. plants that have thorns.
   c. plants that grow in the desert.

3. *Specific ideas:* Band-Aids, gauze, smelling salts, aspirin

   The general idea is:

   a. supplies.
   b. first-aid supplies.
   c. supplies for treating a headache.

4. *Specific ideas:* trout, whales, salmon, frogs

   The general idea is:

   a. animals.
   b. fish.
   c. animals living in water.

5. *Specific ideas:* Hershey bar, lollipop, mints, fudge

   The general idea is:

   a. food.
   b. candy.
   c. chocolate.

6. *Specific ideas:* "Go to bed," "Pick up that trash," "Run twenty laps," "Type this letter."

   The general idea is:

   a. remarks.
   b. orders.
   c. the boss's orders.

7. *Specific ideas:* "I had no time to study," "The questions were unfair," "I had a headache," "The instructor didn't give us enough time."

   The general idea is:

   a. statements.
   b. excuses for being late.
   c. excuses for not doing well on a test.

8. *Specific ideas:* candle, sun, headlight, flashlight

   The general idea is:

   a. things that are very hot.

   b. light sources for a home.

   (c.) sources of light.

9. *Specific ideas:* driving with expired license plates, driving over the speed limit, parking without putting money in the meter, driving without a license

   The general idea is:

   a. ways to cause a traffic accident.

   b. traffic problems.

   (c.) ways to get a ticket.

10. *Specific ideas:* "Do you come here often?" "Would you like to dance?" "Let me buy you a drink," "What's your zodiac sign?"

    The general idea is:

    a. things that people say to one another.

    b. things people commonly say to one another at a wedding.

    (c.) things people say in a singles bar.

Activity 4

In the following items, the specific ideas are given but the general ideas are unstated. Fill in the blanks with the unstated general ideas.

Example *General idea:* car problems
Specific ideas: flat tire, dented bumper, cracked windshield, dirty oil filter

Wording of answers may vary.

1. *General idea:* relatives
   Specific ideas: nephew, grandmother, aunt, cousin

2. *General idea:* footwear
   Specific ideas: boots, sneakers, moccasins, slippers

3. *General idea:* outdoor activities
   Specific ideas: camping, hiking, fishing, hunting

4. *General idea:* cleaning supplies
Specific ideas: broom, sponge, mop, glass cleaner

5. *General idea:* weather conditions
Specific ideas: cloudy, sunny, snowy, rainy

6. *General idea:* steps in making a sandwich
Specific ideas: Spread mustard on slice of bread
Add turkey and cheese
Put lettuce on top of cheese
Cover with another slice of bread

7. *General idea:* picnic items
Specific ideas: thermos of lemonade, insect repellent, basket of food, blanket

8. *General idea:* drawbacks of owning a dog
Specific ideas: fleas in carpeting, loud barking, tangled fur, veterinary bills

9. *General idea:* conditions requiring medical attention
Specific ideas: diabetes, cancer, appendicitis, broken leg

10. *General idea:* effects of rain
Specific ideas: flooded basements, wet streets, rainbow, overflowing rivers

2 Understanding the Paragraph

A *paragraph* is made up of a main idea and a group of related sentences developing the main idea. The main idea often appears in a sentence known as the *topic sentence.*

It is helpful to remember that a topic sentence is a *general* statement. The other sentences provide specific support for the general statement.

Activity

Each group of sentences below could be written as a short paragraph. Circle the letter of the topic sentence in each case. To find the topic sentence, ask yourself, "Which is a general statement supported by the specific details in the other three statements?"

Begin by trying the example item below. First circle the letter of the sentence you think expresses the main idea. Then read the explanation.

Example
a. Newspapers are a good source of local, national, and world news.
b. The cartoons and crossword puzzles in newspapers are entertaining.
(c.) Newspapers have a lot to offer.
d. Newspapers often include coupons worth far more than the cost of the paper.

Explanation: Sentence *a* explains one important benefit of newspapers. Sentences *b* and *d* provide other specific advantages of newspapers. In sentence *c*, however, no one specific benefit is explained. Instead, the words "a lot to offer" refer only generally to such benefits. Therefore sentence *c* is the topic sentence; it expresses the main idea. The other sentences support that idea by providing examples.

1. a. Even when Food City is crowded, there are only two cash registers open.
   b. The frozen foods are often partially thawed.
   (c.) I will never shop at Food City again.
   d. The market is usually out of sale items within a few hours.
2. a. Buy only clothes that will match what's already in your closet.
   b. To be sure you're getting the best price, shop in a number of stores before buying.
   c. Avoid trendy clothes; buy basic pieces that never go out of style.
   (d.) By following a few simple rules, you can have nice clothes without spending a fortune.
3. a. Once my son said a vase jumped off the shelf by itself.
   (b.) When my son breaks something, he always has an excuse.
   c. He claimed that my three-month-old daughter climbed out of her crib and knocked a glass over.
   d. Another time, he said an earthquake must have caused a mirror to crack.
4. (a.) Mars should be the first planet explored by astronauts.
   b. Astronauts could mine Mars for aluminum, magnesium, and iron.
   c. The huge volcano on Mars would be fascinating to study.
   d. Since Mars is close to Earth, we might want to have colonies there one day.

5. a. Instead of talking on the telephone, we leave messages on answering machines.
   (b.) People rarely talk to one another these days.
   c. Rather than talking with family members, we sit silently in front of our TV sets all evening
   d. In cars, we ignore our traveling companions to listen to the radio.

3 Understanding the Topic Sentence

As already explained, most paragraphs center on a main idea, which is often expressed in a topic sentence. An effective topic sentence does two things. First, it presents the topic of the paragraph. Second, it expresses the writer's attitude or opinion or idea about the topic. For example, look at the following topic sentence:

Professional athletes are overpaid.

In the topic sentence, the topic is *professional athletes;* the writer's idea about the topic is that professional athletes *are overpaid.*

Activity

For each topic sentence below, underline the topic and double-underline the point of view that the writer takes toward the topic.

Examples Living in a small town has many advantages.

Car phones should be banned.

1. The apartments on Walnut Avenue are a fire hazard.
2. Losing my job turned out to have benefits.
3. Blues is the most interesting form of American music.
4. Our neighbor's backyard is a dangerous place.
5. Paula and Jeff are a stingy couple.
6. Snakes do not deserve their bad reputation.
7. Pollution causes many problems in American cities.
8. New fathers should receive "paternity leave."
9. People with low self-esteem often need to criticize others.
10. Learning to write effectively is largely a matter of practice.

4 Identifying Topics, Topic Sentences, and Support

The following activity will sharpen your sense of the differences between topics, topic sentences, and supporting sentences.

Activity

Each group of items below includes one topic, one main idea (expressed in a topic sentence), and two supporting details for that idea. In the space provided, label each item with one of the following:

T — Topic
MI — main idea
SD — supporting details

1. SD a. The weather in the summer is often hot and sticky.
   MI b. Summer can be an unpleasant time of year.
   T c. Summer.
   SD d. Bug bites, poison ivy, and allergies are a big part of summertime.
2. MI a. The new Ultimate sports car is bound to be very popular.
   SD b. The company has promised to provide any repairs needed during the first three years at no charge.
   SD c. Because it gets thirty miles per gallon of gas, it offers real savings on fuel costs.
   T d. The new Ultimate sports car.
3. MI a. Decorating an apartment doesn't need to be expensive.
   SD b. A few plants add a touch of color without costing a lot of money.
   SD c. Inexpensive braided rugs can be bought to match nearly any furniture.
   T d. Decorating an apartment.

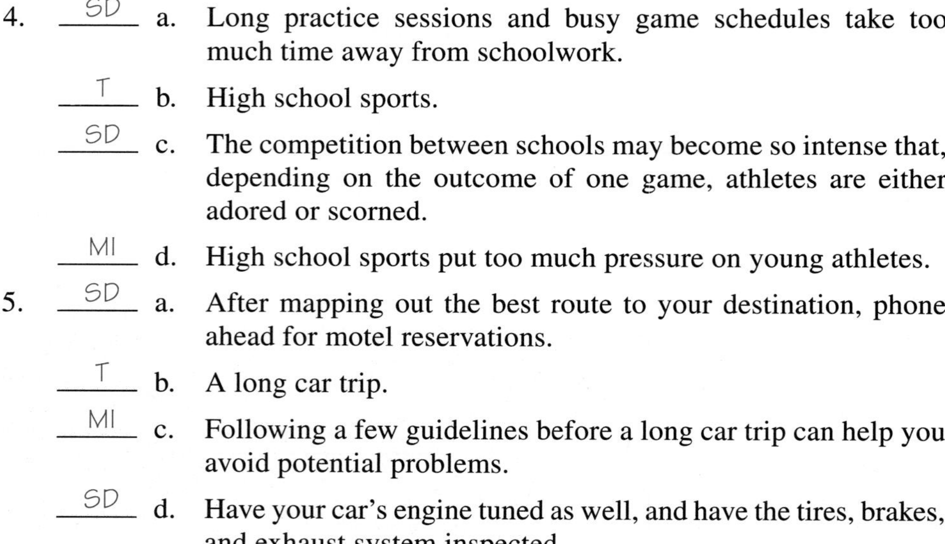

4. ___SD___ a. Long practice sessions and busy game schedules take too much time away from schoolwork.

___T___ b. High school sports.

___SD___ c. The competition between schools may become so intense that, depending on the outcome of one game, athletes are either adored or scorned.

___MI___ d. High school sports put too much pressure on young athletes.

5. ___SD___ a. After mapping out the best route to your destination, phone ahead for motel reservations.

___T___ b. A long car trip.

___MI___ c. Following a few guidelines before a long car trip can help you avoid potential problems.

___SD___ d. Have your car's engine tuned as well, and have the tires, brakes, and exhaust system inspected.

5 Recognizing Specific Details I

Specific details are examples, reasons, particulars, and facts. Such details are needed to support and explain a topic sentence effectively. They provide the evidence needed for us to understand, as well as to feel and experience, a writer's point.

Below is a topic sentence followed by two sets of supporting sentences. Write a check mark next to the set that provides sharp, specific details.

Topic sentence: Ticket sales for a recent Rolling Stones concert proved that the classic rock band is still very popular.

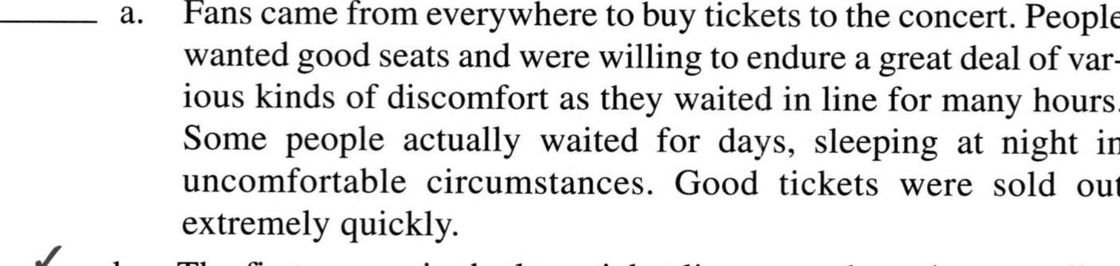

______ a. Fans came from everywhere to buy tickets to the concert. People wanted good seats and were willing to endure a great deal of various kinds of discomfort as they waited in line for many hours. Some people actually waited for days, sleeping at night in uncomfortable circumstances. Good tickets were sold out extremely quickly.

___✓___ b. The first person in the long ticket line spent three days standing in the hot sun and three nights sleeping on the concrete without even a pillow. The man behind her waited equally long in his wheelchair. The ticket window opened at 10:00 A.M., and the tickets for the good seats—those in front of the stage—were sold out an hour later.

Explanation: The second set (*b*) provides specific details. Instead of a vague statement about fans who were "willing to endure a great deal of various kinds of discomforts," we get vivid details we can see and picture clearly: "three days standing in the hot sun," "three nights sleeping on the concrete without even a pillow," "The man behind her waited equally long in his wheelchair."

Instead of a vague statement that tickets were "sold out extremely quickly," we get exact and vivid details: "The ticket window opened at 10:00 A.M., and the tickets for the good seats—those in front of the stage—were sold out an hour later."

Specific details are often like a movie script. They provide us with such clear pictures that we could make a film of them if we wanted to. You would know just how to film the information given in the second set of sentences. You would show the fans in line under a hot sun and, later, sleeping on the concrete. The first person in line would be shown sleeping without a pillow under her head. You would show tickets finally going on sale, and after an hour you could show the ticket seller explaining that all of the seats in front of the stage were sold out.

In contrast, the writer of the first set of sentences (*a*) fails to provide the specific information needed. If you were asked to make a film based on set *a,* you would have to figure out on your own just what particulars to show.

When you are working to provide specific supporting information in a paper, it might help to ask yourself, "Could someone easily film this information?" If the answer is yes, your supporting details are specific enough for your readers to visualize.

Activity

Each topic sentence below is followed by two sets of supporting details, Write *S* (for *specific*) in the space next to the set that provides specific support for the point. Write *G* (for *general*) next to the set that offers only vague, general support.

1. *Topic sentence:* The West Side shopping mall is an unpleasant place.

   __S__ a. The floors are covered with cigarette butts, dirty paper plates, and spilled food. The stores are so crowded I had to wait twenty minutes just to get a dressing room to try on a shirt.

   __G__ b. It's very dirty, and not enough places are provided for trash. The stores are not equipped to handle the large number of shoppers that often show up.

   Hint: Which set of supporting details could you more readily use in a film?

2. *Topic sentence:* Our golden retriever is a wonderful pet for children.

   __G__ a. He is gentle, patient, eager to please, and affectionate. Capable of following orders, he is also ready to think for himself and find solutions to a problem. He senses children's moods and goes along with their wishes.

__S__ b. He doesn't bite, even when children pull his tail. After learning to catch a ball, he will bring it back again and again, seemingly always ready to play. If the children don't want to play anymore, he will just sit by their side, gazing at them with his faithful eyes.

3. *Topic sentence:* My two-year-old daughter's fearlessness is a constant source of danger to her.

__G__ a. She doesn't realize that certain activities are dangerous. Even when I warn her, she will go ahead and do something that could hurt her. I have to constantly be on the lookout for dangerous situations and try to protect her from them.

__S__ b. For instance, she loves going to the swimming pool. That's great. But she will jump into water that is way over her head. She likes animals and will run to pet any dog that wanders by, no matter how unfriendly.

4. *Topic sentence:* People's views of scientists are often more fiction than fact.

__S__ a. Scientists are portrayed in movies as crazy guys with long hair, thick glasses, and shabby clothes. Incapable of remembering the time of day, these imaginary scientists skip meals and prefer the company of laboratory animals to that of their own children. In reality, scientists get hungry at mealtime, love their children, and go to work in suits.

__G__ b. People don't know exactly what scientists do and fantasize a lot about their work. Instead of thinking of scientists as real people who do a particular type of work, people think of them as weird, antisocial geniuses whom one could spot a mile away. In reality, most scientists look and act much like their neighbors.

5. *Topic sentence:* Early theories of child raising were very different from today's theories.

__G__ a. The first books on child raising came out hundreds of years ago. The advice they contained was based almost entirely on superstitions and other untrue beliefs. Some of the advice was harmless, but some could lead to long-term effects. They told parents to do things to their children that seem to us to make no sense at all.

__S__ b. One early book, for example, advised mothers not to breast-feed their babies right after feeling anger because the anger would go into the milk and injure the child. Another told parents to begin toilet-training their children at the age of three weeks and to tie their babies' arms down for several months to prevent thumb sucking.

6 Recognizing Specific Details II

Activity

At several points in each of the following paragraphs, you are given a choice of two sets of supporting details. Write *S* (for *specific*) in the space next to the set that provides specific support for the point. Write *G* (for *general*) next to the set that offers only vague, general support.

Paragraph 1

My daughter is as shy as I am, and it breaks my heart to see her dealing with the same problems I had to deal with in my childhood because of my shyness. I feel very sad for her when I see the problems she has making friends.

__G__ a. It takes her a long time to begin to do the things other children do to make friends, and her feelings get hurt very easily over one thing and another. She is not at all comfortable about making connections with her classmates at school.

__S__ b. She usually spends Christmas vacation alone because by that time of year she doesn't have friends yet. Only when her birthday comes in the summer is she confident enough to invite school friends to her party. Once she sends out the invitations, she almost sleeps by the telephone, waiting for the children to respond. If they say they can't come, her eyes fill with tears.

I recognize very well her signs of shyness, which make her look smaller and more fragile than she really is.

__S__ c. When she has to talk to someone she doesn't know well, she speaks in a whisper and stares sideways. Pressing her hands together, she lifts her shoulders as though she wished she could hide her head between them.

__G__ d. When she is forced to talk to anyone other than her family and her closest friends, the sound of her voice and the position of her head change. Even her posture changes in a way that makes it look as if she's trying to make her body disappear.

It is hard for me to watch her passing unnoticed at school.

__G__ e. She never gets chosen for a special job or privilege, even though she tries her best, practicing in privacy at home. She just doesn't measure up. Worst of all, even her teacher seems to forget her existence much of the time.

S f. Although she rehearses in our basement, she never gets chosen for a good part in a play. Her voice is never loud or clear enough. Worst of all, her teacher doesn't call on her in class for days at a time.

Paragraph 2

It is said that the dog is man's best friend, but I strongly believe that the honor belongs to the telephone directory. A directory can't play ball with me, but it can help me find many ways to entertain myself.

G a. If I am bored, tired, or out of ideas, the telephone directory can tell me where to go for dinner, recreation, and entertainment.

S b. The other day the directory guided me to a charming restaurant, The China Bowl. I frequently use the directory to find movies, theaters, concerts, and museums.

While the dog is a faithful friend, the telephone directory helps me be a good citizen.

S c. I use the phone numbers in the directory's blue pages to learn the guidelines of my town's recycling programs, the rules for garbage disposal, and the procedures of the snow emergency program.

G d. The directory's blue pages help me perform my duties as a citizen because they list telephone numbers of agencies and departments in my town and state. I can find out a great deal about a variety of types of rules and guidelines.

A dog might help me meet people I see in the park, but the directory helps me meet other important people.

G e. When I need to find someone to provide some sort of service for me, I know that I can find help in the Yellow Pages. Looking at the Yellow Pages, I can find someone to call. The Yellow Pages have been especially helpful when I have moved to a new city.

S f. I moved to Chicago two years ago, and the Yellow Pages helped me quickly find Dr. Morris, a very good family physician; Mrs. DeJames, the best hairstylist I've ever used; and Mr. Henderson, a wonderful repairman.

7 Providing Specific Details

Activity

Each of the following sentences contains a general word or words, set off in *italic* type. Substitute sharp, specific words in each case.

Example After the parade, the city street was littered with *garbage*.

After the parade, the city street was littered with multicolored confetti, dirty popcorn, and lifeless balloons.

Answers will vary.

1. If I had enough money, I'd visit *several places*.

2. It took her *a long time* to get home.

3. Ron is often stared at because of his *unusual hair color and hairstyle*.

4. After you pass *two buildings*, you'll see my house on the left.

5. Nia's purse is crammed with *lots of stuff*.

6. I bought *some junk food* for the long car trip.

7. The floor in the front of my car is covered with *things*.

8. When his mother said no to his request for a toy, the child *reacted strongly*.

9. Devan gave his girlfriend a *surprise present* for Valentine's Day.

____

____

10. My cat can *do a wonderful trick.*

____

____

8 Selecting Details That Fit

The details in your paper must all clearly relate to and support your opening point. If a detail does not support your point, leave it out. Otherwise, your paper will lack unity. For example, see if you can circle the letter of the two sentences that do *not* support the topic sentence below.

Topic sentence: Mario is a very talented person.

(a.) Mario is always courteous to his professors.
b. He has created beautiful paintings in his art course.
c. Mario is the lead singer in a local band.
d. He won an award in a photography contest.
(e.) He is hoping to become a professional photographer.

Explanation: Being courteous may be a virtue, but it is not a talent, so sentence *a* does not support the topic sentence. Also, Mario's desire to become a professional photographer tells us nothing about his talent; thus sentence *e* does not support the topic sentence either. The other three statements all clearly back up the topic sentence. Each in some way supports the idea that Mario is talented—in art, as a singer, or as a photographer.

Activity

In each group below, circle the two items that do *not* support the topic sentence.

1. *Topic sentence:* Carla seems attracted only to men who are unavailable.
   a. She once fell in love with a man serving a life sentence in prison.
   (b.) Her parents worry about her inability to connect with a nice single man.
   (c.) She wants to get married and have kids before she is thirty.

d. Her current boyfriend is married.

e. Recently she had a huge crush on a Catholic priest.

2. *Topic sentence:* Some dog owners have little consideration for other people.

(a.) Obedience lessons can be a good experience for both the dog and the owner.

b. Some dog owners let their dogs leave droppings on the sidewalk or in other people's yards.

c. They leave the dog home alone for hours, barking and howling and waking the neighbors.

(d.) Some people keep very large dogs in small apartments.

e. Even when small children are playing nearby, they let their bad-tempered dogs run loose.

3. *Topic sentence:* Dr. Eliot is a very poor teacher.

a. He cancels class frequently with no explanation.

b. When a student asks a question that he can't answer, he becomes irritated with the student.

(c.) He got his Ph.D at a university in another country.

(d.) He's taught at the college for many years and is on a number of faculty committees.

e. He puts off grading papers until the end of the semester, and then returns them all at once.

4. *Topic sentence:* Some doctors seem to think it is all right to keep patients waiting.

(a.) Pharmaceutical sales representatives sometimes must wait hours to see a doctor.

b. The doctors stand in the hallway chatting with nurses and secretaries even when they have a waiting room full of patients.

(c.) Patients sometimes travel long distances to consult with a particular doctor.

d. When a patient calls before an appointment to see if the doctor is on time, the answer is often yes even when the doctor is two hours behind schedule.

e. Some doctors schedule appointments in a way that ensures long lines, to make it appear that they are especially skillful.

5. *Topic sentence:* Several factors were responsible for the staggering loss of lives when the *Titanic* sank.

(a.) Over 1,500 people died in the *Titanic* disaster; only 711 survived.

b. Despite warnings about the presence of icebergs, the captain allowed the *Titanic* to continue at high speed.

c. If the ship had hit the iceberg head on, its watertight compartments might have kept it from sinking; however, it hit on the side, resulting in a long, jagged gash through which water poured in.

(d.) The *Titanic,* equipped with the very best communication systems available in 1912, sent out SOS messages.

e. When the captain gave orders to abandon the *Titanic,* many passengers refused because they believed the ship was unsinkable, so many lifeboats were only partly filled.

9 Providing Details That Fit

Activity 1

Each topic sentence below is followed by one supporting detail. See if you can add a second detail in each case. Make sure your detail supports the topic sentence.
Answers will vary.

1. *Topic sentence:* There are good reasons why the video store is losing so many customers.
   a. The store stocks only one copy of every movie, even the most popular titles.
   b. ______________________________
2. *Topic sentence:* The little boy did some dangerous stunts on his bicycle.
   a. He rode down a flight of steps at top speed.
   b. ______________________________
3. *Topic sentence:* Craig has awful table manners.
   a. He stuffs his mouth with food and then begins a conversation.
   b. ______________________________
4. *Topic sentence:* There are many advantages to living in the city.
   a. One can meet many new people with interesting backgrounds.
   b. ______________________________
5. *Topic sentence:* All high school students should have summer jobs.
   a. Summer jobs help teens learn to handle a budget.
   b. ______________________________

Activity 2

See if you can add *two* supporting details for each of the topic sentences below.
Answers will vary.

1. *Topic sentence:* The managers of this apartment building don't care about their renters.
   a. Mrs. Harris has been asking them to fix her leaky faucet for two months.
   b. ______________________________
   c. ______________________________
2. *Topic sentence:* None of the shirts for sale were satisfactory.
   a. Some were attractive but too expensive.
   b. ______________________________
   c. ______________________________
3. *Topic sentence:* After being married for forty years, Mr. and Mrs. Lambert have grown similar in odd ways.
   a. They both love to have a cup of warm apple juice just before bed.
   b. ______________________________
   c. ______________________________
4. *Topic sentence:* It is a special time for me when my brother is in town.
   a. We always go bowling together and then stop for pizza.
   b. ______________________________
   c. ______________________________
5. *Topic sentence:* Our neighbor's daughter is very spoiled.
   a. When anyone else in the family has a birthday, she gets several presents too.
   b. ______________________________
   c. ______________________________

10 Providing Details in a Paragraph

Activity

The following paragraph needs specific details to back up its three supporting points. In the spaces provided, write two or three sentences of convincing details for each supporting point.

Answers will vary.

A Disappointing Concert

Although I had looked forward to seeing my favorite musical group in concert, the experience was disappointing. For one thing, our seats were terrible, in two ways. ______________________________

____

____

____

In addition, the crowd made it hard to enjoy the music. ______________

____

____

____

____

____

And finally, the band members acted as if they didn't want to be there. ____

____

____

____

____

11 Omitting and Grouping Details in Planning a Paper

One common way to develop material for a paper involves three steps: (1) First, make up a list of details about your point. (2) Then omit details that don't truly support your point. (3) Finally, group remaining details together in logical ways. Omitting details that don't fit and grouping related details together are part of learning how to write effectively.

See if you can figure out a way to put the following details into three groups. Write *A* in front of the details that go with one group, *B* in front of the details that go with a second group, and *C* in front of the details that make up a third group. Cross out the four details that do not relate to the topic sentence.

Topic sentence: My brother Sean caused our parents lots of headaches when he was a teenager.

__A__ In constant trouble at school

__A__ While playing a joke on his lab partner, nearly blew up the chemistry lab

__B__ Girlfriend was eight years older than he and had been married twice

______ ~~Girlfriend had a very sweet four-year-old son~~

__B__ Parents worried about people Sean spent his time with

__C__ Several signs that he was using drugs

__A__ Failed so many courses that he had to go to summer school in order to graduate

__A__ Was suspended twice for getting into fights between classes

______ ~~Our father taught math at the high school we attended~~

__C__ His money just disappeared, and he never had anything to show for it

__B__ His best pal had been arrested for armed robbery

__C__ Often looked glassy-eyed

__B__ Hung around with older kids who had dropped out of school

______ ~~Until he was in eighth grade, he had always been on the honor roll~~

__C__ No one was allowed in his room, which he kept locked whenever he was away from home

______ ~~Has managed to turn his life around now that he's in college~~

Explanation: After thinking about the list for a while, you probably realized that the details about Sean's trouble at school form one group. He got in trouble at school for nearly blowing up the chemistry lab, failing courses, and fighting between classes. Another group of details has to do with his parents' worrying about the people he spent time with. His parents were worried because he had an older girlfriend, a best friend who was arrested for armed robbery, and older friends who were school dropouts. Finally, there are the details about signs that he was using drugs: his money disappearing, his glassy-eyed appearance, and not allowing others in his room.

The main idea—that as a teenager, the writer's brother caused their parents lots of headaches—can be supported with three kinds of evidence: the trouble he got into at school, his friends, and the signs indicating he was on drugs. The other four items in the list do not logically go with any of these three types of evidence and so should be omitted.

Activity

This activity will give you practice in omitting and grouping details. See if you can figure out a way to put the following details into three groups. Write *A* in front of the details that go with one group, *B* in front of the details that go with a second group, and *C* in front of the details that make up a third group. Cross out the four details that do not relate to the topic sentence.

Topic sentence: There are interesting and enjoyable ways for children to keep their classroom skills strong over summer vacation.

___C___ Kids can help figure out how big a tip to leave in a restaurant.

___A___ They can keep their reading skills sharp in various ways.

______ ~~Summer is a good time for learning to swim.~~

___A___ Reading the newspaper with Mom or Dad will keep kids in touch with challenging reading.

___C___ Adults can ask a child to do such tasks as count their change.

___B___ Kids can have fun improving their writing skills.

___B___ A child might enjoy writing a diary of his or her summer activities.

___A___ Weekly visits to the library will keep them in touch with good books.

______ ~~After returning to school, children can write about their summer vacation.~~

______ ~~Kids should also have plenty of physical exercise over the summer.~~

___C___ Arithmetic skills can be polished over the summer.

___B___ Parents can encourage kids to write letters to relatives.

______ ~~Parents should take children to the library during the school year too.~~

___C___ In the grocery store, a child can compare prices and choose the best bargains.

___A___ Even the comic strips provide reading practice for a young child.

___B___ Getting a pen-pal in another state can give a child an enjoyable reason to write over the summer.

12 Using Transitions

As already stated, transitions are signal words that help readers follow the direction of the writer's thought. To see the value of transitions, look at the two versions of the short paragraph below. Check the version that is easier to read and understand.

______ a. Where will you get the material for your writing assignments? There are several good sources. Your own experience is a major resource. For an assignment about childhood, for instance, you can draw on your own numerous memories of childhood. Other people's experience is extremely useful. You may have heard people you know or even people on TV or radio talking about their childhood. Or you can interview people with a specific writing assignment in mind. Books and magazines are a good source of material for assignments. Many experts, for example, have written about various aspects of childhood.

__✓__ b. Where will you get the material for your writing assignments? There are several good sources. First of all, your own experience is a major resource. For an assignment about childhood, for instance, you can draw on your own numerous memories of childhood. In addition, other people's experiences are extremely useful. You may have heard people you know or even people on TV or radio talking about their childhood. Or you can interview people with a specific writing assignment in mind. Finally, books and magazines are a good source of material for assignments. Many experts, for example, have written about various aspects of childhood.

Explanation: You no doubt chose the second version, *b.* The listing transitions—*first of all, in addition,* and *finally*—make it clear when the author is introducing a new supporting point. The reader of paragraph *b* is better able to follow the author's line of thinking and to note that three main sources of material for assignments are being listed: your own experience, other people's experience, and books and magazines.

Activity

The following paragraphs use listing order or time order. In each case, fill in the blanks with appropriate transitions from the box above the paragraph. Use each transition once.

1.

after	now	first	soon	while

My husband has developed an involving hobby, in which I, unfortunately, am unable to share. He ___first___ enrolled in ground flight instruction classes at the local community college. The lessons were all about air safety regulations and procedures. ___After___ passing a difficult exam, he decided to take flying lessons at the city airport. Every Monday he would wake at six o'clock in the morning and drive happily to the airport, eager to see his instructor. ___While___ he was taking lessons, he started to buy airplane magazines and talk about them constantly. "Look at that Cessna 150," he would say. "Isn't she a beauty?" ___Now___, after many lessons, he is flying by himself. ___Soon___ he will be able to carry passengers. That is my biggest nightmare. I know he will want me to fly with him, but I am not a lover of heights. I can't understand why someone would leave the safety of the ground to be in the sky, defenseless as a kite.

2.

finally	for one thing	second

The home economics class I took in high school convinced me that homemaking would never be my strong point. ___For one thing___, there was my experience making chocolate cookies. I gathered the ingredients, including a big chunk of semisweet chocolate, and threw them into the mixing bowl. As I started the mixer, there was a terrible grinding sound. Miss Hooley, my teacher, pointed out that I was supposed to *melt* the chocolate before mixing it in. ___Second___, I didn't do so well making out menus for a week's nutritious meals. Miss Hooley didn't think it was funny that I filled my menu with comments like "Invite Mom over to cook" and "Send out for Chinese food." ___Finally___, there was my lack of success in sewing. Actually, I thought sewing was fun. I loved to stomp on the sewing machine's foot pedal and make it roar loudly. I finished sewing my blouse before anyone else in the class. Unfortunately, I had sewed the armholes and neck opening shut.

3.

later	soon	when	then

At the age of thirty-one I finally had the opportunity to see snow for the first time in my life. It was in New York City on a cloudy afternoon in November.

My daughter and I had gone to the American Museum of Natural History. ___When___ we left the museum, snow was falling gently. I thought that it was so beautiful! It made me remember movies I had seen countless times in my native Brazil. We decided to find a taxi. ___Soon___ we were crossing Central Park, snuggled in the cozy cab, watching the snow cover trees, bushes, branches, and grass. We were amazed to see the landscape quickly change from fall to winter. ___Then___ we arrived in front of our hotel, and I still remember stepping on the crisp snow and laughing like a child who is touched by magic. ___Later___ that day, I heard on the radio that another snowstorm was coming. I was naive enough to wait for thunder and the other sounds of a rainstorm. I did not know yet that snow, even a snowstorm, is silent and soft.

4.

last of all	another	first of all	in addition

Public school students who expect to attend school from September to June, and then have a long summer vacation, may be in for a big surprise before long. For a number of reasons, many schools are switching to a year-round calendar. ___First of all___, many educators point out that the traditional school calendar was established years ago when young people had to be available during the summer months to work on farms, but this necessity has long since passed. ___Another___ reason is that a longer school year accommodates individual learning rates more effectively. That is, fast learners can go into more depth about a subject that interests them, while those who learn at a slower pace have more time to master the essential material. ___In addition___, many communities have gone to year-round school to relieve overcrowding, since students can be put on different schedules throughout the year. ___Last of all___, and perhaps most important, educators feel that year-round schools eliminate the loss of learning that many students experience over a long summer break.

13 Organizing Details in a Paragraph

The supporting details in a paragraph must be organized in a meaningful way. The two most common methods of organizing details are listing order and time order. The activities that follow will give you practice in both methods of organization.

Activity 1

Use *listing order* to arrange the scrambled list of sentences below. Number each supporting sentence 1, 2, 3, . . . so that you go from the least important item to what is presented as the most important item.

Note that transitions will help by making clear the relationships between some of the sentences.

Topic sentence: I am no longer a big fan of professional sports, for a number of reasons.

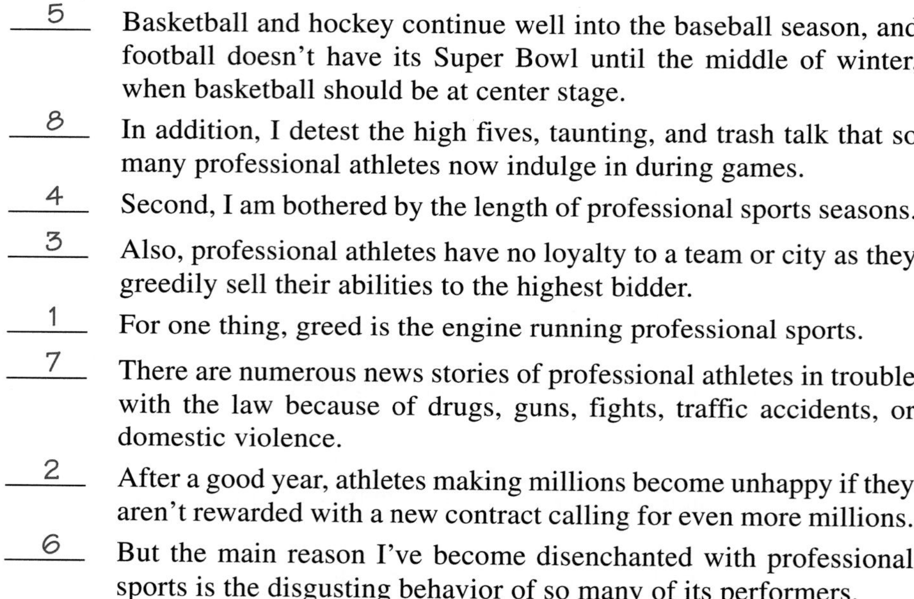

__5__ Basketball and hockey continue well into the baseball season, and football doesn't have its Super Bowl until the middle of winter, when basketball should be at center stage.

__8__ In addition, I detest the high fives, taunting, and trash talk that so many professional athletes now indulge in during games.

__4__ Second, I am bothered by the length of professional sports seasons.

__3__ Also, professional athletes have no loyalty to a team or city as they greedily sell their abilities to the highest bidder.

__1__ For one thing, greed is the engine running professional sports.

__7__ There are numerous news stories of professional athletes in trouble with the law because of drugs, guns, fights, traffic accidents, or domestic violence.

__2__ After a good year, athletes making millions become unhappy if they aren't rewarded with a new contract calling for even more millions.

__6__ But the main reason I've become disenchanted with professional sports is the disgusting behavior of so many of its performers.

Activity 2

Use *time order* to arrange the scrambled sentences below. Number the supporting sentences in the order in which they occur in time (1, 2, 3, . . .).

Note that transitions will help by making clear the relationships between sentences.

Topic sentence: If you are a smoker, the following steps should help you quit.

__4__ Before your "quit day" arrives, have a medical checkup to make sure it will be all right for you to begin an exercise program.

__2__ You should then write down on a card your decision to quit and the date of your "quit day."

5 When your "quit day" arrives, stop smoking and start your exercise program.

8 Finally, remind yourself repeatedly how good you will feel when you can confidently tell yourself and others that you are a non-smoker.

3 Place the card in a location where you will be sure to see it every day.

6 When you begin this exercise program, be sure to drink plenty of water every day and to follow a sensible diet.

1 After making a definite decision to stop smoking, select a specific "quit day."

7 Eventually, your exercise program should include activities strenuous enough to strengthen your lung capacity and your overall stamina.

14 Understanding the Plan of Development in an Essay

Activity

Complete each thesis statement below by adding a third supporting idea. Use wording that is parallel to the two supporting ideas already provided.

Answers will vary.

1. The people who have given me the best advice are my father, my grandmother, and my ______.
2. The qualities I most admire in my best friend are her sense of humor, her loyalty, and her ______.
3. Reading a novel, taking a warm bath, and ______ are excellent ways to relax at the end of a long day.
4. Fights with my wife usually stem from disagreements about money, child raising, and ______.
5. Sticking to a diet, keeping a schedule , and ______ are the most difficult challenges I face.
6. My three favorite possessions are my photograph albums, my letters from friends, and my ______.
7. To find work in a day care center satisfying, a person should enjoy teaching, have lots of patience, and ______.

8. My neighbors are most annoying when they play music late at night, borrow items and never return them, and ____.
9. New college students need advice on managing their time, communicating with their instructors, and ____.
10. Three weeks of vacation, an exercise center, and __________________________ are among the great benefits I receive at work.

15 Recognizing Specific Details in an Essay

Activity

For each supporting paragraph in the essay below, there are two sets of supporting details. Write *S* (for *specific*) in the blank next to the set that provides specific support for the topic sentence. Write *G* (for *general*) in the blank next to the set with only vague, general support.

Introduction

What would you do if one of your friends—a terrific guy who is good-natured, generous, and outgoing—invited you over for dinner? You're probably thinking, "I'd certainly go. Why not?" Would you still go if your friend, a prince of a fellow, was a lousy host? Well, that's the dilemma my old college friend Ben presents. Everybody likes Ben, but nobody wants to be invited to his place for the evening because he doesn't manage his time well, he's an awful cook, and he's messy.

Supporting Paragraph 1

The first problem is that Ben has no sense of how to plan a schedule.

__G__ a. He doesn't seem to think ahead when he invites people over for the evening. When you show up at the time he invited you, you find that he isn't ready for you at all. In fact, he hasn't even begun to prepare dinner. Because he's so busy preparing dinner, he is unable to give his attention to his guests. He expects his guests to take care of themselves or follow him around the kitchen while he prepares dinner. His inability to manage his time can cause his guests a lot of inconvenience and result in a pretty boring evening.

__S__ b. For example, say he invites you over for dinner at six. When you show up at that hour, you will probably meet him just getting home from work. Then you will watch him wander around his kitchen for a while, wondering aloud what to make for dinner. Likely as not, he'll decide to try something that takes a great deal of time, like eggplant Parmesan, leaving you to entertain yourself either watching him prepare dinner or watching TV. By nine o'clock, you'll be begging him for a few carrot sticks, an apple—anything.

Supporting Paragraph 2

Second, Ben is a truly awful cook.

__S__ a. If he does manage to come up with something to eat before you die of hunger, it will probably be so terrible it'll make your tongue curl. He has dreamed up such creative dishes as pork chops with lime sauce and potatoes mashed with sardines. After the first bite, most guests try to find a way to hide the rest under their napkins. Once he stood in front of the cupboard for twenty minutes, muttering, "Well, now let's see what we've got here." Then he fussed like a mad scientist over ingredients he found and came up with something he called "cereal burgers."

__G__ b. Although it doesn't seem that hard to find some tasty-sounding recipes and follow them, Ben doesn't seem capable of doing that. In fact, he prefers not to use recipes at all. He likes to make up his own food combinations. This sounds like a good idea, but it rarely turns out well when Ben does it. The main reasons are that he has such bad taste and also he often has very few ingredients in the apartment. He considers it a challenge to come up with an edible meal based on whatever happens to remain on his cupboard shelves. The idea of shopping with guests in mind never enters his mind.

Supporting Paragraph 3

Finally, Ben's apartment is so messy it's unpleasant to spend time there.

__G__ a. It is challenging to find a place to sit in his apartment, and you may have something on the floor get on your shoes. Ben doesn't seem to notice that he can't find anything and doesn't have any room to sit down. The truth is, it doesn't bother him to be surrounded by all types of things that most people would have thrown in the garbage can or recycled ages ago. Even people who are not terribly neat themselves are shocked by the jumbled environment in Ben's apartment.

__S__ b. When you cross his living room floor, a half-eaten lollipop may stick to the soles of your shoes. When you sit on the sofa, you hear the crunch of hidden crackers. You'd like to move, but all the other seats are buried under mountains of papers, laundry, and pizza boxes. One measure of Ben's messiness is the reaction of our friend Cruz. Cruz's bedroom floor is covered with underwear and empty Chinese food containers. His living room rug, once green, is gray with dust. Last time I spoke to Cruz, he observed, "I had dinner at Ben's last night. Boy, is his apartment a mess."

Conclusion

As I said, Ben is a heck of a guy. He is kind to old people and children. He doesn't have a bad thing to say about anyone. In December, he collects toys for the poor. He tells wonderful jokes and is extremely well read. His friends can't say enough good things about him. They love to spend time with him—anywhere except at his place.

16 Providing Details in an Essay

Activity

The supporting paragraphs of the following essay need more specific details. In the spaces provided, add a sentence or two of convincing details for each idea.
Answers will vary.

Introduction

I remember the September morning that I first laid eyes on Jill. I'd been calling clients at my desk at work when I heard a warm, musical laugh. There was something so attractive about the sound that I got up to get a cup of coffee and to find the source of that laugh. I discovered the voice to be that of a young, auburn-haired woman we had just hired from a temporary agency. Soon after, Jill and I began going out, and we spent the next two years together. Only recently have we decided to break up because of disagreements about finances, about children, and about our relationship with her family.

Supporting Paragraph 1

First of all, Jill and I have very different ideas about how to handle money. She likes to spend a lot of money on entertainment, and I don't. __________

____

____

____

In addition, while I think saving for the future is essential, she thinks it's silly.

Also, I feel she uses credit cards too freely.

Supporting Paragraph 2

Second, our thoughts about children are quite different. One conflict we had was over whether or not we should have any children.

If we did have children, her ideas about how they should be cared for are different from mine.

Her ideas about how children should be educated also differ greatly from my own.

____

____

____

____

Supporting Paragraph 3

Finally, we disagreed about how to deal with her family. Jill expected us to spend a lot of time with her parents, a prospect that horrifies me. ________

____

____

____

____

She also expected us to consult her parents before we made any major decisions; I haven't found their advice all that wise. ________________

____

____

____

____

Conclusion

I care a lot about Jill, and I miss having her in my life. But I am convinced that our marriage would have been a mistake because of our conflicting views on finances, children, and family. I have no regrets about the decision to break off our relationship.

17 Providing Transitions in an Essay

Activity 1

The following essay uses time order. Fill in the blanks with appropriate transitions from the box. Use every transition once. You will probably find it helpful to check off (✓) each transition as you use it.

then	finally	first	as
before	often	soon	when
until	while	next	after

Most mornings at my office pass in a rather typical—and peaceful—fashion. ____First____ , I go over the calendar and write reminders to myself about my day's schedule. I also go through the list of orders that were taken the day before, checking to be sure everything is clear. Other tasks follow ____until____ it's time for lunch. However, life at my office was not so typical this morning because of a black cloud, a loud alarm, and a visitor wearing a mask.

The surprises began with a mistake made by our office boy. ____As____ I was working at my computer, I suddenly heard cursing behind me. ____While____ trying to replace the toner cartridge in our copying machine, Greg, the office boy, had dropped the cartridge, and a cloud of black toner dust was rising in the air above the copier. ____Before____ the dust could begin to subside, it started to go into an air conditioning duct nearby. Someone ran to turn off the air conditioning, but some dust still got into the duct system. We all became aware of a fine black powder on our bodies and all the surfaces in the office.

The ____next____ episode of the morning was equally upsetting. Suddenly a very loud clanging filled the offices, as if a giant telephone were ringing. It took us a few seconds to realize that it was the fire alarm. Everyone ____then____ herded quickly down the stairs. In short order, there were around two hundred people on the front sidewalk wondering where the smoke and hot flames were. As it turned out, there were none. Someone on another floor had burned some toast in a toaster that he had, against the rules, brought into the building. As a result, he triggered the alarm system. We all returned to our desks, hoping to get some work done.

____Finally____ we had to deal with a third unexpected event: a visitor wearing a mask. Our office is in the same building as a veterinarian. We ____often____ hear the yipping of dogs and the yowling of cats as they are carried in to see the doctor. However, we had never actually had a visitor from the vet's office. But ____when____ a secretary heard some scratching and opened the office door to check, something large and furry dashed in between her legs. It hid under a desk where we couldn't really get a good look at it, but we could hear it snarling and spitting at us. Fortunately, it was ____soon____ followed by its owner, who told us the angry animal was a raccoon. "Don't worry," he assured us. "We're almost sure it doesn't have rabies, but we're just having it tested to be certain." ____After____ his announcement, the office once again cleared out very quickly.

After the black cloud, the false alarm, and the surprise visitor, I decided I had had enough for one day. I've been home all afternoon with a cold cloth on my forehead, and I'm hoping for a boring day tomorrow.

Activity 2

The following essay uses listing order. Fill in the blanks with appropriate transitions from the box. Use every transition once. You will probably find it helpful to check off (✓) each transition as you use it.

other	another	one	also
furthermore	third	moreover	

Does your will to study collapse when someone suggests getting a pizza? Does your social life compete with your class attendance? Is there a huge gap between your intentions and your actions? If the answers to these questions are yes, yes, and yes, read on. You can benefit from three powerful ways to motivate yourself: setting goals and working consciously to reach them, using rational thinking, and developing a positive personality.

____One____ key to self-motivation is deciding on your goals—both long- and short-term—and then really working to reach them. Do you want to be an accountant or a nurse in a few years? Do you want to raise your grade point average this semester? Do you want to get at least a B on a paper this week? Whatever your goal, keep it in mind; it is the future you're working toward. ____Also____ keep in mind that the great majority of students who can be classified as failures have no goals. Once you've got some goals firmly in mind, decide how to reach them. Perhaps you'll need to study for at least two hours a day. Then think about the reward you'll give yourself for reaching a goal. Maybe for every hour of study, you'll eat a special snack or listen to your favorite music.

___Other___ rewards for achieving short-term goals might be going to the park, seeing a movie, calling a friend on the phone, and taking a nap.

Along with setting goals, ___another___ key to self-motivation is learning to think rationally. Instead of seeking shortcuts, do things right. If you're not sure about an important point on an assignment, ask instead of guessing. Don't rationalize about why you don't need to study for a math quiz. Instead, remind yourself that you need a passing grade in math to graduate. Also, rationally examine the benefits of good study habits. When you develop good study habits, studying takes less time and you get more out of it. ___Furthermore___, as your studying becomes more and more productive, your self-image improves.

A ___third___ key to self-motivation is developing a positive personality. A positive personality includes attitudes that bring success. For instance, a positive person is enthusiastic, dependable, and supportive of others. ___Moreover___, a positive student has an upbeat, can-do self-image. "I can't," "It's too tough," and "Why bother?" aren't in this student's vocabulary.

So get your willpower in gear and use the three keys to self-motivation—set goals and work to reach them, think rationally, and develop a positive personality. You will find that a firm commitment to this approach becomes easier and easier. Progress will come more often and more readily, strengthening your resolve even further.

Note: "Furthermore" and "moreover" could be reversed.

18 Introductory and Concluding Paragraphs

Activity 1

Four common methods of introducing an essay are as follows:

a Begin with a broad statement and narrow it down to your thesis statement.

b Present an idea or situation that is the opposite of the one you will develop.

c Tell a brief story.

d Ask one or more questions.

Following are four introductions. In the space provided, write the letter of the method of introduction used in each case.

___c___ 1. One morning twenty-nine years ago, my father backed out of his parking space, smashed into the Cadillac parked across the street, put the gear into forward, and kept going. "Take it easy, Floyd," yelled Mom. "Better to be late than to die!" But that didn't keep him from accelerating, weaving in and out of traffic, and running into a telephone booth. As a result, I was born in my parents' old green-and-white Chevy instead of at Bradley Hospital. Perhaps it's no surprise, then, that my own car was the location of other key events in my life—an accident that almost killed me, the place where I made a crucial job decision, and my proposal to my wife.

___a___ 2. I have had a lot on interesting teachers through the years. Some have taught me useful and interesting facts. Even better, some have shown me how to learn. Some have even inspired me. But of all the wonderful teachers I've had, my favorite is Mrs. Rogers, who taught me how to write, showed me the pleasures of reading, and most important, helped me realize I could do just about anything I put my mind to.

___b___ 3. Most mornings at my office pass in a rather typical—and peaceful—fashion. First, I go over the calendar and write reminders to myself about my day's schedule. I also go through the list of orders that were taken the day before, checking to be sure everything is clear. Other tasks follow until it's time for lunch. However, life at my office was not so typical this morning because of a black cloud, a loud alarm, and a visitor wearing a mask.

___d___ 4. Does your will to study collapse when someone suggests getting a pizza? Does your social life compete with your class attendance? Is there a huge gap between your intentions and your actions? If the answers to these questions are yes, yes, and yes, read on. You can benefit from three powerful ways to motivate yourself: setting goals and working consciously to reach them, using rational thinking, and developing a positive personality.

Activity 2

Two common methods of concluding an essay are as follows:

a Provide a summary and a final thought.

b Focus on the future.

Following are two conclusions. In the space provided, write the letter of the method of conclusion used in each case.

___a___ 1. I care a lot about Jill, and I miss having her in my life. But I am convinced that our marriage would have been a mistake because of our conflicting views on finances, children, and family. I have no regrets about the decision to break off our relationship.

___b___ 2. So get your willpower in gear and use the three keys to self-motivation—set goals and work to reach them, think rationally, and develop a positive personality. You will find that a firm commitment to this approach becomes easier and easier. Progress will come more often and more readily, strengthening your resolve even further.

19 Prewriting

These activities will give you practice in some of the prewriting strategies you can use to generate material for a paper. While the focus here is on writing a paragraph, the strategies apply to writing an essay as well. See if you can do two or more of these prewriting activities.

Note: Responses to these activities will vary.

Activity 1: Freewriting

On a sheet of paper, freewrite for several minutes about the best or most disappointing friend you ever had. Don't worry about grammar, punctuation, or spelling. Try to write, without stopping, about whatever comes into your head concerning your best or most disappointing friend.

Activity 2: Questioning

On another sheet of paper, answer the following questions about the friend you've started to write about.

1. When did this friendship take place?
2. Where did it take place?
3. What is one reason you liked or were disappointed in this friend? Give one quality, action, comment, etc. Also, give some details to illustrate this quality.
4. What is another reason that you liked or were disappointed in your friend? What are some details that support the second reason?
5. Can you think of a third thing about your friend that you liked or were disappointed in? What are some details that support the third reason?

Activity 3: Clustering

In the center of a blank sheet of paper, write and circle the words *best friend* or *most disappointing friend.* Then, around the circle, add reasons and details about the friend. Use a series of boxes, circles, or other shapes, along with connecting lines, to set off the reasons and details. In other words, try to think about and explore your topic in a very visual way.

Activity 4: Making a List

On separate paper, make a list of details about the friend. Don't worry about putting them in a certain order. Just get down as many details about the friend as occur to you. The list can include specific reasons you liked or were disappointed in the person and specific details supporting those reasons.

20 Outlining, Drafting, and Revising

Here you will get practice in the writing steps that follow prewriting: outlining, drafting, revising, editing, and proofreading.

Note: Responses to these activities will vary.

Activity 1: Scratch Outline

On the basis of your prewriting, see if you can prepare a scratch outline made up of your main idea and the three main reasons you liked or were disappointed in your friend. Use the form below:

________________________________ was my best *or* most disappointing friend.

Reason 1: ________________________________

Reason 2: ________________________________

Reason 3: ________________________________

Activity 2: First Draft

Now write a first draft of your paper. Begin with your topic sentence, stating that a certain friend was the best or most disappointing one you ever had. Then state the first reason to support your main idea, followed by specific details supporting that reason. Next, state the second reason, followed by specific details supporting that reason. Finally, state the third reason, followed by support.

Don't worry about grammar, punctuation, or spelling. Just concentrate on getting down on paper the details about your friend.

Activity 3: Revising the Draft

Ideally, you will have a chance to put your paper aside for a while before writing the second draft. In your second draft, try to do all of the following:

1. Add transition words such as *first of all, another,* and *finally* to introduce each of the three reasons you liked or were disappointed in the friend you're writing about.

2. Omit any details that do not truly support your topic sentence.
3. Add more details as needed, making sure you have plenty of support for each of your three reasons.
4. Check to see that your details are vivid and specific. Can you make a supporting detail more concrete? Are there any persuasive, colorful specifics you can add?
5. Try to eliminate wordiness (see page 391) and clichés (see page 388).
6. In general, improve the flow of your writing.
7. Be sure to include a final sentence that rounds off the paper, bringing it to a close.

Activity 4: Editing and Proofreading

When you have your almost-final draft of the paper, proofread it as follows:

1. Using your dictionary, check any words that you think might be misspelled. Or use a spell-check program on your computer.
2. Using Part Two of this book, check your paper for mistakes in grammar, punctuation, and usage.
3. Read the paper aloud, listening for awkward or unclear spots. Make the changes needed for the paragraph to read smoothly and clearly. Even better, see if you can get another person to read the draft aloud to you. The spots that this person has trouble reading are spots where you may have to do some rewriting.
4. Take a sheet of paper and cover your writing so that you can expose and carefully check one line at a time. Or read your writing backward, from the end of the paragraph to the beginning. Look for typing errors, omitted words, and other remaining errors.

Don't fail to edit and proofread carefully. You may be tired of working on your paper at this point, but you want to give the extra effort needed to make it as good as possible. A final push can mean the difference between a higher and a lower grade.

21 Paragraph and Essay Writing Assignments

Your instructor may ask you to do some of the following paragraph and essay writing assignments. Be sure to refer to the activities above as you write. Also, check the rules for paper format on page 266.

Note: Responses to these activities will vary.

Five Paragraph Assignments

■ Paragraph Assignment 1: A Sharp Memory of Your Mother or Father

Think of a particularly clear memory you have of your mother or father. It might be a happy memory that warms your heart. Or it could be humorous, frightening, or enraging. The important thing is that it is a sharp, specific recollection that produces a strong emotional response in you. Then write a paragraph about your memory.

Your goal will be to let the reader see exactly what happened and understand what you felt. To accomplish this, you must provide very specific details. Remember that your reader will have no prior knowledge of your mother or father. You are responsible for painting a "word picture" that will let your reader see your parent the way you saw him or her.

Before you begin writing the paragraph itself, do some prewriting. You might jot down answers to the kind of questions a curious reader would have about your memory. Here are a few such questions: Where did this event take place? When? Who was present? How old was your parent when this occurred? How old were you? What did your parent look like? What did he or she say? How did he or she say it? Why is this memory so vivid for you? The answers to questions like these will provide the kind of concrete detail that will make your paragraph come alive.

Begin your paragraph with a summary statement, such as these:

> One of my family's most amusing experiences took place when I found my father sleepwalking in the kitchen.
>
> Seeing my mother trip on the sidewalk was the beginning of a difficult morning for me.

Your paragraph will probably be organized in time order, describing the events that occurred from beginning to end. You can help your reader understand the sequence of events if you use time transitions such as *first, next, then, later,* and *finally.*

If you prefer, write instead about a memory of another relative.

■ Paragraph Assignment 2: A Disagreeable Characteristic

Even the most saintly person has one or more unpleasant traits. Write a paragraph about a particularly disagreeable characteristic of someone you know. Your topic sentence will be a general statement about that person and the quality you've chosen to write about. For example, if you decide to write about your own extreme impatience, your topic sentence might be:

> When I let my impatience get out of hand, I often damage my relationships with others.

A paragraph with this topic sentence might list two or three experiences supporting that main idea. Here are two other examples of topic sentences for this paper:

> Our neighbor Mr. Nagle is a cruel person.
>
> While my minister is basically a kind man, he much prefers hearing his own voice to anyone else's.

■ Paragraph Assignment 3: A Special Goal

We all have goals, long-term and short-term. Write a paragraph about one of your important goals. It might be something you hope to achieve over the next few months or the next few years.

Perhaps you plan to overcome a bad habit or get a better job. Begin your paragraph with a topic sentence that clearly states the goal and when you expect to reach it, such as "I hope to have quit smoking by the end of this year" or "After I graduate, I hope to get a nursing job at a local hospital." Then go on to list and explain two or three reasons you wish to reach the goal. To generate some reasons, make a list, and then choose the three you feel are the strongest. Save the most important reason for last.

■ Paragraph Assignment 4: In Praise of Something

We all are fans of something that we feel greatly enriches our life, such as a pet, basketball, or chocolate. Write a paragraph in which your supporting details show the benefits or virtues of something you adore. For instance, you could write about the advantages of having a dog around the house. Use whatever prewriting strategy you choose to help you come up with more benefits or virtues than you need. Then choose two or three you feel you can explain in colorful detail.

One benefit you might list, for instance, is that a dog makes one feel loved. You could illustrate this benefit by describing an experience such as the following:

> A week ago, I spilled hot coffee on a customer's lap. He was not amused. After the customer left—without leaving a tip, of course—the manager walked past me and said quietly, "Strike one!" When I got home that day and collapsed on a chair, my friend Goldie, a cocker spaniel, hopped onto my lap and licked my face with his broad, warm tongue. I could feel the knot in my stomach loosening.

Here's a sample scratch outline for this assignment.

Topic sentence: Having a dog around the house is one of life's rich pleasures.

(1) A dog is entertaining.

(2) A dog brings out the best in a person.

(3) A dog makes a person feel loved.

■ Paragraph Assignment 5: A Popular Saying

It seems there are sayings to cover every type of experience, from our sleeping habits ("Early to bed, early to rise, makes a man healthy, wealthy and wise") to our expectations ("Hope for the best but expect the worst"). Write a paragraph in which you demonstrate through an experience you have had that a particular saying is either true or false.

Begin your paragraph with a clear statement supporting or opposing the saying, such as "When I painted my house last summer, I learned the truth of the saying 'Haste makes waste'" or "When it comes to escaping a fire, the saying 'Haste makes waste' doesn't apply." Then go on to tell your experience in vivid detail. To help your reader follow the sequence of events involved, use a few time transitions (*before, then, during, now,* and so on). Below are some other popular sayings you might wish to consider using in your paper—or use some other popular saying.

Here today, gone tomorrow.

If you don't help yourself, nobody will.

A penny saved is a penny earned.

The early bird catches the worm.

Curiosity killed the cat.

You get what you pay for.

A rolling stone gathers no moss.

Don't count your chickens before they're hatched.

An ounce of prevention is worth a pound of cure.

A journey of a thousand miles must begin with a single step.

Whatever can go wrong will go wrong.

Don't judge someone until you've walked a mile in his shoes.

Five Essay Assignments

■ Essay Assignment 1: The Place Where You Live

Write an essay about the best or worst features of your apartment or house. In your introduction, you might begin with a general description of where you live. Then end the paragraph with your thesis statement and plan of development.

Here are some thesis statements that may help you think about and develop your own paper.

Thesis statement: I love my apartment because of its wonderful location, its great kitchen, and my terrific neighbors.

(A supporting paragraph on the apartment's location, for example, might focus on the fact that it's in the middle of a lively, interesting neighborhood with a good supermarket, a drugstore, a variety of restaurants, and so on.)

Thesis statement: My house has three key advantages: a wonderful landlord, a beautiful yard, and housemates that are like family.

(A supporting paragraph about the landlord might explain how he or she fixes things promptly and once, in a special circumstance, allowed you to pay your rent late.)

Thesis statement: A tiny kitchen, dismal decor, and noisy neighbors are the three main disadvantages of my apartment.

(A supporting paragraph on the apartment's dismal decor could begin with this topic sentence: "The dark and poorly kept walls and floorings are ugly and, even worse, gloomy." Such a sentence might then be followed by some very carefully worded, concrete specifics and perhaps a revealing anecdote.)

Note that listing transitions such as *first of all, second, another, also, in addition, finally,* and so on may help you introduce your supporting paragraphs as well as set off different supporting details within those paragraphs.

Essay Assignment 2: What Children Really Need

There are many theories about what children need from the adults in their lives. Give some thought to your own childhood, your own children, or your observations of children you know. Decide on three things that *you* believe are essential to a child's growth and development. Then write a five-paragraph essay on those three qualities.

Your introductory paragraph should arouse your readers' interest. For instance, you might explain how important a person's childhood is to the rest of his or her life. The introductory paragraph should also include a thesis statement made up of your central idea and the three necessities you think are so important. For instance, one student's thesis was this: "I feel that three things all children need are love, approval, and a sense of belonging."

Devote each of the following three supporting paragraphs to one of these important things. Begin each paragraph with a clearly stated topic sentence, and use concrete examples to show how adults can provide each quality to children.

Be equally specific in showing what you believe happens when children are not provided with these things. To help your reader make the transition from paragraph to paragraph, use such words as *another thing, in addition,* and *a final quality.* You may wish to consider writing about some of the following things many people feel children need for healthy growth and development:

Unconditional love

Approval

Sense of belonging

Opportunities to experiment

Feeling of safety

Clearly defined limits to behavior

Sense of responsibility

In a concluding paragraph, provide a summary of the points in your paper as well as a final thought to round off your discussion.

■ Essay Assignment 3: Something Special

Imagine that your apartment or house is burning down. Of course, the best strategy would be to get yourself and others out of the building as quickly as possible. But suppose you knew for sure that you had time to rescue three of your possessions. Which three would you choose? Write an essay in which you discuss the three things in your home that you would most want to save from a fire.

Begin by doing some prewriting to find the items you want to write about. You could, for instance, try making a list and then choosing several of the most likely candidates. Then you could freewrite about each of those candidates. In this way, you are likely to find three possessions that will make strong subjects for this essay. Each will be the basis of a supporting paragraph. Each supporting paragraph will focus on why the object being discussed is so important to you. Make your support as specific and colorful as possible, perhaps using detailed descriptions, anecdotes, or quotations to reveal the importance of each object.

In planning your introduction, consider beginning with a broad, general idea and then narrowing it down to your thesis statement. Here, for example, is one such introduction for this paper:

> I have many possessions that I would be sad to lose. Because I love to cook, I would miss various kitchen appliances that provide me with so many happy cooking adventures. I would also miss the wonderful electronic equipment that entertains me every day, including my large-screen television set and my VCR. I would miss the various telephones on which I have spent

many interesting hours chatting in every part of my apartment, including the bathtub. But if my apartment were burning down, I would most want to rescue three things that are irreplaceable and hold great meaning for me—the silverware set that belonged to my grandmother, my mother's wedding gown, and my giant photo album.

Essay Assignment 4: Teaching the Basics

What are you experienced in? Fixing cars? Growing flowers? Baking? Waiting on customers? Giving children's birthday parties? Write an essay teaching readers the basics of an activity in which you have some experience. If you're not sure about which activity to choose, use prewriting to help you find a topic you can support strongly. Once you've chosen your topic, continue to prewrite as a way to find your key points and organize them into three supporting paragraphs. The key details of waiting on customers in a diner, for instance, might be divided according to time order, as seen in the following topic sentences:

Topic sentence for supporting paragraph 1: Greeting customers and taking their orders should not be done carelessly.

Topic sentence for supporting paragraph 2: There are right and wrong ways to bring customers their food and to keep track of them during their meal.

Topic sentence for supporting paragraph 3: The final interaction with customers may be brief, but it is important.

To make your points clear, be sure to use detailed descriptions and concrete examples throughout your essay. Also, you may want to use transitional words such as *first, then, also, another, when, after, while,* and *finally* to help organize your details.

Essay Assignment 5: Advantages or Disadvantages of Single Life

More and more people are remaining single longer, and almost half of the people who marry eventually divorce and become single again. Write an essay on the advantages or disadvantages of single life. Each of your three supporting paragraphs will focus on one advantage or one disadvantage. To decide which approach to take, begin by making two lists. A list of advantages might include:

More freedom of choice

Lower expenses

Fewer responsibilities

Dating opportunities

A list of disadvantages could include:

Loneliness

Depression on holidays

Lack of support in everyday decisions

Disapproval of parents and family

Go on to list as many specific details as you can think of to support your advantages and disadvantages. Those details will help you decide whether you want your thesis to focus on benefits or drawbacks. Then create a scratch outline made up of your thesis statement and each of your main supporting points. Put the most important or most dramatic supporting point last.

In your introduction, you might gain your reader's interest by asking several questions or by telling a brief, revealing story about single life. As you develop your supporting paragraphs, make sure that each paragraph begins with a topic sentence and focuses on one advantage or disadvantage of single life. While writing the essay, continue developing details that vividly support each of your points.

In a concluding paragraph, provide a summary of the points in your paper as well as a final thought to round off your discussion. Your final thought might be in the form of a prediction or a recommendation.

Additional Writing Assignments

Detailed writing assignments follow each of the ten readings in Part Four. As you work on these assignments, you will find it helpful to turn back to the writing activities on pages 75–77.

Part Two

Sentence Skills

Introduction

Part Two explains the basic skills needed to write clear, error-free sentences. While the skills are presented within five traditional categories (sentences; verbs, pronouns, and agreement; modifiers and parallelism; punctuation and mechanics; word use), each section is self-contained so that you can go directly to the skills you need to work on. Note, however, that you may find it helpful to cover "Subjects and Verbs" before turning to other skills. Typically, the main features of a skill are presented on the first pages of a section; secondary points are developed later. Numerous activities are provided so that you can practice skills enough to make them habits. The activities are varied and range from underlining answers to writing complete sentences involving the skill in question. One or more review tests at the end of each section offer additional practice activities.

4 Subjects and Verbs

Introductory Activity

Understanding subjects and verbs is a big step toward mastering many sentence skills. As a speaker of English, you already have an instinctive feel for these basic building blocks of English sentences. See if you can insert an appropriate word in each space below. The answer will be a subject.

Answers will vary.

1. The ______________ will soon be over.
2. ______________ cannot be trusted.
3. A strange ______________ appeared in my backyard.
4. ______________ is one of my favorite activities.

Now insert an appropriate word in the following spaces. Each answer will be a verb.

5. The prisoner ______________ at the judge.
6. My sister ______________ much harder than I do.
7. The players ______________ in the locker room.
8. Rob and Marilyn ______________ with the teacher.

Finally, insert appropriate words in the following spaces. Each answer will be a subject in the first space and a verb in the second.

9. The ______________ almost ______________ out of the tree.
10. Many ______________ today ______________ sex and violence.
11. The ______________ carefully ______________ the patient.
12. A ______________ quickly ______________ the ball.

The basic building blocks of English sentences are subjects and verbs. Understanding them is an important first step toward mastering a number of sentence skills.

Every sentence has a subject and a verb. Who or what the sentence speaks about is called the *subject;* what the sentence says about the subject is called the *verb.* In the following sentences, the subject is underlined once and the verb twice:

People gossip.
The truck belched fumes.
He waved at me.
Alaska contains the largest wilderness area in the United States.
That woman is a millionaire.
The pants feel itchy.

A Simple Way to Find a Subject

To find a subject, ask *who* or *what* the sentence is about. As shown below, your answer is the subject.

Who is the first sentence about? People
What is the second sentence about? The truck
Who is the third sentence about? He
What is the fourth sentence about? Alaska
Who is the fifth sentence about? That woman
What is the sixth sentence about? The pants

It helps to remember that the subject of a sentence is always a *noun* (any person, place, or thing) or a pronoun. A *pronoun* is simply a word like *he, she, it, you,* or *they* used in place of a noun. In the preceding sentences, the subjects are persons (*People, He, woman*), a place (*Alaska*), and things (*truck, pants*). And note that one pronoun (*He*) is used as a subject.

A Simple Way to Find a Verb

To find a verb, ask what the sentence *says about* the subject. As shown below, your answer is the verb.

What does the first sentence *say about* people? They gossip.

What does the second sentence *say about* the truck? It belched (fumes).

What does the third sentence *say about* him? He waved (at me).

What does the fourth sentence *say about* Alaska? It contains (the largest wilderness area in the United States).

What does the fifth sentence *say about* that woman? She is (a millionaire).

What does the sixth sentence *say about* the pants? They feel (itchy).

A second way to find the verb is to put *I, you, he, she, it,* or *they* in front of the word you think is a verb. If the result makes sense, you have a verb. For example, you could put *they* in front of *gossip* in the first sentence above, with the result, *they gossip,* making sense. Therefore, you know that *gossip* is a verb. You could use the same test with the other verbs as well.

Finally, it helps to remember that most verbs show action. In "People gossip," the action is gossiping. In "The truck belched fumes," the action is belching. In "He waved at me," the action is waving. In "Alaska contains the largest wilderness area in the United States," the action is containing.

Certain other verbs, known as *linking verbs,* do not show action. They do, however, give information about the subject of the sentence. In "That woman is a millionaire," the linking verb *is* tells us that the woman is a millionaire. In "The pants feel itchy," the linking verb *feel* gives us the information that the pants are itchy.

Practice 1

In each of the following sentences, draw one line under the subject and two lines under the verb.

To find the subject, ask *who* or *what* the sentence is about. Then to find the verb, ask what the sentence *says about* the subject.

1. Carl spilled cocoa on the pale carpet.
2. A ladybug landed on my shoulder.
3. Nick eats cold pizza for breakfast.
4. The waitress brought someone else's meal by mistake.

5. I found a blue egg under the tree in my backyard.
6. Diane stapled her papers together.
7. The audience applauded before the song was finished.
8. My boss has a lot of patience.
9. I tasted poached eggs today for the first time.
10. The new paperboy threw our newspaper under the car.

Practice 2

Follow the directions given for Practice 1. Note that all the verbs here are linking verbs.

1. I am always nervous on the first day of classes.
2. My parents are not very sociable.
3. Tri Lee was the first person to finish the exam.
4. Our dog becomes friendly after a few minutes of growling.
5. Estelle seems ready for a nervous breakdown.
6. That plastic hot dog looks good enough to eat.
7. Overweight people appear slimmer in clothes with vertical stripes.
8. Many students felt exhausted after finishing the placement exam.
9. A cheeseburger has more than seven times as much sodium as French fries.
10. Yesterday, my telephone seemed to be ringing constantly.

Practice 3

Follow the directions given for Practice 1.

1. The rabbits ate more than their share of my garden.
2. My father prefers his well-worn jeans to new ones.
3. A local restaurant donated food for the homeless.
4. Stanley always looks ready for a fight.
5. An elderly couple relaxed on a bench in the shopping mall.
6. Lightning brightened the dark sky for a few seconds.
7. Our town council voted for a curfew on Halloween.
8. Lola's sore throat kept her home from work today.
9. Surprisingly, Vonda's little sister decided not to go to the circus.
10. As usual, I chose the slowest checkout line in the supermarket.

More about Subjects and Verbs

Distinguishing Subjects from Prepositional Phrases

The subject of a sentence never appears within a prepositional phrase. A *prepositional phrase* is simply a group of words beginning with a preposition and ending with the answer to the question *what, when,* or *where.* Here is a list of common prepositions.

Common Prepositions

about	before	by	inside	over
above	behind	during	into	through
across	below	except	of	to
among	beneath	for	off	toward
around	beside	from	on	under
at	between	in	onto	with

When you are looking for the subject of a sentence, it is helpful to cross out prepositional phrases.

~~In the middle of the night~~, we heard footsteps ~~on the roof~~.

The magazines ~~on the table~~ belong ~~in the garage~~.

~~Before the opening kickoff~~, a brass band marched ~~onto the field~~.

The hardware store ~~across the street~~ went ~~out of business~~.

~~In spite of our advice~~, Sally quit her job ~~at Burger King~~.

Practice

Cross out prepositional phrases. Then draw a single line under subjects and a double line under verbs.

1. ~~By accident~~, Anita dropped her folder ~~into the mailbox~~.
2. ~~Before the test~~, I glanced ~~through my notes~~.
3. My car stalled ~~on the bridge at rush hour~~.

4. I hung a photo ~~of Whitney Houston above my bed~~.
5. ~~On weekends~~, we visit my grandmother ~~at a nursing home~~.
6. ~~During the movie~~, some teenagers giggled ~~at the love scenes~~.
7. A pedestrian tunnel runs ~~beneath the street to the train station~~.
8. The parents hid their daughter's Christmas gifts ~~in the garage~~.
9. All the teachers, ~~except Mr. Blake~~, wear ties ~~to school~~.
10. The strawberry jam ~~in my brother's sandwich~~ dripped ~~onto his lap~~.

Verbs of More Than One Word

Many verbs consist of more than one word. Here, for example, are some of the many forms of the verb *help:*

Some Forms of the Verb Help

helps	should have been helping	will have helped
helping	can help	would have been helped
is helping	would have been helping	has been helped
was helping	will be helping	had been helped
may help	had been helping	must have helped
should help	helped	having helped
will help	have helped	should have been helped
does help	has helped	had helped

Below are sentences that contain verbs of more than one word:

Yolanda is working overtime this week.
Another book has been written about the Kennedy family.
We should have stopped for gas at the last station.
The game has just been canceled.

Notes

1 Words like *not, just, never, only,* and *always* are not part of the verb although they may appear within the verb.

Yolanda is not working overtime next week.

The boys should just not have stayed out so late.

The game has always been played regardless of the weather.

2 No verb preceded by *to* is ever the verb of a sentence.

Sue wants to go with us.

The newly married couple decided to rent a house for a year.

The store needs extra people to help out at Christmas.

3 No *-ing* word by itself is ever the verb of a sentence. (It may be part of the verb, but it must have a helping verb in front of it.)

We planning the trip for months. (This is not a sentence, because the verb is not complete.)

We were planning the trip for months. (This is a complete sentence.)

Practice

Draw a single line under subjects and a double line under verbs. Be sure to include all parts of the verb.

1. Ellen has chosen blue dresses for her bridesmaids.
2. You should plan your weekly budget more carefully.
3. Felix has been waiting in line for tickets all morning.
4. We should have invited Terri to the party.
5. I would have preferred a movie with a happy ending.
6. Classes were interrupted three times today by a faulty fire alarm.
7. Sam can touch his nose with his tongue.
8. I have been encouraging my mother to quit smoking.
9. Tony has just agreed to feed his neighbor's fish over the holiday.
10. Many students have not been giving much thought to selecting a major.

Compound Subjects and Verbs

A sentence may have more than one verb:

> The dancer stumbled and fell.
> Lola washed her hair, blew it dry, and parted it in the middle.

A sentence may have more than one subject:

> Cats and dogs are sometimes the best of friends.
> The striking workers and their bosses could not come to an agreement.

A sentence may have several subjects and several verbs:

> Holly and I read the book and reported on it to the class.
> Pete, Nick, and Fran caught the fish in the morning, cleaned them in the afternoon, and ate them that night.

Practice

Draw a single line under subjects and a double line under verbs. Be sure to mark *all* the subjects and verbs.

1. Boards and bricks make a nice bookcase.
2. We bought a big bag of peanuts and finished it by the movie's end.
3. A fly and a bee hung lifelessly in the spider's web.
4. The twins look alike but think, act, and dress quite differently.
5. Canned salmon and tuna contain significant amounts of calcium.
6. I waited for the bubble bath to foam and then slipped into the warm tub.
7. The little girl in the next car waved and smiled at me.
8. The bird actually dived under the water and reappeared with a fish.
9. Singers, dancers, and actors performed for the heart-association benefit.
10. The magician and his assistant bowed and disappeared in a cloud of smoke.

■ Review Test 1

Draw one line under the subjects and two lines under the verbs. To help find subjects, cross out prepositional phrases as necessary. Underline all the parts of a verb. You may find more than one subject and verb in a sentence.

1. Most breakfast cereals contain sugar.
2. The drawer ~~of the bureau~~ sticks ~~on rainy days~~.
3. Our local bus company offers special rates ~~for senior citizens~~.
4. Drunk drivers ~~in Norway~~ must spend three weeks ~~in jail at hard labor~~.
5. ~~On weekends~~, the campus bookstore closes ~~at five o'clock~~.
6. We wrapped and labeled all the Christmas gifts ~~over the weekend~~.
7. Motorcycles have been banned ~~from the expressway~~.
8. Episodes ~~of this old television series~~ are ~~in black and white~~.
9. The computer sorted, counted, and recorded the ballots ~~within minutes after the closing of the polls.~~
10. Eddie stepped ~~to the foul line~~ and calmly sank both free throws to win the basketball game.

■ Review Test 2

Follow the directions given for Review Test 1.

1. Gasoline ~~from the broken fuel line~~ dripped ~~onto the floor of the garage~~.
2. All the carrot tops ~~in the garden~~ had been eaten ~~by rabbits~~.
3. An old man ~~with a plastic trash bag~~ collected aluminum cans ~~along the road~~.
4. The majority ~~of people~~ wait ~~until April 15~~ to file their income tax.
5. My mother became a college freshman ~~at the age of forty-two~~.
6. ~~At the delicatessen~~, Linda and Paul ate corned beef sandwiches and drank root beer.
7. The window fan made a clanking sound ~~during the night~~ and kept us ~~from sleeping~~.
8. An umbrella tumbled ~~across the street in the gusty wind~~ and landed ~~between two cars~~.
9. Telephones ~~in the mayor's office~~ rang continuously ~~with calls from angry citizens about the city tax increase~~.
10. A teenager pushed a woman, grabbed her purse, and ran off ~~through the crowd~~.

5 Fragments

Introductory Activity

Every sentence must have a subject and a verb and must express a complete thought. A word group that lacks a subject or a verb and does not express a complete thought is a *fragment.*

Listed below are a number of fragments and sentences. See if you can complete the statement that explains each fragment.

1. Telephones. *Fragment*
   Telephones ring. *Sentence*

"Telephones" is a fragment because, while it has a subject (*Telephones*), it lacks a __verb__ (*ring*) and so does not express a complete thought.

2. Explains. *Fragment*
   Darrell explains. *Sentence*

"Explains" is a fragment because, while it has a verb (*Explains*), it lacks a __subject__ (*Darrell*) and does not express a complete thought.

3. Scribbling notes in class. *Fragment*
   Jayne was scribbling notes in class. *Sentence*

"Scribbling notes in class" is a fragment because it lacks a __subject__ (*Jayne*) and also part of the __verb__ (*was*). As a result, it does not express a complete thought.

4. When the dentist began drilling. *Fragment*
   When the dentist began drilling, I closed my eyes. *Sentence*

"When the dentist began drilling" is a fragment because we want to know *what happened when* the dentist began drilling. The word group does not follow through and __express a complete thought__.

Answers are on page 676.

What Fragments Are

Every sentence must have a subject and a verb and must express a complete thought. A word group that lacks a subject or a verb and does not express a complete thought is a *fragment*. Following are the most common types of fragments that people write:

1. Dependent-word fragments
2. *-ing* and *to* fragments
3. Added-detail fragments
4. Missing-subject fragments

Once you understand the specific kind or kinds of fragments that you might write, you should be able to eliminate them from your writing. The following pages explain all four types of fragments.

1 Dependent-Word Fragments

Some word groups that begin with a dependent word are fragments. Here is a list of common dependent words:

Common Dependent Words

after	unless
although, though	until
as	what, whatever
because	when, whenever
before	where, wherever
even though	whether
how	which, whichever
if, even if	while
in order that	who
since	whose
that, so that	

Whenever you start a sentence with one of these dependent words, you must be careful that a dependent-word fragment does not result. The word group beginning with the dependent word *After* in the selection below is a fragment.

After I stopped drinking coffee. I began sleeping better at night.

A *dependent statement*—one starting with a dependent word like *After*—cannot stand alone. It depends on another statement to complete the thought. "After I stopped drinking coffee" is a dependent statement. It leaves us hanging. We expect in the same sentence to find out *what happened after* the writer stopped drinking coffee. When a writer does not follow through and complete a thought, a fragment results.

To correct the fragment, simply follow through and complete the thought:

After I stopped drinking coffee, I began sleeping better at night.

Remember, then, that *dependent statements by themselves* are fragments. They must be attached to a statement that makes sense standing alone.*

Here are two other examples of dependent-word fragments.

Brian sat nervously in the dental clinic. While waiting to have his wisdom tooth pulled.

Maria decided to throw away the boxes. That had accumulated for years in the basement.

"While waiting to have his wisdom tooth pulled" is a fragment; it does not make sense standing by itself. We want to know in the same statement *what Brian did* while waiting to have his tooth pulled. The writer must complete the thought. Likewise, "That had accumulated for years in the basement" is not in itself a complete thought. We want to know in the same statement what *that* refers to.

How to Correct Dependent-Word Fragments

In most cases, you can correct a dependent-word fragment by attaching it to the sentence that comes after it or to the sentence that comes before it:

After I stopped drinking coffee, I began sleeping better at night.
(The fragment has been attached to the sentence that comes after it.)

*Some instructors refer to a dependent-word fragment as a *dependent clause*. A *clause* is simply a group of words having a subject and a verb. A clause may be *independent* (expressing a complete thought and able to stand alone) or *dependent* (not expressing a complete thought and not able to stand alone). A dependent clause by itself is a fragment. It can be corrected simply by adding an independent clause.

Brian sat nervously in the dental clinic while waiting to have his wisdom tooth pulled.

(The fragment has been attached to the sentence that comes before it.)

Maria decided to throw away the boxes that had accumulated for years in the basement.

(The fragment has been attached to the sentence that comes before it.)

Another way of correcting a dependent-word fragment is to eliminate the dependent word and make a new sentence:

I stopped drinking coffee.

He was waiting to have his wisdom tooth pulled.

They had accumulated for years in the basement.

Do not use this second method of correction too frequently, however, for it may cut down on interest and variety in your writing style.

Notes

1 Use a comma if a dependent-word group comes at the *beginning* of a sentence (see also page 321):

After I stopped drinking coffee, I began sleeping better at night.

However, do not generally use a comma if the dependent-word group comes at the end of a sentence:

Brian sat nervously in the dental clinic while waiting to have his wisdom tooth pulled.

Maria decided to throw away the boxes that had accumulated for years in the basement.

2 Sometimes the dependent words *who, that, which,* or *where* appear not at the very start but *near* the start of a word group. A fragment often results.

Today I visited Hilda Cooper. <u>A friend who is in the hospital.</u>

"A friend who is in the hospital" is not in itself a complete thought. We want to know in the same statement *who* the friend is. The fragment can be corrected by attaching it to the sentence that comes before it:

Today I visited Hilda Cooper, a friend who is in the hospital.

(Here a comma is used to set off "a friend who is in the hospital," which is extra material placed at the end of the sentence.)

Practice 1

Turn each of the dependent-word groups into a sentence by adding a complete thought. Put a comma after the dependent-word group if a dependent word starts the sentence.

Examples After I got out of high school
After I got out of high school, I spent a year traveling.

The watch which I got fixed
The watch which I got fixed has just stopped working again.

Answers will vary.

1. Before I go to work

____

____

2. Because I have a test tomorrow

____

____

3. Since it was such a hot day

____

____

4. The dentist that I go to

____

____

5. When the department store closed

____

____

Practice 2

Underline the dependent-word fragment (or fragments) in each selection. Then correct each fragment by attaching it to the sentence that comes before or the sentence that comes after—whichever sounds more natural. Put a comma after the dependent-word group if it starts the sentence.

1. When the waitress coughed in his food. Frank lost his appetite. He didn't even take home a doggy bag.

   When the waitress coughed in his food, Frank lost his appetite.

2. Our power went out. During a thunderstorm. I lost the paper I was writing on the computer.

   Our power went out during a thunderstorm.

3. Tony doesn't like going to the ballpark. If he misses an exciting play. There's no instant replay.

   If he misses an exciting play, there's no instant replay.

4. After the mail carrier comes. I run to our mailbox. I love to get mail. Even if it is only junk mail.

   After the mail carrier comes, I run to our mailbox. I love to get mail even if it is only junk mail.

5. Even though she can't read. My little daughter likes to go to the library. She chooses books with pretty covers. While I look at the latest magazines.

   Even though she can't read, my daughter likes to go to the library. She chooses books with pretty covers while I look at the latest magazines.

2 *-ing* and *to* Fragments

When a word ending in *-ing* or the word *to* appears at or near the start of a word group, a fragment may result. Such fragments often lack a subject and part of the verb.

Underline the word groups in the examples below that contain *-ing* words. Each is an *-ing* fragment.

Example 1

I spent all day in the employment office. Trying to find a job that suited me. The prospects looked bleak.

Example 2

Lola surprised Tony on the nature hike. Picking blobs of resin off pine trees. Then she chewed them like bubble gum.

Example 3

Mel took an aisle seat on the bus. His reason being that he had more legroom.

People sometimes write *-ing* fragments because they think the subject in one sentence will work for the next word group as well. In the first selection above, they might think the subject *I* in the opening sentence will also serve as the subject for "Trying to find a job that suited me." But the subject must actually be *in* the sentence.

How to Correct *-ing* Fragments

1. Attach the fragment to the sentence that comes before it or the sentence that comes after it, whichever makes sense. Example 1 above could read, "I spent all day in the employment office, trying to find a job that suited me." (Note that here a comma is used to set off "trying to find a job that suited me," which is extra material placed at the end of the sentence.)
2. Add a subject and change the *-ing* verb part to the correct form of the verb. Example 2 could read, "She picked blobs of resin off pine trees."
3. Change *being* to the correct form of the verb *be (am, are, is, was, were).* Example 3 could read, "His reason was that he had more legroom."

How to Correct *to* Fragments

As noted above, when *to* appears at or near the start of a word group, a fragment sometimes results.

To remind people of their selfishness. Otis leaves handwritten notes on cars that take up two parking spaces.

The first word group in the example above is a *to* fragment. It can be corrected by adding it to the sentence that comes after it.

To remind people of their selfishness, Otis leaves handwritten notes on cars that take up two parking spaces.

(Note that here a comma is used to set off "To remind people of their selfishness," which is introductory material in the sentence.)

Practice 1

Underline the *-ing* fragment in each of the three items below. Then make the fragment a sentence by rewriting it, using the method described in parentheses.

Example The dog eyed me with suspicion. Not knowing whether its master was at home. I hesitated to open the gate.
(Add the fragment to the sentence that comes after it.)
Not knowing whether its master was at home, I hesitated to open the gate.

1. Vince sat nervously in the dentist's chair. Waiting for his x-rays to be developed. He prayed there would be no cavities. (Add fragment to the preceding sentence.)
   Vince sat nervously in the dentist's chair, waiting for his x-rays to be developed.
2. Looking through the movie ads for twenty minutes. Lew and Marian tried to find a film they both wanted to see.
   (Add fragment to the sentence that comes after it.)
   Looking through the movie ads for twenty minutes, Lew and Marian tried to find a film they both wanted to see.
3. The jeep went too fast around the sharp curve. As a result, tipping over.
   (Add the subject *It* and change the verb *tipping* to the correct form, *tipped.)*
   The jeep went too fast around the sharp curve. As a result, it tipped over.

Practice 2

Underline the *-ing* or *to* fragment in each selection. Then rewrite each selection correctly, using one of the methods of correction described on page 103.
Correction methods may vary.

1. Some workers dug up the street near our house. Causing frequent vibrations inside. By evening, all the pictures on our walls were crooked.
   Some workers dug up the street near our house, causing frequent vibrations inside.
2. I had heard about the surprise party for me. I therefore walked slowly into the darkened living room. Preparing to look shocked.
   I therefore walked slowly into the darkened living room, preparing to look shocked.

3. Dribbling skillfully up the court. Luis looked for a teammate who was open. Then he passed the ball.

   Dribbling skillfully up the court, Luis looked for a teammate who was open.

4. As I was dreaming of a sunny day at the beach, the alarm clock rang. Wanting to finish the dream. I pushed the snooze button.

   Wanting to finish the dream, I pushed the snooze button.

5. To get back my term paper. I went to see my English instructor from last semester. I also wanted some career advice.

   To get back my term paper, I went to see my English instructor from last semester.

3 Added-Detail Fragments

Added-detail fragments lack a subject and a verb. They often begin with one of the following words.

also	except	including
especially	for example	such as

See if you can underline the one added-detail fragment in each of these examples:

Example 1

Tony has trouble accepting criticism. Except from Lola. She has a knack for tact.

Example 2

My apartment has its drawbacks. For example, no hot water in the morning.

Example 3

I had many jobs while in school. Among them, busboy, painter, and security guard.

People often write added-detail fragments for much the same reason they write *-ing* fragments. They think the subject and verb in one sentence will serve for the next word group as well. But the subject and verb must be in *each* word group.

How to Correct Added-Detail Fragments

1 Attach the fragment to the complete thought that precedes it. Example 1 could read: "Tony has trouble accepting criticism, except from Lola." (Note that here a comma is used to set off "except from Lola," which is extra material placed at the end of the sentence.)

2 Add a subject and a verb to the fragment to make it a complete sentence. Example 2 could read: "My apartment has its drawbacks. For example, there is no hot water in the morning."

3 Change words as necessary to make the fragment part of the preceding sentence. Example 3 could read: "Among the many jobs I had while in school have been busboy, painter, and security guard."

Practice 1

Underline the fragment in each selection below. Then make it a sentence by rewriting it, using the method described in parentheses.

Example My husband and I share the household chores. Including meals. I do the cooking and he does the eating.
(Add the fragment to the preceding sentence.)
My husband and I share the household chores, including meals.

1. Denise puts things off until the last minute. For example, waiting until the night before a test to begin studying.
(Correct the fragment by adding the subject *she* and changing *waiting* to the proper form of the verb, *waits*.)
For example, she waits until the night before a test to begin studying.

2. My eleventh-grade English teacher picked on everybody. Except the athletes. They could do no wrong.
(Add the fragment to the preceding sentence.)
My eleventh-grade English teacher picked on everybody except the athletes.

3. Bernardo always buys things out of season. For example, an air conditioner in December. He saves a lot of money this way.

   (Correct the fragment by adding the subject and verb *he bought.)*

   For example, he bought an air conditioner in December.

Practice 2

Underline the added-detail fragment in each selection. Then rewrite that part of the selection needed to correct the fragment. Use one of the three methods of correction described on page 106.

Rewritten versions may vary.

1. I find all sorts of things in my little boy's pockets. Including crayons, stones, and melted chocolate. Luckily, I haven't found anything alive there yet.

   I find all sorts of things in my little boy's pockets, including crayons, stones, and melted chocolate.

2. There are certain chores I hate to do. Especially cleaning windows. So I clean only the windows I look out of.

   There are certain chores I hate to do, especially cleaning windows.

3. Some of the foods in our school cafeteria should not be eaten. The meat loaf, for instance. It is as tender and tasty as shoe leather.

   The meat loaf, for instance, is as tender and tasty as shoe leather.

4. By midnight, the party looked like the scene of an accident. With people stretched out on the floor.

   By midnight, the party looked like the scene of an accident, with people stretched out on the floor.

5. Some people on television really annoy me. For example, game show hosts. Their smiles look pasted on their faces.

   For example, the smiles of game show hosts look pasted on their faces.

4 Missing-Subject Fragments

In each example below, underline the word group in which the subject is missing.

Example 1

One example of my father's generosity is that he visits sick friends in the hospital. And takes along get-well cards with a few dollars folded in them.

Example 2

The weight lifter grunted as he heaved the barbells into the air. Then, with a loud groan, dropped them.

People write missing-subject fragments because they think the subject in one sentence will apply to the next word group as well. But the subject, as well as the verb, must be in *each* word group to make it a sentence.

How to Correct Missing-Subject Fragments

1 Attach the fragment to the preceding sentence. Example 1 could read: "One example of my father's generosity is that he visits sick friends in the hospital and takes along get-well cards with a few dollars folded in them."

2 Add a subject (which can often be a pronoun standing for the subject in the preceding sentence). Example 2 could read: "Then, with a loud groan, he dropped them."

Practice

Underline the missing-subject fragment in each selection. Then rewrite that part of the selection needed to correct the fragment. Use one of the two methods of correction described above.

Rewritten versions may vary.

1. Artie tripped on his shoelace. Then looked around to see if anyone had noticed.

   Then he looked around to see if anyone had noticed.

2. I started the car. And quickly turned down the blaring radio.

   I started the car and quickly turned down the blaring radio.

3. The fire in the fireplace crackled merrily. Its orange-red flames shot high in the air. And made strange shadows all around the dark room.

   Its orange-red flames shot high in the air and made strange shadows all around the dark room.

4. The receptionist at that office is not very well trained. She was chewing gum and talking with a co-worker at the same time she took my call. And forgot to take my name.

   She also forgot to take my name.

5. My elderly aunt never stands for long on a bus ride. She places herself in front of a seated young man. And stands on his feet until he gets up.

   She places herself in front of a seated young man and stands on his feet until he gets up.

A Review: How to Check for Fragments

1 Read your paper aloud from the *last* sentence to the *first.* You will be better able to see and hear whether each word group you read is a complete thought.

2 If you think any word group is a fragment, ask yourself: Does this contain a subject and a verb and express a complete thought?

3 More specifically, be on the lookout for the most common fragments.

- Dependent-word fragments (starting with words like *after, because, since, when,* and *before)*
- *-ing* and *to* fragments (*-ing* or *to* at or near the start of a word group)
- Added-detail fragments (starting with words like *for example, such as, also,* and *especially)*
- Missing-subject fragments (a verb is present but not the subject)

Collaborative Activity

Part A: Editing and Rewriting

Working with a partner, read the short paragraph below and underline the five fragments. Then use the space provided to correct the fragments. Feel free to discuss the rewrite quietly with your partner and refer back to the chapter when necessary.

Wording of answers may vary.

[1]I can't remember a time when my sister didn't love to write. [2]In school, when teachers assigned a composition or essay. [3]Her classmates often groaned. [4]She would join them in their protests. [5]Because she didn't want to seem different. [6]Secretly, though, her spirit would dance. [7]Words were special to her. [8]I remember an incident when she was in third grade. [9]She wrote a funny story. [10]About the time my dog made a mess of our kitchen. [11]The teacher made my sister stand in front of the class and read it aloud. [12]By the time she finished. [13]The classroom was bedlam. [14]Even the teacher wiped away tears of laughter. [15]It was a magic moment. [16]Which made my sister more in love with writing than ever.

2–3 In school, when teachers assigned a composition or essay, her classmates often groaned. 4–5 She would join them in their protests because she didn't want to seem different. 9–10 She wrote a funny story about the time my dog made a mess of our kitchen. 12–13 By the time she finished, the classroom was bedlam. 15–16 It was a magic moment, which made my sister more in love with writing than ever.

Part B: Creating Sentences

Working with a partner, make up your own short fragments test as directed.

Continued

Answers will vary.

1. Write a dependent-word fragment in the space below. Then correct the fragment by making it into a complete sentence. You may want to begin your fragment with the word *before*, *after*, *when*, *because*, or *if*.

   Fragment ______________________________

   Sentence ______________________________

   ____

2. In the space below, write a fragment that begins with a word that has an *-ing* ending. Then correct the fragment by making it into a complete sentence. You may want to begin your fragment with the word *laughing*, *walking*, *shopping*, or *talking*.

   Fragment ______________________________

   Sentence ______________________________

   ____

3. Write an added-detail fragment in the space below. Then correct the fragment by making it into a complete sentence. You may want to begin your fragment with the word *also*, *especially*, *except*, or *including*.

   Fragment ______________________________

   Sentence ______________________________

   ____

Reflective Activity

Answers will vary.

1. Look at the paragraph that you revised above. How has removing fragments affected the paragraph? Explain.
2. Explain what it is about fragments that you find most difficult to remember and apply. Use an example to make your point clear. Feel free to refer to anything in this chapter.

■ Review Test 1

Turn each of the following word groups into a complete sentence. Use the space provided.

Examples Feeling very confident
Feeling very confident, I began my speech.

Until the rain started
We played softball until the rain started.

Answers will vary.

1. After we ate dinner
2. Whenever the instructor is late
3. Under the bed
4. If the weather is bad
5. Dave, who is not very organized
6. To get to know each other better
7. Which was annoying
8. Will meet me later
9. Staring at the computer screen
10. Waiting in the long line

■ Review Test 2

Underline the fragment in each item below. Then correct the fragment in the space provided.

Example Sam received all kinds of junk mail. Then complained to the post office. Eventually, some of the mail stopped coming.
Then he complained to the post office.

1. Fascinated, Nina stared at the stranger. Who was standing in the doorway. She wondered if she could convince him they had met before.

   Fascinated, Nina stared at the stranger who was standing in the doorway.

2. Trees can survive on a steep mountain slope if they obey two rules. They must grow low to the ground. And bend with the wind.

   They must grow low to the ground and bend with the wind.

3. While waiting in line at the supermarket. I look in people's baskets. Their food choices give hints about their personalities.

   While waiting in line at the supermarket, I look in people's baskets.

4. I saw spectacular twin rainbows through the kitchen window. So I rushed to get my camera. To take a picture before they vanished.

   So I rushed to get my camera to take a picture before they vanished.

5. Whenever you buy cotton clothes, get them one size too large. By allowing for shrinkage. You will get a longer life out of them.

   By allowing for shrinkage, you will get a longer life out of them.

6. My nutty cousin cuts the address labels off his magazines. Then pastes them on envelopes. This way, he doesn't have to write his return address.

   Then he pastes them on envelopes.

7. Marian never has to buy ketchup or mustard. Because she saves the extra packets that come with fast-food orders.

   Marian never has to buy ketchup or mustard because she saves the extra packets that come with fast-food orders.

8. The soccer players were amazing. Using their feet as well as most people use their hands.

   The soccer players were amazing, using their feet as well as most people use their hands.

9. My husband climbed his first mountain yesterday. Now he's calling all our friends. To tell them about his peak experience.

   Now he's calling all our friends to tell them about his peak experience.

10. The trivia book listed some interesting facts about Babe Ruth. For instance, he spoke German fluently. Also, kept cool on hot days by putting wet cabbage leaves under his cap.

    Also, he kept cool on hot days by putting wet cabbage leaves under his cap.

Review Test 3

In the space provided, write *C* if a word group is a complete sentence; write *frag* if it is a fragment. The first two are done for you.

frag 1. When the bus drivers went on strike.

C 2. I saw many people giving rides to strangers.

C 3. Some even drove out of their way for others.

frag 4. Especially when the weather was bad.

C 5. One rainy day, I saw an elderly woman pull her cab over to the curb.

frag 6. Yelling and waving for five shivering students to get into her car.

frag 7. Until the strike finally ended.

C 8. Scenes like that were not uncommon.

C 9. It seems that community problems bring people together.

frag 10. By weakening the feeling that we live very separate lives.

Now correct the *fragments* you have found. Attach each fragment to the sentence that comes before or after it, or make whatever other change is needed to turn the fragment into a sentence. Use the space provided. The first one is corrected for you.

Wording of answers may vary.

1. When the bus drivers went on strike, I saw many people giving rides to strangers.
2. Some even drove out of their way for others, especially when the weather was bad.
3. One rainy day, I saw an elderly woman pull her cab over to the curb, yelling and waving for five shivering students to get into her car.

4. Until the strike finally ended, scenes like that were not uncommon.

5. It seems that community problems bring people together by weakening the feeling that we live very separate lives.

■ Review Test 4

Answers will vary.

Write quickly for five minutes about the house or apartment where you live. Don't worry about spelling, punctuation, finding exact words, or organizing your thoughts. Just focus on writing as many words as you can without stopping.

After you have finished, go back and make whatever changes are needed to correct any fragments in your writing.

6 Run-Ons

Introductory Activity

A run-on occurs when two sentences are run together with no adequate sign given to mark the break between them. Shown below are four run-on sentences, each followed by a correct sentence. See if you can complete the statement that explains how each run-on is corrected.

1. A man coughed in the movie theater the result was a chain reaction of copycat coughing.

   A man coughed in the movie theater. The result was a chain reaction of copycat coughing.

The run-on has been corrected by using a ___period___ and a capital letter to separate the two complete thoughts.

2. I heard laughter inside the house, no one answered the bell.

   I heard laughter inside the house, but no one answered the bell.

The run-on has been corrected by using a joining word, ___but___, to connect the two complete thoughts.

3. A car sped around the corner, it sprayed slush all over the pedestrians.

   A car sped around the corner; it sprayed slush all over the pedestrians.

The run-on has been corrected by using a ___semicolon___ to connect the two closely related thoughts.

4. I had a campus map, I still could not find my classroom building.

   Although I had a campus map, I still could not find my classroom building.

The run-on has been corrected by using the subordinating word ___Although___ to connect the two closely related thoughts.

Answers are on page 677.

What Are Run-Ons?

A *run-on* is two complete thoughts that are run together with no adequate sign given to mark the break between them. As a result of the run-on, the reader is confused, unsure of where one thought ends and the next one begins. Two types of run-ons are fused sentences and comma splices.

Some run-ons have no punctuation at all to mark the break between the thoughts. Such run-ons are known as *fused sentences:* they are fused or joined together as if they were only one thought.

Fused Sentence

Rita decided to stop smoking she didn't want to die of lung cancer.

Fused Sentence

The exam was postponed the class was canceled as well.

In other run-ons, known as *comma splices*, a comma is used to connect or "splice" together the two complete thoughts.* However, a comma alone is *not enough* to connect two complete thoughts. Some connection stronger than a comma alone is needed.

Comma Splice

Rita decided to stop smoking, she didn't want to die of lung cancer.

Comma Splice

The exam was postponed, the class was canceled as well.

Comma splices are the most common kind of run-on. Students sense that some kind of connection is needed between thoughts, and so they put a comma at the dividing point. But the comma alone is *not sufficient.* A stronger, clearer mark is needed between the two thoughts.

**Notes*:

1. Some instructors feel that the term *run-ons* should be applied only to fused sentences, not to comma splices. But for many other instructors, and for our purposes in this book, the term *run-on* applies equally to fused sentences and comma splices.The bottom line is that you do not want either fused sentences or comma splices in your writing.

2. Some instructors refer to each complete thought in a run-on as an *independent clause.* A *clause* is simply a group of words having a subject and a verb. A clause may be *independent* (expressing a complete thought and able to stand alone) or *dependent* (not expressing a complete thought and not able to stand alone). A run-on is two independent clauses that are run together with no adequate sign given to mark the break between them.

A Warning: Words That Can Lead to Run-Ons

People often write run-ons when the second complete thought begins with one of the following words. Be on the alert for run-ons whenever you use these words:

I	we	there	now
you	they	this	then
he, she, it		that	next

Correcting Run-Ons

Here are four common methods of correcting a run-on:

1 Use a period and a capital letter to separate the two complete thoughts. (In other words, make two separate sentences of the two complete thoughts.)

Rita decided to stop smoking. She didn't want to die of lung cancer.

The exam was postponed. The class was canceled as well.

2 Use a comma plus a joining word (*and, but, for, or, nor, so, yet*) to connect the two complete thoughts.

Rita decided to stop smoking, for she didn't want to die of lung cancer.

The exam was postponed, and the class was canceled as well.

3 Use a semicolon to connect the two complete thoughts.

Rita decided to stop smoking; she didn't want to die of lung cancer.

The exam was postponed; the class was canceled as well.

4 Use subordination.

Because Rita didn't want to die of lung cancer, she decided to stop smoking.

When the exam was postponed, the class was canceled as well.

The following pages will give you practice in all four methods of correcting run-ons. The use of subordination will be explained further on page 143, in a chapter that deals with sentence variety.

Method 1: Period and a Capital Letter

One way of correcting a run-on is to use a period and a capital letter at the break between the two complete thoughts. Use this method especially if the thoughts are not closely related or if another method would make the sentence too long.

Practice 1

Locate the split in each of the following run-ons. Each is a *fused sentence*—that is, each consists of two sentences fused or joined together with no punctuation at all between them. Reading each sentence aloud will help you "hear" where a major break or split in the thought occurs. At such a point, your voice will probably drop and pause.

Correct the run-on by putting a period at the end of the first thought and a capital letter at the start of the second thought.

Example Gary was not a success at his job. His mouth moved faster than his hands.

1. The fern hadn't been watered in a month its leaves looked like frayed brown shoelaces.
2. Newspapers are piled up on the neighbors' porch they must be out of town.
3. Joyce's recipe for chocolate fudge is very easy to make it is also very expensive.
4. Watching television gave the old man something to do he didn't have many visitors anymore.
5. Jon accidentally dyed his underwear gray a black sock fell into his load of white clothes.
6. The first Olympic Games were held in 776 B.C. the only event was a footrace.
7. Gloria decorated her apartment creatively and cheaply she papered her bedroom walls with magazine covers.
8. There were papers scattered all over Lena's desk she spent twenty minutes looking for a missing receipt.

9. Spring rain dripped into the fireplace the room smelled like last winter's fires.
10. The car swerved dangerously through traffic its rear bumper sticker read, "School's Out—Drive Carefully."

Practice 2

Locate the split in each of the following run-ons. Some of the run-ons are fused sentences, and some of them are *comma splices*—run-ons spliced or joined together only with a comma. Correct each run-on by putting a period at the end of the first thought and a capital letter at the start of the next thought.

1. My father is a very sentimental man he still has my kindergarten drawings.
2. Sue dropped the letter into the mailbox then she regretted mailing it.
3. Certain street names are very common the most common is "Park."
4. Bacteria are incredibly tiny, a drop of liquid may contain fifty million of them.
5. The fastest dog in the world is the greyhound it can run over forty-one miles an hour.
6. Mandy's parents speak only Chinese, she speaks Chinese, English, and French.
7. My portable CD player stopped working, its batteries were worn out.
8. A shadow on the kitchen wall was lovely it had the shape of a plant on the windowsill.
9. The little girl hated seeing her father drink one day, she poured all his liquor down the kitchen drain.
10. Children have been born at odd times for instance, one child was born during his mother's funeral.

Practice 3

Write a second sentence to go with each sentence below. Start the second sentence with the word given at the left.

Example He My dog's ears snapped up. He had heard a wolf howling on television.

Answers will vary.

He 1. Carlos likes going to the mall.

____

____

They 2. Ants marched across our kitchen floor.

____

____

Now 3. Our car just broke down.

____

____

There 4. Raccoons knocked over our garbage cans.

____

____

Then 5. First I stopped at the bakery.

____

____

Method 2: Comma and a Joining Word

Another way of correcting a run-on is to use a comma plus a joining word to connect the two complete thoughts. Joining words (also called *coordinating conjunctions)* include *and, but, for, or, nor, so,* and *yet.* Here is what the four most common joining words mean:

and in addition, along with

Lola was watching Monday night football, and she was doing her homework as well.

(*And* means *in addition:* Lola was watching Monday night football; *in addition,* she was doing her homework as well.)

but however, except, on the other hand, just the opposite

I voted for the president two years ago, but I would not vote for him today.

(*But* means *however:* I voted for the president two years ago; *however,* I would not vote for him today.)

for because, the reason why, the cause for something

Saturday is the worst day to shop, for people jam the stores.

(*For* means *because:* Saturday is the worst day to shop *because* people jam the stores.) If you are not comfortable using *for*, you may want to use *because* instead of *for* in the activities that follow. If you do use *because*, omit the comma before it.

so as a result, therefore

Our son misbehaved again, so he was sent upstairs without dessert.

(*So* means *as a result*: Our son misbehaved again; *as a result,* he was sent upstairs without dessert.)

Practice 1

Insert the comma and the joining word (*and, but, for, so*) that logically connects the two thoughts in each sentence.

Example A trip to the zoo always depresses me, for I hate to see animals in cages.

1. I want to stop smoking, but I don't want to gain weight.
2. Packages are flown to distant cities during the night, and vans deliver them the next morning.
3. The grass turned brown in the summer's heat, and the grapes shriveled and died on the vine.
4. Woody wanted to buy his girlfriend a ring, so he began saving ten dollars a week.
5. I enjoy watching television, but I feel guilty about spending so much time in front of the tube.
6. It was too hot indoors to study, so I decided to go down to the shopping center for ice cream.
7. I don't like to go to the doctor's office, for I'm afraid one of the other patients will make me really sick.
8. This world map was published only three years ago, but the names of some countries are already out of date.
9. Nate is color-blind, so his wife lays out his clothes every morning.
10. We knew there had been a power failure, for all the clocks were forty-five minutes slow.

Practice 2

Add a complete, closely related thought to each of the following statements. When you write the second thought, use a comma plus the joining word shown at the left.

Example but I was sick with the flu, but I still had to study for the test.

Answers will vary.

but 1. We have the same taste in clothes

____

____

so 2. Keisha needed a little break from studying

____

____

and 3. I hammered two nails into the wall

____

____

for 4. The house was unusually quiet

____

____

but 5. Harry meant to stick to his diet

____

____

Method 3: Semicolon

A third method of correcting a run-on is to use a semicolon to mark the break between two thoughts. A *semicolon* (;) is made up of a period above a comma and is sometimes called a *strong comma.* The semicolon signals more of a pause than a comma alone but not quite the full pause of a period.

Occasional use of semicolons can add variety to sentences. For some people, however, the semicolon is a confusing mark of punctuation. Keep in mind that if you are not comfortable using it, you can and should use one of the first two methods of correcting a run-on sentence.

Semicolon Alone

Here are some earlier sentences that were connected with a comma plus a joining word. Now they are connected with a semicolon. Notice that a semicolon, unlike a comma, can be used alone to connect the two complete thoughts in each sentence.

Lola was watching Monday night football; she was doing her homework as well.

I voted for the president two years ago; I would not vote for him today.

Saturday is the worst day to shop; people jam the stores.

Practice

Insert a semicolon where the break occurs between the two complete thoughts in each of the following sentences.

Example She had a wig on; it looked more like a hat than a wig.

1. The problem with pound cake is obvious;I gain a pound every time I eat a piece.
2. The puppy quickly ate;the baby watched with interest.
3. The elderly woman smiled at me;her face broke into a thousand wrinkles.
4. The park has become a dumping ground;old freezers and washing machines are abandoned there.
5. The first birthday parties in history were for kings and queens;birth records were not yet kept for common people.

Semicolon with a Transition

A semicolon is sometimes used with a transitional word and a comma to join two complete thoughts:

I figured that the ball game would cost me about ten dollars; however, I didn't consider the high price of food and drinks.

Fred and Martha have a low-interest mortgage on their house; otherwise, they would move to another neighborhood.

Sharon didn't understand the instructor's point; therefore, she asked him to repeat it.

Note Sometimes transitional words do not join complete thoughts but are merely interrupters in a sentence (see page 322):

My parents, moreover, plan to go on the trip.
I believe, however, that they'll change their minds.

Transitional Words

Here is a list of common transitional words (also known as *adverbial conjunctions*).

Common Transitional Words

however	moreover	therefore
on the other hand	in addition	as a result
nevertheless	also	consequently
instead	furthermore	otherwise

Practice 1

For each item, choose a logical transitional word from the box above and write it in the space provided. In addition, put a semicolon *before* the transition and a comma *after* it.

Example It was raining harder than ever __; however,__ Bobby was determined to go to the amusement park.

1. A new car is always fun to drive __; however,__ the payments are never fun to make.
2. The fork that fell into our garbage disposal looks like a piece of modern art __; otherwise,__ it is useless.
3. Auto races no longer use gasoline __; as a result,__ spectators have nothing to fear from exhaust fumes.
4. We got to the stadium two hours before the game started __;however,__ all the parking spaces were already taken.
5. Mice use their sensitive whiskers as feelers __; consequently,__ they scurry along close to walls.

Practice 2

Punctuate each sentence by using a semicolon and a comma.

Example Our tap water has a funny taste; consequently, we buy bottled water to drink.

1. Nora lives two blocks from the grocery store;nevertheless,she always drives there.
2. The little boy ate too much Halloween candy;as a result,he got a stomachache.
3. Our dog protects us by barking at strangers;however,he also barks at our friends.
4. Jeff cut back a few hours on his work schedule;otherwise,he would have had very little time for studying.
5. My sister invited her ex-husband over to celebrate the holiday with the children;furthermore,she bought a gift for him from the children.

Method 4: Subordination

A fourth method of joining related thoughts is to use subordination. *Subordination* is a way of showing that one thought in a sentence is not as important as another thought. Here are three sentences where one idea is subordinated to (made less emphatic than) the other idea:

Because Rita didn't want to die of lung cancer, she decided to stop smoking.

The wedding reception began to get out of hand when the guests started to throw food at each other.

Although my brothers wanted to watch a *Star Trek* rerun, the rest of the family insisted on turning to the network news.

Dependent Words

Notice that when we subordinate, we use dependent words like *because, when,* and *although.* Following is a brief list of common dependent words (see also the list on page 98). Subordination is explained in full on page 143.

Common Dependent Words		
after	before	unless
although	even though	until
as	if	when
because	since	while

Practice 1

Choose a logical dependent word from the box above and write it in the space provided.

Example ___Until___ I was six, I thought chocolate milk came from brown cows.

1. Will hasn't had a cigarette ___since___ July 4, 2000.
2. ___Unless___ you're willing to work hard, don't sign up for Professor Dunn's class.
3. The lines at that supermarket are so long ___because___ there are too few cashiers.
4. ___After___ reading the scary novel, my sister had nightmares for days.
5. My boss gave me smoked salmon for my birthday ___although___ he knows I'm a vegetarian.

Practice 2

Rewrite the five sentences below (all taken from this chapter) so that one idea is subordinate to the other. Use one of the dependent words in the box above.

Example Auto races no longer use gasoline; spectators have nothing to fear from exhaust fumes.

Since auto races no longer use gasoline, spectators have nothing to fear from exhaust fumes.

Answers may vary.

1. I want to stop smoking; I don't want to gain weight.

   Although I want to stop smoking, I don't want to gain weight.

   ____

2. It was too hot indoors to study; I decided to go down to the shopping center for ice cream.

   Because it was too hot indoors to study, I decided to go down to the shopping center for ice cream.

3. The puppy quickly ate; the baby watched with interest.

   While the puppy quickly ate, the baby watched with interest.

4. The elderly woman smiled at me; her face broke into a thousand wrinkles.

   When the elderly woman smiled at me, her face broke into a thousand wrinkles.

5. This world map was published only three years ago; the names of some countries are already out of date.

   Although this world map was published only three years ago, the names of some countries are already out of date.

Collaborative Activity

Part A: Editing and Rewriting

Wording of answers may vary.

Working with a partner, read carefully the short paragraph below and underline the five run-ons. Then use the space provided to correct the five run-ons. Feel free to discuss the rewrite quietly with your partner and refer back to the chapter when necessary.

[1]When Mark began his first full-time job, he immediately got a credit card, a used sports car was his first purchase. [2]Then he began to buy expensive clothes that he could not afford he also bought impressive gifts for his parents and his girlfriend. [3]Several months passed before Mark realized that he owed an enormous amount of money. [4]To make matters worse, his car broke down, a stack of bills suddenly seemed to be due at once. [5]Mark tried to cut back on his purchases, he soon realized he had to cut up his credit card to prevent himself from using it. [6]He also began keeping a careful record of his spending he had no idea where his money had gone till then. [7]He hated to admit to his family and friends that he

Continued

had to get his budget under control. [8]However, his girlfriend said she did not mind inexpensive dates, and his parents were proud of his growing maturity.

1 When Mark began his first full-time job, he immediately got a credit card. A used sports car was his first purchase. 2 Then he began to buy expensive clothes that he could not afford. He also bought impressive gifts for his parents and his girlfriend. 4 To make matters worse, his car broke down, and a stack of bills suddenly seemed to be due at once. 5 Although Mark tried to cut back on his purchases, he soon realized he had to cut up his credit card to prevent himself from using it. 6 He also began keeping a careful record of his spending, for he had no idea where his money had gone till then.

Part B: Creating Sentences

Answers will vary.

Working with a partner, make up your own short run-ons test as directed.

1. Write a run-on sentence. Then rewrite it, using a period and capital letter to separate the thoughts into two sentences.

   Run-on

   ____

   Rewrite

   ____

2. Write a sentence that has two complete thoughts. Then rewrite it, using a comma and a joining word to correctly join the complete thoughts.

   Two complete thoughts

   ____

   Rewrite

   ____

Continued

3. Write a sentence that has two complete thoughts. Then rewrite it, using a semicolon to correctly join the complete thoughts.

Two complete thoughts

____

Rewrite

____

Reflective Activity

Answers may vary.

1. Look at the paragraph that you revised above. Explain how run-ons affect the paragraph.
2. In your own written work, which type of run-on are you most likely to write: comma splices or fused sentences? Why do you tend to make this kind of mistake?
3. Which method for correcting run-ons are you most likely to use in your own writing? Which are you least likely to use? Why?

Review Test 1

Answers will vary.

Correct the following run-ons by using either (1) a period and a capital letter or (2) a comma and the joining word *and, but, for,* or *so.* Do not use the same method of correction for each sentence.

Example Fred pulled the cellophane off the cake, and the icing came along with it.

1. I put seventy-five cents in the soda machine, but all I got was an empty cup.
2. I tore open a ketchup packet. A bright red streak flew across the front of my new white shirt.
3. Yolanda wanted to sleep late, but her dog woke her up at dawn.
4. The theater's parking lot was full, so we missed the first ten minutes of the movie.
5. Helen bites her nails, so she tries to keep her hands hidden.

6. The waiter cheerfully filled our coffee cups three times. We left him a generous tip.
7. I love to wander through old cemeteries. I enjoy reading the gravestones and taking pictures of them.
8. Travel to distant planets has long been a dream of humanity, and the technology to achieve that dream will soon be available.
9. Gordon no longer has to worry about missing the bus, for he rides to work in a car pool.
10. The baby wouldn't stop crying. All the passengers on the bus gave the mother dirty looks.

Review Test 2

Answers may vary.

Correct each run-on by using subordination. Choose from among the following dependent words.

after	before	unless
although	even though	until
as	if	when
because	since	while

Example Tony hated going to a new barber, he was afraid of butchered hair.
Because Tony was afraid of butchered hair, he hated going to a new barber.

1. Mom was frying potatoes, the heat set off the smoke alarm.
While Mom was frying potatoes, the heat set off the smoke alarm.

2. I love animals I'm not ready to take on the responsibility of a pet.
Even though I love animals, I'm not ready to take on the responsibility of a pet.

3. Lani leaves a lecture class, she reviews and clarifies her notes.
After Lani leaves a lecture class, she reviews and clarifies her notes.

4. Matthew jogs, he thinks over his day's activities.
While Matthew jogs, he thinks over his day's activities.

5. My mother puts apples in the fruit bowl she first washes the wax off them.
Before my mother puts apples in the fruit bowl, she first washes the wax off them.

6. I began to shake on the examining table the nurse reached out and held my hand.
When I began to shake on the examining table, the nurse reached out and held my hand.

7. Some pets are easy to care for, others require patience and lots of hard work.
Some pets are easy to care for, while others require patience and lots of hard work.

8. Molly microwaved her egg too long it exploded all over the inside of the oven.
Because Molly microwaved her egg too long, it exploded all over the inside of the oven.

9. A wheel hit a crack in the sidewalk the skateboard shot out from under Danny.
As a wheel hit a crack in the sidewalk, the skateboard shot out from under Danny.

10. John Grisham and Stephen King make huge fortunes with their novels most writers barely make a living.
While John Grisham and Stephen King make huge fortunes with their novels, most writers barely make a living.

■ Review Test 3

On separate paper, write six sentences, each of which has two complete thoughts. In two of the sentences, use a period and a capital letter between the thoughts. In another two sentences, use a comma and a joining word (*and, but, or, nor, for, so, yet*) to join the thoughts. In the final two sentences, use a semicolon to join the thoughts.

Review Test 4

Write for five minutes about something that makes you angry. Don't worry about spelling, punctuation, finding exact words, or organizing your thoughts. Just focus on writing as many words as you can without stopping.

After you have finished, go back and make whatever changes are needed to correct any run-on sentences in your writing.

7 Sentence Variety I

This chapter will show you how to write effective and varied sentences. You'll learn more about two techniques—subordination and coordination—you can use to expand simple sentences, making them more interesting and expressive. You'll also reinforce what you have learned in Chapters 5 and 6 about how subordination and coordination can help you correct fragments and run-ons in your writing.

Four Traditional Sentence Patterns

Sentences in English are traditionally described as *simple, compound, complex,* or *compound-complex.* Each is explained below.

The Simple Sentence

A simple sentence has a single subject-verb combination.

Children play.
The game ended early.
My car stalled three times last week.
The lake has been polluted by several neighboring streams.

A simple sentence may have more than one subject:

Lola and Tony drove home.
The wind and water dried my hair.

or more than one verb:

> The children smiled and waved at us.
>
> The lawn mower smoked and sputtered.

or several subjects and verbs:

> Manny, Moe, and Jack lubricated my car, replaced the oil filter, and cleaned the spark plugs.

Practice

Answers will vary.

On separate paper, write:

> Three sentences, each with a single subject and verb
>
> Three sentences, each with a single subject and a double verb
>
> Three sentences, each with a double subject and a single verb

In each case, underline the subject once and the verb twice. (See pages 88–89 if necessary for more information on subjects and verbs.)

The Compound Sentence

A compound, or "double," sentence is made up of two (or more) simple sentences. The two complete statements in a compound sentence are usually connected by a comma plus a joining word (*and, but, for, or, nor, so, yet*).

A compound sentence is used when you want to give equal weight to two closely related ideas. The technique of showing that ideas have equal importance is called *coordination.*

Following are some compound sentences. Each sentence contains two ideas that the writer considers equal in importance.

> The rain increased, so the officials canceled the game.
>
> Martha wanted to go shopping, but Fred refused to drive her.
>
> Hollis was watching television in the family room, and April was upstairs on the phone.
>
> I had to give up wood carving, for my arthritis had become very painful.

Practice 1

Combine the following pairs of simple sentences into compound sentences. Use a comma and a logical joining word (*and, but, for, so*) to connect each pair.

Note If you are not sure what *and, but, for,* and *so* mean, review pages 122–123.

Example • We hung up the print.
• The wall still looked bare.
We hung up the print, but the wall still looked bare.

Answers may vary; possible answers are given.

1. • Cass tied the turkey carcass to a tree.
   • She watched the birds pick at bits of meat and skin.
   Cass tied the turkey carcass to a tree, and she watched the birds pick at bits of meat and skin.

2. • I ran the hot water faucet for two minutes.
   • Only cold water came out.
   I ran the hot water faucet for two minutes, but only cold water came out.

3. • Nathan orders all his Christmas gifts through the Internet.
   • He dislikes shopping in crowded stores.
   Nathan orders all his Christmas gifts through the Internet, for he dislikes shopping in crowded stores.

4. • I need to buy a new set of tires.
   • I will read *Consumer Reports* to learn about various brands.
   I need to buy a new set of tires, so I will read *Consumer Reports* to learn about various brands.

5. • I asked Cecilia to go out with me on Saturday night.
   • She told me she'd rather stay home and watch TV.
   I asked Cecilia to go out with me on Saturday night, but she told me she'd rather stay home and watch TV.

Practice 2

Answers will vary.

On separate paper, write five compound sentences of your own. Use a different joining word (*and, but, for, or, nor, so, yet*) to connect the two complete ideas in each sentence.

The Complex Sentence

A complex sentence is made up of a simple sentence (a complete statement) and a statement that begins with a dependent word.* Here is a list of common dependent words:

Dependent Words

after	if, even if	when, whenever
although, though	in order that	where, wherever
as	since	whether
because	that, so that	which, whichever
before	unless	while
even though	until	who
how	what, whatever	whose

A complex sentence is used when you want to emphasize one idea over another in a sentence. Look at the following complex sentence:

Because I forgot the time, I missed the final exam.

The idea that the writer wants to emphasize here—*I missed the final exam*—is expressed as a complete thought. The less important idea—*Because I forgot the time*—is subordinated to the complete thought. The technique of giving one idea less emphasis than another is called *subordination.*

Following are other examples of complex sentences. In each case, the part starting with the dependent word is the less emphasized part of the sentence.

While Aisha was eating breakfast, she began to feel sick.

I checked my money *before* I invited Pedro for lunch.

When Jerry lost his temper, he also lost his job.

Although I practiced for three months, I failed my driving test.

*The two parts of a complex sentence are sometimes called an independent clause and a dependent clause. A *clause* is simply a word group that contains a subject and a verb. An *independent clause* expresses a complete thought and can stand alone. A *dependent clause* does not express a complete thought in itself and "depends on" the independent clause to complete its meaning. Dependent clauses always begin with a dependent or subordinating word.

Practice 1

Use logical dependent words to combine the following pairs of simple sentences into complex sentences. Place a comma after a dependent statement when it starts the sentence.

Example
- I obtained a credit card.
- I began spending money recklessly.

When I obtained a credit card, I began spending money recklessly.

- Alan dressed the turkey.
- His brother greased the roasting pan.

Alan dressed the turkey while his brother greased the roasting pan.

Answers may vary; possible answers are given.

1. • Cindy opened the cutlery drawer.
   • A bee flew out.

   When Cindy opened the cutlery drawer, a bee flew out.

2. • I washed the windows thoroughly.
   • They still looked dirty.

   Although I washed the windows thoroughly, they still looked dirty.

3. • I never opened a book all semester.
   • I guess I deserved to flunk.

   Because I never opened a book all semester, I guess I deserved to flunk.

4. • Manny gets up in the morning.
   • He does stretching exercises for five minutes.

   When Manny gets up in the morning, he does stretching exercises for five minutes.

5. • My son spilled the pickle jar at dinner.
   • I had to wash the kitchen floor.

   After my son spilled the pickle jar at dinner, I had to wash the kitchen floor.

Practice 2

Rewrite the following sentences, using subordination rather than coordination. Include a comma when a dependent statement starts a sentence.

Example The hair dryer was not working right, so I returned it to the store.

Because the hair dryer was not working right, I returned it to the store.

Answers may vary; possible answers are given.

1. Carlo set the table, and his wife finished cooking dinner.

   As Carlo set the table, his wife finished cooking dinner.

2. Maggie could have gotten good grades, but she did not study enough.

   Although Maggie could have gotten good grades, she did not study enough.

3. I watered my drooping African violets, and they perked right up.

   After I watered my drooping African violets, they perked right up.

4. The little boy kept pushing the down button, but the elevator didn't come any more quickly.

   Though the little boy kept pushing the down button, the elevator didn't come any more quickly.

5. I never really knew what pain is, and then I had four impacted wisdom teeth pulled at once.

   I never really knew what pain is until I had four impacted wisdom teeth pulled at once.

Practice 3

Combine the following simple sentences into complex sentences. Omit repeated words. Use the dependent words *who, which,* or *that.*

Notes

a The word *who* refers to persons.

b The word *which* refers to things.

c The word *that* refers to persons or things.

Use commas around the dependent statement only if it seems to interrupt the flow of thought in the sentence. (See pages 322–323.)

Examples
- Clyde picked up a hitchhiker.
- The hitchhiker was traveling around the world.

Clyde picked up a hitchhiker who was traveling around the world.

- Larry is a sleepwalker.
- Larry is my brother.

Larry, who is my brother, is a sleepwalker.

Answers may vary; possible answers are given.

1. • Karen just gave birth to twins.
   • Karen is an old friend of mine.

   Karen, who is an old friend of mine, just gave birth to twins.

2. • The tea burned the roof of my mouth.
   • The tea was hotter than I expected.

   The tea, which was hotter than I expected, burned the roof of my mouth.

3. • I dropped the camera.
   • My sister had just bought the camera.

   I dropped the camera that my sister had just bought.

4. • Ernie brought us some enormous oranges.
   • Ernie is visiting from California.

   Ernie, who is visiting from California, brought us some enormous oranges.

5. • Liz used a steam cleaner to shampoo her rugs.
   • The rugs were dirtier than she realized.

   Liz used a steam cleaner to shampoo her rugs, which were dirtier than she realized.

Practice 4

Answers will vary.

On separate paper, write eight complex sentences, using, in turn, the dependent words *unless, if, after, because, when, who, which,* and *that.*

The Compound-Complex Sentence

A compound-complex sentence is made up of two (or more) simple sentences and one or more dependent statements. In the following examples, there is a solid line under the simple sentences and a dotted line under the dependent statements.

> When the power line snapped, Jack was listening to the stereo, and Linda was reading in bed.
>
> After I returned to school following a long illness, the math teacher gave me makeup work, but the history teacher made me drop her course.

Practice 1

Read through each sentence to get a sense of its overall meaning. Then insert a logical joining word (*and, or, but, for,* or *so*) and a logical dependent word (*because, since, when,* or *although*).

Answers may vary.

1. __After__ you paint the closet, remember to open the bedroom window, __for__ you might get a headache from the smell.
2. __When__ I get into bed at night, I try to read a book, __but__ I always fall asleep within minutes.
3. Russell ate less butter __when__ he learned that his cholesterol level was a little too high, __and__ he also included some bran in his diet.
4. __Because__ she made the honor roll, Molly received a library pass from the principal, __so__ she didn't have to sit in study hall the whole semester.
5. We planned to go to a rock concert tonight, __but__ it was canceled __because__ the lead singer was arrested.

Practice 2

Answers will vary.

On separate paper, write five compound-complex sentences.

Review of Subordination and Coordination

Subordination and coordination are ways of showing the exact relationship of ideas within a sentence. Through **subordination** we show that one idea is less important than another. When we subordinate, we use dependent words like *when, although, while, because,* and *after.* (A list of common dependent words has been given on page 138.) Through **coordination** we show that ideas are of equal importance. When we coordinate, we use the words *and, but, for, or, nor, so, yet.*

Practice

Use subordination or coordination to combine the following groups of simple sentences into one or more longer sentences. Be sure to omit repeated words. Since various combinations are possible, you might want to jot down several combinations on separate paper. Then read them aloud to find the combination that sounds best.

Keep in mind that, very often, the relationship among ideas in a sentence will be clearer when subordination rather than coordination is used.

Example

- My car does not start on cold mornings.
- I think the battery needs to be replaced.
- I already had it recharged once.
- I don't think charging it again would help.

Because my car does not start on cold mornings, I think the battery needs to be replaced. I already had it recharged once, so I don't think charging it again would help.

Comma Hints

a Use a comma at the end of a word group that starts with a dependent word (as in "Because my car does not start on cold mornings, . . .").

b Use a comma between independent word groups connected by *and, but, for, or, nor, so, yet* (as in "I already had it recharged once, so . . .").

Answers will vary.

1. - Sidney likes loud music.
   - His parents can't stand it.
   - He wears earphones.

   Though Sidney likes loud music, his parents can't stand it, so he wears earphones.

2. • The volcano erupted.
   • The sky turned black with smoke.
   • Nearby villagers were frightened.
   • They clogged the roads leading to safety.

   After the volcano erupted, the sky turned black with smoke. Nearby villagers were frightened, so they clogged the roads leading to safety.

3. • Glenda had a haircut today.
   • She came home and looked in the mirror.
   • She decided to wear a hat for a few days.
   • She thought she looked like a bald eagle.

   After Glenda had a haircut today, she came home and looked in the mirror. Then she decided to wear a hat for a few days because she thought she looked like a bald eagle.

4. • I ran out of gas on the way to work.
   • I discovered how helpful strangers can be.
   • A passing driver saw I was stuck.
   • He drove me to the gas station and back to my car.

   When I ran out of gas on the way to work, I discovered how helpful strangers can be. A passing driver saw I was stuck, so he drove me to the gas station and back to my car.

5. • Our dog often rests on the floor in the sunshine.
   • He waits for the children to get home from school.
   • The sunlight moves along the floor.
   • He moves with it.

   Our dog often rests on the floor in the sunshine while he waits for the children to get home from school. As the sunlight moves along the floor, he moves with it.

6. • My father was going to be late from work.
   • We planned to have a late dinner.
   • I was hungry before dinner.
   • I ate a salami and cheese sandwich.
   • I did this secretly.

   Because my father was going to be late from work, we planned to have a late dinner. But I was hungry before dinner, so I secretly ate a salami and cheese sandwich.

7. • A baseball game was scheduled for early afternoon.
   • It looked like rain.
   • A crew rolled huge tarps to cover the field.
   • Then the sun reappeared.

   A baseball game was scheduled for early afternoon, but it looked like rain. So a crew rolled huge tarps to cover the field, and then the sun reappeared.

8. • Cassy worries about the sprays used on fruit.
   • She washes apples, pears, and plums in soap and water.
   • She doesn't rinse them well.
   • They have a soapy flavor.

   Cassy worries about the sprays used on fruit, so she washes apples, pears, and plums in soap and water. Because she doesn't rinse them well, they have a soapy flavor.

9. • Charlene needed to buy stamps.
   • She went to the post office during her lunch hour.
   • The line was long.
   • She waited there for half an hour.
   • She had to go back to work without stamps.

   Charlene needed to buy stamps, so she went to the post office during her lunch hour, when the line was long. After she waited there for half an hour, she had to go back to work without stamps.

10. • The weather suddenly became frigid.
  • Almost everyone at work caught a cold.
  • Someone brought a big batch of chicken soup.
  • She poured it into one of the office coffeepots.
  • The pot was empty by noon.

  After the weather suddenly became frigid, almost everyone at work caught a cold, so someone brought a big batch of chicken soup. She poured it into one of the office coffeepots, and the pot was empty by noon.

Review Test 1

Combine each group of short sentences into one sentence. Various combinations are possible. Choose the combination that reads most smoothly and clearly and that sounds most appropriate in the context of surrounding sentences.

Here is an example of a group of sentences and some possible combinations:

Example
- Martha moved in the desk chair.
- Her moving was uneasy.
- The chair was hard.
- She worked at the assignment.
- The assignment was for her English class.

Martha moved uneasily in the hard desk chair, working at the assignment for her English class.

Moving uneasily in the hard desk chair, Martha worked at the assignment for her English class.

Martha moved uneasily in the hard desk chair as she worked at the assignment for her English class.

While she worked at the assignment for her English class, Martha moved uneasily in the hard desk chair.

Note In combining short sentences into one sentence, omit repeated words where necessary. Use separate paper.

Doctor's Waiting Room

Answers may vary; possibilities appear below.

- People visit the doctor.
- Their ordeal begins.

When people visit the doctor, their ordeal begins.

- A patient has an appointment for 2:00.
- He is told he will have to wait.
- The wait will be at least one hour.

A patient who has an appointment for 2:00 is told he will have to wait for at least one hour.

- Other people arrive.
- Everyone takes a seat.
- Soon the room becomes crowded.

As other people arrive and everyone takes a seat, the room soon becomes crowded.

- Some people read old magazines.
- Others count the stripes.
- The stripes are in the wallpaper.

Some people read old magazines, while others count the stripes in the wallpaper.

- Some people look at each other.
- Some people may smile.
- No one talks to anyone else.

Some people look at each other and may smile, but no one talks to anyone else.

- Some people are very sick.
- They cough a lot.
- They hold tissues to their noses.

Some people, who are very sick, cough a lot and hold tissues to their noses.

- The people around them turn away.
- They hold their breath.
- They are afraid of becoming infected.

The people around them, who are afraid of becoming infected, turn away and hold their breath.

- Time passes.
- It passes slowly.
- All the people count.
- They count the number of people ahead of them.

Time passes slowly as all the people count the number of people ahead of them.

- The long-awaited moment finally arrives.
- The receptionist comes into the waiting area.

The long-awaited moment finally arrives when the receptionist comes into the waiting area.

- She looks at the patient.
- She says the magic words.
- "The doctor will see you now."

She looks at the patient and says the magic words, "The doctor will see you now."

Review Test 2

Combine each group of short sentences into one sentence. Various combinations are possible. Choose the combination that reads most smoothly and clearly and that sounds most appropriate in the context of surrounding sentences.

Notes In combining short sentences into one sentence, omit repeated words where necessary. Use separate paper.

A Remedy for Shyness

Answers may vary; possibilities appear below.

- Linda Nelson was shy.
- She seldom met new people.
- She spent a lot of time alone.

Linda Nelson was shy, so she seldom met new people, and she spent a lot of time alone.

- Too often Linda avoided speaking.
- She did not want to take a risk.
- The risk was embarrassing herself.

Too often Linda avoided speaking because she did not want to take the risk of embarrassing herself.

- Luckily, Linda got some advice.
- The advice was good.
- She got the advice from her cousin Rose.
- Linda decided to try to change.
- She would change her behavior.

Luckily, Linda got some good advice from her cousin Rose, and Linda decided to try to change her behavior.

- Rose told Linda not to blame herself for being shy.
- She told her the shyness made her seem attractive.
- She told her the shyness made her seem modest.

Rose told Linda not to blame herself for being shy, for the shyness made her seem attractive and modest.

- Rose encouraged her to talk to others.
- Linda began to join conversations at school.
- Linda began to join conversations at work.

After Rose encouraged her to talk to others, Linda began to join conversations at school and at work.

- Gradually, Linda learned something.
- She could start conversations.
- She could start them herself.
- She could do this even though her heart pounded.
- She could do this even though her stomach churned.

Gradually, Linda learned that she could start conversations by herself, even though her heart pounded and her stomach churned.

- Linda still feels uncomfortable sometimes.
- She is doing things that once seemed impossible.

Although Linda still feels uncomfortable sometimes, she is doing things that once seemed impossible.

- Linda joined a bowling league.
- She did this recently.
- Some of her new friends invited her to join.
- The friends were from work.

Linda recently joined a bowling league when some of her new friends from work invited her to join.

- She is not the best bowler on the team.
- She is winning a victory over shyness.
- She is winning, thanks to her cousin's help.
- She is winning, thanks to her own determination.

She is not the best bowler on the team, but she is winning a victory over shyness, thanks to her cousin's help and her own determination.

- Linda is a happier person today.
- She has taken charge of her life.
- She has made herself a more interesting person.

Linda is a happier person today because she has taken charge of her life and made herself a more interesting person.

8 Standard English Verbs

Introductory Activity

Underline what you think is the correct form of the verb in each pair of sentences below.

That radio station once (play, played) top-forty hits.
It now (play, plays) classical music.

When Jean was a little girl, she (hope, hoped) to become a movie star.
Now she (hope, hopes) to be accepted at law school.

At first, my father (juggle, juggled) with balls of yarn.
Now that he is an expert, he (juggle, juggles) raw eggs.

On the basis of the above examples, see if you can complete the following statements.

1. The first sentence in each pair refers to an action in the (past time, present time), and the regular verb has an -ed or -d ending.
2. The second sentence in each pair refers to an action in the (past time, present time), and the regular verb has an -s ending.

Answers are on page 679.

Many people have grown up in communities where nonstandard verb forms are used in everyday life. Such nonstandard forms include *they be, it done, we has, you was, she don't,* and *it ain't.* Community dialects have richness and power but are a drawback in college and the world at large, where standard English verb forms must be used. Standard English helps ensure clear communication among English-speaking people everywhere, and it is especially important in the world of work.

This chapter compares the community dialect and the standard English forms of a regular verb and three common irregular verbs.

Regular Verbs: Dialect and Standard Forms

The chart below compares community dialect (nonstandard) and standard English forms of the regular verb *talk.*

TALK

Community Dialect (Do not use in your writing)		*Standard English* (Use for clear communication)	
Present Tense			
I talks	we talks	I talk	we talk
you talks	you talks	you talk	you talk
he, she, it talk	they talks	he, she, it talks	they talk
Past Tense			
I talk	we talk	I talked	we talked
you talk	you talk	you talked	you talked
he, she, it talk	they talk	he, she, it talked	they talked

One of the most common nonstandard forms results from dropping the endings of regular verbs. For example, people might say "Rose work until ten o'clock tonight" instead of "Rose work*s* until ten o'clock tonight." Or they'll say "I work overtime yesterday" instead of "I work*ed* overtime yesterday." To avoid such nonstandard usage, memorize the forms shown above for the regular verb *talk.* Then do the activities that follow. These activities will help you make it a habit to include verb endings in your writing.

Present Tense Endings

The verb ending *-s* or *-es* is needed with a regular verb in the present tense when the subject is *he, she, it,* or any one person or thing.

He	He lifts weights.
She	She runs.
It	It amazes me.
One person	Their son Ted swims.
One person	Their daughter Terry dances.
One thing	Their house jumps at night with all the exercise.

Practice 1

All but one of the ten sentences that follow need *-s* or *-es* endings. Cross out the nonstandard verb forms and write the standard forms in the spaces provided. Mark the one sentence that needs no change with a *C*.

ends Example The sale ~~end~~ tomorrow.

drives 1. Tim ~~drive~~ too fast for me.

gets 2. Our washing machine always ~~get~~ stuck at the rinse cycle.

practices 3. Roberto ~~practice~~ his saxophone two hours each day.

makes 4. Whenever I serve meat loaf, my daughter ~~make~~ a peanut butter sandwich.

brushes 5. My grandfather ~~brush~~ his teeth with baking soda.

falls 6. While watching television in the evening, Kitty usually ~~fall~~ asleep.

C 7. Mom always wakes me by saying, "Get up, the day is growing older."

comes 8. On my old car radio, a static sound ~~come~~ from every station but one.

watches 9. My little sister ~~watch~~ fireworks with her hands over her ears.

buzzes 10. The broken computer ~~buzz~~ like an angry wasp.

Practice 2

Rewrite the short selection below, adding present tense *-s* verb endings in the ten places where they are needed.

My little sister want to be a country singer when she grow up. She constantly hum and sing around the house. Sometimes she make quite a racket. When she listen to music on the radio, for example, she sing very loudly in order to hear herself over the radio. And when she take a shower, her voice ring though the whole house because she think nobody can hear her from there.

My little sister wants to be a country singer when she grows up. She constantly hums and sings around the house. Sometimes she makes quite a racket. When she listens to music on the radio, for example, she sings very loudly in order to hear herself over the radio. And when she takes a shower, her voice rings through the whole house because she thinks nobody can hear her from there.

Past Tense Endings

The verb ending *-d* or *-ed* is needed with a regular verb in the past tense.

Yesterday we finished painting the house.

I completed the paper an hour before class.

Fred's car stalled on his way to work this morning.

Practice 1

All but one of the ten sentences that follow need *-d* or *-ed* endings. Cross out the nonstandard verb forms and write the standard forms in the spaces provided. Mark the one sentence that needs no change with a *C*.

jumped — Example The cat ~~jump~~ onto my lap when I sat down.

spilled — 1. A waiter at the new restaurant accidentally ~~spill~~ ice water into Phil's lap.

jailed — 2. In a prim Indiana town, a couple was actually ~~jail~~ for kissing in public.

burned — 3. While ironing my new shirt this morning, I ~~burn~~ a hole right through it.

tied — 4. Fran wrapped the gag gift in waxed paper and ~~tie~~ it with dental floss.

measured 5. Pencil marks dotted Matt's bedroom wall where he ~~measure~~ his height each month.

C 6. My brother was eating too fast and almost choked on a piece of bread.

smashed 7. Last summer, a burglar ~~smash~~ my car window and stole my jacket.

constructed 8. The kids ~~construct~~ an obstacle course in the basement out of boxes and toys.

leveled 9. The rain came down so hard it ~~level~~ the young cornstalks in our garden.

realized 10. As Alfonso pulled up to the red light, he suddenly ~~realize~~ his brakes were not working.

Practice 2

Rewrite this selection, adding past tense *-d* or *-ed* verb endings in the fifteen places where they are needed.

My cousin Joel complete a course in home repairs and offer one day to fix several things in my house. He repair a screen door that squeak, a dining room chair that wobble a bit, and a faulty electrical outlet. That night when I open the screen door, it loosen from its hinges. When I seat myself in the chair Joel had fix, one of its legs crack off. Remembering that Joel had also fool around with the electrical outlet, I quickly call an electrician and ask him to stop by the next day. Then I pray the house would not burn down before he arrive.

My cousin Joel complet<u>ed</u> a course in home repairs and offer<u>ed</u> one day to fix several things in my house. He repair<u>ed</u> a screen door that squeak<u>ed</u>, a dining room chair that wobbl<u>ed</u> a bit, and a faulty electrical outlet. That night when I open<u>ed</u> the screen door, it loosen<u>ed</u> from its hinges. When I seat<u>ed</u> myself in the chair Joel had fix<u>ed</u>, one of its legs crack<u>ed</u> off. Remembering that Joel had also fool<u>ed</u> around with the electrical outlet, I quickly call<u>ed</u> an electrician and ask<u>ed</u> him to stop by the next day. Then I pray<u>ed</u> the house would not burn down before he arriv<u>ed</u>.

Three Common Irregular Verbs: Dialect and Standard Forms

The following charts compare the community dialect (nonstandard) and standard English forms of the common irregular verbs *be, have,* and *do.* (For more on irregular verbs, see Chapter 9, beginning on page 161.)

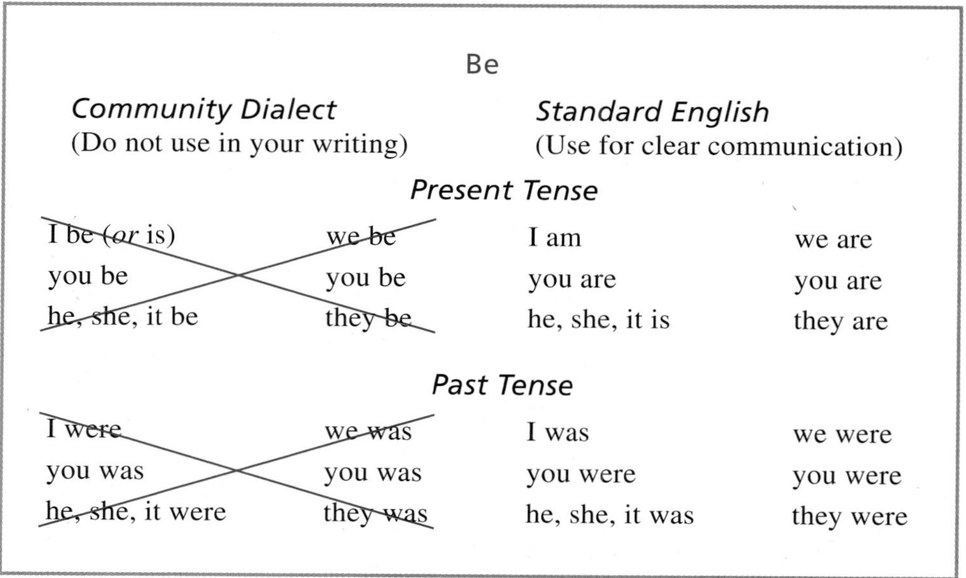

Be

Community Dialect (Do not use in your writing)		*Standard English* (Use for clear communication)	
Present Tense			
I be (*or* is)	we be	I am	we are
you be	you be	you are	you are
he, she, it be	they be	he, she, it is	they are
Past Tense			
I were	we was	I was	we were
you was	you was	you were	you were
he, she, it were	they was	he, she, it was	they were

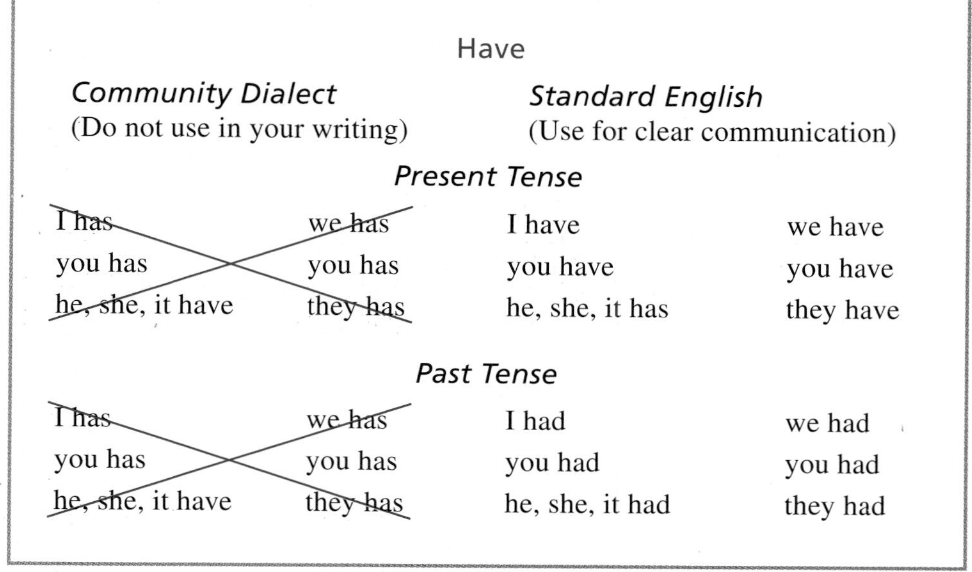

Have

Community Dialect (Do not use in your writing)		*Standard English* (Use for clear communication)	
Present Tense			
I has	we has	I have	we have
you has	you has	you have	you have
he, she, it have	they has	he, she, it has	they have
Past Tense			
I has	we has	I had	we had
you has	you has	you had	you had
he, she, it have	they has	he, she, it had	they had

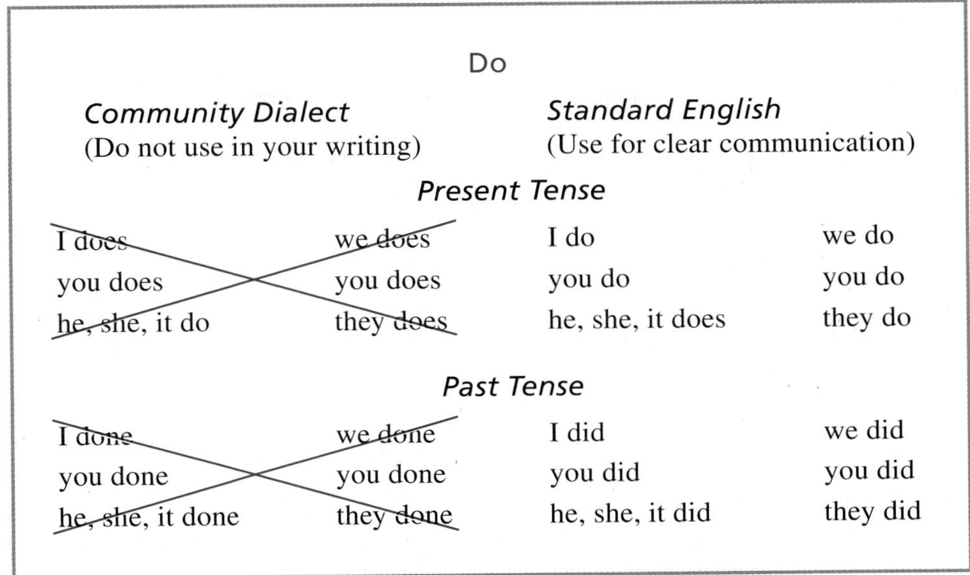

Do

Community Dialect (Do not use in your writing)		*Standard English* (Use for clear communication)	
Present Tense			
I does	we does	I do	we do
you does	you does	you do	you do
he, she, it do	they does	he, she, it does	they do
Past Tense			
I done	we done	I did	we did
you done	you done	you did	you did
he, she, it done	they done	he, she, it did	they did

Note Many people have trouble with one negative form of *do.* They will say, for example, "She don't listen" instead of "She doesn't listen," or they will say "This pen don't work" instead of "This pen doesn't work." Be careful to avoid the common mistake of using *don't* instead of *doesn't.*

Practice 1

Underline the standard form of the irregular verbs *be, have,* or *do.*

1. The piranha (be, is) a fish that lives in South American rivers.
2. Only eight to twelve inches long, piranhas (do, does) not look very frightening.
3. But the smell of blood in the water (have, has) the effect of driving piranhas crazy with excitement.
4. Even the tiny drop of blood produced by a single mosquito bite (be, is) enough to attract the vicious fish.
5. Piranhas (has, have) double rows of teeth which make them dangerous hunters.
6. Those teeth (be, are) so sharp that some Indian tribes use them as arrowheads.
7. A single piranha's bite (has, have) the potential to cause severe injury, such as the loss of a finger or toe.
8. However, piranhas (does, do) their greatest damage when they attack in large numbers.

9. Some travelers (was, were) boating on the Amazon when they saw a school of piranhas strip a four-hundred pound hog to a skeleton in minutes.
10. "What the piranha (does, do) is believable only if you see it," reported one witness.

Practice 2

Cross out the nonstandard verb form in each sentence. Then write the standard form of *be, have,* or *do* in the space provided.

do 1. If you ~~does~~ your assignments on time, you may not understand my friend Albert.
is 2. Albert ~~be~~ the world's worst procrastinator.
are 3. Procrastinators ~~be~~ people who always put things off.
have 4. They ~~has~~ problems with deadlines of all kinds.
was 5. Albert ~~were~~ a procrastinator at the age of six.
had 6. The boy next door ~~have~~ a few friends over for lunch one day.
were 7. Albert's parents ~~was~~ upset when they learned Albert got there three hours late.
did 8. They ~~done~~ the neighbors a favor by taking Albert home at once.
does 9. Today, Albert still ~~do~~ everything at the last minute or even later.
has 10. He ~~have~~ plans to join Procrastinators Anonymous—when he gets around to it.

Practice 3

Fill in each blank with the standard form of *be, have,* or *do.*

My cousin Rita __has__ decided to lose thirty pounds, so she __has__ put herself on a rigid diet that __does__ not allow her to eat anything that she enjoys. Last weekend, while the family __was__ at Aunt Jenny's house for dinner, all Rita __had__ to eat __was__ a can of Diet Delight peaches. We __were__ convinced that Rita meant business when she joined an exercise club whose members __have__ to work out on enormous machines and __do__ twenty sit-ups just to get started. If Rita __does__ reach her goal, we __are__ all going to be very proud of her. But I would not be surprised if she __does__ not succeed, because this __is__ her fourth diet this year.

Review Test 1

Underline the standard verb form.

1. A cake in the oven (make, makes) the whole house smell good.
2. My brother deliberately (wear, wears) socks that clash with his clothes.
3. Our boss (don't, doesn't) want us to take any extra coffee breaks.
4. After I got home from the movie theater, I (realize, realized) I had lost my wallet.
5. The cheap ballpoint pen (leak, leaked) ink on my favorite shirt.
6. If they (was, were) my children, I wouldn't let them play near that creek.
7. We have to be quiet, because my sister (is, be) studying for her sociology test.
8. A neighbor (watch, watched) our house while we were away on vacation.
9. When the sculptor (unveil, unveiled) his work, no one could figure out what it was.
10. *Consumer Reports* (did, done) a report last month on cars, and mine was the lowest-rated model on the list.

Review Test 2

Cross out the nonstandard verb form in each of the sentences that follow. Then write the standard English verb form in the space at the left, as shown.

played Example Yesterday morning, the children ~~play~~ quietly in the sandbox.

is 1. Making promises ~~be~~ easier than keeping them.

don't 2. Baked potatoes ~~doesn't~~ have as many calories as I thought.

was 3. The game ~~were~~ lost when the other team scored a fourth-quarter touchdown.

rides 4. Our psychology professor ~~ride~~ a motorcycle to school.

covered 5. The mayor ~~cover~~ his face from photographers as he was escorted to jail.

growled 6. The large dog ~~growl~~ fiercely when I approached my neighbor's house.

caused 7. Lightning struck a nearby building last night and ~~cause~~ a major fire.

have 8. Many childhood diseases, such as scarlet fever and whooping cough, ~~has~~ almost vanished in the United States.

sounded 9. Stanley turned the television on during the day because the house ~~sound~~ too quiet without it.

is 10. That restaurant offers free nonalcoholic drinks to the person who ~~be~~ the driver for a group.

9 Irregular Verbs

Introductory Activity

You may already have a sense of which common English verbs are regular and which are not. To test yourself, fill in the past tense and past participle of the verbs below. Five are regular verbs and so take *-d* or *-ed* in the past tense and past participle. For these verbs, write *R* under *Verb Type* and then write their past tense and past participle verb forms. Five are irregular verbs and will probably not sound right when you try to add *-d* or *-ed*. For these verbs, write *I* under *Verb Type*. Also, see if you can write in their irregular verb forms.

Present	*Verb Type*	*Past*	*Past Participle*
fall	I	fell	fallen
1. scream	R	screamed	screamed
2. write	I	wrote	written
3. steal	I	stole	stolen
4. ask	R	asked	asked
5. kiss	R	kissed	kissed
6. choose	I	chose	chosen
7. ride	I	rode	ridden
8. chew	R	chewed	chewed
9. think	I	thought	thought
10. dance	R	danced	danced

Answers are on page 680.

A Brief Review of Regular Verbs

Every verb has four principal parts: present, past, past participle, and present participle. These parts can be used to build all the verb tenses (the times shown by a verb).

Most verbs in English are regular. The past and past participle of a regular verb are formed by adding *-d* or *-ed* to the present. The *past participle* is the form of the verb used with the helping verbs *have, has,* or *had* (or some form of *be* with passive verbs, which are explained on page 192). The *present participle* is formed by adding *-ing* to the present.

Here are the principal forms of some regular verbs:

Present	*Past*	*Past Participle*	*Present Participle*
laugh	laughed	laughed	laughing
ask	asked	asked	asking
touch	touched	touched	touching
decide	decided	decided	deciding
explode	exploded	exploded	exploding

List of Irregular Verbs

Irregular verbs have irregular forms in the past tense and past participle. For example, the past tense of the irregular verb *grow* is *grew*; the past participle is *grown*.

Almost everyone has some degree of trouble with irregular verbs. When you are unsure about the form of a verb, you can check the following list of irregular verbs. (The present participle is not shown on this list, because it is formed simply by adding *-ing* to the base form of the verb.) Or you can check a dictionary, which gives the principal parts of irregular verbs.

Present	*Past*	*Past Participle*
arise	arose	arisen
awake	awoke *or* awaked	awoke *or* awaked
be (am, are, is)	was (were)	been
become	became	become
begin	began	begun
bend	bent	bent
bite	bit	bitten
blow	blew	blown
break	broke	broken
bring	brought	brought
build	built	built
burst	burst	burst
buy	bought	bought
catch	caught	caught
choose	chose	chosen
come	came	come
cost	cost	cost
cut	cut	cut
do (does)	did	done
draw	drew	drawn
drink	drank	drunk
drive	drove	driven
eat	ate	eaten
fall	fell	fallen
feed	fed	fed
feel	felt	felt
fight	fought	fought
find	found	found
fly	flew	flown
freeze	froze	frozen
get	got	got *or* gotten
give	gave	given
go (goes)	went	gone
grow	grew	grown
have (has)	had	had
hear	heard	heard
hide	hid	hidden
hold	held	held
hurt	hurt	hurt
keep	kept	kept
know	knew	known

Present	*Past*	*Past Participle*
lay	laid	laid
lead	led	led
leave	left	left
lend	lent	lent
let	let	let
lie	lay	lain
light	lit	lit
lose	lost	lost
make	made	made
meet	met	met
pay	paid	paid
ride	rode	ridden
ring	rang	rung
rise	rose	risen
run	ran	run
say	said	said
see	saw	seen
sell	sold	sold
send	sent	sent
shake	shook	shaken
shrink	shrank	shrunk
shut	shut	shut
sing	sang	sung
sit	sat	sat
sleep	slept	slept
speak	spoke	spoken
spend	spent	spent
stand	stood	stood
steal	stole	stolen
stick	stuck	stuck
sting	stung	stung
swear	swore	sworn
swim	swam	swum
take	took	taken
teach	taught	taught
tear	tore	torn
tell	told	told
think	thought	thought
wake	woke *or* waked	woken *or* waked
wear	wore	worn
win	won	won
write	wrote	written

Practice 1

Cross out the incorrect verb form in the following sentences. Then write the correct form of the verb in the space provided.

began Example When the mud slide started, the whole neighborhood ~~begun~~ going downhill.

came 1. The coach caught Otto when he ~~come~~ in two hours after curfew.

stood 2. We ~~standed~~ out in the rain all night to buy tickets to the concert.

built 3. The Romans had ~~builded~~ a network of roads so the army could travel more quickly from place to place.

swum 4. Our championship team has ~~swam~~ in every important meet this year.

held 5. The nervous mother ~~holded~~ her child's hand tightly as they crossed the busy street.

drove 6. Hakeem ~~drived~~ in circles for an hour before he admitted that he was lost.

written 7. He had ~~wrote~~ the answers to all the questions before anyone else had finished the first page.

blew 8. The tornado ~~blowed~~ the sign from the top of the bank, and it landed five blocks away in the motel swimming pool.

bought 9. Kathy ~~buyed~~ school clothes with the money she earned from her summer job.

knew 10. The poker players ~~knowed~~ they were in trouble when the stranger shuffled the cards with one hand.

Practice 2

For each of the italicized verbs in the following sentences, fill in the three missing forms in the order shown in the box:

a. Present tense, which takes an *-s* ending when the subject is *he, she, it,* or any *one person* or *thing* (see page 153)
b. Past tense
c. Past participle—the form that goes with the helping verb *have, has,* or *had.*

Example My little nephew loves to *break* things. Every Christmas he (a) ___breaks___ his new toys the minute they're unwrapped. Last year he (b) ___broke___ five toys in seven minutes and then went on to smash his family's new china platter. His mother says he won't be happy until he has (c) ___broken___ their hearts.

1. Did you ever go to *sleep* on a water bed? My cousin Nancy (a) ___sleeps___ on one. Last year I spent the weekend at Nancy's apartment, and I (b) ___slept___ on it. Since then I have (c) ___slept___ on it several more times, without once getting seasick.
2. A dreadful little boy in my neighborhood loves to *ring* my doorbell and run away. Sometimes he (a) ___rings___ it several times a day. The last time it (b) ___rang___ over and over, I finally refused to answer the door. Then I found out that United Parcel had (c) ___rung___ the doorbell to deliver a gift from my boyfriend.
3. Why does every teacher ask us to *write* about our summer vacations? Most students (a) ___write___ about what really happened, but that is usually too dull. I (b) ___wrote___ an essay about being taken aboard an alien spacecraft. I bet it was the most interesting essay anybody has ever (c) ___written___ for my teacher's English class.
4. My sister never has to *stand* in line for a movie very long. She always (a) ___stands___ for a few minutes and then walks straight to the entrance. "I (b) ___stood___ in line as long as I could," she tells the ticket taker. "In fact," she continues in a weak voice, "I have (c) ___stood___ in line too long already. I feel faint." She is always ushered inside immediately.
5. As usual, Ron planned to *swim* at least a hundred laps before breakfast. He knew that an Olympic hopeful (a) ___swims___ while others sleep. That morning he (b) ___swam___ with a deliberate stroke, counting the rhythm silently. He had (c) ___swum___ this way daily for the last two years. It was a price he was willing to pay to be one of the best.
6. I know a woman who likes to *buy* things and return them after she uses them. For example, she always (a) ___buys___ new shoes to wear for special occasions. Then she wears them for the event and returns them the next day. Once

she (b) ___bought___ a complete outfit, wore it twice, and returned it a week later. Whenever I shop, I worry that I have (c) ___bought___ something that she has used and returned.

7. Craig sat in his car at the rural crossroads and wondered which direction to *choose*. Should he (a) ___choose___ left or right? He sighed and turned right, knowing that if he (b) ___chose___ the wrong way, he would run out of gas before finding his way back to the highway. After several anxious minutes, he spotted an Exxon sign. He pulled into the service station, grateful that he had (c) ___chosen___ the right direction after all.

8. My friend Alice loves to *eat.* But no matter how much she (a) ___eats___, she stays thin. Her husband, on the other hand, is fat. "Why?" he jokingly complains. "I (b) ___ate___ very little today. In fact," he adds with a grin, "all my life I have (c) ___eaten___ just one meal a day. Of course, it usually lasts from morning till night."

9. All the kids in the neighborhood waited each winter for Mahoney's pond to *freeze.* They knew that a sudden cold snap (a) ___freezes___ only the surface. It took at least a week of low temperatures before the pond (b) ___froze___ more than a few inches deep. Mr. Mahoney checked the ice each day. When it had finally (c) ___frozen___ to a depth of six inches, he gave his permission for the children to skate on it.

10. It is important for people to *give* blood. A healthy person can (a) ___give___ a pint of blood in less than fifteen minutes with little or no discomfort. The first time I (b) ___gave___ blood, I was afraid the needle would hurt, but all I felt was a slight pinch. I have (c) ___given___ blood many times since then. Each time I do, I feel good, knowing that my gift will help other people.

Troublesome Irregular Verbs

Three common irregular verbs that often give people trouble are *be, have,* and *do.* See pages 156–157 for a discussion of these verbs. Three sets of other irregular verbs that can lead to difficulties are *lie-lay, sit-set,* and *rise-raise.*

Lie-Lay

The principal parts of *lie* and *lay* are as follows:

Present	*Past*	*Past Participle*
lie	lay	lain
lay	laid	laid

To lie means *to rest* or *recline*. *To lay* means *to put something down.*

To Lie	*To Lay*
Tony *lies* on the couch.	I *lay* the mail on the table.
This morning he *lay* in the tub.	Yesterday I *laid* the mail on the counter.
He has *lain* in bed all week with the flu.	I have *laid* the mail where everyone will see it.

Practice

Underline the correct verb. Use a form of *lie* if you can substitute *recline.* Use a form of *lay* if you can substitute *place.*

1. On warm sunny days, Serena's kitten often (lies, lays) on the bedroom windowsill.
2. The waitress found a fifty-dollar bill (lying, laying) on the table after her two customers left.
3. The Magna Carta (lay, laid) the foundation for the establishment of the English Parliament.
4. Betsy was embarrassed when she realized that her boyfriend's love letter had (lain, laid) open in the living room all day.
5. I (lay, laid) down on the couch and pressed my face into the pillow.

Sit-Set

The principal parts of *sit* and *set* are as follows:

Present	*Past*	*Past Participle*
sit	sat	sat
set	set	set

To sit means *to take a seat* or *to rest. To set* means *to put* or *to place.*

To Sit	*To Set*
I *sit* down during work breaks.	Tony *sets* out the knives, forks, and spoons.
I *sat* in the doctor's office for three hours.	His sister already *set* out the dishes.
I have always *sat* in the last desk.	They have just *set* out the dinnerware.

Practice

Underline the correct form of the verb. Use a form of *sit* if you can substitute *rest.* Use a form of *set* if you can substitute *place.*

1. When I'm on a bus, I like (sitting, setting) in front.
2. The movers have (sat, set) all the smaller boxes on the kitchen table.
3. The aircraft carrier (sat, set) five miles offshore as helicopters shuttled to and from the island.
4. (Sit, Set) the plant on the windowsill so it will get the morning sun.
5. Lupe helped decorate for the party by (sitting, setting) vases of fresh flowers on each of the tables.

Rise-Raise

The principal parts of *rise* and *raise* are as follows:

Present	*Past*	*Past Participle*
rise	rose	risen
raise	raised	raised

To rise means *to get up* or *to move up. To raise* (which is a regular verb with simple *-ed* endings) means *to lift up* or *to increase in amount.*

To Rise	*To Raise*
The soldiers *rise* at dawn.	I'm going to *raise* the stakes in the card game.
The crowd *rose* to applaud the batter.	I *raised* the shades to let in the sun.
Dracula has *risen* from the grave.	I would have quit if the company had not *raised* my salary.

Practice

Underline the correct verb. Use a form of *rise* if you can substitute *get up* or *move up.* Use a form of *raise* if you can substitute *lift up* or *increase.*

1. It is usually warmer upstairs because heat (rises, raises).
2. The new owner (rose, raised) the rent, so now I will have to look for another apartment.
3. We (rose, raised) at three o'clock in the morning to watch the meteor shower.
4. After four days of rain, the river had (risen, raised) over its banks and threatened to flood the highway.
5. A single sailboat made them (rise, raise) the drawbridge, stopping traffic in both directions for fifteen minutes.

Review Test 1

Cross out the incorrect verb form. Then write the correct form of the verb in the space provided.

fell 1. The spare key under the mat ~~falled~~ through a crack in the porch floor.

blew 2. When he ~~blowed~~ out the dozens of candles on his cake, the old man used a hair dryer.

fought 3. Many residents ~~fighted~~ the city's plan to build a new stadium in their neighborhood.

swum 4. Oscar said he could have ~~swam~~ ten more laps if he hadn't gotten leg cramps.

broken 5. After he had ~~broke~~ the vase, the little boy hid the pieces under the sofa.

lying 6. People looked away from the homeless man who was ~~laying~~ on the sidewalk.

seen 7. You should have ~~saw~~ Ann's face when she passed her driving test.

lent 8. After I ~~lended~~ Dave money, I remembered that he seldom pays people back.

grown 9. My grandmother has ~~growed~~ tomatoes and peppers in her backyard for many years.

came 10. The health inspector ~~come~~ into the kitchen as the cook picked up a hamburger from the floor.

Review Test 2

Write short sentences using the form noted for the following irregular verbs.

Example Past of *ride* The Lone Ranger rode into the sunset.

Answers will vary, but these forms of the verbs should be used:

1. Present of *shake* shake or shakes
2. Past participle of *write* written
3. Past participle of *begin* begun
4. Past of *go* went
5. Past participle of *grow* grown
6. Present of *speak* speak or speaks
7. Past of *bring* brought
8. Present of *do* do or does
9. Past participle of *give* given
10. Past of *drink* drank

10 Subject-Verb Agreement

Introductory Activity

As you read each pair of sentences below, write a check mark beside the sentence that you think uses the underlined word correctly.

The pictures in that magazine is very controversial. _____
The pictures in that magazine are very controvesial. __✓__

There was many applicants for the job. _____
There were many applicants for the job. __✓__

Everybody usually watch the lighted numbers in an elevator. _____
Everybody usually watches the lighted numbers in an elevator. __✓__

On the basis of the above examples, see if you can complete the following statements.

1. In the first two pairs of sentences, the subjects are __pictures__ and __applicants__. Since both these subjects are plural, the verb must be plural.
2. In the last pair of sentences, the subject, *Everybody,* is a word that is always (singular, plural), and so its accompanying verb must be (singular, plural).

Answers are on page 680.

A verb must agree with its subject in number. A *singular subject* (one person or thing) takes a singular verb. A *plural subject* (more than one person or thing) takes a plural verb. Mistakes in subject-verb agreement are sometimes made in the following situations:

1. When words come between the subject and the verb
2. When a verb comes before the subject
3. With indefinite pronouns
4. With compound subjects
5. With *who, which,* and *that*

Each situation is explained on the following pages.

Words between the Subject and the Verb

Words that come between the subject and the verb do not change subject-verb agreement. In the following sentence,

> The breakfast cereals in the pantry are made mostly of sugar.

the subject (*cereals*) is plural, and so the verb (*are*) is plural. The words *in the pantry* that come between the subject and the verb do not affect subject-verb agreement. To help find the subject of certain sentences, you should cross out prepositional phrases (explained on page 91):

> One ~~of the crooked politicians~~ was jailed for a month.
>
> The posters ~~on my little brother's wall~~ include rock singers, monsters, and blond television stars.

Following is a list of common prepositions.

Common Prepositions

about	before	by	inside	over
above	behind	during	into	through
across	below	except	of	to
among	beneath	for	off	toward
around	beside	from	on	under
at	between	in	onto	with

Practice

Draw one line under the subject. Then lightly cross out any words that come between the subject and the verb. Finally, draw two lines under the correct verb in parentheses.

Example The price of the stereo speakers (is, are) too high for my wallet.

1. A trail of bloodstains (leads, lead) to the spot where the murder was committed.
2. The winter clothes in the hall closet (takes, take) up too much room.
3. A basket of fancy fruit and nuts (was, were) delivered to my house.
4. The garbled instructions for assembling the bicycle (was, were) almost impossible to follow.
5. Smoke from the distant forest fires (is, are) visible from many miles away.
6. Workers at that automobile plant (begins, begin) each day with a period of exercise.
7. The earliest date on any of the cemetery gravestones (appears, appear) to be 1804.
8. The line of cars in the traffic jam (seems, seem) to extend for miles.
9. Several boxes in the corner of the attic (contains, contain) old family pictures.
10. Sleeping bags with the new insulation material (protects, protect) campers even in subzero temperatures.

Verb before the Subject

A verb agrees with its subject even when the verb comes *before* the subject. Words that may precede the subject include *there, here,* and, in questions, *who, which, what,* and *where.*

> Inside the storage shed are the garden tools.
>
> At the street corner were two panhandlers.
>
> There are times when I'm ready to quit my job.
>
> Where are the instructions for the microwave oven?

If you are unsure about the subject, ask *who* or *what* of the verb. With the first sentence above, you might ask, "What is inside the storage shed?" The answer, garden *tools*, is the subject.

Practice

Draw one line under the subject. Then draw two lines under the correct verb in parentheses.

1. There (is, are) a scratching noise coming from behind this wall.
2. On the bottom of the jar of preserves (is, are) the berries.
3. Floating near the base of the dock (was, were) several discarded aluminum cans.
4. In the middle of the woods behind our home (sits, sit) an abandoned cabin.
5. There (was, were) so many students talking at once that the instructor shouted for quiet.
6. Outside the novelty shop at the mall (stands, stand) a life-size cutout of W. C. Fields.
7. Coming out of the fog toward the frightened boys (was, were) the menacing shape of a large dog.
8. In the rear of the closet (was, were) the basketball sneakers that I thought I had lost.
9. On the table in the doctor's office (is, are) some magazines that are five years old.
10. Lining one wall of the gym (was, were) a row of lockers for the team members.

Indefinite Pronouns

The following words, known as *indefinite pronouns,* always take singular verbs.

Indefinite Pronouns

(-one words)	*(-body words)*	*(-thing words)*	
one	nobody	nothing	each
anyone	anybody	anything	either
everyone	everybody	everything	neither
someone	somebody	something	

Note *Both* always takes a plural verb.

Practice

Write the correct form of the verb in the space provided.

keeps, keep — 1. Something always keeps me from getting to bed on time.

works, work — 2. Nobody that I know works as hard as Manuel.

pays, pay — 3. Neither of the jobs offered to me pays more than five dollars an hour.

has, have — 4. Both of the speakers have told us more than we care to know about the dangers of water pollution.

slips, slip — 5. Someone in Inez's apartment house slips an unsigned valentine under her door every year.

leans, leans — 6. Anything sitting on the old wooden floor leans to one side.

expects, expect — 7. Each of my friends expects to be invited to my new backyard pool.

was, were — 8. Not one of the three smoke detectors in the house was working properly.

stops, stop — 9. Only one of all the brands of waxes stops the rust on my car from spreading.

has, have — 10. Just about everybody who hates getting up early for work has jumped out of bed at 6 A.M. to go on vacation.

Compound Subjects

Subjects joined by *and* generally take a plural verb.

> Yoga and biking are Lola's ways of staying in shape.
> Ambition and good luck are the keys to his success.

When subjects are joined by *either . . . or, neither . . . nor, not only . . . but also,* the verb agrees with the subject closer to the verb.

> Either the restaurant manager or his assistants deserve to be fired for the spoiled meat used in the stew.

The nearer subject, *assistants,* is plural, and so the verb is plural.

Practice

Write the correct form of the verb in the space provided.

saddens, sadden — 1. The shivering and crying of animals in pet stores __sadden__ me very much.

needs, need — 2. The floor and cabinets in the kitchen __need__ to be cleaned.

has, have — 3. Her best friend and her coach __have__ more influence on Sally than her parents do.

continues, continue — 4. Crabgrass and dandelions __continue__ to spread across the lawn despite my efforts to wipe them out.

tears, tear — 5. Either the neighborhood kids or an automatic car-wash machine always __tears__ the antenna off my car.

Who, Which, and *That*

When *who, which,* and *that* are used as subjects of verbs, they take singular verbs if the word they stand for is singular and plural verbs if the word they stand for is plural. For example, in the sentence

> Gary is one of those people who are very private.

the verb is plural because *who* stands for *people*, which is plural. On the other hand, in the sentence

Gary is a person who is very private.

the verb is singular because *who* stands for *person*, which is singular.

Practice

Write the correct form of the verb in the space provided.

has, have	1. The young man who __has__ mowed my grass for years just left for college.
goes, go	2. The jacket that __goes__ with those pants is at the cleaners.
becomes, become	3. Women who __become__ police officers often have to prove themselves more capable than the men they work with.
tastes, taste	4. The restaurant serves hamburgers which __taste__ like dry cereal.
is, are	5. The ceiling in Kevin's bedroom is covered with stars which __are__ arranged in the shape of the constellations.

Collaborative Activity

Part A: Editing and Rewriting

Working with a partner, read the short paragraph below and see if you can underline the five mistakes in subject-verb agreement. Then use the space provided to correct these five errors. Feel free to discuss the rewrite quietly with your partner and refer back to the chapter when necessary.

When most people think about cities, they do not thinks about wild animals. But in my city apartment, there is enough creatures to fill a small forest. In the daytime, I must contend with the pigeons. These unwanted guests at my apartment makes a loud feathery mess on my bedroom windowsill. In the evening, my apartment is visited by roaches. These large insects creep onto my kitchen floor and walls after dark and frighten me with their shiny glistening bodies. Later at night, my apartment is invaded by mice. Waking from sleep, I can hear their little feet tapping as they

Continued

scurry behind walls and above my ceiling. Everybody I know think I should move into a new apartment. What I really need is to go somewhere that have less wild creatures—maybe a forest!

they do not think

there are enough creatures

guests . . . make

Everybody . . . thinks

somewhere that has

Part B: Creating Sentences

Answers will vary.

Working with a partner, write sentences as directed. Use separate paper. For each item, pay special attention to subject-verb agreement.

1. Write a sentence in which the words *in the cafeteria* or *on the table* come between the subject and verb. Underline the subject of your sentence and circle the verb.
2. Write a sentence that begins with the words *There is* or *There are*. Underline the subject of your sentence and circle the verb.
3. Write a sentence in which the indefinite pronoun *nobody* or *anything* is the subject.
4. Write a sentence with the compound subjects *manager* and *employees*. Underline the subject of your sentence and circle the verb.

Reflective Activity

Answers will vary.

1. Look at the paragraph about the apartment that you revised above. Which rule involving subject-verb agreement gave you the most trouble? How did you figure out the correct answer?
2. Five situations involving subject-verb agreement have been discussed in this chapter. Explain which one is most likely to cause you problems.

■ Review Test 1

Complete each of the following sentences, using *is, are, was, were, have,* or *has.* Underline the subject of each of these verbs. In some cases you will need to provide that subject.

Example The hot dogs in that luncheonette are hazardous to your health.
Answers will vary.

1. In my glove compartment ______
2. The cat and her three kittens ______
3. I frequently see people who ______
4. Neither of the wrestlers ______
5. Scattered across the parking lot ______
6. The dust balls under my bed ______
7. There are ______
8. My friend and his brother ______
9. The newspapers that accumulate in my garage ______
10. It was one of those movies that ______

■ Review Test 2

Draw one line under the subject. Then draw two lines under the correct verb in parentheses.

1. The plants in the window (grows, grow) quickly because they have plenty of sunlight.
2. Nobody (walks, walk) on the streets of this neighborhood at night.
3. Here (is, are) the keys you need to get into the apartment.
4. A talking computerized car and several stunt people (was, were) the true stars of the movie.
5. There (is, are) billboards all along the road warning drivers to stay sober.
6. A paper plate fitted over the dog's head (prevents, prevent) the animal from biting its stitches.
7. Since I gained weight, neither my old suits nor my new shirt (fits, fit) me.

8. What (does, do) my marital status have to do with my qualifications for the job?
9. Sitting silently off in the distance in the bright moonlight (was, were) the wolf and his mate.
10. Neither the security guard nor the police officer (was, were) able to figure out how the thief got into the building.

Review Test 3

There are ten mistakes in subject-verb agreement in the following passage. Cross out each incorrect verb and write the correct form above it. In addition, underline the subject of each of the verbs that must be changed.

After more than twenty years on television, there ~~is~~ are few honors that *Sesame Street* has not won. The awards are deserved, for *Sesame Street* is a show that ~~treat~~ treats children with respect. Most children's programs ~~consists~~ consist of cheaply made cartoons that ~~is~~ are based on the adventures of a superhero or a video-game character. Unfortunately, children's TV programs are generally so poor because quality kids' shows ~~does~~ do not make the profits which the networks demand. Both the superhero story and the video-game story ~~is~~ are easy to slap together. By contrast, the producers of *Sesame Street* ~~spends~~ spend enormous amounts of time and money researching how children learn. Another reason for the low profits ~~are~~ is the nature of the audience. Because children have little money to spend on sponsors' products, each of the networks ~~charge~~ charges bottom rates for advertising during children's programs. *Sesame Street*, a nonprofit show, does not even accept ads. And income from the sale of *Sesame Street* products ~~are~~ is used to do an even better job of producing the show.

11 Consistent Verb Tense

Introductory Activity

See if you can find and underline the two mistakes in verb tense in the following selection.

When Computer Warehouse had a sale, Alex decided to buy a new personal computer. He planned to set up the machine himself and hoped to connect it to the Internet right away. When he arrived home, however, Alex discovers that hooking up the wires to the computer could be complicated and confusing. The directions sounded as if they had been written for electrical engineers. After two hours of frustration, Alex gave up and calls a technician for help.

Now try to complete the following statement:

Verb tenses should be consistent. In the selection above, two verbs have to be changed because they are mistakenly in the (*present, past*) __present__ tense while all the other verbs in the selection are in the (*present, past*) __past__ tense.

Answers are on page 681.

Keeping Tenses Consistent

Do not shift tenses unnecessarily. If you begin writing a paper in the present tense, don't shift suddenly to the past. If you begin in the past, don't shift without reason to the present. Notice the inconsistent verb tenses in the following example:

> Smoke spilled from the front of the overheated car. The driver opens up the hood, then jumped back as steam billows out.

The verbs must be consistently in the present tense:

> Smoke spills from the front of the overheated car. The driver opens up the hood, then jumps back as steam billows out.

Or the verbs must be consistently in the past tense:

> Smoke spilled from the front of the overheated car. The driver opened up the hood, then jumped back as steam billowed out.

Practice

In each item, one verb must be changed so that it agrees in tense with the other verbs. Cross out the incorrect verb and write the correct form in the space at the left.

looked **Example** I gave away my striped sweater after three people told me I ~~look~~ like a giant bee.

rolled 1. The wet dog, delighted that its bath was over, raced madly around the living room and ~~rolls~~ all over the carpet.

purchased 2. On vacation, I couldn't face another restaurant meal, so I ~~purchase~~ cheese and crackers and ate in my room.

stepped 3. The excited crowd clapped and cheered when the performers ~~step~~ onto the stage.

crashed 4. Before the rain stopped, mud slid down the hill and ~~crashes~~ into the houses in the valley.

snatched 5. When my little brother found my new box of markers, he ~~snatches~~ one and made green circles all over our front steps.

covered 6. The old house looked as if it hadn't been cleaned in years. Dust ~~cover~~ everything, and the smell of mildew hung in the air.

lifted 7. The outfielder tumbled, made a spectacular catch, and ~~lifts~~ the ball up for the umpire to witness.

argues 8. Annie talks aloud to her favorite soap opera character; she ~~argued~~ and fights with the woman over her decisions.

swallowed 9. At the pie-eating contest, Leo stuffed in the last piece of blueberry pie, ~~swallows~~ it all, and then flashed a purple grin for the photographer.

glowed 10 The supermarket seemed empty on Sunday morning; shopping carts stood in long lines, bakery shelves were bare, and the lights over the meat counter ~~glow~~ dimly.

Review Test 1

Change the verbs where needed in the following selection so that they are consistently in the past tense. Cross out each incorrect verb and write the correct form above it, as shown in the example. You will need to make nine corrections.

[1]Years ago, I ~~live~~ lived in an old apartment house where I got little peace and quiet. [2]For one thing, I often heard the constant fights that went on in the adjoining apartment. [3]The husband ~~yells~~ yelled about killing his wife, and she screamed right back about leaving him or having him arrested. [4]In addition, the people in the apartment above me ~~have~~ had four noisy kids. [5]Sometimes it ~~seem~~ seemed as if football games were going on upstairs. [6]The noise ~~reach~~ reached a high point when I got home from work, which also happened to be the time the kids ~~return~~ returned from school. [7]If the kids and neighbors were not disturbing me, I always had one other person to depend on—the superintendent, who ~~visits~~ visited my apartment whenever he felt like it. [8]He always had an excuse, such as checking the water pipes or caulking the windows. [9]But each time he came, I ~~suspect~~ suspected he just ~~wants~~ wanted to get away from his noisy family, which occupied the basement apartment. [10]I ~~move~~ moved out of that apartment as soon as I was able to.

Review Test 2

Change verbs as necessary in the following selection so that they are consistently in the past tense. Cross out each incorrect verb and write the correct form above it. You will need to make ten corrections in all.

[1]As a kid, I never really enjoyed the public swimming pool. [2]First, there were all sorts of rules that ~~prevent~~ prevented me from having much fun in the water. [3]One was that children under the age of fourteen had to be accompanied by an adult. [4]I didn't like having to beg a parent or a neighbor to take me swimming every time I ~~want~~ wanted to go. [5]Another rule was that girls ~~are~~ were not allowed in the water without bathing caps. [6]The required bathing cap was so tight that it ~~cause~~ caused a heavy pressure mark on my forehead. [7]Also, it often ~~gives~~ gave me a headache. [8]Second, I wasn't a very good swimmer then. [9]Most of the time I ~~find~~ found myself hanging on to the side of the pool. [10]And whenever I attempted a graceful dive, I ~~end~~ ended up doing a belly flop. [11]Finally, many of the kids ~~tease~~ teased me. [12]Some of them liked splashing water into my face, which ~~force~~ forced me to swallow chlorine and a dead bug or two. [13]Even worse was the boy who ~~sneaks~~ sneaked up behind me all summer long to dump ice cubes down the back of my swimsuit.

12 Additional Information about Verbs

The purpose of this special chapter is to provide additional information about verbs. Some people will find the grammatical terms here a helpful reminder of earlier school learning about verbs. For them, these terms will increase their understanding of how verbs function in English. Other people may welcome more detailed information about terms used elsewhere in the text. In either case, remember that the most common mistakes people make when writing verbs have been treated in earlier sections of the book.

Verb Tense

Verbs tell us the time of an action. The time that a verb shows is usually called *tense.* The most common tenses are the simple present, past, and future. In addition, there are nine other tenses that enable us to express more specific ideas about time than we could with the simple tenses alone. Following are the twelve verb tenses, with examples. Read them to increase your sense of the many different ways of expressing time in English.

Tenses	*Examples*
Present	I *work.* Jill *works.*
Past	Howard *worked* on the lawn.
Future	You *will work* overtime this week.
Present perfect	Gail *has worked* hard on the puzzle. They *have worked* well together.
Past perfect	They *had worked* eight hours before their shift ended.
Future perfect	The volunteers *will have worked* many unpaid hours.
Present progressive	I *am* not *working* today. You *are working* the second shift. The clothes dryer *is* not *working* properly.
Past progressive	She *was working* outside. The plumbers *were working* here this morning.
Future progressive	The sound system *will be working* by tonight.
Present perfect progressive	Married life *has* not *been working* out for that couple.
Past perfect progressive	I *had been working* overtime until recently.
Future perfect progressive	My sister *will have been working* at that store for eleven straight months by the time she takes a vacation next week.

The perfect tenses are formed by adding *have, has,* or *had* to the past participle (the form of the verb that ends, usually, in *-ed*). The progressive tenses are formed by adding *am, is, are, was,* or *were* to the present participle (the form of the verb that ends in *-ing*). The perfect progressive tenses are formed by adding *have been, has been,* or *had been* to the present participle.

Certain tenses are explained in more detail on the following pages.

Present Perfect
(*have* or *has* + past participle)

The present perfect tense expresses an action that began in the past and has recently been completed or is continuing in the present.

The city *has* just *agreed* on a contract with the sanitation workers.

Tony's parents *have lived* in that house for twenty years.

Lola *has watched Star Trek* reruns since she was a little girl.

Past Perfect
(*had* + past participle)

The past perfect tense expresses a past action that was completed before another past action.

Lola *had learned* to dance by the time she was five.

The class *had* just *started* when the fire bell rang.

Bad weather *had* never *been* a problem on our vacations until last year.

Present Progressive
(*am, is,* or *are* + the *-ing* form)

The present progressive tense expresses an action still in progress.

I *am taking* an early train into the city every day this week.

Karl *is playing* softball over at the field.

The vegetables *are growing* rapidly.

Past Progressive
(*was* or *were* + the *-ing* form)

The past progressive expresses an action that was in progress in the past.

I *was spending* twenty dollars a week on cigarettes before I quit.

Last week, the store *was selling* many items at half price.

My friends *were driving* over to pick me up when the accident occurred.

Practice

For the sentences that follow, fill in the present or past perfect or the present or past progressive of the verb shown. Use the tense that seems to express the meaning of each sentence best.

Example park This summer, Mickey is parking cars at a French restaurant.

Some answers may vary.

dry 1. The afternoon sun was so hot it had dried our jeans in less than an hour.

plan 2. My parents were planning/had planned a trip to the seashore until they heard about the sharks.

grow 3. This year, Aunt Anita is growing tomatoes; she must have two hundred already.

throw 4. The pitcher had thrown the ball to second; unfortunately, the runner was on third.

carve 5. Everyone at the dinner table continued to complain about the way Henry was carving the Thanksgiving turkey.

open 6. The excited child had opened all her birthday presents before her father could load his camera.

care 7. Erica answered an ad for a baby-sitter and now is caring for three children, two dogs, and twenty houseplants.

watch 8. Helen is a television athlete; she has watched almost every football and baseball game televised this year.

walk 9. The hiker had walked for over twenty miles before she stopped for a short rest.

try 10. Last winter my brothers were trying to get a job bagging groceries at the supermarket.

Verbals

Verbals are words formed from verbs. Verbals, like verbs, often express action. They can add variety to your sentences and vigor to your writing style. The three kinds of verbals are *infinitives, participles,* and *gerunds.*

Infinitive

An infinitive is *to* plus the base form of the verb.

I started *to practice.*
Don't try *to lift* that table.
I asked Russ *to drive* me home.

Participle

A participle is a verb form used as an adjective (a descriptive word). The present participle ends in *-ing*. The past participle ends in *-ed* or has an irregular ending.

Favoring his *cramped* leg, the *screaming* boy waded out of the pool.
The *laughing* child held up her *locked* piggy bank.
Using a shovel and a bucket, I scooped water out of the *flooded* basement.

Gerund

A gerund is the *-ing* form of a verb used as a noun.

Studying wears me out.
Playing basketball is my main pleasure during the week.
Through *jogging,* you can get yourself in shape.

Practice

In the space beside each section, identify the italicized word as a participle (*P*), an infinitive (*I*), or a gerund (*G*).

P ________ 1. Carmine preferred the *reclining* chair for his bad back.
G ________ 2. Doctors believe that *walking* is one of the most beneficial forms of exercise.
I ________ 3. Once the pan was hot enough, Granddad was ready *to cook* his famous blueberry pancakes.
G ________ 4. It isn't *flying* that makes Elsa anxious but the airline food.
P ________ 5. *Scratching* its back against a tree, the bear looked deceptively harmless.

I 6. *To make* the room more cheerful, Alice painted the dark cabinets yellow.

G 7. *Observing* gorillas' mating behavior is part of that zookeeper's job.

I 8. During the entire movie, the couple continued *to talk* loudly.

P 9. My brother's *receding* hairline makes him look older than he really is.

P 10. At the front door of the hospital, workers found a blanket *containing* a healthy newborn baby.

Active and Passive Verbs

When the subject of a sentence performs the action of a verb, the verb is in the *active voice.* When the subject of a sentence receives the action of a verb, the verb is in the *passive voice.*

The passive form of a verb consists of a form of the verb *be* plus the past participle of the main verb. Look at the active and passive forms of the verbs below.

Active	*Passive*
Lola *ate* the vanilla pudding. (The subject, *Lola*, is the doer of the action.)	The vanilla pudding *was eaten* by Lola. (The subject, *pudding*, does not act. Instead, something happens to it.)
The plumber *replaced* the hot water heater. (The subject, *plumber*, is the doer of the action.)	The hot water heater *was replaced* by the plumber. (The subject, *heater*, does not act. Instead, something happens to it.)

In general, active verbs are more effective than passive verbs. Active verbs give your writing a simpler and more vigorous style. The passive form of verbs is appropriate, however, when the performer of an action is unknown or is less important than the receiver of the action. For example:

My house was vandalized last night.
(The performer of the action is unknown.)

Mark was seriously injured as a result of your negligence.
(The receiver of the action, *Mark,* is being emphasized.)

Practice

Change the following sentences from passive voice to active voice. Note that in some cases you may have to add a subject.

Examples The moped bicycle was ridden by Tony.

Tony rode the moped bicycle.

The basketball team was given a standing ovation.

The crowd gave the basketball team a standing ovation.

(Here a subject had to be added.)

1. The bus was boarded by a man with a live parrot on his shoulder.
   A man with a live parrot on his shoulder boarded the bus.

2. The stained-glass window was broken by a large falling branch.
   A large falling branch broke the stained-glass window.

3. Baseballs for hospitalized children were autographed by the entire team.
   The entire team autographed baseballs for hospitalized children.

4. The hotel was destroyed by a fire that started with a cigarette.
   A fire that started with a cigarette destroyed the hotel.

5. The pressures of dealing with life and death must be faced by doctors.
   Doctors must face the pressures of dealing with life and death.

6. The missile was directed to its target by a sophisticated laser system.
   A sophisticated laser system directed the missile to its target.

7. The kitchen shelves were covered by a thick layer of yellowish grease.
   A thick layer of yellowish grease covered the kitchen shelves.

8. Trash in the neighborhood park was removed by a group of volunteers.
   A group of volunteers removed trash in the neighborhood park.

9. Most of the escaped convicts were captured within a mile of the jail by the state police.
   The state police captured most of the escaped convicts within a mile of the jail.

10. Prizes were awarded by the judges for hog-calling and stone-skipping.
    The judges awarded prizes for hog-calling and stone-skipping.

Review Test

On separate paper, write three sentences for each of the following forms:
Answers will vary.

1. Present perfect tense
2. Past perfect tense
3. Present progressive tense
4. Past progressive tense
5. Infinitive
6. Participle
7. Gerund
8. Passive voice (when the performer of the action is unknown or is less important than the receiver of an action—see page 192)

13 Pronoun Reference, Agreement, and Point of View

Introductory Activity

Read each pair of sentences below, noting the underlined pronouns. Then see if you can circle the correct letter in each of the statements that follow.

1. a. None of the nominees for "best actress" showed their anxiety as the names were being read.
   b. None of the nominees for "best actress" showed her anxiety as the names were being read.
2. a. At the mall, they are already putting up Christmas decorations.
   b. At the mall, shop owners are already putting up Christmas decorations.
3. a. I go to the steak house often because you can get inexpensive meals there.
   b. I go to the steak house often because I can get inexpensive meals there.

In the first pair, (a, b) uses the underlined pronoun correctly because the pronoun refers to *None,* which is a singular word.
In the second pair, (a, b) is correct because otherwise the pronoun reference would be unclear.
In the third pair, (a, b) is correct because the pronoun point of view should not be shifted unnecessarily.

Answers are on page 681.

Pronouns are words that take the place of nouns (persons, places, or things). In fact, the word *pronoun* means *for a noun*. Pronouns are shortcuts that keep you from unnecessarily repeating words in writing. Here are some examples of pronouns:

> Martha shampooed *her* dog. (*Her* is a pronoun that takes the place of *Martha*.)
>
> As the door swung open, *it* creaked. (*It* replaces *door*.)
>
> When the motorcyclists arrived at McDonald's, *they* removed *their* helmets. (*They* and *their* replace *motorcyclists*.)

This section presents rules that will help you avoid three common mistakes people make with pronouns. The rules are as follows:

1 A pronoun must refer clearly to the word it replaces.
2 A pronoun must agree in number with the word or words it replaces.
3 Pronouns should not shift unnecessarily in point of view.

Pronoun Reference

A sentence may be confusing and unclear if a pronoun appears to refer to more than one word, as in this sentence:

> I locked my suitcase in my car, and then it was stolen.

What was stolen? It is unclear whether the suitcase or the car was stolen.

> I locked my suitcase in my car, and then my car was stolen.

A sentence may also be confusing if the pronoun does not refer to any specific word. Look at this sentence:

> We never buy fresh vegetables at that store because they charge too much.

Who charges too much? There is no specific word that *they* refers to. Be clear.

> We never buy fresh vegetables at that store because the owners charge too much.

Here are additional sentences with unclear pronoun reference. Read the explanations of why they are unclear and look carefully at the ways they are corrected.

Unclear	*Clear*
Lola told Gina that she had gained weight. (*Who* had gained weight: Lola or Gina? Be clear.)	Lola told Gina, "You've gained weight." (Quotation marks, which can sometimes be used to correct an unclear reference, are explained in Chapter 25.)
My older brother is an electrician, but I'm not interested in it. (There is no specific word that *it* refers to. It would not make sense to say, "I'm not interested in electrician.")	My older brother is an electrician, but I'm not interested in becoming one.
Our instructor did not explain the assignment, which made me angry. (Does *which* mean that the instructor's failure to explain the assignment made you angry, or that the assignment itself made you angry. Be clear.)	I was angry that our instructor did not explain the assignment.

Practice

Rewrite each of the following sentences to make clear the vague pronoun reference. Add, change, or omit words as necessary.

Example Lana thanked Amy for the gift, which was very thoughtful of her.
Lana thanked Amy for the thoughtful gift.

Answers may vary.

1. The defendant told the judge he was mentally ill.
The defendant told the judge, "I am mentally ill."

2. Fran removed the blanket from the sofa bed and folded it up.
Fran removed the blanket from the sofa bed and folded the blanket up.

3. Before the demonstration, they passed out signs for us to carry.
Before the demonstration, the leaders passed out signs for us to carry.

4. Cindy complained to Rachel that her boyfriend was being dishonest.
Cindy complained to Rachel, "Your boyfriend is being dishonest."

5. Because I didn't rinse last night's dishes, it smells like a garbage can.
Because I didn't rinse last night's dishes, my kitchen smells like a garbage can.

6. The students watched a film on endangered species, which really depressed them.
A film on endangered species really depressed the students.

7. The veterinarian said that if I find a tick on my dog, I should get rid of it immediately.
The veterinarian said that if I find a tick on my dog, I should get rid of the tick immediately.

8. My sister removed the curtains from the windows so that she could wash them.
So that she could wash the curtains, my sister removed them from the windows.

9. Richard said his acupuncture therapist could help my sprained shoulder, but I don't believe in it.
Richard said his acupuncture therapist could help my sprained shoulder, but I don't believe in acupuncture.

10. I discovered when I went to sell my old textbooks that they've put out new editions, and nobody wants to buy them.
I discovered when I went to sell my old textbooks that nobody wants to buy them because publishers have put out new editions.

Pronoun Agreement

A pronoun must agree in number with the word or words it replaces. If the word a pronoun refers to is singular, the pronoun must be singular; if the word is plural, the pronoun must be plural. (Note that the word a pronoun refers to is known as the *antecedent.)*

Lola agreed to lend me her Jewel albums.

The gravediggers sipped coffee during their break.

In the first example, the pronoun *her* refers to the singular word *Lola*; in the second example, the pronoun *their* refers to the plural word *gravediggers*.

Practice

Write the appropriate pronoun (*they, their, them, it*) in the blank space in each of the following sentences.

Example My credit cards got me into debt, so I burned them.

1. The two girls in identical dresses were surprised when they saw each other at the prom.
2. It annoys me when disk jockeys play their favorite songs all the time.
3. I put my family pictures in a photo album, but then I lost it.
4. I used to collect baseball cards and comic books, but then I gave them to my little brother.
5. When the children are watching television, it's impossible to get their attention.

Indefinite Pronouns

The following words, known as *indefinite pronouns,* are always singular.

Indefinite Pronouns

(*-one* words)	(*-body* words)	
one	nobody	each
anyone	anybody	either
everyone	everybody	neither
someone	somebody	

Either of the apartments has its drawbacks.

One of the girls lost her skateboard.

Everyone in the class must hand in his paper tomorrow.

In each example, the pronoun is singular because it refers to one of the indefinite pronouns. There are two important points to remember about indefinite pronouns.

Point 1 The last example above suggests that everyone in the class is male. If the students were all female, the pronoun would be *her.* If the students were a mixed group of males and females, the pronoun form would be *his or her.*

Everyone in the class must hand in *his or her* paper tomorrow.

Some writers still follow the traditional practice of using *his* to refer to both men and women. Many now use *his or her* to avoid an implied sexual bias. Perhaps the best practice, though, is to avoid using either *his* or the somewhat awkward *his or her*. This can often be done by rewriting a sentence in the plural:

All students in the class must hand in *their* papers tomorrow.

Here are some examples of sentences that can be rewritten in the plural.

A young child is seldom willing to share her toys with others.
Young children are seldom willing to share their toys with others.

Anyone who does not wear his seat belt will be fined.
People who do not wear their seat belts will be fined.

A newly elected politician should not forget his or her campaign promises.
Newly elected politicians should not forget their campaign promises.

Point 2 In informal spoken English, *plural* pronouns are often used with indefinite pronouns. Instead of saying

Everybody has *his or her* own idea of an ideal vacation.

we are likely to say

> Everybody has *their* own idea of an ideal vacation.

Here are other examples:

> Everyone in the class must pass in *their* papers.
>
> Everybody in our club has *their* own idea about how to raise money.
>
> No one in our family skips *their* chores.

In such cases, the indefinite pronouns are clearly plural in meaning. Also, the use of such plurals helps people avoid the awkward *his or her*. In time, the plural pronoun may be accepted in formal speech or writing. Until that happens, however, you should use the grammatically correct singular form in your writing.

Practice

Underline the correct pronoun.

Example Neither of those houses has (its, their) own garage.

1. Neither of the men was aware that (his, their) voice was being taped.
2. One of the waiters was fired for failing to report all (his, their) tips.
3. We have three dogs, and each of them has (its, their) own bowl.
4. During the intermission, everyone had to wait a while for (her, their) turn to get into the ladies' room.
5. All the boxes of old clothing need to have labels attached to (it, them).
6. Mr. Alvarez refuses to let anyone ride in his car without using (his or her, their) seat belt.
7. It seems that neither of the mothers is comfortable answering (her, their) teenager's questions about sex.
8. If anybody in the men's club objects to the new rules, (he, they) should speak up now.
9. Nobody on the women's basketball team had enough nerve to voice (her, their) complaints to the coach.
10. Before being allowed to go on the class trip, each student had to have (his or her, their) parents sign a permission form.

Pronoun Point of View

Pronouns should not shift their point of view unnecessarily. When writing a paper, be consistent in your use of first-, second-, or third-person pronouns.

Type of Pronoun	*Singular*	*Plural*
First-person pronouns	I (my, mine, me)	we (our, us)
Second-person pronouns	you (your)	you (your)
Third-person pronouns	he (his, him)	they (their, them)
	she (her)	
	it (its)	

Note Any person, place, or thing, as well as any indefinite pronoun like *one, anyone, someone,* and so on (see page 199), is a third-person word.

For instance, if you start writing in the first-person *I*, don't jump suddenly to the second-person *you*. Or if you are writing in the third-person *they*, don't shift unexpectedly to *you*. Look at the examples.

Inconsistent

One reason that *I* like living in the city is that *you* always have a wide choice of sports events to attend.

(The most common mistake people make is to let a *you* slip into their writing after they start with another pronoun.)

Consistent

One reason that *I* like living in the city is that *I* always have a wide choice of sports events to attend.

Inconsistent

Someone who is dieting should have the help of friends; *you* should also have plenty of willpower.

Consistent

Someone who is dieting should have the help of friends; *he* or *she* should also have plenty of willpower.

Inconsistent

Students who work while *they* are going to school face special problems. For one thing, *you* seldom have enough study time.

Consistent

Students who work while *they* are going to school face special problems. For one thing, *they* seldom have enough study time.

Practice

Cross out inconsistent pronouns in the following sentences and write the correction above the error.

Example I work much better when the boss doesn't hover over ~~you~~ me with instructions on what to do.

1. A good horror movie makes my bones feel like ice and gets ~~your~~ my blood running cold.
2. People buy groceries from that supermarket because ~~you~~ they know it has the best prices in the area.
3. One experience that almost everyone fears is when ~~you~~ they have to speak in front of a crowd of people.
4. If students attend class regularly and study hard, ~~you~~ they should receive a good grade.
5. I drive on back roads instead of major highways because ~~you~~ I can avoid traffic.
6. Many men and women have problems meeting people, especially if ~~you~~ they don't like singles' bars.
7. Andy enjoys watching soap operas because then ~~you~~ he can worry about someone else's problems instead of ~~your~~ his own.
8. Our street was so slippery after the ice storm that ~~you~~ we could barely take a step without falling down.
9. Mrs. Almac enjoys working the three-to-eleven shift because that way ~~you~~ she can still have a large part of ~~your~~ her day free.
10. All of us at work voted to join the union because we felt it would protect ~~your~~ our rights.

■ Review Test 1

Underline the correct word in the parentheses.

1. Devan slammed the phone down on the table so hard that (it, the phone) broke.
2. During the boring movie, people started to squirm in (his or her, their) seats.

3. I love living alone because (you, I) never have to answer to anyone else.
4. Almost all the magazines I subscribe to arrive with (its, their) covers torn.
5. My father disagrees with my husband about almost everything because (he, my father) is so stubborn.
6. I like driving on that turnpike because (they, state officials) don't allow billboards there.
7. Neither one of the umpires wanted to admit that (he, they) had made a mistake.
8. When Ed went to the bank for a home improvement loan, (they, the loan officers) asked him for three credit references.
9. Even if you graduate from that business school, (they, the placement officers) don't guarantee they will find you a job.
10. Not one of the women in the audience was willing to raise (her, their) hand when the magician asked for a female volunteer.

■ Review Test 2

Cross out the pronoun error in each sentence and write the correction in the space provided. Then circle the letter that correctly describes the type of error that was made.

Examples ~~Anyone~~ turning in their papers late will be penalized.

Students

Mistake in: a. pronoun reference (b.) pronoun agreement

When Clyde takes his son Paul to the park, ~~he~~ enjoys himself.

Paul

Mistake in: (a.) pronoun reference b. pronoun point of view

From where we stood, ~~you~~ could see three states.

we

Mistake in: a. pronoun agreement (b.) pronoun point of view

1. A good salesperson knows that ~~you~~ should be courteous to customers.

   he or she

   Mistake in: a. pronoun agreement (b.) pronoun point of view

2. Neither of the girls who flunked bothered to bring ~~their~~ report card home.

   her

   Mistake in: a. pronoun reference (b.) pronoun agreement

3. When the shabbily dressed woman walked into the fancy hotel, ~~they~~ weren't very polite to her.
   the hotel employees

   Mistake in: a. pronoun agreement (b.) pronoun reference

4. Nobody seems to add or subtract without ~~their~~ pocket calculator anymore.
   his or her

   Mistake in: (a.) pronoun agreement b. pronoun point of view

5. Denise went everywhere with Nita until ~~she~~ moved to Texas last year.
   Denise (or Nita)

   Mistake in: a. pronoun agreement (b.) pronoun reference

6. Everyone on my street believes ~~they~~ saw a strange glow in the sky last night.
   he or she

   Mistake in: (a.) pronoun agreement b. pronoun point of view

7. In baking desserts, people should follow the directions carefully or ~~you~~ are likely to end up with something strange.
   they

   Mistake in: a. pronoun reference (b.) pronoun point of view

8. When Jerry added another card to the delicate structure, ~~it~~ fell down.
   the structure (or the card)

   Mistake in: (a.) pronoun reference b. pronoun point of view

9. Anyone who wants to join the car pool should leave ~~their~~ name with me.
   his or her

   Mistake in: (a.) pronoun agreement b. pronoun reference

10. Any working mother knows that ~~you need~~ at least a twenty-five hour day.
    she needs

    Mistake in: a. pronoun agreement (b.) pronoun point of view

Hint In item 10, you will also need to correct a verb form.

14 Pronoun Types

Introductory Activity

In each pair, write a check beside the sentence that you think uses pronouns correctly.

Andy and *I* enrolled in a computer course. ✓

Andy and *me* enrolled in a computer course. ____

The police officer pointed to my sister and *me*. ✓

The police officer pointed to my sister and *I*. ____

Lola prefers men *whom* take pride in their bodies. ____

Lola prefers men *who* take pride in their bodies. ✓

The players are confident that the league championship is *theirs'*. ____

The players are confident that the league championship is *theirs*. ✓

Them concert tickets are too expensive. ____

Those concert tickets are too expensive. ✓

Our parents should spend some money on *themself* for a change. ____

Our parents should spend some money on *themselves* for a change. ✓

Answers are on page 682.

This chapter describes some common types of pronouns: subject and object pronouns, possessive pronouns, demonstrative pronouns, and reflexive pronouns.

Subject and Object Pronouns

Pronouns change their form depending on the place they occupy in a sentence. Here is a list of subject and object pronouns:

Subject Pronouns	*Object Pronouns*
I	me
you	you (no change)
he	him
she	her
it	it (no change)
we	us
they	them

Subject Pronouns

Subject pronouns are subjects of verbs.

They are getting tired. (*They* is the subject of the verb *are getting*.)

She will decide tomorrow. (*She* is the subject of the verb *will decide.)*

We women organized the game. (*We* is the subject of the verb *organized.)*

Several rules for using subject pronouns, and mistakes people sometimes make, are explained starting below.

Rule 1 Use a subject pronoun in a sentence with a compound (more than one) subject.

Incorrect	*Correct*
Nate and *me* went shopping yesterday.	Nate and *I* went shopping yesterday.
Him and *me* spent lots of money.	*He* and *I* spent lots of money.

If you are not sure which pronoun to use, try each pronoun by itself in the sentence. The correct pronoun will be the one that sounds right. For example, "*Me* went shopping yesterday" does not sound right; "*I* went shopping yesterday" does.

Rule 2 Use a subject pronoun after forms of the verb *be*. Forms of *be* include *am, are, is, was, were, has been, have been,* and others.

It was *I* who telephoned.

It may be *they* at the door.

It is *she.*

The sentences above may sound strange and stilted to you, since this rule is seldom actually followed in conversation. When we speak with one another, forms such as "It was me," "It may be them," and "It is her" are widely accepted. In formal writing, however, the grammatically correct forms are still preferred. You can avoid having to use a subject pronoun after *be* simply by rewording a sentence. Here is how the preceding examples could be reworded:

I was the one who telephoned.

They may be at the door.

She is here.

Rule 3 Use subject pronouns after *than* or *as* when a verb is understood after the pronoun.

You read faster than I (read). (The verb *read* is understood after *I.*)

Tom is as stubborn as I (am). (The verb *am* is understood after *I.*)

We don't go out as much as they (do). (The verb *do* is understood after *they.*)

Notes

a Avoid mistakes by mentally adding the "missing" verb at the end of the sentence.

b Use object pronouns after *as* or *than* when a verb is not understood after the pronoun.

The law applies to you as well as me.

Our boss paid Monica more than me.

Object Pronouns

Object pronouns (*me, him, her, us, them*) are objects of verbs or prepositions. (Prepositions are connecting words like *for, at, about, to, before, by, with,* and *of.* See also page 91.)

Raisa chose *me*. (*Me* is the object of the verb *chose*.)

We met *them* at the ballpark. (*Them* is the object of the verb *met*.)

Don't mention UFOs to *us*. (*Us* is the object of the preposition *to*.)

I live near *her*. (*Her* is the object of the preposition *near.*)

People are sometimes uncertain about what pronoun to use when two objects follow the verb.

Incorrect	*Correct*
I spoke to George and *he*.	I spoke to George and *him*.
She pointed at Linda and *I*.	She pointed at Linda and *me*.

Hint If you are not sure which pronoun to use, try each pronoun by itself in the sentence. The correct pronoun will be the one that sounds right. For example, "I spoke to he" doesn't sound right; "I spoke to him" does.

Practice 1

Underline the correct subject or object pronoun in each of the following sentences. Then show whether your answer is a subject or an object pronoun by circling the *S* or *O* in the margin. The first one is done for you as an example.

S O 1. I left the decision to (her, she).

S O 2. (She, Her) and Louise look enough alike to be sisters.

S O 3. Just between you and (I, me), these rolls taste like sawdust.

S O 4. The certified letter was addressed to both (she, her) and (I, me).

S O 5. If (he, him) and Vic are serious about school, why are they absent so much?

S O 6. Practically everyone is better at crossword puzzles than (I, me).

S O 7. It was (they, them) who left the patio furniture outside during the rainstorm.

S O 8. The creature that climbed out of the coffin scared Boris and (I, me) half to death.

S O 9. (We, Us) tenants are organizing a protest against the dishonest landlord.

S O 10. When we were little, my sister and (I, me) invented a secret language.

Practice 2

For each sentence, in the space provided, write an appropriate subject or object pronoun. Try to use as many different pronouns as possible. The first one is done for you as an example.

Answers will vary; below are some possibilities.

1. It was ___I___ who forgot to lock the door on the night our house was robbed.
2. The referee disqualified Tyray and ___him (or me)___ for fighting.
3. I have seldom met two people as boring as ___they___.
4. If you and ___I (or we)___ don't lose patience, we'll finish sanding this floor by tonight.
5. Our professor told ___us___ students that our final exam would be a take-home test.
6. Ernie and ___she (or I or he or they or we)___ drove on the interstate highway for ten hours with only one stop.
7. We don't use our VCR as much as ___they (or he or she)___.
8. You know better than ___I (or he or she or they or we)___ how to remove lipstick stains.
9. Maggie and ___I (or he or she or they or we)___ spent several hours yesterday looking for the lost puppy.
10. The store manager praised ___us (or them)___ for being the best cashiers in the department.

Relative Pronouns

Relative pronouns do two things at once. First, they refer to someone or something already mentioned in the sentence. Second, they start a short word group which gives additional information about this someone or something. Here is a list of relative pronouns:

Relative Pronouns	
who	which
whose	that
whom	

Here are some sample sentences:

> The only friend *who* really understands me is moving away.
>
> The child *whom* Ben and Arlene adopted is from Korea.
>
> Chocolate, *which* is my favorite food, upsets my stomach.
>
> I guessed at half the questions *that* were on the test.

In the example sentences, *who* refers to *friend*, *whom* refers to *child*, *which* refers to *chocolate*, and *that* refers to *questions*. In addition, each of the relative pronouns begins a group of words that describes the person or thing being referred to. For example, the words *whom Ben and Arlene adopted* tell which child the sentence is about, and the words *which is my favorite food* give added information about chocolate.

Points to Remember about Relative Pronouns

Point 1 *Whose* means *belonging to whom.* Be careful not to confuse *whose* with *who's,* which means *who is.*

Point 2 *Who, whose,* and *whom* all refer to people. *Which* refers to things. *That* can refer to either people or things.

> I don't know *whose* book this is.
>
> Don't sit on the chair *which* is broken.
>
> Let's elect a captain *that* cares about winning.

Point 3 *Who, whose, whom,* and *which* can also be used to ask questions. When they are used in this way, they are called *interrogative* pronouns:

> *Who* murdered the secret agent?
>
> *Whose* fingerprints were on the bloodstained knife?
>
> To *whom* have the detectives been talking?
>
> *Which* suspect is going to confess?

Note In informal usage, *who* is generally used instead of *whom* as an interrogative pronoun. Informally, we can say or write, "*Who* are you rooting for in the game?" or "*Who* did the instructor fail?" More formal usage would call for *whom*: "Whom are you rooting for in the game?" "Whom did the instructor fail?"

Point 4 *Who* and *whom* are used differently. *Who* is a subject pronoun. Use *who* as the subject of a verb:

> Let's see *who* will be teaching the course.

Whom is an object pronoun. Use *whom* as the object of a verb or a preposition:

> Dr. Kelsey is the instructor *whom* I like best.
>
> I haven't decided for *whom* I will vote.

You may want to review the material on subject and object pronouns on pages 208–210.

Here is an easy way to decide whether to use *who* or *whom*. Find the first verb after the place where the *who* or *whom* will go. See if it already has a subject. If it does have a subject, use the object pronoun *whom*. If there is no subject, give it one by using the subject pronoun *who*. Notice how *who* and *whom* are used in the sentences that follow:

> I don't know *who* sideswiped my car.
>
> The suspect *whom* the police arrested finally confessed.

In the first sentence, *who* is used to give the verb *sideswiped* a subject. In the second sentence, the verb *arrested* already has a subject, *police*. Therefore, *whom* is the correct pronoun.

Practice 1

Underline the correct pronoun in each of the following sentences.

1. One activity (<u>that</u>, who) my father and I both enjoy is cooking.
2. On a bright, sunny day, some office buildings (who, <u>that</u>) have glass walls look like giant icicles.
3. My sister, (<u>who</u>, whom) loves ballet, walks around the house on her toes.
4. The new highway, (who, <u>which</u>) was supposed to lessen traffic jams, only made them worse.
5. The supervisor (who, <u>whom</u>) everybody dislikes was just given thirty days' notice.

Practice 2

Answers will vary.

On separate paper, write five sentences using *who, whose, whom, which,* and *that.*

Possessive Pronouns

Possessive pronouns show ownership or possession.

Clyde shut off the engine of *his* motorcycle.
The keys are *mine*.

Here is a list of possessive pronouns:

Possessive Pronouns	
my, mine	our, ours
your, yours	your, yours
his	their, theirs
her, hers	
its	

Points to Remember about Possessive Pronouns

Point 1 A possessive pronoun *never* uses an apostrophe. (See also page 299.)

Incorrect	*Correct*
That coat is *hers'*.	That coat is *hers*.
The card table is *theirs'*.	The card table is *theirs*.

Practice

Cross out the incorrect pronoun form in each of the sentences that follow. Write the correct form in the space at the left.

My Example: ~~Me~~ car has broken down again.

yours 1. Is this pen ~~yours'~~ or mine?

his 2. Only relatives of ~~him~~ are allowed to visit while he is in the hospital.

theirs 3. My sisters think that every new dress I buy is ~~theirs'~~ too.

your 4. Are you going to eat all of ~~you~~ hamburger, or can I have half?

mine 5. The thermos that is ~~mines~~ is held together with duct tape.

Demonstrative Pronouns

Demonstrative pronouns point to or single out a person or thing. There are four demonstrative pronouns:

Demonstrative Pronouns	
this	these
that	those

Generally speaking, *this* and *these* refer to things close at hand; *that* and *those* refer to things farther away.

Is anyone using *this* spoon?

I am going to throw away *these* magazines.

I just bought *that* white Volvo at the curb.

Pick up *those* toys in the corner.

Note Do not use *them, this here, that there, these here*, or *those there* to point out. Use only *this, that, these*, or *those.*

Incorrect	*Correct*
Them tires are badly worn.	*Those* tires are badly worn.
This here book looks hard to read.	*This* book looks hard to read.
That there candy is delicious.	*That* candy is delicious.
Those there squirrels are pests.	*Those* squirrels are pests.

Practice 1

Cross out the incorrect form of the demonstrative pronoun and write the correct form in the space provided.

Those Example ~~Them~~ clothes need washing.

This 1. ~~This here~~ town isn't big enough for both of us, Tex.

those 2. Let's hurry and get ~~them~~ seats before someone else does.

That 3. ~~That there~~ dress looked better on the hanger than it does on you.

those 4. Let me try one of ~~those there~~ candies before they're all gone.

those 5. Watch out for ~~them~~ potholes the next time you drive my car.

Practice 2

Write four sentences using *this, that, these* and *those.*

Answers will vary.

Reflexive Pronouns

Reflexive pronouns are pronouns that refer to the subject of a sentence. Here is a list of reflexive pronouns:

Reflexive Pronouns

myself	ourselves
yourself	yourselves
himself	themselves
herself	
itself	

Sometimes a reflexive pronoun is used for emphasis:

You will have to wash the dishes *yourself.*

We *ourselves* are willing to forget the matter.

The president *himself* turns down his living room thermostat.

Points to Remember about Reflexive Pronouns

Point 1 In the plural *-self* becomes *-selves.*

Lola covered *herself* with insect repellent.

They treated *themselves* to a Bermuda vacation.

Point 2 Be careful that you do not use any of the following incorrect forms as reflexive pronouns.

Incorrect	*Correct*
He believes in *hisself.*	He believes in *himself.*
We drove the children *ourself.*	We drove the children *ourselves.*
They saw *themself* in the fun house mirror.	They saw *themselves* in the fun house mirror.
I'll do it *meself.*	I'll do it *myself.*

Practice

Cross out the incorrect form of the reflexive pronoun and write the correct form in the space at the left.

themselves — Example: She believes that God helps those who help ~~themself~~.

themselves — 1. Shoppers stop and stare when they see ~~themself~~ on the closed-circuit TV overhead.

herself — 2. The restaurant owner ~~herselve~~ came out to apologize to us.

himself — 3. When my baby brother tries to dress ~~hisself~~, the results are often funny.

ourselves — 4. The waiter was busy, so we poured ~~ourself~~ coffee from a nearby pot.

themselves — 5. These housepainters seem to be making more work for ~~theirselves~~ than is necessary.

Review Test 1

Underline the correct word in the parentheses.

1. The waitress finally brought Dolores and (I, me) our order.
2. I hope my son behaves (hisself, himself) at preschool.
3. Hand me (that, that there) fiddle and I'll play you a tune.
4. If it were up to (she, her), men wouldn't have the right to vote.
5. Roger, (who, whom) has worked here for almost thirty years, is ready to retire.
6. Vera dressed much more casually than (I, me) for the party.
7. You won't get very far on the bike unless you add more air to (its, it's) tires.
8. We'll be reading (this, this here) stack of books during the semester.
9. The apartment of (his, him) is next to a chemical processing plant.
10. The ducks circled the lake until they were sure that no one was around but (theirselves, themselves).

Review Test 2

Cross out the pronoun error in each sentence and write the correct form in the space at the left.

I ______ Example Terry and ~~me~~ have already seen the movie.

us ______ 1. The chili that Manny prepared was too spicy for ~~we~~ to eat.

those ______ 2. I checked ~~them~~ wires, but I couldn't find any faulty connections.

which ______ 3. The old Chevy, ~~who~~ has 110,000 miles on it, is still running well.

he ______ 4. When ~~him~~ and his partner asked me to step out of my car, I knew I was in trouble.

himself ______ 5. Omar realized that he would have to change the tire ~~hisself~~.

I ______ 6. My husband is much more sentimental than ~~me~~.

its ______ 7. I hope you'll come visit us in July while the garden is looking ~~its'~~ best.

mine ______ 8. The CDs are ~~mines~~, but you can listen to them whenever you wish.

This ______ 9. ~~This here~~ telephone works only if you have a credit card.

I ______ 10. Vicky and ~~me~~ are going to the concert at the fairgrounds.

■ Review Test 3

On separate paper, write sentences that use each of the following words.
Answers will vary.

Example Peter and him *The coach suspended Peter and him.*

1. yourselves
2. Jasmine and me
3. these
4. the neighbors and us
5. Victor and he
6. slower than I
7. its
8. which
9. you and I
10. Maria and them

15 Adjectives and Adverbs

Introductory Activity

Write in an appropriate word or words to complete each of the sentences below.

Answers will vary.

1. The teenage years were a __________ time for me.
2. The mechanic listened __________ while I described my car problem.
3. Basketball is a __________ game than football.
4. My brother is the __________ person in our family.

Now see if you can complete the following sentences.

The word inserted in the first sentence is an (adjective, adverb); it describes the word *time.*

The word inserted in the second sentence is an (adjective, adverb); it probably ends in the two letters ly and describes the word *listened.*

The word inserted in the third sentence is a comparative adjective; it may be preceded by *more* or end in the two letters er.

The word inserted in the fourth sentence is a superlative adjective; it may be preceded by *most* or end in the three letters est.

Answers are on page 683.

Adjectives and adverbs are descriptive words. Their purpose is to make the meaning of the words they describe more specific.

Adjectives

What Are Adjectives?

Adjectives describe nouns (names of persons, places, or things) or pronouns.

Charlotte is a *kind* woman. (The adjective *kind* describes the noun *woman*.)

He is *tired*. (The adjective *tired* describes the pronoun *he*.)

An adjective usually comes before the word it describes (as in *kind woman*). But it can also come after forms of the verb *be (is, are, was, were*, and so on). Less often, an adjective follows verbs such as *feel, look, smell, sound, taste, appear, become*, and *seem*.

The bureau is *heavy*. (The adjective *heavy* describes the bureau.)

These pants are *itchy*. (The adjective *itchy* describes the pants.)

The children seem *restless*. (The adjective *restless* describes the children.)

Using Adjectives to Compare

For most short adjectives, add *-er* when comparing two things and *-est* when comparing three or more things.

I am *taller* than my brother, but my father is the *tallest* person in the house.

The farm market sells *fresher* vegetables than the corner store, but the *freshest* vegetables are the ones grown in my own garden.

For most *longer* adjectives (two or more syllables), add *more* when comparing two things and *most* when comparing three or more things.

Backgammon is *more enjoyable* to me than checkers, but chess is the *most enjoyable* game of all.

My mother is *more talkative* than my father, but my grandfather is the *most talkative* person in the house.

Points to Remember about Adjectives

Point 1 Be careful not to use both an *-er* ending and *more*, or both an *-est* ending and *most*.

Incorrect	*Correct*
Football is a *more livelier* game than baseball.	Football is a *livelier* game than baseball.
Tod Traynor was voted the *most likeliest* to succeed in our high school class.	Tod Traynor was voted the *most likely* to succeed in our high school class.

Point 2 Pay special attention to the following words, each of which has irregular forms.

	Comparative (Two)	*Superlative (Three or More)*
bad	worse	worst
good, well	better	best
little	less	least
much, many	more	most

Practice 1

Fill in the comparative or superlative forms for the following adjectives. Two are done for you as examples.

	Comparative (Two)	*Superlative (Three or More)*
firm	firmer	firmest
organized	more organized	most organized
tough	tougher	toughest
practical	more practical	most practical
quiet	quieter	quietest
aggressive	more aggressive	most aggressive
clear	clearer	clearest

Practice 2

Add to each sentence the correct form of the adjective in the margin.

Example *bad* The ___worst___ day of my life was the one when my house caught fire.

good 1. I hope the ___best___ days of my life are still to come.

dirty 2. The water in Mudville is ___dirtier___ than the name of the town.

considerate 3. If Tyrone were ___more considerate___, he would have more friends.

bad 4. The announcement of a surprise quiz gave me a ___worse___ headache than this morning's traffic did.

scary 5. The ___scariest___ scene in the horror movie was when dead people began crawling out of their graves.

little 6. As hard as it is to believe, he is an even ___less___ dependable worker than his brother.

stylish 7. In an effort to look ___more stylish___, Bob replaced his big glasses with small lightweight ones.

silly 8. June is even ___sillier___ than her sister; she once burst out laughing at a wedding and had to run out of the church.

soft 9. I don't understand why people in commercials are so concerned with finding the ___softest___ toilet paper.

fattening 10. Estella ordered a tossed salad as her main course, so she could have the ___most fattening___ dessert on the menu.

Adverbs

What Are Adverbs?

Adverbs describe verbs, adjectives, or other adverbs. An adverb usually ends in *-ly*.

Charlotte spoke *kindly* to the confused man. (The adverb *kindly* describes the verb *spoke*.)

The man said he was *completely* alone in the world. (The adverb *completely* describes the adjective *alone*.)

Charlotte listened *very* sympathetically to his story. (The adverb *very* describes the adverb *sympathetically.)*

A Common Mistake with Adjectives and Adverbs

Perhaps the most common mistake that people make with adjectives and adverbs is to use an adjective instead of an adverb after a verb.

Incorrect	*Correct*
Tony breathed *heavy.*	Tony breathed *heavily.*
I rest *comfortable* in that chair.	I rest *comfortably* in that chair.
She learned *quick.*	She learned *quickly*.

Practice

Underline the adjective or adverb needed.

1. I need a vacation (bad, badly).
2. The police reacted (harsh, harshly) to the noisy demonstrators.
3. The truck groaned as it crept up the (steep, steeply) grade.
4. My boss tells me (frequent, frequently) that I do a good job.
5. Did you answer every question in the interview (truthful, truthfully)?
6. If you think your decision was right, you'll sleep (peaceful, peacefully).
7. Walter the werewolf smiled at the (bright, brightly) moonlight shining through his bedroom window.
8. Nate was playing the stereo so (loud, loudly) that both the dog and the cat were cowering in the basement.
9. The surgeon stitched the wound very (careful, carefully), so that the scar would not be noticeable.
10. Eli dressed (nice, nicely) for his first meeting with his girlfriend's parents.

Well and *Good*

Two words often confused are *well* and *good. Good* is an adjective; it describes nouns. *Well* is usually an adverb; it describes verbs. *Well* (rather than *good)* is also used when referring to a person's health.

Here are some examples:

I became a *good* swimmer. *(Good* is an adjective describing the noun *swimmer.*)

For a change, two-year-old Rodney was *good* during the church service. *(Good* is an adjective describing Rodney and comes after *was*, a form of the verb *be*.)

Maryann did *well* on that exam. (*Well* is an adverb describing the verb *did.)*

I explained that I wasn't feeling *well.* (*Well* is used in reference to health.)

Practice

Write *well* or *good* in the sentences that follow.

1. Fortunately, the new stepbrothers and stepsisters get along __well__.
2. The dog did a __good__ job of chewing our sofa.
3. Crystal did so __well__ on her placement exam that she was put into an advanced math course.
4. My idea of a __good__ date is to talk over dinner.
5. Although I didn't feel __well__, I tried to keep doing my work.

Review Test 1

Underline the correct word in the parentheses.

1. When I found out that the landlord intended to increase my rent, I moved back in with my parents (immediate, <u>immediately</u>).
2. During the massage, the therapist pressed (deep, <u>deeply</u>) into the muscles of my neck and shoulders.
3. For as long as I can remember, my teachers have tried to get me to write more (neat, <u>neatly</u>).
4. Judy's parents were deeply disturbed that her grades were (<u>worse</u>, more worse) than ever.
5. My grandfather says that teenagers acted just as (unpredictable, <u>unpredictably</u>) when he was a boy as they do today.
6. The plane taxied (rapid, <u>rapidly</u>) down the runway but then came to a complete stop.
7. The crowd booed (loud, <u>loudly</u>) when the referee ejected the player from the game.
8. Although Al thought his accounting test was the (difficultest, <u>most difficult</u>) test he had ever taken, he got an A on it.
9. Holding the purple felt-tipped pen (loose, <u>loosely</u>), Gina drew graceful spirals in her notebook.
10. I did so (good, <u>well</u>) on my first visit to the racetrack that I unwisely decided to try my luck a second time.

■ Review Test 2

Write a sentence that uses each of the following adjectives and adverbs correctly.
Answers will vary.

1. confident ______________________________
2. nervously ______________________________
3. well ______________________________
4. more impulsive ______________________________
5. better ______________________________
6. cleverly ______________________________
7. worst ______________________________
8. rough ______________________________
9. most annoying ______________________________
10. sweeter ______________________________

16 Misplaced Modifiers

Introductory Activity

Because of misplaced words, each of the sentences below has more than one possible meaning. In each case, see if you can explain both the intended meaning and the unintended meaning.

1. The farmers sprayed the apple trees wearing masks.

   Intended meaning: The farmers were wearing masks.

   Unintended meaning: The apple trees were wearing masks.

2. The woman reached out for the faith healer who had a terminal disease.

   Intended meaning: The woman had a terminal disease.

   Unintended meaning: The faith healer had a terminal disease.

Answers are on page 683.

What Misplaced Modifiers Are and How to Correct Them

Misplaced modifiers are words that, because of awkward placement, do not describe the words the writer intended them to describe. Misplaced modifiers often confuse the meaning of a sentence. To avoid them, place words as close as possible to what they describe.

Misplaced Words	*Correctly Placed Words*
They could see the Goodyear blimp *sitting on the front lawn.* (The *Goodyear blimp* was sitting on the front lawn?)	Sitting on the front lawn, they could see the Goodyear blimp. (The intended meaning—that the Goodyear blimp was visible from the front lawn—is now clear.)
We had a hamburger after the movie, *which was too greasy for my taste.* (The *movie* was too greasy for your taste?)	After the movie, we had a hamburger, which was too greasy for my taste. (The intended meaning—that the hamburger was greasy—is now clear.)
Our phone *almost rang* fifteen times last night. (The phone *almost rang* fifteen times, but in fact did not ring at all?)	Our phone rang almost fifteen times last night. (The intended meaning—that the phone rang a little under fifteen times—is now clear.)

Other single-word modifiers to watch out for include *only, even, hardly, nearly,* and *often.* Such words should be placed immediately before the word they modify.

Practice 1

Underline the misplaced word or words in each sentence. Then rewrite the sentence, placing related words together to make the meaning clear.

Example Anita returned the hamburger to the supermarket that was spoiled.
Anita returned the hamburger that was spoiled to the supermarket.

1. The tiger growled at a passerby at the back of his cage.

   At the back of his cage, the tiger growled at a passerby.

2. Lee hung colorful scarves over her windows made of green and blue silk.

   Lee hung colorful scarves made of green and blue silk over her windows.

3. We watched the fireworks standing on our front porch.

   Standing on our front porch, we watched the fireworks.

4. Jason almost has two hundred baseball cards.

   Jason has almost two hundred baseball cards.

5. The salesclerk exchanged the blue sweater for a yellow one with a smile.

   With a smile, the salesclerk exchanged the blue sweater for a yellow one.

6. We all stared at the man in the front row of the theater with curly purple hair.

   We all stared at the man with curly purple hair in the front row of the theater.

7. I love the cookies from the bakery with the chocolate frosting.

   I love the cookies with the chocolate frosting from the bakery.

8. The faculty decided to strike during their last meeting.

   During their last meeting, the faculty decided to strike.

9. Larry looked on as his car burned with disbelief.

   Larry looked on with disbelief as his car burned.

10. My cousin sent me instructions on how to get to her house in a letter.

    My cousin sent me instructions in a letter on how to get to her house.

Practice 2

Rewrite each sentence, adding the *italicized* words. Make sure that the intended meaning is clear and that two different interpretations are not possible.

Example I borrowed a pen for the essay test. (insert *that ran out of ink.*)
For the essay test, I borrowed a pen that ran out of ink.

Answers may vary slightly.

1. My mother sat lazily in the hot sun watching her grandchildren play. (Insert *with a glass of lemonade.*)
   My mother sat lazily with a glass of lemonade in the hot sun, watching her grandchildren play.
2. My father agreed to pay for the car repairs. (Insert *over the phone.*)
   My father agreed over the phone to pay for the car repairs.
3. I found a note on the kitchen bulletin board. (Insert *from Jeff.*)
   I found a note from Jeff on the kitchen bulletin board.
4. The fires destroyed the entire forest. (Insert *almost.*)
   The fires destroyed almost the entire forest.
5. Jon read about how the American Revolution began. (Insert *during class.*)
   During class, Jon read about how the American Revolution began.

■ Review Test 1

Write *M* for *misplaced* or *C* for *correct* in front of each sentence.

M 1. I keep a ten-dollar bill under the car seat for emergencies.
C 2. I keep a ten-dollar bill for emergencies under the car seat.
M 3. This morning, I planned my day in the shower.
C 4. In the shower this morning, I planned my day.
C 5. While skating, Bert ran over a dog's tail.
M 6. Bert ran over a dog's tail skating.

M 7. I could hear my neighbors screaming at each other through the apartment wall.

C 8. Through the apartment wall, I could hear my neighbors screaming at each other.

C 9. For the family reunion, we cooked hamburgers and hot dogs on an outdoor grill.

M 10. For the family reunion on an outdoor grill we cooked hamburgers and hot dogs.

M 11. Virgil visited the old house, still weak with the flu.

C 12. Virgil, still weak with the flu, visited the old house.

C 13. While still weak with the flu, Virgil visited the old house.

M 14. My teenage son nearly grew three inches last year.

C 15. My teenage son grew nearly three inches last year.

M 16. The instructor explained how to study for the final exam at the end of her lecture.

M 17. The instructor explained how to study at the end of her lecture for the final exam.

C 18. At the end of her lecture, the instructor explained how to study for the final exam.

C 19. In the library, I read that a deadly virus was spread through an air-conditioning system.

M 20. I read that a deadly virus was spread through an air-conditioning system in the library.

■ Review Test 2

Underline the five misplaced modifiers in the passage below. Then, in the spaces that follow, show how you would correct them.

1The young teenagers who almost hang out in our town library every night are becoming a major nuisance. 2They show up every weeknight and infuriate the otherwise mild librarians throwing spitballs and paper airplanes. 3Some of the kids hide out behind stacks of bookcases; others indulge in continual adolescent flirting games. 4The noise many of these teenagers make is especially offensive to some of the older library patrons, who often give looks to the clusters of young people that are disapproving. 5One time there was so much noise that a librarian lost her temper and yelled at some boys to be quiet or leave the library at the top of her lungs. 6The worst recent offense took place when a soaking-wet dog was led into the middle of the library by a junior high school boy with a stubby tail and the meanest-looking face one could ever imagine.

Sentence number: 1

Correction:

almost every night

Sentence number: 2

Correction:

every weeknight throwing spitballs and paper airplanes

Sentence number: 4

Correction:

looks that are disapproving

Sentence number: 5

Correction:

yelled at the top of her lungs

Sentence number: 6

Correction:

dog with a stubby tail and the meanest-looking face one could ever imagine

17 Dangling Modifiers

Note for the Introductory Activity below: Some instructors might consider the first example a misplaced modifier, since the subject of the phrase *munching leaves from a tall tree*—the giraffe—does appear later in the sentence. However, correcting the error would involve changing words:

Munching leaves from a tall tree, the eighteen-foot-tall giraffe *fascinated* the children.

or

The children were fascinated by the eighteen-foot-tall giraffe, *which was* munching leaves from a tall tree.

Thus this type of error is classified as a dangling modifier in *Sentence Skills with Readings*. In general, if a word group is a participial phrase, and if the phrase occurs at the beginning of the sentence but modifies a subject that does not appear until later in the sentence, it is labeled a dangling rather than a misplaced modifier.

Introductory Activity

Because of dangling words, each of the sentences below has more than one possible meaning. In each case, see if you can explain both the intended meaning and the unintended meaning.

1. Munching leaves from a tall tree, the children were fascinated by the eighteen-foot-tall giraffe.

   Intended meaning: The giraffe was munching leaves.

   Unintended meaning: The children were munching leaves.

2. Arriving home after ten months in the army, Michael's neighbors threw a block party for him.

   Intended meaning: Michael was arriving home after ten months in the army.

   Unintended meaning: The neighbors were arriving home after ten months in the army.

Answers are on page 684.

What Dangling Modifiers Are and How to Correct Them

A modifier that opens a sentence must be followed immediately by the word it is meant to describe. Otherwise, the modifier is said to be *dangling*, and the sentence takes on an unintended meaning. For example, look at this sentence:

While sleeping in his backyard, a Frisbee hit Bill on the head.

The unintended meaning is that the *Frisbee* was sleeping in his backyard. What the writer meant, of course, was that *Bill* was sleeping in his backyard. The writer should have placed *Bill* right after the modifier, revising the rest of the sentence as necessary:

While sleeping in his backyard, *Bill* was hit on the head by a Frisbee.

The sentence could also be corrected by adding the missing subject and verb to the opening word group:

While *Bill* was sleeping in his backyard, a Frisbee hit him on the head.

Other sentences with dangling modifiers follow. Read the explanations of why they are dangling and look carefully at how they are corrected.

Dangling	*Correct*
Having almost no money, my survival depended on my parents. (*Who* has almost no money? The answer is not *survival* but *I*. The subject *I* must be added.)	Having almost no money, *I* depended on my parents for survival. *Or:* Since *I* had almost no money, I depended on my parents for survival.
Riding his bike, a German shepherd bit Tony on the ankle. (*Who* is riding the bike? The answer is not *German shepherd*, as it unintentionally seems to be, but *Tony*. The subject *Tony* must be added.)	Riding his bike, *Tony* was bitten on the ankle by a German shepherd. *Or:* While *Tony* was riding his bike, a German shepherd bit him on the ankle.

When trying to lose weight, all snacks are best avoided.

(*Who* is trying to lose weight? The answer is not *snacks* but *you*. The subject *you* must be added.)

When trying to lose weight, *you* should avoid all snacks.

Or: When *you* are trying to lose weight, avoid all snacks.

These examples make clear two ways of correcting a dangling modifier. Decide on a logical subject and do one of the following:

1 Place the subject *within* the opening word group:

Since *I* had almost no money, I depended on my parents for survival.

Note In some cases an appropriate subordinating word such as *since* must be added, and the verb may have to be changed slightly as well.

2 Place the subject right *after* the opening word group:

Having almost no money, *I* depended on my parents for survival.

Sometimes even more rewriting is necessary to correct a dangling modifier. What is important to remember is that a modifier must be placed as close as possible to the word that it modifies.

Practice 1

Rewrite each sentence to correct the dangling modifier. Mark the one sentence that is correct with a C.

Wording of answers may vary slightly.

1. Having turned sour, I would not drink the milk.

   Since the milk had turned sour, I would not drink it.

2. At the age of five, my mother bought me a chemistry set.

   When I was five, my mother bought me a chemistry set.

3. While it was raining, shoppers ran into the stores.

   C

4. Hanging safely on a wall, a security guard pointed to the priceless painting.
A security guard pointed to the priceless painting that was hanging safely on a wall.

5. Talking on the phone, my hot tea turned cold.
While I was talking on the phone, my hot tea turned cold.

6. Piled high with dirty dishes, Pete hated to look at the kitchen sink.
Pete hated to look at the kitchen sink, which was piled high with dirty dishes.

7. Having locked my keys in the car, the police had to open it for me.
Because I locked my keys in the car, the police had to open it for me.

8. Drooping and looking all dried out, the children watered the plants.
Because the plants were drooping and looking all dried out, the children watered them.

9. After sitting through a long lecture, my foot was asleep.
After I sat through a long lecture, my foot was asleep.

10. Being late, stopping for coffee was out of the question.
Since I was late, stopping for coffee was out of the question.

Practice 2

Complete the following sentences. In each case, a logical subject should follow the opening words.

Example Checking the oil stick, I saw that my car was a quart low.

Answers will vary.

1. While taking a bath, __________
2. Before starting the car, __________
3. Frightened by the noise in the basement, __________
4. Realizing it was late, __________
5. Though very expensive, __________

■ Review Test 1

Write *D* for *dangling* or *C* for *correct* in front of each sentence. Remember that the opening words are a dangling modifier if they are not followed immediately by a logical subject.

__D__ 1. Burning quickly, the firefighters turned several hoses on the house.

__C__ 2. Because it was burning quickly, the firefighters turned several hoses on the house.

__D__ 3. While focusing the camera, several people wandered out of view.

__C__ 4. While I focused the camera, several people wandered out of view.

__C__ 5. When I peered down from the thirtieth floor, the cars looked like toys.

__D__ 6. Peering down from the thirtieth floor, the cars looked like toys.

__D__ 7. The cars looked like toys peering down from the thirtieth floor.

__D__ 8. Riding in the rear of the bus, the sudden starts and stops were sickening.

__C__ 9. For passengers riding in the rear of the bus, the sudden starts and stops were sickening.

__D__ 10. Thundering loudly, the dog trembled.

__C__ 11. As it thundered loudly, the dog trembled.

__D__ 12. In a sentimental frame of mind, the music brought tears to Beth's eyes.

__C__ 13. As Beth was in a sentimental frame of mind, the music brought tears to her eyes.

__C__ 14. When Helen suddenly became sick, I drove her to the doctor's office.

__D__ 15. Suddenly sick, I drove Helen to the doctor's office.

__C__ 16. The pancake was browned on one side, so Mark flipped it over.

__D__ 17. Browned on one side, Mark flipped the pancake over.

__D__ 18. Hanging by her teeth, the acrobat's body swung back and forth.

__C__ 19. Hanging by her teeth, the acrobat swung back and forth.

__D__ 20. While hanging by her teeth, the acrobat's body swung back and forth.

■ Review Test 2

Underline the five dangling modifiers in this passage. Then correct them in the spaces provided.

[1]Have you ever thought about what life was like for the first generation of your family to come to America? [2]Or have you wondered what your grandparents did for fun when they were your age? [3]Family stories tend to

be told for two or three generations and then disappear because no one ever records them. [4]Using a tape recorder, these stories can be saved for the future. [5]Here are some hints for conducting interviews with older members of your family. [6]Thinking hard about what you really want to know, good questions can be prepared in advance. [7]Try to put the people you interview at ease by reassuring them that you value what they have to say. [8]Nervous about the tape recorder, stories might not come so easily to them otherwise. [9]Remember that most people have never been interviewed before. [10]Listening carefully to everything the person says, your interview will be more successful. [11]By respecting their feelings, your older relatives will be delighted to share their stories. [12]The tapes you make will be valued by your family for many years to come.

Wording of answers may vary.

Sentence number: 4

Correction:

With the use of a tape recorder, the stories . . .

Sentence number: 6

Correction:

If you think hard about what you really want to know, you can prepare good questions in advance.

Sentence number: 8

Correction:

Since people may be nervous about the tape recorder, stories . . .

Sentence number: 10

Correction:

If you listen carefully to everything the person says, your interview . . .

Sentence number: 11

Correction:

By respecting their feelings, you can make your older relatives . . .

18 Faulty Parallelism

Introductory Activity

Read aloud each pair of sentences below. Write a check mark beside the sentence that reads more smoothly and clearly and sounds more natural.

Pair 1

_____ I use my TV remote control to change channels, to adjust the volume, and for turning the set on and off.

__✓__ I use my TV remote control to change channels, to adjust the volume, and to turn the set on and off.

Pair 2

_____ One option the employees had was to take a cut in pay; the other was longer hours of work.

__✓__ One option the employees had was to take a cut in pay; the other was to work longer hours.

Pair 3

_____ The refrigerator has a cracked vegetable drawer, one of the shelves is missing, and a strange freezer smell.

__✓__ The refrigerator has a cracked vegetable drawer, a missing shelf, and a strange freezer smell.

Answers are on page 684.

Parallelism Explained

Words in a pair or a series should have parallel structure. By balancing the items in a pair or a series so that they have the same kind of structure, you will make the sentence clearer and easier to read. Notice how the parallel sentences that follow read more smoothly than the nonparallel ones.

Nonparallel (Not Balanced)	*Parallel (Balanced)*
Fran spends her free time reading, listening to music, and she works in the garden.	Fran spends her free time reading, listening to music, and working in the garden. (A balanced series of *-ing* words: *reading, listening, working*.)
After the camping trip I was exhausted, irritable, and wanted to eat.	After the camping trip I was exhausted, irritable, and hungry. (A balanced series of descriptive words: *exhausted, irritable, hungry*.)
My hope for retirement is to be healthy, to live in a comfortable house, and having plenty of money.	My hope for retirement is to be healthy, to live in a comfortable house, and to have plenty of money. (A balanced series of *to* verbs: *to be, to live, to have*.)
Nightly, Fred puts out the trash, checks the locks on the doors, and the burglar alarm is turned on.	Nightly, Fred puts out the trash, checks the locks on the doors, and turns on the burglar alarm. (Balanced verbs and word order: *puts out the trash, checks the locks, turns on the burglar alarm.)*

Balanced sentences are not a skill you need to worry about when you are writing first drafts. But when you rewrite, you should try to put matching words and ideas into matching structures. Such parallelism will improve your writing style.

Practice 1

The one item in each list that is not parallel in form to the other items is crossed out. In the space provided, rewrite that item in parallel form. The first one has been done for you as an example.

1. fresh food
   attractive setting
   ~~service that is fast~~
   fast service

2. screaming children
   ~~dogs that howl~~
   blaring music
   howling dogs

3. slow
   ~~speaks rudely~~
   careless
   rude

4. ~~to hike~~
   swimming
   boating
   hiking

5. noisy neighbors
   high rent
   ~~security that is poor~~
   poor security

6. ~~cleaning of the apartment~~
   paid the bills
   did the laundry
   cleaned the apartment

7. looking good
   ~~to have fun~~
   feeling fine
   having fun

8. healthy soups
   tasty sandwiches
   ~~desserts that are inexpensive~~
   inexpensive desserts

9. under the desk drawers
   ~~the floor of the closet~~
   behind the bedroom curtains
   on the closet floor

10. works at the supermarket
    ~~member of the church choir~~
    coaches the Little League team
    sings in the church choir

Practice 2

The unbalanced part of each sentence is *italicized*. Rewrite this part so that it matches the rest of the sentence.

Example In the afternoon, I changed two diapers, ironed several shirts, and *was watching* soap operas. watched

1. Annie put a coin into the slot machine, pulled the lever, and *was waiting* to strike it rich.
   waited

2. Studying a little each day is more effective than *to cram*.
   cramming

3. Many old people fear loneliness, *becoming ill*, and poverty.
   illness

4. My pet peeves are screeching chalk, *buses that are late*, and dripping sinks.
late buses

5. The magazine cover promised stories on losing weight quickly, *how to attract* a rich spouse, and finding the perfect haircut.
attracting

6. As smoke billowed around her, Paula knew her only choices were to jump or *suffocation.*
to suffocate

7. The principal often pestered students, yelled at teachers, and *was interrupting* classes.
interrupted

8. People immigrate to America with hopes of finding freedom, happiness, and *in order to become financially secure*.
financial security

9. Once inside the zoo gates, Julio could hear lions roaring, *the chirping of birds*, and elephants trumpeting.
birds chirping

10. As a child I had nightmares about a huge monster that came out of a cave, *was breathing fire*, and wanted to barbecue me.
breathed fire

Practice 3

Complete the following statements. The first two parts of each statement are parallel in form; the part that you add should be parallel in form as well.

Example Three things I like about myself are my sense of humor, my thoughtfulness, and my self-discipline.

Answers will vary.

1. Celebrating my birthday means sleeping late, eating a good dinner, and ______

2. When Anita gets home from work, she likes to kick off her shoes, turn on some soft music, and ______

3. Despite the salesman's pitch, I could see that his "wonderful" used car had worn tires, rusting fenders, and ______________________________

____

4. Trying to realize that it was only a machine, Tina sat down in front of the computer, took a deep breath, and ______________________________

____

5. Three qualities I look for in a friend are loyalty, a sense of humor, and

____

Collaborative Activity

Part A: Editing and Rewriting

Working with a partner, read carefully the short paragraph below and cross out the five instances of faulty parallelism. Then use the space provided to correct the instances of faulty parallelism. Feel free to discuss the rewrite quietly with your partner and refer back to the chapter when necessary.

> [1]Running is an exercise that can be good for you mentally, physically, and ~~also be helpful for your emotions~~. [2]A beginning runner should keep three things in mind: the warm-up session, ~~the actual time that you are running~~, and the cool-down period. [3]Never start a run without first having warmed up through stretching exercises. [4]Stretching reduces muscle stiffness, decreases the possibility of injury, ~~and it's a good method to gradually increase the heart rate~~. [5]During the run itself, move at a comfortable pace. [6]Your breathing should be steady and ~~with depth~~. [7]Finally, remember to cool down after a run. [8]An adequate cool-down period allows time for the body to relax and the ~~normalizing of the heart rate~~.

1. Running is an exercise that can be good for you mentally, physically, and emotionally.

2. A beginning runner should keep three things in mind: the warm-up session, the run, and the cool-down period.

Continued

4. Stretching reduces muscle stiffness, decreases the possibility of injury, and gradually increases the heart rate.

6. Your breathing should be steady and deep.

8. An adequate cool-down period allows time for the body to relax and the heart rate to normalize.

Part B: Creating Sentences

Working with a partner, make up your own short test on faulty parallelism, as directed.

Answers will vary.

1. Write a sentence that includes three things you want to do tomorrow. One of those things should not be in parallel form. Then correct the faulty parallelism.

   Nonparallel ____________________

   Parallel ____________________

2. Write a sentence that names three positive qualities of a person you like or three negative qualities that you don't like.

   Nonparallel ____________________

   Parallel ____________________

3. Write a sentence that includes three everyday things that annoy you.

   Nonparallel ____________________

   Parallel ____________________

Reflective Activity

Answers will vary.

1. Look at the paragraph that you revised above. How does parallel form improve the paragraph?
2. How would you evaluate your own use of parallel form? When you write, do you use it almost never, at times, or often? How would you benefit from using it more?

Review Test 1

Cross out the unbalanced part of each sentence. Then rewrite the unbalanced part so that it matches the other item or items in the sentence.

Example I enjoy watering the grass and ~~to work~~ in the garden.
working

1. When someone gives you advice, do you listen, laugh, or ~~are you just ignoring it?~~
just ignore it?
2. After finding an apartment, we signed a lease, made a deposit, and ~~preparing~~ to move in.
prepared
3. The little girl came home from school with a tear-streaked face, a black eye, and ~~her shirt was torn~~.
a torn shirt.
4. Ruby watched television, ~~was talking on the phone~~, and studied all at the same time.
talked on the phone
5. My Halloween shopping list included one bottle of blue nail polish, fake blood, and ~~a wig that was colored purple~~.
a purple wig.
6. Carmen went to class prepared to take notes, to volunteer answers, and ~~with questions to ask~~.
to ask questions.

7. The severe thunderstorm brought ~~winds that were strong~~, dangerous lightning, and heavy rain to the entire county.
strong winds

8. When I got back from vacation, my refrigerator contained rotting vegetables, ~~milk that was soured~~, and moldy cheese.
sour milk

9. The guide demonstrated how colonial Americans made iron tools, crushed grain for flour, and ~~were making their own cloth~~.
made their own cloth

10. When my roommate's rock records blast, I shut her door, put cotton in my ears, and ~~am running~~ the vacuum cleaner.
run

■ Review Test 2

Each group of sentences contains two errors in parallelism. Underline these errors. Then, on the lines below, rewrite each item that doesn't match to make it parallel with the other item or items in the sentence.

1. When Phil left for work, he felt bright and cheerful. But by midafternoon he was coughing, wheezing, and shivers ran throughout his body. He left work, drove home, and was crawling into bed, where he stayed for the next four days.
   a. shivering
   b. crawled

2. I never spend money on fancy wrapping paper. When people get a present, they generally want to rip off the paper and be looking at what's inside. So I wrap my gifts in either plain brown grocery bags or Sunday comics that are colorful.
   a. look
   b. colorful Sunday comics

3. Failing students can be kinder than to pass them. There is little benefit to passing a student to a level of work he or she can't do. In addition, it is cruel to graduate a student from high school who has neither the communication skills nor the skills at math needed to get along in the world.
   a. passing
   b. math skills

4. The little boy drew back from his new baby-sitter. Her long red nails, black eye makeup, and jewelry that jangled all frightened him. He was sure she was either a bad witch or a queen that was evil.

   a. jangling jewelry

   b. an evil queen

5. An actress stopped in the middle of a Broadway show and scolded flash photographers in the audience. She said they can either have a photo session or they can be enjoying the show, but they can't do both. The photographers sank down in their seats, their cameras were put away, and quietly watched the show.

   a. enjoy

   b. put their cameras away

■ Review Test 3

Cross out the five nonparallel parts in the following passage. Correct them in the spaces between the lines.

[1]When a few people in one community decided to form a homeowners' association, many of their neighbors were skeptical. [2]Some objected to stirring things up, and others felt ~~were feeling~~ the dues were too high. [3]But many neighbors joined, and their first big success was a garage sale. [4]They scheduled a day for everybody in the neighborhood to bring unwanted items to a community center. [5]Big appliances and other heavy items ~~items that are heavy~~ were picked up by volunteers with trucks. [6]The association promoted the sale by placing ads in newspapers and distributing ~~with the distribution of~~ fliers at local shopping centers. [7]Dozens of families took part. [8]After that, the association helped plant trees, start a Crime Watch Program, and repair ~~in repairing~~ cracked sidewalks. [9]Members now receive discounts from local merchants and theater owners. [10]This association's success has inspired many more neighbors to join and people in other neighborhoods to start ~~who are starting~~ their own organizations.

19 Sentence Variety II

Like Chapter 7, this chapter will show you a variety of ways to write effective and varied sentences. You will increase your sense of the many ways available to you for expressing your ideas. The practices here will also reinforce much of what you have learned in this section about modifiers and the use of parallelism.

-ing Word Groups

Use an *-ing* word group at some point in a sentence. Here are examples:

The doctor, *hoping* for the best, examined the x-rays.

Jogging every day, I soon raised my energy level.

More information about *-ing* words, also known as *present participles,* appears on page 191.

Practice 1

Combine each pair of sentences below into one sentence by using an *-ing* word and omitting repeated words. Use a comma or commas to set off the *-ing* word group from the rest of the sentence.

Example
- The diesel truck chugged up the hill.
- It spewed out smoke.

Spewing out smoke, the diesel truck chugged up the hill.

or The diesel truck, spewing out smoke, chugged up the hill.

1. • The tourists began to leave the bus.
   • They picked up their cameras.
   Picking up their cameras, the tourists began to leave the bus.

2. • I was almost hit by a car.
   • I was jogging on the street.
   Jogging on the street, I was almost hit by a car.

3. • Barbara untangled her snarled hair from the brush.
   • She winced with pain.
   Wincing with pain, Barbara untangled her snarled hair from the brush.

4. • The singer ran to the front of the stage.
   • She waved her arms at the excited crowd.
   Waving her arms at the excited crowd, the singer ran to the front of the stage.

5. • The team braced itself for a last-ditch effort.
   • It was losing by one point with thirty seconds left to play.
   Losing by one point with thirty seconds left to play, the team braced itself for a last-ditch effort.

Practice 2

Answers will vary.

On separate paper, write five sentences of your own that contain *-ing* word groups.

-ed Word Groups

Use an *-ed* word group at some point in a sentence. Here are examples:

> *Tired* of studying, I took a short break.
>
> Mary, *amused* by the joke, told it to a friend.
>
> I opened my eyes wide, *shocked* by the red "F" on my paper.

More information about *-ed* words, also known as *past participles,* appears on page 191.

Practice 1

Combine each of the following pairs of sentences into one sentence by using an *-ed* word and omitting repeated words. Use a comma or commas to set off the *-ed* word group from the rest of the sentence.

Example
- Tim woke up with a start.
- He was troubled by a dream.

Troubled by a dream, Tim woke up with a start.

or Tim, troubled by a dream, woke up with a start.

Answers may vary.

1. • Mary sat up suddenly in bed.
   • She was startled by a thunderclap.

   Mary, startled by a thunderclap, sat up suddenly in bed.

2. • My parents decided to have a second wedding.
   • They have been married for fifty years.

   Married for fifty years, my parents decided to have a second wedding.

3. • Erica wouldn't leave her car.
   • She was frightened by the large dog near the curb.

   Frightened by the large dog near the curb, Erica wouldn't leave her car.

4. • The old orange felt like a marshmallow.
   • It was dotted with mold.

   Dotted with mold, the old orange felt like a marshmallow.

5. • Ernie made a huge sandwich and popped popcorn.
   • He was determined to have plenty to eat during the movie.

   Ernie, determined to have plenty to eat during the movie, made a huge sandwich and popped popcorn.

Practice 2

Answers will vary.

On separate paper, write five sentences of your own that contain *-ed* word groups.

-ly Openers

Use an *-ly* word to open a sentence. Her are examples:

Gently, he mixed the chemicals together.
Anxiously, the contestant looked at the game clock.
Skillfully, the quarterback rifled a pass to his receiver.

More information about *-ly* words, which are also known as *adverbs,* appears on page 224.

Practice 1

Combine each of the following pairs of sentences into one sentence by starting with an *-ly* word and omitting repeated words. Place a comma after the opening *-ly* word.

Example
- I gave several yanks to the starting cord of the lawn mower.
- I was angry.

Angrily, I gave several yanks to the starting cord of the lawn mower.

1. - We ate raw carrots and celery sticks.
   - We were noisy.

   Noisily, we ate raw carrots and celery sticks.

2. - Cliff spoke to his sobbing little brother.
   - He was gentle.

   Gently, Cliff spoke to his sobbing little brother.

3. - The newspaper boy threw our paper into a thornbush.
   - He was careless.

   Carelessly, the newspaper boy threw our paper into a thornbush.

4. • I paced up and down the hospital corridor.
   • I was anxious.
   Anxiously, I paced up and down the hospital corridor.

5. • Anita repeatedly dived into the pool to find her engagement ring.
   • She was frantic.
   Frantically, Anita repeatedly dived into the pool to find her engagement ring.

Practice 2

Answers will vary.

On separate paper, write five sentences of your own that begin with *-ly* words.

To Openers

Use a *to* word group to open a sentence. Here are examples.

> *To* succeed in that course, you must attend every class.
>
> *To* help me sleep better, I learned to quiet my mind through meditation.
>
> *To* get good seats, we went to the game early.

The combination of *to* and a verb, also known as an *infinitive,* is explained on page 191.

Practice 1

Combine each of the following pairs of sentences into one sentence by starting with a *to* word group and omitting repeated words. Use a comma after the opening *to* word group.

Example • I fertilize the grass every spring.
• I want to make it greener.
To make the grass greener, I fertilize it every spring.

1. • Sally put a thick towel on the bottom of the tub.
   • She did this to make the tub less slippery.
   To make the tub less slippery, Sally put a thick towel on the bottom.

2. • We now keep our garbage in the garage.
   • We do this to keep raccoons away.

   To keep raccoons away, we now keep our garbage in the garage.

3. • Bill pressed two fingers against the large vein in his neck.
   • He did this to count his pulse.

   To count his pulse, Bill pressed two fingers against the large vein in his neck.

4. • My aunt opens her dishwasher when it begins drying.
   • She does this to steam her face.

   To steam her face, my aunt opens her dishwasher when it begins drying.

5. • We looked through our closets for unused clothing.
   • We did this to help out the homeless.

   To help out the homeless, we looked through our closets for unused clothing.

Practice 2

Answers will vary.

On separate paper, write five sentences of your own that begin with *to* word groups.

Prepositional Phrase Openers

Use prepositional phrase openers. Here are examples:

From the beginning, I disliked my boss.

In spite of her work, she failed the course.

After the game, we went to a movie.

Prepositional phrases include words like *in, from, of, at, by,* and *with.* A list of common prepositions appears on page 91.

Practice 1

Combine each of the following groups of sentences into one sentence by omitting repeated words. Start each sentence with a suitable prepositional phrase and put the other prepositional phrases in places that sound right. Generally, you should use a comma after the opening prepositional phrase.

Example
- A fire started.
- It did this at 5 A.M.
- It did this inside the garage.

At 5 A.M., a fire started inside the garage.

Answers may vary.

1. - We have dinner with my parents.
   - We do this about once a week.
   - We do this at a restaurant.

   About once a week, we have dinner with my parents at a restaurant.

2. - I put the dirty cups away.
   - I did this before company came.
   - I put them in the cupboard.

   Before company came, I put the dirty cups away in the cupboard.

3. - My eyes roamed.
   - They did this during my English exam.
   - They did this around the room.
   - They did this until they met the instructor's eye.

   During my English exam, my eyes roamed around the room until they met the instructor's eye.

4. - The little boy drew intently.
   - He did this in a comic book.
   - He did this for twenty minutes.
   - He did this without stopping once.

   For twenty minutes, the little boy drew intently in a comic book without stopping once.

5. • A playful young orangutan wriggled.
   • He did this at the zoo.
   • He did this in a corner.
   • He did this under a paper sack.

   At the zoo, a playful young orangutan wriggled in a corner under a paper sack.

Practice 2

Answers will vary.

On separate paper, write five sentences of your own, each beginning with a prepositional phrase and containing at least one other prepositional phrase.

Series of Items

Use a series of items. Following are two of the many items that can be used in a series: adjective and verbs.

Adjectives in Series

Adjectives are descriptive words. Here are examples:

> The *husky young* man sanded the *chipped, weather-worn* paint off the fence.

Husky and *young* are adjectives that describe *man; chipped* and *weather-worn* are adjectives that describe *paint.* More information about adjectives appears on page 222.

Practice 1

Combine each of the following groups of sentences into one sentence by using adjectives in a series and omitting repeated words. Use a comma between adjectives only when *and* inserted between them sounds natural.

Example
- I sewed a set of buttons onto my coat.
- The buttons were shiny.
- The buttons were black.
- The coat was old.
- The coat was green.

I sewed a set of shiny black buttons onto my old green coat.

1. • The shingles blew off the roof during the storm.
   • The shingles were old.
   • The shingles were peeling.
   • The storm was blustery.

   The old, peeling shingles blew off the roof during the blustery storm.

2. • The dancer whirled across the stage with his partner.
   • The dancer was lean.
   • The dancer was powerful.
   • The partner was graceful.
   • The partner was elegant.

   The lean, powerful dancer whirled across the stage with his graceful, elegant partner.

3. • The model in the bleach ad wore high heels in the laundry room.
   • The model was well dressed.
   • The model was glamorous.
   • The high heels were three-inch.

   The well-dressed, glamorous model in the bleach ad wore three-inch high heels in the laundry room.

4. • The moon lit up the sky like a street lamp.
   • The moon was full.
   • The moon was golden.
   • They sky was cloudy.
   • The street lamp was huge.
   • The street lamp was floating.

   The full, golden moon lit up the cloudy sky like a huge floating street lamp.

5. • The doorbell of the house played a tune.
   • The doorbell was oval.
   • The doorbell was plastic.
   • The house was large.
   • The house was ornate.
   • The tune was loud.
   • The tune was rock.

   The oval plastic doorbell of the large, ornate house played a loud rock tune.

Practice 2

Answers will vary.

On separate paper, write five sentences of your own that contain a series of adjectives.

Verbs in Series

Verbs are words that express action. Here are examples:

> In my job as a cook's helper, I *prepared* salads, *sliced* meat and cheese, and *made* all kinds of sandwiches.

Basic information about verbs appears on pages 88–89.

Practice 1

Combine each group of sentences below into one sentence by using verbs in a series and omitting repeated words. Use a comma between verbs in a series.

Examples
- In the dingy bar Sam shelled peanuts.
- He sipped a beer.
- He talked up a storm with friends.

In the dingy bar Sam shelled peanuts, sipped a beer, and talked up a storm with friends.

1. • I put my homework on the table.
   • I made a cup of coffee.
   • I turned the radio up full blast.

   I put my homework on the table, made a cup of coffee, and turned the radio up full blast.

2. • The flea-ridden dog rubbed itself against the fence.
   • It bit its tail.
   • It scratched its neck with its hind leg.

   The flea-ridden dog rubbed itself against the fence, bit its tail, and scratched its neck with its hind leg.

3. • The driver stopped the school bus.
   • He walked to the back.
   • He separated two children.

   The driver stopped the school bus, walked to the back, and separated two children.

4. • I rolled up my sleeve.
   • I glanced at the nurse nervously.
   • I shut my eyes.
   • I waited for the worst to be over.

   I rolled up my sleeve, glanced at the nurse nervously, shut my eyes, and waited for the worst to be over.

5. • The parents applauded politely at the program's end.
   • They looked at their watches.
   • They exchanged looks of relief.
   • They reached for their coats.

   The parents applauded politely at the program's end, looked at their watches, exchanged looks of relief, and reached for their coats.

Practice 2

Answers will vary.

On separate paper, write five sentences of your own that use verbs in a series.

Note The section on parallelism (pages 241–249) gives you practice in some of the other kinds of items that can be used in a series.

Review Test 1

Combine each group of short sentences into one sentence. Various combinations are possible. Choose the combination that reads most smoothly and clearly and that sounds most appropriate in the context of surrounding sentences.

Note In combining short sentences into one sentence, omit repeated words where necessary. Use separate paper. The story continues in the next review test.

Dracula's Revenge

- Mickey Raines had a dislike.
- The dislike was of horror movies.
- His friends were different.
- They loved to see such movies.

While Mickey Raines had a dislike of horror movies, his friends loved to see them.

- They would always invite Mickey to go with them.
- He would always refuse.

Mickey's friends would always invite him to go with them, but he would always refuse.

- He thought horror films were stupid.
- The actors were covered with fake blood.
- They were pretending to writhe in agony.

He thought horror films, in which actors were covered with fake blood and pretended to writhe in agony, were stupid.

- Mickey thought their behavior was disgusting.
- He did not think their behavior was frightening.

While Mickey thought their behavior was disgusting, he did not think it was frightening.

- Once his friends persuaded him to come with them.
- They went to see a movie.
- The movie was called *Halloween 14—The Horror Continues.*

Once his friends persuaded him to come with them to see Halloween 14—The Horror Continues.

- Mickey found it ridiculous.
- He laughed aloud through parts of the movie.
- They were the scariest parts.

Mickey found it ridiculous and laughed aloud through the scariest parts of the movie.

- His friends were embarrassed.
- They were so embarrassed they moved.
- They moved away from him.
- They moved to another part of the theater.

His friends were so embarrassed that they moved away from him to another part of the theater.

- Then one night Mickey was alone.
- He was alone in his house.
- His mother was out for the evening.
- He turned on the television.

Then one night when Mickey was alone in his house because his mother was out for the evening, he turned on the television.

- A movie was playing.
- It was called *Nosferatu.*

A movie called Nosferatu was playing.

- It was the original film version of the Dracula story.
- The film version was silent.
- It was made in Germany.
- It was made in 1922.

It was the original silent film version of the Dracula story, made in Germany in 1922.

Review Test 2

Combine each group of short sentences into one sentence. Various combinations are possible. Choose the combination that reads most smoothly and clearly and that sounds most appropriate in the context of surrounding sentences.

Note In combining short sentences into one sentence, omit repeated words where necessary. Use separate paper. The story continues from the previous review test.

- The movie was not gory at all.
- There were no teenage girls in it getting chased.
- There were no teenage girls in it getting murdered.

The movie, which had no teenage girls getting chased or murdered. was not gory at all.

- The villain was a vampire.
- He was hideous.
- He was shriveled.
- He was terrifying.

The villain was a hideous, shriveled, terrifying vampire.

- His victims did not die.
- His victims grew weaker.
- They grew weaker after every attack.

His victims did not die but grew weaker after every attack.

- The vampire reminded Mickey of a parasite.
- The parasite was terrible.
- It was a dead thing.
- It was feeding off the living.

The vampire reminded Mickey of a terrible dead parasite feeding off the living.

- Mickey trembled.
- He was trembling at the thought of such a creature.
- It could be lurking just out of sight.
- It could be lurking in the darkness.

Mickey trembled at the thought of such a creature lurking just out of sight in the darkness.

- Then he heard a scraping noise.
- The noise was at the front door.
- He almost cried out in terror.

Then he heard a scraping noise at the front door and almost cried out in terror.

- The door opened quickly.
- Cold air rushed in.
- His mother appeared.
- She was back from her date.

As the door opened quickly and cold air rushed in, his mother appeared, back from her date.

- His mother smiled at him.
- She called out "Hello."
- She paused in the foyer to take off her coat.

His mother smiled at him, called out "Hello," and paused in the foyer to take off her coat.

- Mickey was relieved to see her.
- His relief was enormous.
- He rushed up to greet her.

Mickey, enormously relieved to see her, rushed up to greet her.

- The spell of the movie was broken.
- Mickey locked the door on the night.

The spell of the movie was broken, and Mickey locked the door on the night.

20 Paper Format

Introductory Activity

Check the paper opening below that seems clearer and easier to read.

✓ A

	Dangers of Prescription Drugs
	Careless consumers can harm themselves with
	prescription drugs. To begin with, consumers should always
	be aware of the possible side effects of a prescription drug.

___ B

	"dangers of prescription drugs"
	Careless consumers can harm themselves with prescription drugs.
	To begin with, consumers should always be aware of the possib-
	le side effects of a prescription drug. They should take the time

What are four reasons for your choice?

In "A," the title is capitalized and centered and has no quotation marks around it; there is a blank line between the title and the body of the paper; there are left and right margins around the body of the paper; no words are incorrectly hyphenated.

Answers are on page 686.

Guidelines for Preparing a Paper

Here are guidelines to follow in preparing a paper for an instructor.

1 Use full-sized theme or typewriter paper, 8½ by 11 inches.

2 Leave wide margins (1 to 1½ inches) all around the paper. In particular, do not crowd the right-hand or bottom margin. This white space makes your paper more readable; also, the instructor has room for comments.

3 If you write by hand:

- Use a pen with blue or black ink (*not* a pencil).
- Be careful not to overlap letters and not to make decorative loops on letters.
- On narrow-ruled paper, write on every other line.
- Make all your letters distinct. Pay special attention to *a, e, i, o,* and *u*—five letters that people sometimes write illegibly.

4 Center the title of your paper on the first line of the first page. Do not put quotation marks around the title. Do not underline the title. Capitalize all the major words in a title, including the first word. Short connecting words within a title, such as *of, for, the, in*, and *to,* are not capitalized.

5 Skip a line between the title and the first line of your text. Indent the first line of each paragraph about five spaces (half an inch) from the left-hand margin.

6 Make commas, periods, and other punctuation marks firm and clear. Leave a slight space after each period. When you type, leave a double space after a period.

7 If you break a word at the end of a line, break only between syllables (see page 341). Do not break words of one syllable.

8 Put your name, date, and course number where your instructor asks for them.

Remember these points about the title and the first sentence of your paper.

9 The title should be several words that tell what the paper is about. It should usually *not* be a complete sentence. For example, if you are writing a paper about your jealous sister, the title could simply be "My Jealous Sister."

10 Do not rely on the title to help explain the first sentence of your paper. The first sentence must be independent of the title. For instance, if the title of your paper is "My Jealous Sister," the first sentence should *not* be, "She has been this way as long as I can remember." Rather, the first sentence might be, "My sister has always been a jealous person."

Practice 1

Identify the mistakes in format in the following lines from a student composition. Explain the mistakes in the spaces provided. One mistake is described for you as an example.

	"Being a younger sister"
	When I was young, I would gladly have donated my older si-
	ster to another family. First of all, most of my clothes were
	hand-me-downs. I rarely got to buy anything new to wear. My
	sister took very good care of her clothes, which only made the
	problem worse. Also, she was always very critical of everything.

1. Break words at correct syllable divisions (sis-ter).
2. Do not use quotation marks around the title.
3. Capitalize the major words in the title ("Being a Younger Sister").
4. Skip a line between the title and the first line of the paper.
5. Indent the first line of the paper.
6. Keep margins on both sides of the paper.

Practice 2

As already stated, a title should tell in several words what a paper is about. Often a title can be based on the sentence that expresses the main idea of a paper.

Following are five main-idea sentences from student papers. Write a suitable specific title for each paper, basing the title on the main idea.

Example Title: Aging Americans as Outcasts

Our society treats aging Americans as outcasts in many ways.

Answers may vary slightly.

1. Title: Benefits of Pets

   Pets offer a number of benefits to their owners.

2. Title: Learning How to Budget

   Since I have learned to budget carefully, I no longer run out of money at the end of the week.

3. Title: The Value of a Study Group

   Studying regularly with a study group has helped me raise my grades.

4. Title: A Special Relationship (or Grandparents and Grandchildren)

   Grandparents have a special relationship with their grandchildren.

5. Title: A Wise Decision

   My decision to eliminate junk food from my diet has been good for my health and my budget.

Practice 3

In four of the five following sentences, the writer has mistakenly used the title to help explain the first sentence. But as has been noted, you must *not* rely on the title to explain your first sentence. Rewrite the sentences so that they are independent of the title. Write *Correct* under the one sentence that is independent.

Example Title: Flunking an Exam
First sentence: I managed to do this because of several bad habits.
Rewritten: I managed to flunk an exam because of several bad habits.

Answers will vary slightly.

1. Title: The Best Children's Television Shows

   First sentence: They educate while they entertain, and they are not violent.

   Rewritten: The best children's television shows educate while they entertain, and they are not violent.

2. Title: Women in the Workplace

   First sentence: They have made many gains there in the last decade.

   Rewritten: Women have made many gains in the workplace in the last decade.

3. Title: The Generation Gap

   First sentence: It results from differing experiences of various age groups.

   Rewritten: The generation gap results from differing experiences of various age groups.

4. Title: My Ideal Job

   First sentence: My ideal job would be to manage a rock group and make a lot of money.

   Rewritten: Correct

5. Title: Important Accomplishments

   First sentence: One of them was to finish high school despite my parents' divorce.

   Rewritten: One of my important accomplishments was to finish high school despite my parents' divorce.

■ Review Test

Use the space provided below to rewrite the following sentences from a student paper, correcting the mistakes in format.

	"my nursing-home friends"
	I now count some of them among my good friends. I fi-
	rst went there just to keep a relative of mine company.
	That is when I learned some of them rarely got any visitors.
	Many were starved for conversation and friendship.
	At the time, I did not want to get involved. But what I

	My Nursing-Home Friends
	I now count residents of a nursing home among my
	good friends. I first went there just to keep a relative of
	mine company. That is when I learned some of them rarely
	got any visitors. Many were starved for conversation and

21 Capital Letters

Introductory Activity

You probably know a good deal about the uses of capital letters. Answering the questions below will help you check your knowledge.

Answers will vary, but all should be capitalized.

1. Write the full name of a person you know: ______
2. In what city and state were you born? ______
3. What is your present street address? ______
4. Name a country where you would like to travel: ______
5. Name a school that you attended: ______
6. Give the name of a store where you buy food: ______
7. Name a company where you or anyone you know works: ______
8. Which day of the week gives you the best chance to relax? ______
9. What holiday is your favorite? ______
10. Which brand of toothpaste do you use? ______
11. Give the brand name of a candy or chewing gum you like: ______
12. Name a song or a television show you enjoy: ______
13. Write the title of a magazine or newspaper you read: ______

Items 14 –16 Three capital letters are needed in the example below. Underline the words you think should be capitalized. Then write them, capitalized, in the spaces provided.

on Super Bowl Sunday, my roommate said, "let's buy some snacks and invite a few friends over to watch the game." i knew my plans to write a term paper would have to be changed.

14. On 15. Let's 16. I

Answers are on page 686.

Main Uses of Capital Letters

Capital letters are used with:

1 First word in a sentence or direct quotation
2 Names of persons and the word *I*
3 Names of particular places
4 Names of days of the week, months, and holidays
5 Names of commercial products
6 Titles of books, magazines, articles, films, television shows, songs, poems, stories, papers that you write, and the like
7 Names of companies, associations, unions, clubs, religious and political groups, and other organizations

Each use is illustrated on the pages that follow.

First Word in a Sentence or Direct Quotation

Our company has begun laying people off.

The doctor said, "This may hurt a bit."

"My husband," said Martha, "is a light eater. When it's light, he starts to eat."

Note In the third example above, *My* and *When* are capitalized because they start new sentences. But *is* is not capitalized, because it is part of the first sentence.

Names of Persons and the Word *I*

At the picnic, I met Tony Curry and Lola Morrison.

Names of Particular Places

After graduating from Gibbs High School in Houston, I worked for a summer at a nearby Holiday Inn on Clairmont Boulevard.

But Use small letters if the specific name of a place is not given.

After graduating from high school in my hometown, I worked for a summer at a nearby hotel on one of the main shopping streets.

Names of Days of the Week, Months, and Holidays

This year, Memorial Day falls on the last Thursday in May.

But Use small letters for the seasons—summer, fall, winter, spring.

In the early summer and fall, my hay fever bothers me.

Names of Commercial Products

The consumer magazine gave high ratings to Cheerios breakfast cereal, Breyer's ice cream, and Progresso chicken noodle soup.

But Use small letters for the *type* of product (breakfast cereal, ice cream, chicken noodle soup, and the like).

Titles of Books, Magazines, Articles, Films, Television Shows, Songs, Poems, Stories, Papers That You Write, and the Like

My oral report was on *The Diary of a Young Girl,* by Anne Frank.

While watching *The Young and the Restless* on television, I thumbed through *Cosmopolitan* magazine and the *New York Times.*

Names of Companies, Associations, Unions, Clubs, Religious and Political Groups, and Other Organizations

A new bill before Congress is opposed by the National Rifle Association.

My wife is Jewish; I am Roman Catholic. We are both members of the Democratic Party.

My parents have life insurance with Prudential, auto insurance with Allstate, and medical insurance with Blue Cross and Blue Shield.

Practice

In the sentences that follow, cross out the words that need capitals. Then write the capitalized forms of the words in the space provided. The number of spaces tells you how many corrections to make in each case.

Example Rhoda said, "~~why~~ should I bother to *eat* this ~~hershey~~ bar? I should just apply it directly to my hips." ___Why___ ___Hershey___

1. Sometimes ~~i~~ still regret not joining the ~~boy~~ ~~scouts~~ when I was in grade school.
___I___ ___Boy___ ___Scouts___

2. After Carol went to ~~smokenders~~ in ~~july~~, she threw away her last pack of ~~marlboro~~ cigarettes.
___Smokenders___ ___July___ ___Marlboro___

3. In the box office of the ~~regal~~ ~~cinema~~ is a sign saying, "~~if~~ you plan to see an R-rated movie, be ready to show your ID."
___Regal___ ___Cinema___ ___If___

4. In many ~~new~~ ~~england~~ towns, ~~republicans~~ outnumber ~~democrats~~ five to one.
___New___ ___England___ ___Republicans___ ___Democrats___

5. Nelson was surprised to learn that both ~~state~~ ~~farm~~ and ~~nationwide~~ have insurance offices in the ~~prudential~~ ~~building~~.
___State___ ___Farm___ ___Nationwide___ ___Prudential___ ___Building___

6. When John F. Kennedy Jr. died in a plane crash off the coast of ~~massachusetts~~, ~~time~~ and ~~newsweek~~ magazines put his photograph on their covers.
___Massachusetts___ ___Time___ ___Newsweek___

7. The rose grower whom Manny works for said that the biggest rose-selling holidays are ~~valentine's~~ ~~day~~ and ~~mother's~~ ~~day~~.
___Valentine's___ ___Day___ ___Mother's___ ___Day___

8. With some ~~pepsis~~ and ~~fritos~~ nearby, the kids settled down to play a game on the ~~macintosh~~ computer.
___Pepsis___ ___Fritos___ ___Macintosh___

9. Bob's ~~ford~~ ~~taurus~~ was badly damaged when he struck a deer last ~~saturday~~.
___Ford___ ___Taurus___ ___Saturday___

10. Though Julie Andrews excelled in the ~~broadway~~ version of ~~*my fair lady*~~, Audrey Hepburn was cast as the female lead in the movie version.
___Broadway___ ___My___ ___Fair___ ___Lady___

Other Uses of Capital Letters

Capital letters are also used with:

1 Names that show family relationships
2 Titles of persons when used with their names
3 Specific school courses
4 Languages
5 Geographic locations
6 Historical periods and events
7 Races, nations, and nationalities
8 Opening and closing of a letter

Each use is illustrated on the pages that follow.

Names That Show Family Relationships

Aunt Fern and Uncle Jack are selling their house.

I asked Grandfather to start the fire.

Is Mother feeling better?

But Do not capitalize words like *mother, father, grandmother, grandfather, uncle, aunt,* and so on when they are preceded by *my* or another possessive word.

My aunt and uncle are selling their house.

I asked my grandfather to start the fire.

Is my mother feeling better?

Titles of Persons When Used with Their Names

I wrote an angry letter to Senator Blutt.

Can you drive to Dr. Stein's office?

We asked Professor Bushkin about his attendance policy.

But Use small letters when titles appear by themselves, without specific names.

I wrote an angry letter to my senator.

Can you drive to the doctor's office?

We asked our professor about his attendance policy.

Specific School Courses

My courses this semester include Accounting I, Introduction to Data Processing, Business Law, General Psychology, and Basic Math.

But Use small letters for general subject areas.

This semester I'm taking mostly business courses, but I have a psychology course and a math course as well.

Languages

Lydia speaks English and Spanish equally well.

Geographic Locations

I lived in the South for many years and then moved to the West Coast.

But Use small letters in giving directions.

Go south for about five miles and then bear west.

Historic Periods and Events

One essay question dealt with the Battle of the Bulge in World War II.

Races, Nations, and Nationalities

The census form asked whether I was African American, Native American, Hispanic, or Asian.

Last summer I hitchhiked through Italy, France, and Germany.

The city is a melting pot for Koreans, Vietnamese, and Mexican Americans.

But Use small letters when referring to *whites* or *blacks*.

Both whites and blacks supported our mayor in the election.

Opening and Closing of a Letter

Dear Sir:	Sincerely yours,
Dear Madam:	Truly yours,

Note Capitalize only the first word in a closing.

Practice

Cross out the words that need capitals in the following sentences. Then write the capitalized forms of the words in the spaces provided. The number of spaces tells you how many corrections to make in each case.

1. The nervous game show contestant couldn't remember how long the ~~hundred~~ ~~year's~~ ~~war~~ lasted.
   Hundred ______ Years' ______ War ______
2. My sister and I always plead with ~~aunt~~ ~~sophie~~ to sing ~~polish~~ songs whenever she visits us.
   Aunt ______ Sophie ______ Polish ______
3. While in Philadelphia, we visited ~~independence~~ ~~hall~~ and saw the ~~liberty~~ ~~bell~~.
   Independence ______ Hall ______ Liberty ______ Bell ______
4. The readings for the first semester of ~~world~~ ~~history~~ end with the ~~middle~~ ~~ages~~.
   World ______ History ______ Middle ______ Ages ______
5. The Miami area has many fine ~~cuban~~ restaurants, several ~~spanish~~-language newspapers, and annual ~~hispanic~~ cultural festivals.
   Cuban ______ Spanish ______ Hispanic ______

Unnecessary Use of Capitals

Practice

Many errors in capitalization are caused by adding capitals where they are not needed. Cross out the incorrectly capitalized letters in the following sentences and write the correct forms in the spaces provided. The number of spaces tells you how many corrections to make in each sentence.

1. Antonio's ~~Grandmother~~ makes the best ~~Spaghetti~~ with ~~Meatballs~~ I've ever tasted.

   grandmother ___ spaghetti ___ meatballs ___

2. In our ~~High~~ ~~School~~, the American history teacher was also the ~~Basketball~~ ~~Coach~~.

   high ___ school ___ basketball ___ coach ___

3. A ~~Shop~~ at Westville Mall sells copies of all the trendy clothes shown in various ~~Fashion~~ ~~Magazines~~.

   shop ___ fashion ___ magazines ___

4. Several ~~Parents~~' ~~Groups~~ protested the ~~Ads~~ for the new horror movie, which showed Santa Claus as a ~~Maniac~~ with a knife.

   parents' ___ groups ___ ads ___ maniac ___

5. When I complained to the ~~Manager~~ of the ~~Restaurant~~ about the poor service, she gave me a free ~~Dessert~~.

   manager ___ restaurant ___ dessert ___

Collaborative Activity

Part A: Editing and Rewriting

Working with a partner, read the short paragraph below and mark off the fifteen spots where capital letters are missing. Then use the space provided to rewrite the passage, adding capital letters where needed. Feel free to discuss the passage quietly with your partner and refer back to the chapter when necessary.

[1]The morning that I visited the lincoln memorial, it was raining. [2]It was a quiet thursday in late october, and the air was cold. [3]I was with my uncle walt, and we had spent the morning visiting the smithsonian institution together. [4]After lunch, my uncle said to me, "now we're going to go someplace that you'll never forget." [5]When we arrived, I was overwhelmed by lincoln's massive statue, which dwarfed everything around it—just as the man had done in life. [6]To my left I was aware of the silently flowing potomac river. [7]Engraved on one of the marble walls was the gettysburg address. [8]I read those familiar words and remained there for a time in

Continued

silence, touched by the simple eloquence of that speech. [9]I then snapped just one picture with my kodak camera and walked down the stone steps quietly. [10]The photograph still sits on my desk today as a reminder of that special visit.

1: Lincoln, Memorial 2: Thursday, October

3: Uncle, Walt, Smithsonian, Institution

4: Now 5: Lincoln's 6: Potomac, River

7: Gettysburg, Address 9: Kodak

Part B: Creating Sentences

Answers will vary.

Working with a partner, write a sentence (or two) as directed. Pay special attention to capital letters.

1. Write about a place you like (or want) to visit. Be sure to give the name of the place, including the city, state, or country where it is located.
2. Write a sentence (or two) in which you state the name of your elementary school, your favorite teacher or subject, and your least favorite teacher or subject.
3. Write a sentence (or two) which includes the names of three brand-name products that you often use. You may begin the sentence with the words, "Three brand-name products I use every day are . . ."
4. Think of the name of your favorite musical artist or performer. Then write a sentence in which you include the musician's name and the title of one of his or her songs.
5. Write a sentence in which you describe something you plan to do two days from now. Be sure to include the date and day of the week.

Reflective Activity

Answers will vary.

1. What would writing be like without capital letters? Use an example or two to help show how capital letters are important to writing.
2. What three uses of capital letters are most difficult for you to remember? Explain, giving examples.

Review Test 1

Cross out the words that need capitals in the following sentences. Then write the capitalized forms of the words in the spaces provided. The number of spaces tells you how many corrections to make in each sentence.

Example During halftime of the ~~saturday~~ afternoon football game, my sister said, "~~let's~~ get some hamburgers from ~~wendy's~~ or put a pizza in the oven."

Saturday ______ Let's ______ Wendy's ______

1. When he saw the exercise commercial that said "~~just~~ do it," Lance put on his ~~nike~~ running shoes and went to the store to get some ice cream.

   Just ______ Nike ______

2. Millions of years ago, ~~america's~~ ~~midwest~~ was covered by a great inland sea.

   America's ______ Midwest ______

3. One of our ~~thanksgiving~~ traditions is sending a check to an organization such as ~~care~~, which helps relieve world hunger.

   Thanksgiving ______ Care ______

4. If you drive onto ~~route~~ 10 in ~~tallahassee~~, ~~florida~~, and stay on that road, you'll eventually end up in ~~california~~.

   Route ______ Tallahassee ______ Florida ______ California ______

5. Just before ~~english~~ class this morning, Arlene titled her final paper "~~my~~ ~~argument~~ for an A."

   English ______ My ______ Argument ______

6. I read in the book ~~*royal*~~ ~~*lives*~~ that when an ancient ~~egyptian~~ king died, his servants were often killed and buried with him.

   Royal ______ Lives ______ Egyptian ______

7. ~~dear~~ ~~mr.~~ Bradford:

This is the third and final time I will write to complain about the leak in my bathroom.

~~sincerely~~,

Anne Morrison

Dear | Mr. | Sincerely

8. "After age eighty," ~~grandma~~ ~~ida~~ would say, "time passes very quickly. ~~it~~ seems as though it's time for breakfast every fifteen minutes."

Grandma | Ida | It

9. Dr. Green, who teaches a course called ~~cultural~~ ~~anthropology~~, spent last summer on an archaeological dig in ~~israel~~.

Cultural | Anthropology | Israel

10. During the singing of "~~the~~ ~~star~~-~~spangled~~ ~~banner~~," many fans at ~~veterans'~~ ~~stadium~~ drank sodas, read their programs, or chatted with each other.

The | Star- | Spangled

Banner | Veterans' | Stadium

■ Review Test 2

Answers will vary.

On separate paper, write:

- Seven sentences demonstrating the seven main uses of capital letters.
- Eight sentences demonstrating the eight other uses of capital letters.

22 Numbers and Abbreviations

Introductory Activity

Write a check mark beside the item in each pair that you think uses numbers correctly.

I finished the exam by 8:55, but my grade was only 65 percent. ___✓___

I finished the exam by eight-fifty-five, but my grade was only sixty-five percent. ______

9 people are in my biology lab, but there are 45 in my lecture group. ______

Nine people are in my biology lab, but there are forty-five in my lecture group. ___✓___

Write a check mark beside the item in each pair that you think uses abbreviations correctly.

Both of my bros. were treated by Dr. Lewis after the mt. climbing accident. ______

Both of my brothers were treated by Dr. Lewis after the mountain climbing accident. ___✓___

I spent two hrs. finishing my Eng. paper and handed it to my teacher, Ms. Peters, right at the deadline. ______

I spent two hours finishing my English paper and handed it to my teacher, Ms. Peters, right at the deadline. ___✓___

Answers are on page 686.

Numbers

Rule 1 Spell out numbers that take no more than two words. Otherwise, use numerals—the numbers themselves.

> Last year Tina bought nine new records.
>
> Ray struck out fifteen batters in Sunday's softball game.
>
> *But*
>
> Tina now has 114 records in her collection.
>
> Already this season Ray has recorded 168 strikeouts.

You should also spell out a number that begins a sentence.

> One hundred fifty first-graders throughout the city showed flu symptoms today.

Rule 2 Be consistent when you use a series of numbers. If some numbers in a sentence or paragraph require more than two words, then use numbers themselves throughout the selection.

> This past spring, we planted 5 rhodos, 15 azaleas, 50 summersweet, and 120 myrtle around our house.

Rule 3 Use numbers to show dates, times, addresses, percentages, exact sums of money, and parts of a book.

> John F. Kennedy was killed on November 22, 1963.
>
> My job interview was set for 10:15. (*But*: Spell out numbers before *o'clock*. For example: The time was then changed to eleven o'clock.)
>
> Janet's new address is 118 North 35 Street.
>
> Almost 40 percent of my meals are eaten at fast-food restaurants.
>
> The cashier rang up a total of $18.35. (*But:* Round amounts may be expressed as words. For example: The movie has a five-dollar admission charge.)
>
> Read Chapter 6 in your math textbook and answer questions 1 to 5 on page 250.

Practice

Use the three rules to make the corrections needed in these sentences.

1. Almost every morning I get up at exactly six-fifteen.

2. But on Sunday mornings, I sleep until 9 o'clock.
3. The Challenger space shuttle tragedy took place on January twenty-eight, 1986.
4. Joanne got really nervous when she saw there were only 6 other people in her English class.
5. Please send your complaints to sixteen hundred Pennsylvania Avenue.
6. 43 stores in the New England area were closed by a retail workers' strike.
7. Martin's computer system, including a printer, cost nine hundred thirty dollars and twenty cents.
8. Pages sixty through sixty-four of my biology book are stuck together.
9. Hanging in Hollywood starlet Fifi LaFlamme's closet are twenty-seven evening gowns, fifty-two designer suits, and 132 pairs of shoes.
10. Since over fifty percent of the class failed the midterm exam, the instructor decided not to count the grades.

Abbreviations

While abbreviations are a helpful time-saver in note-taking, you should avoid most abbreviations in formal writing. Listed below are some of the few abbreviations that are acceptable in compositions. Note that a period is used after most abbreviations.

1 Mr., Mrs., Ms., Jr., Sr., Dr., when used with proper names:

Mr. Rollin   Ms. Peters   Dr. Coleman

2 Time references:

A.M. or a.m.   P.M. or p.m.   B.C. or A.D.

3 First or middle initial in a name:

T. Alan Parker   Linda M. Evans

4 Organizations, technical words, and trade names known primarily by initials:

ABC   CIA   UNESCO   GM   AIDS   DNA

Practice

Cross out the words that should not be abbreviated and correct them in the spaces provided.

1. After I placed the "bike for sale" ad in the ~~newsp~~., the ~~tele~~. rang nonstop for a week.

   newspaper telephone

2. Sharon bought two ~~bush~~. of ripe tomatoes at the farm ~~mkt~~. on ~~Rt~~. 73.

   bushels market Route

3. On ~~Mon~~., NASA will announce its plans for a ~~Sept~~. flight to Mars.

   Monday September

4. The ~~psych~~. class was taught by Dr. Aronson, a noted psychiatrist from ~~Eng~~.

   psychology England

5. The best things on the menu are the ~~chick~~. pot pie and the ~~mac~~. and cheese.

   chicken macaroni

6. Several baby opossums (each of which weighs less than an ~~oz~~.) can fit into a ~~tbsp~~.

   ounce tablespoon

7. I didn't have time to study for my ~~chem~~. test on ~~Sun~~., but I studied for four ~~hrs~~. yesterday.

   chemistry Sunday hours

8. Every ~~Jan~~., our ~~co~~. gives awards for the best employee suggestions of the previous ~~yr~~.

   January company year

9. Lawrence T. Johnson lost his ~~lic~~. to practice medicine when the state board discovered he never went to ~~med~~. school.

   license medical

10. Mick, a Gulf War ~~vet~~., started his own photography ~~bus~~. after graduating from a community ~~coll~~.

    veteran business college

■ Review Test

Cross out the mistake or mistakes in numbers and abbreviations and correct them in the spaces provided.

1. Sears' 4-day sale starts this coming Thurs.

   four ______ Thursday ______

2. One suspect had blue eyes and brn. hair and was over 6 ft. tall.

   brown ______ six ______ feet ______

3. Answers to the chpt. questions start on p. two hundred and ninety-three.

   chapter ______ page ______ 293 ______

4. With Dec. twenty-fifth only hrs. away, little Rhonda couldn't eat or sleep.

   December ______ 25 ______ hours ______

5. Over 200 children helped in the collection of seven hundred and thirty-two dollars for UNICEF.

   two hundred ______ $732 ______

6. My growing 15-year-old son wears sz. 11 shoes that look like boats.

   fifteen ______ size ______

7. My 3 years of Spanish in h.s. helped me to get a job in the city health clinic.

   three ______ high ______ school ______

8. The robber was sentenced to 10 yrs. in prison for holding up a bank on Pacific Blvd.

   ten ______ years ______ Boulevard ______

9. I canceled my appt. when I got an emerg. call that my mother had been taken to the hosp.

   appointment ______ emergency ______ hospital ______

10. When city employees staged a strike on Mon., more than 70 pct. of them didn't show up for work.

    Monday ______ percent ______

23 End Marks

Introductory Activity

Add the end mark needed in each of the following sentences.

1. All week I have been feeling depressed.
2. What is the deadline for handing in the paper?
3. The man at the door wants to know whose car is double-parked.
4. That truck ahead of us is out of control!

Answers are on page 687.

A sentence always begins with a capital letter. It always ends with a period, a question mark, or an exclamation point.

Period (.)

Use a period after a sentence that makes a statement.

More single parents are adopting children.
It has rained for most of the week.

Use a period after most abbreviations.

Mr. Brady	B.A.	Dr. Ballard
Ms. Peters	A.M.	Tom Ricci, Jr.

Question Mark (?)

Use a question mark after a *direct* question.

When is your paper due?
How is your cold?
Tom asked, "When are you leaving?"
"Why can't we all stop arguing?" Rosa asked.

Do *not* use a question mark after an *indirect* question (a question not in the speaker's exact words).

She asked when the paper was due.
He asked how my cold was.
Tom asked when I was leaving.
Rosa asked why we couldn't all stop arguing.

Exclamation Point (!)

Use an exclamation point after a word or sentence that expresses strong feeling.

Come here!

Ouch! This pizza is hot!

That truck just missed us!

Note Be careful not to overuse exclamation points.

Practice

Add a period, question mark, or exclamation point as needed to each of the following sentences.

1. Is it possible for a fish to drown?
2. Thomas Jefferson was a redhead.
3. I asked Jill for the time of day, but she wouldn't give it to me.
4. When Eva learned she had won the lottery, she jumped up and down, yelling, "I don't believe it!"
5. Because Americans watch so much television, one writer has called us a nation of "vidiots."
6. I questioned whether the police officer's report was accurate.
7. If you had one year left to live, what would you do with the rest of your life?
8. The last thing I heard before waking up in the hospital was someone screaming, "Look out for that truck!"
9. On the plane from New York to Chicago, Dominic said, "Must I turn my watch back one hour—or forward?"
10. Carlos asked himself on the way to his wedding whether he was sure he wanted to get married.

Review Test

Add a period, question mark, or exclamation point as needed to each of the following sentences.

1. My birthday present was wrapped in old newspapers and yellowed Scotch tape.
2. Did you know that washing in very hot water can dry out your skin?
3. The bride stunned everyone when she appeared in a purple lace gown.
4. Don't eat that poisonous mushroom!
5. How did you get a wad of gum in your hair?
6. That boy is waving a loaded gun!
7. All through the interview, my stomach grumbled and my hands shook.
8. If you won the lottery, what would you do with the prize money?
9. I wonder if we should have a New Year's Eve party this year.
10. Look out for that swerving car!

24 Apostrophe

Introductory Activity

Look carefully at the three items below. Then see if you can answer the questions that follow each item.

1. the desk of the manager = the manager's desk
   the car of Hakim = Hakim's car
   the teeth of my dog = my dog's teeth
   the smile of the woman = the woman's smile
   the briefcase of my mother = my mother's briefcase

   What is the purpose of the apostrophe in the examples above?
   To show ownership or possession

2. He is my best friend. = He's my best friend.
   I am afraid of spiders. = I'm afraid of spiders.
   Do not watch too much TV. = Don't watch too much TV.
   They are an odd couple. = They're an odd couple.
   It is a wonderful movie. = It's a wonderful movie.

   What is the purpose of the apostrophe in the examples above?
   To indicate missing letters and shortened spellings

3. Several buildings were damaged by the severe storm. One building's roof was blown off and dropped in a nearby field.

   Why does the apostrophe belong in the second sentence but not the first?
   "Buildings" signals a plural noun, while "building's" indicates ownership or possession.

Answers are on page 687.

The two main uses of the apostrophe are:

1 To show the omission of one or more letters in a contraction
2 To show ownership or possession

Each use is explained on the pages that follow.

Apostrophe in Contractions

A contraction is formed when two words are combined to make one word. An apostrophe is used to show where letters are omitted in forming the contraction. Here are two contractions:

have + not = haven't (the *o* in *not* has been omitted)
I + will = I'll (the *wi* in *will* has been omitted)

The following are some other common contractions:

I	+ am	= I'm	it	+ is	= it's
I	+ have	= I've	it	+ has	= it's
I	+ had	= I'd	is	+ not	= isn't
who	+ is	= who's	could	+ not	= couldn't
do	+ not	= don't	I	+ would	= I'd
did	+ not	= didn't	they	+ are	= they're
let	+ us	= let's	there	+ is	= there's

Note The combination *will* + *not* has an unusual contraction: *won't.*

Practice 1

Combine the following words into contractions. One is done for you.

she	+ is	= *she's*	you	+ will	= you'll
you	+ have	= you've	we	+ would	= we'd
have	+ not	= haven't	could	+ not	= couldn't
he	+ has	= he's	they	+ will	= they'll
we	+ are	= we're	does	+ not	= doesn't

Practice 2

Write the contraction for the words in parentheses.

Example He (could not) couldn't come.

1. I (did not) didn't like the movie, but the popcorn (was not) wasn't bad.
2. Tara (does not) doesn't hide her feelings well, so if (she is) she's angry you will know it.
3. (You are) You're taking the wrong approach with Len, as he (cannot) can't stand being lectured.
4. This (is not) isn't the first time (you have) you've embarrassed me in public.
5. (We would) We'd love to have you stay for dinner if you (do not) don't mind eating leftovers.

Note Even though contractions are common in everyday speech and in written dialogue, usually it is best to avoid them in formal writing.

Practice 3

Write five sentences using the apostrophe in different contractions.
Answers will vary.

1. ______
2. ______
3. ______
4. ______
5. ______

Four Contractions to Note Carefully

Four contractions that deserve special attention are *they're, it's, you're,* and *who's.* Sometimes these contractions are confused with the possessive words *their, its, your,* and *whose.* The following list shows the difference in meaning between the contractions and the possessive words.

Contractions	*Possessive Words*
they're (means *they are*)	their (means *belonging to them*)
it's (means *it is* or *it has*)	its (means *belonging to it*)
you're (means *you are*)	your (means *belonging to you*)
who's (means *who is*)	whose (means *belonging to whom*)

Note Possessive words are explained further on page 299.

Practice

Underline the correct form (the contraction or the possessive word) in each of the following sentences. Use the contraction whenever the two words of the contraction (*they are, it is, you are, who is*) would also fit.

1. (It's, Its) wonderful that (you're, your) grandmother is still so strong and active at eighty.
2. I don't know (who's, whose) fault it is that the car battery is dead, but I know (who's, whose) the primary suspect.
3. (You're, Your) feeling nauseated because you did not open any windows while staining (you're, your) living-room floor.
4. (They're, There) are some people who insist on acting gloomy no matter how well (they're, their) lives are going.
5. (It's, Its) hard to be pleasant to neighbors who always keep (they're, their) stereo on too loud.

Apostrophe to Show Ownership or Possession

To show ownership or possession, we can use such words as *belongs to, owned by,* or (most commonly) *of.*

the knapsack *that belongs to* Lola
the grades *possessed by* Travis
the house *owned by* my mother
the sore arm *of* the pitcher

But the apostrophe plus *s* (if the word does not end in *-s*) is often the quickest and easiest way to show possession. Thus we can say:

Lola's knapsack
Travis's grades
my mother's house
the pitcher's sore arm

Points to Remember

1 The *'s* goes with the owner or possessor (in the examples given, *Lola, Travis, mother,* and *pitcher).* What follows is the person or thing possessed (in the examples given, *knapsack, grades, house,* and *sore arm).* An easy way to determine the owner or possessor is to ask the question "Who owns it?" In the first example, the answer to the question "Who owns the knapsack?" is *Lola.* Therefore, the *'s* goes with *Lola.*

2 In handwriting, there should always be a break between the word and the *'s.*

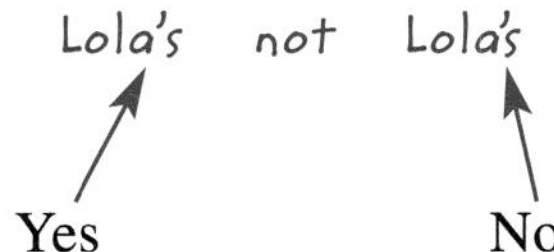

3 A singular word ending in *-s* (such as *Travis* in the earlier example) also shows possession by adding an apostrophe plus *s* (Travis's).

Practice 1

Rewrite the italicized part of each sentence below, using *'s* to show possession. Remember that the *'s* goes with the owner or possessor.

Examples *The motorcycle owned by Clyde* is a frightening machine.
Clyde's motorcycle

The roommate of my brother is a sweet and friendly person.
My brother's roommate

1. The *voice of the singer* had a relaxing effect on the crowd.
   singer's voice
2. *The garage of Dawn* has so much furniture stored in it that there's no room for her car.
   Dawn's garage

3. *The law of Murphy* states, "Anything that can go wrong will go wrong."
   Murphy's law

4. All the financial-planning information has been stored in the *memory of the computer.*
   computer's memory

5. Because *the mother of my wife* is in jail for forgery, I call her my mother-outlaw.
   my wife's mother

6. Where is the rest of *the meat loaf of yesterday,* which I was planning to eat for lunch?
   yesterday's meat loaf

7. *The promotion of my sister* to vice president of the company was well earned.
   My sister's promotion

8. *The bratty little brother of Alexis* has grown up to become a charming young man.
   Alexis's bratty little brother

9. The judges reversed *the call of the referee* after they viewed the videotaped replay.
   the referee's call

10. Thousands of gallons of crude oil spilled into the ocean when *the hull of the tanker* ruptured in the storm.
    the tanker's hull

Practice 2

Underline the word in each sentence that needs *'s*. Then write the word correctly in the space at the left. One is done for you as an example.

horse's 1. The trainer removed a nail from the horse hoof.

brother's 2. My brother appetite is like a bottomless pit.

son's 3. Arnie pulled his young son hand away from the kerosene heater.

comedian's 4. The comedian trademarks were long cigars and red socks.

landlord's 5. No matter when you dial the landlord number, nobody answers the phone.

Ted's 6. The assistant manager always takes credit for Ted ideas.

teller's 7. We all froze when the bank teller wig fell off.

people's 8. Some people never feel other people problems are their concern.

studio's 9. Nita hires an accountant to prepare her dance studio tax returns each year.

girl's 10. The screen door slammed on the little girl fingers.

Practice 3

Add *'s* to each of the following words to make it the possessor or owner of something. Then write sentences using the words. Your sentences can be serious or playful. One is done for you as an example.

Answers for sentences will vary.

1. Cary Cary's
   Cary's hair is bright red.
2. teacher teacher's
3. insect insect's
4. husband husband's
5. salesperson salesperson's

Apostrophe versus Possessive Pronouns

Do not use an apostrophe with possessive pronouns. They already show ownership. Possessive pronouns include *his, hers, its, yours, ours,* and *theirs.*

Incorrect	*Correct*
The bookstore lost its' lease.	The bookstore lost its lease.
The racing bikes were theirs'.	The racing bikes were theirs.
The change is yours'.	The change is yours.
His' problems are ours', too.	His problems are ours, too.
His' skin is more tanned than hers'.	His skin is more tanned than hers.

Apostrophe versus Simple Plurals

When you want to make a word plural, just add *s* at the end of the word. Do *not* add an apostrophe. For example, the plural of the word *movie* is *movies,* not *movie's* or *movies'*.

Look at this sentence:

When Sally's cat began catching birds, the neighbors called the police.

The words *birds* and *neighbors* are simple plurals, meaning more than one bird, more than one neighbor. The plural is shown by adding *-s* only. (More information about plurals starts on page 352.) On the other hand, the *'s* after *Sally* shows possession—that Sally owns the cat.

Practice

In the spaces provided under each sentence, add the one apostrophe needed and explain why the other words ending in *s* are simple plurals.

Example Originally, the cuffs of mens pants were meant for cigar ashes.

cuffs: simple plural meaning more than one cuff

mens: men's, meaning "belonging to men"

ashes: simple plural meaning more than one ash

1. The pizza parlor's aromas seeped through the vents to our second-floor apartment.

   parlors: parlor's, meaning "belonging to the parlor"

   aromas: simple plural meaning more than one aroma

   vents: simple plural meaning more than one vent

2. A police car's siren echoed through the streets and buildings of the city.

   cars: car's, meaning "belonging to the car"

   streets: simple plural meaning more than one street

   buildings: simple plural meaning more than one building

3. Karen's tomato plants are taller than the six-foot stakes she used to support them.

   Karens: Karen's, meaning "belonging to Karen"

   plants: simple plural meaning more than one plant

   stakes: simple plural meaning more than one stake

4. Because of the lake's high bacteria level, officials prohibited boating, swimming, and fishing there.

   lakes: lake's, meaning "belonging to the lake"

   officials: simple plural meaning more than one official

5. I have considered applying for many positions, but an exterminator's job is not one of them.

   positions: simple plural meaning more than one position

   exterminators: exterminator's, meaning "belonging to an exterminator"

6. The candlelight's glow fell gently on the pale white plates and ruby-red goblets.

   candelights: candlelight's, meaning "belonging to candlelight"

   plates: simple plural meaning more than one plate

   goblets: simple plural meaning more than one goblet

7. Crackers layered with cheese and apple slices are my father's favorite snack.

   Crackers: simple plural meaning more than one cracker

   slices: simple plural meaning more than one slice

   fathers: father's, meaning "belonging to my father"

8. Within a day that insect's eggs will turn into glistening white worms.

   insects: insect's, meaning "belonging to the insect"

   eggs: simple plural meaning more than one egg

   worms: simple plural meaning more than one worm

9. Seabirds skidding along the ocean's edge at midnight looked like miniature moonlight surfers.

   Seabirds: simple plural meaning more than one seabird

   oceans: ocean's, meaning "belonging to the ocean"

   surfers: simple plural meaning more than one surfer

10. My daughter's prayers were answered when the heavy snow caused all the schools in the area to close for the rest of the week.

    daughters: daughter's, meaning "belonging to my daughter"

    prayers: simple plural meaning more than one prayer

    schools: simple plural meaning more than one school

Apostrophe with Plural Words Ending in -*s*

Plurals that end in -*s* show possession simply by adding the apostrophe, rather than an apostrophe plus *s*.

> Both of my *neighbors'* homes have been burglarized recently.
>
> The many *workers'* complaints were ignored by the company.
>
> All the *campers'* tents were damaged by the hailstorm.

Practice

Add an apostrophe where needed.

1. The nurses' union protested my layoff.
2. My two sisters' feet are the same size, so they share their shoes.
3. The lions' keeper has worked with those lions since birth.
4. The Tylers' new television set was mistakenly delivered to our house.
5. The photo album that was lost contained my parents' wedding pictures.

Collaborative Activity

Part A: Editing and Rewriting

Working with a partner, read the short paragraph below. Underline ten places where you could rewrite, using apostrophes to indicate contractions and possessives. Then rewrite those parts in the spaces that follow. Feel free to discuss the rewrite quietly with your partner and refer back to the chapter when necessary.

> [1]The dog of my neighbor is evil. [2]For one thing, it barks constantly, even when there is nothing to bark at. [3]Because of the constant barking of the dog, I can not sleep at night. [4]The dog also growls menacingly whenever it sees me. [5]One time, it tried to charge at me through the fence of my landlord. [6]Luckily for me, the fence was strong enough to restrain the dog. [7]I have tried to talk to my neighbor about the problem, but he refuses to listen. [8]He thinks there is nothing wrong with the behavior of the dog. [9]But that is because the dog does not show its fangs to him.

Continued

1 My neighbor's dog 2 there's

3 the dog's constant barking . . . can't

5 my landlord's fence 7 I've

8 there's . . . the dog's behavior

9 that's . . . doesn't

Part B: Creating Sentences

Working with a partner, write sentences that use apostrophes as directed.
Answers will vary.

1. Write a sentence describing something a friend owns. For instance, you might mention a pet or a material possession.

2. Using an apostrophe to show a contraction, write a sentence about something at school or work that you feel is wrong and needs to be changed.

3. Write a sentence that correctly uses the word *teachers*. Then write a second sentence that correctly uses the word *teacher's*.

Reflective Activity

Answers will vary.

1. Look at the paragraph about the dog that you revised above. How has adding apostrophes affected the paragraph?
2. Explain what it is about apostrophes that you find most difficult to remember and apply. Use an example to make your point clear.

Review Test 1

In each sentence, cross out the two words that need apostrophes. Then write the words correctly in the spaces provided.

1. That ~~authors~~ latest horror novel ~~isnt~~ so horrifying.
   author's ___ isn't ___
2. "I ~~dont~~ get it," I confessed after hearing ~~Pams~~ long, complicated joke.
   don't ___ Pam's ___
3. Luckily, the ~~motorcycles~~ gas tank ~~hadnt~~ been scratched in the collision.
   motorcycle's ___ hadn't ___
4. ~~Whos~~ been stealing the Sunday papers from my doorstep before ~~Im~~ awake?
   Who's ___ I'm ___
5. ~~Nadias~~ aunts never start the day without asking an ~~astrologers~~ advice.
   Nadia's ___ astrologer's ___
6. I too would like to take a shower, if ~~theres~~ any water left by the time ~~youre~~ finished.
   there's ___ you're ___
7. Olivia watched sadly as the highway ~~departments~~ bulldozer demolished the house ~~shed~~ grown up in.
   department's ___ she'd ___
8. Sylvia ~~wasnt~~ on time for her first day of work because her ~~mothers~~ car broke down on the highway.
   wasn't ___ mother's ___
9. ~~Ive~~ heard that electric "bug zappers" ~~dont~~ kill more than a few mosquitoes and do kill many beneficial insects.
   I've ___ don't ___
10. The ~~authorities~~ guess is that a radical protest group put the toxic chemical in the ~~towns~~ water supply.
    authorities' ___ town's ___

Review Test 2

Rewrite the following sentences, changing the underlined words into either a contraction or a possessive.

1. Joe was not happy to hear the high-pitched sound of the drill of the dentist.

   wasn't . . . dentist's drill

2. The weather forecast of today assured us that it is definitely going to be sunny, cloudy, or rainy.

   Today's weather forecast . . . it's

3. The enthusiasm of my brother Manny for baseball is so great that he will even wear his glove and cap when he watches a game on TV.

   My brother Manny's enthusiasm . . . he'll

4. Many parents think the influence of television is to blame for the poor performance of their children in school.

   television's influence . . . their children's poor performance

5. I was shocked by the announcement of my friend that he was going to marry a girl he had dated for only two months.

   my friend's announcement . . . he'd

25 Quotation Marks

Introductory Activity

Read the following scene and underline all the words enclosed within quotation marks. Your instructor may also have you dramatize the scene with one person reading the narration and three persons acting the speaking parts—Clyde, Charlotte, and Sam. The two speakers should imagine the scene as part of a stage play and try to make their words seem as real and true-to-life as possible.

At a party that Clyde and his wife Charlotte recently hosted, Clyde got angry at a guy named Sam who kept bothering Charlotte. "Listen, man," Clyde said, "what's this thing you have for my wife? There are lots of other women at this party."

"Relax," Sam replied. "Charlotte is very attractive, and I enjoy talking with her."

"Listen, Sam," Charlotte said. "I've already told you three times that I don't want to talk to you anymore. Please leave me alone."

"Look, there's no law that says I can't talk to you if I want to," Sam challenged.

"Sam, I'm only going to say this once," Clyde warned. "Lay off my wife, or leave this party *now*."

Sam grinned at Clyde smugly. "You've got good liquor here. Why should I leave? Besides, I'm not done talking with Charlotte."

Clyde went to his basement and was back a minute later holding a two-by-four. "I'm giving you a choice," Clyde said. "Leave by the door or I'll slam you out the window."

Sam left by the door.

1. On the basis of the above selection, what is the purpose of quotation marks?

   Quotation marks set off the exact words of a speaker.

2. Do commas and periods that come after a quotation go inside or outside the quotation marks?

   They go inside the quotation marks.

Answers are on page 688.

The two main uses of quotation marks are as follows. Each use is explained here.

1 To set off the exact words of a speaker or writer
2 To set off the titles of short works

Quotation Marks to Set Off the Words of a Speaker or Writer

Use quotation marks when you want to show the exact words of a speaker or writer.

"Who left the cap off the toothpaste?" Lola demanded.

(Quotation marks set off the exact words that Lola spoke.)

Ben Franklin wrote, "Keep your eyes wide open before marriage, half shut afterward."

(Quotation marks set off the exact words that Ben Franklin wrote.)

"You're never too young," Aunt Fern told me, "to have a heart attack."

(Two pairs of quotation marks are used to enclose the aunt's exact words.)

Maria complained, "I look so old some days. Even makeup doesn't help. I feel as though I'm painting a corpse!"

(Note that the end quotes do not come until the end of Maria's speech. Place quotation marks before the first quoted word of a speech and after the last quoted word. As long as no interruption occurs in the speech, do not use quotation marks for each new sentence.)

Punctuation Hint In the four examples above, notice that a comma sets off the quoted part from the rest of the sentence. Also observe that commas and periods at the end of a quotation always go *inside* quotation marks.

Complete the following statements, which explain how capital letters, commas, and periods are used in quotations. Refer to the four examples as guides.

- Every quotation begins with a ___capital___ letter.
- When a quotation is split (as in the sentence about Aunt Fern), the second part does not begin with a capital letter unless it is a ___new___ sentence.

- Commas are typically used to separate the quoted part of a sentence from the rest of the sentence.
- Commas and periods that come at the end of a quotation go inside quotation marks.

The answers are *capital, new, Commas,* and *inside.*

Practice 1

Insert quotation marks where needed in the sentences that follow.

1. The chilling bumper sticker read, "You can't hug children with nuclear arms."
2. "One day we'll look back on this argument, and it will seem funny," Bruce assured Rosa.
3. "Hey, lady, this is an express line!" shouted the cashier to the woman with a full basket.
4. My grandfather was fond of saying, "Happiness is found along the way, not at the end of the road."
5. "When will I be old enough to pay the adult fare?" the child asked.
6. On his deathbed, Oscar Wilde is supposed to have said, "Either this wallpaper goes or I do."
7. The sign on my neighbor's front door reads, "Never mind the dog. Beware of owner."
8. "I'm not afraid to die," said Woody Allen. "I just don't want to be there when it happens."
9. My son once told me, "Sometimes I wish I were little again. Then I wouldn't have to make so many decisions."
10. "I don't feel like cooking tonight," Eve said to Adam. "Let's just have fruit."

Practice 2

Rewrite the following sentences, adding quotation marks where needed. Use a capital letter to begin a quotation and use a comma to set off a quoted part from the rest of the sentence.

Example I'm getting tired Sally said.
"I'm getting tired," Sally said.

1. Simon said take three giant steps forward.
Simon said, "Take three giant steps forward."

2. Please don't hang up before leaving a message stated the telephone recording.
"Please don't hang up before leaving a message," stated the telephone recording.

3. Clark Kent asked a man on the street where is the nearest phone booth?
Clark Kent asked a man on the street, "Where is the nearest phone booth?"

4. You dirtied every pan in the kitchen just to scramble some eggs Rico said in disgust.
"You dirtied every pan in the kitchen just to scramble some eggs," Rico said in disgust.

5. Nothing can be done for your broken little toe, the doctor said. You have to wait for it to heal.
"Nothing can be done for your broken little toe," the doctor said. "You have to wait for it to heal."

Practice 3

Answers will vary.

1. Write three quotations that appear in the first part of a sentence.

   Example "Let's go shopping," I suggested.

   a. ______

   b. ______

   c. ______

2. Write three quotations that appear at the end of a sentence.

   Example Bob asked, "Have you had lunch yet?"

   a. ______

   b. ______

   c. ______

3. Write three quotations that appear at the beginning and end of a sentence.

   Example "If the bus doesn't come soon," Mary said, "we'll freeze."

   a. ______

   b. ______

   c. ______

Indirect Quotations

An indirect quotation is a rewording of someone else's comments rather than a word-for-word direct quotation. The word *that* often signals an indirect quotation.

Direct Quotation	*Indirect Quotation*
George said, "My son is a daredevil." (George's exact spoken words are given, so quotation marks are used.)	George said that his son is a daredevil. (We learn George's words indirectly, so no quotation marks are used.)
Carol's note to Arnie read, "I'm at the neighbors'. Give me a call." (The exact words that Carol wrote in the note are given, so quotation marks are used.)	Carol left a note for Arnie saying that she would be at the neighbors' and he should give her a call. (We learn Carol's words indirectly, so no quotation marks are used.)

Practice 1

Rewrite the following sentences, changing words as necessary to convert the sentences into direct quotations. The first one is done for you as an example.

1. Agnes told me as we left work that Herb got a raise.
   Agnes said to me as we left work, "Herb got a raise."
2. I said that it was hard to believe, since Herb is a do-nothing.
   I said, "That's hard to believe, since Herb is a do-nothing."
3. Agnes replied that even so, he's gone up in the world.
   Agnes replied, "Even so, he's gone up in the world."
4. I told her that she must be kidding.
   I told her, "You must be kidding."
5. Agnes laughed and said that Herb was moved from the first to the fourth floor today.
   Agnes laughed and said, "Herb was moved from the first to the fourth floor today."

Practice 2

Rewrite the following sentences, converting each direct quotation into an indirect statement. In each case you will have to add the word *that* or *if* and change other words as well.

Example The barber asked Fred, "Have you noticed how your hair is thinning?"
The barber asked Fred if he had noticed how his hair was thinning.

1. My doctor said, "You need to lose weight."
My doctor said that I need to lose weight.

2. Lola asked Tony, "Don't you ever wash your car?"
Lola asked Tony if he ever washes his car.

3. The operator asked, "Have you tried to look up the number yourself?"
The operator asked if I had tried to look up the number myself.

4. Jane whispered, "Harold's so boring he lights up a room when he leaves it."
Janie whispered that Harold's so boring he lights up a room when he leaves it.

5. The instructor said, "Movies are actually a series of still pictures."
The instructor said that movies are actually a series of still pictures.

Quotation Marks to Set Off the Titles of Short Works

Titles of short works are usually set off by quotation marks, while titles of long works are underlined. Use quotation marks to set off the titles of short works such as articles in books, newspapers, or magazines; chapters in a book; and short stories, poems, and songs. On the other hand, you should underline the titles of books, newspapers, magazines, plays, movies, music albums, and television shows. See the following examples.

Quotation Marks	*Underlines*
the article "The Toxic Tragedy"	in the book Who's Poisoning America
the article "New Cures for Headaches"	in the newspaper the New York Times
the article "When the Patient Plays Doctor"	in the magazine Family Health
the chapter "Connecting with Kids"	in the book Straight Talk
the story "The Dead"	in the book Dubliners
the poem "Birches"	in the book The Complete Poems of Robert Frost
the song "Some Enchanted Evening"	in the album South Pacific
	the television show Friends
	the movie Rear Window

Note In printed form, the titles of long works are set off by italics—slanted type that looks *like this.*

Practice

Use quotation marks or underlines as needed.

1. My sister just bought a VCR so she won't have to miss any more episodes of General Hospital.
2. Rita grabbed the National Enquirer and eagerly began to read the article "I Had a Space Alien's Baby."
3. Our exam will cover two chapters, "The Study of Heredity" and "The Origin of Diversity," in our biology textbook, Life.
4. The last song on the bluegrass program was called "I Ain't Broke but I'm Badly Bent."
5. A short story like Edgar Allan Poe's "The Pit and the Pendulum" is more exciting to me than a full-length action film like Armageddon.
6. At last night's performance of Annie Get Your Gun, the audience joined the cast in singing "There's No Business Like Show Business."
7. A typical article in Cosmopolitan will have a title like "How to Hook a Man without Letting Him Know You're Fishing."

8. One way Joanne deals with depression is to get out her Man of La Mancha album and play the song"The Impossible Dream."
9. I read the article"How Good Is Your Breakfast?"in Consumer Reports while munching a doughnut this morning.
10. According to a Psychology Today article titled"Home on the Street,"there are 36,000 people living on New York City's sidewalks.

Other Uses of Quotation Marks

Here are two more uses of quotation marks.

1 To set off special words or phrases from the rest of a sentence (when italic is not used for this purpose):

> Many people spell the words "all right" as one word, "alright," instead of correctly spelling them as two words.
>
> I have trouble telling the difference between "principal" and "principle."

2 To mark off a quotation within a quotation. For this purpose, single quotation marks (' ') are used:

> Ben Franklin said, "The noblest question in the world is, 'What good may I do in it?'"
>
> "If you want to have a scary experience," Nick told Fran, "read Stephen King's story 'The Mangler' in his book *Night Shift.*"

Collaborative Activity

Part A: Editing and Rewriting

Working with a partner, read the short paragraph below and circle the places where quotation marks are needed. Then use the space provided to rewrite the paragraph, adding quotation marks where needed. Feel free to discuss the rewrite quietly with your partner and refer back to the chapter when necessary.

Continued

[1]Harry and his friend Susan got stuck in an elevator. [2]Another man was stuck with them. [3]Harry turned to Susan and asked, Has this ever happened to you before?

[4]Once, she said. [5]About ten years ago in a department store. [6]We weren't stuck long.

[7]Harry took a deep breath. [8]We're lucky only three of us are here. [9]I don't like being closed up in small places, especially crowded ones.

[10]Then the other man asked, Is there a phone or something here so we can talk to somebody?

[11]Susan looked around and noticed a small panel in the corner of the elevator. [12]A sign just over the panel read Open in Case of Emergency.

[13]I think it might be in there, she said, pointing to the sign.

[14]The man opened the panel, found a telephone, and dialed the security number written nearby. [15]Can anyone hear me? he asked.

[16]A voice on the phone said, Yes, and we know you're stuck. [17]Just wait a few minutes.

[18]When Harry heard that people knew about their problem, he let out a sigh. [19]I sure hope they can fix this quickly, he said softly, wringing his hands.

[20]Susan put her arm around him and smiled. [21]Don't worry. [22]We'll be out of here in no time.

3 . . . asked, "Has . . . before?" 4 "Once," she said.

5-6 "About . . . long." 8-9 "We're . . . ones."

10 asked, "Is . . . somebody?" 12 read, "Open . . . Emergency."

13 "I . . . there," she said, pointing to the sign.

15 "Can anyone hear me?" he asked. 16-17 "Yes, . . . minutes."

19 "I . . . quickly," he said softly, wringing his hands.

21–22 "Don't . . . time."

Continued

Part B: Creating Sentences

Working with a partner, write sentences that use quotation marks as directed.

Answers will vary.

1. Write a sentence in which you quote a favorite expression of someone you know. Identify the person's relationship to you.

   Example My brother Sam often says after a meal, "That wasn't bad at all."

   ____

   ____

2. Write a quotation that contains the words *Tony asked Lola*. Write a second quotation that includes the words *Lola replied*.

   ____

   ____

3. Write a sentence that interests or amuses you from a book, magazine, or newspaper. Identify the title and author of the book, magazine, or newspaper article.

   Example In her book At Wit's End, Emma Bombeck advises, "Never go to a doctor whose office plants have died."

   ____

   ____

Reflective Activity

Answers will vary.

1. Look at the paragraph about the elevator that you revised above. Explain how adding quotation marks has affected the paragraph.
2. What would writing be like without quotation marks? Explain, using an example, how quotation marks are important to understanding writing.
3. Explain what it is about quotation marks that is most difficult for you to remember and apply. Use an example to make your point clear. Feel free to refer back to anything in this chapter.

■ Review Test 1

Place quotation marks around the exact words of a speaker or writer in the sentences that follow.

1. "Give me a break!" Charlie shouted to no one in particular.
2. My mother always says, "Some are wise, and some are otherwise."
3. "Why do men continue to wear ties when they serve no purpose?" asked Paul.
4. "Take all you want, but eat all you take," read the sign in the cafeteria.
5. One of Mark Twain's famous lines is, "Man is the only animal that blushes—or needs to."
6. "My friend the radio announcer loses his voice every time we drive under a bridge," said the comedian.
7. The first time my daughter had a headache, she told me, "Mommy, I have a pain in my brain."
8. "If your parachute doesn't open," the skydiving instructor joked, "bring it back, and we'll give you a new one."
9. The novelist ended a letter to his brother by saying, "I'm sorry for writing such a long letter. I didn't have time for a shorter one."
10. "I don't apologize for my weight," said the comedian Roseanne Barr. "An important woman should take up some room."

■ Review Test 2

Place quotations around the exact words of a speaker in the sentences that follow. Three of the sentences contain indirect quotations and do not require quotation marks.

Example: Soon after moving into their new house, Mike said to Marian, "Why don't we have a party? It'd be a good way to meet all our neighbors."

1. "Nice idea," said Marian, "but way too much work."
2. "It won't be that bad. We'll grill hamburgers and ask everybody to bring a side dish," Mike answered.
3. Marian said that she would agree to the idea if Mike called all the guests.
4. "Hi, this is Mike Josephs, your new neighbor in 44B," Mike said each time he called someone.
5. Afterward he told Marian that everything was under control.
6. "I told them we'd provide burgers and plenty of drinks," Mike explained, "and they'll bring everything else."

7. When the party started, the first guests arrived saying,"We brought potato salad—we hope that's all right!"
8. Then guests number two, three, and four arrived, also announcing that they had brought potato salad.
9. As the sixth bowl of potato salad arrived, Mike mumbled to Marian,"Maybe I should have made some more suggestions about what people should bring."
10. "Oh, well, I really love potato salad,"Marian said.

■ Review Test 3

Answers will vary.

Go through the comics section of a newspaper to find a comic strip that amuses you. Be sure to choose a strip where two or more characters are speaking to each other. Write a full description that will enable people who have not read the comic strip to visualize it clearly and appreciate its humor. Describe the setting and action in each panel and enclose the words of the speakers in quotation marks.

26 Comma

Introductory Activity

Commas often (though not always) signal a minor break or pause in a sentence. Each of the six pairs of sentences below illustrates one of six main uses of the comma. Read each pair of sentences aloud and place a comma wherever you feel a slight pause occurs. Then choose the rule that applies from the box at the bottom of the page, and write its letter on the line provided.

_a_ 1. You can use a credit card, write out a check, or provide cash.
The old house was infested with red ants, roaches, and mice.

_b_ 2. To start the car, depress the accelerator and turn the ignition key.
Before you go hiking, buy a comfortable pair of shoes.

_c_ 3. Leeches, creatures which suck human blood, are valuable to medical science.
George Derek, who was just arrested, was a classmate of mine.

_d_ 4. Our professor said the exam would be easy, but I thought it was difficult.
Wind howled through the trees, and rain pounded against the window.

_e_ 5. Emily asked, "Why is it so hard to remember your dreams the next day?"
"I am so tired after work," Lily said, "that I fall asleep right away."

_f_ 6. Bert has driven 1,500,000 accident-free miles in his job as a trucker.
The Gates Trucking Company of Newark, New Jersey, gave Bert an award on August 26, 2000, for his superior safety record.

- a. separate items in a list
- b. separate introductory material from the sentence
- c. separate words that interrupt the sentence
- d. separate complete thoughts in a sentence
- e. separate direct quotations from the rest of the sentence
- f. separate numbers, addresses, and dates in everyday writing

Answers are on page 689.

Six Main Uses of the Comma

Commas are used mainly as follows:

1 To separate items in a series
2 To set off introductory material
3 On both sides of words that interrupt the flow of thought in a sentence
4 Between two complete thoughts connected by *and, but, for, or, nor, so, yet*
5 To set off a direct quotation from the rest of a sentence
6 For certain everyday material

You may find it helpful to remember that the comma often marks a slight pause, or break, in a sentence. These pauses or breaks occur at the points where the six main comma rules apply. Sentence examples for each of the comma rules are given on the following pages; read these sentences aloud and listen for the minor pauses or breaks that are signaled by commas.

However, you should keep in mind that commas are far more often overused than underused. As a general rule, you should *not* use a comma unless a given comma rule applies or unless a comma is otherwise needed to help a sentence read clearly. A good rule of thumb is that "when in doubt" about whether to use a comma, it is often best to "leave it out."

After reviewing each of the comma rules that follow, you will practice adding commas that are needed and omitting commas that are not needed.

1 Comma between Items in a Series

Use a comma to separate items in a series.

Magazines, paperback novels, and textbooks crowded the shelves.

Hard-luck Sam needs a loan, a good-paying job, and a close friend.

Pat sat in the doctor's office, checked her watch, and flipped nervously through a magazine.

Lola bit into the ripe, juicy apple.

More and more people entered the crowded, noisy stadium.

Note A comma is used between two descriptive words in a series only if *and* inserted between the words sounds natural. You could say:

Lola bit into the ripe *and* juicy apple.

More and more people entered the crowded *and* noisy stadium.

But notice in the following sentences that the descriptive words do not sound natural when *and* is inserted between them. In such cases, no comma is used.

> The model wore a light sleeveless blouse. ("A light *and* sleeveless blouse" doesn't sound right, so no comma is used.)
>
> Dr. Van Helsing noticed two tiny puncture marks on the patient's neck. ("Two *and* tiny puncture marks" doesn't sound right, so no comma is used.)

Practice 1

Place commas between items in a series.

1. Many of the refugees wandered around without work food or a place to live.
2. Ice cream crushed candy Pepsi and popcorn formed a glue-like compound on the movie theater's floor.
3. We finally drove across the Arizona–New Mexico border after eight hours four hundred miles and three rest stops.

Practice 2

For each item, cross out the one comma that is not needed. Add the one comma that is needed between items in a series.

1. I discovered gum wrappers, pennies and a sock hidden, under the seats when I vacuumed my car.
2. Squirrels Canada geese, two white swans, and clouds of mosquitoes, populate Farwell Park.
3. Lewis dribbled twice, spun to his left and lofted his patented hook shot over the outstretched arms, of the Panthers' center.

2 Comma after Introductory Material

Use a comma to set off introductory material.

> Fearlessly, Lola picked up the slimy slug.
>
> Just to annoy Tony, she let it crawl along her arm.
>
> Although I have a black belt in karate, I decided to go easy on the demented bully who had kicked sand in my face.
>
> Mumbling under her breath, the woman picked over the tomatoes.

Note If the introductory material is brief, the comma is sometimes omitted. In the activities here, you should include the comma.

Practice 1

Place commas after introductory material.

1. When all is said and done, a lot more is said than done.
2. If you mark your suitcase with colored tape, it will be easier to find at the baggage counter.
3. Feeling brave and silly at the same time, Anita volunteered to go onstage and help the magician.

Practice 2

For each item, cross out the one comma that is not needed. Add the one comma that is needed after introductory material.

1. Using metallic cords from her Christmas presents, young Ali made several bracelets for herself. After that, she took a long ribbon$_{x}$ and tied a bow around her dog's head.
2. As the bride smiled and strolled past me down the aisle, I saw a bead of sweat roll$_{x}$ from her forehead down her cheek. Remembering my own wedding, I knew she wasn't sweating from the heat.
3. When my children were young, I wrote interesting anecdotes about them in a notebook. For example, I wrote a note to remind me$_{x}$ that my son once wanted to be a yo-yo maker.

3 Comma around Words Interrupting the Flow of Thought

Use a comma before and after words that interrupt the flow of thought in a sentence.

> The car, cleaned and repaired, is ready to be sold.
>
> Martha, our new neighbor, used to work as a bouncer at Rexy's Tavern.
>
> Taking long walks, especially after dark, helps me sort out my thoughts.

Usually you can "hear" words that interrupt the flow of thought in a sentence. However, when you are not sure if certain words are interrupters, remove them from the sentence. If it still makes sense without the words, you know that the words are interrupters and that the information they give is nonessential. Such nonessential information is set off with commas. In the following sentence,

> Susie Hall, who is my best friend, won a new car in the *Reader's Digest* sweepstakes.

the words *who is my best friend* are extra information, not needed to identify the subject of the sentence, *Susie Hall.* Put commas around such nonessential information. On the other hand, in the sentence

> The woman who is my best friend won a new car in the *Reader's Digest* sweepstakes.

The words *who is my best friend* supply essential information that we need to identify the woman. If the words were removed from the sentence, we would no longer know which woman won the sweepstakes. Commas are not used around such essential information.

Here is another example:

> *The Shining,* a novel by Stephen King, is the scariest book I've ever read.

Here the words *a novel by Stephen King* are extra information, not needed to identify the subject of the sentence, *The Shining.* Commas go around such nonessential information. On the other hand, in the sentence

> Stephen King's novel *The Shining* is the scariest book I've ever read.

the words *The Shining* are needed to identify the novel. Commas are not used around such essential information.

Most of the time you will be able to "hear" words that interrupt the flow of thought in a sentence and will not have to think about whether the words are essential or nonessential.*

Practice 1

Add commas to set off interrupting words.

1. The dancer, aided by members of the chorus, hobbled across the stage toward the wings.
2. Mr. and Mrs. Anderson, who were married on the Fourth of July, named their first child "Freedom."
3. The repairman, unaware of the grease on his shoes, left a black trail from our front door to the washing machine.

*Some instructors refer to nonessential or extra information that is set off by commas as a *nonrestrictive clause.* Essential information that interrupts the flow of thought is called a *restrictive clause.* No commas are used to set off a restrictive clause.

Practice 2

For each item, cross out the one comma that is not needed. Add the comma that is needed to complete the setting off of interrupting words.

1. All trees, even the most gigantic, are only 1 percent living tissue; the rest is deadwood.
2. The city council, in a rare fit of wisdom, established a series of bicycle paths around town.
3. John Adams and Thomas Jefferson, the second and third presidents of the United States, died on the same day in 1826.
4. My aunt, a talkative woman, married a patient man who is a wonderful listener.

4 Comma between Complete Thoughts Connected by a Joining Word

Use a comma between two complete thoughts connected by *and, but, for, or, nor, so, yet.*

My parents threatened to throw me out of the house, so I had to stop playing the drums.

The polyester bedsheets had a gorgeous design, but they didn't feel as comfortable as plain cotton sheets.

The teenage girls walked along the hot summer streets, and the teenage boys drove by in their shined-up cars.

Notes

a The comma is optional when the complete thoughts are short:

Hal relaxed but Bob kept working.

The soda was flat so I poured it away.

We left school early for the furnace had broken down.

b Be careful not to use a comma in sentences having *one* subject and a *double* verb. The comma is used only in sentences made up of two complete thoughts (two subjects and two verbs). In the sentence

Mary lay awake that stormy night and listened to the thunder crashing.

there is only one subject (*Mary*) and a double verb (*lay* and *listened*). No comma is needed. Likewise, the sentence

The quarterback kept the ball and plunged across the goal line for a touchdown.

has only one subject (*quarterback)* and a double verb (*kept* and *plunged*); therefore, no comma is needed.

Practice

Place a comma before a joining word that connects two complete thoughts (two subjects and two verbs). Remember, do *not* place a comma within sentences that have only one subject and a double verb. Mark sentences that are correct with a *C*.

1. The apartment Kate looked at was clean and spacious, but the rent was too expensive for her budget.
2. Our power went out during the thunderstorm, so we decided to eat dinner by candlelight.
3. C Eddie is building a kayak in his garage and plans to take it down the Columbia River next year.
4. I desperately need more storage space, for I can't seem to throw anything away.
5. C The helicopter hovered overhead and lowered a rescue line to the downed pilot.
6. Travis was going to quit his job at the supermarket, but he changed his mind after getting a raise.
7. C One of the men got ready to leave work at four but put his coat away upon seeing his boss.
8. The family expected Valerie to go to college, but she went to work after eloping with her boyfriend.
9. Bobby pleaded with his parents to buy him a personal computer for his schoolwork, but he spends most of his time playing games on it.
10. C The doctor examined me for less than ten minutes and then presented me with a bill for ninety dollars.

5 Comma with Direct Quotations

Use a comma to set off a direct quotation from the rest of a sentence.

"Please take a number," said the deli clerk.

Fred told Martha, "I've just signed up for a course on web-page design."

"Those who sling mud," a famous politician once said, "usually lose ground."

"Reading this book," complained Stan, "is about as interesting as watching paint dry."

Note Commas and periods at the end of a quotation go inside quotation marks. See also page 308.

Practice 1

In each sentence, add the one or more commas needed to set off the quoted material.

1. The five-year-old boy said, "Mommy, I have a bad headache in my tummy."
2. "The best way to get rid of a temptation," Oscar Wilde advised, "is to yield to it."
3. "The movie will scare the whole family," wrote the reviewer.

Practice 2

In each item, cross out the one comma that is not needed to set off a quotation. Add the comma that is needed to set off a quotation from the rest of the sentence.

1. "If you're smoking a cigarette," read the poster in the chemistry lab, "you shouldn't be in this room."
2. "Your arms look fine," said the swimming instructor, "but you keep forgetting to kick."
3. "Did you really think," the judge asked the defendant, "you could kill both your parents and then ask for mercy because you're an orphan?"

6 Comma with Everyday Material

Use a comma with certain everyday material, as shown in the following sections.

Persons Spoken To

I think, Sally, that you should go to bed.

Please turn down the stereo, Mark.

Please, sir, can you spare a dollar?

Dates

Our house was burglarized on June 28, 2000, and two weeks later on July 11, 2000.

Addresses

Lola's sister lives at 342 Red Oak Drive, Los Angeles, California 90057.
She is moving to Manchester, Vermont, after her divorce.

Note No comma is used before a zip code.

Openings and Closings of Letters

Dear Marilyn,	Sincerely,
Dear John,	Truly yours,

Note In formal letters, a colon is used after the opening:

Dear Sir:
Dear Madam:

Numbers

Government officials estimate that Americans spend about 785,000,000 hours a year filling out federal forms.

Practice

Place commas where needed.

1. Excuse me, madam, but your scarf is in my soup.
2. Before age eighteen the average child spends 6,000 hours in school and 15,000 hours watching television.
3. The famous ocean liner *Titanic* sank in the Atlantic Ocean on April 15, 1912.
4. Dear Teresa,

   What do you think of this psychology lecture? Will you meet me for lunch after class? I'll treat. Pass me your answer right away.

   Love,
   Jeff
5. The zoo in Washington, D.C., purchases 50,000 pounds of meat; 6,500 loaves of bread; 114,000 live crickets; and other foods for its animals each year.

Unnecessary Use of Commas

Remember that if no clear rule applies for using a comma, it is usually better not to use a comma. As stated earlier, "When in doubt, leave it out." Following are some typical examples of unnecessary commas.

Incorrect

Sharon told me, that my socks were different colors.

(A comma is not used before *that* unless the flow of thought is interrupted.)

The union negotiations, dragged on for three days.

(Do not use a comma between a simple subject and verb.)

I waxed all the furniture, and cleaned the windows.

(Use a comma before *and* only with more than two items in a series or when *and* joins two complete thoughts.)

Sharon carried, the baby into the house.

(Do not use a comma between a verb and its object.)

I had a clear view, of the entire robbery.

(Do not use a comma before a prepositional phrase.)

Practice

Cross out commas that do not belong. Some commas are correct. Do not add any commas.

1. We grew a pumpkin last year,$_x$ that weighed over one hundred pounds.
2. Anyone with a failing grade,$_x$ must report to the principal.
3. Last weekend a grizzly bear attacked a hiker,$_x$ who got too close to its cubs.
4. After watching my form,$_x$ on the high diving board, Mr. Riley, my instructor, asked me if I had insurance.
5. Rosa flew first to Los Angeles, and then she went to visit her parents,$_x$ in Mexico City.
6. The tall, thin man who bought the red socks,$_x$ is a nightclub comedian.
7. Onions, radishes, and potatoes,$_x$ seem to grow better in cooler climates.
8. Whenever Vincent is in Las Vegas, you can find him at the blackjack table,$_x$ or the roulette wheel.

9. While I watched in disbelief, my car rolled down the hill and through the front window of a Chinese restaurant.
10. The question, sir, is not whether you committed the crime but when you committed the crime.

Collaborative Activity

Part A: Editing and Rewriting

Working with a partner, read carefully the short paragraph below and cross out the five misplaced commas. Then insert the ten additional commas needed. Feel free to discuss the rewrite quietly with your partner and refer back to the chapter when necessary.

Dear Teresa,

On Tuesday, May 1, 2000, my husband and I were unable to sleep because of the loud music coming from your apartment. When I first heard the music, I didn't say anything to you because it was still early. But the music, along with loud laughter and talking, continued until around four o'clock in the morning. At midnight, my husband went into the hallway to see what was happening, and he ran into one of your guests. The man, who seemed very drunk, stared at him and said, "Go back to bed, old man." The next morning, we found beer cans, pizza boxes, and cigarette butts piled outside our door. This is unacceptable. We have written this letter to you as a warning. The next time something like this happens, we will call the police and the building manager. We don't want to cause trouble with you, but we will not tolerate another incident like what happened that night.

Sincerely,

Rose Connelly

Continued

Part B: Creating Sentences

Working with a partner, write sentences that use commas as directed.

Answers will vary.

1. Write a sentence mentioning three items you want to get the next time you go to the store.

____

____

2. Write two sentences describing how you relax after getting home from school or work. Start the first sentence with *After* or *When*. Start the second sentence with *Next*.

____

____

3. Write a sentence that tells something about your favorite movie, book, television show, or song. Use the words *which is my favorite movie* (or *book, television show,* or *song*) after the name of the movie, book, television show, or song.

____

____

4. Write two complete thoughts about a person you know. The first thought should mention something that you like about the person. The second thought should mention something you don't like. Join the two thoughts with *but*.

____

____

5. Invent a line that Lola might say to Tony. Use the words *Lola said* in the sentence. Then include Tony's reply, using the words *Tony responded.*

____

____

6. Write a sentence about an important event in your life. Include the day, month, and year of the event.

____

____

Reflective Activity

Answers will vary.

1. Look at the letter that you revised above. Explain how adding commas has affected the paragraph.
2. What would writing be like without the comma? How do commas help writing?
3. What is the most difficult comma rule for you to remember and apply? Explain, giving an example.

Review Test 1

Insert commas where needed. In the space provided under each sentence, summarize briefly the rule that explains the use of the comma or commas.

1. As the usher turned his head, two youngsters darted into the movie theater.
   Comma after introductory material
2. My boss, it is rumored, is about to be fired.
   Set off words interrupting the flow of thought
3. I found my father's dusty, water-stained yearbook behind some pipes in the basement.
   Separate items in a series
4. "Be careful what you wish for," an old saying goes, "or you may get it."
   Set off a direct quotation
5. My final mortgage payment on December 3, 2011, seems light-years away.
   Set off everyday material
6. We sat together on the riverbank, watched the sun disappear, and made plans for our divorce.
   Separate items in a series
7. I panicked when I saw the flashing red lights behind me, but the policeman just wanted to pass.
   Separate two complete thoughts
8. The burly umpire, his shoes and trousers now covered with dirt, pulled off his mask and angrily ejected the St. Louis manager from the game.
   Set off words interrupting the flow of thought

9. "Knock off the noise," Sam yelled to the children. "I'm talking long distance to your grandmother."

   Set off a direct quotation

10. Rubbing her eyes and clearing her throat, Stella tried to sound human as she answered the early-morning call.

    After introductory material

Review Test 2

Insert commas where needed. One sentence does not need commas.

1. Some people believe that television can be addictive, but I think they're wrong.
2. While there are people who turn on their sets upon waking up in the morning, I don't do that.
3. I turn on my set only upon sitting down for breakfast, and then I watch the *Today* show with Katie Couric and Matt Lauer.
4. I don't need to watch game shows, soap operas, and situation comedies to get through the day.
5. Instead, I watch all these programs simply because I enjoy them.
6. I also keep the television turned on all evening because, thanks to cable, there is always something decent to watch.
7. If I did not have good viewing choices, I would flick the set off without hesitation.
8. C Lots of people switch channels rapidly to preview what is on.
9. I, on the other hand, turn immediately to the channel I know I want.
10. In other words, I am not addicted; I am a selective viewer who just happens to select a lot of shows.

Review Test 3

Answers will vary.

On separate paper, write six sentences, with each sentence demonstrating one of the six main comma rules.

27 Other Punctuation Marks

Introductory Activity

Each sentence below needs one of the following punctuation marks.

; — - ( ) :

See if you can insert the correct mark in each case.

1. The following items were on my mother's grocery list: eggs, tomatoes, milk, and cereal.
2. A life-size statue of her cat adorns the living room of Diana's penthouse.
3. Sigmund Freud, the pioneer of psychoanalysis (1856–1939), was a habitual cocaine user.
4. As children, we would put pennies on the railroad track; we wanted to see what they would look like after being run over by a train.
5. The stuntwoman was battered, broken, barely breathing—but alive.

Answers are on page 690.

Colon (:)

The colon is a mark of introduction. Use the colon at the end of a complete statement to do the following:

1 Introduce a list.

My little brother has three hobbies: playing video games, racing his Hot Wheels cars all over the floor, and driving me crazy.

2 Introduce a long quotation.

Janet's paper was based on a passage from George Eliot's novel *Middlemarch:* "If we had a keen vision and feeling of all ordinary human life, it would be like hearing the grass grow and the squirrel's heart beat, and we should die of that roar which lies on the other side of silence. As it is, the quickest of us walk about well wadded with stupidity."

3 Introduce an explanation.

There are two ways to do this job: the easy way and the right way.

Two minor uses of the colon are after the opening in a formal letter (*Dear Sir or Madam:*) and between the hour and the minute in writing the time (*The bus will leave for the game at 11:45*).

Practice

Place colons where needed.

1. Roger is on a "see-food" diet:if he sees food, he eats it.
2. Brenda had some terrible problems last summer:her mother suffered a heart attack, her husband lost his job, and one of her children was arrested for shoplifting.
3. Andy Rooney wrote in one of his columns:"Doctors should never talk to ordinary people about anything but medicine. When doctors talk politics, economics, or sports, they reveal themselves to be ordinary mortals, idiots just like the rest of us. That isn't what any of us wants our doctors to be."

Semicolon (;)

The semicolon signals more of a pause than the comma alone but not quite the full pause of a period. Use a semicolon to do the following:

1 Join two complete thoughts that are not already connected by a joining word such as *and, but, for,* or *so.*

The chemistry lab blew up; Professor Thomas was fired.

I once stabbed myself with a pencil; a black mark has been under my skin ever since.

2 Join two complete thoughts that include a transitional word such as *however, otherwise, moreover, furthermore, therefore*, or *consequently.*

I cut and raked the grass; moreover, I weeded the lawn.

Sally finished typing the paper; however, she forgot to bring it to class.

Note The first two uses of the semicolon are treated in more detail on pages 124–127.

3 Separate items in a series when the items themselves contain commas.

This fall I won't have to work on Labor Day, September 7; Veterans Day, November 11; or Thanksgiving Day, November 26.

At the final Weight Watchers' meeting, prizes were awarded to Sally Johnson, for losing 20 pounds; Irving Ross, for losing 26 pounds; and Betty Mills, the champion loser, who lost 102 pounds.

Practice

Place semicolons where needed.

1. Manny worked four extra hours at his job last night; consequently, he has been like a zombie in class today.
2. We could tell it was still raining; all the puddles looked as if they were being shot at.
3. My grocery shopping has to take into account my daughter, who's a vegetarian; my mother, who is diabetic; and my husband, who wants meat at every meal.

Dash (—)

A dash signals a degree of pause longer than a comma but not as complete as a period. Use the dash to set off words for dramatic effect.

> I suggest—no, I insist—that you stay for dinner.
>
> The prisoner walked toward the electric chair—grinning.
>
> A meaningful job, a loving wife, and a car that wouldn't break down all the time—these are the things he wanted in life.

Practice

Place dashes where needed.

1. The members of the Polar Bear Club marched into the icy sea shivering.
2. The actress's wedding her third in three years included a dozen bridesmaids and a flock of white doves.
3. My sociology class meets at the worst possible time eight o'clock on Monday morning.

Hyphen (-)

Use a hyphen in the following ways:

1 With two or more words that act as a single unit describing a noun.

> The society ladies nibbled at the deep-fried grasshoppers.
>
> A white-gloved waiter then put some snails on their table.
>
> Your dictionary will often help when you are unsure about whether to use a hyphen between words.

2 To divide a word at the end of a line of writing or typing.

> Although it had begun to drizzle, the teams decided to play the champion-ship game that day.

Notes

a Divide a word only between syllables. Use your dictionary (see page 339) to be sure of correct syllable divisions.

b Do not divide words of one syllable.

c Do not divide a word if you can avoid dividing it.

Practice

Place hyphens where needed.

1. Why do I always find myself behind a slow-moving car when I'm in a no-passing zone?
2. To convince herself that she was still on a diet, Paula ordered a sugar-free cola with her double-cheese pizza.
3. Twirling his mustache, the hard-hearted villain chuckled as he tied the teary-eyed heroine to the railroad tracks.

Parentheses ( )

Use parentheses to do the following:

1 Set off extra or incidental information from the rest of a sentence.

> The chapter on drugs in our textbook (pages 234–271) contains some frightening statistics.
>
> The normal body temperature of a cat (101° to 102°) is 3° higher than the temperature of its owner.

2 Enclose letters or numbers that signal items in a series.

> Three steps to follow in previewing a textbook are to (1) study the title, (2) read the first and last paragraphs, and (3) study the headings and subheadings.

> **Note** Do not use parentheses too often in your writing.

Practice

Add parentheses where needed.

1. Only a minority of Americans (22 percent) can remember what life was like before television.
2. That instructor's office hours (3 to 4 P.M.) are impossible for any student with an afternoon job.
3. Since I am forgetful, I often (1) make a list and then (2) check off items I have done. Now where did I put my list?

Review Test 1

At the appropriate spot or spots, insert the punctuation mark shown in the margin.

Example ; The singles dance was a success; I met several people I wanted to see again.

: 1. That catalog lists some unusual items: a sausage stuffer, an electric foot warmer, and a remote-control car starter.

— 2. My brother's jokes—none of which I can repeat—are unfunny and tasteless.

- 3. These days, many two-career couples have decided not to have children.

( ) 4. The section on space travel in my daughter's science book (Chapters 10–11) is sadly out of date.

: 5. Anne Frank wrote in her diary: "It's a wonder I haven't abandoned all my ideals; they seem so absurd and impractical. Yet I cling to them because I still believe, in spite of everything, that people are truly good at heart."

; 6. The frightened hamster darted from room to room; finally, it crawled under a dresser.

— 7. Credit card bills, the mortgage payment, and car repairs—no wonder my paycheck doesn't last till the end of the month.

- 8. Someone once defined a self-confident person as one who does crossword puzzles in pen instead of pencil.

( ) 9. Three ways to save money on home repairs are (1) get several estimates, (2) avoid costly designer products, and (3) do it yourself.

; 10. I ordered several items from Sears: two suitcases, one maroon and one blue; an extra-large, machine-washable sweater; and a canvas gym bag.

Review Test 2

Answers will vary.

On separate paper, write two sentences using each of the following punctuation marks: colon, semicolon, dash, hyphen, parentheses.

28 Dictionary Use

Introductory Activity

The dictionary is an indispensable tool, as will be apparent if you try to answer the following questions *without* using the dictionary.

1. Which one of the following words is spelled incorrectly?

   fortuitous
   fortutious   macrobiotics   stratagem

2. If you wanted to hyphenate the following word correctly, at which points would you place the syllable divisions?

   h i/e r/o/g l y p h/i c s

3. What common word has the sound of the first *e* in the word *chameleon*? be

4. Where is the primary accent in the following word?

   o c/t o/g e/n a r/i/a n

5. What are the two separate meanings of the word *earmark*?

   (1) Identifying mark on the ear of a domestic animal

   (2) Identifying feature or characteristic

Your dictionary is a quick and sure authority on all these matters: spelling, syllabication, pronunciation, and word meanings. And as this chapter will show, it is also a source for many other kinds of information.

Answers are on page 690.

The dictionary is a valuable tool. To take advantage of it, you need to understand the main kinds of information that a dictionary gives about a word. Look at the information provided for the word *dictate* in the following entry from the *American Heritage Dictionary*, third paperback edition.*

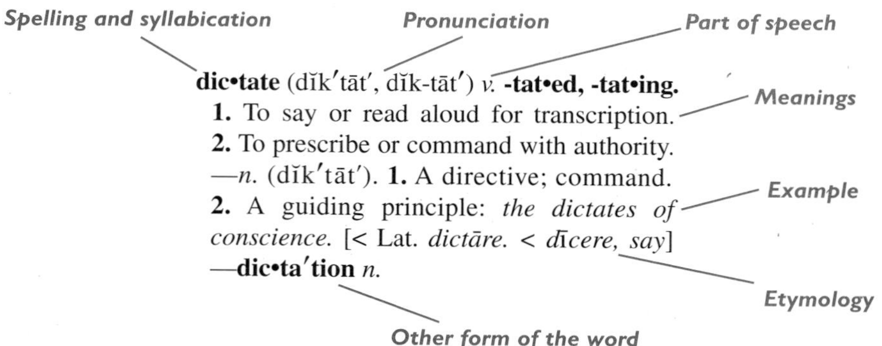

Spelling

The first bit of information, in the **boldface** (heavy type) entry itself, is the spelling of *dictate*. You probably already know the spelling of *dictate,* but if you didn't, you could find it by pronouncing the syllables in the word carefully and then looking it up in the dictionary.

Use your dictionary to correct the spelling of the following words:

wellcome welcome
quiting quitting
consentration concentration
perfessional professional
recieving receiving
aranged arranged
extremly extremely
nesasary necessary
exciteing exciting

persistant persistent
proformance performance
oppurtinity opportunity
desision decision
roomate roommate
envolvment involvement
diferance difference
catagory category
priveledge privilege

Syllabication

The second bit of information that the dictionary gives, also within the boldface entry, is the syllabication of *dic•tate*. Note that a dot separates each syllable (or part) of the word. Use your dictionary to mark the syllable divisions in the following words. Also indicate how many syllables are in each word.

v e n•t u r e	(__2__ syllables)
o b•s e s•s i o n	(__3__ syllables)
e n•e r•g e t•i c	(__4__ syllables)
i n•s p i•r a•t i o n•a l	(__5__ syllables)

Noting syllable divisions will enable you to *hyphenate* a word: divide it at the end of one line of writing and complete it at the beginning of the next line. You can correctly hyphenate a word only at a syllable division, and you may have to check your dictionary to make sure of the syllable divisions for a particular word.

Pronunciation

The third bit of information in the dictionary entry is the pronunciation of *dictate: (dik'tat')* or *(dik-tat')*. You already know how to pronounce *dictate,* but if you did not, the information within the parentheses would serve as your guide. Use your dictionary to complete the pronunciation exercises on page 343.

Vowel Sounds

You will probably use the pronunciation key in your dictionary mainly as a guide to pronouncing different vowel sounds (*vowels* are the letters *a, e, i, o,* and *u*). Here is the pronunciation key that appears on every other page of the paperback *American Heritage Dictionary:*

> ă pat ā pay â care ä father ĕ pet ē be ĭ pit ī tie î pier ŏ pot ō toe ô paw, for oi noise o͝o took o͞o boot ou out th thin *th* this ŭ cut û urge yo͞o abuse zh vision ə about, item, edible, gallop, circus

This key tells you, for example, that the short *a* is pronounced like the *a* in *pat*, the long *a* is like the *a* in *pay*, and the short *i* is like the *i* in *pit*.

Now look at the pronunciation key in your own dictionary. The key is probably located in the front of the dictionary or at the bottom of every page. What common word in the key tells you how to pronounce each of the following sounds?

Answers may vary.

ĕ	pet	ō	toe
ī	pie	ŭ	cut
ŏ	pot	o͞o	boot

(Note that a long vowel always has the sound of its own name.)

The Schwa (ə)

The symbol ə looks like an upside-down *e*. It is called a *schwa,* and it stands for the unaccented sound in such words as *about, item, edible, gallop*, and *circus*. More approximately, it stands for the sound *uh*—like the *uh* that speakers sometimes make when they hesitate. Perhaps it would help to remember that *uh,* as well as ə, could be used to represent the schwa sound.

Here are three of the many words in which the schwa sound appears*: socialize* (sō′shə līz or sō′shuh līz); *legitimate* (lə jĭt′ə mĭt or luh jĭt′uh mĭt); *oblivious* (ə blĭv′ē əs or uh blĭv′ē uhs). Open your dictionary to any page, and you will almost surely be able to find three words that make use of the schwa in the pronunciation in parentheses after the main entry. Write three such words and their pronunciations in the following spaces:

Answers will vary.

1. ____________________
2. ____________________
3. ____________________

Accent Marks

Some words contain both a primary accent, shown by a heavy stroke (′), and a secondary accent, shown by a lighter stroke (′). For example, in the word *vicissitude* (vĭ sĭs′ĭ to͞od′), the stress, or accent, goes chiefly on the second syllable (sĭs′), and, to a lesser extent, on the last syllable (to͞od′).

Use your dictionary to add stress marks to the following words:

notorious (nō tôr′ē əs)
instigate (ĭn′stĭ gāt)
equivocate (ĭ kwĭv′ə kāt)
millennium (mə lĕn′ē əm)
enterprise (ĕn′tər prīz)
irresistible (ĭr′ĭ zĭs′tə bəl)
probability (prŏb′ə bĭl′ĭ tē)
representative (rĕp′rĭ zen′tə tĭv)

Full Pronunciation

Use your dictionary to write out the full pronunciation (the information given in parentheses) for each of the following words:

1. magnate (măg′ nāt′,-nĭt)
2. semblance (sĕm′ bləns)
3. satiate (sā′ shē-āt′)
4. bastion (băs′ chən, -tē-ən)
5. celestial (sə-lĕs′ chəl)
6. extraneous (ĭk-strā′ nē-əs)
7. edifice (ĕd′ə-fĭs)
8. incipient (ĭn-sĭp′ ē-ənt)
9. fallacious (fə-lā′ shəs)
10. ostracize (ŏs′ trə-sīz′)
11. phlegmatic (flĕg-măt′ĭk)
12. proximity (prŏk-sĭm′ ĭ-tē)
13. anachronism (ə-năk′-rə-nĭz′əm)
14. felicitous (fĭ-lĭs′ĭt-əs)
15. extemporaneous (ĭk-stĕm′-pə-rā′ nē-əs)

Now practice pronouncing each word. Use the pronunciation key in your dictionary as an aid to sounding out each syllable. Do *not* try to pronounce a word all at once; instead, work on mastering *one syllable at a time.* When you can pronounce each of the syllables in a word successfully, then say them in sequence, add the accent, and pronounce the entire word.

Other Information about Words

Parts of Speech

The dictionary entry for *dictate* includes the abbreviation *v.* This indicates that the meanings of *dictate* as a verb will follow. The abbreviation *n.* is then followed by the meaning of *dictate* as a noun.

At the front of your dictionary, you will probably find a key that will explain the meanings of abbreviations used in the dictionary. Use the key to fill in the meanings of the following abbreviations:

pl. = plural
sing. = singular
adj. = adjective
adv. = adverb

Principal Parts of Irregular Verbs

Dictate is a regular verb and forms its principal parts by adding *-d, -d,* and *-ing* to the stem of the verb. When a verb is irregular, the dictionary lists its principal parts. For example, with *begin* the present tense comes first (the entry itself, *begin).* Next comes the past tense (*began*), and then the past participle (*begun*)—the form of the verb used with such helping words as *have, had*, and *was.* Then comes the present participle (*beginning*)—the *-ing* form of the word.

Look up the principal parts of the following irregular verbs and write them in the spaces provided. The first one has been done for you.

Present	*Past*	*Past Participle*	*Present Participle*
see	saw	seen	seeing
choose	chose	chosen	choosing
know	knew	known	knowing
speak	spoke	spoken	speaking

Plural Forms of Irregular Nouns

The dictionary supplies the plural forms of all irregular nouns. (Regular nouns form the plural by adding *-s* or *-es.*) Write the plurals of the following nouns:

thief	thieves
cavity	cavities
hero	heroes
thesis	theses

Note See page 352 for more information about plurals.

Meanings

When a word has more than one meaning, its meanings are numbered in the dictionary, as with the verb *dictate.* In many dictionaries, the most common meanings are presented first. The introductory pages of your dictionary will explain the order in which meanings are presented.

Use the sentence context to try to explain the meaning of the underlined word in each of the following sentences. Write your definition in the space provided. Then look up and record the dictionary meaning of the word. Be sure to select the meaning that fits the word as it is used in the sentence.

Students' own definitions may vary.

1. Honesty is a <u>cardinal</u> rule in my family.

   Your definition: ______________________________

   Dictionary definition: of foremost importance; paramount

2. The union strike put management in a <u>ticklish</u> situation.

   Your definition: ______________________________

   Dictionary definition: requiring skillful or tactful handling

3. Ben lacks confidence, probably because his parents constantly <u>railed</u> at him.

   Your definition: ______________________________

   Dictionary definition: expressed objections or criticisms in bitter, harsh, or abusive language

Etymology

Etymology refers to the history of a word. Many words have origins in foreign languages, such as Greek (abbreviated Gk in the dictionary) or Latin (L). Such information is usually enclosed in brackets and is more likely to be present in a hardbound desk dictionary than in a paperback one. A good desk dictionary will tell you, for example, that the word *cannibal* derives from the name of the man-eating tribe, the Caribs, that Christopher Columbus discovered on Cuba and Haiti.

The following are good desk dictionaries:

The American Heritage Dictionary
Random House College Dictionary
Webster's New Collegiate Dictionary
Webster's New World Dictionary

See if your dictionary says anything about the origins of the following words.

magazine from a French word meaning "storehouse"

anatomy from the Greek <u>anatomē</u>, meaning "dissection"

frankfurter after Frankfurt, Germany

Usage Labels

As a general rule, use only standard English words in your writing. If a word is not standard English, your dictionary will probably give it a usage label such as *informal, nonstandard, slang, vulgar, obsolete, archaic,* or *rare.*

Look up the following words and record how your dictionary labels them. Remember that a recent hardbound desk dictionary will always be the best source of information about usage.

Students' answers may vary.

sharp (meaning *attractive)*

informal

hard-nosed

informal

sass (meaning *to talk impudently*)

informal

ain't

nonstandard

put-down

slang

Synonyms

A *synonym* is a word that is close in meaning to another word. Using synonyms helps you avoid unnecessary repetition of the same word in a paper. A paperback dictionary is not likely to give you synonyms for words, but a good desk dictionary will. (You might also want to own a *thesaurus*, a book that lists synonyms and antonyms. An *antonym* is a word approximately opposite in meaning to another word.)

Consult a desk dictionary that gives synonyms for the following words, and write some of the synonyms in the spaces provided.

Answers may vary.

desire covet, crave, want, wish

ask question, inquire, query, interrogate, examine, quiz

cry weep, wail, whimper, sob, blubber

Review Test

Items 1–5 Use your dictionary to answer the following questions.

1. How many syllables are in the word *neurosurgery*? five
2. Where is the primary accent in the word *elevation?* el ə vā′ shən
3. In the word *evasion*, the *a* is pronounced like
   a. short *o*
   b. short *a*
   c. schwa
   d. long *a*
4. In the word *nobility,* the *y* is pronounced like
   a. schwa
   b. short *a*
   c. long *e*
   d. short *e*
5. In the word *data*, the second *a* is pronounced like
   a. short *a*
   b. schwa
   c. short *i*
   d. long *e*

Items 6–10 There are five misspelled words in the following sentence. Cross out each misspelled word and write the correct spelling in the spaces provided.

Some ~~freinds~~ and I are planning to go to the ~~libary~~ on ~~Wensday~~ to do some research for an ~~importent~~ paper for our ~~litrature~~ class.

6. friends
7. library
8. Wednesday
9. important
10. literature

29 Spelling Improvement

Introductory Activity

See if you can circle the word that is misspelled in each of the following pairs:

akward	*or*	awkward
exercise	*or*	exercize
business	*or*	buisness
worried	*or*	worryed
shamful	*or*	shameful
begining	*or*	beginning
partys	*or*	parties
sandwichs	*or*	sandwiches
heroes	*or*	heros

Answers are on page 690.

Poor spelling often results from bad habits developed in the early school years. With work, such habits can be corrected. If you can write your name without misspelling it, there is no reason why you can't do the same with almost any word in the English language. Following are seven steps you can take to improve your spelling.

Step 1: Using the Dictionary

Get into the habit of using the dictionary. When you write a paper, allow yourself time to look up the spelling of all the words you are unsure about. Do not underestimate the value of this step just because it is such a simple one. By using the dictionary, you can probably make yourself a 95 percent better speller.

Step 2: Keeping a Personal Spelling List

Keep a list of words you misspell, and study those words regularly. Use the chart on the inside front cover of this book as a starter. When you accumulate additional words, you may want to use a back page of your English notebook.

Hint When you have trouble spelling long words, try to break each word into syllables and see whether you can spell the syllables. For example, *misdemeanor* can be spelled easily if you can hear and spell in turn its four syllables: *mis-de-mean-or.* The word *formidable* can be spelled easily if you hear and spell in turn its four syllables: *for-mi-da-ble.* Remember, then: try to see, hear, and spell long words in terms of their syllables.

Step 3: Mastering Commonly Confused Words

Master the meanings and spellings of the commonly confused words on pages 365–383. Your instructor may assign twenty words for you to study at a time and give you a series of quizzes until you have mastered all the words.

Step 4: Using Electronic Aids

There are three electronic aids that may help your spelling. First, many *electronic typewriters* on the market today will beep automatically when you misspell or mistype a word. They include built-in dictionaries that will then give you the correct spelling. Smith-Corona, for example, has a series of portable typewriters with an "Auto-Spell" feature that start at around $100 at discount stores.

Second, a *computer with a spell-checker* will identify incorrect words and suggest correct spellings. If you know how to write on a computer, you will have no trouble learning how to use the spell-check feature.

Third, *electronic spell-checkers* are pocket-size devices that look much like the pocket calculator you may carry to your math class. They are the latest example of how technology can help the learning process. Electronic spellers can be found in the typewriter or computer section of any discount store, at prices in the $100 range. The checker has a tiny keyboard. You type out the word the way you think it is spelled, and the checker quickly provides you with the correct spelling of related words. Some of these checkers even *pronounce* the word aloud for you.

Step 5: Understanding Basic Spelling Rules

Explained briefly here are three rules that may improve your spelling. While exceptions sometimes occur, these rules hold true most of the time.

1 ***Change y to i.*** When a word ends in a consonant plus *y,* change *y* to *i* when you add an ending.

try + ed = tried	marry + es = marries
worry + es = worries	lazy + ness = laziness
lucky + ly = luckily	silly + est = silliest

2 ***Final silent e.*** Drop a final *e* before an ending that starts with a vowel (the vowels are *a, e, i, o,* and *u*).

hope + ing = hoping	sense + ible = sensible
fine + est = finest	hide + ing = hiding

Keep the final *e* before an ending that starts with a consonant.

use + ful = useful	care + less = careless
life + like = lifelike	settle + ment = settlement

3 ***Doubling a final consonant.*** Double the final consonant of a word when all the following are true:

a The word is one syllable or is accented on the last syllable.

b The word ends in a single consonant preceded by a single vowel.

c The ending you are adding starts with a vowel.

sob + ing = sobbing
drop + ed = dropped
admit + ing = admitting

big + est = biggest
omit + ed = omitted
begin + ing = beginning

Practice

Combine the following words and endings by applying the three rules above.

1. hurry + ed = hurried
2. admire + ing = admiring
3. deny + es = denies
4. jab + ing = jabbing
5. magnify + ed = magnified
6. commit + ed = committed
7. dive + ing = diving
8. hasty + ly = hastily
9. propel + ing = propelling
10. nudge + es = nudges

Step 6: Understanding Plurals

Most words form their plurals by adding *-s* to the singular.

Singular	*Plural*
blanket	blankets
pencil	pencils
street	streets

Some words, however, form their plurals in special ways, as shown in the rules that follow.

1 Words ending in *-s, -ss, -z, -x, -sh,* or *-ch* usually form the plural by adding *-es*.

kiss	kisses	inch	inches
box	boxes	dish	dishes

2 Words ending in a consonant plus *y* form the plural by changing *y* to *i* and adding *-es*.

party	parties	county	counties
baby	babies	city	cities

3 Some words ending in *f* change the *f* to *v* and add *-es* in the plural.

leaf	leaves	life	lives
wife	wives	yourself	yourselves

4 Some words ending in *o* form their plurals by adding *-es.*

potato	potatoes	mosquito	mosquitoes
hero	heroes	tomato	tomatoes

5 Some words of foreign origin have irregular plurals. When in doubt, check your dictionary.

antenna	antennae	crisis	crises
criterion	criteria	medium	media

6 Some words form their plurals by changing letters within the word.

man	men	foot	feet
tooth	teeth	goose	geese

7 Combined words (words made up of two or more words) form their plurals by adding *-s* to the main word.

brother-in-law	brothers-in-law
passerby	passersby

Practice

Complete these sentences by filling in the plural of the word at the left.

bus — 1. No buses are permitted on the Channel Bridge.

grocery — 2. Many of the groceries spilled out of the bags in my trunk when I braked suddenly.

potato — 3. Baked potatoes complement almost any main dish.

taxi — 4. Just after I decided to take the crowded bus, four taxis passed us on Market Street.

themself — 5. The owners of the failed curried-pizza restaurant have no one but themselves to blame.

theory — 6. The essay question asked us to describe two theories of evolution.

passerby 7. When I had a flat tire after work, several ___passersby___ stopped to ask if they could help.

alumnus 8. More presidents of the United States were ___alumni___ of Harvard than of any other university.

sandwich 9. The best short-order cook I ever met could make thirty bacon, lettuce, and tomato ___sandwiches___ in ten minutes.

mouse 10. During the sanitation workers' strike, ___mice___ scurried along the street between bags of uncollected trash.

Step 7: Mastering a Basic Word List

Make sure you can spell all the words in the following list. They are some of the words used most often in English. Again, your instructor may assign twenty words for you to study at a time and give you a series of quizzes until you have mastered the words.

ability		anxious		breathe	
absent		apply		building	
accident		approve		business	
across		argue		careful	
address		around		careless	
advertise		attempt		cereal	
advice		attention		certain	
after		awful		change	
again		awkward		cheap	
against		balance		chief	
all right		bargain		children	
almost		beautiful		church	
a lot		because		cigarette	
although		become		clothing	
always		before		collect	
among		begin		color	
angry		being		comfortable	
animal		believe		company	
another		between		condition	
answer	**20**	bottom	**40**	conversation	**60**

daily
danger
daughter
death
decide
deposit
describe
different
direction
distance
doubt
dozen
during
each
early
earth
education
either
English
enough 80
entrance
everything
examine
exercise
expect
family
flower
foreign
friend
garden
general
grocery
guess
happy
heard

heavy
height
himself
holiday
house 100
however
hundred
hungry
important
instead
intelligence
interest
interfere
kitchen
knowledge
labor
language
laugh
leave
length
lesson
letter
listen
loneliness
making 120
marry
match
matter
measure
medicine
middle
might
million
minute
mistake

money
month
morning
mountain
much
needle
neglect
newspaper
noise
none 140
nothing
number
ocean
offer
often
omit
only
operate
opportunity
original
ought
pain
paper
pencil
people
perfect
period
personal
picture
place 160
pocket
possible
potato
president
pretty

problem
promise
property
psychology
public
question
quick
raise
ready
really
reason
receive
recognize
remember
repeat 180
restaurant
ridiculous
said
same
sandwich
send
sentence
several
shoes
should
since
sleep
smoke
something
soul
started
state
straight
street
strong 200
student
studying
success
suffer
surprise
teach
telephone
theory
thought
thousand
through
ticket
tired
today
together
tomorrow
tongue
tonight
touch
travel 220
truly
understand
unity
until
upon
usual
value
vegetable
view
visitor
voice
warning
watch
welcome
window
would
writing
written
year
yesterday 240

Review Test

Items 1–10 Use the three spelling rules to spell the following words.

1. admire + able = admirable
2. drop + ing = dropping
3. big + est = biggest
4. gamble + ing = gambling
5. luxury + es = luxuries
6. immediate + ly = immediately

7. imply + es = implies
8. plan + ed = planned
9. involve + ment = involvement
10. refer + ed = referred

Items 11–14 Circle the correctly spelled plural in each pair.

11. daisies daisys
12. bookshelfs bookshelves
13. mosquitos mosquitoes
14. crisis crises

Items 15 – 20 Circle the correctly spelled word (from the basic word list) in each pair.

15. tommorrow tomorrow
16. height hieght
17. needel needle
18. visiter visitor
19. hungry hungery
20. writting writing

30 Omitted Words and Letters

Introductory Activity

Some people drop small connecting words such as *of, and,* or *in* when they write. They may also drop the *-s* endings of plural nouns. See if you can find the six places in the passage below where letters or words have been dropped. Supply whatever is missing.

Two glass bottle^s of apple juice lie broken ^in the supermarket aisle. Suddenly, a toddler who has gotten away from his parents appears at the head of the aisle. He spots the broken bottles and begins to run toward them. His chubby body lurches along like ^a wind-up toy, and his arm^s move excitedly up and down. Luckily, ^an alert shopper quickly reacts to the impending disaster and blocks the toddler's path. Then the shopper waits with ^the crying, frustrated little boy until his parents show up.

Answers are on page 691.

Be careful not to leave out words or letters when you write. The omission of words like *a, an, of, to,* or *the* or the *-s* ending needed on nouns or verbs may confuse and irritate your readers. They may not want to read what they regard as careless work.

Finding Omitted Words and Letters

Finding omitted words and letters, like finding many other sentence-skills mistakes, is a matter of careful proofreading. You must develop your ability to look carefully at a page to find places where mistakes may exist.

The exercises here will give you practice in finding omitted words and omitted *-s* endings on nouns. Another section of this book (pages 153–154) gives you practice in finding omitted *-s* endings on verbs.

Omitted Words

Practice

Add the missing word (*a, an, the, of,* or *to*) as needed.

Example Some people regard television as ^a tranquilizer that provides temporary relief from ^the pain and anxiety ^of modern life.

1. I grabbed ^a metal bar on ^the roof of ^the subway car as the train lurched into ^the station.
2. For most ^of our country's history, gold was ^the basis ^of the monetary system.
3. Maggie made about a quart ^of French-toast batter—enough ^to soak ^a few dozen slices.
4. Several pairs ^of sneakers tumbled around in ^the dryer and banged against ^the glass door.
5. To err is human and to forgive is divine, but never ^to make a mistake in the first place takes ^a lot of luck.
6. Raccoons like ^to wash their food in ^a stream with their nimble, glove-like hands before eating.
7. When I got ^to the grocery store, I realized I had left my shopping list in ^the glove compartment ^of my car.

8. Game shows are inexpensive way for networks make high profit.
9. Soap operas, on other hand, are very expensive to produce because the high salaries of many cast members.
10. One memorable Friday the thirteenth, a friend mine bought black cat, broke mirror, and walked under ladder. He had a wonderful day!

Omitted *-s* Ending

The plural form of regular nouns usually ends in *-s*. One common mistake that some people make with plurals is to omit this *-s* ending. People who drop the ending from plurals when speaking also tend to do it when writing. This tendency is especially noticeable when the meaning of the sentence shows that a word is plural.

> Ed and Mary pay two hundred dollar a month for an apartment that has only two room.

The *-s* ending has been omitted from *dollars* and *rooms*.

The activities that follow will help you correct the habit of omitting the *-s* endings from plurals.

Practice 1

Add *-s* endings where needed.

Example Bill beat me at several game of darts.

1. Many sightseer flocked around the disaster area like ghoul.
2. Martha has two set of twins, and all of their name rhyme.
3. Dozen of beetle are eating away at the rosebush in our yard.
4. Since a convention of dentist was in town, all the restaurant had waiting line.
5. Until the first of the year, worker in all department will not be permitted any overtime.
6. Blinking light, such as those on video game or police car, can trigger seizures in person with epilepsy.

7. Ray and his friends invented several game using an old rubber radiator hose and two plastic ball.
8. My thirteen-year-old has grown so much lately that she doesn't fit into the shoe and jean I bought for her a couple of month ago.
9. While cleaning out her desk drawers, Ann found a page of postage stamp stuck together and a couple of dried-up pen.
10. Worker fed large log and chunk of wood into the huge machine, which spit out chip and sawdust from its other end.

Practice 2

Write sentences that use plural forms of the following pairs of words.

Example girl, bike *The little girls raced their bikes down the street.*

Answers will vary.

1. college, student

 ____

2. shopper, bargain

3. car, driver

4. instructor, grade

5. vampire, victim

Note People who drop the *-s* ending on nouns also tend to omit endings on verbs. Pages 153–155 will help you correct the habit of dropping endings on verbs.

■ Review Test 1

Insert the two small connecting words needed in each sentence.

1. When I opened [the] freezer door, [a] box of ice cream fell out.
2. Hiking along [the] trail next to the lake, we came to [a] very muddy stretch.
3. The newlyweds rented [an] apartment with two rooms and [a] bath.
4. I had [to] walk all the way up to our fifth-floor office because [the] elevator was broken.
5. Unfortunately, the road leading [to] wealth is a lot longer than [the] one leading to poverty.

■ Review Test 2

Insert the two *-s* endings needed in each sentence.

1. The tallest building in the city has 67 floor[s] and 75,010 doorknob[s].
2. Student[s] who receive the highest grades are usually the one[s] who study the most.
3. The trash cans by the picnic benches attracted dozen[s] of bee[s].
4. Grimy fingerprint[s] had turned all the electric switch plate[s] black.
5. The fruit basket we received included instruction[s] for ripening fresh fruit and a booklet of recipe[s].

31 Commonly Confused Words

Introductory Activity

Circle the five words that are misspelled in the following passage. Then write their correct spellings in the spaces provided.

If your a resident of a temperate climate, you may suffer from feelings of depression in the winter and early spring. Scientists are now studying people who's moods seem to worsen in winter, and there findings show that the amount of daylight a person receives is an important factor in "seasonal depression." When a person gets to little sunlight, his or her mood darkens. Its fairly easy to treat severe cases of seasonal depression; the cure involves spending a few hours a day in front of full-spectrum fluorescent lights that contain all the components of natural light.

1. you're
2. whose
3. their
4. too
5. It's

Answers are on page 691.

Homonyms

The commonly confused words shown below are known as *homonyms;* they have the same sounds but different meanings and spellings. Complete the activities for each set of words, and check off and study the words that give you trouble.

Common Homonyms

all ready already	pair pear	threw through
brake break	passed past	to too two
coarse course	peace piece	wear where
hear here	plain plane	weather whether
hole whole	principal principle	whose who's
its it's	right write	your you're
knew new	than then	
know no	their there they're	

all ready completely prepared
already previously, before

We were *all ready* to go, for we had eaten and packed *already* that morning.

Fill in the blanks: Phil was ___all ready___ for his driver's test, since he had ___already___ memorized the questions and regulations.

Write sentences using *all ready* and *already.*

Students' sentences throughout this section will vary.
____
____

brake stop
break come apart

Dot slams the *brake* pedal so hard that I'm afraid I'll *break* my neck in her car.

Fill in the blanks: While attempting to ___break___ a speed record, the racecar driver had to ___brake___ for a spectator who had wandered onto the track.

Write sentences using *brake* and *break.*

____

____

coarse rough
course part of a meal; a school subject; direction; certainly (with *of*)

During the *course* of my career as a waitress, I've dealt with some very *coarse* customers.

Fill in the blanks: The instructor in my electronics ___course___ is known to use ___coarse___ language.

Write sentences using *coarse* and *course.*

____

____

hear perceive with the ear
here in this place

If I *hear* another insulting ethnic joke *here,* I'll leave.

Fill in the blanks: Unless you sit right ___here___ in one of the front rows, you won't be able to ___hear___ a single thing the soft-spoken lecturer says.

Write sentences using *hear* and *here.*

____

____

hole empty spot
whole entire

If there is a *hole* in the tailpipe, I'm afraid we will have to replace the *whole* exhaust assembly.

Fill in the blanks: If you eat the __whole__ portion of chili, it will probably burn a __hole__ in your stomach.

Write sentences using *hole* and *whole.*

____

____

its belonging to it
it's contraction of *it is* or *it has*

The kitchen floor has lost *its* shine because *it's* been used as a roller skating rink by the children.

Fill in the blanks: Our living-room carpet has lost __its__ vivid color since __it's__ been exposed to so much sunlight.

Write sentences using *its* and *it's.*

____

____

knew past tense of *know*
new not old

We *knew* that the *new* television comedy would be canceled quickly.

Fill in the blanks: As soon as we brought our __new__ microwave home, we __knew__ it wouldn't fit where we planned to put it.

Write sentences using *knew* and *new.*

____

____

know to understand
no a negative

I never *know* who might drop in even though *no* one is expected.

Fill in the blanks: I ___know___ there are ___no___ openings in your company at present, but please keep my résumé in case anything turns up.

Write sentences using *know* and *no.*

____

____

pair set of two
pear fruit

The dessert consisted of a *pair* of thin biscuits topped with vanilla ice cream and poached *pear* halves.

Fill in the blanks: We spotted a ___pair___ of bluejays on our dwarf ___pear___ tree.

Write sentences using *pair* and *pear.*

____

____

passed went by; succeeded in; handed to
past time before the present; by, as in "I drove past the house."

After Edna *passed* the driver's test, she drove *past* all her friends' houses and honked the horn.

Fill in the blanks: Norman couldn't understand why he'd been ___passed___ over for the promotion, because his ___past___ work had been very good.

Write sentences using *passed* and *past.*

____

____

peace calm
piece part

The *peace* of the little town was shattered when a *piece* of a human body was found in the town dump.

Fill in the blanks: We ate in ___peace___ until my two brothers started fighting over who would get the last ___piece___ of blueberry pie.

Write sentences using *peace* and *piece*.

____

____

plain simple
plane aircraft

The *plain* box contained a very expensive model *plane* kit.

Fill in the blanks: The ___plain___ truth is that unless you can land this ___plane___ within the next twenty minutes, it will run out of fuel and crash.

Write sentences using *plain* and *plane.*

____

____

principal main; a person in charge of a school; amount of money borrowed
principle law or standard

My *principal* goal in child rearing is to give my daughter strong *principles* to live by.

Fill in the blanks: My ___principal___ reason for turning down the part-time job is that it's against my ___principle___s to work on weekends.

Write sentences using *principal* and *principle.*

____

____

Note It might help to remember that the *e* in *principle* is also in *rule*—the meaning of *principle.*

right correct; opposite of *left;* something to which one is entitled
write to put words on paper

It is my *right* to refuse to *write* my name on your petition.

Fill in the blanks: The instructor said if the students' outlines were not ___right___, they would have to ___write___ them again.

Write sentences using *right* and *write.*

____

____

than used in comparisons
then at that time

I glared angrily at my boss, and *then* I told him our problems were more serious *than* he suspected.

Fill in the blanks: Felix hiked seven miles and ___then___ chopped firewood; he was soon more tired ___than___ he'd been in years.

Write sentences using *than* and *then.*

____

____

Note It might help to remember that *then* (the word spelled with an *e*) is a time signal (*time* also has an *e*).

their belonging to them
there at that place; a neutral word used with verbs like *is, are, was, were, have,* and *had*
they're contraction of *they are*

The tenants *there* are complaining because *they're* being cheated by *their* landlords.

Fill in the blanks: The music next door is so loud that I'm going over ___there___ to tell my neighbors to turn ___their___ stereo down before ___they're___ arrested for disturbing the peace.

Write sentences using *their, there,* and *they're.*

____

____

threw past tense of *throw*
through from one side to the other; finished

When a character in a movie *threw* a cat *through* the window, I had to close my eyes.

Fill in the blanks: When Lee was finally __through__ studying for her psychology final, she __threw__ her textbook and notes into her closet.

Write sentences using *threw* and *through.*

____

____

to verb part, as in *to smile;* toward, as in "I'm going to school."
too overly, as in "The pizza was too hot"; also, as in "The coffee was hot, too."
two the number 2

Lola drove *to* the store *to* get some ginger ale. (The first *to* means *toward*; the second *to* is a verb part that goes with *get*.)

The sport jacket is *too* tight; the slacks are tight, *too.* (The first *too* means *overly;* the second *too* means *also.*)

The *two* basketball players leaped for the jump ball. (2)

Fill in the blanks: My __two__ daughters are __too__ young __to__ wear much makeup.

Write sentences using *to, too,* and *two.*

____

____

wear to have on
where in what place

I work at a nuclear reactor, *where* one must *wear* a radiation-detection badge at all times.

Fill in the blanks: At the college ___where___ Ann goes, almost all the students ___wear___ very casual clothes to class.

Write sentences using *wear* and *where.*

weather atmospheric conditions
whether if it happens that; in case; if

Because of the threatening *weather,* it's not certain *whether* the game will be played.

Fill in the blanks: After I hear the ___weather___ report, I'll decide ___whether___ I'll drive or take a train to my sister's house.

Write sentences using *weather* and *whether.*

whose belonging to whom
who's contraction of *who is* and *who has*

The man *who's* the author of the latest diet book is a man *whose* ability to cash in on the latest craze is well known.

Fill in the blanks: The cousin ___who's___ visiting us is the one ___whose___ car was just demolished by a tractor trailer.

Write sentences using *whose* and *who's.*

your belonging to you
you're contraction of *you are*

Since *your* family has a history of heart disease, *you're* the kind of person who should take extra health precautions.

Fill in the blanks: If you're not going to eat any more, could I have what's left on your plate?

Write sentences using *your* and *you're.*

____

____

Other Words Frequently Confused

Following is a list of other words that people frequently confuse. Complete the activities for each set of words, and check off and study the ones that give you trouble.

Commonly Confused Words

a an	among between	desert dessert	learn teach
accept except	beside besides	does dose	loose lose
advice advise	can may	fewer less	quiet quite
affect effect	clothes cloths	former latter	though thought

a
an

Both *a* and *an* are used before other words to mean, approximately, *one.*

Generally you should use *an* before words starting with a vowel (*a, e, i, o, u*):

an absence an exhibit an idol an offer an upgrade

Generally you should use *a* before words starting with a consonant (all other letters):

a pen a ride a digital clock a movie a neighbor

Fill in the blanks: When it comes to eating, I am lucky; I can eat like ___an___ elephant and stay as thin as ___a___ snake.

Write sentences using *a* and *an.*

Students' sentences throughout this section will vary.

____

accept receive; agree to
except exclude; but

If I *accept* your advice, I'll lose all my friends *except* you.

Fill in the blanks: Everyone ___except___ my parents was delighted when I decided to ___accept___ the out-of-town job offer.

Write sentences using *accept* and *except.*

____

____

advice noun meaning *an opinion*
advise verb meaning *to counsel, to give advice*

Jake never listened to his parents' *advice,* and he ended up listening to a cop *advise* him of his rights.

Fill in the blanks: My father once gave me some good ___advice___; never ___advise___ people on anything unless they ask you to.

Write sentences using *advice* and *advise.*

____

____

affect verb meaning *to influence*
effect verb meaning *to bring about something;* noun meaning *result*

My sister Sally cries for *effect,* but her act no longer *affects* my parents.

Fill in the blanks: Some school officials think suspension will ___affect___ students positively, buy many students think its main ___effect___ is time off from school.

Write sentences using *affect* and *effect.*

____

____

among implies three or more
between implies only two

We selfishly divided the box of candy *between* the two of us rather than *among* all the members of the family.

Fill in the blanks: ___Among___ my souvenirs from high school is a scrapbook with a large pink rose pressed ___between___ two of its pages.

Write sentences using *among* and *between.*

____

____

beside along the side of
besides in addition to

Fred sat *beside* Martha. *Besides* them, there were ten other people at the Tupperware party.

Fill in the blanks: Elena refused to sit ___beside___ Carlos in class because he always fidgeted, and, ___besides___, he couldn't keep his mouth shut.

Write sentences using *beside* and *besides.*

____

____

can refers to the ability to do something
may refers to permission or possibility

If you *can* work overtime on Saturday, you *may* take Monday off.

Fill in the blanks: Joanne certainly ___can___ handle the project, but she ___may___ not have time to complete it by the deadline.

Write sentences using *can* and *may.*

____

____

clothes articles of dress
cloths pieces of fabric

I tore up some old *clothes* to use as polishing *cloths.*

Fill in the blanks: I keep a bag of dust ___cloths___ in the corner of my ___clothes___ closet.

Write sentences using *clothes* and *cloths.*

____

____

desert a stretch of dry land; to abandon one's post or duty
dessert last part of a meal

Don't *desert* us now; order a sinful *dessert* along with us.

Fill in the blanks: I know my willpower will ___desert___ me whenever there are brownies for ___dessert___.

Write sentences using *desert* and *dessert.*

____

____

does form of the verb *do*
dose amount of medicine

Martha *does* not realize that a *dose* of brandy is not the best medicine for the flu.

Fill in the blanks: A ___dose___ of aspirin ___does___ wonders for Sally's arthritis.

Write sentences using *does* and *dose.*

____

____

fewer used with things that can be counted
less refers to amount, value, or degree

I missed *fewer* writing classes than Rafael, but I wrote *less* effectively than he did.

Fill in the blanks: Florence is taking __fewer__ courses this semester because she has __less__ free time than she did last year.

Write sentences using *fewer* and *less.*

____

____

former refers to the first of two items named
latter refers to the second of two items named

I turned down both the job in the service station and the job as a shipping clerk; the *former* involved irregular hours and the *latter* offered very low pay.

Fill in the blanks: My mother does both calisthenics and yoga; the __former__ keeps her weight down while the __latter__ helps her relax.

Write sentences using *former* and *latter.*

____

____

Note Be sure to distinguish *latter* from *later* (meaning *after some time*).

learn to gain knowledge
teach to give knowledge

After Roz *learns* the new dance, she is going to *teach* it to me.

Fill in the blanks: My dog is very smart; she can __learn__ any new trick I __teach__ her in just minutes.

Write sentences using *learn* and *teach.*

____

____

loose not fastened; not tight-fitting
lose misplace; fail to win

I am afraid I'll *lose* my ring; it's too *loose* on my finger.

Fill in the blanks: Those slippers are so __loose__ that every time I take a step, I __lose__ one.

Write sentences using *loose* and *lose.*

____

____

quiet peaceful
quite entirely; really; rather

After a busy day, the children were not *quiet,* and their parents were *quite* tired.

Fill in the blanks: After moving furniture all day, Vince was __quite__ exhausted, so he found a __quiet__ place and lay down for a nap.

Write sentences using *quiet* and *quite.*

____

____

though despite the fact that
thought past tense of *think*

Though I enjoyed the dance, I *thought* the cover charge of ten dollars was too high.

Fill in the blanks: Even __though__ my paper was two weeks late, I __thought__ the instructor would accept it.

Write sentences using *though* and *thought.*

____

____

Incorrect Word Forms

Following is a list of incorrect word forms that people sometimes use in their writing. Complete the activities for each word, and check off and study the words that give you trouble.

Incorrect Word Forms		
being that	could of	would of
can't hardly	must of	irregardless
couldn't hardly	should of	

being that Incorrect! Use *because* or *since.*

I'm going to bed now ~~being that~~ because I must get up early tomorrow.

Correct the following sentences.

1. ~~Being that~~ Since our stove doesn't work, we'll have tuna salad for dinner.
2. I never invite both of my aunts over together, ~~being that~~ since they don't speak to each other.
3. I'm taking a day off tomorrow, ~~being that~~ since it's my birthday.

can't hardly
couldn't hardly Incorrect! Use *can hardly* or *could hardly.*

Small store owners ~~can't~~ can hardly afford to offer large discounts.

Correct the following sentences.

1. I ~~can't~~ can hardly concentrate when the teacher looks over my shoulder.
2. James ~~couldn't~~ could hardly believe the bill for fixing his car's brakes.
3. You ~~couldn't~~ could hardly hear the music, because the audience was so loud.

could of Incorrect! Use *could have.*

I could ~~of~~ have done better in that test.

Correct the following sentences.

1. The sidewalk was so hot you could ~~of~~ have toasted bread on it.
2. The moon was so bright you could ~~of~~ have read by it.
3. The peach pie was so good that I could ~~of~~ have eaten it all.

irregardless Incorrect! Use *regardless.*

~~Irregardless~~ Regardless of what anyone says, he will not change his mind.

Correct the following sentences.

1. ~~Irregardless~~ Regardless of your feelings about customers, you must treat them with courtesy.
2. Jay jogs every day ~~irregardless~~ regardless of the weather.
3. Anyone can learn to read ~~irregardless~~ regardless of age.

must of
should of
would of Incorrect! Use *must have, should have, would have.*

I should ~~of~~ have applied for a loan when my credit was good.

Correct the following sentences.

1. I must ~~of~~ have dozed off during the movie.
2. If Marty hadn't missed class yesterday, he would ~~of~~ have known about today's test.
3. You should ~~of~~ have told me to stop at the supermarket.

Review Test 1

These sentences check your understanding of *its, it's; there, their, they're; to, too, two;* and *your, you're*. Underline the correct word in the parentheses. Rather than guess, look back at the explanations of the words when necessary.

1. It seems whenever (your, you're) at the doctor's office, (your, you're) symptoms disappear.
2. The boss asked his assistant (to, too, two) rearrange the insurance files, placing each in (its, it's) proper sequence.
3. You'll get (your, you're) share of the pizza when (its, it's) cool enough (to, too, two) eat.
4. (Its, It's) a terrible feeling when (your, you're) (to, too, two) late (to, too, two) help someone.
5. (To, Too, Two) eat insects, most spiders use their (to, too, two) fangs to inject a special poison which turns (there, their, they're) victim's flesh into a soupy liquid they can drink.
6. (Its, It's) a fact that (there, their, they're) are (to, too, two) many violent shows on TV.
7. (There, Their, They're) is no valid reason for the (to, too, two) of you (to, too, two) have forgotten about turning in (your, you're) assignments.
8. If you (to, too, two) continue (to, too, two) drive so fast, (its, it's) likely you'll get ticketed by the police.
9. "My philosophy on guys is that (there, their, they're) just like buses," said Lola. "If you miss one, (there, their, they're) is always another one coming by in a little while."
10. "(Its, It's) about time you (to, too, two) showed up," the manager huffed. "(There, Their, They're) is already a line of customers waiting outside."

Review Test 2

The sentences that follow check your understanding of a variety of commonly confused words. Underline the correct word in the parentheses. Rather than guess, look back at the explanations of the words when necessary.

1. When (your, you're) (plain, plane) arrives, call us (weather, whether) (its, it's) late or not.
2. You (should have, should of) first found out (whose, who's) really (to, too, two) blame before coming in (hear, here) and making false accusations.
3. When Jack drove (threw, through) his old neighborhood, he (could hardly, couldn't hardly) recognize some of the places he (knew, new) as a child.

4. The (affect, effect) of having drunk (to, too, two) much alcohol last night was something like having (a, an) jackhammer drilling (among, between) my ears.
5. I was (quiet, quite) surprised to learn that in the (passed, past), (our, are) town was the site of (a, an) Revolutionary War battle.
6. Of (coarse, course) (its, it's) important to get good grades while (your, you're) in school, but it (does, dose) not hurt to (know, now, no) the (right, write) people when (your, you're) looking for a job.
7. If (your, you're) interested in listening to a great album, take my (advice, advise) and pick up a copy of *Sgt. Pepper's Lonely Hearts Club Band;* (its, it's) been voted the most popular rock album in history.
8. (Being that, Since) Barry has failed all five quizzes and one major exam and didn't hand in the midterm paper, he (though, thought) it would be a good idea (to, too, two) drop the (coarse, course).
9. (Their, There, They're) is (know, no) greater feeling (than, then) that of walking (threw, through) a forest in the spring.
10. I spent the (hole, whole) day looking (threw, through) my history notes, but when it came time to take the exam, I still (could hardly, couldn't hardly) understand the similarities (among, between) the Korean War, World War I, and World War II.

■ Review Test 3

On separate paper, write short sentences using the ten words shown below.

Answers will vary.

their	effect
your	passed
it's	here
then	brake
too (meaning *also*)	whose

32 Effective Word Choice

Introductory Activity

Put a check beside the sentence in each pair that makes more effective and appropriate use of words.

1. After a bummer of a movie, we pigged out on a pizza. ______
   After a disappointing movie, we devoured a pizza. ___✓___
2. Feeling blue about the death of his best friend, Tennyson wrote the tearjerker "In Memoriam." ______
   Mourning the death of his best friend, Tennyson wrote the moving poem "In Memoriam." ___✓___
3. The personality adjustment inventories will be administered on Wednesday in the Student Center. ______
   Psychological tests will be given on Wednesday in the Student Center. ___✓___
4. The referee in the game, in my personal opinion, made the right decision in the situation. ______
   I think the referee made the right decision. ___✓___

Now see if you can circle the correct number in each case:

Pair (1, 2, 3, 4) contains a sentence with slang; pair (1, 2, 3, 4) contains a sentence with a cliché; pair (1, 2, 3, 4) contains a sentence with pretentious words; and pair (1, 2, 3, 4) contains a wordy sentence.

Answers are on page 692.

Choose your words carefully when you write. Always take the time to think about your word choices, rather than simply using the first word that comes to mind. You want to develop the habit of selecting words that are appropriate and exact for your purposes. One way you can show sensitivity to language is by avoiding slang, clichés, pretentious words, and wordiness.

Slang

We often use slang expressions when we talk because they are so vivid and colorful. However, slang is usually out of place in formal writing. Here are some examples of slang expressions:

The party was a *real horror show.*

I don't want to *lay a guilt trip* on you.

Our boss is not *playing with a full deck.*

Dad *flipped out* when he learned that Jan had *totaled* the car.

Someone *ripped off* Ken's new Adidas running shoes from his locker.

After the game, we *stuffed our faces* at the diner.

I finally told my parents to *get off my case.*

The movie really *grossed me out.*

Slang expressions have a number of drawbacks. They go out of date quickly, they become tiresome if used excessively in writing, and they may communicate clearly to some readers but not to others. Also, the use of slang can be an evasion of the specific details that are often needed to make one's meaning clear in writing. For example, in "The party was a real horror show," the writer has not provided the specific details about the party necessary for us to understand the statement clearly. Was it the setting, the food and drink (or lack of them), the guests, the music, or the hosts that made the party such a dreadful experience? In general, then, you should avoid slang in your writing. If you are in doubt about whether an expression is slang, it may help to check a recently published hardbound dictionary.

Practice

Rewrite the following sentences, replacing the italicized slang words with more formal ones.

Example I was *so beat* Friday night that I decided *to ditch* the birthday party.
I was so exhausted Friday night that I decided not to go to the birthday party.

Answers may vary.

1. If you keep *putting it away,* you're going to be *a blimp.*
   If you keep overeating, you're going to be fat.

2. My parents always *shoot me down* when I ask them for some *bucks* to buy new CDs.
   My parents always refuse when I ask them for some money to buy new CDs.

3. The entire city was *psyched up* when the basketball team *creamed* its opponent in the playoffs.
   The entire city was excited when the basketball team beat its opponent in the playoffs.

4. If Ellen would *lighten up* and stop talking about her troubles, a date with her wouldn't be such a *downer.*
   If Ellen would get less serious and stop talking about her troubles, a date with her wouldn't be so depressing.

5. I'm going to have to *sweat it out* for the next couple of days, hoping the boss doesn't discover the *goof* I made.
   I'm going to have to wait anxiously for the next couple of days, hoping the boss doesn't discover the mistake I made.

Clichés

Clichés are expressions that have been worn out through constant use. Some typical clichés are listed below.

Common Clichés

all work and no play	sad but true
at a loss for words	saw the light
better late than never	short and sweet
drop in the bucket	sigh of relief
easier said than done	singing the blues
had a hard time of it	taking a big chance
in the nick of time	time and time again
in this day and age	too close for comfort
it dawned on me	too little, too late
it goes without saying	took a turn for the worse
last but not least	under the weather
make ends meet	where he (*or* she) is coming from
needless to say	word to the wise
on top of the world	work like a dog

Clichés are common in speech but make your writing seem tired and stale. Also, they are often an evasion of the specific details that you must work to provide in your writing. You should, then, avoid clichés and try to express your meaning in fresh, original ways.

Practice 1

Underline the cliché in each of the following sentences. Then substitute specific, fresh words for the trite expression.

Example My parents supported me through some trying times.
rough years
____

1. To make a long story short, my sister decided to file for divorce.
   In brief,
2. As quick as a wink, the baby tipped over the open box of oatmeal.
   Very quickly,
3. Any advice my friends give me goes in one ear and out the other.
   is ignored
4. I felt like a million dollars when I got my first A on a college test.
   was delighted
5. These days, well-paying jobs for high school graduates are few and far between.
   rare

Practice 2

Write a short paragraph describing the kind of day you had yesterday. Try to put as many clichés as possible into your writing. For example, "I had a long hard day. I had a lot to get done, and I kept my nose to the grindstone." By making yourself aware of clichés in this way, you should lessen the chance that they will appear in your writing.

Pretentious Words

Some people feel that they can improve their writing by using fancy, elevated words rather than simpler, more natural words. They use artificial and stilted language that more often obscures their meaning than communicates it clearly.

Here are some unnatural-sounding sentences:

The football combatants left the gridiron.

His instructional technique is a very positive one.

At the counter, we inquired about the arrival time of the aircraft.

I observed the perpetrator of the robbery depart from the retail establishment.

The same thoughts can be expressed more clearly and effectively by using plain, natural language, as below:

The football players left the field.

He is a good teacher.

At the counter, we asked when the plane would arrive.

I saw the robber leave the store.

Following is a list of some other inflated words and the simple words that could replace them.

Inflated Words	*Simpler Words*
component	part
delineate	describe
facilitate	help
finalize	finish
initiate	begin
manifested	shown
subsequent to	after
to endeavor	to try
transmit	send

Practice

Cross out the two pretentious words in each sentence. Then substitute clear, simple language for the pretentious words.

Example Sally was ~~terminated~~ from her ~~employment~~.
Sally was fired from her job.

1. Please ~~query~~ one of our sales ~~associates~~.
   Please ask one of our salespeople.

2. The ~~meteorological~~ ~~conditions~~ are terrible today.
   The weather is terrible today.

3. My parents ~~desire~~ me to ~~obtain~~ a college degree.
   My parents want me to get a college degree.

4. Do not ~~protrude~~ your arm out of the car, or an accident might ~~ensue~~.
   Do not put your arm out of the car, or an accident might happen.

5. Many ~~conflagrations~~ are caused by the careless ~~utilization~~ of portable heaters.
Many fires are caused by the careless use of portable heaters.

Wordiness

Wordiness—using more words than necessary to express a meaning—is often a sign of lazy or careless writing. Your readers may resent the extra time and energy they must spend when you have not done the work needed to make your writing direct and concise.

Here is a list of some wordy expressions that could be reduced to single words.

Wordy Form	*Short Form*
a large number of	many
a period of a week	a week
arrive at an agreement	agree
at an earlier point in time	before
at the present time	now
big in size	big
due to the fact that	because
during the time that	while
five in number	five
for the reason that	because
good benefit	benefit
in every instance	always
in my opinion	I think
in the event that	if
in the near future	soon
in this day and age	today
is able to	can
large in size	large
plan ahead for the future	plan
postponed until later	postponed
red in color	red
return back	return

Here are examples of wordy sentences:

At this point in time in our country, the amount of violence seems to be increasing every day.

I called to the children repeatedly to get their attention, but my shouts did not get any response from them.

Omitting needless words improves these sentences:

Violence is increasing in our country.

I called to the children repeatedly, but they didn't respond.

Practice

Rewrite the following sentences, omitting unnecessary words.

Example Starting as of the month of June, I will be working at the store on a full-time basis.

As of June, I will be working at the store full time.

Answers may vary.

1. It is a well-known and proven fact that there is no cure as yet for the common cold.

   There is no cure for the common cold.

2. The main point that I will try to make in this paper is that our state should legalize and permit gambling.

   My main point is that our state should legalize gambling.

3. Due to the fact that Chen's car refused to start up, he had to take public transportation by bus to his place of work.

   Because Chen's car wouldn't start, he took a bus to work.

4. When I was just a little boy, I already knew in my mind that my goal was to be a stockbroker in the future of my life.

   Even when I was a boy, my goal was to be a stockbroker.

5. The exercises that Susan does every day of the week give her more energy with which to deal with the happenings of everyday life.

   Susan's daily exercises energize her.

Review Test 1

Certain words are italicized in the following sentences. In the space provided, identify whether the words are slang (*S*), clichés (*C*), or pretentious words (*PW*). Then replace them with more effective words.

C 1. Donna *came out of her shell* after she joined a singing group at school.
overcame her shyness

S 2. I *totally lost it* when my little brother *got busted* for underage drinking.
was very upset . . . was arrested

PW 3. I'm *suffering from a temporary depletion of all cash reserves.*
I have no money.

S 4. Our manager *flipped out* when a cashier gave the wrong change to a customer.
got upset

PW 5. I got angry at the park visitors who did not put their *waste materials* in the *trash receptacle.*
garbage . . . trash

C 6. Hearing I had passed the accounting final really *took a load off my mind.*
was a relief

C 7. We all thought it was *too good to be true* when the instructor said that most of us would get A's in the course.
unbelievable

PW 8. Fred *asserted to* the collection agency that he had sent the *remuneration.*
told . . . payment

S 9. My old Toyota just *bit the dust,* so I'm *checking out* new cars.
stopped running . . . looking at

C 10. This book was written by a millionaire who *didn't have a dime to his name* as a boy.
was poor

Review Test 2

Rewrite the following sentences, omitting unnecessary words.

Answers will vary; possibilities are shown.

1. At 6 A.M. early this morning, I suddenly heard a loud and noisy banging by someone at the front door of my apartment.

   AT 6 A.M., I heard a loud banging at my front door.

2. The fact of the matter is that I did not remember until, of course, just now that I had an appointment to meet you.

   I forgot my appointment with you.

3. We are very pleased to have the opportunity to inform you that your line of credit on your credit card with us has just been increased.

   We have increased your credit.

4. At this point in time, the company has no plan of adding to anyone's salary by giving a raise in pay in the near or distant future.

   The company plans no pay raises.

5. If you are out on the job market seeking a job, you just might benefit from professional help to assist you in your search for employment.

   If you are looking for a job, you might benefit from professional help.

Part Three

Reinforcement of the Skills

Introduction

To reinforce the sentence skills presented in Part Two, this part of the book—Part Three—provides mastery tests, combined mastery tests, proofreading tests, and editing tests. There are four *mastery tests* for each of the skills where errors occur most frequently and two *mastery tests* for each of the remaining skills. A series of *combined mastery tests* will reassure your understanding of important related skills. Editing and proofreading tests offer practice in finding and correcting one kind of error in a brief passage. *Combined editing tests* then offer similar practice—except that each of these passages contains a variety of mistakes. Both the editing and the proofreading tests will help you become a skilled editor and proofreader. All too often, students can correct mistakes in practice sentences but are unable to do so in their own writing. You must learn to look carefully for sentence-skills errors and to make close checking a habit.

Appendix F at the end of the book provides progress charts that will help you keep track of your performance on these tests.

Mastery Tests

Subjects and Verbs

■ Mastery Test 1

Draw one line under subjects and two lines under verbs. Cross out prepositional phrases as necessary to help find subjects. (Be sure to underline all the parts of a verb. Also, remember that you may find more than one subject and one verb in a sentence.)

1. The sailboat drifted ~~for hours on the calm sea~~.
2. Career Day ~~at my high school~~ was a big success.
3. Tall pine trees hid the farmhouse ~~from view~~.
4. Sandy's revealing swimsuit attracted stares ~~from everyone at the swimming pool~~.
5. Televisions, radios, and microwave ovens are ~~on sale at greatly reduced prices~~.
6. All the fish ~~in that lake~~ have become contaminated.
7. Several garbage cans lined the weathered fence ~~behind the old hotel~~.
8. Gloria often buys secondhand clothes and brightens them up ~~by dyeing or embroidering them~~.
9. Weapons ~~from police raids~~ are kept ~~under lock and key~~.
10. The old lady got back ~~on her feet~~ and surprised her attacker ~~with a karate chop~~.

Score Number correct ______ × 10 = ______ %

Subjects and Verbs

Mastery Test 2

Draw one line under subjects and two lines under verbs. Cross out prepositional phrases as necessary to help find subjects. (Be sure to underline all the parts of a verb. Also, remember that you may find more than one subject and one verb in a sentence.)

1. Sharks swim continuously ~~in their search for food~~.
2. The spider floated down ~~from the ceiling~~ and landed ~~on my arm~~.
3. Most ~~of the applicants for office jobs~~ type about thirty words ~~per minute~~.
4. The elderly man sat ~~on the park bench~~ and carefully opened his newspaper.
5. The shrubs are growing too close ~~to the side of the house~~.
6. Andrew wants to learn to repair watches but does not have enough time ~~on his hands~~.
7. All my friends, ~~except my boyfriend~~, like my new hairstyle.
8. Carl washed his sports car every weekend and polished it once a month to protect the finish.
9. ~~With only a day~~ ~~till the wedding~~, the bride and groom were having second thoughts.
10. Astrologers and astronomers agree ~~on the importance of the stars~~ but disagree ~~on almost everything else~~.

Score Number correct ________ × 10 = ________ %

Subjects and Verbs

■ Mastery Test 3

Draw one line under subjects and two lines under verbs. Cross out prepositional phrases as necessary to help find subjects. (Be sure to underline all the parts of a verb. Also, remember that you may find more than one subject and one verb in a sentence.)

1. Blue wildflowers fill the empty lot.
2. No quarrel ~~between good friends~~ lasts ~~for very long~~.
3. We borrowed my uncle's truck to move the refrigerator.
4. A young boy paid ~~for the lollipop with a fistful of pennies~~.
5. Fewer people have been attending the school games this year.
6. ~~Toward evening~~, my appetite seems to increase ~~by the minute~~.
7. The woman ~~in front of me~~ was wearing a straw hat ~~with a large daisy~~.
8. ~~After a long search~~, I found my sweater ~~in my sister's closet~~.
9. Giant lions and camels once roamed the American West.
10. An ancient footbridge formerly spanned the narrow stream but now lies ~~under water~~.

Score Number correct ______ × 10 = ______ %

Subjects and Verbs

■ Mastery Test 4

Draw one line under subjects and two lines under verbs. Cross out prepositional phrases as necessary to help find subjects. (Be sure to underline all the parts of a verb. Also, remember that you may find more than one subject and one verb in a sentence.)

1. The sharp edge ~~of a book page~~ slit my finger.
2. Floyd should have waxed his car ~~in the shade~~.
3. A maze ~~of gopher tunnels~~ winds ~~under our lawn~~.
4. I am planning to protest the school's suspension policy.
5. The thick coating ~~on the fried chicken~~ slipped off ~~like a jacket~~.
6. My sister and I have agreed to share only our everyday clothes.
7. A ghostly image appeared ~~on the instant print~~ and slowly turned ~~into a portrait of Nick and Fran~~.
8. Canned salmon and tuna contain significant amounts ~~of calcium~~.
9. A small dog followed me home and waited on my doorstep.
10. Dexter and Gale are taking their vacations ~~at the same time~~ and will rent a cottage ~~on the lake for two weeks~~.

Score Number correct ________ × 10 = ________ %

Fragments

Mastery Test 1

Each word group in the student paragraph below is numbered. In the space provided, write *C* if a word group is a complete sentence; write *frag* if it is a fragment. You will find ten fragments in the paragraph.

1. frag
2. C
3. frag
4. C
5. frag
6. frag
7. C
8. C
9. C
10. frag
11. C
12. C
13. frag
14. frag
15. C
16. C
17. frag
18. C
19. frag
20. frag

[1]If an advertisement captures your interest. [2]It may be because some proven psychological methods of gaining attention are being used. [3]Such as change. [4]A flashing light, for example, is more noticeable than a continuously lit one. [5]Which is why many signs flash on and off. [6]And change colors and shapes. [7]Another advertising device is repetition. [8]We remember many advertising slogans and jingles because we have heard them so often. [9]In a thirty-second commercial, for instance, a message to use a certain toothpaste might be repeated five or six times. [10]In addition, frequent appearances of such ads. [11]Contrast, too, gains people's interest. [12]An advertiser may make a bright gold bracelet more appealing by placing it on a black velvet background. [13]Creating a dramatic visual effect. [14]Finally, to grab our attention. [15]Advertisers also use novelty. [16]Since people are drawn to the new and different, companies often change their products slightly. [17]Or make new products that are just variations of the old ones. [18]Then they emphasize the newness in their ads with various slogans. [19]Including "new and improved" and "different from anything you've ever tried before." [20]Even if the products are not very new and different.

Score Number correct ________ × 5 = ________ %

Fragments

■ Mastery Test 2

Underline the fragment in each item. Then make whatever changes are needed to turn the fragment into a sentence.

Example In grade school, I didn't want to wear glasses. And avoided having to get them by memorizing the Snellen eye chart.

1. Lee went to the beauty parlor. To have her nails done for the vampire party.
2. When the Millers moved away last winter. The entire town was mystified. They had left all their furniture behind.
3. Nobody knew when the next train would arrive. Impatient commuters waited in line. And checked their watches every few minutes.
4. Richard brought a stepladder to the parade. Planning to sell seats on the top rungs. Several police officers vetoed that idea.
5. I don't like to go to the bank. Except on Friday. That's when I deposit money.
6. Dawn is almost always early for work. But was late this morning. The boss told her not to worry.
7. Sitting on the boat dock. Jesse was lost in thought. The rising sun climbed slowly in the sky.
8. Nan felt around for the scissors at the back of the crowded drawer. She realized she had found them. When they stabbed her.
9. The battery in Frank's Chevy is five years old. And barely able to start the engine on a cold morning. He is waiting to buy a new battery on sale.
10. We had to wait at the airport for quite a while. All departing flights were delayed. Because a small private plane had to make an emergency landing.

Score Number correct _______ × 10 = _______ %

Fragments

■ Mastery Test 3

Underline the fragment in each item. Then make whatever changes are needed to turn the fragment into a sentence.

1. The police recruits lined up on the practice range. And loaded their pistols with bullets. Then they began firing at the targets in the distance.
2. Having gone on an all-day hike. We walked into the restaurant with dusty clothes and dirty faces. The hostess led us to a table in back by the kitchen.
3. The sanitation workers made quite a racket this morning. Also bent my new metal trash can. If they continue to be so rough, the can will soon be trash.
4. Sometimes my boss disappoints me. He can be very rude. For example, interrupting me while I'm making excuses.
5. My son wants to buy all the toys advertised on TV. Even if we had the money for them all. We wouldn't have the space.
6. I put off studying for the test until the last minute. As a result, being up all night. During the test the next morning, I was too tired to think clearly.
7. Nancy likes to be a know-it-all. She pretends to identify the stars on camping trips. But consults her map when no one is looking.
8. George and Charlotte got up at four this morning. To stand in line at the box office. They wanted front-row seats for the rock concert.
9. The boss gave all the secretaries bonuses at Christmas. Even Ms. Foster, who just joined the company in November. Many people felt he was too generous.
10. The newest ride at the amusement park is the "Elevator." You are hauled to the top of a tall shaft. And then dropped four stories to the ground. Fortunately, the brakes prevent your death.

Score Number correct ______ × 10 = ______ %

Fragments

■ Mastery Test 4

Underline and then correct the ten fragments in the following passage.

My cousin Darryl is the worst driver I know. When he picks me up for school in the morning, he screeches to a halt outside my door. And peels away again in a cloud of blue exhaust fumes. Before hitting the highway, we speed through several narrow streets. Doing forty-five in twenty-miles-an-hour zones. On the four-lane road, Darryl weaves from lane to lane, tailgating cars six inches from their rear bumpers. Then passes them with a burst of stomach-flattening acceleration. To pass a car that's moving somewhat slowly in the passing lane. Darryl will get behind it, beep his horn, and even flash his high beams. Nothing infuriates him more than the "idiots," as he calls them. Who ignore these hints to move over. As we approach the jug-handle turn leading to school, Darryl speeds up. He is determined to make the light allowing cars to cross the highway into campus. If the light turns red and a car has already stopped. Darryl tromps on the brake pedal at the last possible second before impact and curses various things. Such as the red light and the car that stopped for it. Once in the parking lot, he finishes with a flourish. Pulling into a parking space at thirty-five miles an hour. As I reach out a limp hand to open the car door. I usually vow that I soon will buy my own car. Or find another ride to school.

Score Number correct _______ × 10 = _______ %

Run-Ons

Mastery Test 1

In the space provided, write *R-O* beside run-on sentences. Write *C* beside the one sentence that is punctuated correctly. Some of the run-ons have no punctuation between the two complete thoughts; others have only a comma.

Correct each run-on by using (1) a period and a capital letter, (2) a comma and a joining word, or (3) a semicolon. Do not use the same method of correction for every sentence.

Examples

R-O I applied for the job, but I never got called in for an interview.

R-O Carla's toothache is getting worse. She should go to a dentist soon.

Methods of correction will vary.

R-O 1. He enjoys watching a talk show. She prefers watching a late movie.

R-O 2. Elena tried an herbal shampoo; her hair smelled like a meadow.

R-O 3. My last vacation trip was very broadening. I gained five pounds.

R-O 4. Some people prefer very loud music; their bodies vibrate with the sound.

C 5. Lorenzo is determined to find a new job, for his old one has given him an ulcer.

R-O 6. The rain fell softly outside. It was a relaxing day to stay indoors.

R-O 7. A little girl toddled down the street; she was attached to her mother by a chest harness and leash.

R-O 8. The school bus stopped at the corner, and children scattered like leaves in the wind.

R-O 9. The restaurant was closing. Waiters were already stacking chairs on the tables for the night.

R-O 10. His nose had become very cold, so he pressed the warm underside of his forearm against it.

Score Number correct _______ × 10 = _______ %

Run-Ons

■ Mastery Test 2

In the space provided, write *R-O* beside run-on sentences. Write *C* beside the one sentence that is punctuated correctly. Some of the run-ons have no punctuation between the two complete thoughts; others have only a comma.

Correct each run-on by using (1) a period and capital letter, (2) a comma and a joining word, or (3) a semicolon. Do not use the same method of correction for every sentence.

Methods of correction will vary.

R-O 1. This semester our instructor gained a lot of weight; he opened his belt another notch every two weeks.

R-O 2. First Darlene washes her hair, and then she goes to the hairdresser.

R-O 3. The blue whale is an endangered animal. Its population has been reduced to near extinction by whaling.

R-O 4. Barbara saw a funeral on television; she thought of her brother's recent death.

C 5. I began to get sleepy during the long ride, so I opened all the windows and pinched myself.

R-O 6. A flock of crows settled on a dimly lit tree. Their silhouettes stood out against the moon.

R-O 7. The average American teenager spends thirty-eight hours a week on schoolwork; the average Japanese teenager spends about sixty.

R-O 8. Many people complained that the proposed apartment building would obstruct the scenery. The water tower was bad enough.

R-O 9. I spoke to the growling dog in a friendly tone; I hoped his owner would show up soon.

R-O 10. At the crack of dawn, our neighbor started his lawnmower. Our "Saturday morning symphony" had begun.

Score Number correct ______ × 10 = ______ %

Run-Ons

■ Mastery Test 3

In the space provided, write *R-O* beside run-on sentences. Write *C* beside the two sentences that are punctuated correctly. Some of the run-ons have no punctuation between the two complete thoughts; others have only a comma.

Correct each run-on by using (1) a period and capital letter, (2) a comma and a joining word, or (3) a semicolon. Do not use the same method of correction for every sentence.

Methods of correction will vary.

R-O 1. The early bird catches the worm, [but] the early worm is not so lucky.

R-O 2. A mountain of garbage bags stood on the curb[, and] I wondered about the fate of all that plastic.

R-O 3. Some cities sponsor odd food festivals[. O]ne celebrates spring with a dandelion-eating spree.

C 4. Confinement in bed was the worst part of my illness, for I had to use a bedpan.

R-O 5. At first, Regina forgot to serve the dinner rolls[;] the smoke from the oven reminded her.

R-O 6. The roadside trees were infested[. W]ebbed caterpillar nests filled the tree branches.

R-O 7. Al slammed the New York City phone book down with disgust[;] it was impossible to find the right John Smith in it.

R-O 8. Few trout live in the stream[. I]ts once-clear waters are cloudy with the runoff from the new subdivision.

R-O 9. The dashboard lights flickered on and off[, for] there was a short in the electrical system.

C 10. The children enjoyed seeing the animals at the zoo, but the high points of their visit were the cotton candy and popcorn.

Score Number correct ______ × 10 = ______ %

Run-Ons

■ Mastery Test 4

In the space provided, write *R-O* beside run-on sentences. Write *C* beside the one sentence that is punctuated correctly. Some of the run-ons have no punctuation between the two complete thoughts; others have only a comma.

Correct each run-on by using (1) a period and capital letter, (2) a comma and a joining word, or (3) a semicolon. Do not use the same method of correction for every sentence.

Methods of correction will vary.

R-O 1. The sky in the country seems to have more stars, for no city pollution blocks the view.

R-O 2. An old engraving of New York City shows a startling fact; pigs once ran loose on Broadway.

R-O 3. Sandy sat quietly in the empty church. It was better than any tranquilizer.

R-O 4. On the way home, Linda wanted get her gas tank filled, but the stations she passed were all closed.

R-O 5. Numerous shrubs lined the driveway. They were a pruner's nightmare.

R-O 6. Victor turned to look at the unexpected face in the window; it was his own reflection.

R-O 7. An elephant's thin ears cool the animal in two ways. They fan the body and cool blood on its way to the heart.

R-O 8. A vigorous wind lashed through the forest. Trees nodded and bowed toward each other like old men in conversation.

C 9. Theo chose a bad time to teach his tardy wife a lesson, for he showed up four hours late for dinner on the night of his surprise birthday party.

R-O 10. Soldiers in the Revolutionary Army had to be at least sixteen, and they also had to have good teeth in order to tear the paper cartridges filled with gunpowder.

Score Number correct ______ × 10 = ______ %

Sentence Variety I

■ Mastery Test 1

Combine each group of short sentences into one sentence. Various combinations are possible. Choose the combination that reads most smoothly and clearly and that sounds most appropriate in the context of surrounding sentences.

Note In combining short sentences into one sentence, omit repeated words where necessary. Use separate paper. The story about the mother's advice continues in the next mastery test.

Answers may vary.

Helpful Advice

- People repeat common sayings.
- People do this often.
- People do this without thinking about them.

People often repeat common sayings without thinking about them.

- These sayings are old proverbs.
- They are based on a lot of experience.
- They can be good advice.

These old proverbs, which are based on a lot of experience, can be good advice.

- My mother told me a proverb.
- My mother told it to me many years ago.
- My mother lived by this proverb.

Many years ago, my mother told me a proverb which she lived by.

- This old saying still rings in my ears.
- The ringing is often.
- The saying is "Don't sweat the small stuff."

This old saying, which often still rings in my ears, is, "Don't sweat the small stuff."

- My mother realized she worried about problems.
- My mother realized she worried for too long.
- The problems were trivial.
- The problems were soon forgotten.

My mother realized she worried for too long about trivial problems that were soon forgotten.

Score Number correct _______ × 20 = _______ %

Sentence Variety I

■ Mastery Test 2

Combine each group of short sentences into one sentence. Various combinations are possible. Choose the combination that reads most smoothly and clearly and that sounds most appropriate in the context of surrounding sentences.

Note In combining short sentences into one sentence, omit repeated words where necessary. Use separate paper. The story about the mother's advice continues from the previous mastery test.

Answers may vary.

- She kept this saying in mind.
- The saying reminded her not to fret about little things.
- The fretting was needless.

She kept this saying in mind because it reminded her not to fret needlessly about little things.

- I lie in bed sleepless.
- I do this sometimes.
- I worry about the dent in my car.
- I worry about the way my clothes fit.
- I worry about a remark someone made.

Sometimes I lie in bed sleepless worrying about the dent in my car, the way my clothes fit, or a remark someone made.

- I do something then.
- I put things in perspective.
- I do this by remembering my mother's words.
- I decide not to "sweat the small stuff."

Then I put things in perspective by remembering my mother's words, and I decide not to "sweat the small stuff."

- My mother's advice is like a pill.
- The pill is for sleeping.
- The pill allows me to rest.

My mother's advice is like a sleeping pill that allows me to rest.

- I am able to save my worrying.
- My worrying will be for important matters.
- My worrying will not be for the small stuff.

I am able to save my worrying for important matters, not the small stuff.

Score Number correct ______ × 20 = ______ %

Standard English Verbs

■ Mastery Test 1

Underline the correct words in the parentheses.

1. Bert's car (have, has) a horn that (play, plays) six different tunes.
2. When the pile of rags (start, started) to catch on fire, Dave (reach, reached) for the hose.
3. I (don't, doesn't) think my mother (has, have) gone out to a movie in years.
4. When she (is, be) upset, Mimi (tell, tells) her troubles to her houseplants.
5. The play (was, were) ruined when the quarterback (fumble, fumbled) the handoff.
6. My husband (think, thinks) more clearly in the morning than he (do, does) at night.
7. I (want, wanted) to take off my rings, but they (was, were) stuck on my swollen fingers.
8. Dolores (has, have) only three more courses before she (earn, earns) her degree.
9. Sometimes I (think, thinks) the happiest people (be, are) those with the lowest expectations of life.
10. The street musician (count, counted) the coins in his donations basket and (pack, packed) his trumpet in its case.

Score Number correct ________ × 10 = ________ %

Standard English Verbs

Mastery Test 2

Cross out the nonstandard verb form and write the correct form in the space provided.

seems Example The job offer ~~seem~~ too good to be true.

clowns 1. Billy always ~~clown~~ around in the back of the class.

were 2. When the last guests left our party, we ~~was~~ exhausted but happy.

keeps 3. The computer in the library ~~keep~~ saying, "No such file."

advised 4. Today my counselor ~~advise~~ me to drop one of my courses.

walks 5. My sister Louise ~~walk~~ a mile to the bus stop every day.

has 6. I don't think that Juan ~~have~~ thought enough about his future.

cheered 7. The fans all stood up and ~~cheer~~ when the home team made a goal-line stand.

doesn't 8. Dora's husband ~~don't~~ like to talk about his experiences in Vietnam.

pronounced 9. After fumbling with his papers, the nervous announcer ~~pronounce~~ the president's name wrong.

head 10. Some students ~~heads~~ for the parking lot between classes to sit in their cars and blast their radios.

Score Number correct _______ × 10 = _______ %

Standard English Verbs

Mastery Test 3

Part 1 Fill in each blank with the appropriate standard verb form of *be, have,* or *do* in the present or past tense.

I have (1) this problem called a little brother. Though I am (2) always nice to him, he enjoys embarrassing me. The other night, for example, I had (3) my boyfriend over to the house. The lights were turned down low, and my boyfriend and I were (4) alone on the living-room couch. At least I thought so. That Dennis-the-Menace clone who is (5) my brother crawled into the living room with a portable cassette recorder. My boyfriend and I did (6) not notice him because we had (7) started getting "friendly." It was (8) the next night when I discovered what that little brat had (9) been up to. In front of my parents, he played the tape. His plan was (10) a big success, because I felt embarrassed to death.

Part 2 Fill in the correct form of the regular verb in parentheses.

Shopping at a convenience store isn't always so convenient. The other night I (stop) stopped (1) off at the local Seven-Eleven to pick up a two-liter bottle of diet soda and a package of chips. After I had (park) parked (2) my car and gone inside, I was (greet) greeted (3) by the sight of a long line of customers, which was (back) backed (4) up down one aisle. Since Seven-Eleven was the only place still open at that time of night, I (decide) decided (5) to stay. I (pick) picked (6) up my soda and potato chips and (walk) walked (7) to the end of the line. I saw that the delay was (cause) caused (8) by a woman who had (place) placed (9) a large order for lunch meat. And the teenage boy waiting on her (move) moved (10) like someone in a slow-motion film.

Score Number correct ______ × 5 = ______ %

Standard English Verbs

■ Mastery Test 4

Part 1 Fill in each blank with the appropriate standard verb form of *be, have,* or *do* in the present or past tense.

There ____is____ (1) one thing my mother does better than anybody else in the world—make requests. It seems she ____has____ (2) to start right in as soon as I wake up. "____Did____ (3) you make your bed, Arnold?" she always asks me. "____Are____ (4) you going to wear that nice sport shirt I pressed for you last night? ____Do____ (5) not forget to put out the trash before you leave for school, dear. ____Are____ (6) you still going to paint the basement this weekend? ____Did____ (7) you remember to stop by the grocery on your way home from school?" She ____has____ (8) an endless supply of such appeals. I think I ____have____ (9) to get out of here. Maybe it ____is____ (10) time to get married, which happens to be another thing she wants me to do.

Part 2 Fill in each blank with the appropriate form of the regular verb shown in parentheses. Use present or past tense as needed.

Driving on trips with my three-year-old son has its drawbacks. For one thing he (find) ____finds____ (1) it difficult to sit still for long. Besides that, when he (eat) ____eats____ (2) in the car, which is frequently, he (scatter) ____scatters____ (3) crumbs all over the backseat and floor. And after each time he (snack) ____snacks____ (4) on something, he (insist) ____insists____ (5) on touching everything in sight with his dirty hands. My mother (believe) ____believes____ (6) he actually (enjoy) ____enjoys____ (7) smudging the windows with grease. Last week, driving (affect) ____affected____ (8) his stomach, which (require) ____required____ (9) an unpleasant stop at the side of the road. The only good thing about traveling with my son is that he still (take) ____takes____ (10) naps a couple of times a day.

Score Number correct ________ × 5 = ________ %

Irregular Verbs

■ Mastery Test 1

Underline the correct word in the parentheses.

1. (Lying, Laying) in the hot sun is bad for the skin.
2. Last night I (saw, seen) a dead collie on the road.
3. My girlfriend (teached, taught) me how to make curtains for my van.
4. The judge reminded Daniel that he had (sworn, swore) to tell the truth.
5. My boss has (chosen, chose) to treat me the way a baby treats a diaper.
6. Whenever I had an important date, my brother (lended, lent) me his good jacket.
7. Molly has finally (took, taken) aspirin for the headache she's had all day.
8. Five different people had (bringed, brought) huge bowls of potato salad to the barbecue.
9. I scratched the spot where the hornet (stinged, stung) me till I bled.
10. The picture I (drawed, drew) in art class ended up looking like a plate of spaghetti.
11. Taking care of two of the neighbor's children this week has (worn, wore) me out.
12. I left the wine in the freezer to cool, and it (froze, freezed) into wine slush.
13. Our cat (stoled, stole) home in the middle of the night after being gone for a week.
14. Stan's truck (rises, raises) a cloud of dust when it comes down the dirt road.
15. My research paper is due in two weeks, and I haven't even (begun, began) to work on it.
16. Having (slept, sleeped) all day, Dracula looked forward to a bite to eat.
17. I accidentally (throwed, threw) away the parking ticket when I cleaned out my glove compartment.
18. After playing touch football all afternoon, Jake (drunk, drank) a quart of Gatorade.
19. Since Carol left a third of the answer spaces blank, she (knew, knowed) she had failed the psychology exam.
20. After you have (broke, broken) up with a boyfriend or girlfriend, every day feels like a cloudy, cold Monday morning.

Score Number correct ______ × 5 = ______ %

Irregular Verbs

■ Mastery Test 2

Cross out the incorrect verb form in each sentence. Write the correct form in the space provided.

rang 1. The phone ~~rung~~ once and then stopped.

spent 2. Rosie ~~spended~~ an entire week's salary on a new pair of boots.

broken 3. No one had ~~broke~~ the news to Rich that he had not made the team.

blew 4. The hurricane winds ~~blowed~~ several beach houses off their foundations.

swum 5. I've ~~swam~~ in this lake for years, and I've never seen it so shallow.

driven 6. That trucker has ~~drove~~ over a million accident-free miles.

hidden 7. How did the police know where the kidnappers had ~~hid~~ their victim?

shrank 8. My cotton sweater ~~shranked~~ so much in the wash that I gave it to my daughter.

taken 9. If I had ~~took~~ more notes in that class, I would have done better on the exam.

threw 10. The second baseman fielded the grounder, stepped on the bag, and then ~~throwed~~ to first for a double play.

Score Number correct _______ × 10 = _______ %

Irregular Verbs

■ Mastery Test 3

Write in the space provided the correct form of the verb shown at the left.

grow	1. My nephew must have ___grown___ six inches since last summer.
drive	2. We ___drove___ almost seven hundred miles before pulling over for a break.
fall	3. Frowning, the building inspector stood where the store's sign had ___fallen___.
fight	4. My parents ___fought___ with the IRS for a year before finally paying the additional tax.
break	5. During last night's storm, lightning ___broke___ the clock over the town hall.
write	6. The police found the hit-and-run driver because Aunt Edith had ___written___ the license number down.
eat	7. Hank's dog climbed onto the kitchen table at night and ___ate___ most of the chocolate chip cookies.
tear	8. After he ___tore___ the cartilage in his knee for the third time, Bubba decided to retire from football.
take	9. The orchestra arrived two hours late for the New Year's Eve party because the bus driver had ___taken___ a wrong turn.
go	10. When his boss caught him sleeping at his desk, Norman wished he had ___gone___ to bed earlier the night before.

Score Number correct ______ × 10 = ______ %

Irregular Verbs

■ Mastery Test 4

Write in the space provided the correct form of the verb shown at the left.

see	1. My roommate and I ___saw___ a double feature this weekend.
bring	2. I should have ___brought___ a gift to the office Christmas party.
speak	3. Has the supervisor ___spoken___ to Marcia yet about being late for work?
come	4. Just as we were talking about Rob's new pickup truck, Rob ___came___ up the driveway.
throw	5. Huey ___threw___ out his back trying to put a new air conditioner in his bedroom window.
sing	6. I could have ___sung___ professionally, but I lacked the determination to pursue a career.
sit	7. When I have company for dinner, I ___sit___ in the middle of the table rather than at one end.
speak	8. Our guest is a former police detective who has ___spoken___ all over the country on the subject of teenage drug abuse.
choose	9. I know I should have ___chosen___ a different major, but I don't want to start from the beginning now.
give	10. The state trooper ___gave___ Harley a warning for riding his motorcycle on the interstate without a safety helmet.

Score Number correct ______ × 10 = ______ %

Subject-Verb Agreement

■ Mastery Test 1

Underline the correct verb in the parentheses. Note that you will first have to determine the subject in each sentence. To help find subjects in certain sentences, you may find it helpful to cross out prepositional phrases.

1. Many stories in the *National Enquirer* (seems, seem) hard to believe.
2. Where (has, have) all the pens gone in this house?
3. One of my sweaters (has, have) moth holes in the sleeves.
4. There (is, are) plenty of reasons for not going to the party tonight.
5. Each of the marathon runners (receives, receive) a special T-shirt.
6. The records in my collection (is, are) arranged alphabetically.
7. Football players who (scores, score) touchdowns get most of the glory.
8. The major story on all the news programs (concerns, concern) the president's operation.
9. Both of the drive-in windows at the bank (closes, close) at three o'clock.
10. Here (is, are) my address and phone number, so you can get in touch.
11. On the front page of the newspaper (was, were) a story about my accident.
12. Someone (keeps, keep) calling me and hanging up when I answer.
13. How (does, do) the weather forecasters determine if it's partly sunny or partly cloudy?
14. Growing in the middle of our flower bed (was, were) a single stalk of wild asparagus.
15. Every one of the boxers (seems, seem) to follow a different training regimen.
16. Each of my little boys (needs, need) a warmer jacket for the winter.
17. The level of water in local reservoirs (has, have) dropped dramatically recently.
18. The figure that intrigues Wayne most in his geometry class (belongs, belong) to the girl sitting next to him.
19. Why (does, do) many appliances stop working as soon as their warranties expire?
20. Orange slices and ginger ale still (needs, need) to be added to the punch.

Score Number correct _______ × 5 = _______ %

Subject-Verb Agreement

■ Mastery Test 2

In the space provided, write the correct form of the verb shown in the margin.

cares, care 1. Gina seems like the kind of person who ___cares___ more about style than about substance.

was, were 2. There ___were___ only two handkerchiefs left in the drawer.

runs, run 3. The portable television and the radio ___run___ on batteries or house current.

snarls, snarl 4. Either construction work or accidents ___snarl___ expressway traffic every morning.

has, have 5. Along with the two graduate assistants, the professor ___has___ conducted the experiment hundreds of times.

is, are 6. At least a few of the gray hairs on your poor father's head ___are___ due to you and that no-good brother of yours.

finds, find 7. Each runner, summoning all the courage and adrenaline he has left, ___finds___ that the ultimate challenger is himself.

is, are 8. Lined up outside the movie theater ___are___ dozens of impatient children and their angry parents.

seems, seem 9. Politicians, I have noticed, often ___seem___ to choose words very carefully, as if selecting stones to step on while crossing a stream.

was, were 10. I found it almost impossible to believe that this seventy-year-old man, with his rumpled clothes, ___was___ a mass murderer.

Score Number correct ______ × 10 = ______ %

Subject-Verb Agreement

■ Mastery Test 3

Cross out the incorrect form of the verb. In addition, underline the subject that goes with the verb. Then write the correct form of the verb in the space provided. Mark the one sentence that is correct with a *C*.

works 1. Each of the secretaries ~~work~~ from nine to five.

seems 2. The price of the theater tickets ~~seem~~ much too high.

accompany 3. A salad, beverage, and dessert ~~accompanies~~ the meal.

were 4. There ~~was~~ only three pieces of wood left in the pile.

make 5. The new tenant and her little boy ~~makes~~ a lot of noise.

are 6. Corn on the cob, iced tea, and watermelon ~~is~~ symbolic of summer.

is 7. One of the most regal-looking animals in the zoo ~~are~~ the big-horned sheep.

C 8. The picture on the cover of that paperback gives the wrong idea of the book's story.

have 9. Neither Brenda nor her sisters ~~has~~ enough money to go to the movies tonight.

were 10. The roots of the tree on the beach ~~was~~ exposed by erosion from the surf.

Score Number correct ______ × 10 = ______ %

Subject-Verb Agreement

■ Mastery Test 4

Cross out the incorrect form of the verb. In addition, underline the subject that goes with the verb. Then write the correct form of the verb in the space provided. Mark the one sentence that is correct with a *C*.

are 1. When is Kay and her parents going on vacation?

wanders 2. One of the patients wander aimlessly down the halls.

take 3. My sister and her husband takes my father bowling every Thursday night.

has 4. Each of the fast-food restaurants now have a breakfast special.

was 5. Next to the newborn chicks were one of the barn rats.

curl 6. Whenever the coach gets angry, both sides of his mouth curls up in a sneer.

C 7. The clouds part, and the warming rays of the sun shine through, bringing instant heat with them.

has 8. Anyone who comes in late to Mr. Barker's class have to have a good excuse.

feels 9. Snuggling under the covers feel wonderful on Saturday mornings.

lasts 10. A box of shredded wheat last about a year in our house, since the kids call it "shredded steel wool."

Score Number correct ______ × 10 = ______ %

Consistent Verb Tense

■ Mastery Test 1

In each item, one verb must be changed so that it agrees in tense with the other verb or verbs. Cross out the inconsistent verb and write the correct form in the space provided.

counted 1. Sofia asked the grouchy cashier for change, and he ~~counts~~ out twenty-five pennies.

cleared 2. After dinner, my parents watched the news while the children ~~clear~~ the table and washed the dishes.

called 3. I walked through town yesterday, and a friend from grade school ~~calls~~ to me.

sprayed 4. Rose tried to avoid breathing the fumes as she ~~sprays~~ her houseplants with pesticide.

remembered 5. When we arrived at the theater, I suddenly ~~remember~~ that I had left the oven turned on at home.

guided 6. Annie sighed as her little boy repeatedly ~~guides~~ the spoonful of mashed carrots to his ear.

rushed 7. I drank the ice water too quickly; sharp pains ~~rush~~ to my temple and forced me to stop walking for a minute.

turned 8. Upon finding a seat on the bus, Victor unfolded his newspaper, ~~turns~~ to the sports section, and began to read.

face 9. Polar bear cubs stay with their mothers for two years; then they leave home and ~~faced~~ the Arctic winter alone.

was 10. Our family car was in sad shape; the tires were worn, the chrome ~~is~~ pitted, and the paint came off if you rubbed it too hard.

Score Number correct ______ × 10 = ______ %

Consistent Verb Tense

■ Mastery Test 2

In each item, one verb must be changed so that it agrees in tense with the other verb or verbs. Cross out the inconsistent verb and write the correct form in the space provided.

skips 1. Hana eats a nutritious breakfast, ~~skipped~~ lunch, and then enjoys a big dinner.

saluted 2. The wrestler stepped into the ring, ~~salutes~~ the crowd, and banged on his chest like Tarzan.

combed 3. Tears streamed down little Heather's face as her father ~~combs~~ her tangled hair.

opens 4. The restaurant near the wharf ~~opened~~ in May, stays busy all summer, and then closes for the winter.

hummed 5. At the game, Danny ~~hums~~ along with the national anthem when he forgot some of the words.

wants 6. Terri buys and reads several romance novels every month, for she ~~wanted~~ to escape from her dull daily routine.

sliced 7. When he prepared the omelet, the chef grated fresh cheese, chopped an onion, and ~~slices~~ a crisp green pepper.

tightened 8. To make the dress fit, Inez shortened the shoulder straps, moved a button, and ~~tightens~~ the waist.

passed 9. Stu got his driver's license after he had an eye exam, took a written quiz, and ~~passes~~ a driving-skills test.

turned 10. Before she decided to buy the wall calendar, Magda ~~turns~~ its pages and looked at all the pictures.

Score Number correct ______ × 10 = ______ %

Pronoun Reference, Agreement, and Point of View

■ Mastery Test 1

Underline the correct word in the parentheses.

1. As Jill argued with her mother, (she, Jill) became more and more upset.
2. One of the female astronauts will take (her, their) first space walk during the flight.
3. If you stay up too late watching television, (one, you) may walk around like a zombie the next day.
4. At the library, (they, the librarian) showed me how to use the microfilm machines.
5. Everyone who works in this company must have (his or her, their) chest x-rayed every two years.
6. The nurse finally penetrated my vein with a large needle, although (it, the vein) had been hard to find.
7. I like living in a large apartment house because (I, you) have more chances to meet people.
8. Jesse's brother called to say that (he, Jesse) had gotten bad news from the doctor.
9. Although I was an announcer on my college radio station, I wouldn't want to make a career of (announcing, it).
10. Anybody who lives to (their, his or her) ninetieth year is eligible to receive a birthday card from the president.

Score Number correct _______ × 10 = _______ %

Pronoun Reference, Agreement, and Point of View

■ Mastery Test 2

In the space provided, write *PE* beside sentences that contain pronoun errors. Write *C* beside the two sentences that use pronouns correctly. Then cross out each pronoun error and write the correction above it.

Corrections may vary somewhat.

PE **Example** Each of the boys explained ~~their~~ *his* project.

PE 1. Vincent doesn't like visiting his in-laws because ~~you~~ *he* never feel*s* like part of the family.

PE 2. Nadine told her niece that ~~she~~ *the niece (or Nadine)* would be famous someday.

PE 3. I ordered three albums from the record store, but ~~they~~ *the store* never sent them.

PE 4. We are treated horribly at work; ~~they~~ *our bosses* must think we're slaves.

C 5. Someone on the team shared his complaints with a reporter.

PE 6. Ernie placed the ladder against the wall of the garage and then leaned against ~~it~~ *the wall (or the ladder)* for a moment.

C 7. Each of these jobs has its advantages: one has good pay, and the other has short hours.

PE 8. I like to watch TV quiz shows because ~~you~~ *I* can learn a lot from their questions.

PE 9. The college instructors made sure the students understood that ~~they~~ *the students* were bright and capable.

PE 10. Any salesperson in our office will win a free trip to Hawaii if ~~they~~ *he or she* can sell one house in the next twenty-four hours.

Score Number correct ______ × 10 = ______ %

Pronoun Reference, Agreement, and Point of View

■ Mastery Test 3

In the spaces provided, write *PE* beside sentences that contain pronoun errors. Write *C* beside the two sentences that use pronouns correctly. Then cross out each pronoun error and write the correction above it.

PE 1. When the car banged into the wall, ~~it~~ [the car (or the wall)] was damaged.

PE 2. One of my friends entered ~~their~~ [his (or her)] dog in a Frisbee tournament.

PE 3. One of the floorboards is warped, and I keep tripping on ~~them~~ [it].

PE 4. As I slowed down at the scene of the accident, ~~you~~ [I] could see long black skid marks on the highway.

C 5. As we looked out the plane window, we could see roads and buildings get smaller and smaller.

C 6. All visitors should stay in their cars while driving through the wild animal park.

PE 7. Tisha avoids office parties because ~~one~~ [she] always has to watch out for the office Romeos.

PE 8. I always shopped at that market because ~~they~~ [it] had such a large selection.

PE 9. A person who likes to criticize others often objects when someone teases ~~them~~ [him or her].

PE 10. If anyone works with an irresponsible lab partner, ~~you~~ [he or she] will find it difficult to complete experiments successfully.

Score Number correct _______ × 10 = _______ %

Pronoun Reference, Agreement, and Point of View

■ Mastery Test 4

In the spaces provided, write *PE* beside sentences that contain pronoun errors. Write *C* beside the two sentences that use pronouns correctly. Then cross out each pronoun error and write the correction above it. One item needs to be rewritten altogether. Identify it and rewrite it in the space at the bottom.

Corrections may vary somewhat.

PE 1. Bill spent a half hour complaining to Gary about ~~his~~ [Bill's (or Gary's)] girlfriend.

PE 2. As I watched the pro wrestling match, ~~you~~ [I] could tell the violence was faked.

C 3. Each gymnast has to develop his or her own floor routine.

PE 4. I arrived late for the final exam in English, which is why I failed ~~it~~ [the exam (or English)].

PE 5. Anybody willing to volunteer ~~their~~ [his or her] time to work at the shelter for the homeless should sign up here.

PE 6. My sister and I fought a lot as children, but ~~you~~ [we] learned to get along better as grown-ups.

C 7. Sally received an ad in the mail that said she could make six hundred dollars a month addressing envelopes.

PE 8. One of the players on the women's basketball team scored ~~their~~ [her] thousandth point yesterday.

PE 9. Mr. Penge invited his students to his home to meet a famous scientist, ~~which~~ made them feel special.

PE 10. During my first year in college, I stayed in a dorm where ~~they~~ [dormitory officials] chose a roommate for me.

Rewritten Version of Item : 9

Mr. Penge made his students feel special by inviting them to his home to meet a famous scientist. (Rewritten version may vary.)

Score Number correct ______ × 10 = ______ %

Pronoun Types

Mastery Test 1

Underline the correct word in parentheses.

1. Paul is a much faster typist than (I, me).
2. (That, That there) tree will probably fall over with the next strong wind.
3. Since I'm about to get sick, that last drink is (yours, yours') if you want it.
4. My neighbor asked Eric and (I, me) to help him unload his new living-room furniture.
5. The students raised the money for the class trip (theirselves, themselves).
6. Our neighbors take (they, their) dog with them whenever they go for a ride.
7. My sister and (I, me) have gotten part-time jobs at the same store.
8. I feel certain that Steven will speak for (hisself, himself) at the meeting tonight.
9. Before I dated Don, I dated a number of friends of (his, his').
10. It was up to Kelly and (I, me) to fix the loose handrail on the back porch.
11. (Them, Those) strawberries we picked should taste delicious on our homemade ice cream.
12. After the riot, the members of the rock group (theirselves, themselves) decided to go on with the concert.
13. My father always said to remember to give each man the respect due to (he, him).
14. Julie is the one student (who, whom) is doing well in that class.
15. The audience laughed when Mario and (he, him) walked onstage in the carrot costumes.
16. Terry left some old books of (her's, hers) when she moved out of the apartment.
17. The encyclopedia salesman insisted on talking to my wife and (I, me) at the same time.
18. If any of you want tickets to the play-offs, you will have to pick them up (yourselfs, yourselves).
19. I couldn't decide to (who, whom) I should tell the secret.
20. If we don't get overtime pay for working on the holiday, (we, us) employees are going to file a complaint.

Score Number correct ______ × 5 = ______ %

Pronoun Types

■ Mastery Test 2

Cross out the incorrect pronoun in each sentence and write the correct form in the space provided at the left.

That 1. ~~That there~~ house across the street has been vacant for two years now.

hers 2. The wallet that was stolen from the health club is ~~hers'~~.

me 3. Give Chet and ~~I~~ a few hours, and we'll have that washing machine running again.

himself 4. Rodney convinced ~~hisself~~ he would win the bowling match, and he did.

he 5. If I have to be marooned on a desert island with someone, I hope it is ~~him.~~

yours 6. Carla has put everything of ~~yours'~~ in the hall closet.

me 7. Just between you and ~~I~~, the mayor is a horrible womanizer.

themselves 8. The coaches ~~themself~~ took full blame for the loss of the football game.

they 9. You two have a better attitude about school than ~~them~~.

these 10. Please clear your books off the table, so I can set ~~these here~~ dishes down.

us 11. At the meeting, the store buyers told ~~we~~ salespeople about the new fall line.

its 12. The tornado destroyed everything in ~~its'~~ path.

he 13. If you were as nervous as ~~him~~, your forehead would be sweating too.

me 14. When our whispering started to annoy her, the librarian asked Paula and ~~I~~ to leave.

those 15. You can tell ~~them~~ plants haven't been watered in ages because their leaves are turning brown.

me 16. After the police released us from the station, Father read my brother and ~~I~~ the riot act.

who 17. Margo did not recognize the man ~~whom~~ stood at her apartment door.

theirs 18. Our students seem to have less school spirit than ~~theirs'~~.

ourselves 19. We asked ~~ourself~~ why such a young girl would try to take her own life.

I 20. Although we got a late start, Herbie and ~~me~~ collected enough aluminum cans along the highway to fill three plastic trash bags.

Score Number correct _______ × 5 = _______ %

Adjectives and Adverbs

Mastery Test 1

Part 1 Cross out the incorrect adjectival and adverbial form in each sentence. Then write the correct form in the space provided.

1. I did my work ~~silent~~, but I was seething inside.

   silently

2. The children's smiles were so ~~sweetly~~ that I knew they were up to something.

   sweet

3. Sarita was proud that she had stuck to her diet ~~faithful~~ for two weeks.

   faithfully

4. The students gazed ~~longing~~ at the clock as the instructor's voice droned on.

   longingly

5. Signs warn motorists to drive ~~slow~~ near the school.

   slowly

Part 2 Cross out the error in comparison in each sentence. Then write the correct form in the space provided.

6. Roy can't pitch, but he catches ~~good~~.

   well

7. You gave me a ~~more smaller~~ slice of pizza than you gave Bud.

   smaller

8. A king-size bed is much ~~comfortabler~~ than a single bed.

   more comfortable

9. Mrs. Patridge owns several banks, but she's the ~~most stingiest~~ person I know.

   stingiest

10. My coach said I had the ~~most good~~ chance of any person on the team of becoming a professional ballplayer.

    best

Score Number correct ______ × 10 = ______ %

Adjective and Adverbs

Mastery Test 2

Part 1 Cross out the incorrect adjectival and adverbial form in each sentence. Then write the correct form in the space provided.

1. Too many children complain that their parents don't take them ~~serious~~.
   seriously
2. The president's spouse greeted all the guests at the reception ~~warm~~.
   warmly
3. He is the most ~~fiendishly~~ culprit the police have ever encountered.
   fiendish
4. Fran polished the dull chrome tabletop until she could see her face ~~clear~~ in it.
   clearly
5. The doctor said I wasn't ~~good~~ enough to travel, but I stubbornly refused to listen to him.
   well

Part 2 Add to each sentence the correct form of the word at the left.

good 6. Of the two hundred applicants, Olivia was easily the ___best___.

few 7. ___Fewer___ people live in Los Angeles than in New York.

boring 8. Of all the new television shows I have watched this year, that comedy is the ___most boring___.

high 9. Since my car is twelve years old, it requires a ___higher___-octane gasoline than yours.

scary 10. *The Night of the Living Dead* is the ___scariest___ movie I have ever seen.

Score Number correct ______ × 10 = ______ %

Misplaced Modifiers

■ Mastery Test 1

Underline the misplaced word or words in each sentence. Then rewrite the sentence, placing related words together and making the meaning clear.

Rewritten sentences may vary somewhat.

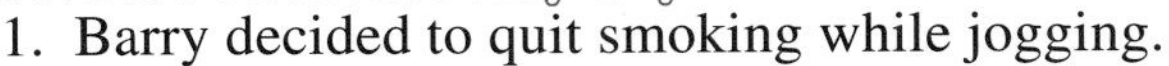

1. Barry decided to quit smoking while jogging.

   While jogging, Barry decided to quit smoking.

2. The suburbs nearly had five inches of rain.

   The suburbs had nearly five inches of rain.

3. I decided to send fewer Christmas cards out this year in October.

   I decided in October to send fewer Christmas cards out this year.

4. My mother talked about her plans to start a garden while preparing dinner.

   While preparing dinner, my mother talked about her plans to start a garden.

5. The car was parked along the side of the road with a flat tire.

   The car with a flat tire was parked along the side of the road.

6. Olivia stretched out on the lounge chair wearing her bathing suit.

   Wearing her bathing suit, Olivia stretched out on the lounge chair.

7. Caryl read an article about starting your own business in the dentist's office.

   In the dentist's office, Caryl read an article about starting your own business.

8. A cake baked by my brother covered with coconut and candies was the prizewinner.

   Covered with coconut and candies, a cake baked by my brother was the prizewinner.

Score Number correct _____ × 12.5 = _____ %

Misplaced Modifiers

■ Mastery Test 2

Underline the misplaced word or words in each sentence. Then rewrite the sentence, placing related words together and making the meaning clear.

Rewritten sentences may vary somewhat.

1. I replaced the shingle on the roof that was loose.

   I replaced the shingle that was loose on the roof.

2. The instructor explained why cheating was wrong on Friday.

   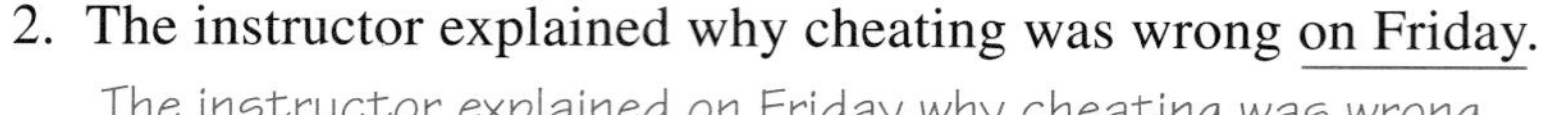

   The instructor explained on Friday why cheating was wrong.

3. Jamal ordered a large pizza for his family topped with extra cheese.

   Jamal ordered for his family a large pizza topped with extra cheese.

4. The helicopter filmed the migrating antelope hovering overhead.

   Hovering overhead, the helicopter filmed the migrating antelope.

5. We bought a television set at our neighborhood video store that has stereo sound.

   At our neighborhood video store, we bought a television set that has stereo sound.

6. The magician almost held his breath for five minutes while escaping from the submerged trunk.

   The magician held his breath for almost five minutes while escaping from the submerged trunk.

7. Neighborhood children watched the new family move in from the street corner.

   From the street corner, neighborhood children watched the new family move in.

8. Newspapers ran the story of the congressman's lies in every part of the country.

   Newspapers in every part of the country ran the story of the congressman's lies.

Score Number correct ______ × 12.5 = ______ %

Dangling Modifiers

■ Mastery Test 1

Underline the dangling modifier in each sentence. Then rewrite the sentence, correcting the dangling modifier.

Answers may vary.

1. Being on a diet, my pie had no whipped cream.

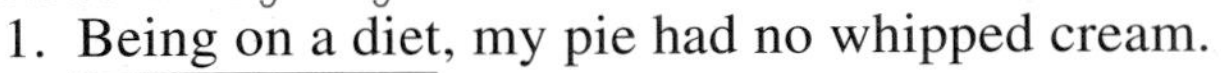

Being on a diet, I had no whipped cream on my pie.

2. Running as fast as I could, the bus waited for me.

While I ran as fast as I could, the bus waited for me.

3. After a nap in my room, my mother always gave me a snack.

After a nap in my room, I always got a snack from my mother.

4. Running to catch the ball at full speed, my cap went flying into the wind.

As I ran to catch the ball at full speed, my cap went flying into the wind.

5. While looking for bargains at Sears, an exercise bike caught my eye.

While I looked for bargains at Sears, an exercise bike caught my eye.

6. Filled with sand, Debbie took off her shoes before going into the house.

Debbie took off her shoes, which were filled with sand, before going into the house.

7. Pedaling as fast as possible, Todd's bike pulled away from the snapping dog.

Pedaling as fast as possible, Todd pulled his bike away from the snapping dog.

8. Punctured by a pin, Dexter mended his water bed with a plastic bandage.

Punctured by a pin, Dexter's water bed was mended with a plastic bandage.

Score Number correct ______ × 12.5 = ______ %

Dangling Modifiers

■ Mastery Test 2

Underline the dangling modifier in each sentence. Then rewrite the sentence, correcting the dangling modifier.

Rewritten sentences may vary.

1. Being hungry as a bear, my dinner was enormous.

   Because I was as hungry as a bear, my dinner was enormous.

2. Feet spread, the police frisked the suspects for weapons.

   Feet spread, the suspects were frisked for weapons by the police.

3. Blown over in the hurricane, Roberto had to build a new garage.

   Because his garage blew over in the hurricane, Roberto had to build a new one.

4. Stolen from the mall parking lot, my girlfriend spotted my sports car the next day.

   My sports car was stolen from the mall parking lot, and my girlfriend spotted it the next day.

5. Even before being housebroken, I thought the beagle was lovable.

   Even before it was housebroken, I thought the beagle was lovable.

6. Walking down the weedy path, the old, weathered house loomed larger than I had remembered.

   As I walked down the weedy path, the old, weathered house loomed larger than I had remembered.

7. While dreaming about the beach, the alarm suddenly woke Lynn up.

   While Lynn was dreaming about the beach, the alarm suddenly woke her up.

8. After spending most of the night outdoors in a tent, the sun rose, and we went into the house.

   We spent most of the night outdoors in a tent and went into the house after the sun rose.

Score Number correct _______ × 12.5 = _______ %

Faulty Parallelism

■ Mastery Test 1

The unbalanced part of each sentence is italicized. Rewrite this part so that it matches the rest of the sentence.

1. The theater popcorn was greasy, stale, and *had too much salt.*
   salty
2. I would rather have you call me on the phone than *sending me a letter.*
   send me a letter
3. The orchestra leader had slick black hair, a long thin nose, and *eyes that were dark blue.*
   dark blue eyes
4. Whenever I get home, my dog barks, *is running to get his ball,* and drops it at my feet.
   runs to get his ball
5. The job applicant—well dressed, well spoken, and *with a good education*—impressed the interviewer.
   well educated
6. I stood for two hours in the hot sun in my heavy wool dress, long-sleeved jacket, and *shoes that were tight.*
   tight shoes
7. After his family's weekend visit ended, Enrique was exhausted and relieved but *was feeling lonely.*
   lonely (or felt lonely)
8. Before assembling the casserole, Marty had to sauté the onions and *stirring them into the ground meat.*
   stir them into the ground meat
9. As they neared the ocean, they could hear the waves, smell the salt water, and *the dampness was felt by them.*
   feel the dampness
10. They spent a relaxing afternoon enjoying the view from their balcony, eating lunch at an old inn, and *window-shopped* in the village square.
    window-shopping

Score Number correct ________ × 10 = ________ %

Faulty Parallelism

Mastery Test 2

Draw a line under the unbalanced part of each sentence. Then rewrite the unbalanced part so that it matches the other items in the sentence.

Rewritten portions may vary somewhat.

1. The movie contains adult language, nudity, and it is violent.
   violence
2. My doctor told me to stop smoking and that I should lose weight.
   to lose weight (or lose weight)
3. Holly was frightened, upset, and a nervous wreck; she had three exams in the next two days.
   nervous
4. We had a choice of chocolate-flavored coffee or coffee flavored with cinnamon.
   cinnamon-flavored coffee
5. After moving the furniture, spreading a drop cloth, and the wall edges were taped, we were ready to paint.
   taping the wall edges
6. Toshio promised his girlfriend he would be more reliable, less moody, and jealous less often.
   less jealous
7. I've tried several cures for my headaches, including medication, exercise, meditation, and massaging my head.
   massage for my head
8. The astronauts' concerns were landing on the satellite, to take off again, and reentering the earth's atmosphere.
   taking off again
9. I'm attending college to gain knowledge, to meet people, and preparation for a good job.
   to prepare for a good job
10. My aunt believes that the moon landing was a hoax, in the invasion of earth by aliens, and that Hitler is living in South America.
    that the earth has been invaded by aliens

Score Number correct ________ × 10 = ________ %

Sentence Variety II

■ Mastery Test 1

Combine each group of short sentences into one sentence. Various combinations are possible. Choose the combination that reads most smoothly and clearly and that sounds most appropriate in the context of surrounding sentences.

Note In combining short sentences into one sentence, omit repeated words where necessary. Use separate paper. The story about the snake continues in the next mastery test.

Answers may vary.

The Snake and the Frog

- An unusual thing happened.
- It happened in my backyard.
- It happened while I was mowing the grass.

An unusual thing happened in my backyard while I was mowing the grass.

- There is an old wall in the yard.
- It is a stone wall.
- It is bordered by high weeds.

There is an old stone wall in the yard, bordered by high weeds.

- I approached the wall with the mower.
- I saw a snake.
- The snake was yellow and black.
- I saw it in the weeds.

When I approached the wall with the mower, I saw a yellow and black snake in the weeds.

- I thought the snake had been crushed.
- I thought this at first.
- The snake's "neck" was widened and bulging.

At first I thought the snake had been crushed because its "neck" was widened and bulging.

- I grabbed my metal hoe.
- I slid it under the snake.
- I began to lift the snake.
- I did this carefully.

I grabbed my metal hoe, slid it under the snake, and began to lift the snake carefully.

Score Number correct ________ × 20 = ________ %

Sentence Variety II

■ Mastery Test 2

Combine each group of short sentences into one sentence. Various combinations are possible. Choose the combination that reads most smoothly and clearly and that sounds most appropriate in the context of surrounding sentences.

Note In combining short sentences into one sentence, omit repeated words where necessary. Use separate paper. The story about the snake continues from the previous mastery test.

Answers may vary.

- The snake shuddered.
- The snake opened its mouth wide.
- The snake began to regurgitate something.

Shuddering, the snake opened its mouth wide and began to regurgitate something.

- I watched in horror.
- The snake coughed up a frog.
- The frog was large.
- The frog was green.

As I watched in horror, the snake coughed up a large, green frog.

- I had interrupted the snake.
- He had been digesting a fresh meal.
- I did this unknowingly.

Unknowingly, I had interrupted the snake as it digested a fresh meal.

- The snake crawled away.
- The snake was suddenly slim.
- The snake slithered into a cranny in the stone wall.

The snake, suddenly slim, crawled away and slithered into a cranny in the stone wall.

- I was amazed.
- I was shocked.
- I stood staring at the frog.
- The frog was dead.

Amazed and shocked, I stood staring at the dead frog.

Score Number correct ________ × 20 = ________ %

Capital Letters

■ Mastery Test 1

Cross out the two capitalization errors in each of the following sentences. Then write the corrections in the spaces provided.

Thanksgiving
world

1. One of our ~~thanksgiving~~ traditions is sending a check to an organization dedicated to relieving ~~World~~ hunger.

Academy
mascot

2. Josh couldn't understand why the U.S. Naval ~~academy~~ would want to have a goat for a ~~Mascot~~.

brother
Monopoly

3. Until he actually walked on the boardwalk in Atlantic City, my ~~Brother~~ thought it was just a blue strip on the ~~monopoly~~ game board.

Grandmom
Grandpop

4. I spent my vacation visiting ~~grandmom~~ and ~~grandpop~~ in New York City.

lake
west

5. To get to the ~~Lake~~, go ~~West~~ for five miles until you see a Honda billboard.

Cajun
French

6. There are only a few people in Louisiana who still speak ~~cajun~~, a language similar to ~~french~~.

Uncle
South

7. In ~~uncle~~ Charlie's last letter, he wrote that he was thinking of retiring and moving to the ~~south~~.

Chevy
Wendy's

8. Vern's old ~~chevy~~ finally broke down outside a ~~wendy's~~ a few blocks from his home.

Dracula
Doctor

9. Count ~~dracula~~ asked ~~doctor~~ Frankenstein to make a donation to the annual blood drive.

Red
Cross

10. When the ~~red~~ ~~cross~~ arrived, many of the flood victims were wandering the muddy streets in a daze.

Score Number correct ______ × 5 = ______ %

Capital Letters

■ Mastery Test 2

Cross out the two capitalization errors in each of the following sentences. Then write the corrections in the spaces provided.

Center
Out

1. A sign on a closed office door at the Kennedy Space ~~center~~ read, "~~out~~ to launch."

Toyota
Canada

2. While I was driving my ~~toyota~~ to ~~canada~~, the state police stopped me for speeding.

Quinn
heart

3. Dr. ~~quinn~~ told me that if I didn't lose twenty pounds, I'd be risking a ~~Heart~~ attack.

Technical
Writing

4. Laura was happy that Mr. Armstrong would be teaching ~~technical writing~~ II this semester.

Mr.
Live

5. It was *Star Trek's* ~~mr.~~ Spock who said, "~~live~~ long and prosper."

Service
West

6. Lena and I wrote to the National Park ~~service~~ for information on camping sites out ~~west~~.

James
Scrabble

7. My brother ~~james~~ benefits from my poor spelling whenever we play ~~scrabble~~.

Latin
summer

8. Carlos, an exchange student from ~~latin~~ America, spent last ~~Summer~~ living with our family.

Paramount
holiday

9. Each Christmas, big motion picture studios such as MGM and ~~paramount~~ release new films aimed at attracting huge ~~Holiday~~ audiences.

cigarettes
Eve

10. The maker of ~~Cigarettes~~ such as ~~eve~~ and Virginia Slims try to lure women consumers by using pastel colors and slender shapes.

Score Number correct _______ × 5 = _______ %

Capital Letters

■ Mastery Test 3

Cross out the two capitalization errors in each of the following sentences. Then write the corrections in the spaces provided.

steak Chinese	1. Is it possible to order a ~~Steak~~ sandwich at a ~~chinese~~ restaurant?
spring September	2. Many romances that blossom in ~~Spring~~ wilt by ~~september~~.
Jekyll Mr.	3. Doctor ~~jekyll~~ seemed to do better with the women when he turned into ~~mr.~~ Hyde.
Beatles' Yesterday	4. Nicole feels sentimental every time the ~~beatles'~~ song "~~yesterday~~" is played on the radio.
sale Tuesday	5. At Bloomingdale's there is a ~~Sale~~ on Calvin Klein jeans until ~~tuesday~~.
brother's Snickers	6. My ~~Brother's~~ idea of a balanced meal is pizza followed by a ~~snickers~~ bar.
Hindus reincarnation	7. I've been thinking of converting to Hinduism, because ~~hindus~~ believe in ~~Reincarnation~~.
Washington Vietnam	8. My father died for his country, so we regularly visit ~~washington~~, D.C., to see his name carved on the ~~vietnam~~ memorial.
By computer	9. The instructor explained, "~~by~~ the end of the course, you should be very comfortable writing on a ~~Computer~~."
I Superman	10. ~~i~~ never could understand how every time Clark Kent decides to become ~~superman~~, he can find an empty phone booth.

Score Number correct ________ × 5 = ________ %

Capital Letters

■ Mastery Test 4

Cross out the two capitalization errors in each of the following sentences. Then write the corrections in the spaces provided.

February
summer

1. Do you think ~~february~~ is too early to start planning a ~~Summer~~ vacation?

I
weeks

2. After ~~i~~ heard about John Lennon's death, I cried for ~~Weeks~~.

herself
Girl

3. Before she could stop ~~Herself~~, Clarice had bought three boxes of ~~girl~~ Scout cookies.

Introduction
advanced

4. Since I did so well in ~~introduction~~ to Sociology, my adviser suggested I take an ~~Advanced~~ course.

Scrabble
because

5. "I can never win at ~~scrabble~~," Nellie complained, "~~Because~~ I'm always at a loss for words."

news
telephone

6. It seems the minute I turn on the television to watch the ~~News~~, my ~~Telephone~~ rings.

films
Cinderella

7. Many Walt Disney ~~Films~~, such as ~~*cinderella*~~, are timeless.

video
Avenue

8. The ~~Video~~ store on Baltimore ~~avenue~~ will let us rent as many as four cassettes at a time.

Ocean
City

9. The Knights of Columbus convention was the reason all the motels along the beach in ~~ocean city~~, Maryland, were so crowded last weekend.

Eve
he

10. My little brother's favorite Bible story is the one about Adam and ~~eve~~; ~~He~~ loves hearing about other people who get into trouble.

Score Number correct _______ × 5 = _______ %

Numbers and Abbreviations

■ Mastery Test 1

Cross out the mistake in numbers or abbreviations in each sentence and correct it in the space provided.

eighty 1. Robert was arrested for doing ~~80~~ miles an hour on Skyline Drive.

telephone 2. Our ~~tel~~. bill listed three long-distance calls to someone in Australia.

10:30 3. When I retire, I want to sleep until ~~ten-thirty~~ every morning.

license 4. Convicted speeders will lose their driver's ~~lic.~~ in this state.

two 5. The corn crop was cut in half this year owing to ~~2~~ months of hot, dry weather.

high school 6. Three different classmates called Francisco and urged him to attend the ten-year reunion of his ~~h.s.~~ class.

station 7. I never seem to be able to find a gas ~~sta.~~ open before six o'clock in the morning.

1,000 8. Billy has about 250 baseball cards and almost ~~one thousand~~ clippings from *Sports Illustrated.*

Wednesday 9. Dr. Goldsmith's secretary called to confirm my ~~Wed.~~ dental appointment.

$25.50 10. I won ~~twenty-five dollars and fifty cents~~ in the lottery after spending at least five times that much to buy tickets.

Score Number correct ______ × 10 = ______ %

Numbers and Abbreviations

■ Mastery Test 2

Cross out the mistake in numbers or abbreviations in each sentence and correct it in the space provided. Mark the one sentence that is correct with a C.

doctor 1. My ~~dr.~~ told me the best way to lose weight is little by little.

C 2. The third baseman struck out ten of his last eleven times at bat.

1776 3. My aunt has a patriotic address: ~~seventeen seventy six~~ North Street.

hour 4. My car performs very well if I don't go over thirty miles an ~~hr.~~

three 5. I enjoy watching shows on the ~~3~~ major networks, but I prefer the shows on PBS.

1901 6. Grandma Belle jokingly gives her birth date as ~~nineteen hundred and one~~ B.C.

1986 7. I started working as a part-time salesperson at Sears in ~~nineteen eighty-six~~.

sandwich 8. At about 1:30 last night I woke up and made myself a ham ~~sand~~. on rye.

11 9. The instructor said our class is bankrupt when it comes to Chapter ~~Eleven~~ in our economics text.

brother 10. My little ~~bro~~. wants to join the FBI so he can snoop into other people's business.

Score Number correct ______ × 10 = ______ %

End Marks

■ Mastery Test 1

Add a period, question mark, or exclamation point, as needed, to each of the following sentences.

Note End marks always go *inside* the quotation marks that appear in some sentences.

1. Sometimes I wonder why I always seem to learn lessons the hard way.
2. Look out or you'll smash the car!
3. When you finish with the dishes, please put them neatly in the cupboards.
4. Do you always find time to read the Sunday newspaper?
5. I asked Heather where her club's party is being held.
6. Claudio had to cut one of his sneakers to make room for his swollen toe.
7. All the game show contestant could do was yell, "I won, I won!"
8. People often buy through a mixture of rational and irrational motives.
9. Jerry looked up from the stack of bills and asked, "Whose idea was it to have teenagers?"
10. Staci shouted, "If that's the way you feel, you can take back your ring!"
11. There's a woman at the door asking if we want to save our souls.
12. Will you still need me, and will you still feed me, when I'm sixty-four?
13. If it's noon here, what time is it in Tokyo?
14. The patriot Tom Paine wrote: "These are the times that try men's souls."
15. Barbara always gets terrific bargains the day after Christmas.
16. The larger pieces of farm equipment stood next to the empty barn, waiting for the auction to begin.
17. "But Mr. Wilson," Ling said to the bank manager, "how can I be overdrawn when I still have four checks left?"
18. In the early part of the twenty-first century, half the population of the United States will be senior citizens.
19. For the convenience of our customers, employees will no longer park in the spaces near the front entrance of the store.
20. As the members of the cast took their bows, a woman called from the back of the audience, "That's my Bernie up there!"

Score Number correct ________ × 5 = ________ %

End Marks

■ Mastery Test 2

Add a period, questions mark, or exclamation point, as needed, to each of the following sentences.

Note End marks always go *inside* the quotation marks that appear in some sentences.

1. The dog's bite is worse than its bark.
2. Please run down to the store and buy a loaf of rye bread.
3. Hurry, Alan, the movie will be starting any minute!
4. I wonder what Beethoven would think of the Beatles.
5. What do you think about before you fall asleep?
6. The young apprentice was inspired by the skill of the master carpenter.
7. Judging by all the television ads, Americans are in great need of pain relief.
8. Which is better, one long vacation a year or several shorter ones?
9. Erica cried out in her sleep, "Please—somebody help me!"
10. Len keeps a mug full of pencils on his desk, but every one of them has a broken point.
11. Why do I always pick the slowest checkout line in the supermarket?
12. If I catch you kids in my yard again, I'm calling the police!
13. Because of a printing error, each month in the calendar had thirty-five days.
14. The sign in front of Buckingham Palace seemed to scream, "Don't even think of parking here!"
15. "Dear Abby," wrote Lana, "do you think you can love someone too much?"
16. The first time I saw your car, I thought you must have strayed into the wrong neighborhood.
17. Taylor sat for over an hour watching a pair of robins building a nest in the tree outside his bedroom window.
18. The player won the championship game with a half-court basket, and the sportscaster shouted, "What a shot!"
19. Because of the increase in sexually transmitted diseases, monogamous relationships are becoming more popular.
20. Dried grapes are raisins, and dried plums are prunes, but dried apricots are always called "dried apricots."

Score Number correct ______ × 5 = ______ %

Apostrophe

■ Mastery Test 1

In each sentence, cross out the word that needs an apostrophe. Then write the word correctly in the space provided.

store's 1. That department ~~stores~~ prices are too high.

Christine's 2. ~~Christines~~ aunt has a very deep voice for such a small woman.

won't 3. The black rhino will eventually become extinct, because it ~~wont~~ breed in captivity.

tomorrow's 4. As the snow fell harder, the children began to plan for ~~tomorrows~~ holiday from school.

doesn't 5. When lost on the road, Carl will never ask questions or admit that he ~~doesnt~~ know the way.

mother's 6. The TV program dealt with a ~~mothers~~ concern about drugs and alcohol.

he'd 7. Matt stood silently in the darkened hallway and tried to remember why ~~hed~~ come there.

cat's 8. "If you pull that ~~cats~~ tail one more time," Rhona told her little daughter, "you will be very sorry."

pilot's 9. Spectators were thrilled by the stunt ~~pilots~~ ability to put the biplane through breathtaking loops and rolls.

attorney's 10. The district ~~attorneys~~ address to the jury was so convincing that Perry Mason resigned from the case on the spot.

Score Number correct _______ × 10 = _______ %

Apostrophe

■ Mastery Test 2

In the spaces provided under each sentence, add the one apostrophe needed and explain why the other word ending in *s* is a simple plural.

1. Sallys grades in math began to improve after a session or two with a tutor.

   Sallys: Sally's, meaning "belonging to Sally"

   grades: simple plural meaning more than one grade

2. Before the boys were halfway across the lake, their grandfathers old canoe sprang a leak.

   boys: simple plural meaning more than one boy

   grandfathers: grandfather's, meaning "belonging to their grandfather"

3. Garys mother woke him and his sisters in the middle of the night to watch the meteor shower.

   Garys: Gary's, meaning "belonging to Gary"

   sisters: simple plural meaning more than one sister

4. The squeaking of the elevators outside Williams hotel room kept the poor man awake half the night.

   elevators: simple plural meaning more than one elevator

   Williams: William's, meaning "belonging to William"

5. Marie and her sister often watch music videos at Terrys house, since they aren't allowed to see them at home.

   videos: simple plural meaning more than one video

   Terrys: Terry's, meaning "belonging to Terry"

Score Number correct ______ × 10 = ______ %

Apostrophe

■ Mastery Test 3

In each sentence two apostrophes are missing or are used incorrectly. Cross out the two errors and write the corrections in the spaces provided.

invitations / aren't — 1. The ~~invitation's~~ to the wedding ~~arent~~ being mailed until the bride and groom start speaking to each other again.

you're / boys' — 2. On Wednesday morning, ~~youre~~ supposed to report to the ~~boys~~ gym for your physical.

Toby's / his — 3. ~~Tobys~~ parents gave him a new leather briefcase on the morning he started ~~his'~~ new job at the insurance agency.

things / didn't — 4. Looking through the classified ads only reminded Roger of the many ~~thing's~~ he ~~didnt~~ know how to do.

provides / town's — 5. My cousins, Sharon and Ben, work for Meals on Wheels, a volunteer organization that ~~provide's~~ hot food to many of the ~~towns~~ senior citizens.

Lola's / men's — 6. The sight of ~~Lolas~~ tanned body in a black bikini was enough to make young ~~mens~~ heads spin around as if they were on ball bearings.

university's / slips — 7. With each new scandal in the athletic department, the ~~universitys~~ reputation for integrity ~~slips'~~ another notch.

Grandmother's / eyes — 8. ~~Grandmothers~~ ~~eye's~~ were misty as she remembered the nights Grandfather called for her in a Model T Ford.

whale's / weighs — 9. A blue ~~whales~~ tongue ~~weighs'~~ as much as forty men.

Rick's / semester's — 10. ~~Ricks~~ decision to begin attending classes so close to the ~~semesters~~ end is like turning off the faucets on the sinking *Titanic*.

Score Number correct ______ × 5 = ______ %

Apostrophe

■ Mastery Test 4

In each sentence two apostrophes are missing or are used incorrectly. Cross out the two errors and write the corrections in the spaces provided.

What's / yours — 1. ~~Whats~~ mine is ~~your's~~, darling, including the bills.

brother's / don't — 2. "Stay away from my ~~brothers~~ stuff if you ~~dont~~ want your face removed," said Gladys.

I'd / diamonds — 3. Slivers from the glass ~~Id~~ broken glistened like ~~diamond's~~ on the kitchen tile.

man's / Colleen's — 4. The young ~~mans~~ hands were shaking as he dialed ~~Colleens~~ number on the phone.

Craig's / he's — 5. ~~Craigs~~ medical exam revealed that he has high blood pressure and that ~~hes~~ twenty pounds overweight.

who'd / spectators — 6. The pitcher ~~whod~~ given up the home run doffed his cap to the jeering ~~spectator's~~ as he exited.

applicant's / scores — 7. In considering new admissions, most colleges look at each ~~applicants~~ grades, extracurricular activities, test ~~score's~~, and personal recommendations.

weekend's / people's — 8. If this ~~weekends~~ forecast for heavy rain and flash floods comes true, many ~~peoples~~ houses are in danger.

haven't / she's — 9. Nick and Ellen ~~havent~~ seen their friends much since having the baby; they say ~~shes~~ more work than a full-time job.

would've / Annemarie's — 10. We ~~wouldve~~ won the sardine race after stuffing fifteen people into ~~Annemaries~~ Volkswagen, but she couldn't budge the gearshift to drive the car.

Score Number correct ______ × 5 = ______ %

Quotation Marks

■ Mastery Test 1

Place quotation marks or underlines where needed.

1. A sign in a cluttered hardware store read, "We've got it if we can find it."
2. "Go ahead, make my day!" snarled Dirty Harry.
3. "I can't do the dishes," Tyrone said, "because the cat is sitting on my lap."
4. "This machine will do half your work for you," the salesclerk promised.
5. "That's terrific," I replied. "I'll take two of them."
6. Robert Frost's poem "The Road Not Taken" influenced Gordon's decision to be an architect.
7. When someone asked Willie Sutton why he kept robbing banks, he replied, "Because that's where the money is."
8. "I'd never date him," Celia said. "He switches girlfriends at the blink of an eyelid."
9. One of Murphy's laws states: "An optimist believes we live in the best of all possible worlds; a pessimist fears this is true."
10. The bittersweet song "At the Ballet" is one of several showstoppers in <u>A Chorus Line</u>, the longest-running musical in Broadway history.

Score Number correct _______ × 10 = _______ %

Quotation Marks

■ Mastery Test 2

Place quotation marks or underlines where needed.

1. "Get back behind the railing!" the zookeeper yelled to the little boy.
2. A New York subway sign showing little confidence in the public reads, "No spitting."
3. "The job is yours," Ms. Washburn said, "as long as you're willing to work a fifty-hour week."
4. Mae West once said, "It's better to be looked over than overlooked."
5. The only part of the income-tax form I like to read is the one called "How to Claim Your Refund."
6. "Why don't you watch where you're going?" the drunk mumbled to the lamppost.
7. In a special section of Harper's magazine called "Tools for Living," I saw an ad for a gadget that triples the life of a lightbulb.
8. Turning to his father during the ball game, Joey mimicked the nearby vendor and said, "Hot dogs! Hot dogs! Get your son a hot dog right here."
9. One letter to Abigail Van Buren from a man named Henry read, "Dear Abby: Between you and me, the people who write to you are either morons or just plain stupid."
10. Abby's response was, "Dear Henry: Which are you?"

Score Number correct _______ × 10 = _______ %

Quotation Marks

■ Mastery Test 3

Place quotation marks or underlines where needed.

1. "If life's a bowl of cherries," sighed Reggie, "mine are canned."
2. "My friends are mistaken when they say I'm afraid of flying," said my aunt.
3. Then she added, "It's crashing I'm afraid of."
4. Stephen King's short story "The Body" was the basis for the successful movie Stand by Me.
5. The comedian said, "I took a cab to the drive-in; the movie cost me ninety-five dollars."
6. "If a tree falls in the forest and nobody is there to hear it," asked the philosophy instructor, "is there a noise?"
7. The late Spencer Tracy's advice on acting was, "Remember your lines and don't bump into the furniture."
8. "Here's some sound financial advice," Mr. Green said to his son, who was dressing for a date. "Take her to a place that has a cook, not a chef."
9. Many music critics consider the Beatles' song "Sgt. Pepper's Lonely Hearts Club Band" to be a turning point in the history of rock.
10. "The different between that weatherman and us," my father said as he watched the news, "is that when it comes to telling the weather he has to stick his neck out, but we only have to stick our heads out."

Score Number correct _______ × 10 = _______ %

Quotation Marks

■ Mastery Test 4

Place quotation marks or underlines where needed.

1. On our way to the doctor's office, Dad said, "Dr. Cobb has been practicing medicine for forty years."
2. "Hasn't he learned how to do it yet?" my little brother asked.
3. "No onions on that sandwich, please," Sharon told the deli clerk. "I'm on my way to an interview."
4. Ever since my sixth-grade teacher made me memorize Carl Sandburg's poem "The Grass," I've hated it.
5. A judge asked Oscar Wilde during Wilde's trial, "Are you trying to show contempt for this court?"
6. "On the contrary—I'm trying to conceal it," Wilde replied.
7. "Either that painting is crooked or our house is leaning," Teresa said to her husband. "Please fix one of them."
8. "The lion may be king of the beasts, but the majestic elegance of the giraffe certainly makes it part of the royal court," asserted the zoo tour guide.
9. "Of course, I saw the play under unfortunate conditions," wrote the drama critic in the morning paper. "The curtain was up."
10. "I'm determined to grow roses this summer," my Aunt Freda said. "So I bought a copy of <u>McCall's Garden Book</u> and began reading the first chapter, 'How to Cultivate Your Green Thumb.'"

Score Number correct ________ × 10 = ________ %

Comma

Mastery Test 1

Add commas where needed. Then refer to the box below and write, in the space provided, the letter of the comma rule that applies in each sentence.

a. Between items in a series	d. Between complete thoughts
b. After introductory material	e. With direct quotations
c. Around interrupters	

a 1. The witness swore to tell the truth, the whole truth, and nothing but the truth.

b 2. When Mona loses her temper, she speaks in a very subdued voice.

d 3. The coach told me it was his way or the highway, so I hit the road.

e 4. The undertaker's sign stated, "We're the last ones in the world to let you down."

c 5. Three sets of twins, a hospital record, were born on the same day.

e 6. "Park your car over there," the attendant said, "and leave the keys in the ignition."

b 7. Entering the crystal blue ocean like a pin, the cliff diver caused barely a ripple on the surface.

a 8. Helen's new food processor slices, dices, chops, and makes mounds of julienne fries.

c 9. The next time you dare use language like that in my presence, young man, will be your last day in this school.

d 10. Rob is forty-one years old and runs his own business, but his mother still wants to know when he's going to settle down.

Score Number correct ______ × 10 = ______ %

Comma

■ Mastery Test 2

Add commas where needed. Then refer to the box below to write, in the space provided, the letter of the one comma rule that applies in each sentence.

a. Between items in a series	d. Between complete thoughts
b. After introductory material	e. With direct quotations
c. Around interrupters	

b 1. As I opened the car door, a wave of hot air spilled out of the baking interior.

a 2. Cindy bought two lamps, a beach chair, and plastic salt and pepper shakers at a yard sale.

e 3. Hal's instructions to the prospective models were, "Don't just do something, stand there."

d 4. Ved realized checkmate was inevitable, so he conveniently knocked over the four pawns closest to him.

c 5. Cary Grant, a symbol of sophisticated charm for many moviegoers, never won an Oscar, the film industry's highest honor.

b 6. After the wild dog had devoured my pet rabbits, it disappeared into the woods behind our house.

e 7. "This is the worst coffee I've ever had," protested Rochelle.

c 8. The wrestler's face, fleshy and pockmarked and dominated by big green eyes, seemed too small for such a colossal body.

d 9. Mrs. Evans scooped Tommy up as he headed for the mouthwash display, but her unattended shopping cart smashed into a mountain of cereal boxes.

a 10. The lifeguard had white-blond hair, piercing blue eyes, a deep bronze tan, and a scraggly beard that the teenage girl mistook for a sign of maturity.

Score Number correct _______ × 10 = _______ %

Comma

■ Mastery Test 3

Add commas where needed. Then refer to the box below to write, in the space provided, the letter of the one comma rule that applies in each sentence.

a.	Between items in a series	d.	Between complete thoughts
b.	After introductory material	e.	With direct quotations
c.	Around interrupters		

c 1. The dean of the law school, I am told, was arrested for fraud and embezzlement.

d 2. The accident outside the mall destroyed both cars, but no one was killed.

b 3. After I flunked out of school, I realized that studying might have been a good idea.

a 4. The thirsty, sore, and exhausted marathon runner collapsed as she staggered across the finish line.

c 5. The professor's stare, so disconcertingly frank that it caused me to blush, made me forget my question.

d 6. Mother tried to probe my eyes for the truth, but I avoided her penetrating gaze.

e 7. "He's greyhound lean and wolf-pack mean," the sportscaster said in describing the middleweight boxing contender.

c 8. Ted Kelly, one of my high school friends, was nicknamed "Gingersnap" for the large freckles on his face.

b 9. Because the convict showed no remorse for his brutal crime, the judge imposed the maximum sentence allowed under law.

a 10. The construction workers had already torn down the fence, uprooted the trees, and dug a trench across the front yard before they realized they were at the wrong address.

Score Number correct ______ × 10 = ______ %

Comma

Mastery Test 4

Add commas where needed. Then refer to the box below to write, in the space provided, the letter of the one comma rule that applies in each sentence.

a. Between items in a series	d. Between complete thoughts
b. After introductory material	e. With direct quotations
c. Around interrupters	

c 1. I sat there, open-mouthed and embarrassed, listening to the class laugh at my answer.

a 2. Calvin couldn't sleep because the baby upstairs was crying, a neighborhood dog was barking, and someone nearby kept racing a car engine.

d 3. Franco has taken trumpet lessons for five years, but most people agree they have been in vain.

d 4. The defendant had to be extremely careful of his testimony, for the prosecutor was clever and determined.

e 5. "Stay tuned," said the announcer, "for an important message for everyone who would like to become a millionaire."

a 6. My father shut his eyes, put his hands of his lap, and said a quiet prayer as he waited for the news from the doctor.

b 7. With the utmost care, little Jenny placed the kitten in her coat pocket and headed for the school playground.

d 8. Tom Zydakis became tired of spelling his name over the telephone, so he now orders all his pizzas for "Smith."

c 9. Irving Berlin composed "White Christmas," one of the most popular Christmas songs of all time, while sitting by his swimming pool.

b 10. Realizing that every one of the six lottery numbers matched her ticket, Roxanne could hear a surge of blood to her temples.

Score Number correct _______ × 10 = _______ %

Other Punctuation Marks

■ Mastery Test 1

At the appropriate spot (or spots), place the punctuation mark shown in the margin.

— 1. He's so rich he doesn't count his money—he weighs it.

; 2 Ruby's savings have dwindled to nothing; she's been borrowing from me to pay her rent.

\- 3. The quick-witted little boy called the rescue squad for help.

: 4. Martha likes only two kinds of books: cookbooks and bankbooks.

( ) 5. The size of the lot (two acres) was just what Bob had been looking for.

\- 6. The anti-nuclear activists staged a rally to protest the opening of the new power plant.

— 7. I think—as a matter of fact, I'm positive—I returned your power drill last week.

: 8. The novelist Jessamyn West once defined irony as follows: "Irony is when you buy a suit with two pairs of pants and then burn a hole in the coat."

( ) 9. If you're running out of storage space, there are only two solutions: (1) store your possessions more efficiently or (2) get rid of some of the junk you never use.

; 10. An old Chinese proverb says, "If you are planting for a year, sow rice; if you are planting for a decade, plant trees; and if you are planting for a lifetime, educate a person."

Score Number correct _______ × 10 = _______ %

Other Punctuation Marks

■ Mastery Test 2

Each sentence below needs one of the following punctuation marks:

colon :	hyphen -	semicolon ;
dash —	parentheses ( )	

Insert the correct mark (or pair of marks) as needed.

1. Call the toll-free number for quick service from our catalogue.
2. My sister is allergic to cats and dogs;therefore, we never could have any pets when we were little.
3. The counseling center's hours(9:00 A.M. to 5:00 P.M.)are inconvenient, since all my classes are at night.
4. My distinguished opponent is a highly qualified person—if you ignore his long prison record.
5. There are two basic rules for travelers:take half as many clothes and take twice as much money as you think you will need.
6. A sixty-year-old woman is entered in the marathon.
7. The crippled airliner landed safely;the passengers and crew walked away unharmed.
8. Lola said, "My first boyfriend—I'll never forget him—proposed to me fifteen minutes after we met."
9. Before the party, Alicia had to stop at the cleaner's, where her dress was ready; at the bakery, where she had ordered a decorated cake;and at the convenience store for ice, so they'd have plenty for punch.
10. In his book *On Writing Well,* William Zinssser wrote about wordiness:"If you give me an article that runs to eight pages and I tell you to cut it to four, you'll howl and say it can't be done. Then you will go home and do it, and it will be infinitely better. After that comes the hard part: cutting it to three."

Score Number correct ______ × 10 = ______ %

Dictionary Use

Mastery Test 1

Items 1–5 Use your dictionary to answer the following questions.

1. How many syllables are in the word *inconsequential?* 5
2. Where is the primary accent in the word *contemplation?* con tem pla´ tion
3. In the word *frivolity,* the first *i* is pronounced like
   a. long *e*
   b. long *i*
   c. schwa
   d. short *i*
4. In the word *rudiment,* the *u* is pronounced like
   a. short *u*
   b. long *u*
   c. short *a*
   d. schwa
5. In the word *inhalation,* the first *a* is pronounced like
   a. schwa
   b. short *i*
   c. short *a*
   d. long *a*

Items 6–10 There are five misspelled words in the following sentence. Cross out each misspelled word and write in the correct spelling in the spaces provided.

I had a chance to work thirty hours a week at a ~~restarant~~ this ~~semestir~~, but my ~~parants~~ told me that it was more ~~importent~~ to have ~~sufficent~~ time for studying.

6. restaurant
7. semester
8. parents
9. important
10. sufficient

Score Number correct ______ × 10 = ______ %

Dictionary Use

■ Mastery Test 2

Items 1–5 Use your dictionary to answer the following questions.

1. How many syllables are in the word *subsequently?* 4
2. Where is the primary accent in the word *fastidious?* fa stid′ i ous
3. In the word *cantankerous,* the *e* is pronounced like
   a. short *i*
   b. short *e*
   c. long *e*
   (d.) schwa
4. In the word *demoniac,* the *o* is pronounced like
   a. short *a*
   b. short *i*
   c. short *o*
   (d.) long *o*
5. In the word *malleable,* the first *a* is pronounced like
   a. schwa
   (b.) short *a*
   c. long *a*
   d. short *e*

Items 6–10 There are five misspelled words in the following sentences. Cross out each misspelled word and write the correct spelling in the space provided.

My ~~dauhter~~ Judy wants to ~~legaly~~ change her name to "Violet" because she thinks "Judy" is too ~~commen~~ and "Violet" has a ~~senee~~ of mystery and ~~glamer~~ to it.

6. daughter
7. legally
8. common
9. sense
10. glamour (or glamor)

Score Number correct ______ × 10 = ______ %

Spelling Improvement

■ Mastery Test 1

Items 1–8 Use the three spelling rules to spell the following words.

1. inflate + able	= inflatable	5. trim + er	= trimmer
2. ban + ing	= banning	6. plenty + ful	= plentiful
3. thrifty + est	= thriftiest	7. concern + ed	= concerned
4. refer + ed	= referred	8. derive + ing	= deriving

Items 9–14 Circle the correctly spelled plural in each pair.

9. sheafs	(sheaves)	12. quarrys	(quarries)
10. (pitches)	pitchs	13. echos	(echoes)
11. (pastries)	pastrys	14. (relays)	relais

Items 15–20 Circle the correctly spelled word (from the basic word list) in each pair.

15. (direction)	direcion	18. awkwerd	(awkward)
16. wellcome	(welcome)	19. (believe)	beleive
17. generel	(general)	20. comfortible	(comfortable)

Score Number correct ______ × 5 = ______ %

Spelling Improvement

■ Mastery Test 2

Items 1–8 Use the three spelling rules to spell the following words.

1. grip + ed = gripped
2. fancy + ful = fanciful
3. imply + ed = implied
4. curve + ing = curving
5. date + ing = dating
6. employ + er = employer
7. spine + less = spineless
8. duty + ful = dutiful

Items 9–14 Circle the correctly spelled plural in each pair.

9.	(embargoes)	embargos	12. hobbys	(hobbies)
10.	(wolves)	wolfs	13. (guards)	guardes
11.	attorney-at-laws	(attorneys-at-law)	14. reflexs	(reflexes)

Item 15–20 Circle the correctly spelled word (from the basic word list) in each pair.

15.	atempt	(attempt)	18. (several)	severel
16.	attenshun	(attention)	19. alot	(a lot)
17.	(personal)	perssonal	20. diferent	(different)

Score Number correct ______ × 5 = ______ %

Omitted Words and Letters

■ Mastery Test 1

Part 1 Write in the two short connecting words needed in each sentence. Use carets (^) within the sentences to show where these words belong.

1. A carton ^of milk leaked all over ^the floor of my car.
2. I'd like ^to introduce you to ^the man I'm going to marry.
3. The supermarket was full ^of shoppers who heard about ^the big sale.
4. When spring is ^in the air, most people seem ^to feel especially happy.
5. After the torrents ^of rain turned to ice, ^the condition of the streets was treacherous.

Part 2 Add the two *-s* endings needed in each sentence. Use carets.

6. Between you and me, raisin^s make a better pie than apple^s do.
7. Darien spent forty-five minute^s balancing his checkbook and found four error^s.
8. The member^s of the sixth grade collected Christmas toy^s for needy children.
9. Together, my daughter^s and my husband have twenty-seven mateless socks^s.
10. There is little doubt remaining that many student^s cheated on several final examination^s.

Score Number correct _______ × 5 = _______ %

Omitted Words and Letters

■ Mastery Test 2

Part 1 In the spaces provided, write in the two short connecting words needed in each sentence. Use carets (^) within the sentences to show where these words belong.

1. I noticed number of anthills our backyard while I was mowing the lawn.
2. Please put timer on so you remember take the cookies out of the oven.
3. Without a doubt, Jenny's drawing was best all the students' art projects today.
4. My brother couldn't remember the name of book on which he had to write book report.
5. At first, the mountains looked like a foggy dream off the distance; then, as we approached, they seemed be almost too real.

Part 2 Add the two *-s* endings needed in each sentence. Use carets.

6. All the houseplant on my sun porch have aphid.
7. In our basic math course, the final exam covers statistic and graph.
8. At the beginning of the football season, most of the defensive player got Mohawk haircut.
9. Your children left their coat on the sidewalk about two block away from here.
10. Too many cook may spoil the broth, but I still want as many helper in the kitchen as possible.

Score Number correct ______ × 5 = ______ %

Commonly Confused Words

Mastery Test 1

Choose the correct words in each sentence and write them in the spaces provided.

advice
right
1. If you want my (advice, advise), the (right, write) thing to do is apologize.

Because
already
2. (Being that, Because) Leon had (all ready, already) dropped off his last assignment, he prepared to leave campus for spring vacation.

knew
whose
3. I wish I (knew, new) (whose, who's) dog is responsible for the mess in my front yard.

two
through
4. You (to, too, two) troublemakers are (threw, through) with this team as of right this minute.

course
principles
5. The reason I signed up for an accounting (coarse, course) is that I want to know the basic (principals, principles) of bookkeeping.

here
you're
6. If you intend to continue living (hear, here), young man, (your, you're) going to have to follow my rules.

passed
they're
7. Ann and George's friendship developed into love as the years (passed, past), and now, in midlife, (their, there, they're) newlyweds.

Besides
its
8. (Beside, Besides) the fact that this car runs like a dream, (its, it's) trade-in value remains quite high.

hole
write
9. Randy, you must have a (hole, whole) in your head if you really believe you can (right, write) a term paper in one night.

There
quite
10. (Their, There, They're) was so much alcohol served with dinner that the noise at our table became (quite, quiet) loud.

Score Number correct ________ × 5 = ________ %

Commonly Confused Words

■ Mastery Test 2

Choose the correct words in each sentence and write them in the spaces provided.

there peace	1. When my son's stereo broke, (their, there, they're) was finally some (peace, piece) around the house.
clothes effect	2. By using pieces of her children's old (clothes, cloths), Lois gave her quilt a wonderfully colorful (affect, effect).
passed among	3. The hosts of the New Year's Eve party (passed, past) glasses of champagne among, between) the guests just after midnight.
knew should have	4. If you (knew, new) you weren't feeling well this morning, you (should have, should of) called in sick and stayed home.
fewer desserts	5. An easy way to eat (fewer, less) calories is to simply eliminate all (deserts, desserts) from your diet.
whether may	6. Is it important (weather, whether) I use up all my vacation this year, or (can, may) I apply this year's leftover days to next year?
would have break	7. I think I (would have, would of) collapsed any minute if the coach hadn't given us a (brake, break) from those wind sprints when he did.
know plain	8. I don't (know, no) a nicer couple than the Wenofs, who are just (plain, plane) folks despite their wealth.
can hardly lose	9. You (can't hardly, can hardly) blame people for avoiding you when you (loose, lose) your temper all the time.
teach than	10. Our English professor is a tough grader, but students like her because she can (learn, teach) better (than, then) anyone else in the school.

Score Number correct ______ × 5 = ______ %

Commonly Confused Words

■ Mastery Test 3

Cross out the two mistakes in usage in each sentence. Then write the correct words in the spaces provided.

your than	1. If ~~you're~~ family is starving, is it better to become a beggar ~~then~~ a thief?
fewer lose	2. If you ate ~~less~~ snacks between meals, you probably would ~~loose~~ some weight.
all ready except	3. We're ~~already~~ for our vacation, ~~accept~~ for the usual last-minute packing.
Whose its	4. ~~Who's~~ job was it to give the dog ~~it's~~ bath?
desert to	5. In the ~~dessert,~~ plant life has learned ~~too~~ survive with very little rainfall.
Right new	6. ~~Write~~ from the beginning, we could tell the ~~knew~~ professor was going to be a pushover.
could hardly brake	7. The fog was so thick that Aaron ~~couldn't hardly~~ see the ~~break~~ lights of the car ahead of him.
would have taught	8. Denzel ~~would of~~ ~~learned~~ his brother to play the drums, but their mother hid the drumsticks.
principal whole	9. The acting ~~principle~~ of the new high school addressed the ~~hole~~ student body on the first day of school.
quiet pair	10. As Wilma paddled along the ~~quite~~ stream, the only sounds she heard were the calls of a ~~pear~~ of mourning doves.

Score Number correct ________ × 5 = ________ %

Commonly Confused Words

■ Mastery Test 4

Cross out the two mistakes in usage in each sentence. Then write the correct words in the spaces provided.

accept / a — 1. Charlotte has never learned to ~~except~~ ~~an~~ compliment without blushing.

fewer / affect — 2. I'd have ~~less~~ worries if I didn't let the opinions of others ~~effect~~ me so much.

principle / through — 3. Scott holds to the ~~principal~~ that true wisdom comes only ~~threw~~ experience.

should have / there — 4. I ~~should of~~ mowed the lawn as soon as I heard ~~their~~ was going to be a thunderstorm tonight.

would have / except — 5. Chuck's car ~~would of~~ passed inspection ~~accept~~ for the hole in its muffler.

Because / two — 6. ~~Being that~~ the airport bus was late, we missed our flight and had to wait ~~too~~ hours for the next one.

knew / plain — 7. I ~~new~~ there was something questionable about the magazine when it arrived in a ~~plane~~ brown wrapper.

it's / already — 8. Some guys think ~~its~~ a lot easier to break up with a girlfriend when they ~~all ready~~ have a replacement lined up.

must have / passed — 9. The friends ~~must of~~ ~~past~~ four theaters before they spotted a movie they all wanted to see.

course / than — 10. A California man once rode a skateboard down a mountainside ~~coarse~~ at speeds greater ~~then~~ seventy miles an hour.

Score Number correct ________ × 5 = ________ %

Effective Word Choice

■ Mastery Test 1

Certain words are italicized in the following sentences. In the spaces at the left, identify whether those words are slang (*S*), clichés (*C*), or pretentious words (*PW*). Then replace the words with more effective diction.

Answers may vary for rewritten portions.

S 1. I *get off* on horror *flicks*.
enjoy . . . movies

PW 2. You should file all office *memorandums* after *perusing* them.
memos . . . reading

C 3. Building your own house is *easier said than done.*
hard

C 4. Because Ben realized he *had had one too many,* he decided to take a taxi home.
was drunk

PW 5. My little brother's *demeanor* always *ameliorates* just before Christmas.
behavior . . . improves

S 6. Often when I am called on in school, *my brain is out to lunch.*
I can't think of the answers.

S 7. When Flora tried to *bum* a *cancer stick* from me, I told her I quit smoking a week ago.
borrow . . . cigarette

PW 8. The committee's *mission* is to *alleviate* scheduling problems.
job . . . relieve

C 9. Because Marita kept forgetting to clean her room, our mother decided to *put her foot down.*
be firm

PW 10. The students *manifested* delight at the *communication* that classes would be canceled Tuesday morning.
showed . . . news

Score Number correct _______ × 10 = _______ %

Effective Word Choice

Mastery Test 2

Certain words are italicized in the following sentences. In the spaces at the left, identify whether those words are slang (*S*), clichés (*C*), or pretentious words (*PW*). Then replace the words with more effective diction.

Answers may vary for rewritten portions.

C 1. Receiving an A on my final was *as sweet as pie.*
very satisfying

S 2. If you don't *get off my case,* I'll *punch your lights out.*
stop bothering me . . . hit you

C 3. The school board's decision to drop football *had many parents up in arms.*
angered many parents

PW 4. The interviewer *inquired as to the location of my permanent residence.*
asked where I lived

S 5. Too many people *get hung up on* the way teenagers look, instead of trying to understand *where they're coming from.*
focus on . . . the way they think

PW 6. Our *refuse* cans were bent up by the *sanitation personnel.*
trash . . . garbage collectors

S 7. John, your mother and I *have had it up to here* with your careless attitude.
are disgusted

S 8. The instructor *raked him over the coals* for missing class, but Jed *kept his cool.*
scolded him harshly . . . stayed calm

PW 9. *An excess of precipitation* has caused crop failure.
Too much rain

C 10. I *let out a sigh of relief* when I saw my grade for the paper.
was relieved

Score Number correct ______ × 10 = ______ %

Effective Word Choice

■ Mastery Test 3

The following sentences include examples of wordiness. Rewrite the sentences in the spaces provided, omitting needless words.

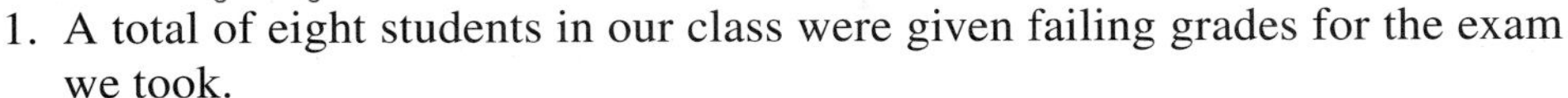

Answers may vary.

1. A total of eight students in our class were given failing grades for the exam we took.

   Eight students failed the exam.

2. During the time that the Millers were off on vacation somewhere, their home was burglarized by unknown persons.

   While the Millers were on vacation, their home was burglarized.

3. Holly took three hundred dollars from her bank account for the purpose of buying a television in the near future.

   Holly withdrew three hundred dollars to buy a television.

4. At this point in time, I have not as yet fully and completely made my decision concerning just what it is that I should do.

   I don't know what to do yet.

5. If you want to make sure that the answer you have come up with is correct, you should refer to the answer key that you will find by turning to the back of the book.

   To check your answer, refer to the answer key in the back of the book.

Score Number correct ______ × 20 = ______ %

Effective Word Choice

■ Mastery Test 4

The following sentences include examples of wordiness. Rewrite the sentences in the spaces provided, omitting needless words.

Answers may vary.

1. Owing to the fact that I was half an hour late, I did not do very well on the test and failed it.

   Because I was late, I failed the test.

2. The actual true reason I don't watch much television is that there are too many television commercials to look at.

   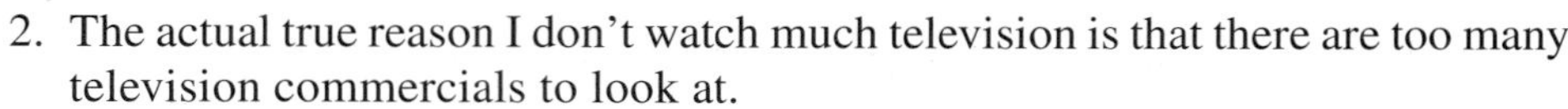

   I don't watch much television because there are too many commercials.

3. After a great deal of driving practice that she had with the family car, my sister said she felt she was finally ready to take and pass her driver's test.

   After much practice, my sister felt ready to take her driving test.

4. In this day and age, the majority of people seem more than ever to want to get something of value in return for the money they pay out.

   Today people want to get value for their money.

5. Because of the fact that the amount of my salary is less than the total sum of my expenses, it has been necessary for me to find a second job in addition to my present one.

   Because I earned less than I spent, I have taken a second job.

Score Number correct ______ × 20 = ______ %

Combined Mastery Tests

Fragments and Run-Ons

■ Combined Mastery Test 1

Each of the word groups below is numbered. In the space provided, write *C* if a word group is a complete sentence, write *F* if it is a fragment, and write *R-O* if it is a run-on.

1. C
2. F
3. C
4. F
5. R-O
6. F
7. C
8. F
9. F
10. R-O
11. F
12. C
13. C
14. F
15. C
16. C
17. R-O
18. F
19. R-O
20. F

[1]Richard was an angry young man a few years ago. [2]And still has some scars to prove it. [3]He once became so furious. [4]That he broke a window with his fist and cut his hand on the glass. [5]Another time, he threw a plate of spaghetti across a room through the years, his temper got him into many arguments. [6]And even fistfights. [7]Richard finally realized he had to bring his anger under control, or it would defeat him. [8]Making him the biggest victim of his own fury. [9]To get some perspective on the problem. [10]He asked his uncle Jay for help, Jay pointed out that Richard's explosions only made bad situations worse. [11]When a person has a lot of rage inside, Jay said. [12]His explosions often have little to do with the incidents that seem to cause the anger. [13]Jay suggested that Richard might get some insight into the problem. [14]By keeping a diary of his feelings and of his temper tantrums. [15]Jay also advised Richard to ask himself a question whenever he began to feel angry. [16]The question was, "Is it really important enough to get upset about?" [17]Richard took his uncle's advice, he began to seek new responses to situations that frustrated and angered him. [18]Although it hasn't been easy. [19]He has gradually learned how to control his temper even more important is that by examining his feelings, Richard has changed his outlook on life. [20]Which has resulted in less temper to control.

Score Number correct ________ × 5 = ________ %

Fragments and Run-Ons

■ Combined Mastery Test 2

In the space provided, indicate whether each item below contains a fragment (*F*) or a run-on (*R-O*). Then correct the error.

R-O 1. A pungent odor filled the house; cabbage was simmering on the stove. I suddenly felt hungry.

F 2. Stella clips out many recipes. That she finds in the newspaper. However, she rarely tries them out.

F 3. Hummingbirds eat half their weight every day. They are tiny, colorful creatures. Weighing no more than a dime.

R-O 4. The impatient driver could hardly wait for the green light. He kept edging his car into the intersection then he accelerated when the light turned green.

F 5. Using Tupperware containers as molds. The children built an elaborate sand castle on the beach. A helpful wave filled in their moat.

R-O 6. Pauline has taught in many elementary classes, she finds first-graders the most rewarding to teach. Most of them still think school is fun.

F 7. Some people feel we should bring our own bags to the supermarket. We could save millions of trees. Instead of throwing away usable paper.

F 8. When I got home. I stuffed my wet shoes with newspaper. I didn't want the toes to curl up as they dried.

R-O 9. On my way to class, I spied a dollar bill on the ground of course, I stooped to pick it up. But as I bent over, I dropped and broke my twelve-dollar thermos.

F 10. Andrea decorated her home with purchases from the novelty store where she worked. She put a red satin pillow shaped like a pair of lips on the couch. And a pink and green rug with a watermelon design on the floor.

Score Number correct _______ × 10 = _______ %

Verbs

■ Combined Mastery Test 1

Each sentence contains a mistake involving (1) standard English or irregular verb forms, (2) subject-verb agreement, or (3) consistent verb tense. Cross out the incorrect verb and write the correct form in the space provided.

remain 1. Only two pieces of lemon meringue pie ~~remains~~ on the plate.

tunes 2. Every morning, he starts the car, ~~tuned~~ in the radio, and adjusts the heat.

grew 3. The basketball team's center ~~growed~~ almost five inches between his freshman and sophomore seasons.

flown 4. Uncle Edwin became frightened as we approached the airport, for he had never ~~flew~~ before.

was 5. Each of the cupcakes for Jenny's birthday ~~were~~ decorated with blue roses.

slept 6. I came home, settled down for a short nap, and ~~sleep~~ for three hours.

had 7. On my way home, an oncoming car's headlights were so bright I ~~have~~ to slow down till it passed.

lie 8. When the accident victim complained of dizziness, the paramedics told him to ~~lay~~ on the stretcher.

realized 9. After I checked my bank balance, I ~~realize~~ I did not have enough money for a new stereo.

covers 10. The full moon ~~covered~~ the beach with a cool blue light, and the water shimmers as a soft breeze blows off the lake.

Score Number correct ______ × 10 = ______ %

Verbs

■ Combined Mastery Test 2

Each sentence contains a mistake involving (1) standard English or irregular verb forms, (2) subject-verb agreement, or (3) consistent verb tense. Cross out the incorrect verb and write the correct form in the space provided.

stacked 1. Travis chopped the wood from the dead maple tree and ~~stack~~ it against the shed.

are 2. School closings because of bad weather ~~is~~ announced on the radio.

begun 3. By the time we reached our seats in the upper deck, the game had already ~~began~~.

returned 4. Jasmine took down some books, thumbed through their indexes, and then ~~returns~~ them to the library shelf.

smoke 5. Every morning, several people on the bus ~~smokes~~ cigarettes.

rise 6. He makes me so angry I can feel my blood pressure ~~raise~~ every time he's nearby.

are 7. There ~~is~~ two fat pigeons strutting back and forth on my windowsill.

asked 8. An elderly, poorly dressed man came up to us on the sidewalk and ~~asks~~ if we had any spare change.

taken 9. Anne had not ~~took~~ the hamburger out of the freezer, so we had peanut butter sandwiches for dinner.

hauled 10. Members of the rescue team climbed down the cliff, grabbed the frightened boy, and ~~haul~~ him to safety.

Score Number correct ______ × 10 = ______ %

Pronouns

Combined Mastery Test 1

Choose the sentence in each pair that uses pronouns correctly. Then write the letter of that sentence in the space provided at the left.

b 1. a. The five students in our lab group developed a closeness that you could feel grow as the semester progressed.
b. The five students in our lab group developed a closeness that we could feel grow as the semester progressed.

a 2. a. Carrie and he have a surprise for everyone at the dance tonight.
b. Carrie and him have a surprise for everyone at the dance tonight.

b 3. a. This here fudge is the creamiest I've ever tasted.
b. This fudge is the creamiest I've ever tasted.

b 4. a. Though we started our diets at the same time, Hal has lost twice as much weight as me.
b. Though we started our diets at the same time, Hal has lost twice as much weight as I.

a 5. a. The teacher told the children that everyone could choose his or her partner for the class trip to the zoo.
b. The teacher told the children that everyone could choose their partner for the class trip to the zoo.

Score Number correct _______ × 20 = _______ %

Pronouns

■ Combined Mastery Test 2

In the spaces provided, write *PE* for each of the nine sentences that contain pronoun errors. Write *C* for the sentence that uses pronouns correctly. Then cross out each pronoun error and write the correction in the space provided.

PE 1. Alma doesn't like ~~them~~ [those] jelly-filled doughnuts.

PE 2. Neither of the candidates writes ~~their~~ [his or her] own speeches.

PE 3. Mary asked her friend why ~~she~~ [the friend (or Mary)] wasn't invited to the party.

PE 4. Most people who know my brother and me think I am more shy than ~~him~~ [he].

PE 5. What I don't like about eating a heavy lunch is that ~~you~~ [I] always feel sleepy afterward.

PE 6. People who work with young children must have ~~his or her~~ [their] share of patience.

PE 7. I want to get a part-time restaurant job, but ~~they~~ [the restaurant owners] just won't give me a chance.

PE 8. Quincy decided to add a porch onto the house by ~~hisself~~ [himself].

PE 9. Last Halloween, ~~him~~ [he] and Anita went to the neighborhood center's party dressed as Mr. Ed, the talking horse.

C 10. If you want to get along with others, you have to know how to be a good listener.

Score Number correct ______ × 20 = ______ %

Faulty Modifiers and Parallelism

Combined Mastery Test 1

In the spaces at the left, indicate whether each sentence contains a misplaced modifier (*MM*), a dangling modifier (*DM*), or faulty parallelism (*FP*). Then correct the error in the space under the sentence.

Rewritten sentences may vary.

DM 1. Being frightened, the skunk's odor filled the air.
The frightened skunk's odor filled the air.

MM 2. We watched the traffic pile up bumper to bumper from the window.
From the window, we watched the traffic pile up bumper to bumper.

FP 3. A police officer needs an open mind, sharp eyes, and to be cool-headed.
A police officer needs an open mind, sharp eyes, and a cool head.

DM 4. Wondering if my hair is naturally blond, I told Jim the truth.
I told Jim, who was wondering if my hair is naturally blond, the truth.

MM 5. The biology students saw one-celled animals squirming through their microscopes.
Through their microscopes, the biology students saw one-celled animals squirming.

DM 6. Snuggling under the warm comforter, the cold room didn't bother me.
Snuggling under the warm comforter, I wasn't bothered by the cold room.

DM 7. After sitting through a long class, my foot was asleep.
After I sat through a long class, my foot was asleep.

FP 8. My lasagna recipe includes chopped spinach, grated cheese, and onions that have been sliced.
My lasagna recipe includes chopped spinach, grated cheese, and sliced onions.

DM 9. While learning to shift gears, the Toyota crashed into the garage door.
While learning to shift gears, I crashed the Toyota into the garage door.

FP 10. The new employee is not only intelligent but also friendly, dedicated, and can be relied on.
The new employee is not only intelligent but also friendly, dedicated, and reliable.

Score Number correct ______ × 10 = ______ %

Faulty Modifiers and Parallelism

Combined Mastery Test 2

In the spaces at the left, indicate whether each sentence contains a misplaced modifier (*MM*), a dangling modifier (*DM*), or faulty parallelism (*FP*). Then correct the error in the space under the sentence.

Rewritten sentences may vary.

FP 1. The guests were hungry, noisy, and they messed up the room.
The guests were hungry, noisy, and messy.

DM 2. The last of a set, I used the old cup as a pencil holder.
I used the old cup, which was the last of a set, as a pencil holder.

MM 3. Leroy and Ella watched the stars lying on their backs in the grass at dusk.
Lying on their backs in the grass at dusk, Leroy and Ella watched the stars.

DM 4. Waiting in the icy rain for twenty minutes, the bus finally arrived.
After I waited in the icy rain for twenty minutes, the bus finally arrived.

DM 5. After bragging so much, Lester's friends became impatient with him.
After Lester bragged so much, his friends became impatient with him.

FP 6. The receptionist opens the mail, sorts it, and it is piled neatly on her boss's desk.
The receptionist opens the mail, sorts it, and piles it neatly . . .

MM 7. At the zoo, Hazel watched a hippopotamus that sat near a stone wall and ate a sandwich.
At the zoo, Hazel ate a sandwich and watched a hippopotamus that sat near a stone wall.

MM 8. Mrs. Sanchez has lived in the area for most of her life, and she almost knows everyone by name.
. . . and she knows almost everyone by name.

DM 9. Grateful for the relief from the heat, the air-conditioned library made it easier for Ruth to study.
Grateful for the relief from the heat, Ruth found that the air-conditioned library made it easier for her to study.

FP 10. We couldn't decide whether taking a ride in the country, barbecuing in the backyard, or to go to the park was how we should spend the afternoon.
. . . or going to the park was how . . .

Score Number correct _______ × 10 = _______ %

Capital Letters and Punctuation

Combined Mastery Test 1

Each of the following sentences contains an error in capitalization or punctuation. Refer to the box below and, in the space provided, write the letter identifying the error. Then correct the error.

a.	missing capital	c.	missing quotation marks
b.	missing apostrophe	d.	missing comma

______ 1. The Texas flight attendant asked “Is everyone tied down to a seat?”

______ 2. Todays paper had a story about a councilman who was arrested for drunk driving.

______ 3. I had to write two papers during my first college english class.

______ 4. “My cellar is so damp,” the comedian said, that when I set a mousetrap there, I caught a herring.”

______ 5. You may not believe this, but I havent watched television in a week.

______ 6. My little brothers worst trick was to hide a dead fish in my closet.

______ 7. “One of the most important things a writer can do, the speaker told his audience, “is to satisfy the reader’s curiosity.”

______ 8. Because of the noise of the dishwasher Emma didn’t hear the doorbell ring.

______ 9. Phan hates winter so much that he wishes he could go to sleep every november and not wake up until spring.

______ 10. The little girl, her eyes filled with desperation believed the shadow on the wall of her bedroom was a monster.

Score Number correct ________ × 10 = ________ %

Capital Letters and Punctuation

■ Combined Mastery Test 2

Each of the following sentences contains an error in capitalization or punctuation. Refer to the box below and, in the space provided, write the letter identifying the error. Then correct the error.

a.	missing capital	c.	missing quotation marks
b.	missing apostrophe	d.	missing comma

___b___ 1. Its often not what you do but how you do it that counts.

___d___ 2. Kwan enjoys reading books of all kinds but she probably spends more time with nonfiction than with fiction.

___a___ 3. An instant polaroid camera will not provide the same sharp pictures as a 35-millimeter camera.

___c___ 4. “The trouble with this office, Darryl confided, “is that the only ones who are sharp are the pencils.”

___d___ 5. Coffee tea, colas, and chocolate all contain caffeine.

___a___ 6. My father always told me, “when you drive, watch out for the other guy.”

___a___ 7. In many rural areas of the west, mail deliveries are made at odd hours.

___b___ 8. My daughters purse is full of jelly beans and dandelions.

___b___ 9. Peter was amazed at his compact cars trunk space when he fit all the camping gear into it with room to spare.

___c___ 10. “It’s not my fault that I’m having trouble with spelling, my little brother insisted. “The teacher keeps changing the words.”

Score Number correct _______ × 10 = _______ %

Word Use

■ Combined Mastery Test 1

Each of the following sentences contains a mistake identified in the left-hand margin. Underline the mistake and then correct it in the space provided.

Answers may vary for the rewritten versions.

Slang — 1. Gene trained to the max for the school marathon.
as much as possible

Wordiness — 2. At this point in time, I haven't decided which courses I'll take next semester.
I haven't decided which courses I'll take next semester.

Cliché — 3. I am so sick and tired of television commercials that I watch only cable shows.
so bored with

Pretentious language — 4. After a year on the job, the foreman received an increase in remuneration.
a raise

Adverb error — 5. Balancing several plates on my arm careful, I turned and bumped into a customer.
carefully

Error in comparison — 6. That last game was the most bad one I ever bowled.
worst

Confusing word — 7. For those who want help with the final exam, their will be a review on Thursday.
there

Confusing word — 8. We must have past ten service stations, but Lennie wouldn't stop until he found one that sold snacks.
passed

Confusing word — 9. San Francisco's Golden Gate Bridge is constructed out of more then eighty thousand miles of wire.
than

Confusing word — 10. The mayor's remarks aggravated the all ready bad feelings that existed among the city's rival street gangs.
already

Score Number correct _______ × 10 = _______ %

Word Use

Combined Mastery Test 2

Each of the following sentences contains a mistake identified in the left-hand margin. Underline the mistake and then correct it in the space provided.

Slang

1. The boss has been on my case for leaving half an hour before quitting time.

   has been angry with me

Wordiness

2. Violence seems to be increasing more and more every day in our cities.

   increase daily

Cliché

3. The championship game slipped through our fingers when our best receiver dropped the ball in the end zone.

   We lost the championship game when our best receiver . . .

Pretentious language

4. My husband and I have lost weight as a result of our reducing regimen.

   on our diet

Adverb error

5. The water was coming out of the hose too slow, so I increased the pressure.

   slowly

Error in comparison

6. Accounting has been the usefulest course that I have ever taken.

   most useful

Confusing word

7. Irregardless of my beliefs, I am willing to listen to your views with an open mind.

   Regardless

Confusing word

8. It's plane to see that nobody in this class studied for the exam.

   plain

Confusing word

9. I asked my doctor what the side affects might be from the medicine he prescribed.

   effects

Confusing word

10. In the passed few years, it seems that adults have become as interested in dressing up for Halloween as their children.

    past

Score Number correct _______ × 10 = _______ %

Editing and Proofreading Tests

The passages in this section can be used in either of two ways:

1 As Editing Tests Each passage contains a number of mistakes involving a single sentence skill. For example, the first passage (on page 491) contains five sentence fragments. Your instructor may ask you to proofread the passage to locate the five fragments. Spaces are provided at the bottom of the page for you to indicate which word groups are fragments. Your instructor may also have you correct the errors, either in the text itself or on separate paper. Depending on how well you do, you may also be asked to edit the second and third passages for fragments.

There are three passages for each skill area, and there are twelve skills covered in all. Here is a list of the skill areas:

Test 1	Fragments
Test 2	Fragments
Test 3	Run-Ons (Fused Sentences)
Test 4	Run-Ons (Comma Splices)
Test 5	Standard English Verbs
Test 6	Irregular Verbs
Test 7	Faulty Parallelism
Test 8	Capital Letters
Test 9	Apostrophes
Test 10	Quotation Marks
Test 11	Commas
Test 12	Commonly Confused Words

2 As Guided Composition Activities To give practice in proofreading as well, your instructor may ask you to do more than correct the skill mistakes in each passage. You may be asked to rewrite the passage, correcting it for skill mistakes *and also* copying the rest of the passage perfectly. Should you miss one skill mistake or make even one copying mistake (for example, omitting a word, dropping a verb ending, misspelling a word, or misplacing an apostrophe), you may be asked to rewrite a different passage that deals with the same skill.

Here is how you would proceed. You would start with sentence fragments, rewriting the first passage, proofreading your paper carefully, and then showing it to your instructor. He or she will check it quickly to see that all the fragments have been corrected and that no copying mistakes have been made. If the passage is error-free, the instructor will mark and initial the appropriate box in the progress chart on pages 697–698 and you can proceed to run-ons.

If even a single mistake is made, the instructor may question you briefly to see if you recognize and understand it. (Perhaps he or she will put a check beside the line in which the mistake appears, and then ask if you can correct it.) You may then be asked to write the second passage under a particular skill.

You will complete the program in guided composition when you successfully work through all twelve skills. Completing the twelve skills will strengthen your understanding of the skills, increase your ability to transfer the skills to actual writing situations, and markedly improve your proofreading.

In working on the passages, note the following points:

a For each skill, you will be told how many mistakes appear in the passages. If you have trouble finding the mistakes, turn back and review the pages in this book that explain the skill in question.

b Here is an effective way to go about correcting a passage. First, read it over quickly. Look for and mark off mistakes in the skill area involved. For example, in your first reading of a passage that has five fragments, you may locate and mark only three fragments. Next, reread the passage carefully so you can find the remaining errors in the skill in question. Finally, make notes in the margin about how to correct each mistake. Only at this point should you begin to rewrite the passage.

c Be sure to proofread with care after you finish a passage. Go over your writing word for word, looking for careless errors. Remember that you may be asked to do another passage involving the same skill if you make even one mistake.

Test 1: Fragments

Mistakes in each passage: 5

Passage A

[1]I can't remember a time when my sister didn't love to write. [2]In school, when teachers assigned a composition or essay. [3]Her classmates often groaned. [4]She would join them in their protests. [5]Because she didn't want to seem different. [6]Secretly, though, her spirit would dance. [7]Words were special to her. [8]I remember an incident when she was in third grade. [9]She wrote a funny story. [10]About the time my dog made a mess out of our kitchen. [11]The teacher made my sister stand in front of the class and read it aloud. [12]By the time she finished. [13]The classroom was bedlam. [14]Even the teacher wiped away tears of laughter. [15]It was a magic moment. [16]Which made my sister more in love with writing than ever.

Word groups that are fragments: 2 5 10 12 16

Corrections (corrections may vary):

Passage A

In school, when teachers assigned a composition or essay, her classmates often . . .
She would join them in their protests because she didn't want to seem different.
She wrote a funny story about the time my dog made a mess out of our kitchen.
By the time she finished, the classroom was bedlam.
It was a magic moment which made my sister more in love with writing than ever.

Passage B

[1]Too little attention is paid to the common household problem of single socks. [2]Although it seems missing socks must have fallen behind the washer or stuck to other clothing. [3]Careful searches always end in failure. [4]Some sock wearers react by buying only one type and color of socks. [5]So that they can deny ever losing any. [6]Accepting the inevitability of single socks is braver. [7]Also, finding uses for them is a creative challenge. [8]They are often transformed into containers for small items in drawers and suitcases. [9]Or used to shine shoes. [10]Many people even wear single socks that are only slightly mismatched. [11]Deluding themselves into thinking the mismatch will go unnoticed. [12]A better strategy is to be bold and wear pairs that do not match at all. [13]Such as a bright red sock and a gray one. [14]This establishes the wearer as a trendsetter and turns the appearance of a single sock into a welcome event.

Word groups that are fragments: 2 5 9 11 13

Corrections (corrections may vary):

Passage B

Although it seems missing socks must have fallen behind the washer or stuck to other clothing, careful searches always end in failure.

Some sock wearers react by buying only one type and color of socks so that they . . .

They are often transformed into containers for small items in drawers and suitcases or used to shine shoes.

Many people even wear single socks that are only slightly mismatched, deluding themselves into thinking . . .

A better strategy is to be bold and wear pairs that do not match at all, such as a bright . . .

Test 2: Fragments

Mistakes in each passage: 5

Passage A

[1]Your friend's new restaurant is a big success. [2]Since it is attracting large numbers of customers. [3]You know you should be thrilled for her. [4]In secret, however, her achievement makes you feel slightly depressed. [5]Maybe in the back of your mind you were secretly hoping that the restaurant would be a flop. [6]If you occasionally have negative thoughts about people you like. [7]You are not alone. [8]Many people are secretly pleased. [9]When their friends fail at something and are tortured with envy when they succeed. [10]Psychologists believe that such feelings are the result of a poor self-image. [11]For example, people who have a poor opinion of themselves are likely to feel threatened. [12]By their friends' success. [13]Instead of feeling happy when a friend is successful. [14]They feel unhappy with themselves—and their friend's achievement.

Word groups that are fragments: 2 6 9 12 13

Corrections (corrections may vary):

Your friend's new restaurant is a big success, since it is attracting large numbers of customers.
If you occasionally have negative thoughts about people you like, you are not alone.
Many people are secretly pleased when their friends fail at something and are tortured with envy when they succeed.
For example, people who have a poor opinion of themselves are likely to feel threatened by their friends' success.
Instead of feeling happy when a friend is successful, they feel unhappy with themselves—and their friend's achievement.

Passage B

[1]Much has been written in newspapers and magazines about fear of heights. [2]As well as fear of open places and of closed spaces. [3]Another phobia, the fear of bridges, is less known but just as disabling. [4]People who have this phobia fear that they will get dizzy and faint. [5]When they drive on a bridge. [6]As a result, they drive very slowly. [7]Staying close to the protective railing. [8]Some people are also afraid they will be pulled through the railing. [9]Down into the water below. [10]One help for such drivers is provided by the police force. [11]On the Chesapeake Bay Bridge, our nation's longest-span bridge. [12]The police will drive motorists' cars for them. [13]The police perform this welcome service many times each day.

Word groups that are fragments: __2__ __5__ __7__ __9__ __11__

Corrections (corrections may vary):

Much has been written in newspapers and magazines about fear of heights as well as fear of open places and of closed spaces.
People who have this phobia fear that they will get dizzy and faint when they drive on a bridge.
As a result, they drive very slowly, staying close to the protective railing.
Some people are also afraid they will be pulled through the railing down into the water below.
One help for such drivers is provided by the police force on the Chesapeake Bay Bridge, our nation's longest-span bridge.

■ Test 3: Run-Ons (Fused Sentences)

Mistakes in each passage: 5

Passage A

1A young girl looks at a fashion magazine she sees clothes modeled by women who weight 115 pounds although they are nearly six feet tall. 2She receives a "teen doll" as a present and studies its proportions. 3The doll has legs nearly two-thirds the length of its body it also has a tiny waist and nonexistent hips and thighs. 4She goes to the movies the screen heroines resemble adolescent boys more than mature women. 5Her favorite television shows are filled with commercials showing attractive men and women. 6The commercials are for weight-loss programs these programs insist that a person must be slender to be desirable. 7By the time the girl reaches her teens, she has been thoroughly brainwashed. 8The media have given her the same messages over and over they all say that to be thin is the only acceptable option.

Word groups that are run-ons: __1__ __3__ __4__ __6__ __8__

Corrections:

A young girl looks at a fashion magazine. She sees clothes modeled . . .
The doll has legs nearly two-thirds the length of its body. It also has a tiny . . .
She goes to the movies, and the screen heroines resemble adolescent boys . . .
The commercials are for weight-loss programs. These programs insist that . . .
The media have given her the same messages over and over. They all say that . . .

Note: Rewritten sentences may vary somewhat.

Passage B

[1]Before there were Hindus, Christians, or Jews, there were Jains. [2]In all of its history, this religious group has avoided violence in fact, it has never fought a war. [3]Today ten million Jains live in India of these millions, not one has a criminal record. [4]Jains restrict themselves to occupations that do not destroy the environment or other living creatures they work as computer operators, teachers, and doctors. [5]In spite of these limitations, the Jains are India's most successful people. [6]They contribute more to charity than any other group they have built schools, hospitals, and shelters for the poor all over India. [7]Their kindness even extends to animals the Jains eat no meat and wear no skins or furs. [8]What is the secret of this remarkable people? [9]They not only teach nonviolence; they also live it.

Word groups that are run-ons: 2 3 4 6 7

Corrections:

In all of its history, this religious group has avoided violence. In fact, it has . . .
Today ten million Jains live in India. Of these millions, not one has a criminal . . .
Jains restrict themselves to occupations that do not destroy the environment or other living creatures.
They work as computer operators . . .
They contribute more to charity than any other group. They have built schools . . .
Their kindness even extends to animals, for the Jains eat no meat . . .

Note: Rewritten sentences may vary somewhat.

Test 4: Run-Ons (Comma Splices)

Mistakes in each passage: 5

Passage A

1In any high school, three subcultures exist within the larger school environment. 2The three groups are quite different, almost every student can be identified with one of them. 3The first one is the delinquent subculture, this one is the least popular of the three groups. 4Members of the delinquent group despise school, they hate the faculty, the staff, and any other symbols of authority. 5The next step up the social ladder is the academic subculture, it is composed of hardworking students who value their education. 6The third major student group is the fun subculture. 7These students care most about looks, clothes, cars, and dates, for this group, social status is the most important thing in the world. 8Needless to say, the fun subculture is the most popular of the three groups.

Word groups that are run-ons: 2 3 4 5 7

Corrections:

The three groups are quite different, but almost every student . . .
The first one is the delinquent subculture. This one is the least popular . . .
Members of the delinquent group despise school. They hate the faculty . . .
The next step up the social ladder is the academic subculture. It is composed . . .
These students care most about looks, clothes, cars, and dates. For this group . . .

Note: Rewritten sentences may vary somewhat.

Passage B

[1]A trip to the supermarket can be quite frustrating, especially if you need only a few items. [2]When you arrive, you look for a parking space close to the store, you can't find one and have to walk half the distance of the parking lot. [3]Then you must find an empty cart, those which don't bounce or squeak are in short supply. [4]When you finally start shopping, you discover that the items you want are "out of stock until Tuesday" or that their prices have gone up since your last visit. [5]Eventually, you approach the so-called express lane. [6]You're supposed to have ten items or fewer for this lane, the person in front of you usually has many more. [7]It also seems that the store's slowest checkout person is assigned to that register. [8]But eventually it is your turn, and you pay for your order and leave. [9]Then, with a bag in each hand, you make the long walk back to your car, you are understandably frazzled at this point. [10]Struggling to unlock the car without dropping your bags, you decide to try the local mini-market next time, it's closer to home anyway.

Word groups that are run-ons: __2__ __3__ __6__ __9__ __10__

Corrections:

When you arrive, you look for a parking space close to the store. You can't . . .
Then you must find an empty cart. Those that don't bounce or squeak are in . . .
You're supposed to have ten items or fewer for this lane. The person in . . .
Then, with a bag in each hand, you make the long walk back to your car. You . . .
Struggling to unlock the car without dropping your bags, you decide to try the local mini-market next time. It's closer . . .

Note: Rewritten sentences may vary somewhat.

Test 5: Standard English Verbs

Mistakes in each passage: 5

Passage A

[1]Few issues generate more heated debate than gun control. [2]Most of the controversy has centered ~~center~~ on the sale of handguns, which, because they can be concealed easily, are usually the weapons used ~~use~~ in armed robberies and murders. [3]For that reason, while it is often easy to buy a rifle, many localities ban private ownership of handguns or require owners to get licenses from the police. [4]Advocates of gun control argue that these restrictions do not go far enough. [5]They feel, for example, that selling handguns through the mail should be abolished ~~abolish~~. [6]Their opponents maintain that further restrictions would prevent law-abiding citizens from buying guns for protection or recreation. [7]Such debates have continued ~~continue~~ for years, with both sides frequently appealing to emotion rather than reason. [8]Opponents of gun-control laws, for example, shout, "Guns don't kill people—people do," which is true enough but has little to do with the issue. [9]And advocates of tougher laws accuse the other side of wanting guns in order to live out childish or macho fantasies. [10]Because neither side attempts ~~attempt~~ to understand the other, it has been difficult to reach a rational public consensus.

Sentences with nonstandard verbs (write down the number of a sentence twice if it has two nonstandard verbs): 2 2 5 7 10

Passage B

[1]When I was a part-time library assistant at our public high school, I work the Friday afternoon shift. [2]In the middle of an unusually hectic and complicated Friday morning of running errands, I realize that I would never make it to work by 12:30. [3]I tried several times to telephone the high school but kept getting a busy signal. [4]So I decided to just keep going and explain later, since I had never been late before. [5]When I finally arrived at the library at 1:10, the librarian shot a glance at me and then look up at the wall clock. [6]"I was in the neighborhood, so I though I'd drop in," I quipped. [7]We both laughed, and I went right to work. [8]The librarian never ask me to explain, but I made a point of getting to work the following Monday forty minutes early.

Sentences with nonstandard verbs (write down the number of a sentence twice if it has two nonstandard verbs): _____ _____ _____ _____ _____

■ Test 6: Irregular Verbs

Mistakes in each passage: 10

Passage A

[1]Although Margo Carbone has hiked and skied in frigid weather, her greatest risk from cold was when her car ~~breaked~~ broke down in a rural area during a winter storm. [2]The temperature had ~~fell~~ fallen below zero. [3]At first she stayed in her car and waited for help, but she was so cold she ~~shaked~~ shook. [4]She hoped that moving would warm her up, so she ~~begun~~ began to walk briskly toward the nearest town. [5]Walking did warm her at first, but it also drained her energy reserves. [6]She ~~knowed~~ knew that her body was losing heat fast. [7]As she struggled against the wind, she started to feel disoriented. [8]She was afraid her low body temperature had begun to affect her brain. [9]If she did not get help soon, she could become too tired and confused to save herself. [10]Luckily, a car soon ~~come~~ came plodding through the snow, and the driver insisted that Margo get in and then ~~taked~~ took her to a nearby diner. [11]Once she ~~drunk~~ drank some hot tea, warmed up, and rested, she felt better. [12]However, she knew that she had been lucky. [13]She could have ~~froze~~ frozen to death. [14]Her experience ~~teached~~ taught her a lesson. [15] Now she carries a blanket and candy bars in her car during the winter and always takes cold weather seriously.

Sentences with mistakes in irregular verbs (write down the number of a sentence twice if it contains two mistakes):

1	2	3	4	6
10	10	11	13	14

Passage B

[1]It was delightful to visit a day care center and watch children at play. [2]In the playground, some ~~throwed~~ threw colorful balls to one another while others ~~swinged~~ swung on the play equipment. [3]Inside, some of the children had ~~took~~ taken coloring books off a shelf. [4]They were ~~laying~~ lying on the floor and giving serious attention to their artwork. [5]Two others had ~~began~~ begun to build a castle with blocks, but it ~~falled~~ fell down when a little girl ~~runned~~ ran into it. [6]Then there was the little girl who played nurse to her doll. [7]She pretended that it had been ~~bit~~ bitten by a dog and put a bandage on its finger. [8]I loved seeing all the children having such a good time while learning to play together. [9]After a while, the bell ~~ringed,~~ rang and all the children ~~wented~~ went to take a nap.

Sentences with mistakes in irregular verbs (write down the number of a sentence twice or more if it contains two or more mistakes):

2 ____ 2 ____ 3 ____ 4 ____ 5 ____

5 ____ 5 ____ 7 ____ 9 ____ 9 ____

Test 7: Faulty Parallelism

Mistakes in each passage: 5

Passage A

[1]For many athletes, life after a sports career is a letdown. [2]While they are in the limelight, the athletes are praised for the records they break and winning games. [3]The public cheers them on and is seeking their autographs. [4]But what happens when a sports figure is no longer able to play? [5]Most athletes, because of the physical demands of the game or injuring themselves, are unable to play into their thirties. [6]While a few former athletes move on to success in other fields, most are not prepared for nonathletic careers and lives that are private. [7]Sadly, many former players are unable to find a second career. [8]Many suffer from depression, and with some there are suicide attempts. [9]Players' associations, having become aware of the problem, are investigating ways to prepare their members for life after athletics.

Sentences with faulty parallelism: 2 3 5 6 8

Corrections:

the games they win (or breaking records)
seeks
injuries to themselves
private lives
some attempt suicide

Passage B

[1]Humanity's longtime dream of flying remained just a dream until two brothers, Joseph and Etienne Montgolfier, built the first hot-air balloon. [2]Joseph had experimented with parachutes and mechanical devices. [3]Then Etienne decided to leave an architectural career and was working with his brother. [4]They came to believe that if one made a sufficiently light container and would fill it with a gas that was lighter than air, the container must rise. [5]Joseph proved this theory by building small paper balloons and filling them with air that was hot. [6]When these small balloons rose, the brothers made larger and larger paper balloons, and then the building of a paper balloon seven hundred cubic feet in size. [7]Eventually, they constructed a silk balloon, which they kept aloft for ten minutes. [8]It carried the first air passengers—a rooster, a duck, and a sheep. [9]The animals were placed in a basket that dangled below the balloon, arousing great interest, and it attracted crowds. [10]That balloon was launched September 19, 1783, and the rest, as they say, is history.

Sentences with faulty parallelism: 3 4 5 6 9

Corrections:

work
filled
hot air
they built
attracting crowds

Note: Rewritten versions may vary somewhat.

Test 8: Capital Letters

Mistakes in each passage: 10

Passage A

[1]Orlando, an area in florida that used to be known primarily for citrus groves, has become one of the most popular vacation spots in the world. [2]It all began with Disney World, a wildly successful theme park far bigger and more lavish than even disneyland in california. [3]Disney World's success has drawn other tourist attractions to the orlando area. [4]Sea World, featuring shamu, the killer whale, is the most successful of these, drawing over one million visitors a year. [5]The Elvis Presley Museum, Flea World (a huge flea market), Reptile World, and the tupperware Museum, which exhibits food containers used through the ages, are other nearby attractions. [6]But perhaps the most striking is Faith world, billed as "god's tourist attraction in central Florida." [7]This church is in a huge red and white airline hangar that was formerly an air museum. [8]In addition, hundreds of hotels, restaurants, and nightclubs have grown up in the area to accommodate an annual eight million visitors. [9]Still, the center of attention remains Disney World itself, bringing millions to America's south to meet such international stars as Donald duck and Goofy.

Sentences with missing capitals (write the number of a sentence as many times as it contains capitalization mistakes):

______ ______ ______ ______ ______

______ ______ ______ ______ ______

Passage B

[1]Most immigrants who came to the United States by ship at the beginning of the century were thrilled at the sight of the Statue of Liberty. [2]But none were delighted with Ellis Island. [3]This drab little island off the southern tip of Manhattan was the primary immigration center from January 1, 1902, until late in 1943. [4]The majority of immigrants came to this island from Europe. [5]On arrival, their first task was to prove they were physically and morally fit. [6]Herded into a big hall with all their possessions, these people were given medical and legal examinations. [7]Doctors had to certify that immigrants were not carrying or suffering from serious diseases; legal inspectors, asking questions in English, had to determine that the immigrants had a place to go, money, and potential employment. [8]Immigrants were asked questions such as "Are you an anarchist?" and "Do you have a criminal record?" [9]For most people, this investigation took three to five hours. [10]The immigrants were then free to join their waiting relatives and begin their new life in America.

Sentences with missing capitals (write the number of a sentence as many times as it contains capitalization mistakes):

1 1 2 2 3

3 7 8 8 10

■ Test 9: Apostrophes

Mistakes in each passage: 10

Passage A

[1]Sharon has worked at a convenience store long enough to spot three types of customers. [2]She recognizes customers of the first type by their haggard faces and bewildered expressions. [3]Such people may buy soft drinks or candy bars, but their main reason for coming in is to ask directions. [4]Unfortunately, they dont know north from south or any of the areas landmarks. [5]Although Sharons city has a population of forty thousand, they ask such questions as, “Do you know where Bill Hendersons house is?” [6]The second type buys more, but people in this category are never satisfied. [7]They complain that the dairy products arent fresh enough or act astonished that the store doesnt stock a product such as plum ketchup. [8]“Im an expert in these matters” seems to be this types attitude. [9]Luckily, Sharon sees many of her favorite customers, the friendly type, who often buy the same things each visit. [10]By the time one of her favorites, Mr. Clauser, reaches her counter each morning, she has gotten his coffee and roll and has begun to ring them up. [11]Mr. Clausers purchases are bagged so quickly that he has time to chat for a moment. [12]Without this type of customer, Sharon is sure she wouldve quit her job by now.

Sentences with missing apostrophes (write down the number of a sentence twice if it contains two missing apostrophes):

4 4 5 5 7

7 8 8 11 12

Passage B

[1]I love all kinds of food, but I've a special fondness for fresh fruit. [2]There are many reasons for this. [3]An apple's chewy skin covers a crispy treat. [4]An orange's rind is bitter, but the fruit beneath is sweet and juicy. [5]Peeling a banana's smooth skin reveals a mushy delight inside. [6]Other fruits offer more of a challenge and more of a reward. [7]It can be almost dangerous to remove a pineapple's prickly exterior or a coconut's tough shell, but it is worth the effort to get to the delicious contents. [8]Another reason for eating fresh fruits is that they're usually a good source of vitamins and fiber. [9]And they're naturally sweet—an ideal substitute for foods with refined sugar. [10]You'll probably find that cake and candy are more popular, but you can't choose anything better for you than fresh fruit.

Sentences with missing apostrophes (write down the number of a sentence twice if it contains two missing apostrophes):

1 3 4 5 7

7 8 9 10 10

■ Test 10: Quotation Marks

Quotation marks needed in each passage: 10 pairs

Passage A

1 Tony and Lola were driving down the interstate highway at about sixty-five miles an hour. 2 "You should slow down, Lola," Tony said. 3 "We can't afford another ticket."

4 "Oh, don't worry," Lola replied. 5 "I haven't seen a police car all morning. 6 Besides, everyone else is driving just as fast."

7 Suddenly, a police car driving in the opposite direction made a quick U-turn, turned on its light and siren, and came up behind their car.

8 "I knew it!" Tony moaned. 9 "Half a week's paycheck down the drain."

10 "Now, this just isn't fair," Lola said to the officer as he walked toward the car. 11 "It's not fair to stop us when everyone else is driving just as fast."

12 "You may be right," the policeman answered, 13 "But what's really unfair is that there's just one of me and so many speeders. 14 I can stop only one car at a time."

Sentences or sentence groups with missing quotation marks:

2 ___ 3 ___ 4 ___ 5–6 ___ 8 ___

9 ___ 10 ___ 11 ___ 12 ___ 13–14 ___

Passage B

1 The phone rang as the Parkers ate dinner. 2"I'll bet that's another nuisance call,"said Mr. Parker, groaning as he got up to answer it.

3"Hello, my name is Marge. 4 May I speak to Mr. or Mrs. Parker?"

5"This is Mr. Parker."6 He rolled his eyes toward the ceiling.

7"Mr. Parker, you are probably aware of changes in the tax laws, inflated prices, and . . ."

8"Yes, but I'm really not interested in buying anything,"said Mr. Parker, trying to be patient.

9 Marge stumbled over a few words, cleared her throat, and said,"I represent a service that will . . ."

10"Perhaps you didn't understand me,"said Mr. Parker, beginning to get angry. 11"I do not want to buy anything from you. 12 Now please hang up, because that's what I'm going to do."

13"But Mr. Parker . . ."

14 The receiver slammed onto its base. 15 Mr. Parker returned to his dinner, sighed, and said,"I hope I wasn't too rough on her. 16 I know she's just trying to earn a living, but I hate being interrupted at dinnertime."

Sentences or sentence groups with missing quotation marks:

2 3–4 5 7 8

9 10 11–12 13 15–16

Test 11: Commas

Mistakes in each passage: 10

Passage A

[1]How many homeless people live in the United States? [2]Estimates range as high as 3,000,000. [3]Today's homeless include not only single people but also families with small children. [4]Run-down boardinghouses and hotels, the places where the poor once lived, have been replaced by expensive houses and condominiums. [5]Although some of the homeless have jobs, they do not make enough money to pay for food, rent, and other necessities. [6]Others are unable to find work. [7]Many of them have been released from mental hospitals but are still ill. [8]A few of the homeless refuse to live in shelters, but most of them live on the street because they have nowhere else to go. [9]They are often seen sleeping in boxes or huddled in doorways. [10]To find enough food, they search through garbage cans or accept handouts. [11]Life on the street is dangerous and short. [12]Our society is slow in realizing that these dirty, poorly dressed people have not brought their problems on themselves. [13]They cannot solve their problems without help.

Sentences with missing commas (write down the number of a sentence as many times as it contains comma mistakes):

2 2 4 4 5

5 5 8 10 12

Passage B

[1]On one bitterly cold day a week ago,I experienced one of the nicest features of rural life—old-fashioned neighborliness. [2]I had gotten a flat tire while driving to work on a back road,so I walked to the nearest house and knocked at the door. [3]An elderly, kind-eyed woman answered. [4]I quickly explained my problem and asked to use her telephone to call my boss and a gas station. [5]The woman graciously led me inside and then said her son might be willing to change the tire. [6]As I started to protest,she left the room. [7]She soon returned to inform me that her son would change it. [8]Then she explained that she had to take her husband to a doctor. [9]She insisted,however,that I sit by the wood stove and have some coffee while I waited. [10]Too astonished and grateful to protest again,I thanked her profusely as she left. [11]About twenty minutes later,I saw from the window that her son was finishing with my tire. [12]I went out to my car. [13]"Thanks so much. [14]Please accept this for your kindness," I said as I offered him a bill from my wallet. [15]He waved it away. [16]"Hope your day gets better," he said as he headed back to his house.

Sentences with missing commas (write down the number of a sentence as many times as it contains comma mistakes):

1 2 3 6 9

9 10 11 14 16

Test 12: Commonly Confused Words

Mistakes in each passage: 10

Passage A

[1]How does a magician saw a woman in half? [2]~~Thought~~ Though this illusion usually makes a strong impression on an audience, ~~its~~ it's an easy one for magicians, ~~irregardless~~ regardless of experience. [3]In fact, it requires more skill on the part of a ~~pear~~ pair of female assistants than the magician. [4]The trick begins when a table holding the coffinlike box is rolled onstage. [5]One assistant is hiding inside that table. [6]When the magician displays the box to the audience, it is, of ~~coarse~~ course, empty. [7]~~Than~~ Then the magician asks an assistant on stage to climb into the box. [8]As she ~~dose~~ does this, the hidden woman enters the box through a trapdoor in the table, sticks her feet out one end, and curls up with her head between her knees. [9]The other woman, drawing her knees up to her chin, puts her head out the other end. [10]Now the box appears to be holding one ~~hole~~ whole woman, and the magician can saw ~~write~~ right through. [11]To complete the ~~affect~~ effect, the woman at the foot end slides back into the table as the magician reopens the box.

Sentences with commonly confused words (write the number of a sentence more than once if it contains more than one commonly confused word):

2 2 2 3 6

7 8 10 10 11

Passage B

[1]Increasing social pressure is encouraging many smokers to try to quit their habit. [2]Many restaurants allow smoking only in special sections, and smoking has been banned in some other public places. [3]When asked ~~weather~~ whether they would mind if a smoker lights up, people are more likely to object ~~then~~ than they once were. [4]At parties, smokers may be forced ~~too~~ to sneak outside for a cigarette while their friends enjoy themselves inside. [5]~~Less~~ Fewer employers tolerate smoking, and family members also complain about smoke that reaches them ~~threw~~ through the air. [6]~~Its~~ It's no wonder that many smokers are trying to quit. [7]Succeeding is easy for a few people, but many find it almost impossible to ~~brake~~ break the habit. [8]Quitting is like ending a dozen habits, ~~being that~~ because people smoke in so many different situations. [9]They may light up when they wake up, when they have coffee or snacks, and when they drive ~~there~~ their cars. [10]In any such familiar situation, a person ~~whose~~ who's quit smoking is at risk of starting again. [11]Luckily, the more times a person tries, the greater his or her chances are of quitting for good the next time.

Sentences with commonly confused words (write down the number of a sentence twice if it contains two commonly confused words):

3	3	4	5	5
6	7	8	9	10

Combined Editing Tests

Editing for Sentence-Skills Mistakes

The twelve editing tests in this section will give you practice in finding a variety of sentence-skills mistakes. People often find it hard to edit a paper carefully. They have put so much work, or so little work, into their writing, that it's almost painful for them to look at the paper one more time. You may simply have to *force* yourself to edit. Remember that eliminating sentence-skills mistakes will improve an average paper and help ensure a high grade on a good paper. Further, as you get into the habit of editing your papers, you will get into the habit of using the sentence skills consistently. They are a basic part of clear, effective writing.

In tests 3 through 7, the spots where errors occur have been underlined; your job is to identify each error. In tests 1 and 2 and 8 through 12, you must locate as well as identify the errors. Use the progress chart on page 699 to keep track of your performance on these tests.

Combined Editing Test 1

Identify the five mistakes in format in the student paper on the opposite page. From the box below, choose the letters that describe the five mistakes and write those letters in the spaces provided.

a. The title should not be underlined.
b. The title should not be set off in quotation marks.
c. There should not be a period at the end of a title.
d. All the major words in a title should be capitalized.
e. The title should be just several words, not a complete sentence.
f. The first line of a paper should stand independent of the title.
g. A line should be skipped between the title and the first line of the paper.
h. The first line of a paper should be indented.
i. The right-hand margin should not be crowded.
j. Hyphenation should occur only between syllables.

1. __b__ 2. __c__ 3. __d__ 4. __f__ 5. __g__

"My worst job."

It was when I was working as a cashier last summer at Morgan's Department Store. Because I was the newest employee, I was given the hours no one else wanted. I usually had to work weekday evenings and weekend afternoons. I also got stuck working nearly every holiday. Further, Morgan's was very disorganized. Each Saturday, the store would run a large advertisement in our local newspaper offering fantastic sales on various products. However, there were usually only five or six of these items in stock. Once, there was a large advertisement offering barbecue grills for only $19.99. Unfortunately, we had sold the last grill within the first two hours of the day. For the rest of the afternoon, I had to deal with irate customers who complained that they had driven out of their way just for our sale. Between the long hours no one else wanted and the irate customers, I was happy when the summer came to a close and I could go back to being a full-time student.

Combined Editing Test 2

Identify the five mistakes in paper format in the student paper on the opposite page. From the box below, choose the letters that describe the five mistakes and write those letters in the spaces provided.

a. The title should not be underlined.
b. The title should not be set off in quotation marks.
c. There should not be a period at the end of a title.
d. All the major words in a title should be capitalized.
e. The title should be just several words, not a complete sentence.
f. The first line of a paper should stand independent of the title.
g. A line should be skipped between the title and the first line of the paper.
h. The first line of a paper should be indented.
i. The right-hand margin should not be crowded.
j. Hyphenation should occur only between syllables.

1. __a__ 2. __c__ 3. __g__ 4. __i__ 5. __j__

Why Tabloids Are Popular.

Tabloids have become famous for such headlines as "Aliens Steal Businessman on his Lunch Break" and "Woman Gives Birth to Fifty-Pound Baby." In fact, the weekly gossip sheets have become a multimillion-dollar business. Yet it is hard to believe that the people who buy these magazines actually believe the stories they read. Why, then, are these tabloids so popular? One reason for their popularity might be their entertainment value. The stories covered in such magazines as the National Enquirer are often so absurd that they are funny. To the weary shopper in a crowded checkout lane at a grocery store, these magazines may provide just the entertainment needed at the end of a long day. But, ce-rtainly, tabloids have not made their millions simply by being funny. In fact, their popularity may be a sad indicator of the state of many Americans' lives. The truth is that day-to-day life is often pathetically mundane. Thus, though the average tabloid reader may consciously know that the stories he or she reads are largely false, the articles may provide just the bit of imagination, the spark of controversy and extravagance, that the reader lacks in his or her everyday life.

Combined Editing Test 3

Identify the sentence-skills mistakes at the underlined spots in the selection that follows. From the box below, choose the letter that describes each mistake and write it in the space provided. (The same kind of mistake may appear more than once.) Then, in the space provided between the lines, correct each mistake.

a. fragment	d. missing capital letter
b. run-on	e. missing apostrophe
c. irregular verb mistake	

Did anyone ever throwed [1] (throw) a surprise party for you? It's supposed to be fun, but I'm not so sure about that anymore. I had one at the house of my girlfriend last week. When I walked into Ellens [2] (Ellen's) living room, people hiding behind doors rushed out in a frenzy and shouted, "surprise!" [3] ("Surprise!") All that noise made me so nervous that I felled [4] (fell) over a chair, I couldn't believe this was happening to me. [5] (chair. I) When everyone calmed down. [6] (down, I) I noticed how dressed up they all were. My girlfriend had told me we were going to plant vegetables in her mothers [7] (mother's) garden, I was wearing old messy clothes. [8] (garden, so I) Everyone elses [9] (else's) clothes were at least clean and nice. I suppose it didn't really matter, but somehow I felt something was wrong. About the guest of honor being dressed like a slob. [10] (wrong about) On my next birthday, I want to go to a nice quiet horror show.

1. c 2. e 3. d 4. c 5. b
6. a 7. e 8. b 9. e 10. a

Combined Editing Test 4

Identify the sentence-skills mistakes at the underlined spots in the selection that follows. From the box below, choose the letter that describes each mistake and write it in the space provided. (The same kind of mistake may appear more than once.) Then, in the spaces provided between the lines, correct each mistake.

a. fragment	d. missing capital letter
b. run-on	e. missing comma
c. dropped verb ending	f. homonym mistake

him after
The best advice I ever got was from a minister. I went to see him. After an episode in
1
which I betrayed my wife. I had been married for a little over a year and felt closed in by
out. I
my marriage. Somehow, seeing my unmarried friends play the field made me feel left out,
2
wanted
I loved my wife but want freedom to have an affair on the side. I thought I had found it with
3 parlor, whom
the owner of a beauty parlor. Whom I met in my job selling supplies to beauty shops. One
4
arranged
day, we arrange to meet at her shop after hours, when I supposedly was to drop off
5
supplies. But we both knew the real purpose of that meeting. I spent an hour with her that
dirty, I shower, but
afternoon. When I left, feeling guilty and dirty. I went home and took a shower but I still
6 7
felt like a traitor. I decided I could cleanse myself only by confessing to my wife. But first
"Don't "There's
I went to talk to my minister the next day. "don't tell your wife," he said. "Their's no reason
8 9 wife. I
to give her pain. You must carry your pain alone and learn from it." I never did tell my wife,
10
I have never betrayed her again either.

1. a 2. b 3. c 4. a 5. c
6. a 7. e 8. d 9. f 10. b

Combined Editing Test 5

Identify the sentence-skills mistakes at the underlined spots in the selection that follows. From the box below, choose the letter that describes each mistake and write it in the space provided. (The same kind of mistake may appear more than once.) Then, in the space provided between the lines, correct each mistake.

a. fragment	d. faulty parallelism
b. run-on	e. mistake in pronoun agreement
c. mistake in subject-verb agreement	f. apostrophe mistake
	g. missing comma

lonely, it

Although living alone can sometimes be lonely. It is very convenient. (1) When you live by yourself, no one ever gives you a hard time for being a slob. You can do Mondays (2) [Monday's] breakfast dishes on Tuesday afternoon. Or even wait until Friday if you have enough spare dishes. (3) [afternoon or] The same is true with the vacuuming and dusting. If you choose to wait until things start growing out of the carpet or the knickknacks are knee-deep in dust before cleaning nobody (4) [cleaning, nobody] will care in the least. Also, you get to watch whichever television shows you want whenever you want. The same is true for the radio and the stereo, you (5) [stereo. You] can play whatever music you wish at any volume and never have to listen to complaints' (6) [complaints.]. Another nice thing about living alone is that there are (7) [is] never an argument about money. You always know exactly who made every phone call, ate everything in the refrigerator, and was running up (8) [ran] the electric bill. And when you do get lonely, you can always call someone up and invite them (9) [him or her] over without being stuck with company for too long. Its (10) [It's] a lot harder to get rid of somebody who lives with you.

1. a 2. f 3. a 4. g 5. b
6. f 7. c 8. d 9. e 10. f

Combined Editing Test 6

Identify the sentence-skills mistakes at the underlined spots in the selection that follows. From the box below, choose the letter that describes each mistake and write it in the space provided. (The same kind of mistake may appear more than once.) Then, in the space provided between the lines, correct each mistake.

a. fragment	d. mistake in pronoun agreement
b. run-on	e. missing comma
c. dangling modifier	f. cliché

days, I
When I worked behind a soda fountain during my high-school days. I loved to make
1 one, I'd base
ice cream sodas. Whenever someone ordered one I'd grab a tall, heavy soda glass by its
and then 2 When I poised my
base. Then move over to where the syrups were kept. Poising my left hand above the syrup
3 4
dispenser, two inches of thick chocolate or vanilla flavoring would squirt into the bottom
them
of the glass. Next, I'd scoop two neat round balls of ice cream and drop it into the glass over
5
the syrup. As the ice cream sank slowly into the syrup, causing curls of color to swirl
around, I
around I would insert a long-handled spoon with a small ladle. I'd briefly stir this mixture
6 spoon, and then glass, taking
with the spoon, then I would squirt seltzer into the glass. Taking care to aim directly onto
7 Finally, 8
the ice cream. Last but by no means least, I'd add a scarlet cherry and serve the soda on a
9 smile, and I'd
paper place mat. Often, the customer would smile, I'd be given a good tip for my creation.
10

1. a 2. e 3. a 4. c 5. d
6. e 7. b 8. a 9. f 10. b

Combined Editing Test 7

Identify the sentence-skills mistakes at the underlined spots in the selection that follows. From the box below, choose the letter that describes each mistake and write it in the space provided. (The same kind of mistake may appear more than once.) Then, in the space provided between the lines, correct each mistake.

a. fragment	d. mistake in pronoun reference
b. run-on	e. apostrophe mistake
c. inconsistent verb tense	f. missing comma

Children of the Night, founded and directed by Lois Lee, is helping many young runaways in Hollywood California.[1] According to a recent segment on *Sixty Minutes* presented by Ed Bradley.[2] Lee, a sociologist, has a twofold job. First, she spent[3] time on the crime-ridden streets of Hollywood. She looks for missing girls between the ages of twelve and seventeen. And passes out a twenty-four-hour hot line number.[4] The girls who seek her assistance are helped back into mainstream society, Lee[5] said that 80 percent of first-time runaways who get help do not return to the streets'.[6] The second aspect of Lees[7] work is fund-raising. Since she refuses government funds because of the restrictions they[8] make Lee[9] solicits money from various civic groups her[10] goal is to establish a shelter for girls who cannot or will not go home to their families.

(Corrections printed between the lines: 1. Hollywood, California, according 3. spends 4. seventeen and passes 5. society. Lee 6. streets. 7. Lee's 8. the officials 9. make, Lee 10. groups. Her)

1. f 2. a 3. c 4. a 5. b
6. e 7. e 8. d 9. f 10. b

Combined Editing Test 8

See if you can locate the ten sentence-skills mistakes in the following passage. The mistakes are listed below. As you find each mistake, write the number of the word group containing it in the space provided. Then, in the space between the lines, correct each mistake.

1 fragment 9
1 run-on 6
1 irregular verb mistake 7
1 mistake in subject-verb agreement 6
1 apostrophe mistake 4
1 missing comma after introductory words 8
2 missing commas in a series 10 10
2 missing commas around an interrupter 1 1

America, an race, starts
1 The Race Across America an annual bicycle race starts in Huntington Beach, California, and ends 3,107 miles later in Atlantic City, New Jersey. 2 One man always trains for this race by pedaling a stationary bike five hours at a time in a totally dark basement.
cyclists
3 Once the race begins, there are no time-outs. 4 The cyclists' go for days without sleeping.
test,
5 Eventually, they grab sixty- or ninety-minute catnaps every day or so. 6 But it is a time test,
and knows
each of the bikers know that every minute of sleep gives someone else the chance to get
rode
ahead. 7 In one of these races, the leader rided for 54 hours and 940 miles without sleep.
bike, his hopped,
8 When he got off his bike his muscles were so cramped that the flesh on his thighs hopped.
as
9 As if Mexican jumping beans were under his skin. 10 The winner of a recent race crossed
eight days, nine hours, and forty-seven minutes.
the continent in eight days nine hours and forty-seven minutes.

■ Combined Editing Test 9

See if you can locate the ten sentence-skills mistakes in the following passage. The mistakes are listed below. As you find each mistake, write the number of the word group containing it in the space provided. Then, in the space between the lines, correct each mistake.

1 fragment __14__

2 run-ons __11__ __15__

1 dangling modifier __5__

2 mistakes in parallelism __6__ __10__

2 missing quotation marks __14__ __14__

1 missing comma around an interrupter __10__

1 homonym mistake __12__

[1]The world seems to be divided into two kinds of people: the patient and the impatient.
[2]People reveal which they are by their behavior in certain situations. [3]While waiting in
line, patient people do constructive activities, such as reading a paperback and taking notes
As they glare at the
on a memo pad. [4]Impatient people treat waiting in line as torture. [5]Glaring at the helpless
and sigh loudly
cashier, their fists are clenched. [6]They tap their feet and sighing loudly. [7]The way people
drive is also revealing. [8]Patient people pass other cars only when necessary. [9]While waiting
people, on
at stoplights, they hum along with the radio and relax. [10]Impatient people on the other
and race their engines
hand, pass other cars at every opportunity and are racing their engines while waiting at
restaurants. The
stoplights. [11]These two types can also be spotted quickly in restaurants, the patient ones
Then,
wait politely for the hostess to seat them and for their waitress to arrive. [12]Than, while
waiting for their food, they converse. [13]Impatient people, however, are outraged if they
They mumble
aren't seated immediately. [14]And mumble such remarks as "I'm never coming here again"
and "If crowded . . . ."
and If I had known it would be this crowded . . . . [15]They eat quickly and want the check
immediately. A good
immediately, a good meal for them is a fast one.

Combined Editing Test 10

See if you can locate the ten sentence-skills mistakes in the following passage. The mistakes are listed below. As you find each mistake, write the number of the word group containing it in the space provided. Then, in the space between the lines, correct each mistake.

1 fragment 3

1 run-on 11

1 dropped verb ending 1

1 irregular verb mistake 10

1 dangling modifier 10

1 missing capital letter 5

1 apostrophe mistake 12

2 missing quotation marks 9

9

1 missing comma between complete thoughts 5

[1]I have just register for my first college math class. [2]The prospect of attending that class must have stirred up my old fears of math. [3]Because I had a nightmare the other night. [4]I was in a math class where the instructor was explaining a complicated theorem. [5]For all I understood, he could have been speaking greek but the other students hung on his every word. [6]Then he asked for volunteers to put their homework on the board. [7]The other students demonstrated their desire for that privilege by waving their hands wildly. [8]I slithered down in my seat, hoping the instructor would forget I was even there. [9]He called on three other students, and then I heard my name—You too, Mr. Oliver. [10]Feeling like a kindergartner, my weak legs somehow brang me to the board. [11]I began to doodle on it, the room suddenly became silent. [12]I turned around to discover every pair of eye's in that room staring at me as if I were insane. [13]Then the school bell rang, but no one budged—until I reached over to turn off my alarm.

■ Combined Editing Test 11

See if you can locate the ten sentence-skills mistakes in the following passage. The mistakes are listed below. As you find each mistake, write the number of the word group containing it in the space provided. Then, in the space between the lines, correct each mistake.

1 fragment ___6___

1 run-on ___12___

2 mistakes in subject-verb agreement ___1___ ___11___

1 apostrophe mistake ___5___

1 mistake in pronoun agreement ___1___

1 missing comma after introductory words ___8___

2 missing commas around an interrupter ___10___ ___10___

1 missing comma between complete thoughts ___13___

show
[1]The numerous ads for cat and dog products shows that Americans are concerned
of their pets.
about the well-being of its pets. [2]The relationship between people and animals, however, is
of as much value to humans as it is to animals. [3]Our pets show us they have feelings and
help create in us a respect for all living creatures. [4]Pets are also important as companions.
people's lives,
[5]According to one study, they can be especially helpful at special times in peoples lives.
including
[6]Including during childhood and periods of depression and illness. [7]Pets can also revitalize
homes, depressed
people. [8]When they are brought into nursing homes depressed and bored elderly patients
demonstrated,
gain a new optimism. [9]Pets can even reduce anxiety. [10]One study demonstrated for
for example,
example that gazing at a fish tank can reduce fear among patients about to undergo medical
is
or dental surgery. [11]Yet another of the benefits of animals are that they provide important
special services for humans. [12]Seeing-eye dogs offer mobility—and companionship—to
people, and trained
many blind people, trained monkeys do chores for the paralyzed. [13]Dogs and horses are
work, and
used in police work and cats are valued for their ability to limit the mouse population.
[14]Clearly, animals do as much for people as people do for them.

Combined Editing Test 12

See if you can locate the ten sentence-skills mistakes in the following passage. The mistakes are listed below. As you find each mistake, write the number of the word group containing it in the space provided. Then, in the space between the lines, correct each mistake.

2 fragments __5__ __10__

2 run-ons __3__ __8__

1 irregular verb mistake __10__

2 mistakes in subject-verb agreement __3__ __6__

1 missing apostrophe __12__

1 missing comma after introductory words __2__

1 missing comma around an interrupter __4__

[1]More young people are living with their parents than ever before. [2]According to the
Bureau, about
United States Census Bureau about 50 percent of people aged eighteen to twenty-four live
appear situation.
either at home or in college dorms. [3]There appears to be several reasons for this situation,
In however,
in the past, children often left home when they got married. [4]Today, however people tend
age than
to get married at an older age. [5]Than they once did. [6]Also, the high divorce rate among
has
Americans have brought many of them back home to their parents. [7]In addition, the high
cost of college keeps many students from moving into their own apartments. [8]However,
home,
even entering the job market does not guarantee that young people will finally leave home,
for many
many simply do not earn incomes that allow them to support themselves. [9]Children from
longer, waiting
well-off families are even more likely to stay home longer. [10]Waiting to be able to support
grew
themselves in the lifestyle they growed up with. [11]Of course, most eventually do leave
Bureau's
home. [12]The Census Bureaus statistics show that only 9 percent of men and 5 percent of
women aged thirty to thirty-four are still living with their parents.

Part Four

Readings for Writing

Introduction

Part Four provides a series of reading selections that should both capture your interest and enlarge your understanding. This part of the book begins by explaining the format of each selection, the four kinds of comprehension questions that accompany each reading, and four hints that can make for effective reading. After you read each selection, work through the reading comprehension, technique, and discussion questions that follow. They will help you understand, appreciate, and think about the selection. Then write a paragraph or essay on one of the three writing assignments provided.

As you work on a paper, refer as needed to the guidelines for effective writing in Part One and the rules of grammar, punctuation, and usage in Part Two. Doing so will help make these basic rules an everyday part of your writing.

Introduction to the Readings

This part of the book will help you become a better reader as well as a stronger writer. Reading and writing are closely connected skills—so practicing one skill helps develop the other. Included here are ten high-interest reading selections that provide inspiration for a wide range of paragraph and essay writing assignments.

The Format of Each Selection

To help you read the selections effectively—and write about them effectively—the following features are included.

Preview

A short preview introduces you to each reading selection and to its author. These previews will help you start thinking about a selection even before you start to read it.

"Words to Watch"

For each selection, there is a list of difficult words in the selection, with their paragraph numbers and their meanings as they are used in the reading. You may find it helpful to read through "Words to Watch" to remind yourself of meanings or to learn new ones. Within the reading itself, each listed word is marked with a small color bullet (•). When you're reading, if you are not sure of the definition of a word marked with this bullet, go back and look it up in "Words to Watch."

Reading Comprehension Questions

Following each selection, a series of questions gives you practice in four reading skills widely recognized as important to comprehension. These skills have to do with (1) vocabulary, (2) main and central ideas, (3) key details, and (4) inferences.

1 Understanding Vocabulary in Context The *context* of a word is the words that surround it. We learn many words by guessing their meanings from their context. For example, look at the sentence below. Can you figure out the meaning of the italicized word? After reading the sentence, try to answer the multiple-choice item.

> Karen was *euphoric* when the college that was her first choice accepted her.
>
> The word *euphoric* in the above sentence means
> a. puzzled.
> b. angry.
> c. overjoyed.
> d. sad.

You can figure out the meaning of *euphoric* on the basis of its context. Since Karen was accepted by the college that was her first choice, we can assume that she was overjoyed (*c*) rather than puzzled, angry, or sad. Understanding vocabulary in context is a very useful skill to develop, since we often meet new words in our reading. If we pay attention to their context, we may not need a dictionary to figure out what they mean.

2 Determining Main Ideas and the Central Idea As you learned in Part One of this book, a paragraph is about a point, or main idea, which is often expressed in a topic sentence; and in an essay, there is an overall main idea, often called the central idea. While the reading selections here are longer than the essays you write for your classes, they follow this same pattern. Sometimes the author of a selection states the central idea directly in one or more sentences; sometimes the reader must figure it out. In either case, to know what an author is really saying, readers must determine the central idea and the main ideas that support it.

3 Recognizing Key Supporting Details Supporting details are reasons, examples, and other kinds of information that help explain or clarify main ideas and the central idea. Recognizing key supporting details is an important part of understanding an author's message.

4 Making Inferences Often, an author does not state a point directly. Instead, he or she may only suggest the point, and the reader must *infer* it—in other words, figure it out. We make inferences every day, basing them on our understanding and experience. For example, suppose you take your seat in a lecture class in which the instructor always reads from notes in a boring tone of voice. A fellow student comments, "Well, this should be another thrilling lecture." You readily infer—you conclude from the circumstances—that your classmate is not saying what he or she means. The meaning is really the opposite of what was said.

Here is another example of inference. Consider the sentence below. What can you infer from it? Circle the letter of the most logical inference.

> Two elderly men silently played chess on a park bench, ignoring both the hot July sun and a fortyish woman who held a red umbrella over her head while watching their game.
>
> The sentence suggests that
>
> a. the men disliked the woman.
>
> b. the woman was related to one of the men.
>
> c. it was raining heavily.
>
> d. the woman wanted to protect herself from the sun.

If the men were concentrating on their game, they would be likely to ignore their surroundings, including the woman, so nothing in the sentence suggests that they disliked her, and *a* is therefore not a logical inference. Also, nothing in the sentence suggests that the men knew the woman, so *b* is not a logical inference either. And *c* is also incorrect, since the sentence mentions only the sun: if it were sunny and raining at the same time, the sentence would surely note such an unusual situation. That leaves only *d* as the correct inference—that the woman was using the umbrella to protect herself from the "hot July sun."

Making inferences like these is often necessary for a full understanding of an author's point.

Technique Questions

Questions about *technique* point to methods writers have used to present their material effectively. In particular, technique questions make you aware of directly stated central ideas, methods of organization, transition words, and vivid details that help writers make their ideas come alive for the reader. Focusing on such techniques will help you use them in your own writing.

Discussion Questions

The discussion questions help you think in detail about ideas raised by the selection and make connections between the selection and your own life. They will help you look closely at what you value, whom you respect, and how you react to people and situations.

Writing Assignments

The writing assignments following each selection are based specifically on that selection. Many assignments provide guidelines on how to proceed, including suggestions about prewriting, possible topic sentences and thesis statements, and methods of development.

Hints for Effective Reading

Effective reading, like effective writing, does not happen all at once. Rather, it is a process. Often you begin with a general impression of what something means, and then, by rereading, you move to a deeper level of understanding of the material.

Here are some hints for becoming a better reader.

1 **Read in the right place.** Ideally, you should get settled in a quiet spot that encourages concentration. If you can focus your attention while lying on a bed or curled up in a chair, that's fine. But if you find that being very comfortable leads to daydreaming or dozing off rather than reading, then avoid getting too relaxed. You might find that sitting in an upright chair promotes concentration and keeps your mind alert.

2 **Preview the selection.** Begin by reading the overview that precedes the selection. Then think for a minute about the title. A good title often hints at a selection's central idea, giving you insight into the piece even before you read it. For example, you can deduce from the title of Donna Barron's essay, "American Family Life: The Changing Picture," that Barron thinks family life has changed. You can also guess that she is likely to suggest why.

3 **Read the selection right through for pleasure.** Allow yourself to be drawn into the world that the author has created. Don't slow down or turn back. Instead, just read to understand as much as you can the first time through. After this reading, sit back for a moment and think about what you enjoyed in the piece.

4 **Deepen your sense of the selection.** Go back and reread it, or at least reread the passages that may not have been clear the first time through. Look up any words that you cannot figure out from context, and write their meanings in the margin. Now ask yourself the following questions:

- What is the central idea of the piece?
- What are the main supporting points for the central idea?
- How does the author explain and illustrate these main supporting points?

Reread carefully the parts of the selection that seem most relevant to answering these questions. By asking yourself the questions and by rereading, you will gradually deepen your understanding of the material.

The Importance of Regular Reading

Chances are that you are not as good a reader as you should be to do well in college. If so, it's not surprising. You live in a culture where people watch an average of *over seven hours of television every day!* All that passive viewing does not allow much time for reading. Reading is a skill that must be actively practiced. The simple fact is that people who do not read very often are not likely to be strong readers.

Another reason for not reading much is that you may have a lot of responsibilities. You may be going to school and working at the same time, and you may have many family duties as well. Given a hectic schedule, you're not going to have much opportunity to read. When you have free time, you may be exhausted and find it easier to turn on the TV than to open a book.

A third reason for not reading is that our public school system may have soured you on it. One government study after another has said that our schools have not done a good job of turning people on to the rewards of reading. If you had to read a lot of uninteresting and irrelevant material in grade school and high school, you may have decided (mistakenly) that reading in general is not for you.

These reasons may help explain why you are not in the habit of regular reading. For people who are unpracticed readers, there is one overall key to becoming a better reader. That key, simple as it may sound, is to do a great deal of reading. The truth of the matter is that *reading is like any other skill. The more you practice, the better you get.*

Regular reading is a habit with many rewards. Research has shown that frequent reading improves vocabulary, spelling, reading speed, and comprehension, as well as grammar and writing style. All of these language and thinking skills develop in an almost painless way for the person who becomes a habitual reader.

The question to ask, then, is "What steps can I take to become a regular reader?" The first step is to develop the right attitude. Recognize that a person who can read well has more potential and more power than a person who cannot. Reading is a source of extraordinary power. Consider the experience of Ben Carson as told on pages 555–561 of this book. After he started reading two books a week, at his mother's insistence, his entire world changed. He moved from the bottom of his class to the head of his class, and he went on to become a world-famous surgeon. And Grant Berry, on pages 544–548, describes how a commitment to reading was the key to his hopes for the future. Increasingly in today's world, jobs involve processing information. More than ever, words are the tools of our trades. The better your command of words, the more success you are likely to have. And nothing else will give you a command of words like regular reading.

A second step toward becoming a regular reader is to subscribe to a daily newspaper and, every day, read the sections that interest you. Remember that it is not what you read that matters—for example, you should not feel obliged to read the editorial section if opinion columns are not your interest. Instead, what matters is *the very fact that you read.* Your favorite section may be the comics, or fashion, or sports, or movie reviews, or the front page. Feel perfectly free to read whatever you decide you want to read.

A third step is to subscribe to one or more magazines. On many college bulletin boards, you'll see displays offering a wide variety of magazines at discount rates for college students. You may want to consider a weekly newsmagazine, such as *Newsweek* or *Time*, or a weekly general-interest magazine such as *People*. You will also be able to choose from a wide variety of monthly magazines, some of which will suit your interests. You may also want to look over the magazine section at any newsstand or bookstore. Most magazines contain postage-paid subscriber cards inside that you can send in to start a subscription. Finally, you may want to visit the magazine section of your library on a regular basis to just sit and read for an hour or so.

A fourth step to regular reading is to create a half hour of reading in your daily schedule. That time might be during your lunch hour, or late afternoon before dinner, or the half hour or so before you turn off your light at night. Find a time that is possible for you and make reading then a habit. The result will be both recreation and personal growth.

A fifth step is to read aloud to your children, which will benefit both them and you. Alternatively, have a family reading time when you and your children take turns reading. There are many books on the market that can be enjoyed by both parents and children. One outstanding choice is *Charlotte's Web,* by E. B. White—a classic story available in any bookstore or library. The children's librarian at your local library may be a good source for books. There are also many choices in the children's section at almost any paperback bookstore. An excellent mail-order source of books for children is the Chinaberry Book Service, 2780 Via Orange Way, Suite B, Spring Valley, California 91978. In its catalog, recommended books are grouped in five levels, from titles suitable for the very young to titles for young adults. Many of the books are pictured, and each book is helpfully described. To get a catalog, you can call a toll-free number: 1-800-776-2242.

The most important step on the road to becoming a regular reader is to read books on your own. Reading is most valuable and most enjoyable when you get drawn into the special world created by a book. You can travel in that world for hours or days, unmindful for a while of everyday concerns. In that timeless zone you will come to experience the joy of reading. You will also add depth to your life and make more sense out of the world. Too many people are addicted to smoking or drugs or television; you should try, instead, to get hooked on books.

The books to read are simply any books that interest you. They might be comic books, science fiction, adventure stories, romances, suspense or detective stories, horror novels, autobiographies, or any other type of book. To select your books, browse in a paperback bookstore, a library, a reading center, or any other place with a large number of books. Or read the short descriptions of the widely popular books in the list that follows. Find something you like and begin your reading journey. If you stick to it and become a regular reader, you may find that you have done nothing less than change your life.

A List of Interesting Books

Autobiographies and Other Nonfiction

I Know Why the Caged Bird Sings, Maya Angelou

The author writes with love, humor, and honesty about her childhood and what it is like to grow up black and female.

Alicia: My Story, Alicia Appleman-Jurman

Alicia was a Jewish girl living with her family in Poland when the Germans invaded in 1941. Her utterly compelling and heartbreaking story shows some of the best and worst of which human beings are capable.

Growing Up, Russell Baker

Russell Baker's mother, a giant presence in his life, insisted that he make something of himself. In his autobiography, the prizewinning journalist shows that he did with an engrossing account of his own family and growing up.

In Cold Blood, Truman Capote

This book, a frightening true story about the murder of a family, is also an examination of what made their killers tick. Many books today tell gripping stories of real-life crimes. *In Cold Blood* was the first book of this type and may still be the best.

Gifted Hands, Ben Carson

This is a the inspiring story of an inner-city kid with poor grades and little motivation who turned his life around. Dr. Carson is now a world-famous neurosurgeon at one of the best hospitals in the world; his book tells how he got there. In *Think Big* and *The Big Picture,* two related books, Dr. Carson tells more of his story and presents the philosophy that helped him make the most of his life.

Move On, Linda Ellerbee

A well-known television journalist writes about the ups and downs of her life, including her stay at the Betty Ford Center for treatment of her alcoholism.

The Diary of a Young Girl, Anne Frank

To escape the Nazi death camps, Anne Frank and her family hid for years in an attic. Her journal tells a story of love, fear, and courage.

Man's Search for Meaning, Viktor Frankl

How do people go on when they have been stripped of everything, including human dignity? In this short but moving book, the author describes his time in a concentration camp and what he learned there about survival.

Angela's Ashes, Frank McCourt

This widely popular autobiography tells the story of an Irish boy whose father was a drunkard and whose mother tried desperately to hold her family together. The poverty described is heartbreaking, and yet the book is wonderfully moving and often funny. You'll shake your head in disbelief at all the hardships, but at other times you'll laugh out loud at the comic touches.

The Story of My Life, Helen Keller

How Miss Keller, a blind and deaf girl who lived in isolation and frustration, discovered a path to learning and knowledge.

The Autobiography of Malcolm X, Malcolm X and Alex Haley

Malcolm X, the controversial black leader who was assassinated by one of his followers, writes about the experiences that drove him to a leadership role in the Black Muslims.

Makes Me Wanna Holler, Nathan McCall

A dramatic first-person account of how a bright young black man went terribly wrong and was lured into a life of crime. McCall, now a reporter for the *Washington Post,* eventually found a basis for self-respect different from that of his peers, who are murdered, commit suicide, become drug zombies, or wind up in prison.

A Hole in the World, Richard Rhodes

Little more than a year old when his mother killed herself, Rhodes has ever since been conscious of "a hole in the world" where his mother's love should have been. In this true and terrifying account of his boyhood, he describes how he managed to survive.

Down These Mean Streets, Piri Thomas

Life in a Puerto Rican ghetto is shown vividly and with understanding by one who experienced it.

Fiction

Watership Down, Richard Adams

A wonderfully entertaining adventure story about rabbits who act a great deal like people. The plot may sound unlikely, but it will keep you on the edge of your seat.

Patriot Games, Tom Clancy

In a story of thrills and suspense, a government agent helps stop an act of terrorism. The terrorists then plot revenge on the agent and his family.

The Cradle Will Fall, Mary Higgins Clark

A country prosecutor uncovers evidence that a famous doctor is killing women, not realizing that she herself is becoming his next target. One typical comment by a reviewer about Clark's books is that they are "a ticket to ride the roller coaster . . . once on the track, we're there until the ride is over."

Note: If you like novels with terror and suspense, many of Mary Higgins Clark's books are good choices.

And Justice for One, John Clarkson

In this adventure-thriller, a former Secret Service agent seeks revenge after his brother is almost killed and his girlfriend is kidnapped. Because of corruption in the police force, the agent must take the law into his own hands.

Deliverance, James Dickey

Several men go rafting down a wild river in Georgia and encounter beauty, violence, and self-knowledge.

Eye of the Needle, Ken Follett

A thriller about a Nazi spy—"The Needle"—and a woman who is the only person who can stop him.

Lord of the Flies, William Golding

Could a group of children, none older than twelve, survive by themselves on a tropical island in the midst of World War Three? In this modern classic, Golding shows us that the real danger is not the war outside but "the beast" within each of us.

Snow Falling on Cedars, David Guterson

This is a unique murder mystery. The story is set in the 1950s in an island community where a fisherman is found dead on his boat and another fisherman is quickly blamed for the death. The accused man is so proud that he refuses to defend himself for a crime he says he did not commit. Like all great stories, this one is about more than itself. It becomes a celebration of the mystery of the human heart.

The Silence of the Lambs, Thomas Harris

A psychotic killer is on the loose, and to find him, the FBI must rely on clues provided by an evil genius. Like some other works on this list, *The Silence of the Lambs* was made into a movie that is not as good as the book.

Flowers for Algernon, Daniel Keyes

A scientific experiment turns a retarded man into a genius. But the results are a mixture of joy and heartbreak.

The Shining, Stephen King

A haunted hotel, a little boy with extrasensory perception, and an insane father—they're all together in a horror tale of isolation and insanity. One review says, "Be prepared to be scared out of your mind. . . . Don't read this book when you are home alone. If you dare—once you get past a certain point, there's no stopping."

Note: If you like novels with terror and suspense, many of Stephen King's books are good choices.

Watchers, Dean Koontz

An incredibly suspenseful story about two dogs that undergo lab experiments. One dog becomes a monster programmed to kill, and it seeks to track down the couple who know its secret.

Note: If you like novels with a great deal of action and suspense, many of Dean Koontz's books are good choices.

To Kill a Mockingbird, Harper Lee

A controversial trial, involving a black man accused of raping a white woman, is the centerpiece of this story about adolescence, bigotry, and justice. One review described the book as "a novel of great sweetness, humor, compassion, and mystery carefully sustained."

The Natural, Bernard Malamud

An aging player makes a comeback that stuns the baseball world.

Waiting to Exhale, Terry McMillan

Four thirty-something black women all hope that Mr. Right will appear, but this doesn't stop them from living their lives. One reviewer wrote that McMillan "has such a wonderful ear for story and dialogue. She gives us four women with raw, honest emotions that breathe off the page."

Gone with the Wind, Margaret Mitchell

The characters and places in this book—Scarlett O'Hara, Rhett Butler, Tara—have become part of our culture because they are unforgettable.

A Day No Pigs Would Die, Robert Peck

A boy raises a pig that is intelligent and affectionate. Will the boy follow orders and send the animal off to be slaughtered? Read this short novel to find out.

Harry Potter and the Sorcerer's Stone, J. K. Rowling

The first in a series of award-winning stories that have captured the hearts of young and old alike, around the world. These funny, action-packed, touching books are about a likable boy who is mistreated by the relatives who take him in after his parents are killed. Then Harry discovers that he is a wizard, and his extraordinary adventures begin.

The Catcher in the Rye, J. D. Salinger

The frustrations and turmoil of being an adolescent have never been captured so well as in this book. The main character, Holden Caulfield, is honest, funny, affectionate, obnoxious, and tormented at the same time.

The Lord of the Rings, J. R. R. Tolkien

Enter an amazing world of little creatures known as Hobbits; you, like thousands of other readers, may never want to leave.

Charlotte's Web, E. B. White

This best-loved story, for children and adults, is about a little pig named Wilbur and his best friend, a spider named Charlotte. Wilbur is being fattened in order to be killed for a holiday meal; Charlotte must come up with a plan to save him.

A Change of Attitude

Grant Berry

Preview

Every college has them: students the same age as some of their professors, students rushing into class after a full day at work, students carrying photographs—not of their boyfriends or girlfriends, but of the children they too seldom see. In many cases, these students are as surprised as anyone to find themselves in college, after an earlier educational experience that was anything but positive. In this essay, one such student describes his development from a bored high-schooler to a committed college student.

Words to Watch

decades (3): periods of ten years

striven (3): tried

suavely (4): in a sophisticated manner

immaculately (4): perfectly clean

tedious (6): boring

trudging (6): moving with great effort

nil (6): zero

smugly (8): in a way that demonstrates self-satisfaction

deprivation (16): state of being without possessions

battering (22): pounding

For me to be in college is highly improbable. That I am doing well in school teeters on the illogical. Considering my upbringing, past educational performance, and current responsibilities, one might say, "This guy hasn't got a chance." If I were a racehorse and college were the track, there would be few who would pick me to win, place, or show. 1

When I told my dad that I was going back to school, the only encouragement he offered was this: "Send me anywhere, but don't send me back to school." For my father, school was the worst kind of prison, so I was raised believing that school at its best was a drag. My dad thought that the purpose of graduating from high school was so you never had to go back to school again, and I adopted this working stiff's philosophy. 2

I followed my dad's example the way a man who double-crosses the mob follows a cement block to the bottom of the river. My dad has been a union 3 factory worker for more than two decades,• and he has never striven• to be anything more than average. Nonetheless, he is a good man; I love him very much, and I respect him for being a responsible husband and father. He seldom, if ever, missed a day of work; he never left his paycheck at a bar, and none of our household appliances were ever carted off by a repo-man. He took his family to church each week, didn't light up or lift a glass, and has celebrated his silver anniversary with his first, and only, wife. However, if he ever had a dream of being more than just a shop rat, I never knew about it.

On the other hand, my dreams were big, but my thoughts were small. I was not raised to be a go-getter. I knew I wanted to go to work each day in a suit and tie; unfortunately, I could not define what it was I wanted to do. I told a few people that I wanted to have a job where I could dress suavely• and carry a briefcase, and they laughed in my face. They said, "You'll never be anything," and I believed them. Even now I am envious of an immaculately• dressed businessman. It is not the angry type of jealousy; it is the "wish it were me" variety. 4 5

Grant Berry looks over a book before class.

Since I knew I was not going to further my education, and I didn't know what I wanted to do except wear a suit, high school was a disaster. I do not know how my teachers can respect themselves after passing me. In every high school there are cliques and classifications. I worked just hard enough to stay above the bottom, but I did not want to work hard enough to get into the clique with the honor roll students.

Also, I had always had a problem with reading. When I was a kid, reading for me was slow and tedious.• My eyes walked over words like a snail trudging• through mud. I couldn't focus on what I was reading, and this allowed my young, active mind to wander far from my reading material. I would often finish a page and not remember a single word I had just read. Not only was reading a slow process, but my comprehension was nil.• I wasn't dumb; in fact, I was at a high English level. However, reading rated next to scraping dog poop from the tread of my sneakers. I didn't yet know that reading could be like playing the guitar: the more you do it, the better you get. As far as reading was concerned, I thought I was stuck in the same slow waltz forever. 6

In junior high and high school, I read only when it was absolutely essential. For example, I had to find out who Spiderman was going to web, or how many chidren Superman was going to save each month. I also had to find out which girls were popular on the bathroom walls. I'm ashamed to say that my mother even did a book report for me, first reading the book. In high school, when I would choose my own classes, I took art and electronics rather than English. 7

Even though I was raised in a good Christian home, the only things I cared about were partying and girls. I spent all of my minimum-wage paycheck on 8 beer, cigarettes, and young ladies. As a senior, I dated a girl who was twenty. She had no restrictions, and I tried to keep pace with her lifestyle. I would stay out drinking until 3:00 A.M. on school nights. The next morning I would sleep through class or just not show up. It became such a problem that the school sent letters to my parents telling them that I would not be joining my classmates for commencement if I didn't show up for class once in a while. This put the fear of the establishment in me because I knew the importance of graduating from high school. Nonetheless, I never once remember doing homework my senior year. Yet in June, they shook my hand and forked over a diploma as I smugly• marched across the stage in a blue gown and square hat.

Since I felt I didn't deserve the piece of paper with the principal's and superintendent's signatures on it, I passed up not only a graduation party but also a class ring and a yearbook. If it were not for my diploma and senior pictures, there would not be enough evidence to convince a jury that I am guilty of attending high school at all. I did, however, celebrate with my friends on graduation night. I got loaded, misjudged a turn, flattened a stop sign, and got my car stuck. When I pushed my car with my girlfriend behind the steering wheel, mud from the spinning tire sprayed all over my nice clothes. It was quite a night, and looking back, it was quite a fitting closure for the end of high school. 9

"For my father, school was the worst kind of prison, so I was raised believing that school at its best was a drag."

After graduation I followed my father's example and went to work, plunging into the lukewarm waters of mediocrity. All I was doing on my job bagging groceries was trading dollars for hours. I worked just hard enough to keep from getting fired, and I was paid just enough to keep from quitting. 10

Considering the way my father felt about school, college was a subject that seldom came up at our dinner table. I was not discouraged, nor was I encouraged, to go to college; it was my choice. My first attempt at college came when I was nineteen. I had always dreamed of being a disk jockey, so I enrolled in a broadcasting class. However, my experience in college was as forgettable as high school. My habit of not doing homework carried over, and the class was such a yawner that I often forgot to attend. Miraculously, I managed to pull a C, but my dream was weak and quickly died. I did not enroll for the next term. My girlfriend, the one who kept me out late in high school, became pregnant with my child. We were married two days after my final class, and this gave me another excuse not to continue my education. 11

My first job, and every job since, has involved working with my hands and not my head. I enjoyed my work, but after the money ran out, the month would keep going. One evening my wife's cousin called and said he had a way that we could increase our income. I asked, "How soon can you get here?" He walked us through a six-step plan of selling and recruiting, and when he was finished, my wife and I wanted in. Fumbling around inside his large briefcase, he told us we needed the proper attitude first. Emerging with a small stack of books, he said, "Read these!" Then he flipped the books into my lap. I groaned at the thought of reading all those volumes. If this guy wanted me 12 to develop a good attitude, giving me books was having the opposite effect. However, I wanted to make some extra cash, so I assured him I would try.

I started reading the books each night. They were self-help, positive-mental-attitude manuals. Reading those books opened up my world; they put me in touch with a me I didn't know existed. The books told me I had potential, possibly even greatness. I took their message in like an old Chevrolet being pumped full of premium no-lead gasoline. It felt so good I started reading more. Not only did I read at night; I read in the morning before I went to work. I read during my breaks and lunch hour, when waiting for signal lights to turn green, in between bites of food at supper, and while sitting on the toilet. One of the books I read said that there is no limit to the amount of information our brains will hold, so I began filling mine up. 13

The process of reading was slow at first, just as it had been when I was a kid, but it was just like playing the guitar. If I struck an unclear chord, I would try it again, and if I read something unclear, I would simply read it again. Something happened: the more I read, the better I got at it. It wasn't long before I could focus in and understand without reading things twice. I began feeling good about my reading skills, and because of the types of books I was reading, I started feeling good about myself at the same time. 14

The income from my day job blossomed while the selling and recruiting business grew demanding, disappointing, and fruitless. We stopped working that soil and our business died, but I was hooked on reading. I now laid aside the self-help books and began reading whatever I wanted. I got my first library card, and I subscribed to *Sports Illustrated*. I found a book of short stories, and I dived into poetry, as well as countless newspaper articles, cereal boxes, and oatmeal packages. Reading, which had been a problem for me, became a pleasure and then a passion. 15

Reading moved me. As I continued to read in a crowded lunchroom, sometimes I stumbled across an especially moving short story or magazine article. For example, a young Romanian girl was saved from starvation and deprivation• by an adoptive couple from the United States. I quickly jerked the reading material to my face to conceal tears when she entered her new home filled with toys and stuffed animals. 16

Not only did reading tug at my emotions; it inspired me to make a move. All those positive-mental-attitude books kept jabbing me in the ribs, so last fall, at age twenty-seven, I decided to give college another try. Now I am back in school, but it's a different road I travel from when I was a teenager. Mom and Dad paid the amount in the right-hand column of my tuition bill then, but now I am determined to pay for college myself, even though I must miss the sound of the pizza delivery man's tires on my blacktop driveway. I hope to work my way out of my blue collar by paying for school with blue-collar cash. 17

As a meat-cutter, I usually spend between 45 and 50 hours a week with a knife in my hand. Some weeks I have spent 72 hours beneath a butcher's cap. In one two-week period I spent 141 hours with a bloody apron on, but in that time I managed to show up for all of my classes and get all of my homework done (except being short a few bibliography cards for my research paper). 18

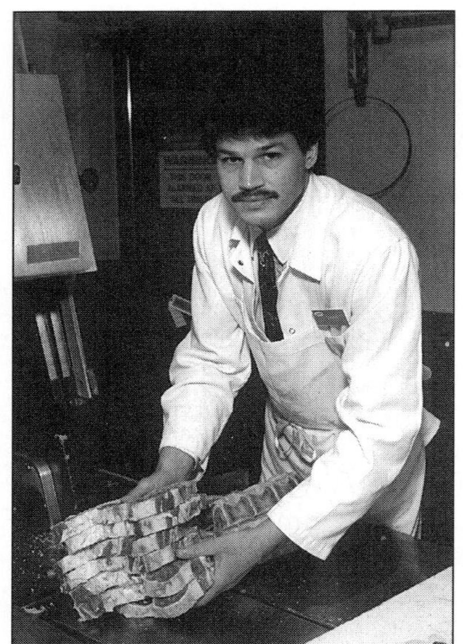

Grant continues to work as a butcher full-time.

Working full time and raising a family leave me little free time. If I am not in class, I'm studying linking verbs or trying to figure out the difference between compound and complex sentences. 19

There are other obstacles and challenges staring me in the face. The tallest hurdle is a lack of time for meeting all my obligations. For instance, my wife works two nights a week, leaving me to care for my two daughters. A twelve-hour day at work can lead to an evening coma at home, so when Mom's punching little square buttons on a cash register, I hardly have the energy to pour cornflakes for my kids, let alone outline a research paper. 20

Going to college means making choices, some of which bring criticism. My neighbors, for example, hate my sickly, brown lawn sandwiched between their lush, green, spotless plots of earth, which would be the envy of any football field. Just walking to my mailbox can be an awful reminder of how pitiful my lawn looks when I receive an unforgiving scowl from one of the groundskeepers who live on either side of me. It is embarrassing to have such a colorless lawn, but it will have to wait because I want more out of life than a half-acre of green turf. Right now my time and money are tied up in college courses instead of fertilizer and weed killer. 21

But the toughest obstacle is having to take away time from those I love most. I am proud of the relationship I have with my wife and kids, so it tears my guts out when I have to look into my daughter's sad face and explain that I can't go to the Christmas program she's been practicing for weeks because I have a final exam. It's not easy to tell my three-year-old that I can't push her on the swings because I have a cause-and-effect paper to write, or tell my seven-year-old that I can't build a snowman because I have an argument essay to polish. As I tell my family that I can't go sledding with them, my wife lets out a big sigh, and my kids yell, "Puleeze, Daddy, can't you come with us?" At these times I wonder if my dream of a college education can withstand such an emotional battering,• or if it is even worth it. But I keep on keeping on because I must set a good example for the four little eyes that are keeping watch over their daddy's every move. I must succeed and pass on to them the right attitude toward school. This time when I graduate, because of the hurdles I've overcome, there will be a celebration—a proper one. 22

In the college computer lab, Grant works on a paper.

Reading Comprehension Questions

1. The word *clique* in "In every high school there are cliques and classifications. I worked just hard enough to stay above the bottom, but I did not want to work hard enough to get into the clique with the honor roll students" (paragraph 5), means
   a. grade.
   b. school.
   c. group.
   d. sports.
2. The word *scowl* in "Just walking to my mailbox can be an awful reminder of how pitiful my lawn looks when I receive an unforgiving scowl from one of the groundskeepers who live on either side of me" (paragraph 21) means
   a. sincere smile.
   b. favor.
   c. angry look.
   d. surprise.
3. Which sentence best expresses the central idea of the selection?
   a. The author was never encouraged to attend college or to challenge himself mentally on the job.
   b. After years of not caring about education, Berry was led by some self-help books to love reading, gain self-esteem, and attend college.
   c. The author's wife and children often do not understand why he is unable to take part in many family activities.
   d. The author was given a high school diploma despite the fact that he did little work and rarely attended class.
4. Which sentence best expresses the main idea of paragraph 13?
   a. Influenced by self-help books, the author developed a hunger for reading.
   b. People who really care about improving themselves will find the time to do it, such as during the early morning, at breaks, and during the lunch hour.
   c. Self-help books send the message that everyone is full of potential and even greatness.
   d. There is no limit to the amount of information the brain can hold.
5. Which sentence best expresses the main idea of paragraph 22?
   a. The author's decision to attend college is hurting his long-term relationship with his wife and daughters.
   b. The author has two children, one age three and the other age seven.
   c. The author enjoys family activities such as attending his children's plays and building snowmen.
   d. Although he misses spending time with his family, the author feels that graduating from college will make him a better role model for his children.

6. The author's reading skills
   a. were strong even when he was a child.
   (b.) improved as he read more.
   c. were strengthened considerably in high school.
   d. were sharpened by jobs he held after high school graduation.
7. The author's father
   a. was rarely home while the author was growing up.
   b. often missed work and stayed out late at bars.
   c. was a college graduate.
   (d.) disliked school.
8. In stating that his graduation night "was quite a fitting closure for the end of high school," Berry implies that
   a. he was glad high school was finally over.
   b. car troubles were a common problem for him throughout high school.
   (c.) his behavior had ruined that night just as it had ruined his high school education.
   d. despite the problems, the evening gave him good memories, just as high school had given him good memories.
9. We can infer from paragraph 21 that the author
   a. does not tend his lawn because he enjoys annoying his neighbors.
   b. receives a lot of mail.
   (c.) is willing to make sacrifices for his college education.
   d. has neighbors who care little about the appearance of their property.
10. We can infer that the author believes children
    a. should be passed to the next grade when they reach a certain age, regardless of their test scores.
    b. should not require a great deal of time from their parents.
    c. fall into two categories: "born readers" and those who can never learn to read very well.
    (d.) benefit from having role models who care about education.

■ Technique Questions

1. In explaining that he followed his father's example, the author compares himself to "a man who double-crosses the mob [and follows] a cement block to the bottom of the river." In this comparison, Berry strikingly makes the point that his own actions led him to an undesirable situation. Find two other places where the author uses a richly revealing comparison. Write those images below, and explain what Berry means by each one.

Image: Answers will vary

Meaning:

Image:

Meaning:

2. In most of his essay, Berry uses time order, but in some places he uses listing order. For example, what does Berry list in paragraphs 20–22?
Obstacles Berry faces as a result of his decision to return to college

3. In closing his essay, Berry writes that at his college graduation, "there will be a celebration—a proper one." With what earlier event is he contrasting this graduation?
His high school graduation

Discussion Questions

1. The author looks back at this period of reading self-help books as one in which his attitude improved, eventually leading to his enrollment in college. Has a particular occurrence ever sharply changed your outlook on life? Was it something that you read, observed, or directly experienced? How did it happen? How did it change your point of view?
2. Berry writes that his father did not encourage him to go on to college. Nevertheless, he sees many positive things about his father. In what ways was his father a positive role model for him? In other words, is Berry's positive behavior as an adult partly a result of his father's influence? What do you see in your own adult behavior that you can attribute to your parents' influence?
3. Berry discusses some of the difficulties he faces as a result of being in college—struggling to find time to meet his obligations, giving up lawn care, spending less time with his family. What difficulties do you face as a result of fitting college into your life? What obligations must you struggle to fulfill? What activities remain undone?

Writing Assignments

1. Children are strongly influenced by the example of their parents (and other significant adults in their lives). For instance, the author of this essay followed his father's example of disliking school and getting a job that did not challenge him mentally.

Think about your growing-up years and about adults who influenced you, both positively and negatively. Then write a paragraph that describes one of these people and his or her influence on you. Supply plenty of vivid examples to help the reader understand how and why this person affected you.

The topic sentence of your paragraph should identify the person (either by name or by relationship to you) and briefly indicate the kind of influence he or she had on you. Here are some examples of topic sentences for this paper:

> My aunt's courage in difficult situations helped me to become a stronger person.
>
> My father's frequent trouble with the law made it necessary for me to grow up in a hurry.
>
> The pastor of our church helped me realize that I was a worthwhile, talented person.

2. Write a paragraph about one way that reading has been important in your life, either positively or negatively. To discover the approach you wish to take, think for a moment about the influence of reading throughout your life. When you were a child, was being read to at bedtime a highlight of your day? Did reading out loud in elementary school cause you embarrassment? Do you adore mysteries or true-crime books? Do you avoid reading whenever possible? Find an idea about the role of reading in your life that you can write about in the space of a paragraph. Your topic sentence will be a clear statement of that idea, such as:

> I first learned to read from watching *Sesame Street.*
>
> One key experience in second grade made me hate reading out loud in class.
>
> My parents' attitude toward reading rubbed off on me.
>
> Reading to my child at bedtime is an important time of day for both of us.
>
> Books have taught me some things I never would have learned from friends and family.
>
> There are several reasons why I am not a good reader.
>
> A wonderful self-help book has helped me build my self-esteem.

Develop your main idea with detailed explanations and descriptions. For example, if you decide to write about reading to your child at bedtime, you might describe the positions you and your child take (Is the child in bed? On the floor? On your lap?), one or two of the stories the child and you have loved, some of the child's reactions, and so on.

3. Berry's graduation-night celebration was a dramatic one and, he states, "a fitting closure for the end of high school." What was your high school graduation

celebration like? Did you participate in any of the planning and preparation for the events? Were finding a date and shopping for clothing for the prom fun or nerve-racking experiences? Was the event itself wonderful or disappointing? Write an essay telling the story of your graduation celebration from start to finish. Use many sharp descriptive details to help your readers envision events, decorations, clothing, cars, the weather, and so on. In addition, add meaning to your story by telling what you were thinking and feeling throughout the event.

You might try making a list as a way of collecting details for this paper. At first, don't worry about organizing your details. Just keep adding to your list, which might at one point look like this:

decorations committee

considered asking my cousin to go with me, if necessary

shopping for prom dress with Mom (and arguing)

afraid I'd be asked first by someone I didn't want to go with

talk of being up all night

pressed orchid corsage afterward

florist busy that week

working on centerpieces

feet hurt

Eventually, you will have enough information to begin thinking about the organization of your essay. Here's what the scratch outline for one such essay looks like:

<u>Central idea:</u> My high school prom was a mixture of fun and disappointment.

(1) Before the dance
Work on the decorations com. (theme: sky's the limit)
Anxiety over getting a date, finally relief
Worn out shopping for a dress
Last-minute preparations (getting flowers, having hair done, decorating ballroom)

(2) Night of the dance
Picture-taking at home
Squeezing gown into car, hem gets stuck in car door and grease rubs on it
Beautiful ballroom
Rotten meal
Great band (even teachers yelling requests)
After two dances had to take off heels
Date kept dancing with others
Danced with my brother, who came with my girlfriend

Early breakfast served at hotel

(3) After the dance
Total exhaustion for two days
Extensive phone analysis of dance with girlfriends
Never went out with that date again
Several years later, prom dress, wrapped in a garbage bag, went to Salvation Army

Perhaps you don't remember your graduation night celebration very well, or don't wish to. Feel free to write about another important social event instead, such as a high school reunion, a family reunion, or your own or someone else's wedding.

Do It Better!

Ben Carson, M.D., with Cecil Murphey

Preview

If you suspect that you are now as "smart" as you'll ever be, then read the following selection, taken from the book *Think Big*. It is about Dr. Ben Carson, who was sure he was "the dumbest kid in the class" in school. Carson tells how he turned his life around from what was a sure path to failure. Today he is a famous neurosurgeon at Johns Hopkins University Hospital in Baltimore, Maryland.

■ Words to Watch

inasmuch as (13): since
potential (18): capacity for development and progress
solely (20): alone
rebellious (46): resisting authority
indifferent (58): uninterested
startled (75): surprised
astonished (81): surprised

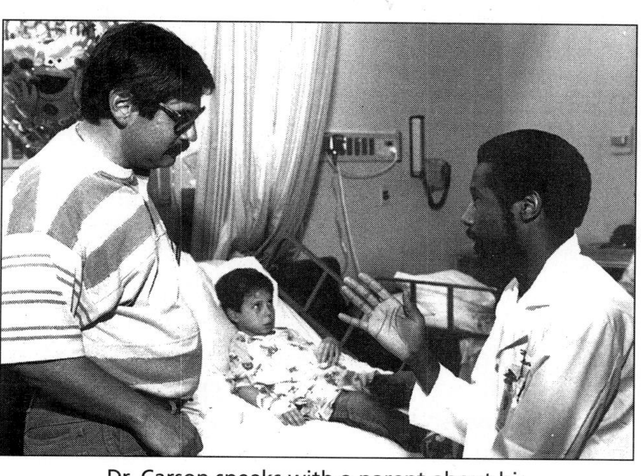

Dr. Carson speaks with a parent about his child's medical condition.

"Benjamin, is this your report card?" my mother asked as she picked up the folded white card from the table. 1

"Uh, yeah," I said, trying to sound casual. Too ashamed to hand it to her, I had dropped it on the table, hoping that she wouldn't notice until after I went to bed. 2

It was the first report card I had received from Higgins Elementary School since we had moved back from Boston to Detroit, only a few months earlier. 3

I had been in the fifth grade not even two weeks before everyone considered me the dumbest kid in the class and frequently made jokes about me. Before long I too began to feel as though I really was the most stupid kid in fifth grade. Despite Mother's frequently saying, "You're smart, Bennie. You can do anything you want to do," I did not believe her. 4

5 No one else in school thought I was smart, either.

6 Now, as Mother examined my report card, she asked, "What's this grade in reading?" (Her tone of voice told me that I was in trouble.) Although I was embarrassed, I did not think too much about it. Mother knew that I wasn't doing well in math, but she did not know I was doing so poorly in every subject.

7 While she slowly read my report card, reading everything one word at a time, I hurried into my room and started to get ready for bed. A few minutes later, Mother came into my bedroom.

8 "Benjamin," she said, "are these your grades?" She held the card in front of me as if I hadn't seen it before.

9 "Oh, yeah, but you know, it doesn't mean much."

10 "No, that's not true, Bennie. It means a lot."

11 "Just a report card."

12 "But it's more than that."

13 Knowing I was in for it now, I prepared to listen, yet I was not all that interested. I did not like school very much and there was no reason why I should. Inasmuch as• I was the dumbest kid in the class, what did I have to look forward to? The others laughed at me and made jokes about me every day.

14 "Education is the only way you're ever going to escape poverty," she said. "It's the only way you're ever going to get ahead in life and be successful. Do you understand that?"

15 "Yes, Mother," I mumbled.

16 "If you keep on getting these kinds of grades you're going to spend the rest of your life on skid row, or at best sweeping floors in a factory. That's not the kind of life that I want for you. That's not the kind of life that God wants for you."

17 I hung my head, genuinely ashamed. My mother had been raising me and my older brother, Curtis, by herself. Having only a third-grade education herself, she knew the value of what she did not have. Daily she drummed into Curtis and me that we had to do our best in school.

18 "You're just not living up to your potential•," she said. "I've got two mighty smart boys and I know they can do better."

19 I had done my best—at least I had when I first started at Higgins Elementary School. How could I do much when I did not understand anything going on in our class?

20 In Boston we had attended a parochial school, but I hadn't learned much because of a teacher who seemed more interested in talking to another female teacher than in teaching us. Possibly, this teacher was not solely• to blame—perhaps I wasn't emotionally able to learn much. My parents had separated just before we went to Boston, when I was eight years old. I loved both my mother and my father and went through considerable trauma over their separating. For months afterward, I kept thinking that my parents would get back together, that my daddy would come home again the way he used to, and that we could be the same old family again—but he never came back. Consequently, we moved to Boston and lived with Aunt Jean and Uncle

William Avery in a tenement building for two years until Mother had saved enough money to bring us back to Detroit.

Mother kept shaking the report card at me as she sat on the side of my bed. "You have to work harder. You have to use that good brain that God gave you, Bennie. Do you understand that?" 21

"Yes, Mother." Each time she paused, I would dutifully say those words. 22

"I work among rich people, people who are educated," she said. "I watch how they act, and I know they can do anything they want to do. And so can you." She put her arm on my shoulder. "Bennie, you can do anything they can do—only you can do it better!" 23

Mother had said those words before. Often. At the time, they did not mean much to me. Why should they? I really believed that I was the dumbest kid in fifth grade, but of course, I never told her that. 24

"I just don't know what to do about you boys," she said. "I'm going to talk to God about you and Curtis." She paused, stared into space, then said (more to herself than to me), "I need the Lord's guidance on what to do. You just can't bring in any more report cards like this." 25

As far as I was concerned, the report card matter was over. 26

The next day was like the previous ones—just another bad day in school, another day of being laughed at because I did not get a single problem right in arithmetic and couldn't get any words right on the spelling test. As soon as I came home from school, I changed into play clothes and ran outside. Most of the boys my age played softball, or the game I liked best, "Tip the Top." 27

We played Tip the Top by placing a bottle cap on one of the sidewalk cracks. Then taking a ball—any kind that bounced—we'd stand on a line and take turns throwing the ball at the bottle top, trying to flip it over. Whoever succeeded got two points. If anyone actually moved the cap more than a few inches, he won five points. Ten points came if he flipped it into the air and it landed on the other side. 28

When it grew dark or we got tired, Curtis and I would finally go inside and watch TV. The set stayed on until we went to bed. Because Mother worked long hours, she was never home until just before we went to bed. Sometimes I would awaken when I heard her unlocking the door. 29

Two evenings after the incident with the report card, Mother came home about an hour before our bedtime. Curtis and I were sprawled out, watching TV. She walked across the room, snapped off the set, and faced both of us. "Boys," she said, "you're wasting too much of your time in front of that television. You don't get an education from staring at television all the time." 30

Before either of us could make a protest, she told us that she had been praying for wisdom. "The Lord's told me what to do," she said. "So from now on, you will not watch television, except for two preselected programs each week." 31

"Just *two* programs?" I could hardly believe she would say such a terrible thing. "That's not—" 32

"And *only* after you've done your homework. Furthermore, you don't play outside after school, either, until you've done all your homework." 33

"Everybody else plays outside right after school," I said, unable to think 34
of anything except how bad it would be if I couldn't play with my friends. "I won't have any friends if I stay in the house all the time—"

"That may be," Mother said, "but everybody else is not going to be as 35
successful as you are—"

"But, Mother—" 36

"This is what we're going to do. I asked God for wisdom, and this is the 37
answer I got."

Dr. Carson and his wife, Candy, are photographed at home with their sons (from left to right) Murry, B.J., and Rhoeyce.

I tried to offer several other arguments, but Mother 38
was firm. I glanced at Curtis, expecting him to speak up, but he did not say anything. He lay on the floor, staring at his feet.

"Don't worry about everybody else. The whole 39
world is full of 'everybody else,' you know that? But only a few make a significant achievement."

The loss of TV and play time was bad enough. I got 40
up off the floor, feeling as if everything was against me. Mother wasn't going to let me play with my friends, and there would be no more television—almost none, anyway. She was stopping me from having any fun in life.

"And that isn't all," she said. "Come back, Bennie." 41

I turned around, wondering what else there 42
could be.

"In addition," she said, "to doing your homework, 43
you have to read two books from the library each week. Every single week."

"Two books? Two?" Even though I was in fifth 44
grade, I had never read a whole book in my life.

"Yes, two. When you finish reading them, you must 45
write me a book report just like you do at school. You're not living up to your potential, so I'm going to see that you do."

Usually Curtis, who was two years older, was the more rebellious•. But this 46
time he seemed to grasp the wisdom of what Mother said. He did not say one word.

She stared at Curtis. "You understand?" 47

He nodded. 48

"Bennie, is it clear?" 49

"Yes, Mother." I agreed to do what Mother told me—it wouldn't have 50
occurred to me not to obey—but I did not like it. Mother was being unfair and demanding more of us than other parents did.

The following day was Thursday. After school, Curtis and I walked to the 51
local branch of the library. I did not like it much, but then I had not spent that much time in any library.

We both wandered around a little in the children's section, not having any 52
idea about how to select books or which books we wanted to check out.

The librarian came over to us and asked if she could help. We explained 53
that both of us wanted to check out two books.

"What kind of books would you like to read?" the librarian asked. 54

"Animals," I said after thinking about it. "Something about animals." 55

"I'm sure we have several that you'd like." She led me over to a section 56
of books. She left me and guided Curtis to another section of the room. I flipped through the row of books until I found two that looked easy enough for me to read. One of them, *Chip, the Dam Builder*—about a beaver—was the first one I had ever checked out. As soon as I got home, I started to read it. It was the first book I ever read all the way through even though it took me two nights. Reluctantly I admitted afterward to Mother that I really had liked reading about Chip.

Within a month I could find my way around the children's section like some- 57
one who had gone there all his life. By then the library staff knew Curtis and me and the kind of books we chose. They often made suggestions. "Here's a delightful book about a squirrel," I remember one of them telling me.

As she told me part of the story, I tried to appear indifferent•, but as soon 58
as she handed it to me, I opened the book and started to read.

Best of all, we became favorites of the librarians. When new books came 59
in that they thought either of us would enjoy, they held them for us. Soon I became fascinated as I realized that the library had so many books—and about so many different subjects.

After the book about the beaver, I chose others about animals—all types 60
of animals. I read every animal story I could get my hands on. I read books about wolves, wild dogs, several about squirrels, and a variety of animals that lived in other countries. Once I had gone through the animal books, I started reading about plants, then minerals, and finally rocks.

My reading books about rocks was the first time the information ever 61
became practical to me. We lived near the railroad tracks, and when Curtis and I took the route to school that crossed by the tracks, I began paying attention to the crushed rock that I noticed between the ties.

As I continued to read more about rocks, I would walk along the tracks, 62
searching for different kinds of stones, and then see if I could identify them.

Often I would take a book with me to make sure that I had labeled each 63
stone correctly.

"Agate," I said as I threw the stone. Curtis got tired of my picking up 64
stones and identifying them, but I did not care because I kept finding new stones all the time. Soon it became my favorite game to walk along the tracks and identify the varieties of stones. Although I did not realize it, within a very short period of time, I was actually becoming an expert on rocks.

"That day—for the first time—I realized that Mother had been right. Reading is the way out of ignorance, and the road to achievement. I did not have to be the class dummy anymore."

Two things happened in the second half of fifth grade that convinced me 65
of the importance of reading books.

66 First, our teacher, Mrs. Williamson, had a spelling bee every Friday afternoon. We'd go through all the words we'd had so far that year. Sometimes she also called out words that we were supposed to have learned in fourth grade. Without fail, I always went down on the first word.

67 One Friday, though, Bobby Farmer, whom everyone acknowledged as the smartest kid in our class, had to spell "agriculture" as his final word. As soon as the teacher pronounced his word, I thought, I can spell that word. Just the day before, I had learned it from reading one of my library books. I spelled it under my breath, and it was just the way Bobby spelled it.

68 *If I can spell "agriculture," I'll bet I can learn to spell any other word in the world. I'll bet I can learn to spell better than Bobby Farmer.*

69 Just that single word, "agriculture," was enough to give me hope.

70 The following week, a second thing happened that forever changed my life. When Mr. Jaeck, the science teacher, was teaching us about volcanoes, he held up an object that looked like a piece of black, glass-like rock. "Does anybody know what this is? What does it have to do with volcanoes?"

71 Immediately, because of my reading, I recognized the stone. I waited, but none of my classmates raised their hands. I thought, *This is strange. Not even the smart kids are raising their hands.* I raised my hand.

72 "Yes, Benjamin," he said.

73 I heard snickers around me. The other kids probably thought it was a joke, or that I was going to say something stupid.

74 "Obsidian," I said.

75 "That's right!" He tried not to look startled•, but it was obvious he hadn't expected me to give the correct answer.

76 "That's obsidian," I said, "and it's formed by the supercooling of lava when it hits the water." Once I had their attention and realized I knew information no other student had learned, I began to tell them everything I knew about the subject of obsidian, lava, lava flow, supercooling, and compacting of the elements.

77 When I finally paused, a voice behind me whispered, "Is that Bennie Carson?"

78 "You're absolutely correct," Mr. Jaeck said, and he smiled at me. If he had announced that I'd won a million-dollar lottery, I couldn't have been more pleased and excited.

79 "Benjamin, that's absolutely, absolutely right," he repeated with enthusiasm in his voice. He turned to the others and said, "That is wonderful! Class, this is a tremendous piece of information Benjamin has just given us. I'm very proud to hear him say this."

80 For a few moments, I tasted the thrill of achievement. I recall thinking, *Wow, look at them. They're all looking at me with admiration. Me, the dummy! The one everybody thinks is stupid. They're looking at me to see if this is really me speaking.*

81 Maybe, though, it was I who was the most astonished• one in the class. Although I had been reading two books a week because Mother told me to, I had not realized how much knowledge I was accumulating. True, I had

Dr. Carson finds time between surgical operations to deliver motivational talks to groups of schoolchildren.

learned to enjoy reading, but until then I hadn't realized how it connected with my schoolwork. That day—for the first time—I realized that Mother had been right. Reading is the way out of ignorance, and the road to achievement. I did not have to be the class dummy anymore.

For the next few days, I felt like a hero at school. The jokes about me stopped. The kids started to listen to me. *I'm starting to have fun with this stuff.* 82

As my grades improved in every subject, I asked myself, "Ben, is there any reason you can't be the smartest kid in the class? If you can learn about obsidian, you can learn about social studies and geography and math and science and everything." 83

That single moment of triumph pushed me to want to read more. From then on, it was as though I could not read enough books. Whenever anyone looked for me after school, they could usually find me in my bedroom—curled up, reading a library book—for a long time, the only thing I wanted to do. I had stopped caring about the TV programs I was missing; I no longer cared about playing Tip the Top or baseball anymore. I just wanted to read. 84

In a year and a half—by the middle of sixth grade—I had moved to the top of the class. 85

Reading Comprehension Questions

1. The word *trauma* in "I loved both my mother and father and went through considerable trauma over their separating. For months afterward, I kept thinking that my parents would get back together, . . . but he never came back" (paragraph 20) means
   a. love.
   b. knowledge.
   c. distance.
   (d) suffering.
2. The word *acknowledged* in "One Friday, though, Bobby Farmer, whom everyone acknowledged as the smartest kid in our class, had to spell 'agriculture' as his final word" (paragraph 67) means
   a. denied.
   (b) recognized.
   c. forgot.
   d. interrupted.

3. Which sentence best expresses the central idea of the selection?
   a. Children who grow up in single-parent homes may spend large amounts of time home alone.
   b. Because of parental guidance that led to a love of reading, the author was able to go from academic failure to success.
   c. Parents should stay committed to their marriage when their children are young.
   d. Today's young people watch too much television day after day.
4. Which sentence best expresses the main idea of paragraph 56?
   a. Bennie's first experience with a library book was positive.
   b. The first book that Bennie ever checked out at a library was about a beaver.
   c. The librarian was very helpful to Bennie and Curtis.
   d. At first, Bennie could not read most of the animal books at the library.
5. Which sentence best expresses the main idea of paragraphs 61–64?
   a. Books about rocks gave the author his first practical benefits from reading.
   b. Curtis took little interest in what his brother had learned about rocks.
   c. The author found a piece of agate by the railroad tracks.
   d. Studying rocks can be a fascinating experience.
6. In Boston, Bennie
   a. had an excellent teacher.
   b. attended a public school.
   c. longed for his parents to get together again.
   d. lived with his father in a tenement building.
7. To get her sons to do better in school, Mrs. Carson insisted that they
   a. watch educational TV.
   b. finish their homework before playing.
   c. read one library book every month.
   d. all of the above.
8. We can conclude that Mrs. Carson believed
   a. education leads to success.
   b. her sons needed to be forced to live up to their potential.
   c. socializing was less important to her sons than a good education.
   d. all of the above.
9. We can infer that Bennie Carson believed he was dumb because
   a. in Boston he had gotten behind in school.
   b. other students laughed at him.
   c. he had done his best when he first started at Higgins Elementary School, but still got poor grades.
   d. all of the above.

10. From paragraphs 70–80, we can infer that
    a. Bennie thought his classmates were stupid because they did not know about obsidian.
    b. Mr. Jaeck knew less about rocks than Bennie did.
    (c.) this was the first time Bennie had answered a difficult question correctly in class.
    d. Mr. Jaeck thought that Bennie had taken too much class time explaining about obsidian.

Technique Questions

1. Instead of pausing to describe Bennie's mother, the author reveals her character through the specific details of her actions and words. For example, what does paragraph 25 tell us about Mrs. Carson?

   Paragraph 25 reveals Mrs. Carson's extreme concern about and devotion to her sons. It also illustrates her wisdom (regarding the value of education) and her powerful spirituality.

2. What is the main order in which the details of this reading are organized—time order or listing order? Locate and write down three of the many transitions that are used as part of that order.

   Time order. Answers include: first, Before long, Now, later, before, afterward, next, then, finally, after, until, following, within a month, soon, in a year and a half.

3. The author states in paragraph 65, "Two things happened in the second half of fifth grade that convinced me of the importance of reading books." In paragraph 66, the first of those two events is introduced with a listing transition. In paragraph 70, the second event is introduced with another listing transition. Write those two transitions on the lines below.

   first ______ second ______

Discussion Questions

1. The author recalls his failure in the classroom as an eight-year-old child by writing, "Perhaps I wasn't emotionally able to learn much." Why does he make this statement? In general, what things in a child's home or social life might interfere with his or her education?
2. Part of Mrs. Carson's plan for helping her sons do better in school was limiting them to two television shows a week. How much of a role do you think this limit played in the success of her plan? Do you agree with her that unrestricted television can be harmful to children? Explain.

3. Reading on a regular basis helped turn Carson's life around. Think about your daily schedule. If you were to do regular reading, where in your day could you find time to relax for half an hour and just read? What would you choose to read? How do you think you might benefit from becoming a regular reader?

■ Writing Assignments

1. The reading tells about some of Carson's key school experiences, both positive and negative. Write a paragraph about one of your key experiences in school. Use concrete details—actions, comments, reactions, and so on—to help your readers picture what happened. (To see how Carson used details to bring classroom scenes to life, look at paragraphs 65–81.)

   To select an event to write about, try asking yourself the following questions:

   - Which teachers or events in school influenced how I felt about myself?
   - What specific incidents stand out in my mind as I think back to elementary school?

   Once you know which experience you'll write about, use freewriting to help you remember and record the details. Here is one student's freewriting for this assignment.

   > In second grade, Richard L. sat next to me. A really good artist. He would draw something, and it really looked like something. He was so good at choosing colors. Good at crayons, good at water paint. His pictures were always picked by teacher. They were shown on bulletin board. I remember his drawing of a circus and acrobats and animals and clowns. Many colors and details. I felt pretty bad in art. But I loved it and couldn't wait for art in class. One day the teacher read a story about a boy who looked at the mountains and wondered what was on the other side, the mountains were huge, dark. After the reading the teacher said "Paint something from the story." I painted those mountains, big purple brown mountains. Watercolor dripped to show slopes and a colored sunset, at the top of the picture a thin slice of blue sky. Next day I sat down in my desk in the morning. Then I saw my picture was on the bulletin board! Later teacher passed by me and put a hand on my shoulder and whispered good job, lovely picture. Made me feel really proud. The feeling lasted a long time.

   After the details of the experience are on paper, you will be free to concentrate on a more carefully constructed version of the event. The author of the freewriting above, for instance, needed to think of a topic sentence. So when writing the first draft, she began with this sentence: "A seemingly small experience in elementary school encouraged me greatly." Writing drafts is also the time to add any persuasive details you may have missed at first. When working on her second draft, the author of the above added at the end: "I felt very proud, which gave me confidence to work harder in all my school subjects."

Before writing out your final version, remember to check for grammar, punctuation, and spelling errors.

2. Reading helped Bennie, and it can do a lot for adults too. Most of us, however, don't have someone around to insist that we do a certain amount of personal reading every week. In addition, many of us don't have the amount of free time that Bennie and Curtis had. How can adults find time to read more? Write a paragraph listing several ways adults can add more reading to their lives.

   A good prewriting strategy for this assignment is making a list. Simply write out as many ways as you can think of. Don't worry about putting them in any special order. You will select and organize the strategies you wish to include in your paper after accumulating as many ideas as you can. Here is an example of a prewriting list for this paper:

   Ways adults can increase the amount of time they spend reading:

   on the bus to and from work/school

   while eating breakfast

   instead of watching some TV

   choose motivating materials (articles, books about hobbies, problems, etc.)

   Feel free to use items from the above list, but add at least one or two of your own points to include in your paper.

3. "Do It Better!" suggests that television can interfere with children's academic progress. Write a paragraph on what you believe is another unfortunate effect of television. You may feel that television includes too much violence, that TV advertising encourages children to want to buy too much, or that TV sitcoms promote poor family values. After deciding what effect you wish to write about, make a list of possible points of support. You may find it helpful to spend a few sessions in front of the TV with a notebook. Following, for instance, is part of a list of notes that can be used to support the point "TV advertising promotes poor nutrition."

   During kids' cartoon show:

   A sugary chocolate cereal in which marshmallow ghosts appear once milk is added. Children are pictured enjoying these ghosts, appearances and loving the cereal.

Chocolate-dipped cookies are included in boxes of another chocolate cereal. Appealing cartoon characters invite children to look for these boxes.

During talk show:

Ad for soda (empty calories) shows symbols of Christmas, making the soda seem like a healthy holiday drink.

An ad for corn chips (high fat) shows happy, healthy faces finishing up a huge bowl of the chips.

Lost Years, Found Dreams

Regina Ruiz

Preview

Divorced, far from home, with three children, not very fluent in English—Regina Ruiz could easily have become a sad statistic, a woman sunk in despair after a failed marriage. But Ruiz decided she had given up enough years of her life; she would reclaim the rest. Her story is hardly a fairy tale with a magical happy ending. But it is perhaps even better; it is the story of a courageous, life-loving commitment to a new and meaningful future.

Words to Watch

regal (2): royal
haze (3): confused state of mind
intervened (7): came in to change a situation
bleak (8): not hopeful
bleary-eyed (18): with blurry vision
preoccupation (18): extreme concern with something
Morpheus (20): the god of dreams in Greek mythology

I feel funny. So very funny, telling you about my life, my feelings, my secrets. I do not know how to welcome you into my heart and soul. You see, nobody ever asked me what I thought or how I felt about life's challenges. Or, maybe, nobody ever really cared about what I thought. 1

My journey to Burlington County College began many years ago in Caracas, Venezuela, where I was born and grew to be a young lady full of energy and life. My parents called me Regina because there was something regal° about the sound. They had high hopes of my marrying a local boy from a good, wealthy family. You know the kind—slick, black hair, long sideburns, driving a sports car. The kind who brings you flowers on every date and swears his undying love for you three days a week, and the other days he is sleeping with Maria, the local social worker. 2

To get even, or because I was in a romantic haze,° I met and married a U.S. Marine from Des Moines, Iowa, who was stationed at our local embassy, where I also worked. 3

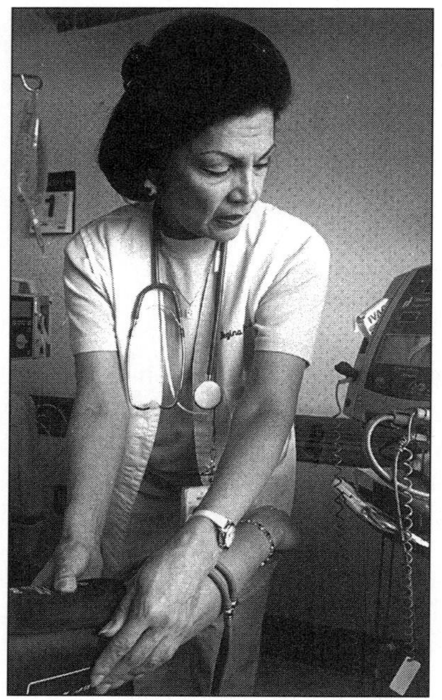

Regina Ruiz's nursing duties include taking a patient's blood pressure.

Marriage, a home in America, and three beautiful children occupied twenty-five years of my life. 4

Where did my life go? It went somewhere. But there is no lost-and-found department for lost years. 5

The marriage was bad. It was so bad that I cried every night for all those years. I would tell myself, "You are in a strange country—maybe the customs are different. The children need you, and you cannot admit failure to your parents back in Venezuela." 6

As luck would have it, fate intervened.• My ex-Marine husband found someone new and left me and the children with no money, very hurt and depressed. 7

I quickly took an inventory—foreign-born, with not a great command of the English language, no money, no job training, and two kids in college. The future looked bleak.• 8

But it did not stop. My father died. I loved him so much, and he was always my source of strength in need. Mother became ill. 9

I felt very hurt, lonely, angry, and very sorry for myself. 10

However, I remembered a saying my Dad would quote to me when things were going wrong and the future looked black. He may have gotten this quotation from the Spanish edition of *Reader's Digest*. He would say, "My dear, it is always the darkest when you are fresh out of matches." 11

"Dad, I am out of matches." Or so I thought. 12

I decided to make my life something worthwhile by helping people. I wanted to help and heal and maybe, at the same time, heal myself. 13

I appeared before the college doors with my knees shaking and full of doubt. I wanted to be a nurse. 14

I enrolled in college. I was proud of myself for not falling into the garbage pit waiting so close by. 15

Then the fun began—subjects which were very hard for me. 16

In order to survive, I managed to get two jobs to keep up with house payments and food. The kids found college money by working and by appealing to their father. I met my challenges on a daily basis. 17

Now, my days are very active and long. Before the sun makes its appearance, I stumble bleary-eyed• to the shower and afterward select the day's outfit. After a quick check in the mirror, I make my way downstairs to prepare a quick breakfast along with my lunch, feed the cat (who happens to be my alarm clock), and do what seem like a million other small chores. Then I drive for forty-five minutes to the Pemberton Campus, while studying my chemistry key notes on index cards before a test. I do this with tears in my eyes. You see, at the same time I am worrying about the situation with my water heater that slowly but surely is leaking and may not last until the new one can be 18

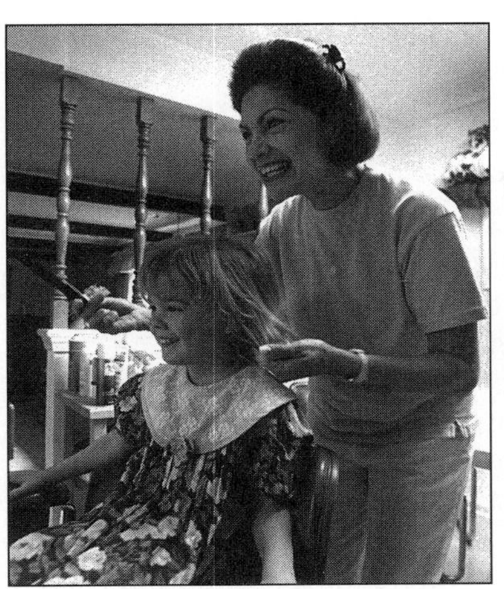
Regina continues to cut hair of her friends and family.

installed. In addition, I am anxious to schedule my exterminator's visit to treat the termites discovered in my basement. My preoccupation• with such household woes is due to a canceled appointment to have my furnace cleaned, which resulted in a periodic spray of soot.

After a hectic morning of classes, I rush to my car for 19
a hurried thirty-minute ride to the office, where a desk piled high with import documents is waiting for me, along with innumerable phone calls from the brokers, customs officials, and suppliers. Meanwhile, an impatient boss wants to know the precise location of one of
the fifty containers traveling between eastern Europe 20
and Burlington, New Jersey.

As the clock winds toward 5 P.M., I get ready to travel back to the Cinnaminson Campus for another round of classes. As I arrive on campus, I waste another thirty minutes searching for that nonexistent parking spot. My class continues until ten o'clock in the evening, and I praise the Lord it doesn't last longer. By that time, I am beginning to see double. I slowly make my way to the car and begin the long commute home, counting in my mind how many customers I will see as a result of my second job—hairdressing. On evenings when I have no classes scheduled, I take appointments to cut hair or give permanents. As I arrive home, I find a hungry son and starving cat, both waiting to be fed. I usually cook something simple for us, then proceed to do the few dishes because I hate the thought of adding one more chore to my early-morning schedule. By the time I finish getting ready for bed, it is midnight; I look up and see the stairway leading to the bedroom, which by then seems longer than the one outside the Philadelphia Museum of Art, and proceed to crawl in bed and into the arms of Morpheus.•

"I decided to make my life something worthwhile by helping people. I wanted to help and heal and maybe, at the same time, heal myself."

On many nights, I do not stay there long. At 3 A.M., maybe 4 A.M., my 21
eyes pop open. The thought, "Am I ready for the test? Do I understand the material?" makes me sit upright in a panic. Rather than toss and turn uneasily for the rest of the night, I get out of bed and open my textbooks for a couple of hours. If fatigue finally wins, I may fall back into bed before getting up for the day.

Without long luxurious stretches of time to study, I must constantly search 22
out such little windows of opportunity to prepare for class. When the laundry is washing, I study. While supper is simmering on the stove, I study. When a customer cancels her appointment for a haircut, I thank the Lord for a free hour, and I study. "Mom, if I studied half as hard as you, I'd be a straight-A student," says my son. But he understands that the life of a working mother

is not designed to make going to college easy. If I do not budget my time carefully, I will fail.

People question the wisdom of my studying to be a nurse. It may take four or five years. 23

"You will never last," they tell me. 24

"You will be too old to lift a bedpan," they mock. 25

But I am not discouraged. There are twenty more courses ahead of me before I get into the nursing area. While all these things challenge me, the greatest of all is to be able to hold my head high. 26

Somehow, just somehow, I think it might be all worth it—if I can hold the hand of someone dying all alone in a cold hospital ward and whisper in the patient's ear, "You are not alone, I am here, I am here, I will never leave you." 27

Maybe, just maybe, I will find that life that was lost. It is out there somewhere. 28

But I know one thing—I am in charge, and I will never let go again. Never. 29

An Update

Regina Ruiz successfully completed her registered nurse degree and is only a few credits away from earning her bachelor's degree at Jefferson University in Philadelphia. She is a nurse at Voorhees Pediatric Rehabilitation Hospital in New Jersey. 30

At the hospital, Regina's patients range in age from newborns to eighteen-year-olds. As she grows attached to particular patients, she requests that they be assigned to her daily shift, giving "extra love" to children battling illness, fear, and loneliness. "To see tiny preemies and children who are so sick grow and get better and be released to their families—it is wonderful to be part of that. School was very difficult, and nursing is a demanding profession, but when I am at work I am in heaven." 31

When she is not working, she takes pride in keeping her home beautiful. "After my divorce and through all those long difficult years, I worried so much about not being able to keep up with things," she said. "The roof leaked so badly at one point I had trash cans sitting in the living room. So I had to learn to budget my money as well as my time. When I had three jobs, one was for tuition and food, and the others were for repairs—a roof, siding, new windows, everything. Now I can look at the house and feel so good. A little neighbor boy told me the other day, 'Mrs. Ruiz, you have the nicest house on the street.'" 32

Regina enjoys reading to her two grandchildren, Rachel and Nicole.

She still does hair for a handful of longtime clients. "They were my friends 33
for so many years," she said. "When I'd come home from a test crying because I was sure I'd failed, they'd be the ones to say, 'No, Regina! You're going to make it.' Now, maybe I don't have to cut hair anymore to earn a living," she says with a chuckle, "but how can I tell them to go jump in the lake?"

■ Reading Comprehension Questions

1. The words *took an inventory* in "I quickly took an inventory—foreign-born, with not a great command of the English language, no money, no job training and two kids in college" (paragraph 8) mean
   a. fell asleep.
   (b) made a detailed list.
   c. formed a plan of action.
   d. got a job.
2. The word *appealing* in "The kids found college money by working and by appealing to their father" (paragraph 17) means
   a. pretending.
   b. refusing.
   c. suggesting an alternative.
   (d) making a request.
3. Which sentence best expresses the central idea of the selection?
   a. Ruiz could not tell her parents back in Venezuela that her marriage was unhappy.
   b. Ruiz should not have married the Marine and moved so far from home.
   (c) After a bad marriage, Ruiz successfully took charge of her own life and future.
   d. Ruiz is often exhausted by her schedule of school and two jobs.
4. A main idea may cover more than one paragraph. Which sentence best expresses the main idea of paragraphs 11–13?
   a. Ruiz remembered a saying her father used to say.
   (b) Ruiz at first saw no way out of a bad situation but then thought of a worthwhile path.
   c. Ruiz's father may have gotten inspiration from the Spanish edition of *Reader's Digest*.
   d. Ruiz thought helping people was a worthwhile goal.
5. Which sentence best expresses the main idea of paragraphs 21–22?
   a. Ruiz never has time to study, so she goes to class unprepared.
   b. Ruiz always chooses to sleep an extra hour or two rather than study for class.
   (c) Ruiz values studying and uses every spare minute for schoolwork.
   d. Because of her excess leisure time, Ruiz always has enough opportunity for study.

6. Ruiz's marriage ended when
   a. she left her husband for another man.
   b. she enrolled in college and her husband divorced her.
   c. her husband left her for another woman.
   d. Ruiz's parents demanded that she come back to Venezuela.
7. According to the "Update," Ruiz now works as a(n)
   a. office worker and baby-sitter.
   b. nurse and occasional hairdresser.
   c. translator and cleaning woman.
   d. parking lot attendant and veterinarian's assistant.
8. We can infer that Ruiz
   a. wishes she had married "a local boy from a good, wealthy family."
   b. believes she married the U.S. Marine too quickly.
   c. regrets having three children.
   d. believes enrolling in the nursing program was not wise.
9. We can infer that in the passage below, the author uses the word *matches* to refer to
   a. heat.
   b. solutions.
   c. the love between a child and a parent.
   d. something that will light a cigarette.

   He would say, "My dear, it is always the darkest when you are fresh out of matches." "Dad, I am out of matches." Or so I thought. (Paragraphs 11–12)
10. We can conclude one reason Ruiz wanted to become a nurse was that
   a. she believed that helping other people would help her too.
   b. Venezuela needed more nurses.
   c. her father always wanted her to be a nurse.
   d. nursing was the easiest course offered by the college she attended.

Technique Questions

1. In paragraph 5, Regina asks the question "Where did my life go?" Where in the essay does she return to the image of her "lost life"? Write here the number of the paragraph in which she returns to this image: 28 What is the difference between how she discusses her lost life in paragraph 5 and in the later paragraph?

   In paragraph 28, she is optimistic about finding her lost life again.

2. Ruiz begins her essay by describing a series of disappointments and her resulting depression. Later, she describes her decision to make something good out of her life and what her life has been like since then. In what paragraph of her essay does she make the transition between those two sections, and what word marks that transition?

   Paragraph 11; the transition word is "However."

3. Who wrote paragraphs 1–29 of the reading? Was the update written by the same person? What evidence supports your answers to these questions?

   Paragraphs 1–29 were written by Ruiz herself; this is indicated by the use of "I." The update was written by someone else—probably the editor of her story or this textbook. This is indicated by the use of "she."

Discussion Questions

1. Ruiz stayed with an unhappy marriage for twenty-five years. During those years, she told herself, "You are in a strange country—maybe the customs are different. The children need you, and you cannot admit failure to your parents back in Venezuela." Judging from your own experience and observations of people around you, are these typical reasons for remaining in an unhappy relationship? Are these *good* reasons?
2. Like Ruiz, adults who return to college often have a difficult time balancing the demands of their work, family, and classes. What challenges do you face as a student? What ways have you found to deal with them?
3. Ruiz briefly explains her decision to become a nurse. Why have you chosen your own course of study? What about it interests you? What do you hope it will offer you after college?

Writing Assignments

1. Ruiz and her parents had very different ideas about whom she should marry. How well have your plans for your life conformed to your parents' hopes for you? Write a paragraph about a decision in your life on which you and your parents have either clashed or agreed. Include concrete details in your paragraph that show exactly what your parents had in mind and how they communicated their hopes to you. Also explain clearly your decision and the reasons for it. Here are some sample topic sentences for this assignment:

   Although my parents urged me to become a teacher, I am studying to be a veterinary assistant.

> My parents did not want me to marry my high school girlfriend, and I surprised them—and myself—by doing what they wanted.

2. In paragraph 18, Regina writes about her typical morning, from stumbling out of bed to getting to and through school. She includes various specific details about getting ready in the morning, studying for a test while driving to school, and thinking about the "household woes" that plague her all the while. Write a paragraph describing your typical morning. To prepare yourself with plenty of concrete details, do some freewriting or make a list. After accumulating enough information about a typical morning, think of a topic sentence that will cover all of the details you will write about. Here, for instance, is one possible topic sentence:

   > A typical morning in my life starts slowly before developing into some very hectic, but productive hours.

   Before writing your final draft, double-check your topic sentence to see if it still covers the details in your paragraph or if it needs adjusting. (Perhaps, for example, you realize that your morning doesn't start so slowly after all.) Also, use a few time transitions to make the sequence of events clear to your reader. You could write, for example, "First I hear my alarm go off at 6 A.M. Then I take a shower, ending with a few seconds of ice-cold water to wake up my body and my brain."

3. Ruiz was proud of herself for taking control of her life and enrolling in college, rather than getting stuck in depression and self-pity after her marriage ended. When have you taken an action that you are proud of? Write an essay about such a time.

   In your first paragraph, state your central idea. Here are some possibilities:

   > I am proud of myself for quitting smoking.
   >
   > I am proud of myself for leaving an abusive marriage and getting my life together afterward.
   >
   > I am proud of myself for confronting a friend about her drinking problem.
   >
   > I am proud of myself for earning my high school diploma.

   Then continue by explaining the situation you faced, how you decided to take the course of action you did, and what the results have been.

   Below is a sample scratch outline for this paper.

Central idea: I am proud of myself for confronting a friend about her drinking problem.

1. Lana's drinking and its effect on her family and job performance
2. The day I told Lana she was hurting herself and her children
3. Lana's decision to join a twelve-step program

A great deal of specific detail would be needed to support each general point in this outline. Freewriting or making a list, or both, would help generate the necessary specific details.

The introduction of the outlined essay might begin with an anecdote dramatizing Lana's problem. The conclusion could restate the central idea and include a brief explanation of how Lana is doing now.

Papa

Leo Buscaglia

■ Preview

Leo Buscaglia gained worldwide fame as a favorite lecturer on public radio and the author of inspirational books including *Living, Loving, and Learning* and *The Fall of Freddie the Leaf.* Here, Buscaglia writes of the man who laid the foundation for his own lively curiosity and love of learning—the uneducated Italian factory worker whom Buscaglia knew as Papa.

■ Words to Watch

fathom (1): understand
insular (3): isolated
credo (4): a belief
complacency (4): self-satisfaction
stagnation (4): failure to develop
forum (5): a time and place for discussion
inevitable (6): sure to happen, unavoidable
pungent (7): strong and sharp
animated (8) lively
analytical (8): carefully examining
potent (11): strong
affirming (23): maintaining the truth of

Papa had a natural wisdom. He wasn't educated in the formal sense. When he was growing up at the turn of the century in a very small village in rural northern Italy, education was for the rich. Papa was the son of a dirt-poor farmer. He used to tell us that he never remembered a single day of his life when he wasn't working. The concept of doing nothing was never a part of his life. In fact, he couldn't fathom• it. How could one do nothing? 1

He was taken from school when he was in the fifth grade, over the protests of his teacher and the village priest, both of whom saw him as a young person with great potential for formal learning. Papa went to work in a factory in a nearby village, the very same village where, years later, he met Mama. 2

For Papa, the world became his school. He was interested in everything. He read all the books, magazines, and newspapers he could lay his hands on. 3

He loved to gather with people and listen to the town elders and learn about "the world beyond" this tiny, insular• region that was home to generations of Buscaglias before him. Papa's great respect for learning and his sense of wonder about the outside world were carried across the sea with him and later passed on to his family. He was determined that none of his children would be denied an education if he could help it.

Papa believed that the greatest sin of which we were capable was to go to bed at night as ignorant as we had been when we awakened that day. The credo• was repeated so often that none of us could fail to be affected by it. "There is so much to learn," he'd remind us. "Though we're born stupid, only the stupid remain that way." To ensure that none of his children ever fell into the trap of complacency•, he insisted that we learn at least one new thing each day. He felt that there could be no fact too insignificant, that each bit of learning made us more of a person and insured us against boredom and stagnation•. 4

So Papa devised a ritual. Since dinnertime was family time and we all came to dinner unless we were dying of malaria, it seemed the perfect forum• for sharing what new things we had learned that day. Of course, as children we thought this was perfectly crazy. There was no doubt, when we compared such paternal concerns with other children's fathers, Papa was weird. 5

It would never have occurred to us to deny Papa a request. So when my brother and sisters and I congregated in the bathroom to clean up for dinner, the inevitable• question was, "What did you learn today?" If the answer was "Nothing," we didn't dare sit at the table without first finding a fact in our much-used encyclopedia. "The population of Nepal is . . . ," etc. 6

Now, thoroughly clean and armed with our fact for the day, we were ready for dinner. I can still see the table piled high with mountains of food. So large were the mounds of pasta that as a boy I was often unable to see my sister sitting across from me. (The pungent• aromas were such that, over a half century later, even in memory they cause me to salivate.) 7

Dinner was a noisy time of clattering dishes and endless activity. It was also a time to review the activities of the day. Our animated• conversations were always conducted in Piedmontese dialect, since Mama didn't speak English. The events we recounted, no matter how insignificant, were never taken lightly. Mama and Papa always listened carefully and were ready with some comment, often profound and analytical•, always right to the point. 8

"That was a smart thing to do." "*Stupido*, how could you be so dumb?" "*Cose sia*, you deserved it." "*E allora*, no one is perfect." "*Testa dura* ('hardhead'), you should have known better. Didn't we teach you anything?" "Oh, that's nice." One dialogue ended and immediately another began. Silent moments were rare at our table. 9

Then came the grand finale to every meal, the moment we dreaded most—the time to share the day's new learning. The mental imprint of those sessions still runs before me like a familiar film clip, vital and vivid. 10

"Without being aware of it, our family was growing together, sharing experiences, and participating in one another's education. Papa was, without knowing it, giving us an education in the most real sense."

Papa, at the head of the table, would push his chair back slightly, a gesture that signified the end of the eating and suggested that there would be a new activity. He would pour a small glass of red wine, light up a thin, potent• Italian cigar, inhale deeply, exhale, then take stock of his family. 11

For some reason this always had a slightly unsettling effect on us as we stared back at Papa, waiting for him to say something. Every so often he would explain why he did this. He told us that if he didn't take the time to look at us, we would soon be grown and he would have missed us. So he'd stare at us, one after the other. 12

Finally, his attention would settle upon one of us. "Felice,"* he would say to me, "tell me what you learned today." 13

"I learned the population of Nepal is . . ." 14

Silence. 15

It always amazed me, and reinforced my belief that Papa was a little crazy, that nothing I ever said was considered too trivial for him. First, he'd think about what was said as if the salvation of the world depended on it. 16

"The population of Nepal. Hmmm. Well." 17

He would look down the table at Mama, who would be ritualistically fixing her favorite fruit in a bit of leftover wine. "Mama, did you know that?" 18

Mama's responses were always astonishing and seemed to lighten the otherwise reverential atmosphere. "Nepal," she'd say. "Nepal? Not only don't I know the population of Nepal, I don't know where in God's world it is!" Of course, this was only playing into Papa's hands. 19

"Felice," he'd say. "Get the atlas so we can show Mama where Nepal is." And the search began. The whole family went on a search for Nepal. This same experience was repeated until each family member had a turn. No dinner at our house ever ended without having been enlightened by at least a half dozen such facts. 20

As children, we thought very little about these educational wonders and even less about how we were being enriched. We couldn't have cared less. We were too impatient to have dinner end so we could join our less-educated friends in a rip-roaring game of kick the can. 21

In retrospect, after years of studying how people learn, I realize what a dynamic educational technique Papa was offering us, reinforcing the value of continual learning. Without being aware of it, our family was growing together, sharing experiences, and participating in one another's education. Papa was, without knowing it, giving us an education in the most real sense. 22

By looking at us, listening to us, hearing us, respecting our opinions, affirming• our value, giving us a sense of dignity, he was unquestionably our most influential teacher. 23

*Buscaglia's real first name.

Reading Comprehension Questions

1. The word *reverential* in "Mama's responses were always astonishing and seemed to lighten the otherwise reverential atmosphere" (paragraph 19) means
   a. relaxed.
   b. respectful.
   c. confusing.
   d. humorous.
2. The word *congregated* in "So when my brother and sisters and I congregated in the bathroom to clean up for dinner" (paragraph 6) means
   a. gathered.
   b. searched.
   c. argued.
   d. listened.
3. The word *retrospect* in "As children, we thought very little about these educational wonders and even less about how we were being enriched. . . . In retrospect, after years of studying how people learn, I realize what a dynamic educational technique Papa was offering us" (paragraph 22) means
   a. looking back.
   b. truth.
   c. imagination.
   d. part.
4. Which sentence best expresses the central idea of this selection?
   a. Buscaglia's father was a natural teacher who encouraged his children to love learning.
   b. Buscaglia's father insisted that his children come to the dinner table with one new fact each day.
   c. Dinnertime at the Buscaglia household was always a lively affair.
   d. The Buscaglia children treated their father with the kind of respect that is rarely seen today.
5. Which statement best expresses the main idea of paragraph 4?
   a. Buscaglia's father was scornful of people of low intelligence.
   b. Buscaglia's father frequently repeated himself.
   c. Believing that ignorance is sinful, Papa insisted that each child should learn one new fact a day.
   d. Papa believed that his children were born stupid and faced a life of boredom and lack of development.

6. A main idea may cover more than one paragraph. Which sentence best expresses the main idea of paragraphs 8 and 9?
   a. Buscaglia's parents listened and responded carefully to their children's conversation.
   b. Over dinner, everyone in the Buscaglia family talked.
   c. Buscaglia's parents were sometimes critical of their children.
   d. Because Mrs. Buscaglia did not speak English, the dinnertime conversation was in Piedmontese dialect.
7. Buscaglia states that he and his brother and sisters would
   a. invent made-up "facts" to satisfy his father.
   b. look up facts in the encyclopedia before dinner.
   c. compete with each other to find the most interesting fact.
   d. refuse to cooperate with his father's request.
8. Paragraphs 1 and 2 suggest that Buscaglia's father left school at a young age because
   a. he was considered too stupid to learn very much.
   b. his village priest recommended it.
   c. he could learn a lot on his own without school.
   d. his family needed him to earn money.
9. *True or false?* F Paragraph 5 suggests that many of the neighborhood fathers played similar learning games with their children over dinner.
10. Buscaglia implies that his mother
    a. approved of her husband's methods and played along with them.
    b. did not understand why her husband thought learning was so important.
    c. thought her husband was making fun of her ignorance.
    d. was better educated than her husband.

■ Technique Questions

1. How does Buscaglia organize most of the material in his essay—through time order or listing order?

   Time order

2. Paragraph 9 consists almost entirely of direct quotations from Buscaglia's parents. Why do you think the author chose to quote their exact words?

   The quotations reveal the Buscaglias' affectionate yet critical attitude toward their children. They demonstrate that each child's remark was heard and responded to. They also indicate the fast pace of the dinner-table conversation. (Wording will vary).

3. In paragraphs 11 and 12, the author provides vivid details. Which do you find most memorable?

   Answers may vary.

   What do these details add to the essay?

   They add vividness to the essay, allowing Buscaglia to communicate exactly how he regarded his father. The details, recalled by Buscaglia after many years, also reveal the impact of the family ritual on Buscaglia.

Discussion Questions

1. If Buscaglia is writing in praise of his father's educational techniques, why does he mention that he and his siblings didn't think much of them at the time (paragraphs 5 and 21)?
2. Buscaglia states that his father gave him "an education in the most real sense." What does he mean? What about his father's teaching style was so real? In what ways was it similar to or different from what happens in a typical classroom?
3. Was it especially important that the Buscaglia children knew, for example, the population of Nepal? What do you think was important to Mr. Buscaglia about the children's learning such facts?

Writing Assignments

1. Write a paragraph in which you describe a typical scene in your own family when you were a child. Make the paragraph as richly detailed as you can. In order to remember details vividly, you might ask yourself the following questions:

   What sights, smells, and sounds were usually part of our dinnertime?

   What were some foods that were frequently served?

   Who was typically present at dinner? Where did each person sit?

   What was the mood usually like at dinner? Rushed? Relaxed? Informal? Argumentative? Quiet?

   Were certain items always on the table—a particular coffee cup, for instance, or a sugar bowl?

2. Buscaglia writes of his father's outstanding characteristic—he was a natural teacher. Think of a person you know who also has one very strong characteristic. It could be a positive characteristic, such as generosity, humor, or

helpfulness. Or it could be a less positive trait, perhaps pessimism, bad temper, or laziness. Write a paragraph that begins with a topic sentence naming the person and stating his or her outstanding characteristic. Then support your topic sentence. Use several brief examples or one extended example of the person's behavior.

3. Buscaglia's essay is an affectionate tribute to a man who helped him realize that learning is a lifelong process. Write an essay about three adults in your life who have each helped you learn something. They may have taught you to *do* something practical—for example, tune up a car, make a dress, or cook. Or they might have taught you how to *be* something you value—kind, hard-working, assertive.

   Your topic sentence should name the three adults you will write about. Here is such a topic sentence:

   > My uncle, my stepmother, and a family friend have each helped me learn something important to me.

   The first sentence of each of your main paragraphs should then specify what each person taught you. For example:

   > My uncle taught me to fly-fish.

   Such a main idea sentence would then be followed by a description of how you observed your uncle fly-fish, how you yourself learned from his example, and why you value what he taught you. Repeat this process for each of the three adults you are writing about.

Let's Get Specific

Beth Johnson

Preview

Some people are better writers than others. That's obvious to anyone who reads. There are writers whose material you just can't put down—and there are writers whose material you can't put down fast enough. One of the biggest differences between the skillful writer and the poor one is this: the successful writer uses specific, concrete language. The journalist and teacher Beth Johnson explains the power of specific language and demonstrates how any writer can become more skilled in its use.

Words to Watch

instinctive (2): natural
prospective (2): expected, or possible
vividly (2): clearly, in lifelike images
glaze (3): become glassy
blandly (7): dully
intuitively (8): naturally
parody (8): imitation meant to be amusing or mocking
crave (9): strongly desire
anecdote (12): story
sustain (17): support

Imagine that you've offered to fix up your sister with a blind date. "You'll like him," you tell her. "He's really nice." Would that assurance be enough to satisfy her? Would she contentedly wait for Saturday night, happily anticipating meeting this "nice" young man? Not likely! She would probably bombard you with questions: "But what's he like? Is he tall or short? Funny? Serious? Smart? Kind? Shy? Does he work? How do you know him?" 1

Such questions reveal the instinctive° hunger we all feel for specific detail. Being told that her prospective° date is "nice" does very little to help your sister picture him. She needs concrete details to help her vividly° imagine this stranger. 2

The same principle applies to writing. Whether you are preparing a research paper, a letter to a friend, or an article for the local newspaper, your writing will be strengthened by the use of detailed, concrete language. Specific 3 language energizes and informs readers. General language, by contrast, makes their eyes glaze• over.

The following examples should prove the point. 4

Dear Sir or Madam:

Please consider my application for a job with your company. I am a college graduate with experience in business. Part-time jobs that I have held during the school year and my work over summer vacations make me well-qualified for employment. My former employers have always considered me a good, reliable worker. Thank you for considering my application.

Sincerely,

Bob Cole

Dear Sir or Madam:

I would like to be considered for an entry-level position in your purchasing department. I graduated in June from Bayside College with a 3.5 GPA and a bachelor's degree in business administration. While at Bayside, I held a part-time job in the college's business office, where I eventually had responsibility for coordinating food purchasing for the school cafeteria. By encouraging competitive bidding among food suppliers, I was able to save the school approximately $2,500 in the school year 1998–1999. During the last three summers (1997–1999), I worked at Bayside Textiles, where I was promoted from a job in the mailroom to the position of assistant purchasing agent, a position that taught me a good deal about controlling costs. Given my background, I'm confident I could make a real contribution to your company. I will telephone you next Tuesday morning to ask if we might arrange an interview.

Sincerely,

Julia Moore

Which of the preceding letters do you think makes a more convincing case for these job seekers? If you're like most people, you would choose the second. Although both letters are polite and grammatically acceptable, the first one suffers badly in comparison with the second for one important reason. It is *general* and *abstract*, while the second is *specific* and *concrete*. 5

Let's look at the letters again. The differing styles of the two are evident in the first sentence. Bob is looking for "a job with your company." He doesn't specify what kind of job—it's for the employer to figure out if Bob wants to work as a groundskeeper, on an assembly line, or as a salesperson. By contrast, Julia is immediately specific about the kind of job she is seeking—"an entry-level position in your purchasing department." Bob tells only that he is "a college graduate." But Julia tells where she went to college, what her grade point average was, and exactly what she studied. 6

The contrast continues as the two writers talk about their work experience. Again, Bob talks in vague, general terms. He gives no concrete evidence to show how the general descriptions "well-qualified" and "good, reliable worker" apply to him. But Julia backs up her claims. She tells specifically what 7 positions she's held (buyer for cafeteria, assistant purchasing clerk for textile company), gives solid evidence that she performed her jobs well (saved the school $2,500, was promoted from mailroom), and explains what skills she has acquired (knows about controlling costs). Julia continues to be clear and concrete as she closes the letter. By saying, "I will telephone you next Tuesday morning," she leaves the reader with a helpful, specific piece of information. Chances are, her prospective employer will be glad to take her call. The chances are equally good that Bob will never hear from the company. His letter was so blandly• general that the employer will hardly remember receiving it.

"Vague, general language is the written equivalent of baby food. It is adequate; it can sustain life. But it isn't very interesting."

Julia's letter demonstrates the power of specific detail—a power that we all appreciate intuitively.• Indeed, although we may not always be aware of it, our opinions and decisions are frequently swayed by concrete language. On a restaurant menu, are you more tempted by a "green salad" or "a colorful salad bowl filled with romaine and spinach leaves, red garden-fresh tomatoes, and crisp green pepper rings"? Would being told that a movie is "good" persuade you to see it as much as hearing that it is "a hilarious parody• of a rock documentary featuring a fictional heavy-metal band"? Does knowing that a classmate has "personal problems" help you understand her as well as hearing that "her parents are divorcing, her brother was just arrested for selling drugs, and she is scheduled for surgery to correct a back problem"? 8

When we read, all of us want—even crave•—this kind of specificity. Concrete language grabs our attention and allows us to witness the writer's world almost firsthand. Abstract language, on the other hand, forces us to try to fill in the blanks left by the writer's lack of specific imagery. Usually we tire of the effort. Our attention wanders. We begin to wonder what's for lunch and whether it's going to rain, as our eyes scan the page, searching for some concrete detail to focus on. 9

Once you understand the power of concrete details, you will gain considerable power as a writer. You will describe events so vividly that readers will feel they experienced them directly. You will sprinkle your essays with nuggets of detail that, like the salt on a pretzel, add interest and texture. 10

Consider the following examples and decide for yourself which came from a writer who has mastered the art of the specific detail. 11

Living at Home

Unlike many college students, I have chosen to live at home with my parents. Naturally, the arrangement has both good and bad points. The most difficult part is that, even though I am an adult, my parents sometimes still think of me as a child. Our worst disagreements occur when they expect me to report to them as though I were still twelve years old. Another drawback to living with my parents is that I don't feel free to have friends over to "my place." It's not that my parents don't welcome my friends in their home, but I can't tell my friends to drop in anytime as I would if I lived alone.

But in other ways, living at home works out well. The most obvious plus is that I am saving a lot of money. I pay room and board, but that doesn't compare to what renting an apartment would cost. There are less measurable advantages as well. Although we do sometimes fall into our old parent-child roles, my parents and I are getting to know each other in new ways. Generally, we relate as adults, and I think we're all gaining a lot of respect for one another.

The Pros and Cons of Living at Home

Most college students live in a dormitory or apartment. They spend their hours surrounded by their own stereos, blaring Pearl Jam or Arrested Development; their own furnishings, be they leaking beanbag chairs or Salvation Army sofas; and their own choice of foods, from tofu-bean sprout casseroles to a basic diet of Cheetos. My life is different. I occupy the same room that has been mine since babyhood. My school pictures, from gap-toothed first-grader to cocky senior, adorn the walls. The music drifting through my door from the living room ranges from Lawrence Welk to . . . Lawrence Welk. The food runs heavily to Mid-American Traditional: meatloaf, mashed potatoes, frozen peas.

Yes, I live with my parents. And the arrangement is not always ideal. Although I am twenty-four years old, my parents sometimes slip into a time warp and mentally cut my age in half. "Where are you going, Lisa? Who will you be with?" my mother will occasionally ask. I'll answer patiently, "I'm going to have pizza with some people from my psych class." "But where?" she continues. "I'm not sure," I'll say, my voice rising just a hair. If the questioning continues, it will often lead to a blowup. "You don't need to know where I'm going, OK?" I'll say shrilly. "You don't have to yell at me," she'll answer in a hurt voice.

Living at home also makes it harder to entertain. I find myself envying classmates who can tell their friends, "Drop in anytime." If a friend of mine "drops in" unexpectedly, it throws everyone into a tizzy. Mom runs for the dustcloth while Dad ducks into the bedroom, embarrassed to be seen in his comfortable, ratty bathrobe.

On the other hand, I don't regret my decision to live at home for a few years. Naturally, I am saving money. The room and board I pay my parents wouldn't rent the tiniest, most roach-infested apartment in the city. And despite our occasional lapses, my parents and I generally enjoy each other's company. They are getting to know me as an adult, and I am learning to see them as people, not just my parents. I realized how true this was when I saw them getting dressed up to go out recently. Dad was putting on a tie, and Mom one of her best dresses. I opened my mouth to ask where they were going when it occurred to me that maybe they didn't care to be checked up on any more than I did. Swallowing my curiosity, I simply waved good-bye and said, "Have a good time!"

Both passages could have been written by the same person. Both make the same basic points. But the second passage is far more interesting because it backs up the writer's points with concrete details. While the first passage merely *tells* that the writer's parents sometimes treat her like a child, the second passage follows this point up with an anecdote• that *shows* exactly what she means. Likewise with the point about inviting friends over: the first passage only states that there is a problem, but the second one describes in concrete terms what happens if a friend does drop in unexpectedly. The first writer simply says that her room and board costs wouldn't pay for an 12 apartment, but the second is specific about just how inadequate the money would be. And while the first passage uses abstract language to say that the writer and her parents are "getting to know each other in new ways," the second shows what that means by describing a specific incident.

Every kind of writing can be improved by the addition of concrete detail. 13
Let's look at one final example: the love letter.

> Dear April,
>
> I can't wait any longer to tell you how I feel. I am crazy about you. You are the most wonderful woman I've ever met. Every time I'm near you I'm overcome with feelings of love. I would do anything in the world for you and am hoping you feel the same way about me.
>
> Love,
>
> *Paul*

Paul has written a sincere note, but it lacks a certain something. That 14
something is specific detail. Although the letter expresses a lot of positive feelings, it could have been written by practically any love-struck man about any woman. For this letter to be really special to April, it should be unmistakably about her and Paul. And that requires concrete details.

Here is what Paul might write instead. 15

> Dear April,
>
> Do you remember last Saturday, as we ate lunch in the park, when I spilled my soda in the grass? You quickly picked up a twig and made a tiny dam to keep the liquid from flooding a busy anthill. You probably didn't think I noticed, but I did. It was at that moment that I realized how totally I am in love with you and your passion for life. Before that I only thought you were the most beautiful woman in the world, with your eyes like sparkling pools of emerald water and your chestnut hair glinting in the sun. But now I recognize what it means when I hear your husky laugh and I feel a tight aching in my chest. It means I could stand on top of the Empire State Building and shout to the world, "I love April Snyder." Should I do it? I'll be waiting for your reply.
>
> *Paul*

There's no guarantee that April is going to return Paul's feelings, but 16
she certainly has a better idea now just what it is about her that Paul finds so lovable, as well as what kind of guy Paul is. Concrete details have made this letter far more compelling.

Vague, general language is the written equivalent of baby food. It is 17
adequate; it can sustain• life. But it isn't very interesting. For writing to have satisfying crunch, sizzle, and color, it must be generously supplied with specifics. Whether the piece is a job application, a student essay, or a love letter, it is concrete details that make it interesting, persuasive, and memorable.

Reading Comprehension Questions

1. The word *swayed* in "our opinions and decisions are frequently swayed by concrete language" (paragraph 8) means
   a. hidden.
   b. repeated.
   c. influenced.
   d. shown to be wrong.
2. The word *compelling* in "she certainly has a better idea now just what it is about her that Paul finds so lovable . . . . Concrete details have made this letter far more compelling" (paragraph 16) means
   a. forceful and interesting.
   b. long and boring.
   c. empty and vague.
   d. silly but amusing.
3. Which sentence best expresses the central idea of the selection?
   a. Communication skills of all types are useful throughout life.
   b. Always be specific when applying for a job.
   c. Specific language will strengthen your writing.
   d. Most people need help with their writing skills.
4. Main ideas may cover more than one paragraph. Which sentence best expresses the main idea of paragraphs 6–7?
   a. In letters of application for a job, Bob and Julia have included their background and job goals.
   b. Bob and Julia have written letters of application for a job.
   c. While Bob says only that he's a college graduate, Julia goes into detail about where and what she studied and her grades.
   d. While Bob's job-application letter is probably too vague to be successful, Julia's very specific one is likely to get a positive response.
5. Which sentence best expresses the main idea of paragraph 8?
   a. Julia's letter is a good example of the power of specific details.
   b. Our opinions and decisions are often influenced by specific language.
   c. We want to hear exactly what's in a salad or movie before spending money on it.
   d. When we know just what someone's "personal problems" are, we understand him or her better.
6. Johnson states that abstract language
   a. is rare.
   b. lets us clearly see what the writer's world is like.
   c. tends to lose our attention.
   d. makes us want to read more of the writer's piece.

7. Johnson feels that concrete language
   a. is hard to follow.
   b. makes readers' eyes glaze over.
   (c) helps readers picture what the author is writing about.
   d. is not appropriate for a menu or a parody.
8. In paragraphs 6–7, the author suggests that Bob Cole
   a. is not qualified to enter the business world.
   b. is lying about his education and work experience.
   c. should have written a less wordy letter.
   (d) should have written a more detailed letter.
9. Which of the following sentences can we assume Beth Johnson would most approve of?
   a. Shore City is an amusing but expensive place.
   b. Shore City is an interesting place to spend a bit of time.
   (c) Shore City has an amusement park and racetrack, but all the hotel rooms cost over $100 a day.
   d. There is a city near the shore which has some interesting attractions, but its hotels are quite expensive.
10. We can infer from the reading that specific details would be very important in
   a. a novel.
   b. a history textbook.
   c. a biography.
   (d) all of the above.

■ Technique Questions

1. Essays often begin with an introduction that prepares readers for the author's central idea. How does Johnson begin her essay? Why do you think she chose this kind of introduction?

   She begins with a brief story about a prospective blind date. This introduction serves as an example of her central idea by vividly demonstrating the need for specific details.

2. The authors of the papers on "living at home" are essentially using listing order. What are they listing?

   Advantages and disadvantages of living at home with parents.

3. Johnson takes her own advice and uses many concrete details in her essay. Locate two particularly strong examples of specific details in the reading that are not in the three pairs of samples, and write them below:

   Answers will vary.
   ____
   ____
   ____

Discussion Questions

1. At some earlier point in school, did you learn the importance of writing specifically? If so, do you remember when? If not, when do you think you should have been taught about the power of specific details in writing?
2. Johnson provides three pairs of examples: two job-application letters, two passages about living at home, and two love letters. Which pair most effectively makes her point for you about the value of writing specifically?
3. What kinds of writing will you be doing over the next few weeks, either in or out of school? Will it be papers for other classes, answers to essay questions, reports at work, letters of application for jobs, letters to friends, or other types of writing? Name one kind of writing you will be doing, and give an example of one way you could make that writing more specific.

Writing Assignments

1. Using the same level of detail as Julia's application letter in the reading, write a one-paragraph letter of application for a part-time or a full-time job. Like Julia Moore, be sure to include the following in your paragraph:

   What kind of job you are applying for
   Where you have worked previously
   What positions you have held
   Evidence that you performed your job well
   Which skills you have acquired

2. In this reading, "The Pros and Cons of Living at Home" is a strong example of a "pro and con" analysis—one that details the advantages and disadvantages of something. Think of a topic about which you have conflicting views. It could be a decision you are struggling with, such as changing jobs or moving to a larger (or smaller) house or apartment. Or it could be a situation in

which you already find yourself, such as attending school while holding a job or having an elderly parent living with you. Write a paragraph in which you explain in detail what the pros and cons of the issue are.

Once you've chosen a topic, do some prewriting. A good strategy is to make two lists; one of the advantages, the other of the disadvantages. Here is a sample:

<u>Advantages of moving to a smaller apartment</u>

Save money on rent ($325 a month instead of $400 a month)

Save money on utilities (smaller heating bill)

Less space to clean (one bedroom instead of two)

<u>Disadvantages of moving to a smaller apartment</u>

Less space for all my furniture (big chest of drawers, sofa bed)

No spare bedroom (can't have friends sleep over)

Will get more cluttered (little space to display all my trophies, souvenirs, and sports equipment)

If you are not sure about which issue to write about, make lists for two or three topics. Then you'll have a better idea of which one will result in a better paper.

Use the lists of advantages and disadvantages as an outline for your paragraph, adding other ideas as they occur to you. Begin with a topic sentence such as "_________ has both advantages and disadvantages" or "I'm having a hard time deciding whether or not to ________." Next, write the supporting sentences, discussing first one side of the issue and then the other.

Be sure to include plenty of specific details. For inspiration, reread "The Pros and Cons of Living at Home" before writing your essay.

3. Johnson uses sharp, concrete details to make a point she feels strongly about—that specific language gives writing real power. Write an essay persuading readers of the importance of something you believe in strongly. Be sure to include at least one or two concrete, convincing examples for every point that you make. You might write about the value of something, such as:

   Regular exercise

   Volunteer work

   Reading for pleasure

   Gardening

   Spending time with young (or grown) children

   Periodic intense housecleaning

Alternatively, you can write about the negative aspects of something, such as:

Excessive television watching
Compulsive shopping
Tabloid journalism
Procrastinating
Smoking

Following is an example of an informal outline for this assignment. As the writer developed this outline into paragraphs, she added, subtracted, and rearranged some of her examples.

Central idea: Cleaning out closets every now and then can be rewarding.

(1) I get rid of things I no longer need, or never needed:

Pair of ten-year-old hiking boots which I kept because they were expensive but which are thoroughly worn out

Portable TV that no longer works

Yogurt maker given to me by my first husband on our anniversary

(2) I make room for things I do need:

All my shoes and pocketbooks, which can be arranged in neat rows on the shelves instead of crammed into cartons

Christmas presents I buy for my family in July and want to hide

(3) I find things that I thought were lost forever or that I forgot I ever had:

Box of photographs from our first family vacation

My bowling trophy

Presents I bought for last Christmas and forgot about

American Family Life: The Changing Picture

Donna Barron

Preview

Mom's in the kitchen baking a cake; Dad's at the office, doing a man's job; Johnny and Susie are having a swell time in the family room. Whether such picture-perfect images of family life were ever realistic, many of us grew up accepting them as "the way it ought to be." As we compare the reality of family life with such old-fashioned images, how does the way we live today stack up? What have our families lost—and gained—along the way?

Words to Watch

self-reliance (8): independence

fantasy (23): unrealistic fiction

It's another evening in an American household. 1

The door swings open at 5:30 sharp. "Hi, honey! I'm home!" In walks dear old Dad, hungry and tired after a long day at the office. He is greeted by Mom in her apron, three happy children, and the aroma of a delicious pot roast. 2

After a leisurely meal together, Mom does the dishes. That, after all, is part of her job. The whole family than moves to the living room. There they spend the evening playing Scrabble or watching TV. 3

Then everyone is off to bed. And the next morning they wake up to the sounds and smells of Mom preparing pancakes and sausage for breakfast. 4

What? You say that doesn't sound like life in your house? Well, you're not alone. In fact, you're probably in the majority. 5

A few years ago, the above household might have been typical. You can still visit such a home—on television. Just watch reruns of old situation comedies. *Leave It to Beaver*, for example, shows Mom doing housework in pearls and high heels. Dad keeps his suit and tie on all weekend. But the families that operate like Beaver Cleaver's are fewer and fewer. They're disappearing because three parts of our lives have changed. These are the way we work, the way we eat, and the way we entertain ourselves. Becoming aware of the effects of those changes may help us improve family life. 6

Let's look first at the changes in the way we work. Today the words, "Hi, honey! I'm home!" might not be spoken by dear old Dad. Dear old Mom is 7 just as likely to be saying them. A generation ago, most households could get by on one paycheck—Dad's. Mom stayed home, at least until the children started school. But today, over half the mothers with young children go to work. Even a greater percentage of mothers of older children are in the workforce. And the number of single-parent homes has mushroomed in the last thirty years.

These changes in work have affected children as well as parents. When only Dad went out to work, children came home from school to Mom. (In TV situation comedies, they came home to Mom and home-baked cookies.) Today, we'll find them at an after-school program or a neighbor's house. Or they may come home to no one at all. In every community, children are caring for themselves until their parents return from work. Are these children missing out on an important part of childhood? Or are they developing a healthy sense of self-reliance•? These are questions that Mrs. Cleaver never had to deal with. 8

"But we might borrow one important lesson from the Cleavers. It is that family life is just as important as work or play."

In addition, Dad and—now—Mom are often gone from home longer than ever. Not too long ago, most men worked closer to home. The office or factory was just downtown. Dad often walked to work or hitched a ride with a friendly neighbor. But no more. 9

Today's working men and women are commuters. They travel distances to work that would have made their parents gasp. Commutes of forty-five minutes or an hour are common. Workers travel on buses, subways, and crowded highways. Many leave their suburban homes at dawn and don't return until dark. No running home for lunch in the 21st century. 10

And speaking of lunch, there's been a second big change in American family life. If both parents are away from home for long hours, who's whipping up those delicious meals in the kitchen? The answer, more and more, is nobody. 11

These days, few people have time to shop for and prepare "home-style" meals. The Cleavers were used to dinners of pot roast or chicken. Potatoes, salad, and vegetables went with the main course, with pie or cake for dessert. But this kind of meal takes several hours to fix. People can't spend hours in the kitchen if they get home at 5:30. 12

So what do working families eat? They choose meals that are easy to prepare or are already prepared. Fast food, take-out, and heat-and-serve dishes make up much of the modern American diet. Dad may arrive home with a bag of Big Macs and shakes. Mom may phone out for Chinese food or ask the local pizzeria to deliver. And more and more people rely on microwaves to thaw out TV dinners in minutes. 13

One consequence of these quickly prepared meals is that families spend less time dining together. It's hard to make single servings on aluminum or microwave trays special. And classic fast foods, like hamburgers and fries, are meant to be eaten on the run, not slowly enjoyed at the dinner table. The family of the 21st century no longer shares the evening meal. As a result, it no longer shares the day's news . . . or the feeling of togetherness. 14

Finally, what about after dinner? Is today's family evening something the Cleavers could relate to? 15

Not a chance. 16

We don't have to look outside the home to see the changes. The modern American family entertains itself in ways the Cleavers would never have dreamed of. 17

Thirty years ago, families gathered around a radio each evening. Later, television took over. Most families had just one set, which they watched together. Today, television and computers bring a dizzying array of entertainments into the home. Cable television provides everything from aerobics classes to Shakespeare. VCRs expand the choices even more. If there's nothing good on network TV or cable, the video store offers the best and worst of Hollywood: recent movies, cartoons, "adult" films, exercise programs, travel, sports, how-to tapes. Computer games, which make up part of the action, also provide excitement. Players can compete in the Olympics, search out aliens, or wipe out entire civilizations on their little screens. 18

With all these choices, it makes sense to own more than one television set. The two-or-more-TV family used to be rare. Nowadays, Dad might want to rent an action movie when Mom's cable shopping service is on. Or Junior is playing a let's-blow-up-Saturn video game while Sis wants to watch MTV. Why not invest in several sets? Then each family member can enjoy himself or herself in peace. 19

What's wrong with this picture of today's family? 20

Only this. Today's Cleavers spend their evenings in front of their separate TV screens. Then they go to bed. The next morning, they rush off to their separate jobs (work and school). They come home at separate times. They eat separately. Finally, they return to their separate TV screens for another evening's entertainment. During all of these times, when do they talk to each other or even see each other? When are they a family? 21

Certain realities of modern life cannot change. One is the need, in most families, for both parents to bring home a paycheck. Another is the distance many of us must travel to work or to school. But must everything change? And must we lose the family structure in the process? 22

No one is suggesting that we go back to the 1950s. The Cleaver household was a fantasy• even then, not reality. But we might borrow one important lesson from the Cleavers. It is that family life is just as important as work or play. If we agree, we'll find ways of spending more time together. We'll find things to share. And then there will be something *right* with the picture. 23

■ Reading Comprehension Questions

1. The word *operate* in "You can still visit such a home—on television. . . . But the families that operate like Beaver Cleaver's are fewer and fewer" (paragraph 6) means
   a. visit.
   b. perform surgery.
   c. function.
   d. eat.
2. The word *mushroomed* in "the number of single-parent homes has mushroomed in the last thirty years" (paragraph 7) means
   a. fallen.
   b. grown rapidly.
   c. remained the same.
   d. disappeared.
3. The word *array* in "Today, television and computers bring a dizzying array of entertainments into the home" (paragraph 18) means
   a. purpose.
   b. loss.
   c. topic.
   d. collection.
4. Which sentence best expresses the central idea of the selection?
   a. Three changes in America have affected family life, which must be strengthened.
   b. Many children take care of themselves while their parents are at work.
   c. American families have many new ways to entertain themselves.
   d. Today, most families need both parents to bring home a paycheck.
5. A main idea may cover more than one paragraph. Which sentence best expresses the main idea of paragraphs 9 and 10?
   a. Most men used to work close to home.
   b. Today, working people don't go home for lunch.
   c. The transportation system in this country today is in poor shape.
   d. Parents are gone from home longer today than ever because of long commutes.
6. Because of the changes in the way we work,
   a. family incomes are lower.
   b. many children are alone after school.
   c. relationships with neighbors are poor.
   d. family members spend their evenings separately.

7. The author states that family life
   a. is more important than work or play.
   (b.) is just as important as work or play.
   c. is less important than work or play.
   d. should be just like that of the Cleavers.

8. *True or false?* __T__ Paragraph 8 suggests that there may be a possible benefit to children caring for themselves.

9. The author suggests that fast foods
   a. are not as nutritious as home-cooked meals.
   b. are too expensive.
   (c.) tend to be eaten on the run.
   d. all of the above.

10. The author implies that the American family has been affected by
   a. the development of suburbs.
   b. the wide availability of prepared foods.
   c. entertainment technology.
   (d.) all of the above.

■ Technique Questions

1. Barron's essay is not really about the Cleavers. She mentions them because they represent something that she is writing about. What do they represent?
   The Cleavers represent the idealized American family of the 1950s. They represent togetherness, which Barron feels must be reemphasized in the 2000s.

2. This essay is basically organized in listing order—it lists three main ways family life has changed. Write below the listing transition used to introduce each of the main types of changes.
   a. Changes in the way we work are introduced in the first sentence of paragraph 7. The transition used there is __first__.
   b. Changes in the way we eat are introduced in the first sentence of paragraph 11. The transition used there is __second__.
   c. Changes in the way we entertain ourselves after dinner are introduced in the first sentence of paragraph 15. The transition used there is __Finally__.

3. Barron includes numerous specific details in her essay. For example, what details does she use to illustrate her point that "Fast food, take-out, and heat-and-serve dishes make up much of the modern American diet"?
   Big Macs and shakes, Chinese takeout food or delivered pizza, TV dinners thawed in microwaves.

   Note: Wording of answers to questions 1 and 3 will vary.

Discussion Questions

1. What changes does Barron describe in the ways we work, eat, and entertain ourselves? How does your lifestyle reflect each of those changes?
2. Think back to your family's lifestyle as you were growing up. Does it differ from the way you live now? If so, in what ways?
3. According to Barron, if we agree that "family life is just as important as work or play," then "we'll find ways of spending more time together." What are some ways that your family spends time together? Are there changes you could make to spend more time together?

Writing Assignments

1. If we agree that "family life is just as important as work or play," Barron says then "we'll find ways of spending more time together." What are some ways today's families can routinely find time together? Write a paragraph beginning with the following topic sentence:

   > There are several ways busy families can spend more time together.

   Then go on to support that point with several ideas. You could, for instance, suggest that families pick one weeknight to do something together. But don't stop there. Go on to give examples of what families could do on that weeknight (take turns reading an exciting mystery out loud, play board games, etc.).

   Use listing transitions to introduce your ideas. (Information on listing order and transitions is on pages 13–15). The first suggestion, for instance, might be worded like this:

   > First of all, parents can encourage everyone to eat dinner together on weeknights.

   (You could then follow this point with ideas about what could be done during dinner—sharing the day's activities, discussing news events, and so on.)

2. As Barron explains, few children "come home from school to Mom" these days. What did you usually do after school when you were young? In a paragraph, describe what it was typically like for you from the time the last school bell rang until dinnertime. Remember to use time transitions to make the sequence of events clear. To think of ways to develop this paper, ask yourself a series of questions such as these:

   What did I do on the way home after school? (Walk alone, daydreaming? Walk home with a best friend, discussing the school day? Run all the way?)

   Where did I go after school? (Home? To a neighbor's house?)

   What was the first thing I did when I got there? (Watch TV game shows? Do homework?)

   Did I have a snack after school? (Peanut-butter sandwich with a quarter-inch of cherry jam?)

   Who was home when I got home? (Nobody? Mom, who worked half a day so she could be there when you got home?)

   Begin by accumulating a great deal of information about your after-school hours. Next, think of a general point supported by the information. Then begin your paragraph with that statement. For instance, you may find that the details of your after-school activities support a point such as one of the following:

   My after-school time as a child was a mixture of relaxation, play, and homework.

   When I was in elementary school, much of my after-school time was dominated by baseball.

   When I was in sixth grade, I had several after-school responsibilities.

3. Barron asks if children who are alone after school are "missing out on an important part of childhood? Or are they developing a healthy sense of self-reliance?" What do you think? Write an essay expressing and supporting your answer to these questions. If you feel those children miss out on something important *and* develop self-reliance, feel free to make and support that point as well. To clarify your points, use detailed, persuasive examples—from your own or other people's experiences or from your imagination.

   One helpful preparation for this assignment is writing an informal outline. Following is one student's scratch outline. Feel free to use it yourself, but note that you will have to add the specific examples a paper needs for clarity and interest.

Central idea: Children who care for themselves after school do miss out on something, but they also develop a useful self-reliance.

(1) Miss out on something:
Nobody there to share day's events with
Nobody there to drive student to special activities
May tend to choose passive activities, such as watching TV
(2) Gain useful self-reliance:
Learn to do household chores
Develop self-discipline
Learn to enjoy one's own company

In your introduction, you might wish to use an anecdote from your own youth or that of your children as a way to gain the reader's interest. Here is an example of how such an introduction might begin:

> After a long day in fifth grade, I could walk home kicking stones and hoping my black cat Lucky would greet me at the door. No one else would. If he wasn't near the back door when I came home, I'd spend as long as necessary to find him, calling out his name and searching on chairs, under beds, and in closets. . . .

Men and Their Hidden Feelings

Richard Cohen

■ Preview

A man and his best friend spend a day fishing. When the man gets home, his wife begins this typical conversation: "How was Barry?" "He was fine." "What did you talk about?" "Nothing." "You were together for five hours. You must have talked about something." "We didn't talk. We just fished." She shakes her head in wonder, and with more than a little frustration. In this essay, the columnist Richard Cohen wonders about men—himself included—and their ability to truly connect with other human beings.

■ Words to Watch

wench (2): spend time with sexually loose women
emerged (3): in full view
anguish (3): great pain
legend (7): popular belief
virtually (8): almost
catty (9): spiteful; wishing to harm others
outmoded (11): no longer fashionable
programmed (11): trained
sentiment (12): thinking influenced by emotion
agenda (15): program of things to be done

My friends have no friends. They are men. They think they have friends, and if you ask them whether they have friends they will say yes, but they don't really. They think, for instance, that I'm their friend, but I'm not. It's OK. They're not my friends either. 1

The reason for that is that we are all men—and men, I have come to believe, cannot or will not have real friends. They have something else—companions, buddies, pals, chums, someone to drink with and someone to wench• with and someone to lunch with, but no one when it comes to saying how they feel—especially how they hurt. 2

Women know this. They talk about it among themselves. I heard one woman describe men as the true Third World people—still not yet emerged.° To women this inability of men to say what they feel is a source of amazement and then anguish° and then, finally, betrayal. Women will tell you all the time that they don't know the men they live with. They talk of long silences and drifting off and of keeping feelings hidden and never letting on that they are troubled or bothered or whatever. 3

If it's any comfort to women, they should know that it's nothing personal. Men treat other men the same way. 4

For instance, I know men who have suffered brutal professional setbacks and never mentioned it to their friends. I know of a guy who never told his best friend that his own son had a rare childhood disease. And I know others who never have sex with their wives but talk to their friends as though they're living in the Playboy Mansion, either pretending otherwise or saying nothing. 5

"To women, the inability of men to say what they feel is a source of amazement and then anguish and then, finally, betrayal."

This is something men learn early. It is something I learned from my father, who taught me, the way fathers teach sons, to keep my emotions to myself. I watched him and learned from him. One day we went to the baseball game, cheered and ate and drank, and the next day he was taken to the hospital with yet another ulcer attack. He had several of them. My mother said he worried a lot, but I saw none of this. 6

Legend° has it that men talk a lot about sex. They don't. They talk about it only in the sense that it is treated like sports. They joke about it and rate women from 1 to 10. But they almost never talk about it in a way that matters—the quality of it. They almost never talk in real terms, in terms other than a cartoon, in terms that apply to them and the woman or women with whom they have a relationship. 7

Women do talk that way. Women talk about fulfillment, and they admit—maybe complain is the better word—to nonexistent sex lives. No man would admit to having virtually° no sex life, yet there are plenty who do. 8

When I was a kid, I believed that it was men who had real friendships and women who did not. This seemed to be the universal belief, and boys would talk about this. We wondered about girls, about what made them so catty° that they could not have friendships, and we really thought we were lucky to be men and have real friends. 9

We thought our friendships would last forever; we talked about them in some sort of Three Musketeers fashion—all for one and one for all. If one of us needed help, all of us would come running. We are still good friends, some of us, anyway, and I still feel that I will fight for them, but I don't think I could confide in them. No—not that. 10

Sometimes I think that men are walking relics—outmoded° and outdated, programmed° for some other age. We have all the essential qualities for 11 survival in the wild and for success in battle, but we run like hell from talking about our feelings. We are, as the poet said in a different context, truly a thing of wonder.

Some women say that they have always had this ability to confide in one 12
another—to talk freely. Others say that this is something relatively new—yet another benefit of the women's movement. I don't know. All I know is that they have it, and most men don't, and even the men who do—the ones who can talk about how they feel—talk to women. Have we been raised to think of feelings and sentiment• as feminine? Can a man talk intimately with another man and not wonder about his masculinity? I don't know. I do know it sometimes makes the other men feel uncomfortable.

I know this is a subject that concerns me, and yet I find myself bottling it 13
all up—keeping it all in. I've been on automatic pilot for years now.

It would be nice to break out of it. It would be nice to join the rest of the 14
human race, connect with others in a way that makes sense, in a way that's meaningful—in a way that's more than a dirty joke and a slap on the back. I wonder whether it can be done.

If it can, it will happen because women will insist on it, because they 15
themselves have shown the way, come out of the closet as women, talked about it, organized, defined an agenda,• set their goals and admitted that as women—just as women—they have problems in common. So do men. It's time to talk about them.

Reading Comprehension Questions

1. The word *relics* in "Sometimes I think that men are walking relics—outmoded and outdated, programmed for some other age" (paragraph 11) means
   a. advertisements.
   b. encyclopedias.
   c. things from the past
   d. good friends

2. The word *intimately* in "Have we been raised to think of feelings and sentiment as feminine? Can a man talk intimately with another man and not wonder about his masculinity?" (paragraph 12) means
   a. roughly.
   b. bravely.
   c. loudly.
   d. personally.

3. Which sentence best expresses the central idea of the selection?
   a. Women and men should be better friends to each other.
   b. Men talk about sex more than women do.
   c. Women are able to talk freely with one another.
   d. Men should learn from women's behavior to overcome their own traditional behavior and confide in each other.

4. A main idea may cover more than one paragraph. The main idea of paragraphs 1 and 2 is
   a. men like to drink and eat with their male friends.
   b. men have buddies, but no friends to share feelings with.
   c. the author and his pals are real men.
   d. if you ask men if they have friends, they will answer yes.
5. The author says he once believed that
   a. sharing feelings is wrong.
   b. his father disliked him.
   c. men are good at sharing feelings.
   d. women are too catty to have real friends.
6. Cohen writes that he learned to hold his emotions from
   a. his friends' behavior.
   b. his mother's scolding.
   c. his father's example.
   d. women.
7. The author implies that while men talk about sex "like sports," women
   a. never talk about sex at all.
   b. talk about sex as part of a relationship.
   c. don't want to hear men talk about sex.
   d. feel sex is not important.
8. When Cohen writes, "My friends have no friends," he means that they
   a. rarely see each other.
   b. are too violent.
   c. don't share feelings.
   d. drink too much.
9. Cohen implies that his father's ulcer attacks were caused in part by
   a. his son's problems.
   b. holding in emotions.
   c. poor hospital care.
   d. marital problems.
10. Cohen implies that
    a. he doesn't get along with his father.
    b. men have very few buddies.
    c. he is uncomfortable keeping his feelings inside.
    d. men have little to learn from women.

Technique Questions

1. Cohen makes some of his points through contrast. Explain below what Cohen is contrasting in paragraphs 7 and 8 and paragraph 12.

In paragraphs 7 and 8, the author contrasts how men and women talk about or view sex.

In paragraph 12, he contrasts women's ability to confide in each other and men's inability to talk about their feelings.

2. The techniques listed below help give a casual, conversational tone to Cohen's piece. In each case, write the number of a paragraph in which an example of the technique appears. Answers include the following:
   a. Contractions 1, 3, 4, 5, 7, 10, 12, 13, 14, 15
   b. First person-pronouns (*I* and *we*) 1, 2, 3, 5, 6, 9, 10, 11, 12, 13, 14
   c. Informal words and phrases 1, 2, 7, 9, 10, 11, 12, 15
3. One way Cohen achieves an interesting, conversational style is by varying sentence length. For instance, paragraph 1 contains this fairly long sentence: "They think they have friends, and if you ask them whether they have friends they will say yes, but they don't really." In contrast, here's another sentence in that paragraph: "It's OK."

   Similar variation in sentence length occurs throughout the reading. For instance, note the varied rhythm in paragraphs 7 and 10. Reread them, and then underline the longest and shortest sentences in each of these paragraphs. Note: See underlining in these paragraphs.

Discussion Questions

1. How do the men you know communicate with male and female friends? Do they—as Cohen suggests—keep their feelings and troubles to themselves?
2. Whether you're male or female, do you have someone you can confide in? What do you feel are the benefits—or drawbacks—of sharing personal feelings and problems?
3. Everything considered, do you feel that men or women are better equipped to deal with the problems of everyday living and survival? Defend your answer.

Writing Assignments

1. Do you agree with Cohen that men don't share their feelings? Write a paragraph about your experience in communicating with men. Use one of the following topic sentences, or a similar one:

   Like Cohen, I learned from my father to keep my feelings inside.

   Unlike Cohen, I learned from my father to communicate how I feel to friends and family.

My brothers learned from my father to keep their feelings to themselves.

My male friends and I do (or don't) share our feelings and troubles with each other.

Although several males have been my pals for years, there is still much I don't know about them.

After stating your topic sentence, support it with one or more examples. (Note how Cohen uses several examples in paragraph 5 to support the point he makes in paragraph 4. In contrast, in paragraph 6 he uses one longer example—to show how he learned from his father to hide his feelings.)

2. Cohen writes about a characteristic of the men he knows. Write a paragraph examining another characteristic of men or women, or both. As examples, use people you know well or have observed. Following are some areas you might consider writing about.

   Household responsibilities

   Attitude toward marriage

   Communication between mates

   Method of arguing

   Attitude toward sports

   When you choose a topic to write about, think of the point you want to make about it. Feel free to use either a serious or a humorous approach. Here are a few topic sentences that express opinions on some of the above topics:

   Many young women are in no rush to get married.

   Women don't always communicate what they really want their husbands to do around the house.

   The men in my family are sports addicts.

   As you work on your topic sentence, keep in mind your need for supporting details. You may find that the first topic sentence you think of is going to be hard to support. Keep working at it until you have an appealing main idea that you can support well. One good way to check for supporting details is to create an informal outline. If your outline is too bare and you can't fill it out, then you'll know you have to find a more supportable point. Here, for instance, is a workable outline:

Topic sentence: Men are more intereseted than ever in cosmetics and fashion.

(1) Greater use of cosmetics
  a. Various lotions
  b. Hair treatments

(2) Greater variety in clothing
  a. Styles of shirts and pants
  b. Color variety

(3) Jewelry
  a. Rings and fashionable watches
  b. Earrings

Once you know you have enough support, you can begin writing your paper with confidence. As you write, you may find an idea here and there in your outline that you wish to change, remove, or add. Also, you'll need to add examples to your paragraph. But once you have done the outline, you will have a feeling of control, a sense that your paper is already taking shape.

3. Write an essay with the following central idea:

There are advantages to sharing one's feelings and problems with a friend.

For each advantage that you name, provide at least one example from your own or other people's experience. Below are a few advantages to write about. Feel free to use any or all of them, but take a few minutes to see if you can add at least one or two more to use in your paper.

Expressing a problem out loud provides some relief.

In discussing a problem with a friend, you may find a solution that you wouldn't have otherwise found.

Sharing your feelings with a friend enriches your friendship with that person.

To prepare for writing this paper, take some time to make up a list of possible examples and details that could be used to develop each advantage.

A Small Victory

Steve Lopez

Preview

There are a million small miseries in a big city, and most of them go unnoticed and unrepaired. But when Steve Lopez, a columnist for the *Philadelphia Inquirer*, wrote about Ruby Knight, a gracious woman caught in a nightmarish tangle of medical red tape, he touched a nerve in his readers. You may or may not be surprised to learn of the outpouring of response to Lopez's article.

Words to Watch

dog days (1): hot humid summer days between early July and early September
metropolis (2): big city
bureaucracy (6): system in which complex rules interfere with effective action
meager (15): very small
inventory (15): amount of goods on hand
recurrence (38): reappearance
exclusively (40): entirely
sprawling (44): spread out (and therefore hard to deal with)
cynical (53): distrustful of people's motives

First Column, Written on July 22

On the dog days* of summer, ten floors about Camden [New Jersey], Ruby Knight sets the fan at the foot of her bed and aims it at Philadelphia. Then she sits in the window, breeze at her back, and lets her thoughts carry her across the river to the city where she grew up. 1

She is seventy-one and has lived—since her husband passed on—in a high-rise near the Ben Franklin Bridge toll plaza. The neighborhood isn't the greatest, but from the tenth floor, Philadelphia is a gleaming metropolis.* The city sprouts above the river, and the sun glances off skyscrapers that shimmer in the July heat. 2

Mrs. Knight watches the boats and ships on the river, the cars on the bridge. She looks to North Philly and thinks back on her eighteen proud years as a crossing guard at Seventeenth and Ridge. And she worries about tomorrow. 3

Mrs. Knight, in the quiet of her home, is slowly starving. 4

She beat cancer: Her doctor calls it a near miracle. But now she's wrestling 5
a worse kind of beast.

Bureaucracy•. 6

Joseph Spiegel, a Philadelphia surgeon, tells the story: 7

In 1986, a tumor filled Mrs. Knight's throat. Spiegel removed her voice box 8
and swallowing mechanism. Mrs. Knight was fed through a tube to her stomach. It was uncomfortable and painful, but she was happy to be alive.

Although she couldn't speak, she learned to write real fast and took to 9
carrying a notepad around. She gets help from an older sister, Elizabeth Woods, who herself beat a form of lung cancer that's often a quick killer.

The doctor was impressed by Mrs. Knight's fight. "She said she was placing 10
her faith in my hands and the Lord's," he says.

"She beat cancer: Her doctor calls it a near miracle. But now she's wrestling a worse kind of beast. Bureaucracy."

Mrs. Knight had several more operations. But over the years, no sign of 11
cancer. And five months ago—she smiles at the memory—Spiegel removed the tube. She was able to swallow again. After four years.

Little did she know the end of one problem was the start of another. 12

Instead of pouring her liquid nutrition down the tube, Mrs. Knight now 13
drank it. The same exact liquid.

But Medicare, which paid when it went down the tube, refused to pay 14
when it went down her throat.

Mrs. Knight, who lives on a fixed and meager• income, kept the liquid 15
cans in the corner of her living room, an open inventory.• She would look at those cans as if they represented the days left in her life. And she began rationing.

Mrs. Knight says her fighting weight is close to one hundred pounds. 16
When it dropped noticeably, she went to the doctor but had trouble making her point.

"I think she was a little embarrassed that she couldn't afford to buy the 17
stuff," Spiegel says.

She had lost about ten pounds since her last visit, down to the high eight- 18
ies. She was on her way, Spiegel says, to starving herself to death.

Spiegel got an emergency supply of the liquid—she goes through about 19
six cans a day at one dollar a can—and began calling Medicare. If she ends up in the hospital, Spiegel argued, it'll cost Medicare a lot more than six dollars a day.

But Medicare, with built-in safeguards against intentional or accidental 20
use of common sense, wouldn't budge.

"This is a federally funded program and we have specific guidelines for 21
what we can pay for and can't pay for," Jan Shumate said in an interview. She's director of "Medicare Part B Services" in the Columbia, South Carolina, claims office.

But it's the same liquid. 22

"Yes, I understand that." 23

It costs less than hospitalization. 24

"Yes, I understand that, but we're mandated to go by the rules." 25

Even if it costs more money? 26

"My only solution I can suggest is if she files again and it gets denied, she 27
can request an informal review."

The reasoning is Medicare can't pay for every substance somebody claims 28
to need for survival.

Spiegel says Mrs. Knight needs this drink. She can't eat or drink much 29
of anything else. He has told her he may have to put the tube back in her stomach, so Medicare will pay again.

At the mere suggestion, Mrs. Knight loses it. No way. Her sister is with her, 30
the two of them confused by it all. They've beaten cancer, cheated the days, and now this.

Mrs. Knight hustles to the bathroom and returns with the scale. She puts 31
it by her bed, gets on. The needle hits eighty-three. She stands at the window, frail against the Philadelphia skyline, grace and dignity showing through her despair.

The two sisters look at the cans in the corner. There's enough for one 32
month, but Mrs. Knight will try to stretch it. One her pad, she writes:

"My trial. God's got to do something." 33

(Dr. Spiegel is at 215-545-3322.) 34

Follow-Up Column, Written on July 29

It's the kind of thing I don't get around to often enough. But today, I think 35
some thanks are in order.

The problem is, I won't be able to get to everyone. I don't even know 36
where to begin.

Maybe with last week's column. 37

Those who looked in this corner last Sunday saw a story about Ruby 38
Knight, a retired crossing guard in North Philadelphia. She had throat cancer real bad at one time, but Dr. Joseph Spiegel removed a tumor and Mrs. Knight has gone nearly five years without a recurrence.°

It took four years for Mrs. Knight, now seventy-one, to learn how to swal- 39
low again. And it was a big day for her about six months ago when Spiegel removed the feeding tube from her stomach. Finally, she could swallow.

Problem was, she couldn't eat or drink regular food because of discomfort. 40
Her diet was still, exclusively,° a nutritional supplement called Ensure Plus.

Now here's the deal. 41

When Mrs. Knight poured it down the tube, it was covered by Medicare. 42
When she drank the same stuff, Medicare refused to cover it.

Medicare reasons that if you don't need a tube, you don't need a special 43
diet. The rule exists to avoid abuse.

"The idea is a good one," Spiegel says. "But Medicare is the biggest, most 44
sprawling• bureaucracy of all." He says its inability to make reasonable excep-
tions often hurts the elderly poor.

Spiegel tried to get Medicare to change its mind, arguing that it would 45
cost the government a lot more if he had to surgically implant the tube back
in Mrs. Knight's stomach. But he got nowhere.

"We're mandated to go by the rules," a Medicare spokeswoman told me 46
when I asked for an explanation.

Meanwhile, Mrs. Knight, without anyone's knowledge, was working on 47
her own solution. She had begun rationing her Ensure Plus.

She kept a careful count of the cans, figuring she needed at least four a 48
day to survive. Mrs. Knight stacked the fifty-one cans in her Camden living
room, measuring the supply each day against her fixed income.

As Spiegel puts it, "she was slowly starving herself." She went from nearly 49
one hundred pounds to eighty-three.

When I went to visit, I found one of the sweetest, most unassuming 50
people I have ever met. Mrs. Knight's sister, Elizabeth Woods, is the same way.
She's seventy-six and also beat cancer. They live in the same high-rise apart-
ment house with a fabulous view of Philadelphia, and they help each other
through the days.

Mrs. Knight can't speak, but she gets her points across just fine. She writes 51
almost as fast as you can talk and she has a world-class hug.

The day after the column, Spiegel and his staff got to their Pine Street 52
office at 8:00 A.M. There were seventy-four messages on the machine. By noon,
there were 150. By closing time Monday, more than four hundred people had
called.

"You can get cynical• about things," Spiegel says, "but then there's this 53
outpouring of help from people. It's just astounding."

People called for two reasons. Compassion and anger. Everyone knows 54
somebody who's been seriously ill. Everyone has had trouble with bureau-
cracy.

Ruby Knight hit the daily double. 55

And I would like to begin now with the thank-yous. First to Dr. Spiegel 56
for his sense of compassion and outrage. To his staff—Lori, Gina, Maria, Sally,
Laura, Monica, and Mike—for patiently handling calls, letters, and donations.
"It was kind of fun," Maria says.

And thanks to readers whose names fill thirteen typed pages compiled by 57
Spiegel's staff. One person gave a year's supply of Ensure Plus. One donated
twenty cases. Some sent prayers, holy cards, religious medals.

Some thanked Mrs. Knight for her years as a crossing guard at Seven- 58
teenth and Ridge. Some people sent as much as four hundred dollars. One
sent three one-dollar bills and a note: "I wish I could send more."

One sent ten dollars and this note: "May God bless you. I lost my dear 59
husband to leukemia two and a half years ago."

Some called Medicare to complain. Some called Ensure Plus, where 60
spokeswoman Sharon Veach said she thought the company could arrange to
provide a lifetime supply, if needed.

Friday at noon, Spiegel, Maria, and Mike drove to Camden and dropped 61
in on Mrs. Knight with thirty cases of Ensure Plus and a list of donors.

Mrs. Knight was beside herself, humble, gracious, overwhelmed. She and 62
her sister kept looking at each other, shaking their heads.

"I'm speechless," Mrs. Knight wrote on her pad, and then laughed. 63

She said she would pray for everyone. She kept scribbling that she wishes 64
there were some way she could express thanks and love for the kindness of
strangers.

And I told her that she had. 65

Reading Comprehension Questions

1. The word *mandated* in "'This is a federally funded program and we have specific guidelines for what we can pay for and can't pay for. . . . we're mandated to go by the rules'" (paragraphs 21 and 25) means
   a. not allowed.
   b. scared.
   c. mistaken.
   d. required.
2. The word *compiled* in "thanks to readers whose names fill thirteen typed pages compiled by Spiegel's staff" (paragraph 57) means
   a. put together.
   b. paid for.
   c. delayed.
   d. remembered.
3. Which sentence best expresses the central idea of the selection?
   a. The elderly poor usually suffer unnecessarily.
   b. Individuals solved an elderly woman's problem that bureaucracy failed to handle.
   c. Mrs. Knight's diet is made up almost completely of a liquid supplement.
   d. Ruby Knight lost her voice box to throat cancer.
4. Which sentence best expresses the main idea of paragraph 15?
   a. Mrs. Knight lives on a fixed income.
   b. Mrs. Knight kept her supply of Ensure Plus in her living room.
   c. Mrs. Knight looked every day at the cans of Ensure Plus in her living room.
   d. Since Mrs. Knight could not afford more Ensure Plus, she began rationing the cans she had.

5. Which sentence best expresses the main idea of paragraph 52?
   a. Many people read the author's column about Mrs. Knight.
   b. Dr. Spiegel and his staff begin their work day at 8:00 A.M.
   c. Dr. Spiegel's office is a busy one.
   (d) Many people called Dr. Spiegel in response to the author's column.
6. *True or false?* __T__ Both Ruby Knight and her sister have been cured of cancer.
7. Even though she could swallow after the tube was removed, Mrs. Knight
   (a) could comfortably take in only Ensure Plus.
   b. lost her taste for regular food.
   c. preferred to feed herself through a tube.
   d. wanted to go to the hospital.
8. Dr. Spiegel's argument to Medicare was that
   a. the government should pay for whatever a person claims to need for survival.
   b. Mrs. Knight had suffered greatly because of her cancer.
   (c) it would cost the government less if Mrs. Knight didn't have a tube in her stomach.
   d. keeping Mrs. Knight out of the hospital would be helpful because the hospitals are already too full.
9. We can assume that Lopez included Dr. Spiegel's phone number
   a. with Dr. Spiegel's permission.
   b. to encourage people to help Mrs. Knight.
   c. because he believed people would want to help Mrs. Knight.
   (d) all of the above.
10. Lopez would probably agree that
    a. all of Medicare's rules are totally senseless.
    b. Ensure Plus is too expensive.
    (c) the Medicare system should find a way to make reasonable exceptions.
    d. people helped Mrs. Knight because they knew they would be praised in the newspaper.

■ Technique Questions

1. Lopez doesn't get directly into Mrs. Knight's problem until the end of paragraph 3. What does he accomplish by providing us with background information about Mrs. Knight?
   She seems more sympathetic and deserving; by contrast, Medicare's denial of her claim appears even more unjust. (Wording of answer may vary.)

2. To emphasize some of his points, Lopez at times uses very short paragraphs. Paragraph 6, in fact, consists of only one word. Find two of Lopez's particularly meaningful one-sentence paragraphs and write them in the spaces below:

   a. Answers will vary.

   b. ______

3. Lopez directly quotes various people in his articles. For example, look at the quotations from Jan Shumate (paragraphs 21, 23, 25, 27), Dr. Spiegel (paragraphs 44 and 49), two of the donors (paragraphs 58–59), and Ruby Knight (paragraphs 33 and 63). Why might Lopez have decided to include some of the exact words people spoke? Why didn't he simply tell Mrs. Knight's story in only his own words?

   The quotations reveal each speaker's personality and add variety and authenticity to Lopez's writing. (Wording of answer will vary.)

Discussion Questions

1. In paragraph 20, Lopez writes that Medicare has "built-in safeguards against intentional or accidental use of common sense." What does he mean by "intentional or accidental use of common sense"?
2. Lopez writes, "People called for two reasons. Compassion and anger" (paragraph 54). What does he mean by that comment? Why do you think so many people reacted with such depth of feeling?
3. Do you know any people who, like Mrs. Knight and her sister, have struggled to live with quiet dignity? How have they been helped or harmed during this time by government programs?

Writing Assignments

1. Lopez writes, "Everyone knows somebody who's been seriously ill. Everyone has had trouble with bureaucracy" (paragraph 54). Write a paragraph about either of these topics. In your paragraph, describe the illness or the trouble with a bureaucratic agency. Then explain what was done to cope with this problem. One useful prewriting strategy for this assignment may be to ask and then answer questions, such as the following questions about illness:

   Who was seriously ill? With what? What were the symptoms?

   What was the effect of this illness on the patient? On the family?

What was done to help the sick person and his or her family cope?

What finally happened? Why?

Your topic sentence for the paragraph might be a sentence like one of the following:

My mother's bout with lung cancer has been a very difficult time for both Mom and the family.

Applying for a grant to help pay for my education has taught me the true meaning of "red tape."

To make the sequence of events in your paragraph clear, remember to use some time transition words such as *first, next, after,* and *finally.*

2. Mrs. Knight "wished there were some way she could express thanks and love for the kindness of strangers." Write a paragraph describing another situation in which one or more people have gone out of their way to help a stranger. Perhaps you know a retired person who tutors children in a shelter for the homeless, a bystander who helped a mugging victim, or simply someone who gave someone else another chance.

   In your paragraph, provide plenty of details about the situation in question and the people involved. (To see how Lopez helps readers "know" Mrs. Knight and her sister, look, for example, at paragraphs 1–3, 31, and 50.)

   Making a list is one way for you to think of a topic for this paper. Following is one student's list:

   Helpful reactions to woman who fainted in church
   People who helped when I ran out of gas
   Helping a neighborhood family whose house burned down
   Kind bus driver when I lost my wallet
   Local family sponsored new immigrants
   Volunteers at soup kitchen

   After making such a list, a writer could choose the topic for which the most interesting, convincing support can be found. The writer could then use freewriting to begin generating material for a paragraph. If it becomes apparent that the support for that topic is weak, he or she could try another topic.

3. In his first column, Steve Lopez wrote about a problem he hoped his readers would help solve. Write an essay for your school newspaper discussing solutions to a problem you hope readers—students, instructors, administrators—will do something about. You might begin by listing some campus problems.

Then, to see which is the most promising topic, you could make a separate rough list of possible solutions for each of those problems.

Once you choose a topic, continue making lists or use freewriting to develop two or three concrete solutions you hope to persuade your readers to support. In your essay, describe the problem and solutions in detail, using examples wherever possible.

Your thesis statement will be a summary statement, such as "There are several ways in which our campus should be made much safer" or "Students should be given more opportunities to get help from instructors and tutors."

Before beginning your first draft, create a rough outline as a guide. Here's one that includes three general ways in which the campus can be made safer, along with specific ways to put them into effect.

Central idea: There are several ways that our campus can be made significantly safer.

(1) Better lighting
    In parking lots
    Along dark walkways
    In all building entranceways
(2) Better coverage by campus police
    Outside in busy and less busy places
    Checking empty hallways, dark doorways, etc.
(3) Safety information to students
    Booklets on safe behavior
    Information on crimes that have happened on campus

The writer who developed this outline enriched her essay by adding examples to emphasize many of her points. For instance, she told how one student was recently raped at night in a closet off an empty hallway. She also told how another student's purse was snatched as she walked back to her car in the middle of the day. In telling these anecdotes, she included concrete details to help readers "see" and "hear" what happened.

Finally, if you prefer, write about solving a problem off campus, such as one in your neighborhood or at a local beach.

The Quiet Hour

Robert Mayer

Preview

Families who do not own a TV set are considered an oddity in modern-day America. "But what do you *do* all day?" they are asked by puzzled friends who cannot imagine life without their electronic companion. According to Robert Mayer, however, getting rid of TV—at least for a brief period each day—could allow family members to do something radical: they could spend more personal time with each other. Of course, many would protest losing any time with the TV. How about you? Read Mayer's ideas with your own family in mind, and then decide what you think of "The Quiet Hour."

Words to Watch

lingering (1): staying
conjure up (2): bring to mind
slack (2): loose
scenario (3): imagined scene
subside (3): quiet down
byword (5): slogan
literate (7): able to read and write
by-product (7): side effect
bugaboo (12): steady source of concern
invalid (12): not effective
saturation (13): state of being totally full
pompous (14): given an exaggerated importance
drivel (14): nonsense
radical (15): extreme

What would you consider an ideal family evening? Call me a romantic, but that question calls up in my mind pictures of parents and children lingering• around the dinner table to cozily discuss the day's events; munching popcorn from a common bowl as they engage in the friendly competition of a board game; or perhaps strolling through their neighborhood on an early summer evening, stopping to chat with friends in their yards. 1

Let me tell you what "an ideal family evening" does not conjure up• for 2
me: the image of a silent group of people—the intimate word "family" seems hardly to apply—bathed in the faint blue light of a television screen that barely illuminates their glazed eyes and slack• jaws.

Yet we all know that such a scenario• is the typical one. I would like to 3
suggest a different scenario. I propose that for sixty to ninety minutes each evening, right after the early-evening news, all television broadcasting in the United States be prohibited by law. Let us pause for a moment while the howls of protest subside.•

Now let us take a serious, reasonable look at what the results might be 4
if such a proposal were adopted.

New Explorations

Without the distraction of the tube, families might sit around together after 5
dinner and actually talk to one another. It is a byword• in current psychology that many of our emotional problems—everything, in fact, from the generation gap to the soaring divorce rate to some forms of mental illness—are caused at least in part by failure to communicate. We do not tell each other what is bothering us. Resentments build. The result is an emotional explosion of one kind or another. By using the quiet family hour to discuss our problems, we might get to know each other better, and to like each other better.

> **"Let me tell you what 'an ideal family evening' does not conjure up for me: the image of a silent group of people—the intimate word 'family' seems hardly to apply—bathed in the faint blue light of a television screen that barely illuminates their glazed eyes and slack jaws."**

On evenings when such talk is unnecessary, families could rediscover more 6
active pastimes. Freed from the chains of the tube, forced to find their own diversions, they might take a ride together to watch the sunset. Or they might take a walk together (remember feet?) and explore the neighborhood with fresh, innocent eyes.

Pros and Cons

With time to kill and no TV to slay it for them, children and adults alike might 7
rediscover reading. There is more entertainment and intellectual nourishment in a decent book than in a month of typical TV programming. Educators report that the generation growing up under television can barely write an English sentence, even at the college level. Writing is often learned from reading. A more literate• new generation could be a major by-product• of the quiet hour.

A different form of reading might also be dug up from the past: reading 8
aloud. Few pastimes bring a family closer together than gathering around and listening to Mother or Father read a good story.

It has been forty years since my mother read to me, a chapter a night, 9
from *Tom Sawyer*. After four decades, the whitewashing of the fence, Tom
and Becky in the cave, Tom at his own funeral remain more vivid in my mind
than any show I have ever seen on TV.

When the quiet hour ends, the networks might even be forced to come up 10
with better shows in order to lure us back from our newly discovered diversions.

Now let us look at the other side of the proposal. What are the negatives? 11

At a time when "big government" is becoming a major political buga- 12
boo,• a television-free hour created by law would be attacked as further intru-
sion by the government on people's lives. But that would not be the case.
Television stations already must be federally licensed. A simple regulation
making TV licenses invalid• for sixty to ninety minutes each evening would
hardly be a major violation of individual freedom.

It will be argued that every television set ever made has an "off" knob; 13
that any family that wants to sit down and talk, or go for a drive, or listen to
music, or read a book need only switch off the set, without interfering with
the freedom of others to watch. That is a strong, valid argument—in theory.
But in practice, it doesn't hold up. Twenty-five years of saturation• television
have shown us the hypnotic lure of the tube. Television viewing tends to
expand to fill the available time. What's more, what is this "freedom to
watch" of which we would be deprived? It is the freedom to watch three or
four quiz shows and mediocre sitcoms. That's all. In practice, the quiet hour
would not limit our freedom; it would expand it. It would revitalize a whole
range of activities that have wasted away in the consuming glare of the tube.

A Radical Notion?

Economically, the quiet hour would produce screams of outrage from the net- 14
works, which would lose an hour or so of prime-time advertising revenues;
and from the sponsors, who would have that much less opportunity to ped-
dle us deodorants and hemorrhoid preparations while we are trying to digest
our dinners. But given the vast sums the networks waste on such pompous•
drivel• as almost any of the TV "mini-series," I'm sure they could make do. The
real question is, how long are we going to keep passively selling our own and
our children's souls to keep Madison Avenue on Easy Street?

At first glance, the notion of a TV-less hour seems radical.• What will par- 15
ents do without the electronic baby-sitter? How will we spend the quiet? But
it is not radical at all. It has been only about thirty-five years since television
came to dominate American free time. Those of us forty-five and older can
remember television-free childhoods, spent partly with radio—which at least
involved the listener's imagination—but also with reading, learning, talking,
playing games, inventing new diversions, creating fantasylands.

It wasn't that difficult. Honest. 16

The truth is, we had a ball. 17

Reading Comprehension Questions

1. The word *diversions* in "Freed from the chain of the tube, forced to find their own diversions, they might take a ride together to watch the sunset. Or they might take a walk together (remember feet?) and explore the neighborhood" (paragraph 6) means
   a. troubles.
   b. facts.
   c. amusements.
   d. friends.
2. The word *revitalize* in "the quiet hour . . . would revitalize a whole range of activities that have wasted away in the consuming glare of the tube" (paragraph 13) means
   a. bring to an end.
   b. give new life to.
   c. upset.
   d. follow.
3. Which sentence best expresses the central idea of the selection?
   a. Television shows need to improve in order to compete with other family activities.
   b. Many people will argue that a "quiet hour" interferes with their basic freedoms.
   c. Americans spend too much time watching television.
   d. Banning TV for an hour each day would enrich our lives.
4. Which sentence best expresses the main idea of paragraph 5?
   a. After dinner, many families watch television instead of talking about their problems.
   b. Three problems of modern society are an increasing generation gap, a soaring divorce rate, and mental illness.
   c. Many of our emotional problems are caused by lack of communication.
   d. A "quiet hour" would improve family life by giving us time to communicate with one another.
5. Which sentence best expresses the main idea of paragraph 14?
   a. The benefits of a "quiet hour" are more important than its disadvantages to networks and sponsors.
   b. Networks and sponsors should stop advertising deodorants and hemorrhoid preparations during dinner.
   c. The networks waste the huge sums of money gained from ads on terrible programs.
   d. The networks will not support a "quiet hour."
6. *True or false?* __T__ Mayer states that reading often improves our writing skills.

7. Mayer feels that an enforced "quiet hour"
   a. would bankrupt TV networks, since fewer commercials could be aired.
   (b.) is not an extreme idea, because TV didn't dominate America's free time thirty-five years ago.
   c. could break families apart as people are forced to spend more time doing things together.
   d. would interfere with our freedom to spend an evening as we please.
8. According to the article, television stations currently
   (a.) must be federally licensed.
   b. make little profit from commercials.
   c. are not regulated by the government.
   d. voluntarily provide a "quiet hour" in many states.
9. We can conclude that the author believes reading
   (a.) involves the imagination more actively than TV does.
   b. should always be done aloud by parents.
   c. is valuable only with nonfiction books.
   d. can easily be done while watching TV.
10. The author implies that our freedom to shut off the TV is limited by
   a. the large number of available quiz shows and mediocre sitcoms.
   (b.) the hypnotic effect of television.
   c. too much time being available for TV watching.
   d. the high quality of certain TV shows.

■ Technique Questions

1. In paragraphs 1 and 2, the author contrasts his ideas of an ideal family evening with an evening spent with TV. By choosing his words carefully, the author conveys two very different images. Below, for instance, are two phrases from paragraph 1 that help to show Mayer's idea of the ideal evening. In the blank spaces, fill in two groups of words from paragraph 2 that suggest what he feels a night spent with TV is like:

   Paragraph 1: cozily discusses the day's events
   friendly competition of a board game

   Paragraph 2: silent group of people
   glazed eyes and slack jaws

2. In which paragraph does Mayer state his central idea? Write the paragraph number here: 3. What is the value of starting this idea at this point?
   Mayer engages readers' interest with two colorful contrasting images of family evenings. (Wording of answer may vary.)

3. How does Mayer organize most of the material in his essay—through time order or listing order? Listing order

Discussion Questions

1. Since the author is trying to persuade his readers that a "quiet hour" would be helpful, why do you think he includes arguments *against* a "quiet hour" (paragraphs 12–14)?
2. Do you think a "quiet hour" would work as Mayer suggests it would? Why or why not?
3. Does television have a "hypnotic lure" for you? If it does, in what ways do you, or could you, control your TV watching?

Writing Assignments

1. Regardless of the merits of Mayer's proposal, it seems clear that a "quiet hour" will not be adopted soon, if ever. What other ways are there to encourage the types of activities Mayer writes about? Write a paragraph of advice to parents on how to limit the influence of television in their homes. Like Mayer, you might focus on one proposal and how it could benefit family life. Or you might list several steps families can take to lessen the interference of television in their lives. In either case, try using transitions such as *first of all, second, another,* and *finally* to introduce some of your supporting points.

2. A major presence in many of our lives, television can be both helpful and harmful. Make up a list of ways you feel TV helps you. Next, make up a list of ways you feel it harms you. Then use those lists as the basis for developing a paragraph with one of these topic sentences:

   Everything considered, TV is more helpful to me than harmful.

   Everything considered, TV is more harmful to me than helpful.

   Your paragraph might simply be a list of the most important ways in which television is helpful or harmful in your life. For each reason, however, be specific. If you feel that TV helps you relax at the end of a day, explain how, using examples. Perhaps, for instance, you count on David Letterman's wacky sense of humor to melt away some of the tensions of the day, allowing you to slip into bed in a good mood. You might even go on to give an example of the sort of thing that delights you on Letterman's show. Or you may feel the temptations of TV often keep you from doing other, more important things. If so, be sure to explain in detail what the temptations are and what exactly they keep you from doing.

3. Mayer's purpose in "The Quiet Hour" is to persuade readers that an hour with no television at all would be beneficial. Write an essay in which you try to persuade your readers of the benefits of another change in their lives. For example, you might try to persuade them to become vegetarians, ride a bike to work instead of driving a car, spend at least one hour a day reading, lose weight, or begin a daily exercise program. Provide at least two or three main points of support for your argument.

   Clustering is one way to generate support for your central idea. One student used clustering to think of ideas for an essay about beginning a daily exercise program. She began by writing "Daily exercise program" in the center of a page. Then she drew a circle around those words and began connecting supporting ideas meant to persuade readers of the benefits of such a program. At one point, her clustering looked like the following.

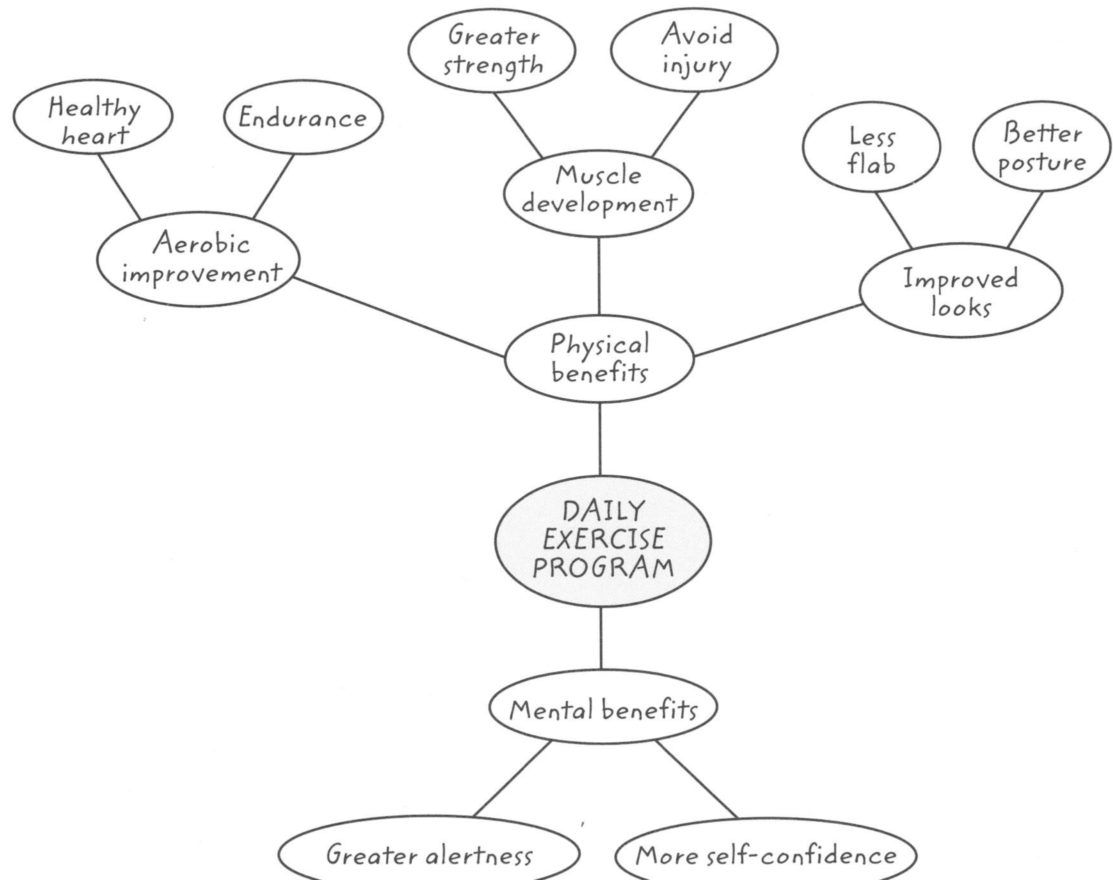

The writer of this essay also did clustering about the ease of establishing a daily exercise program ("can be done in twenty, thirty minutes a day," "no need for much equipment," "doesn't have to be expensive"). Once she felt that clustering had provided plenty of ideas, this student worked on her scratch outline. As she did so, she added many specific details about the points above, including examples from her own experience. For instance, she mentioned how her own improved endurance has made it easy for her to walk up several flights of steps to one of her classes instead of taking the escalator, thereby adding to her fitness program.

Since this essay uses listing order, use listing transitions (*also, next, in addition,* and so on) to introduce some of the benefits you mention.

My Daughter Smokes

Alice Walker

Preview

Alice Walker is a famous writer, probably best known for her novel *The Color Purple*. In "My Daughter Smokes," her daughter's habit is a stepping stone to a broader discussion of smoking than the title suggests. She goes on to also tell of her father's experience with tobacco and from there slips into a discussion of tobacco that moves through the centuries and across continents.

Words to Watch

consort (2): spouse
pungent (3): having a sharp, bitter taste
dapper (4): stylishly dressed
perennially (6): continually
ritual (12): activity done regularly
emaciated (13): thin
futility (16): uselessness
empathy (17): understanding
denatured (17): changed from its natural state
mono-cropping (17): growing of single crops apart from other crops
suppressed (18): kept down
redeem (18): restore the honor of
cajole (20): gently urge

My daughter smokes. While she is doing her homework, her feet on the bench in front of her and her calculator clicking out answers to her algebra problems, I am looking at the half-empty package of Camels tossed carelessly close at hand. Camels. I pick them up, take them into the kitchen, where the light is better, and study them—they're filtered, for which I am grateful. My heart feels terrible. I want to weep. In fact, I do weep a little, standing there by the stove holding one of the instruments, so white, so precisely rolled, that could cause my daughter's death. When she smoked Marlboros and Players I hardened myself against feeling so bad; nobody I knew ever smoked these brands. 1

She doesn't know this, but it was Camels that my father, her grandfather, 2
smoked. But before he smoked "ready-mades"—when he was very young and very poor, with eyes like lanterns—he smoked Prince Albert tobacco in cigarettes he rolled himself. I remember the bright-red tobacco tin, with a picture of Queen Victoria's consort, Prince Albert, dressed in a black frock coat and carrying a cane.

The tobacco was dark brown, pungent, slightly bitter. I tasted it more 3
than once as a child, and the discarded tins could be used for a number of things: to keep buttons and shoelaces in, to store seeds, and best of all, to hold worms for the rare times my father took us fishing.

By the late forties and early fifties no one rolled his own anymore (and 4
few women smoked) in my hometown, Eatonton, Georgia. The tobacco industry, coupled with Hollywood movies in which both hero and heroine smoked like chimneys, won over completely people like my father, who were hopelessly addicted to cigarettes. He never looked as dapper as Prince Albert, though; he continued to look like a poor, overweight, overworked colored man with too large a family; black, with a very white cigarette stuck in his mouth.

I do not remember when he started to cough. Perhaps it was unnotice- 5
able at first. A little hacking in the morning as he lit his first cigarette upon getting out of bed. By the time I was my daughter's age, his breath was a wheeze, embarrassing to hear; he could not climb stairs without resting every third or fourth step. It was not unusual for him to cough for an hour.

It is hard to believe there was a time when people did not understand that 6
cigarette smoking was an addiction. I wondered aloud once to my sister—who is perennially trying to quit—whether our father realized this. I wonder how she, a smoker since high school, viewed her own habit.

It was our father who gave her her first cigarette, one day when she had 7
taken water to him in the fields.

"I always wondered why he did that," she said, puzzled, and with some 8
bitterness.

"What did he say?" I asked. 9

"That he didn't want me to go to anyone else for them," she said, "which 10
never really crossed my mind."

So he was aware it was addictive, I thought, though as annoyed as she 11
that he assumed she would be interested.

I began smoking in eleventh grade, also the year I drank numerous bot- 12
tles of terrible sweet, very cheap wine. My friends and I, all boys for this venture, bought our supplies from a man who ran a segregated bar and liquor store on the outskirts of town. Over the entrance there was a large sign that said COLORED. We were not permitted to drink here, only to buy. I smoked Kools, because my sister did. By then I thought her toxic darkened lips and gums glamorous. However, my body simply would not tolerate smoke. After six months I had a chronic sore throat. I gave up smoking, gladly. Because it was a ritual with my buddies—Murl, Leon, and "Dog" Farley—I continued to drink wine.

My father died from "the poor man's friend," pneumonia, one hard winter when his bronchitis and emphysema had left him low. I doubt he had much lung left at all, after coughing for so many years. He had so little breath that, during his last years, he was always leaning on something. I remembered once, at a family reunion, when my daughter was two, that my father picked her up for a minute—long enough for me to photograph them—but the effort was obvious. Near the very end of his life, and largely because he had no more lungs, he quit smoking. He gained a couple of pounds, but by then he was so emaciated• no one noticed. 13

When I travel to Third World countries I see many people like my father and daughter. There are large billboards directed at them both: the tough, "take-charge," or dapper older man, the glamorous, "worldly" young woman, both puffing away. In these poor countries, as in American ghettos and on reservations, money that should be spent for food goes instead to the tobacco companies; over time, people starve themselves of both food and air, effectively weakening and addicting their children, eventually eradicating themselves. I read in the newspaper and in my gardening magazine that cigarette butts are so toxic that if a baby swallows one, it is likely to die, and that the boiled water from a bunch of them makes an effective insecticide. 14

"It is hard to believe there was a time when people did not understand that cigarette smoking is an addiction."

My daughter would like to quit, she says. We both know the statistics are against her; most people who try to quit smoking do not succeed.* 15

There is a deep hurt that I feel as a mother. Some days it is a feeling of futility.• I remember how carefully I ate when I was pregnant, how patiently I taught my daughter how to cross a street safely. For what, I sometimes wonder; so that she can wheeze through most of her life feeling half her strength, and then die of self-poisoning, as her grandfather did? 16

But, finally, one must feel empathy• for the tobacco plant itself. For thousands of years, it has been venerated by Native Americans as a sacred medicine. They have used it extensively—its juices, its leaves, its roots, its (holy) smoke—to heal wounds and cure diseases, and in ceremonies of prayer and peace. And though the plant as most of us know it has been poisoned by chemicals and denatured• by intensive mono-cropping• and is therefore hardly the plant it was, still, to some modern Indians it remains a plant of positive power. I learned this when my Native American friends, Bill Wahpepah and his family, visited with me for a few days and the first thing he did was sow a few tobacco seeds in my garden. 17

Perhaps we can liberate tobacco from those who have captured and abused it, enslaving the plant on large plantations, keeping it from freedom and its kin, and forcing it to enslave the world. Its true nature suppressed,• no wonder it has become deadly. Maybe by sowing a few seeds of tobacco 18

*Three months after reading this essay, my daughter stopped smoking.

in our gardens and treating the plant with the reverence it deserves, we can redeem• tobacco's soul and restore its self-respect.

Besides, how grim, if one is a smoker, to realize one is smoking a slave. 19

There is a slogan from a battered women's shelter that I especially like: 20
"Peace on earth begins at home." I believe everything does. I think of a slogan for people trying to stop smoking: "Every home a smoke-free zone." Smoking is a form of self-battering that also batters those who must sit by, occasionally cajole• or complain, and helplessly watch. I realize now that as a child I sat by, through the years, and literally watched my father kill himself; surely one such victory in my family, for the rich white men who own the tobacco companies, is enough.

Reading Comprehension Questions

1. The word *eradicating* in "over time, people starve themselves of both food and air, effectively weakening and addicting their children, eventually eradicating themselves" (paragraph 14) means
   a. curing.
   b. feeding.
   c. destroying.
   d. controlling.
2. The word *venerated* in "For thousands of years, it has been venerated by Native Americans as a sacred medicine. They have used it extensively" (paragraph 17) means
   a. honored.
   b. ignored.
   c. ridiculed.
   d. forgotten.
3. Which of the following sentences best expresses the central idea of the essay?
   a. Most people who try to quit smoking are not successful.
   b. Pained by her daughter's cigarette addiction and the misdeeds of the tobacco companies, Walker urges people to stop smoking.
   c. Native Americans have used the tobacco plant for thousands of years as a sacred medicine and in ceremonies of prayer and peace.
   d. Tobacco advertisements that show healthy, attractive people are misleading.
4. Which sentence best expresses the main idea of paragraph 4?
   a. For Walker's father and others, the reality of smoking was very different from the images shown in ads and movies.
   b. Walker's father smoked because he wanted to be as stylish as Prince Albert.
   c. No one rolled his or her own cigarettes by the 1950s.
   d. Walker's father was poor, overweight, and overworked.

5. Which sentence best expresses the main idea of paragraph 5?
   a. Walker does not know when her father began to cough.
   b. When Walker was her daughter's age, she was embarrassed to hear her father wheezing.
   c. Walker's father's cough began quietly but grew to become a major problem.
   d. Walker's father had great difficulty climbing stairs.
6. Walker is especially upset that her daughter smokes Camel cigarettes because
   a. she believes Camels to be especially bad for people's health.
   b. Camels are the brand that Walker herself smoked as a teenager.
   c. Walker's father, who died as a result of smoking, smoked Camels.
   d. Camels' advertisements are glamorous and misleading.
7. When Walker's father picked up his granddaughter at a family reunion, he
   a. burned the child with his cigarette.
   b. put her down quickly so he could have another cigarette.
   c. warned her against smoking.
   d. was too weak to hold her for long.
8. We can infer that Walker
   a. believes people who are poor, uneducated, and nonwhite have been especially victimized by the tobacco industry.
   b. believes that tobacco should be made illegal.
   c. blames her father for her daughter's decision to smoke.
   d. believes Native Americans were wrong to honor the tobacco plant.
9. We can infer that, for Walker, smoking as a teenager
   a. was strictly forbidden by her parents.
   b. was an exciting experiment.
   c. was quickly habit-forming.
   d. was the end of her friendship with Murl, Leon, and "Dog" Farley.
10. We can infer that Walker's daughter
    a. did not care that her mother was concerned about her smoking.
    b. may have been helped to quit smoking by her mother's essay.
    c. remembered her grandfather well.
    d. did not believe that smoking was harmful to people's health.

■ Technique Questions

1. In which parts of her essay does Walker use time order? Paragraphs 2–5 and 12–13

2. Write down what you think are two of the most vivid images in Walker's essay. Then explain how each helps to further her central idea.
(Answers will vary.)

3. How does Walker enlarge the significance of her essay so that it becomes more than the story of her daughter's smoking?
She moves from her daughter's use of Camels to her father, then her and her sister's smoking. In paragraph 14, she uses her daughter and father as a transition to a discussion of Third World countries. Finally, she moves from her feelings for her daughter (16) to feelings for the tobacco plant itself (17). (Wording of answers will vary.)

Discussion Questions

1. How would you deal with a friend who engages in self-destructive behavior, such as smoking, excessive drinking, or taking drugs? Would you ignore the behavior or try to educate the friend about its dangers? Is letting a friend know you are concerned worth risking the friendship?
2. The dangers of smoking are well documented. Study after study shows that smoking leads to a variety of illnesses, including cancer, emphysema, and heart disease. Newer studies are proving that secondhand smoke—smoke that nonsmokers breathe when they are around smokers—is dangerous as well. If you had the power to do so, would you make smoking illegal? Or do you believe that smoking should continue to be an individual's right?
3. Imagine learning that your sixteen-year-old child has begun smoking or drinking, or has become sexually active. Which discovery would worry you most? Would it make a difference if the child were a girl or a boy? What fears would each of these discoveries raise in you? How would you respond to your child?

Writing Assignments

1. Write a paragraph in which you try to persuade a friend to quit smoking. Explain in detail three reasons you think he or she should quit. Use transitions such as *first of all, second, another*, and *finally* as you list the three reasons.

2. In her essay, Walker is critical of the glamorous, healthy image presented by cigarette advertisements. Write a paragraph in which you describe what you think an honest cigarette advertisement would look like. Who would appear in the ad? What would they be doing? What would they be saying? Use the following as a topic sentence, or write one of your own.

   The elements of an honest cigarette "advertisement" would tempt people not to smoke.

   In preparation for this assignment, you might study two or three cigarette ads, using them as inspiration for this assignment. Use the name of a real cigarette or make up a name.

3. What bad habits do *you* have? Write an essay explaining how you believe you acquired one of those habits, how you think it harms you, and how you could rid yourself of it. You might begin by making a list or questioning to help you find a bad habit you wish to write about. (We all have plenty of bad habits, such as smoking, drinking too much, spending money impulsively, biting our nails, eating too much food, and so on.)

   Remember to write an informal outline to guide you in your writing. Here, for example, is one possible outline for this assignment:

   Central idea: A bad habit I intend to change is studying for tests at the last minute.

   (1) I acquired the habit in high school, where studying at the last minute was often good enough.
   For example, I studied for spelling tests in the hallway on the way to class.
   Even history tests were easy to study for because our teacher demanded so little.

   (2) I've learned the hard way that last-minute studying doesn't work well in college.
   During my first quarter, I got the first D I've ever gotten.
   I thought memorizing a few names would get me through my first business class, but was I ever wrong.

   (3) I took a study skills course, and what I learned is helping me get on the right track.
   I learned the benefits of taking class notes, and I'm trying to get better at getting down a written record of each lecture.
   I also learned that keeping up with readings and taking notes on a regular basis are needed for some classes.

The writer of the above outline still has to come up with many more details to expand each of her points. For instance, why did she get the D, and how did that help motivate her to improve her study habits? Also, what techniques is she experimenting with in her effort to improve her note-taking? She could add such details to her outline, or she could begin working them into her essay when she starts writing.

APPENDIXES

Introduction

Six appendixes follow. Appendix A consists of Parts of Speech, and Appendix B is a series of ESL Pointers. Appendixes C and D consist of a diagnostic test and an achievement test that measure many of the skills in this book. The diagnostic test can be taken at the outset of your work; the achievement test can be used to measure your progress at the end of your work. Appendix E supplies answers to the introductory projects and the practice exercises in Part Two. The answers, which you should refer to only after you have worked carefully through each exercise, give you responsibility for testing yourself. (To ensure that the answer key is used as a learning tool only, answers are *not* given for the review tests in Part Two or for the reinforcement tests in Part Three. These answers appear only in the Instructor's Manual; they can be copied and handed out at the discretion of your instructor.) Finally, Appendix F provides handy progress charts that you can use to track your performance on all the tests in the book and the writing assignments as well.

Appendix A

Parts of Speech

Words—the building blocks of sentences—can be divided into eight parts of speech. *Parts of speech* are classifications of words according to their meaning and use in a sentence.

This chapter will explain the eight parts of speech:

nouns	prepositions	conjunctions
pronouns	adjectives	interjections
verbs	adverbs	

Nouns

A *noun* is a word that is used to name something: a person, a place, an object, or an idea. Here are some examples of nouns:

Nouns			
woman	city	pancake	freedom
Alice Walker	street	diamond	possibility
Steve Martin	Chicago	Corvette	mystery

Most nouns begin with a lowercase letter and are known as *common nouns.* These nouns name general things. Some nouns, however, begin with a capital letter. They are called *proper nouns.* While a common noun refers to a person or thing in general, a proper noun names someone or something specific. For example, *woman* is a common noun—it doesn't name a particular woman. On the other hand, *Alice Walker* is a proper noun because it names a specific woman.

Practice 1

Insert any appropriate noun into each of the following blanks.
Answers will vary.

1. The shoplifter stole a(n) __________________ from the department store.
2. __________________ threw the football to me.
3. Tiny messages were scrawled on the __________________.
4. A __________________ crashed through the window.
5. Give the __________________ to Keiko.

Singular and Plural Nouns

A *singular noun* names one person, place, object, or idea. A *plural noun* refers to two or more persons, places, objects, or ideas. Most singular nouns can be made plural with the addition of an *s*.

Some nouns, like *box*, have irregular plurals. You can check the plural of nouns you think may be irregular by looking up the singular form in a dictionary.

Singular and Plural Nouns

Singular	*Plural*
goat	goats
alley	alleys
friend	friends
truth	truths
box	boxes

- For more information on nouns, see "Subjects and Verbs," pages 87–95

Practice 2

Underline the three nouns in each sentence. Some are singular, and some are plural.

1. Two bats swooped over the heads of the frightened children.
2. The artist has purple paint on her sleeve.
3. The lost dog has fleas and a broken leg.

4. Tiffany does her homework in green ink.
5. Some farmers plant seeds by moonlight.

Pronouns

A *pronoun* is a word that stands for a noun. Pronouns eliminate the need for constant repetition. Look at the following sentences:

> The phone rang, and Malik answered the phone.
>
> Lisa met Lisa's friends in the record store at the mall. Lisa meets Lisa's friends there every Saturday.
>
> The waiter rushed over to the new customers. The new customers asked the waiter for menus and coffee.

Now look at how much clearer and smoother these sentences sound with pronouns.

> The phone rang, and Malik answered *it*.
> (The pronoun *it* is used to replace the word *phone*.)
>
> Lisa met *her* friends in the record store at the mall. *She* meets *them* there every Saturday.
> (The pronoun *her* is used to replace the word *Lisa's*. The pronoun *she* replaces *Lisa*. The pronoun *them* replaces the words *Lisa's friends*.)
>
> The waiter rushed over to the new customers. *They* asked *him* for menus and coffee.
> (The pronoun *they* is used to replace the words *the new customers*. The pronoun *him* replaces the words *the waiter*.)

Following is a list of commonly used pronouns known as personal pronouns:

Personal Pronouns

I	you	he	she	it	we	they
me	your	him	her	its	us	them
my	yours	his	hers		our	their

Practice 3

Fill in each blank with the appropriate personal pronoun.

1. André feeds his pet lizard every day before school. ___He___ also gives ___it___ flies in the afternoon.
2. The reporter interviewed the striking workers. ___They___ told ___him (or her)___ about their demand for higher wages and longer breaks.
3. Students should save all returned tests. ___They___ should also keep ___their___ review sheets.
4. The pilot announced that we would fly through some air pockets. ___He (or She)___ said that we should be past ___them___ soon.
5. Adolfo returned the calculator to Sheila last Friday. But Sheila insists that ___she___ never got ___it___ back.

There are several types of pronouns. For convenient reference, they are described briefly in the box below.

Types of Pronouns

Personal pronouns can act in a sentence as subjects, objects, or possessives.

Singular: I, me, my, mine, you, your, yours, he, him, his, she, her, hers, it, its

Plural: we, us, our, ours, you, your, yours, they, them, their, theirs

Relative pronouns refer to someone or something already mentioned in the sentence.

who, whose, whom, which, that

Interrogative pronouns are used to ask questions.

who, whose, whom, which, what

Demonstrative pronouns are used to point out particular persons or things.

this, that, these, those

Note: Do not use *them* (as in *them* shoes), *this here, that there, these here,* or *those there* to point out.

Continued

Reflexive pronouns are those that end in *-self* or *-selves*. A reflexive pronoun is used as the object of a verb (as in *Cary cut **herself***) or the object of a preposition (as in *Jack sent a birthday card to **himself***) when the subject of the verb is the same as the object.

Singular: myself, yourself, himself, herself, itself

Plural: ourselves, yourselves, themselves

Intensive pronouns have exactly the same forms as reflexive pronouns. The difference is in how they are used. Intensive pronouns are used to add emphasis. (*I **myself** will need to read the contract before I sign it.*)

Indefinite pronouns do not refer to a particular person or thing.

each, either, everyone, nothing, both, several, all, any, most, none

Reciprocal pronouns express shared actions or feelings.

each other, one another

- For more information on pronouns, see "Pronoun Types," pages 207–219.

Verbs

Every complete sentence must contain at least one verb. There are two types of verbs: action verbs and linking verbs.

Action Verbs

An *action verb* tells what is being done in a sentence. For example, look at the following sentences:

Mr. Jensen *swatted* at the bee with his hand.

Rainwater *poured* into the storm sewer.

The children *chanted* the words to the song.

In these sentences, the verbs are *swatted, poured*, and *chanted*. These words are all action verbs; they tell what is happening in each sentence.

- For more about action verbs, see "Subjects and Verbs," pages 87–95.

Practice 4

Insert an appropriate word in each blank. That word will be an action verb; it will tell what is happening in the sentence.

Answers will vary.

1. The surgeon ________________ through the first layer of skin.
2. The animals in the cage ________________ all day.
3. An elderly woman on the street ________________ me for directions.
4. The boy next door ________________ our lawn every other week.
5. Our instructor ________________ our papers over the weekend.

Linking Verbs

Some verbs are *linking verbs.* These verbs link (or join) a noun to something that is said about it. For example, look at the following sentence:

> The clouds *are* steel gray.

In this sentence, *are* is a linking verb. It joins the noun *clouds* to words that describe it: *steel gray.*

Other common linking verbs include *am, is, was, were, look, feel, sound, appear, seem,* and *become.*

- For more about linking verbs, see "Subjects and Verbs," pages 87–95.

Practice 5

In each blank, insert one of the following linking verbs: *am, feel, is, look, were.* Use each linking verb once.

1. The important papers ____were____ in a desk drawer.
2. I ____am____ anxious to get my test back.
3. The bananas ____look____ ripe.
4. The grocery store ____is____ open until 11 P.M.
5. Whenever I ____feel____ angry, I go off by myself to calm down.

Helping Verbs

Sometimes the verb of a sentence consists of more than one word. In these cases, the main verb will be joined by one or more *helping verbs*. Look at the following sentence:

The basketball team *will be leaving* for their game at six o'clock.

In this sentence, the main verb is *leaving*. The helping verbs are *will* and *be*.

Other helping verbs include *do, has, have, may, would, can, must, could*, and *should*.

- For more information about helping verbs, see "Subjects and Verbs," pages 87–95, and "Irregular Verbs," pages 161–171.

Practice 6

In each blank, insert one of the following helping verbs: *does, must, should, could, has been*. Use each helping verb once.

1. You __should (or must)__ start writing your paper this weekend.
2. The victim __could__ describe her attacker in great detail.
3. You __must (or should)__ rinse the dishes before putting them into the dishwasher.
4. My neighbor __has been__ arrested for drunk driving.
5. The bus driver __does__ not make any extra stops.

Prepositions

A *preposition* is a word that connects a noun or a pronoun to another word in the sentence. For example, look at the following sentence:

A man *in* the bus was snoring loudly.

In is a preposition. It connects the noun *bus* to *man*. Here is a list of common prepositions:

Prepositions

about	before	down	like	to
above	behind	during	of	toward
across	below	except	off	under
after	beneath	for	on	up
among	beside	from	over	with
around	between	in	since	without
at	by	into	through	

The noun or pronoun that a preposition connects to another word in the sentence is called the *object* of the preposition. A group of words beginning with a preposition and ending with its object is called a *prepositional phrase.* The words *in the bus*, for example, are a prepositional phrase.

Now read the following sentences and explanations.

An ant was crawling *up the teacher's leg*.

The noun *leg* is the object of the preposition *up*. *Up* connects *leg* with the word *crawling*. The prepositional phrase *up the teacher's leg* describes *crawling*. It tells just where the ant was crawling.

The man *with the black moustache* left the restaurant quickly.

The noun *moustache* is the object of the preposition *with*. The prepositional phrase *with the black moustache* describes the word *man*. It tells us exactly which man left the restaurant quickly.

The plant *on the windowsill* was a present *from my mother*.

The noun *windowsill* is the object of the preposition *on*. The prepositional phrase *on the windowsill* describes the word *plant*. It describes exactly which plant was a present.

There is a second prepositional phrase in this sentence. The preposition is *from*, and its object is *mother*. The prepositional phrase *from my mother* explains *present*. It tells who gave the present.

- For more about prepositions, see "Subjects and Verbs," pages 87–95, and "Sentence Variety II," pages 251–264.

Practice 7

In each blank, insert one of the following prepositions: *of, by, with, in, without.* Use each preposition once.

1. The letter from his girlfriend had been sprayed ___with___ perfume.
2. The weedkiller quickly killed the dandelions ___in___ our lawn.
3. ___Without___ giving any notice, the tenant moved out of the expensive apartment.
4. Donald hungrily ate three scoops ___of___ ice cream and an order of French fries.
5. The crates ___by___ the back door contain glass bottles and old newspapers.

Adjectives

An *adjective* is a word that describes a noun (the name of a person, place, or thing). Look at the following sentence.

The dog lay down on a mat in front of the fireplace.

Now look at this sentence when adjectives have been inserted.

The *shaggy* dog lay down on a *worn* mat in front of the fireplace.

The adjective *shaggy* describes the noun *dog*; the adjective *worn* describes the noun *mat*. Adjectives add spice to our writing. They also help us to identify particular people, places, or things.

Adjectives can be found in two places:

1 An adjective may come before the word it describes (a *damp* night, the *moldy* bread, a *striped* umbrella).

2 An adjective that describes the subject of a sentence may come after a linking verb. The linking verb may be a form of the verb *be* (he *is* **furious**, I *am* **exhausted**, they are **hungry**). Other linking verbs include *feel, look, sound, smell, taste, appear, seem,* and *become* (the soup *tastes* **salty**, your hands *feel* **dry**, the dog *seems* **lost**).

Note The words *a, an,* and *the* (called *articles*) are generally classified as adjectives.

- For more information on adjectives, see "Adjectives and Adverbs," pages 221–227.

Practice 8

Write any appropriate adjective in each blank.

Answers will vary.

1. The ____________ pizza was eaten greedily by the ____________ teenagers.
2. Melissa gave away the sofa because it was ____________ and ____________.
3. Although the alley is ____________ and ____________, Jian often takes it as a shortcut home.
4. The restaurant throws away lettuce that is ____________ and tomatoes that are ____________.
5. When I woke up in the morning, I had a(n) ____________ fever and a(n) ____________ throat.

Adverbs

An *adverb* is a word that describes a verb, an adjective, or another adverb. Many adverbs end in the letters *-ly*. Look at the following sentence:

> The canary sang in the pet store window as the shoppers greeted each other.

Now look at this sentence after adverbs have been inserted.

> The canary sang *softly* in the pet store window as the shoppers *loudly* greeted each other.

The adverbs add details to the sentence. They also allow the reader to contrast the singing of the canary and the noise the shoppers are making.

Look at the following sentences and the explanations of how adverbs are used in each case.

> The chef yelled **angrily** at the young waiter.
> (The adverb *angrily* describes the verb *yelled.*)

> My mother has an **extremely** busy schedule on Tuesdays.
> (The adverb *extremely* describes the adjective *busy.*)

The sick man spoke **very** faintly to his loyal nurse.

(The adverb *very* describes the adverb *faintly*.)

Some adverbs do not end in *-ly*. Examples include *very, often, never, always,* and *well.*

- For more information on adverbs, see "Adjectives and Adverbs," pages 221–227.

Practice 9

Fill in each blank with any appropriate adverb.

Answers will vary.

1. The water in the pot boiled ____________.
2. Carla ____________ drove the car through ____________ moving traffic.
3. The telephone operator spoke ____________ to the young child.
4. The game show contestant waved ____________ to his family in the audience.
5. Wes ____________ studies, so it's no surprise that he did ____________ poorly on his finals.

Conjunctions

A *conjunction* is a word that connects. There are two types of conjunctions: coordinating and subordinating.

Coordinating Conjunctions

Coordinating conjunctions join two equal ideas. Look at the following sentence:

Kevin *and* Steve interviewed for the job, *but* their friend Anne got it.

In this sentence, the coordinating conjunction *and* connects the proper nouns *Kevin* and *Steve*. The coordinating conjunction *but* connects the first part of the sentence, *Kevin and Steve interviewed for the job*, to the second part, *their friend Anne got it*.

Following is a list of all the coordinating conjunctions. In this book, they are simply called *joining words*.

Coordinating Conjunctions (Joining Words)			
and	so	nor	yet
but	or	for	

- For more on coordinating conjunctions, see information on joining words in "Run-Ons," pages 117–134, and "Sentence Variety I," pages 135–149.

Practice 10

Write a coordinating conjunction in each blank. Choose from the following: *and, but, so, or, nor*. Use each conjunction once.

1. Either Jerome ____or____ Alex scored the winning touchdown.
2. I expected roses for my birthday, ____but____ I received a vase of plastic tulips from the discount store.
3. The cafeteria was serving liver and onions for lunch, ____so____ I bought a sandwich at the corner deli.
4. Marian brought a pack of playing cards ____and____ a pan of brownies to the company picnic.
5. Neither my sofa ____nor____ my armchair matches the rug in my living room.

Subordinating Conjunctions

When a *subordinating conjunction* is added to a word group, the words can no longer stand alone as an independent sentence. They are no longer a complete thought. For example, look at the following sentence:

> Karen fainted in class.

The word group *Karen fainted in class* is a complete thought. It can stand alone as a sentence. See what happens when a subordinating conjunction is added to a complete thought:

> *When* Karen fainted in class

Now the words cannot stand alone as a sentence. They are dependent on other words to complete the thought:

When Karen fainted in class, we put her feet up on some books.

In this book, a word that begins a dependent word group is called a *dependent word*. Subordinating conjunctions are common dependent words. Below are some subordinating conjunctions.

Subordinating Conjunctions

after	even if	unless	where
although	even though	until	wherever
as	if	when	whether
because	since	whenever	while
before	though		

Following are some more sentences with subordinating conjunctions:

After she finished her last exam, Irina said, "Now I can relax."
(*After she finished her last exam* is not a complete thought. It is dependent on the rest of the words to make up a complete sentence.)

Lamont listens to books on tape **while** he drives to work.
(*While he drives to work* cannot stand by itself as a sentence. It depends on the rest of the sentence to make up a complete thought.)

Since apples were on sale, we decided to make an apple pie for dessert.
(*Since apples were on sale* is not a complete sentence. It depends on *we decided to make an apple pie for dessert* to complete the thought.)

- For more information on subordinating conjunctions, see information on dependent words in "Fragments," pages 97–115; "Run-Ons," pages 117–134; "Sentence Variety I," pages 135–149; and "Sentence Variety II," pages 251–264.

Practice 11

Write a logical subordinating conjunction in each blank. Choose from the following: *even though, because, until, when, before*. Use each conjunction once.

1. The bank was closed down by federal regulators __because__ it lost more money than it earned.
2. __When__ Paula wants to look mysterious, she wears dark sunglasses and a scarf.
3. __Even though__ the restaurant was closing in fifteen minutes, customers sipped their coffee slowly and continued to talk.
4. __Before__ anyone else could answer it, Leon rushed to the phone and whispered, "Is that you?"
5. The waiter was instructed not to serve any food __until__ the guest of honor arrived.

Interjections

An *interjection* is a word that can stand independently and is used to express emotion. Examples are *oh, wow, ouch,* and *oops*. These words are usually not found in formal writing.

> "*Hey!*" yelled Maggie. "That's my bike."
>
> *Oh*, we're late for class.

A Final Note

A word may function as more than one part of speech. For example, the word *dust* can be a verb or a noun, depending on its role in the sentence.

> I *dust* my bedroom once a month, whether it needs it or not. (verb)
>
> The top of my refrigerator is covered with an inch of *dust*. (noun)

Appendix B

ESL Pointers

This section covers rules that most native speakers of English take for granted but that are useful for speakers of English as a second language (ESL).

Articles

Types of Articles

An *article* is a noun marker—it signals that a noun will follow. There are two kinds of articles: indefinite and definite. The indefinite articles are *a* and *an*. Use *a* before a word that begins with a consonant sound:

a desk, **a p**hotograph, **a u**nicycle

(A is used before *unicycle* because the *u* in that word sounds like the consonant *y* plus *u,* not a vowel sound.)

Use *an* before a word beginning with a vowel sound:

an error, **an o**bject, **an h**onest woman

(*Honest* begins with a vowel sound because the *h* is silent.)

The definite article is *the.*

the sofa, **the** cup

An article may come right before a noun:

a magazine, **the** candle

Or an article may be separated from the noun by words that describe the noun:

a popular magazine, **the** fat red candle

Note There are various other noun markers, including quantity words (*a few, many, a lot of*), numerals (*one, thirteen, 710*), demonstrative adjectives (*this, these*), adjectives (*my, your, our*), and possessive nouns (*Raoul's, the school's*).

Articles with Count and Noncount Nouns

To know whether to use an article with a noun and which article to use, you must recognize count and noncount nouns. (A *noun* is a word used to name something—a person, place, thing, or idea.)

Count nouns name people, places, things, or ideas that can be counted and made into plurals, such as *pillow, heater*, and *mail carrier* (*one pillow, two heaters, three mail carriers*).

Noncount nouns refer to things or ideas that cannot be counted and therefore cannot be made into plurals, such as *sunshine, gold,* and *toast*. The box below lists and illustrates common types of noncount nouns.

Common Noncount Nouns

Abstractions and emotions: justice, tenderness, courage, knowledge, embarrassment

Activities: jogging, thinking, wondering, golf, hoping, sleep

Foods: oil, rice, pie, butter, spaghetti, broccoli

Gases and vapors: carbon dioxide, oxygen, smoke, steam, air

Languages and areas of study: Korean, Italian, geology, arithmetic, history

Liquids: coffee, kerosene, lemonade, tea, water, bleach

Materials that come in bulk or mass form: straw, firewood, sawdust, cat litter, cement

Natural occurrences: gravity, sleet, rain, lightning, rust

Other things that cannot be counted: clothing, experience, trash, luggage, room, furniture, homework, machinery, cash, news, transportation, work

The quantity of a noncount noun can be expressed with a word or words called a *qualifier*, such as *some, more, a unit of*, and so on. In the following two examples, the qualifiers are shown in *italic* type, and the noncount nouns are shown in **boldface** type.

How *much* **experience** have you had as a salesclerk?

Our tiny kitchen doesn't have *enough* **room** for a table and chairs.

Some words can be either count or noncount nouns depending on whether they refer to one or more individual items or to something in general:

Three **chickens** are running around our neighbor's yard.

(This sentence refers to particular chickens; *chicken* in this case is a count noun.)

Would you like some more **chicken**?

(This sentence refers to chicken in general; in this case, *chicken* is a noncount noun.)

Using *a* or *an* with Nonspecific Singular Count Nouns Use *a* or *an* with singular nouns that are nonspecific. A noun is nonspecific when the reader doesn't know its specific identity.

A photograph can be almost magical. It saves a moment's image for many years.

(The sentence refers to any photograph, not a specific one.)

An article in the newspaper today made me laugh.

(The reader isn't familiar with the article. This is the first time it is mentioned.)

Using *the* with Specific Nouns In general, use *the* with all specific nouns—specific singular, plural, and noncount nouns. A noun is specific—and therefore requires the article *the*—in the following cases:

- When it has already been mentioned once:

An article in the newspaper today made me laugh. **The** article was about a talking parrot who frightened away a thief.

(*The* is used with the second mention of *article*.)

- When it is identified by a word or phrase in the sentence:

The CD that is playing now is a favorite of mine.

(*CD* is identified by the words *that is playing now*.)

- When its identity is suggested by the general context:

The service at Joe's Bar and Grill is never fast.

(*Service* is identified by the words *at Joe's Bar and Grill.*)

- When it is unique:

  Some people see a man's face in **the** moon, while others see a rabbit. (Earth has only one moon.)

- When it comes after a superlative adjective (for example, *best, biggest*, or *wisest)*:

  The funniest movie I've seen is *Young Frankenstein.*

Omitting Articles Omit articles with nonspecific plurals and nonspecific noncount nouns. Plurals and noncount nouns are nonspecific when they refer to something in general.

Stories are popular with most children.
Service is almost as important as food to a restaurant's success.
Movies can be rented from many supermarkets as well as video stores.

Using *the* with Proper Nouns

Proper nouns name particular people, places, things, or ideas and are always capitalized. Most proper nouns do not require articles; those that do, however, require *the*. Following are general guidelines about when not to use *the* and when to use *the*.

Do not use *the* for most singular proper nouns, including names of the following:

- *People and animals* (Ronald Reagan, Fluffy)
- *Continents, states, cities, streets, and parks* (South America, Utah, Boston, Baker Street, People's Park)
- *Most countries* (Cuba, Indonesia, Ireland)
- *Individual bodies of water, islands, and mountains* (Lake Michigan, Captiva Island, Mount McKinley)

Use *the* for the following types of proper nouns:

- *Plural proper nouns* (the Harlem Globetrotters, the Marshall Islands, the Netherlands, the Atlas Mountains)
- *Names of large geographic areas, deserts, oceans, seas, and rivers* (the Midwest, the Kalahari Desert, the Pacific Ocean, the Sargasso Sea, the Nile River)
- *Names with the format* "the _______ of _______" (the king of Morocco, the Strait of Gibraltar, the University of Illinois)

Practice

Underline the correct word or words in parentheses.

1. (Map, The map) on the wall is old and out of date.
2. To show (affection, the affection), a cat will rub against you and purr.
3. This morning my daughter sang (a song, the song) I had not heard before.
4. She had learned (a song, the song) in her kindergarten class.
5. When Javier takes a test, he always begins by answering (the easiest, easiest) questions.
6. (Nile River, The Nile River) has been used for irrigation in Egypt since 4,000 B.C.
7. Although (Sahara Desert, the Sahara Desert) is very hot during the day, it can get terribly cold at night.
8. The reason we don't fall off the Earth is the pull of (gravity, the gravity).
9. (Patience, The patience) is not always a virtue.
10. Don't forget to put the (garbage, garbages) out to be picked up Wednesday morning.

Subjects and Verbs

Avoiding Repeated Subjects

In English, a particular subject can be used only once in a word group with a subject and a verb (that is, a clause). Don't repeat a subject in the same word group by following a noun with a pronoun.

Incorrect: My *parents they* live in Miami.

Correct: My **parents** live in Miami.

Correct: **They** live in Miami.

Even when the subject and verb are separated by several words, the subject cannot be repeated in the same word group.

Incorrect: The *windstorm* that happened last night *it* damaged our roof.

Correct: The **windstorm** that happened last night **damaged** our roof.

Including Pronoun Subjects and Linking Verbs

Some languages omit a subject that is a pronoun, but in English, every sentence other than a command must have a subject. In a command, the subject *you* is understood: (You) Hand in your papers now.

Incorrect: The soup tastes terrible. *Is* much too salty.

Correct: The soup tastes terrible. **It is** much too salty.

Every English sentence must also have a verb, even when the meaning of the sentence is clear without the verb.

Incorrect: The table covered with old newspapers.

Correct: The table **is** covered with old newspapers.

Including *There* and *Here* at the Beginning of Sentences

Some English sentences begin with *there* or *here* plus a linking verb (usually a form of *to be: is, are,* and so on). In such sentences, the verb comes before the subject.

There are ants all over the kitchen counter.

(The subject is the plural noun *ants*, so the plural verb *are* is used.)

Here is the bug spray.

(The subject is the singular noun *spray*, so the singular verb *is* is used.)

In sentences like those above, remember not to omit *there* or *here*.

Incorrect: *Are* several tests scheduled for Friday.

Correct: **There are** several tests scheduled for Friday.

Not Using the Progressive Tense of Certain Verbs

The progressive tenses are made up of forms of *be* plus the *-ing* form of the main verb. They express actions or conditions still in progress at a particular time.

The garden **will be blooming** when you visit me in June.

However, verbs for mental states, the senses, possession, and inclusion are normally not used in the progressive tense.

Incorrect: I **am knowing** a lot about auto mechanics.

Correct: I **know** a lot about auto mechanics.

Incorrect: Gerald **is having** a job as a supermarket cashier.

Correct: Gerald **has** a job as a supermarket cashier.

Common verbs not generally used in the progressive tense are listed in the following box.

Common Verbs Not Generally Used in the Progressive

Verbs relating to thoughts, attitudes and desires: agree, believe, imagine, know, like, love, prefer, think, understand, want, wish

Verbs showing sense perceptions: hear, see, smell, taste

Verbs relating to appearances: appear, seem, look

Verbs showing possession: belong, have, own, possess

Verbs showing inclusion: contain, include

Using Gerunds and Infinitives after Verbs

Before learning the rules about gerunds and infinitives, you must understand what they are. A *gerund* is the *-ing* form of a verb that is used as a noun:

Reading is a good way to improve one's vocabulary.

(*Reading* is the subject of the sentence.)

An *infinitive* is *to* plus the basic form of the verb (the form in which the verb is listed in the dictionary), as in **to eat**. The infinitive can function as an adverb, an adjective, or a noun.

On weekends, Betsy works at a convenience store **to make** some extra money.

(*To make some extra money* functions as an adverb that describes the verb *works*.)

My advisor showed me a good way **to study** for a test.

(*To study for a test* functions as an adjective describing the noun *way*.)

To forgive can be a relief.

(*To forgive* functions as a noun—it is the subject of the verb *can be*.)

Some verbs can be followed by only a gerund or only an infinitive; other verbs can be followed by either. Examples are given in the following lists. There are many others; watch for them in your reading.

Verb + gerund (*enjoy* + *skiing*)
Verb + preposition + gerund (*think* + *about* + *coming*)

Some verbs can be followed by a gerund but not by an infinitive. In many cases, there is a preposition (such as *for, in*, or *of*) between the verb and the gerund. Following are some verbs and verb-preposition combinations that can be followed by gerunds but not by infinitives:

admit	deny	look forward to
apologize for	discuss	postpone
appreciate	dislike	practice
approve of	enjoy	suspect of
avoid	feel like	talk about
be used to	finish	thank for
believe in	insist on	think about

Incorrect: The governor *avoids to make* enemies.
Correct: The governor **avoids making** enemies.

Incorrect: I *enjoy to go* to movies alone.
Correct: I **enjoy going** to movies alone.

Verb + infinitive (*agree* + *to leave*)

Following are common verbs that can be followed by an infinitive but not by a gerund:

agree	decide	manage
arrange	expect	refuse
claim	have	wait

Incorrect: I *arranged paying* my uncle's bills while he was ill.

Correct: I **arranged to pay** my uncle's bills while he was ill.

Verb + noun or pronoun + infinitive (*cause + them + to flee*)

Below are common verbs that are first followed by a noun or pronoun and then by an infinitive, not a gerund.

cause	force	remind
command	persuade	warn

Incorrect: The flood *forced them leaving* their home.

Correct: The flood **forced them to leave** their home.

Following are common verbs that can be followed either by an infinitive alone or by a noun or pronoun and an infinitive:

ask	need	want
expect	promise	would like

Rita **expects to go** to college.

Rita's parents **expect her to go** to college.

Verb + gerund or infinitive (*begin + packing* or *begin + to pack*)

Following are verbs that can be followed by either a gerund or an infinitive:

begin	hate	prefer
continue	love	start

The meaning of each verb in the box above remains the same or almost the same whether a gerund or an infinitive is used.

I love **to sleep** late.
I love **sleeping** late.

With the verbs below, the gerunds and the infinitives have very different meanings.

forget	remember	stop

Yuri **forgot putting money** in the parking meter.
(He put money in the parking meter, but then he forgot that he had done so.)

Yuri **forgot to put money** in the parking meter.
(He neglected to put money in the parking meter.)

Practice

Underline the correct word or words in parentheses.

1. The coffee table (wobbles, it wobbles) because one leg is loose.
2. The firewood is very dry. (Is, It is) burning quickly.
3. (Are knives and forks, There are knives and forks) in that drawer.
4. Olivia (seems, is seeming) sad today.
5. Our instructor warned us (studying, to study) hard for the exam.
6. When the little boy saw his birthday presents, he (very excited, became very excited).
7. Do you (feel like walking, feel like to walk) home?
8. A vegetarian (refuses eating, refuses to eat) meat.
9. The alarm on my watch (it started beeping, started beeping) in the middle of the church service.
10. I like small parties, but my boyfriend (prefers, is preferring) large noisy ones.

Adjectives

Following the Order of Adjectives in English

Adjectives describe nouns and pronouns. In English, an adjective usually comes directly before the word it describes or after a linking verb (a form of *be* or a "sense" verb such as *look*, *seem,* or *taste*), in which case it modifies the subject of the sentence. In each of the following two sentences, the adjective is **boldfaced** and the noun it describes is *italicized.*

Marta has **beautiful** *eyes.*

Marta's *eyes* are **beautiful**.

When more than one adjective modifies the same noun, the adjectives are usually stated in a certain order, though there are often exceptions. Following is the typical order of English adjectives:

Typical Order of Adjectives in a Series

1 Article or other noun marker: a, an, the, Helen's, this, seven, your
2 Opinion adjective: rude, enjoyable, surprising, easy
3 Size: tall, huge, small, compact
4 Shape: triangular, oval, round, square
5 Age: ancient, new, old, young
6 Color: gray, blue, pink, green
7 Nationality: Greek, Thai, Korean, Ethiopian
8 Religion: Hindu, Methodist, Jewish, Islamic
9 Material: fur, copper, stone, velvet
10 Noun used as an adjective: book (as in *book report*), picture (as in *picture frame*), tea (as in *tea bag*)

Here are some examples of the order of adjectives:

an exciting new movie
the petite young Irish woman
my favorite Chinese restaurant
Greta's long brown leather coat

In general, use no more than two or three adjectives after the article or another noun marker. Numerous adjectives in a series can be awkward: **that comfortable big old green velvet** couch.

Using the Present and Past Participles as Adjectives

The present participle ends in *-ing*. Past participles of regular verbs end in *-ed* or *-d*; a list of the past participles of many common irregular verbs appears on pages 163–164. Both types of participles may be used as adjectives. A participle used as an adjective may come before the word it describes:

There was a **frowning** *security guard.*

A participle used as an adjective may also follow a linking verb and describe the subject of the sentence:

The *security guard* was **frowning**.

While both present and past participles of a particular verb may be used as adjectives, their meanings differ. Use the present participle to describe whoever or whatever causes a feeling:

a **disappointing** *date*
(The date *caused* the disappointment.)

Use the past participle to describe whoever or whatever experiences the feeling:

the **disappointed** *neighbor*
(The neighbor *is* disappointed.)

Here are two more sentences that illustrate the differing meanings of present and past participles.

The waiter was **irritating**.
The diners were **irritated**.
(The waiter caused the irritation; the diners experienced the irritation.)

The following box shows pairs of present and past participles with similar distinctions.

annoying / annoyed	exhausting / exhausted
boring / bored	fascinating / fascinated
confusing / confused	tiring / tired
depressing / depressed	surprising / surprised
exciting / excited	

Practice

Underline the correct word or wording in parentheses.

1. When my grandfather died, he left me his (big old oak, old big oak) seaman's chest.
2. The guest lecturer at today's class was a (young Vietnamese Buddhist, Vietnamese Buddhist young) nun.
3. Yolanda's family lives in a (gray huge stone, huge gray stone) farmhouse.
4. Doesn't working all day and studying at night make you very (tired, tiring)?
5. The (fascinated, fascinating) children begged the magician to tell them how he made a rabbit disappear.

Prepositions Used for Time and Place

The use of a preposition in English is often not based on its common meaning, and there are many exceptions to general rules. As a result, correct use of prepositions must be learned gradually through experience. Following is a chart showing how three of the most common prepositions are used in some customary references to time and place:

Use of *On, In,* and *At* to Refer to Time and Place

Time

On *a specific day:* on Wednesday, on January 11, on Halloween

In *a part of a day:* in the morning, in the daytime (but *at* night)

In *a month or a year:* in October, in 1776

Continued

***In** a period of time:* in a second, in a few days, in a little while

***At** a specific time:* at 11 P.M., at midnight, at sunset, at lunchtime

Place

***On** a surface:* on the shelf, on the sidewalk, on the roof

***In** a place that is enclosed:* in the bathroom, in the closet, in the drawer

***At** a specific location:* at the restaurant, at the zoo, at the school

Practice

Underline the correct preposition in parentheses.

1. May I come see you (on, at) Saturday?
2. We will eat dinner (on, at) 7 P.M.
3. I found this book (on, in) the library.
4. Alex will be leaving for the army (in, at) a week.
5. David and Lisa met one another (on, at) the post office.

Review Test

Underline the correct word or words in parentheses.

1. I had to pull off the road because of the heavy (hail, hails).
2. (Are, There are) fresh cookies on the kitchen table.
3. Theresa does not like living alone—she becomes (frightening, frightened) at every little sound.
4. Have you gotten used to working (in, at) night?
5. Carla (practiced to give, practiced giving) her speech at least ten times.
6. What a (pretty red, red pretty) scarf you are wearing today!
7. That antique car (belongs to, is belonging to) my cousin.
8. Fireworks are set off (on, in) the Fourth of July to commemorate the American Revolution.
9. The newlyweds' apartment does not contain much (furnitures, furniture).
10. Paul's favorite pasttime is going to (the rock concerts, rock concerts).

Appendix C

Sentence-Skills Diagnostic Test

Part 1

This diagnostic test will help check your knowledge of a number of sentence skills. In each item below, certain words are underlined. Write *X* in the answer space if you think a mistake appears at the underlined part. Write *C* in the answer space if you think the underlined part is correct.

The headings within the text ("Fragments," "Run-Ons," and so on) will give you clues to the mistakes to look for. However, you do not have to understand the heading to find a mistake. What you are checking is your own sense of effective written English.

Fragments

X 1. Because I didn't want to get wet. I waited for a break in the downpour. Then I ran for the car like an Olympic sprinter.

C 2. The baby birds chirped loudly, especially when their mother brought food to them. Their mouths gaped open hungrily.

X 3. Trying to avoid running into anyone. Cal wheeled his baby son around the crowded market. He wished that strollers came equipped with flashing hazard lights.

X 4. The old woman combed out her long, gray hair. She twisted it into two thick braids. And wrapped them around her head like a crown.

Run-Ons

X 5. Irene fixed fruits and healthy sandwiches for her son's lunch, he traded them for cupcakes, cookies, and chips.

X 6. Angie's dark eyes were the color of mink they matched her glowing complexion.

C 7. My mother keeps sending me bottles of vitamins, but I keep forgetting to take them.

X 8. The little boy watched the line of ants march across the ground, he made a wall of Popsicle sticks to halt the ants' advance.

Standard English Verbs

C 9. When she's upset, Mary tells her troubles to her houseplants.

X 10. The street musician counted the coins in his donations basket and pack his trumpet in its case.

X 11. I tried to pull off my rings, but they was stuck on my swollen fingers.

X 12. Belle's car have a horn that plays six different tunes.

Irregular Verbs

X 13. I've swam in this lake for years, and I've never seen it so shallow.

X 14. The phone rung once and then stopped.

C 15. Five different people had brought huge bowls of potato salad to the barbecue.

C 16. The metal ice cube trays froze to the bottom of the freezer.

Subject-Verb Agreement

X 17. The records in my collection is arranged in alphabetical order.

C 18. There was only one burner working on the old gas stove.

X 19. My aunt and uncle gives a party every Groundhog Day.

X 20. One of my sweaters have moth holes in the sleeves.

Consistent Verb Tense

C 21. After I turned off the ignition, the engine continued to sputter for several minutes.

X 22. Before cleaning the oven, I lined the kitchen floor with newspapers, open the windows, and shook the can of aerosol foam.

Pronoun Reference, Agreement, and Point of View

C 23. All visitors should stay in their cars while driving through the wild animal park.

X 24. At the library, they showed me how to use the microfilm machines.

X 25. As I slowed down at the scene of the accident, you could see long black skid marks on the highway.

Pronoun Types

X 26. My husband is more sentimental than me.

C 27. Andy and I made ice cream in an old-fashioned wooden machine.

Adjectives and Adverbs

X 28. Brian drives so reckless that no one will join his carpool.

C 29. Miriam pulled impatiently at the rusty zipper.

X 30. I am more happier with myself now that I earn my own money.

C 31. The last screw on the license plate was the most corroded one of all.

Misplaced Modifiers

X 32. I stretched out on the lounge chair wearing my bikini bathing suit.

X 33. I replaced the shingle on the roof that was loose.

Dangling Modifiers

X 34. While doing the dishes, a glass shattered in the soapy water.

C 35. Pedaling as fast as possible, Todd tried to outrace the snapping dog.

Faulty Parallelism

X 36. Before I could take a bath, I had to pick up the damp towels on the floor, gather up the loose toys in the room, and the tub had to be scrubbed out.

X 37. I've tried several cures for my headaches, including drugs, meditation, exercise, and massaging my head.

Capital Letters

C 38. This fall we plan to visit Cape Cod.

X 39. Vern ordered a set of tools from the sears catalog.

C 40. When my aunt visits us, she insists on doing all the cooking.

X 41. Maureen asked, "will you split a piece of cheesecake with me?"

Numbers and Abbreviations

X 42. Before I could stop myself, I had eaten 6 glazed doughnuts.

C 43. At 10:45 A.M., a partial eclipse of the sun will begin.

X 44. Larry, who is now over six ft. tall, can no longer sleep comfortably in a twin bed.

End Marks

C 45. Jane wondered if her husband was telling the truth.

C 46. Does that stew need some salt?

Apostrophe

X 47. Elizabeths thick, curly hair is her best feature.

X 48. I tried to see through the interesting envelope sent to my sister but couldnt.

C 49. Pam's heart almost stopped beating when Roger jumped out of the closet.

X 50. The logs' in the fireplace crumbled in a shower of sparks.

Quotation Marks

C 51. Someone once said, "A lie has no legs and cannot stand."

X 52. "This repair job could be expensive, the mechanic warned."

C 53. "My greatest childhood fear," said Sheila, "was being sucked down the bathtub drain."

X 54. "I was always afraid of everybody's father, said Suzanne, except my own."

Comma

X 55. The restaurant's "sundae bar" featured bowls of whipped cream chopped nuts and chocolate sprinkles.

C 56. My sister, who studies karate, installed large practice mirrors in our basement.

X 57. When I remove my thick eyeglasses the world turns into an out-of-focus movie.

C 58. Gloria wrapped her son's presents in pages from the comics section, and she glued a small toy car atop each gift.

Spelling

X 59. When Terry practises scales on the piano, her whole family wears earplugs.

X 60. I wondered if it was alright to wear sneakers with my three-piece suit.

X 61. The essay test question asked us to describe two different theorys of evolution.

X 62. A theif stole several large hanging plants from Marlo's porch.

Omitted Words and Letters

C 63. After dark, I'm afraid to look in the closets or under the bed.

X 64. I turned on the television, but baseball game had been rained out.

X 65. Polar bear cubs stay with their mother for two year.

Commonly Confused Words

X 66. Before your about to start the car, press the gas pedal to the floor once.

X 67. The frog flicked it's tongue out and caught the fly.

X 68. I was to lonely to enjoy the party.

C 69. The bats folded their wings around them like leather overcoats.

Effective Word Choice

X 70. If the professor gives me a break, I might pass the final exam.

X 71. Harry worked like a dog all summer to save money for his tuition.

X 72. Because Monday is a holiday, sanitation engineers will pick up your trash on Tuesday.

C 73. Our family's softball game ended in an argument, as usual.

X 74. As for my own opinion, I feel that nuclear weapons should be banned.

X 75. This law is, for all intents and purposes, a failure.

Part 2 (Optional)

Do the following at your instructor's request. This second part of the test will provide more detailed information about skills you need to know. On separate paper, number and correct all the items you have marked with an *X*. For example, suppose you had marked the word groups below with an *X*. (Note that these examples are not taken from the actual test.)

4. When I picked up the tire. Something in my back snapped. I could not stand up straight.
7. The phone started ringing, then the doorbell sounded as well.
15. Marks goal is to save enough money to get married next year.
29. Without checking the rearview mirror the driver pulled out into the passing lane.

Here is how you should write your corrections on a separate sheet of paper:

4. When I picked up the tire, something in my back snapped.
7. The phone started ringing, and then the doorbell sounded as well.
15. Mark's
29. mirror, the driver

There are over forty corrections to make in all.

Many answers will vary; see Instructor's Manual for corrected sentences.

Appendix D

Sentence-Skills Achievement Test

Part I

This achievement test will help you check your mastery of a number of sentence skills. In each item below, certain words are underlined. Write *X* in the answer space if you think a mistake appears at the underlined part. Write *C* in the answer space if you think the underlined part is correct.

The headings within the test ("Fragments," "Run-Ons," and so on) will give you clues to the mistakes to look for.

Fragments

X ______ 1. When the town's bully died. Hundreds of people came to his funeral. They wanted to make sure he was dead.

C ______ 2. Suzanne adores junk foods, especially onion-flavored potato chips. She can eat an entire bag at one sitting.

X ______ 3. My brother stayed up all night. Studying the rules in his driver's manual. He wanted to get his license on the first try.

X ______ 4. Hector decided to take a study break. He picked up *TV Guide*. And flipped through the pages to find that night's listings.

Run-Ons

X ______ 5. Ronnie leaned forward in his seat, he could not hear what the instructor was saying.

X ______ 6. Our television set obviously needs repairs the color keeps fading from the picture.

C ______ 7. Nick and Fran enjoyed their trip to Chicago, but they couldn't wait to get home.

X ______ 8. I tuned in the weather forecast on the radio, I had to decide what to wear.

Standard English Verbs

C 9. My sister Louise walks a mile to the bus stop every day.

X 10. The play was ruined when the quarterback fumble the handoff.

X 11. When the last guests left our party, we was exhausted but happy.

X 12. I don't think my mother have gone out to a movie in years.

Irregular Verbs

X 13. My roommate and I seen a double feature this weekend.

X 14. My nephew must have growed six inches since last summer.

C 15. I should have brought a gift to the office Christmas party.

C 16. After playing touch football all afternoon, Al drank a quart of Gatorade.

Subject-Verb Agreement

X 17. The cost of those new tires are more than I can afford.

C 18. Nick and Fran give a New Year's Eve party every year.

X 19. There was only two slices of cake left on the plate.

X 20. Each of the fast-food restaurants have a breakfast special.

Consistent Verb Tense

C 21. After I folded the towels in the basket, I remembered that I hadn't washed them yet.

X 22. Before she decided to buy the wall calendar, Joanne turns its pages and looked at all the pictures.

Pronoun Reference, Agreement, and Point of View

C 23. All drivers should try their best to be courteous during rush hour.

X 24. When Bob went to the bank for a home improvement loan, they asked him for three credit references.

X 25. I like to shop at factory outlets because you can always get brand names at a discount.

Pronoun Types

X 26. My brother writes much more neatly than me.

C 27. Vonnie and I are both taking Introduction to Business this semester.

Adjectives and Adverbs

X 28. When the elevator doors closed sudden, three people were trapped inside.

C 29. The bag lady glared angrily at me when I offered her a dollar bill.

X 30. Frank couldn't decide which vacation he liked best, a bicycle trip or a week at the beach.

C 31. I find proofreading a paper much more difficult than writing one.

Misplaced Modifiers

X 32. The car was parked along the side of the road with a flat tire.

X 33. We bought a television set at our neighborhood video store that has stereo sound.

Dangling Modifiers

X 34. While looking for bargains at Sears, an exercise bike caught my eye.

C 35. Hurrying to catch the bus, Donna fell and twisted her ankle.

Faulty Parallelism

X 36. Before she leaves for work, Agnes makes her lunch, does fifteen minutes of calisthenics, and her two cats have to be fed.

X 37. Three remedies for insomnia are warm milk, taking a hot bath, and sleeping pills.

Capital Letters

C 38. Every Saturday I get up early, even though I have the choice of sleeping late.

X 39. We stopped at the drugstore for some crest toothpaste.

C 40. Rows of crocuses appear in my front yard every spring.

X 41. The cashier said, "sorry, but children under three are not allowed in this theater."

Numbers and Abbreviations

X 42. Our train finally arrived—2 hours late.

C 43. Answers to the chapter questions start on page 293.

X 44. Three yrs. from now, my new car will finally be paid off.

End Marks

C 45. I had no idea who was inside the gorilla suit at the Halloween party.

X 46. Are you taking the makeup exam.

Apostrophe

X 47. My fathers favorite old television program is *Star Trek.*

X 48. I couldnt understand a word of that lecture.

C 49. My dentist's recommendation was that I floss after brushing my teeth.

X 50. Three house's on our street are up for sale.

Quotation Marks

C 51. Garfield the cat is fond of saying, "I never met a carbohydrate I didn't like."

X 52. "This restaurant does not accept credit cards, the waiter said."

X 53. Two foods that may prevent cancer," said the scientist, "are those old stand-bys spinach and carrots."

X 54. "I can't get anything done," Dad complained, if you two insist on making all that noise."

Comma

X 55. The snack bar offered overdone hamburgers rubbery hot dogs and soggy pizza.

C 56. My sister, who regards every living creature as a holy thing, cannot even swat a housefly.

X 57. When I smelled something burning I realized I hadn't turned off the oven.

C 58. Marge plays the musical saw at parties, and her husband does Dracula imitations.

Spelling

X 59. No one will be admited without a valid student identification card.

X 60. Pat carrys a full course load in addition to working as the night manager at a supermarket.

X 61. Did you feel alright after eating Ralph's special chili?

X 62. My parents were disappointed when I didn't enter the family busines.

Omitted Words and Letters

C 63. Both high schools in my hometown offer evening classes for adults.

X 64. I opened new bottle of ketchup and then couldn't find the cap.

X 65. Visiting hour for patients at this hospital are from noon to eight.

Commonly Confused Words

X 66. Shelley has always been to self-conscious to speak up in class.

X 67. Its not easy to return to college after raising a family.

X 68. "Thank you for you're generous contribution," the letter began.

C 69. Nobody knew whose body had been found floating in the swimming pool.

Effective Word Choice

X 70. My roommate keeps getting on my case about leaving clothing on the floor.

X 71. Karla decided to take the bull by the horns and ask her boss for a raise.

X 72. Although Lamont accelerated his vehicle, he was unable to pass the truck.

C 73. When the movie ended suddenly, I felt I had been cheated.

X 74. In light of the fact that I am on a diet, I have stopped eating between meals.

X 75. Personally, I do not think that everyone should be allowed to vote.

Part 2 (Optional)

Do the following at your instructor's request. This second part of the test will provide more detailed information about which skills you have mastered and which skills you still need to work on. On separate paper, number and correct all the items you have marked with an *X*. For example, suppose you had marked the word groups below with an *X*. (Note that these examples were not taken from the actual test.)

4. When I picked up the tire. Something in my back snapped. I could not stand up straight.
7. The phone started ringing, then the doorbell sounded as well.
15. Marks goal is to save enough money to get married next year.
29. Without checking the rearview mirror the driver pulled out into the passing lane.

Here is how you should write your corrections on a separate sheet of paper:

4. When I picked up the tire, something in my back snapped.
7. The phone started ringing, and then the doorbell sounded as well.
15. Mark's
29. mirror, the driver

There are over forty corrections to make in all.

Many answers will vary; see Instructor's Manual for corrected sentences.

Appendix E

Answers to Introductory Activities and Practice Exercises in Part Two

This answer key can help you teach yourself. Use it to find out why you got some answers wrong—you want to uncover any weak spot in your understanding of a given skill. By using the answer key in an honest and thoughtful way, you will master each skill and prepare yourself for many tests in this book that have no answer key.

SUBJECTS AND VERBS

Introductory Activity (page 87)

Answers will vary.

Practice 1 (89)

1. Carl spilled
2. ladybug landed
3. Nick eats
4. waitress brought
5. I found
6. Diane stapled
7. audience applauded
8. boss has
9. I tasted
10. paperboy threw

Practice 2 (90)

1. I am
2. parents are
3. Tri Lee was
4. dog becomes
5. Estelle seems
6. hot dog looks
7. people appear
8. students felt
9. cheeseburger has
10. telephone seemed

Practice 3 (90)

1. rabbits ate
2. father prefers
3. restaurant donated
4. Stanley looks
5. couple relaxed
6. Lightning brightened
7. council voted
8. throat kept
9. sister decided
10. I chose

Practice (91)

1. ~~By accident~~, Anita dropped her folder ~~into the mailbox~~.
2. ~~Before the test~~, I glanced ~~over my notes~~.
3. My car stalled ~~on the bridge at rush hour~~.
4. I hung a photo ~~of Whitney Houston above my bed~~.
5. ~~On weekends~~ we visit my grandmother ~~at a nursing home~~.
6. ~~During the movie~~, some teenagers giggled ~~at the love scenes~~.
7. A pedestrian tunnel runs ~~beneath the street to the train station~~.
8. The parents hid their daughter's Christmas gifts ~~in the garage~~.
9. All the teachers, ~~except Mr. Blake~~, wear ties ~~to school~~.
10. The strawberry jam ~~in my brother's sandwich~~ dripped ~~onto his lap~~.

Practice (93)

1. Ellen has chosen
2. You should plan
3. Felix has been waiting
4. We should have invited
5. I would have preferred
6. Classes were interrupted
7. Sam can touch
8. I have been encouraging
9. Tony has agreed
10. students have been giving

Practice (94)

1. Boards and bricks make
2. We bought and finished
3. fly and bee hung
4. twins look, think, act, and dress
5. salmon and tuna contain
6. I waited and slipped
7. girl waved and smiled
8. bird dived and reappeared
9. Singers, dancers, and actors performed
10. magician and assistant bowed and disappeared

FRAGMENTS

Introductory Activity (97)

1. verb
2. subject
3. subject . . . verb
4. express a complete thought

Practice 1 (101)

Answers will vary.

Practice 2 (102)

Note The underlined part shows the fragment (or that part of the original fragment not changed during correction).

1. When the waitress coughed in his food, Frank lost his appetite. He didn't even take home a doggy bag.
2. Our power went out during a thunderstorm.
3. Tony doesn't like going to the ballpark. If he misses an exciting play, there's no instant replay.
4. After the mail carrier comes, I run to our mailbox. I love to get mail even if it is only junk mail.
5. Even though she can't read, my little daughter likes to go to the library. She chooses books with pretty covers while I look at the latest magazines.

Practice 1 (104)

1. Vince sat nervously in the dentist's chair, waiting for his x-rays to be developed.
2. Looking through the movie ads for twenty minutes, Lew and Marian tried to find a film they both wanted to see.
3. As a result, it tipped over.

Practice 2 (104)

Rewritten versions may vary.

1. Some workers dug up the street near our house, causing frequent vibrations inside.
2. I therefore walked slowly into the darkened living room, preparing to look shocked.
   Or: I was preparing to look shocked.
3. Dribbling skillfully up the court, Luis looked for a teammate who was open.
4. Wanting to finish the dream, I pushed the snooze button.
5. To get back my term paper, I went to see my English instructor from last semester.

Practice 1 (106)

1. For example, she waits until the night before a test to begin studying.
2. My eleventh-grade English teacher picked on everybody except the athletes.
3. For example, he bought an air conditioner in December.

Practice 2 (107)

Rewritten versions may vary.

1. I find all sorts of things in my little boy's pockets, including crayons, stones, and melted chocolate.
2. There are certain chores I hate to do, especially cleaning windows.
3. The meat loaf, for instance, is as tender and tasty as shoe leather.
4. By midnight, the party looked like the scene of an accident, with people stretched out on the floor.
5. For example, the smiles of game show hosts look pasted on their faces.

Practice (108)

Rewritten versions may vary.

1. Artie tripped on his shoelace and then looked around to see if anyone had noticed.
   Or: Then he looked around to see if anyone had noticed.
2. I started the car and quickly turned down the blaring radio.
   Or: And I quickly turned down the blaring radio.
3. Its orange-red flames shot high in the air and made strange shadows all around the dark room.
4. She also forgot to take my name.
5. She places herself in front of a seated young man and stands on his feet until he gets up.
   Or: And she stands on his feet until he gets up.

RUN-ONS

Introductory Activity (117)

1. period
2. *but*
3. semicolon
4. *Although*

Practice 1 (120)

1. month. Its
2. porch. They
3. make. It
4. do. He
5. gray. A
6. B.C. The
7. cheaply. She
8. desk. She
9. fireplace. The
10. traffic. Its

Practice 2 (121)

1. man. He
2. mailbox. Then
3. common. The
4. tiny. A
5. greyhound. It
6. Chinese. She
7. working. Its
8. lovely. It
9. drink. One
10. times. For

Practice 3 (121)

Answers will vary.

Practice 1 (123)

1. , but
2. , and
3. , and
4. , so
5. , but
6. , so
7. , for
8. , but
9. , so
10. , for

Practice 2 (124)

Answers will vary.

Practice (125)

1. obvious; I
2. ate; the
3. me; her
4. ground; old
5. queens; birth

Practice 1 (126)

Answers may vary.

1. drive; however, the
2. art; otherwise, it
3. gasoline; as a result, spectators (*or* thus *or* consequently *or* therefore)
4. started; however, all
5. feelers; consequently, they (*or* as a result *or* thus or therefore)

Practice 2 (127)

1. store; nevertheless, she
2. candy; as a result, he
3. strangers; however, he
4. schedule; otherwise, he
5. children; furthermore, she

Practice 1 (128)

Answers may vary.

1. since
2. Unless
3. because
4. After
5. although

Practice 2 (128)

Answers may vary.

1. Although I want to stop smoking, I don't want to gain weight.
2. Because it was too hot indoors to study, I decided to go down to the shopping center for ice cream.
3. While the puppy quickly ate, the baby watched with interest.
4. When the elderly woman smiled at me, her face broke into a thousand wrinkles.
5. Although this world map was published only three years ago, the names of some countries are already out of date.

SENTENCE VARIETY I

The Simple Sentence

Practice (136)

Answers will vary.

The Compound Sentence

Practice 1 (137)

Answers may vary; possible answers are given.

1. Cass tied the turkey carcass to a tree, and she watched the birds pick at bits of meat and skin.
2. I ran the hot water faucet for two minutes, but only cold water came out.
3. Nathan orders all his Christmas gifts through the Internet, for he dislikes shopping in crowded stores.
4. I need to buy a new set of tires, so I will read *Consumer Reports* to learn about various brands.
5. I asked Cecilia to go out with me on Saturday night, but she told me she'd rather stay home and watch TV.

Practice 2 (137)

Answers will vary.

The Complex Sentence

Practice 1 (139)

Answers may vary; possible answers are given.

1. When Cindy opened the cutlery drawer, a bee flew out.
2. Although I washed the windows thoroughly, they still looked dirty.
3. Because I never opened a book all semester, I guess I deserved to flunk.
4. When Manny gets up in the morning, he does stretching exercises for five minutes.
5. After my son spilled the pickle jar at dinner, I had to wash the kitchen floor.

Practice 2 (140)

Answers may vary; possible answers are given.

1. As Carlo set the table, his wife finished cooking dinner.
2. Although Maggie could have gotten good grades, she did not study enough.
3. After I watered my drooping African violets, they perked right up.
4. Though the little boy kept pushing the down button, the elevator didn't come any more quickly.
5. I never really knew what pain is until I had four impacted wisdom teeth pulled at once.

Practice 3 (141)

Answers may vary; possible answers are given.

1. Karen, who is an old friend of mine, just gave birth to twins.
2. The tea, which was hotter than I expected, burned the roof of my mouth.
3. I dropped the camera that my sister had bought last week.
4. Ernie, who is visiting from California, brought us some enormous oranges.
5. Liz used a steam cleaner to shampoo her rugs, which were dirtier than she realized.

Practice 4 (142)

Answers will vary.

The Compound-Complex Sentence

Practice 1 (142)

Answers may vary.

1. After . . . for
2. When . . . but
3. when . . . and
4. Because . . . so
5. but . . . because

Practice 2 (142)

Answers will vary.

Review of Coordination and Subordination

Practice (143)

Answers will vary.

1. Though Sidney likes loud music, his parents can't stand it, so he wears earphones.
2. After the volcano erupted, the sky turned black with smoke. Nearby villagers were frightened, so they clogged the roads leading to safety.
3. After Glenda had a haircut today, she came home and looked in the mirror. Then she decided to wear a hat for a few days because she thought she looked like a bald eagle.
4. When I ran out of gas on the way to work, I discovered how helpful strangers can be. A passing driver saw I was stuck, so he drove me to the gas station and back to my car.

5. Our dog often rests on the floor in the sunshine while he waits for the children to get home from school. As the sunlight moves along the floor, he moves with it.
6. Because my father was going to be late from work, we planned to have a late dinner. But I was hungry before dinner, so I secretly ate a salami and cheese sandwich.
7. A baseball game was scheduled for early afternoon, but it looked like rain. So a crew rolled huge tarps to cover the field, and then the sun reappeared.
8. Cassy worries about the sprays used on fruit, so she washes apples, pears, and plums in soap and water. Because she doesn't rinse them well, they have a soapy flavor.
9. Charlene needed to buy stamps, so she went to the post office during her lunch hour, when the line was long. After she waited there for half an hour, she had to go back to work without stamps.
10. After the weather suddenly became frigid, almost everyone at work caught a cold, so someone brought a big batch of chicken soup. She poured it into one of the office coffeepots, and the pot was empty by noon.

STANDARD ENGLISH VERBS

Introductory Activity (151)

played . . . plays
hoped . . . hopes
juggled . . . juggles

1. past time . . . *–ed* or *–d*
2. present time . . . -s

Practice 1 (153)

1. drives
2. gets
3. practices
4. makes
5. brushes
6. falls
7. *C*
8. comes
9. watches
10. buzzes

Practice 2 (153)

My little sister wants to be a country singer when she grows up. She constantly hums and sings around the house. Sometimes she makes quite a racket. When she listens to music on the radio, for example, she sings very loudly in order to hear herself over the radio. And when she takes a shower, her voice rings through the whole house because she thinks nobody can hear her from there.

Practice 1 (154)

1. spilled
2. jailed
3. burned
4. tied
5. measured
6. *C*
7. smashed
8. constructed
9. leveled
10. realized

Practice 2 (155)

My cousin Joel completed a course in home repairs and offered one day to fix several things in my house. He repaired a screen door that squeaked, a dining room chair that wobbled a bit, and a faulty electrical outlet. That night when I opened the screen door, it loosened from its hinges. When I seated myself in the chair Joel had fixed, one of its legs cracked off. Remembering that Joel had also fooled around with the electrical outlet, I quickly called an electrician and asked him to stop by the next day. Then I prayed the house would not burn down before he arrived.

Practice 1 (157)

1. is
2. do
3. has
4. is
5. have
6. are
7. has
8. do
9. were
10. does

Practice 2 (158)

1. ~~does~~ do
2. ~~be~~ is
3. ~~be~~ are
4. ~~has~~ have
5. ~~were~~ was
6. ~~have~~ had
7. ~~was~~ were
8. ~~done~~ did
9. ~~do~~ does
10. ~~have~~ has

Practice 3 (158)

My cousin Rita has decided to lose thirty pounds, so she has put herself on a rigid diet that does not allow her to eat anything that she enjoys. Last weekend, while the family was at Aunt Jenny's house for dinner, all Rita had to eat was a can of Diet Delight peaches. We were convinced that Rita meant business when she joined an exercise club whose members have to work out on enormous machines and do twenty sit-ups just to get started. If Rita does reach her goal, we are all going to be very proud of her. But I would not be surprised if she does not succeed, because this is her fourth diet this year.

IRREGULAR VERBS

Introductory Activity (161)

1. *R* . . . screamed . . . screamed
2. *I* . . . wrote . . .written
3. *I* . . . stole . . . stolen
4. *R* . . . asked . . . asked
5. *R* . . . kissed . . .kissed
6. *I* . . . chose . . . chosen
7. *I* . . . rode . . . ridden
8. *R* . . . chewed . . . chewed
9. *I* . . . thought . . . thought
10. *R* . . . danced . . . danced

Practice 1 (165)

1. came
2. stood
3. built
4. swum
5. held
6. drove
7. written
8. blew
9. bought
10. knew

Practice 2 (165)

1. (a) sleeps
   (b) slept
   (c) slept
2. (a) rings
   (b) rang
   (c) rung
3. (a) write
   (b) wrote
   (c) written
4. (a) stands
   (b) stood
   (c) stood
5. (a) swims
   (b) swam
   (c) swum
6. (a) buys
   (b) bought
   (c) bought
7. (a) choose
   (b) chose
   (c) chosen
8. (a) eats
   (b) ate
   (c) eaten
9. (a) freezes
   (b) froze
   (c) frozen
10. (a) give
    (b) gave
    (c) given

Practice (168)

1. lies
2. lying
3. laid
4. lain
5. lay

Practice (169)

1. sitting
2. set
3. sat
4. Set
5. setting

Practice (170)

1. rises
2. raised
3. rose
4. risen
5. raise

SUBJECT-VERB AGREEMENT

Introductory Activity (173)

Correct: The pictures in that magazine are very controversial.
Correct: There were many applicants for the job.
Correct: Everybody usually watches the lighted numbers in an elevator.

1. pictures . . . applicants
2. singular . . . singular

Practice (175)

1. trail ~~of bloodstains~~ leads
2. clothes ~~in the hall closet~~ take
3. basket ~~of fancy fruits and nuts~~ was
4. instructions ~~for assembling the bicycle~~ were
5. Smoke ~~from the distant forest fires~~ is
6. Workers ~~at that automobile plant~~ begin
7. date ~~on any of the cemetery gravestones~~ appears
8. line ~~of cars in the traffic jam~~ seems
9. boxes ~~in the corner of the attic~~ contain
10. bags ~~with the new insulation material~~ protect

Practice (176)

1. is noise
2. are berries
3. were cans
4. sits cabin
5. were students
6. stands cutout
7. was shape
8. were sneakers
9. are magazines
10. was row

Practice (177)

1. keeps
2. works
3. pays
4. have
5. slips
6. leans
7. expects
8. was
9. stops
10. has

Practice (178)

1. sadden
2. need
3. have
4. continue
5. tears

Practice (179)

1. has
2. goes
3. become
4. taste
5. are

CONSISTENT VERB TENSE

Introductory Activity (183)

Mistakes in verb tense: Alex discovers . . . calls . . . present . . . past

Practice (184)

1. rolled
2. purchased
3. stepped
4. crashed
5. snatched
6. covered
7. lifted
8. argues
9. swallowed
10. glowed

ADDITIONAL INFORMATION ABOUT VERBS

Practice (Tense; 190)

1. had dried
2. had planned (or were planning)
3. is growing
4. had thrown
5. was carving (*or* had carved)
6. had opened
7. is caring
8. has watched
9. had walked
10. were trying

Practice (Verbals; 191)

1. *P*
2. *G*
3. *I*
4. *G*
5. *P*
6. *I*
7. *G*
8. *I*
9. *P*
10. *P*

Practice (Active and Passive Verbs; 193)

1. A man with a live parrot on his shoulder boarded the bus.
2. A large falling branch broke the stained-glass window.
3. The entire team autographed baseballs for hospitalized children.
4. A fire that started with a cigarette destroyed the hotel.
5. Doctors must face the pressures of dealing with life and death.
6. A sophisticated laser system directed the missile to its target.
7. A thick layer of yellowish grease covered the kitchen shelves.
8. A group of volunteers removed trash in the neighborhood park.
9. The state police captured most of the escaped convicts within a mile of the jail.
10. The judges awarded prizes for hog-calling and stone-skipping.

PRONOUN REFERENCE, AGREEMENT AND POINT OF VIEW

Introductory Activity (195)

1. b
2. b
3. b

Practice (197)

Note The practice sentences could be rewritten to have meanings other than the ones indicated below.

1. The defendant told the judge, "I am mentally ill."
2. Fran removed the blanket from the sofa bed and folded the blanket up.
3. Before the demonstration, the leaders passed out signs for us to carry.
4. Cindy complained to Rachel, "My (*or* Your) boyfriend is being dishonest."
5. Because I didn't rinse last night's dishes, my kitchen smells like a garbage can.
6. A film on endangered species really depressed the students.
   Or: Watching a film on endangered species really depressed the students.

7. The veterinarian said that if I find a tick on my dog, I should get rid of the tick immediately.
8. My sister removed the curtains from the windows so that she could wash the curtains.
   Or: So that she could wash the curtains, my sister removed them from the windows.
   Or: My sister removed the curtains from the windows so that she could wash the windows.
   Or: So that she could wash the windows, my sister removed the curtains from them.
9. Richard said his acupuncture therapist could help my sprained shoulder, but I don't believe in acupuncture.
10. I discovered when I went to sell my old textbooks that publishers have put out new editions, and nobody wants to buy my textbooks.
    Or: I discovered when I went to sell my old textbooks that nobody wants to buy them because publishers have put out new editions.

Practice (199)

1. they
2. their
3. it
4. them
5. their

Practice (201)

1. his
2. his
3. its
4. her
5. them
6. his or her
7. her
8. he
9. her
10. his or her

Practice (203)

1. my blood
2. they know
3. they have
4. they should receive
5. I can avoid
6. they don't
7. he can worry . . . his own
8. we could
9. she can still have . . . her day
10. our rights

PRONOUN TYPES

Introductory Activity (207)

Correct sentences:

Andy and I enrolled in a computer course.

The police officer pointed to my sister and me.

Lola prefers men who take pride in their bodies.

The players are confident that the league championship is theirs.

Those concert tickets are too expensive.

Our parents should spend some money on themselves for a change.

Practice 1 (210)

2. She (*S*)
3. me (*O*)
4. her and me (*O*)
5. he (*S*)
6. I (*am* is understood) (S)
7. they (*S*)
8. me (*O*)
9. We (*S*)
10. I (*S*)

Practice 2 (211)

Answers will vary.

2. him or me
3. they
4. I *or* we
5. Us
6. I *or* he *or* she *or* they *or* we
7. they *or* he *or* she
8. I *or* he *or* she *or* they *or* we
9. I *or* he *or* she *or* they *or* we
10. us (*or* them)

Practice 1 (213)

1. that
2. that
3. who
4. which
5. whom

Practice 2 (213)

Answers will vary.

Practice (214)

1. yours
2. his
3. theirs
4. your
5. mine

Practice 1 (216)

1. This town
2. those seats
3. That dress
4. those candies
5. those potholes

Practice 2 (216)

Answers will vary.

Practice (217)

1. themselves
2. herself
3. himself
4. ourselves
5. themselves

ADJECTIVES AND ADVERBS

Introductory Activity (221)

Answers will vary for 1-4.

Adjective . . . adverb . . . *ly* . . . *er* . . . *est*

Practice 1 (223)

tougher	toughest
more practical	most practical
quieter	quietest
more aggressive	most aggressive
clearer	clearest

Practice 2 (224)

1. best
2. dirtier
3. more considerate
4. worse
5. scariest
6. less
7. more stylish
8. sillier
9. softest
10. most fattening

Practice (225)

1. badly
2. harshly
3. steep
4. frequently
5. truthfully
6. peacefully
7. bright
8. loudly
9. carefully
10. nicely

Practice (226)

1. well
2. good
3. well
4. good
5. well

MISPLACED MODIFIERS

Introductory Activity (229)

1. Intended: The farmers were wearing masks.
   Unintended: The apple trees were wearing masks.
2. Intended: The woman had a terminal disease.
   Unintended: The faith healer had a terminal disease.

Practice 1 (230)

Note In each of the corrections below, the underlined part shows what was the misplaced modifier.

1. At the back of his cage, the tiger growled at a passerby.
2. Lee hung colorful scarves made of green and blue silk over her windows.
3. Standing on our front porch, we watched the fireworks.
4. Jason has almost two hundred baseball cards.
5. With a smile, the salesclerk exchanged the blue sweater for a yellow one.
6. We all stared at the man with curly purple hair in the front row of the theater.
7. I love the cookies with the chocolate frosting from the bakery.
8. During their last meeting, the faculty decided to strike.
9. Larry looked on with disbelief as his car burned.
10. My cousin sent me instructions in a letter on how to get to her house.

Practice 2 (232)

1. My mother sat lazily with a glass of lemonade in the hot sun, watching her grandchildren play.
2. My father agreed over the phone to pay for the car repairs.
   Or: Over the phone, my father agreed to pay for the car repairs.
3. I found a note from Jeff on the kitchen bulletin board.
4. The fire destroyed almost the entire forest.
5. During class, Jon read about how the American Revolution began.
   Or: Jon read during class about how the American Revolution began.

DANGLING MODIFIERS

Introductory Activity (235)

1. Intended: The giraffe was munching leaves from a tall tree.
   Unintended: The children were munching leaves.
2. Intended: Michael was arriving home after ten months in the army.
   Unintended: The neighbors were arriving home after ten months in the army.

Practice 1 (237)

Wording of answers may vary.

1. Since the milk had turned sour, I would not drink it.
2. When I was five, my mother bought me a chemistry set.
3. *C*
4. A security guard pointed to the priceless painting that was hanging safely on a wall.
5. While I was talking on the phone, my hot tea turned cold.
6. Pete hated to look at the kitchen sink, which was piled high with dirty dishes.
7. Having locked my keys in the car, I had to have the police open it for me.
   Or: Because I locked my keys in the car, the police had to open it for me.
8. Because the plants were drooping and looking all dried out, the children watered them.
9. After I sat through a long lecture, my foot was asleep.
10. Since we were late, stopping for coffee was out of the question.

Practice 2 (238)

Answers will vary.

FAULTY PARALLELISM

Introductory Activity (241)

Correct sentences:

I use my TV remote control to change channels, to adjust the volume, and to turn the set on and off.

One option the employees had was to take a cut in pay; the other was to work longer hours.

The refrigerator has a cracked vegetable drawer, a missing shelf, and a strange freezer smell.

Practice 1 (242)

2. howling dogs
3. rude
4. hiking
5. poor security
6. cleaned the apartment
7. having fun
8. inexpensive desserts
9. on the closet floor
10. sings in the church choir

Practice 2 (243)

1. waited
2. cramming
3. illness
4. late buses
5. attracting
6. to suffocate
7. interrupted
8. financial security
9. birds chirping
10. breathed fire

Practice 3 (244)

Answers will vary.

SENTENCE VARIETY II

-ing Word Groups

Practice 1 (251)

Suggested combinations are shown below.
Other combinations are possible.

1. Picking up their cameras, the tourists began to leave the bus.
2. Jogging on the street, I was almost hit by a car.
3. Wincing with pain, Barbara untangled her snarled hair from the brush.
4. Waving her arms at the excited crowd, the singer ran to the front of the stage.
5. Losing by one point with thirty seconds left to play, the team braced itself for a last-ditch effort.

Practice 2 (252)

Answers will vary.

-ed Word Groups

Practice 1 (253)

Suggested combinations are shown below. Other combinations are possible.

1. Mary, startled by a thunderclap, sat up suddenly in bed.
2. Married for fifty years, my parents decided to have a second wedding.
3. Frightened by the large dog near the curb, Erica wouldn't leave her car.

4. Dotted with mold, the old orange felt like a marshmallow.
5. Ernie, determined to have plenty to eat during the movie, made a huge sandwich and popped popcorn.

Practice 2 (253)

Answers will vary.

-ly Openers

Practice 1 (254)

1. Noisily, we ate raw carrots and celery sticks.
2. Gently, Cliff spoke to his sobbing little brother.
3. Carelessly, the newspaper boy threw our paper into a thornbush.
4. Anxiously, I paced up and down the hospital corridor.
5. Frantically, Anita repeatedly dived into the pool to find her engagement ring.

Practice 2 (255)

Answers will vary.

To Openers

Practice 1 (255)

1. To make the tub less slippery, Sally put a thick towel on the bottom.
2. To keep raccoons away, we now keep our garbage in the garage.
3. To count his pulse, Bill pressed two fingers against the large vein in his neck.
4. To steam her face, my aunt opens her dishwasher when it begins drying.
5. To help out the homeless, we looked through our closets for unused clothing.

Practice 2 (256)

Answers will vary.

Prepositional Phrase Openers

Practice 1 (257)

Suggested combinations are shown below. Other combinations are possible.

1. About once a week, we have dinner with my parents at a restaurant.
2. Before company came, I put the dirty cups away in the cupboard.
3. During my English exam, my eyes roamed around the room until they met the instructor's eye.
4. For twenty minutes, the little boy drew intently in a comic book without stopping once.
5. At the zoo, a playful young orangutan wriggled in a corner under a paper sack.

Practice 2 (258)

Answers will vary.

Series of Items: Adjectives

Practice 1 (259)

1. The old, peeling shingles blew off the roof during the blustery storm.
2. The lean, powerful dancer whirled across the stage with his graceful, elegant partner.
3. The well-dressed, glamorous model in the bleach ad wore three-inch high heels in the laundry room.
4. The full, golden moon lit up the cloudy sky like a huge floating street lamp.
5. The oval plastic doorbell of the large, ornate house played a loud rock tune.

Practice 2 (260)

Answers will vary.

Series of Items: Verbs

Practice 1 (260)

1. I put my homework on the table, made a cup of coffee, and turned the radio up full blast.
2. The flea-ridden dog rubbed itself against the fence, bit its tail, and scratched its neck with its hind leg.
3. The driver stopped the school bus, walked to the back, and separated two children.
4. I rolled up my sleeve, glanced at the nurse nervously, shut my eyes, and waited for the worst to be over.
5. The parents applauded politely at the program's end, looked at their watches, exchanged looks of relief, and reached for their coats.

Practice 2 (261)

Answers will vary.

PAPER FORMAT

Introductory Activity (265)

In "A," the title is capitalized and centered and has no quotation marks around it; there is a blank line between the title and the body of the paper; there are left and right margins around the body of the paper; no words are incorrectly hyphenated.

Practice 1 (267)

2. Do not use quotation marks around the title.
3. Capitalize the major words in the title ("Being a Younger Sister").
4. Skip a line between the title and first line of the paper.
5. Indent the first line of the paper.
6. Keep margins on both sides of the paper.

Practice 2 (267)

Answers may vary slightly.

1. Benefits of Pets
2. Learning How to Budget
3. The Value of a Study Group
4. A Special Relationship *or* Grandparents and Grandchildren
5. A Wise Decision

Practice 3 (268)

Answers may vary slightly.

1. The best children's television shows educate while they entertain, and they are not violent.
2. Women have made many gains in the workplace in the last decade.
3. The generation gap results from differing experiences of various age groups.
4. Correct.
5. One of my important accomplishments was to finish high school despite my parents' divorce.

CAPITAL LETTERS

Introductory Activity (271)

1–13: Answers will vary, but all should be capitalized.
14–16: On . . . "Let's . . . I

Practice (274)

1. I . . . Boy Scouts
2. Smokenders . . . July . . . Marlboro
3. Regal Cinema . . . If
4. New England . . . Republicans . . . Democrats
5. State Farm . . . Nationwide . . . Prudential Building
6. Massachusetts . . . *Time* . . . *Newsweek*
7. Valentine's Day . . . Mother's Day
8. Pepsis . . . Fritos . . . Macintosh
9. Ford Taurus . . . Saturday
10. Broadway . . . *My Fair Lady*

Practice (277)

1. Hundred Years' War
2. Aunt Sophie . . . Polish
3. Independence Hall . . .Liberty Bell
4. World History . . . Middle Ages
5. Cuban . . . Spanish . . . Hispanic

Practice (278)

1. grandmother . . . spaghetti . . . meatballs
2. high school . . . basketball coach
3. shop . . . fashion magazines
4. parents' groups . . . ads . . . maniac
5. manager . . . restaurant . . . dessert

NUMBERS AND ABBREVIATIONS

Introductory Activity (283)

Correct choices:

First sentence: 8:55 . . . 65 percent
Second sentence: Nine . . . forty-five
Second sentence: brothers . . . mountain
Second sentence: hours . . . English

Practice (284)

1. 6:15
2. nine o'clock
3. January 28, 1986
4. Six
5. 1600 Pennsylvania Avenue
6. Forty-three
7. $930.20
8. 60 . . . 64
9. 27 . . . 52
10. 50 percent

Practice (286)

1. newspaper . . . telephone
2. bushels . . . market . . . Route
3. Monday . . . September
4. psychology . . . England
5. chicken . . . macaroni
6. ounce . . . tablespoon
7. chemistry . . . Sunday . . . hours
8. January . . . company . . . year
9. license . . . medical
10. veteran . . . business . . . college

END MARKS

Introductory Activity (289)

1. depressed.
2. paper?
3. parked.
4. control!

Practice (291)

1. drown?
2. redhead.
3. me.
4. it!"
5. "vidiots."
6. accurate.
7. life?
8. truck!"
9. forward?"
10. married.

APOSTROPHE

Introductory Activity (293)

1. In each case, the *'s* indicates possession or ownership.
2. The apostrophes indicate omitted letters and shortened spellings.
3. In the first sentence, *s* indicates a plural noun; in the second sentence, *'s* indicates possession.

Apostrophe in Contractions

Practice 1 (294)

you've	we're	couldn't
haven't	you'll	they'll
he's	we'd	doesn't

Practice 2 (295)

1. didn't . . . wasn't
2. doesn't . . . she's
3. You're . . . can't
4. isn't . . . you've
5. We'd . . . don't

Practice 3 (295)
Answers will vary.

Practice (296)

1. It's . . . your
2. whose . . . who's
3. You're . . . your
4. There . . . their
5. It's . . . their

Apostrophe to Show Ownership or Possession

Practice 1 (297)

1. singer's voice
2. Dawn's garage
3. Murphy's law
4. computer's memory
5. my wife's mother
6. yesterday's meat loaf
7. My sister's promotion
8. Alexis's bratty little brother
9. the referee's call
10. the tanker's hull

Practice 2 (298)

2. brother's
3. son's
4. comedian's
5. landlord's
6. Ted's
7. teller's
8. people's
9. studio's
10. girl's

Practice 3 (299)
Sentences will vary.
2. teacher's
3. insect's
4. husband's
5. salesperson's

Practice (300)

1. parlors: parlor's, meaning "belonging to the parlor"
aromas: simple plural meaning more than one aroma
vents: simple plural meaning more than one vent
2. cars: car's, meaning "belonging to the car"
streets: simple plural meaning more than one street
buildings: simple plural meaning more than one building
3. Karens: Karen's, meaning "belonging to Karen"
plants: simple plural meaning more than one plant
stakes: simple plural meaning more than one stake
4. lakes: lake's, meaning "belonging to the lake"
officials: simple plural meaning more than one official
5. positions: simple plural meaning more than one position
exterminators: exterminator's, meaning "belonging to an exterminator"
6. candlelights: candlelight's, meaning "belonging to the candlelight"
plates: simple plural meaning more than one plate
goblets: simple plural meaning more than one goblet
7. Crackers: simple plural meaning more than one cracker
slices: simple plural meaning more than one slice
fathers: father's, meaning "belonging to my father"
8. insects: insect's, meaning "belonging to the insect"
eggs: simple plural meaning more than one egg
worms: simple plural meaning more than one worm
9. Seabirds: simple plural meaning more than one seabird
oceans: ocean's, meaning "belonging to the ocean"
surfers: simple plural meaning more than one surfer
10. daughters: daughter's, meaning "belonging to my daughter"
prayers: simple plural meaning more than one prayer
schools: simple plural meaning more than one school

Practice (302)

1. nurses' union
2. sisters' feet
3. lions' keeper
4. Tylers' new television set
5. parents' wedding pictures

QUOTATION MARKS

Introductory Activity (307)

1. Quotation marks set off the exact words of a speaker.
2. Commas and periods following quotations go inside quotation marks.

Practice 1 (309)

1. The chilling bumper sticker read, "You can't hug children with nuclear arms."
2. "One day we'll look back on this argument, and it will seem funny," Bruce assured Rosa.
3. "Hey, lady, this is an express line!" shouted the cashier to the woman with a full basket.
4. My grandfather was fond of saying, "Happiness is found along the way, not at the end of the road."
5. "When will I be old enough to pay the adult fare?" the child asked.
6. On his deathbed, Oscar Wilde is supposed to have said, "Either this wallpaper goes or I do."
7. The sign on my neighbor's front door reads, "Never mind the dog. Beware of owner."
8. "I'm not afraid to die," said Woody Allen. "I just don't want to be there when it happens."
9. My son once told me, "Sometimes I wish I were little again. Then I wouldn't have to make so many decisions."
10. "I don't feel like cooking tonight," Eve said to Adam. "Let's just have fruit."

Practice 2 (309)

1. Simon said, "Take three giant steps forward."
2. "Please don't hang up before leaving a message," stated the telephone recording.
3. Clark Kent asked a man on the street, "Where is the nearest phone booth?"
4. "You dirtied every pan in the kitchen just to scramble some eggs," Rico said in disgust.
5. "Nothing can be done for your broken little toe," the doctor said. "You have to wait for it to heal."

Practice 1 (311)

2. I said, "That's hard to believe, since Herb is a do-nothing."
3. Agnes replied, "Even so, he's gone up in the world."
4. I told her, "You must be kidding."
5. Agnes laughed and said, "Herb was moved from the first to the fourth floor today."

Practice 2 (312)

1. My doctor said that I need to lose weight.
2. Lola asked Tony if he ever washes his car.
3. The operator asked if I had tried to look up the number myself.

4. Janie whispered that Harold's so boring he lights up a room when he leaves it.
5. The instructor said that movies are actually a series of still pictures.

Practice (313)

1. My sister just bought a VCR so she won't have to miss any more episodes of General Hospital.
2. Rita grabbed the National Enquirer and eagerly began to read the article "I Had a Space Alien's Baby."
3. Our exam will cover two chapters, "The Study of Heredity" and "The Origin of Diversity," in our biology textbook, Life.
4. The last song on the bluegrass program was called "I Ain't Broke but I'm Badly Bent."
5. A short story like Edgar Allan Poe's "The Pit and the Pendulum" is more exciting to me than a full-length action film like Armageddon.
6. At last night's performance of Annie Get Your Gun, the audience joined the cast in singing "There's No Business Like Show Business."
7. A typical article in Cosmopolitan will have a title like "How to Hook a Man without Letting Him Know You're Fishing."
8. One way Joanne deals with depression is to get out her Man of La Mancha album and play the song "The Impossible Dream."
9. I read the article "How Good Is Your Breakfast?" in Consumer Reports while munching a doughnut this morning.
10. According to a Psychology Today article titled "Home on the Street," there are 36,000 people living on New York City's sidewalks.

COMMA

Introductory Activity (319)

1. a: card, . . . check . . . ; ants, roaches,
2. b: car, . . .; hiking,
3. c: leeches, . . . blood, . . . ; Derek, . . . arrested,
4. d: easy, . . . ; trees,
5. e: asked, . . . ; work, . . . said,
6. f: 1,500,000; Newark, New Jersey, . . . August 26, 2000,

Practice 1 (321)

1. work, food, or a place to live
2. Ice cream, crushed candy, Pepsi, and popcorn
3. eight hours, four hundred miles, and three rest stops

Practice 2 (321)

1. pennies, and a sock hidden under the seats
2. Squirrels, . . . and clouds of mosquitoes populate
3. spun to his left, . . . arms of the Panthers' center

Practice 1 (322)

1. done, 2. tape, 3. time,

Practice 2 (322)

1. presents, . . . ribbon and tied
2. aisle, I saw a bead of sweat roll from her forehead
3. For example, I wrote a note to remind me that

Practice 1 (323)

1. dancer, aided by members of the chorus,
2. Anderson, who were married on the Fourth of July,
3. repairman, unaware of the grease on his shoes,

Practice 2 (324)

1. gigantic, . . . the rest is deadwood
2. council, in a rare fit of wisdom
3. presidents of the Untied States,
4. aunt, a talkative woman,

Practice (325)

1. spacious, but
2. thunderstorm, so
3. *C*
4. space, for
5. *C*
6. supermarket, but
7. *C*
8. college, but
9. schoolwork, but
10. *C*

Practice 1 (326)

1. said,
2. temptation," Oscar Wilde advised,
3. family,"

Practice 2 (326)

1. poster in the chemistry lab,
2. fine,". . . forgetting to kick."
3. think," the judge asked the defendant,

Practice (327)

1. me, madam
2. 6,000 . . . 15,000
3. 15, 1912.
4. Teresa, . . . Love,
5. Washington, D.C., . . . 50,000 . . . 6,500

Practice (328)

1. We grew a pumpkin last year that weighed over one hundred pounds.
2. Anyone with a failing grade must report to the principal.
3. Last weekend a grizzly bear attacked a hiker who got too close to its cubs.
4. After watching my form on the high diving board, Mr. Riley, my instructor, asked me if I had insurance.
5. Rosa flew first to Los Angeles, and then she went to visit her parents in Mexico City.
6. The tall, thin man who bought the red socks is a nightclub comedian.
7. Onions, radishes, and potatoes seem to grow better in cooler climates.
8. Whenever Vincent is in Las Vegas, you can find him at the blackjack table or the roulette wheel.
9. While I watched in disbelief, my car rolled down the hill and through the front window of a Chinese restaurant.
10. The question, sir, is not whether you committed the crime but when you committed the crime.

OTHER PUNCTUATION MARKS

Introductory Activity (333)

1. list:
2. life-size
3. (1856–1939)
4. track;
5. breathing—but alive

Practice (334)

1. diet:
2. summer:
3. columns:

Practice (335)

1. night; consequently,
2. raining; all
3. vegetarian; my . . . diabetic; and

Practice (336)

1. sea—shivering
2. —her third in three years—
3. time—eight

Practice (337)

1. slow-moving . . . no-passing
2. sugar-free . . . double-cheese
3. hard-hearted . . . teary-eyed

Practice (337)

1. Americans (22 percent) can
2. hours (3 to 4 P.M.) are
3. often (1) make a list and then (2) check off items I have done.

DICTIONARY USE

Introductory Activity (339)

1. fortutious (fortuitous)
2. hi/er/o/glyph/ics
3. be
4. oct/to/ge/nar′/i/an (primary accent is on *nar*)
5. (1) identifying mark on the ear of a domestic animal
   (2) identifying feature or characteristic

Answers to the practice activities are in your dictionary. Check with your instructor if you have any problems.

SPELLING IMPROVEMENT

Introductory Activity (349)

Misspellings:

akward . . . exercize . . . buisness . . . worryed . . .
shamful . . . begining . . . partys . . . sandwichs . . .
heros

Practice (352)

1. hurried
2. admiring
3. denies
4. jabbing
5. magnified
6. committed
7. diving
8. hastily
9. propelling
10. nudges

Practice (353)

1. buses
2. groceries
3. potatoes
4. taxis
5. themselves
6. theories
7. passersby
8. alumni
9. sandwiches
10. mice

OMITTED WORDS AND LETTERS

Introductory Activity (359)

bottles . . . in the supermarket . . . like a wind-up toy
his arms . . . an alert shopper . . . with the crying

Practice (360)

1. I grabbed a metal bar on the roof of the subway car as the train lurched into the station.
2. For most of our country's history, gold was the basis of the monetary system.
3. Maggie made about a quart of French-toast batter—enough to soak a few dozen slices.
4. Several pairs of sneakers tumbled around in the dryer and banged against the glass door.
5. To err is human and to forgive is divine, but never to make a mistake in the first place takes a lot of luck.
6. Raccoons like to wash their food in a stream with their nimble, glovelike hands before eating.
7. When I got to the grocery store, I realized I had left my shopping list in the glove compartment of my car.
8. Game shows are an inexpensive way for networks to make a high profit.
9. Soap operas, on the other hand, are very expensive to produce because of the high salaries of many cast members.
10. One memorable Friday the thirteenth, a friend of mine bought a black cat, broke a mirror, and walked under a ladder. He had a wonderful day!

Practice 1 (361)

1. sightseers . . . ghouls
2. sets . . . names
3. Dozens . . . beetles
4. dentists . . . restaurants . . . lines
5. workers . . . departments
6. lights . . . games . . . cars . . . persons
7. games . . . balls
8. shoes . . . jeans . . . months
9. stamps . . . pens
10. Workers . . . logs . . . chunks . . . chips

Practice 2 (362)

Answers will vary.

COMMONLY CONFUSED WORDS

Introductory Activity (365)

1. Incorrect: your Correct: you're
2. Incorrect: who's Correct: whose
3. Incorrect: there Correct: their
4. Incorrect: to Correct: too
5. Incorrect: Its Correct: It's

Homonyms (366–374)

Sentences will vary.

all ready . . . already
break . . . brake
course . . . coarse
here . . . hear
whole . . . hole
its . . . it's
new . . . knew
know . . . no
pair . . . pear
passed . . . past
peace . . . piece
plain . . . plane
principal . . . principle
right . . . write
then . . . than
there . . . their . . . they're

through . . . threw
two . . . too . . . to
where . . . wear
weather . . . whether
who's . . . whose
you're . . . your

Other Words Frequently Confused (375–379)

Sentences will vary.

an . . . a
except . . . accept
advice . . . advise
affect . . . effect
Among . . . between
beside . . . besides
can . . . may
cloths . . . clothes
desert . . . dessert
dose . . . does
fewer . . . less
former . . . latter
learn . . . teach
loose . . . lose
quite . . . quiet
though . . . thought

Incorrect Word Forms (380–381)

being that (380)

1. Since (*or* Because) our stove doesn't work
2. since (*or* because) they don't speak to each other
3. since (*or* because) it's my birthday

can't hardly/couldn't hardly (380)

1. I can hardly
2. James could hardly
3. You could hardly

could of (381)

1. you could have
2. you could have
3. I could have

irregardless (381)

1. Regardless of your feelings
2. regardless of the weather
3. regardless of age

must of/should of/would of (381)

1. I must have
2. he would have
3. You should have

EFFECTIVE WORD CHOICE

Introductory Activity (385)

Correct sentences:

1. After a disappointing movie, we devoured a pizza.
2. Mourning the death of his best friend, Tennyson wrote the moving poem "In Memoriam."
3. Psychological tests will be given on Wednesday in the Student Center.
4. I think the referee made the right decision.

1 . . . 2 . . . 3 . . . 4

Practice (387)

Answers may vary.

1. If you keep overeating, you're going to be fat.
2. My parents always refuse when I ask them for some money to buy new CDs.
3. The entire city was excited when the basketball team beat its opponent in the playoffs.
4. If Ellen would get less serious and stop talking about her troubles, a date with her wouldn't be so depressing.
5. I'm going to have to wait anxiously for the next couple of days, hoping the boss doesn't discover the mistake I made.

Practice 1 (388)

Answers will vary for rewritten versions.

1. Substitute In brief for To make a long story short.
2. Substitute Very quickly for As quick as a wink.
3. Substitute is ignored for goes in one ear and out the other.
4. Substitute was delighted for felt like a million dollars.
5. Substitute rare for few and far between.

Practice 2 (389)

Answers will vary.

Practice (390)

1. Please ask one of our salespeople.
2. The weather is terrible today.
3. My parents want me to get a college degree.
4. Do not put your arm out of the car, or an accident might happen.
5. Many fires are caused by the careless use of portable heaters.

Practice (392)

1. There is no cure for the common cold.
2. My main point is that our state should legalize gambling.
3. Because Chen's car wouldn't start, he took a bus to work.
4. Even when I was a boy, my goal was to be a stockbroker.
5. Susan's daily exercises energize her.

Note The above answers are examples of how the clichés could be corrected. Other answers are possible.

Appendix F

Progress Charts

Progress Charts for Mastery Tests

Enter Your Score for Each Test in the Space Provided

Individual Tests	*1 Mastery*	*2 Mastery*	*3 Mastery*	*4 Mastery*	*5 IM*	*6 IM*
Subjects and Verbs						
Fragments						
Run-Ons						
Sentence Variety I						
Standard English Verbs						
Irregular Verbs						
Subject-Verb Agreement						
Consistent Verb Tense						
Additional Information About Verbs						
Pronoun Reference, Agreement, and Point of View						
Pronoun Types						
Adjectives and Adverbs						
Misplaced Modifiers						
Dangling Modifiers						

Individual Tests Continued	*1 Mastery*	*2 Mastery*	*3 Mastery*	*4 Mastery*	*5 IM*	*6 IM*
Faulty Parallelism						
Sentence Variety II						
Capital Letters						
Numbers and Abbreviations						
End Marks						
Apostrophe						
Quotation Marks						
Comma						
Other Punctuation Marks						
Dictionary Use						
Spelling Improvement						
Omitted Words and Letters						
Commonly Confused Words						
Effective Word Choice						

Combined Tests	*1 Mastery*	*2 Mastery*	*3 Mastery*	*4 Mastery*	*5 IM*	*6 IM*
Fragments and Run-Ons						
Verbs						
Pronouns						
Faulty Modifiers And Parallelism						
Capital Letters and Punctuation						
Word Use						

Progress Chart for Editing and Proofreading Tests

Date	*Step*	*Comments*	*To Do Next*	*Instructor's Initials*
9/27	1a	Missed –ing frag; 3 copying	1b	JL
		mistakes		
9/27	1b	No Mistakes—Good job!	2a	JL

Date	*Step*	*Comments*	*To Do Next*	*Instructor's Initials*

Progress Chart for Combined Editing Tests

Enter Your Score for Each Test in the Space Provided

Combined Test 1		Combined Test 7	
Combined Test 2		Combined Test 8	
Combined Test 3		Combined Test 9	
Combined Test 4		Combined Test 10	
Combined Test 5		Combined Test 11	
Combined Test 6		Combined Test 12	

Progress Chart for Writing Assignments

Date	Paper	Comments	To Do Next
10/15	Worst job	Promising but needs more support.	Rewrite
		Also, 2 frags and 2 run-ons.	

Date	Paper	Comments	To Do Next

Acknowledgments

The American Heritage Dictionary, 3rd edition, Copyright © 1994. The entry for *dictate* and the pronunciation key are reprinted with permission of Houghton Mifflin Company.

Barron, Donna, "American Family Life: The Changing Picture." Copyright © 1995 by Townsend Press. Reprinted by permission.

Berry, Grant, "A Change in Attitude." Copyright © 1995 by Townsend Press. Reprinted by permission.

Buscaglia, Leo, "Papa" from *Papa, My Father.* Copyright © 1980 by Leo F. Buscaglia, Inc. Reprinted by permission.

Carson, Ben, M.D., and Cecil Murphey, "Do It Better!" from *Think Big.* Copyright © 1996 by Zondervan Publishing House.

Cohen, Richard, "Men and Their Hidden Feelings." Copyright © 1983 by The Washington Post Writers Group. Reprinted with permission.

Johnson, Beth, "Let's Get Specific." Copyright © 1995 by Townsend Press. Reprinted with permission.

Kowal, Paul, of Cherry Hill, New Jersey. Photographs of Benjamin Carson on page 561 and Regina Ruiz on pages 568–570.

Lopez, Steve, "A Small Victory," from *The Philadelphia Inquirer*. Copyright © 1990 by The Philadelphia Inquirer. Reprinted with permission of The Philadelphia Inquirer.

Marcus, Larry, of Minneapolis, Minnesota. Photographs of Grant Berry on pages 545–548.

Mayer, Robert, "The Quiet Hour." Reprinted by permission.

Office of Communications and Public Affairs, Johns Hopkins Children's Center, Baltimore, Maryland. Photographs of Benjamin Carson on pages 555 and 558.

Ruiz, Regina, "Taking Charge of My Life." Copyright © 1994, 2000 by Townsend Press. Reprinted by permission.

Walker, Alice, "My Daughter Smokes," from *Living by the Word: Selected Writings 1973–1987.* Copyright © 1987 by Alice Walker. Reprinted by permission of Harcourt, Inc.

Index

D

J

K

L

M

N

O

P

T

U

V